Grits is Groceries

and
other facts of
Southern life

Darrell Huckaby

Contents

Contents

Contents

Contents

Acknowledgments

This book has been a labor of love and is the fulfillment of a dream I've had longer than I care to admit. There are many people responsible for this dream coming to fruition, and I would like to offer a word of acknowledgment and heart felt thanks to each of them.

First, I would like to thank my father, Homer Huckaby, who taught me to love the written word, and my mother, Tommie Huckaby, who provided me with a rich larder of childhood memories upon which to draw inspiration for my stories.

I would be remiss if I didn't acknowledge the dedicated teachers I had at Porterdale School and Newton County High School. They played a major role in shaping my life.

I offer my love, and my thanks, to my wife, Lisa, who has offered me encouragement and support throughout this project and who has spent countless hours, herself, helping to turn *Grits* into a reality. I also extend a special thanks to our children--Jamie, Jackson, and Jenna--and a word of apology for not being as attentive as I should have been while this book was being prepared for press.

To my mother-in-law, Bitzi Potts, I say a special word of gratitude for giving so freely of her time to help me pursue my writing goals.

I can think of no person more instrumental in the publication of this book than the little lady from Montezuma--Alice Queen--editor of the *Rockdale Citizen*. I thank her for giving me a forum in which to share my thoughts and feelings. Without her faith in my talents and abilities, *Grits is Groceries* would not exist.

And lastly, to my readers, whose kind response to my weekly column provided me with the impetus to publish this collection.

Thank you all, and may God bless.
Darrell Huckaby

For

Lisa

1

I'm as Southern as Cotton . . . or grits ain't groceries

I'm as Southern as Cotton . . . or grits ain't groceries

I'm Southern. Make no mistake about it. I'm as Southern as cotton, and proud of it. I was raised in a Georgia mill village, educated in a large Southern university, and have been a lifetime member of the Methodist church. You can't hardly get any more Southern than that.

Barbecue, corn bread, slow cooked vegetables, seasoned with pork, and all manner of battered and fried meats have been and continue to be a part of my diet. Sweet iced tea is a given. I eat dinner in the middle of the day and supper in the evening. Yes, I grew up putting peanuts in my Coca Cola.

I don't live off the land, but I fully understand the attraction for those that do. I don't have a pickup truck or a hound dog or a shotgun, but most of my relatives have all of the above.

I will never live anywhere that doesn't have a red clay motif and I never hope to live among people who don't understand why an inch of snow is a big deal. As far as I'm concerned, Nashville's up north, Florida is the Tropics, and Alabama is out west.

I know my manners. I hold the door open for ladies, take my hat off in the house, and always say "ma'am." I also say "mama" and "ain't" every once in a while. Of course I understand that "y'all" is a perfectly good contraction, always to be used in the second person plural.

I'm not still fighting the War Between the States (there was nothing civil about it), but appreciate those that did, enough to have named my only son Jackson Lee, without apologies to anyone.

I don't like anyone from above the Mason-Dixon line telling me how we should do things down here and I have little patience for those that sit and whine about how much better life was back in Buffalo. Last time I was there, there were no fences keeping folks out.

I know exactly why college football is the greatest spectacle in the world and why pretty women cry and grown men hug total strangers when their team does good.

I hope all readers find a laugh in my book. You may find a tear or two.

Those of you who are as Southern as I am will enjoy this book. It will bring back precious memories of a bygone day. It will make you pause, if only for a moment, and remember how things used to be. It will also cause you to wonder how in the world things got to be how they are now. It will give you cause to celebrate your Southerness.

Those of you who "ain't from around here" might enjoy it, too. Hopefully it will help you gain a little insight into what makes us Southerners tick.

I say again—I'm Southern, and proud of it. In fact, if I ain't Southern, grits ain't groceries.

Facts Every Georgian Should Know

I was born in Porterdale, Georgia. I've never lived out-side the boundaries of the Peach State and never hope to. I have, however, traveled extensively within our state, from Rabun Gap to Tybee Light. I've also devoted a large portion of my life to studying the history and culture of our state. Please, allow me to share a little of what I've learned.

I can't help but notice that there are more and more people in our community that talk funny and turn their nose up at ham hocks and collard greens. Yankees in Georgia! How did they ever get in? As part of my civic duty I want to provide a primer, of sorts, of useful information these folks need in order to live comfortably amongst us. Here are some facts that every Georgian should know.

Coca Cola is ours and unless you've had one in a green tinted six ounce bottle with a slight crust of ice on it—you don't know what the real thing is.

If it weren't for a Georgian—Crawford Long of Jefferson—open heart surgery would hurt like hell.

True Georgians say "ma'am" and "sir" and call their mothers "mama" and their fathers "daddy." Y'all is a perfectly good contraction and never means just one person, and if y'all don't like the way we talk, Delta (which is also ours) is ready when y'all are.

Long before the Olympics brought the world's greatest athletes to Atlanta, we gave the world Ty Cobb, Jackie Robinson, Walt Frazier, Luke Appling, Johnny Mize, Fran Tarkenton, Bobby Jones, Wyomia Tyus and Herschel Walker. If you don't know who those people are you need to find out before you go to bed. Long after the Olympics are forgotten the greatest tournament in golf will still be played in Augusta every April and 80,000 or so red and black faithful will gather for services on autumn Saturdays in Athens. No matter how many we play in, nothing will top the excitement of the first World Series or the first Super Bowl. Turner Field is nice, but I still miss Ponce De Leon Park.

The Stone Mountain carving is LOTS bigger than the one on Mt. Rushmore, and the people honored on it deserve to be. It wasn't just about slavery.

Atlanta was called "the city too busy to hate" during the civil rights era of the '60s because it was, and we should be proud of that.

In 1864 Sherman burned Atlanta, and much of Georgia, on his way to the sea. Crack cocaine is doing more damage in Atlanta than Sherman ever did.

We don't grow the most peaches, but still deserve to be called the *Peach State*, because ours are the best. We do produce the most peanuts, pecans, and poultry.

Elvis wasn't ours, but Otis Redding, James Brown, the Allman Brothers, Johnny Mercer, Joe South, Ray Charles, Bill Anderson, Brenda Lee, Trisha Yearwood, and Alan Jackson are.

So are Sidney Lanier, Joel Chandler Harris, Margaret Mitchell, and Lewis Grizzard. Find something these folks have written and start reading. I'll bet my next cotton crop you're hooked for life.

FDR adopted us. His "Little White House" in Warm Springs is exactly as it was the day he died there, near the end of WW II. Every Georgian needs to visit Warm Springs. FDR's New Deal put Georgians to work and turned an entire generation of our people into "Yellow Dog Democrats." Depression era Georgians would vote for a yellow dog if it were running on the Democratic ticket.

Georgia once had three governors at the same time. Lester Maddox wasn't one of them, but was elected by the legislature without getting a majority of the popular vote. He did a great job, too. Zell Miller was the best governor I never voted for and Jimmy Earl Carter may have had a rough tenure as president, but is the best ex-president we've ever had.

We really ought to change the flag.

Gone With the Wind belongs to us. We own it. It's by one of us and about us. It's one of the world's great novels, an absolute film classic, and we don't need to apologize for liking it.

WSB means "Welcome South Brother"—but she ain't what she used to be. Neither is the Atlanta Constitution, by the way.

The Brown Thrasher, the Cherokee Rose, and the Live Oak are our symbols. Proud, decent people are our heritage. None of the above are as plentiful as they once were, but none are on the endangered list either.

The best barbecue in the world is at either Fresh Air in Jackson or Sprayberry's in Newnan. It's a toss-up. The best fried shrimp is at Archie's in Darien; the best seafood value is Williams in Savannah; the best catfish is served at Henderson's in Covington and the best fried chicken is at my mama's house. Grits is groceries. Sugar doesn't belong in cornbread and God intended for tea to be sweet. If you don't like these foods, you ought to consider moving.

And lastly—Georgia ain't heaven, but it will sure do 'til I get there.

"Accused" of Being Southern; Guilty as Charged.

If I live to be a hundred, I'll never understand why Yankees choose to live among us if life is so much better up north. I can't help but agree with the late Lewis Grizzard when I run across folks like the lady in this column. "Delta is ready when you are, y'all"

In a bizarre incident at the local post office last week, I was "accused" of being Southern. That's right. I wasn't called Southern, I was accused of it. There's a big difference.

I was standing in line behind a rather innocuous looking older lady. Suddenly, she went off on me. She screamed at me to back off and give her more space. Then she plunged the proverbial dagger into my heart. She said, "You're a Southerner, and I'm tired of all this cozy Southern (word that can't appear in the newspaper unless written by Dave Baker.)

I was stunned. Dozens of retorts came to my mind. Thankfully none of them found their way out of my mouth. Instead of retaliating, I did what any other well mannered Southern gentleman, who had been educated in a large Southern university and raised in the Methodist Church, would have done. I politely backed off and said nothing. However, I could not, for the life of me, get the incident out of my mind. I just didn't enter the post office in Conyers, Georgia, expecting to get attacked for being Southern.

My thoughts lingered on the lady's words and I began to wonder, "What, exactly, makes a person Southern?" The obvious answer is living in the South, but we all know that living in the South doesn't make a person Southern any more than living in Alaska makes a person an Eskimo. Got to be more to it than that.

OK. Being born and raised in the South would do it. Nope. I know people who have lived here all their lives who are about as Southern as cream cheese and bagels. Being Southern is not about location or geography. With the blending of culture that has occurred in our great nation over the past three decades, as more and more Americans get the good sense to move to the Sun Belt, Southern has now become a state of mind.

Let me tell you what Southern is.

Southern is saying "yes, ma'am" and "no sir." It's being able to unashamedly talk about your "daddy" and your "mama" instead of your "mother" and "father," or even your "mom" or "dad." If you can't bring yourself to say "mama" you might as well be from New Jersey. It's also, of course, using "y'all" freely and throwing "ain't" into a sentence occasionally, even though you know better.

Southern is the art of slowing down, which, unfortunately, is quickly becoming a lost art, even in the South. It's taking time from a hectic schedule to sit on the porch and visit for a spell. It's bringing home cooked food to a house where there has been a death, and staying long enough to make sure that everyone has had plenty and the dishes are washed.

Southern is wearing overalls without thinking of yourself as cute or as making a fashion statement. It's insisting that your daughter doesn't wear white shoes to church after Labor Day, no matter what the temperature is outside. It's feeling natural in a baseball cap with a heavy equipment logo and it is knowing not to comment on someone's clothes, because they may be the best they can afford.

Southern is grits, fried chicken, cornbread, peas, collards, pulled pork barbecue, and sweet iced tea.

Southern is understanding why college football is life or death and that the NFL is something to pass the time of day, but not anything to get worked up over.

Southern is being enough of a stock car fan to remember when Fireball Roberts crashed into the wall at Daytona, and it's turning up one's nose at the current interest in race car drivers by corporate America and all the new found fans who watch the cars run because it's a trend.

Southern is not wanting to refight "The War," but still being able to understand why Robert E. Lee and Stonewall Jackson are heroes.

Southern is thinking that the people on the Andy Griffith Show reruns are just like the folks you grew up with.

Southern is going to church on Sunday and feeling funny when you head to the mall or the lake or the golf course instead. It's knowing all the words to the old gospel hymns and wondering why the song leader picks all the new fangled songs every Sunday instead of Amazing Grace and the Old Rugged Cross. Southern is driving to the cemetery and standing with the family beside the open grave, even if it's cold or rainy or you're late getting back to work. And it's pulling off on the side of the road when you meet a funeral, even though you don't know the deceased.

Southern is waving at cars that drive by while you're walking on the side of the road. It's smiling at strangers and hugging your friends. I guess Southern must be accidentally standing too close to someone in the post office. Or maybe it was the fact that I smiled at someone I didn't know.

Whatever the case, I am guilty as charged. I think the penalty for being caught being Southern is a weekend of eating barbecued ribs and boiled peanuts while watching three college football games in a row. Let the punishment begin!

The Name's the Game

If you ever find yourself overcome with boredom and need something to do, find a Georgia road map and study all of the colorful, interesting, and unusual place names. Many, such as Hiawassee and Chattahoochee, are beautiful Indian words. Many places are named for people long forgotton, and some are down right common. But a few stories about how Georgia towns got their names are real doozies.

I get many unusual phone calls from many unusual people in many unusual places. I suppose this is only fitting, since I'm a bit unusual myself. I got a call the other day from LuLu Bo Bo of

TyTy. She wanted me to come to her civic league luncheon and talk about the time Sherman marched through Georgia.   In case you don't know, by the way, Ty Ty is in Tift County, which is way below the gnat line.

I told Miss LuLu Bobo that I would have to get back with her on my availability for the particular day she had in mind.   However, her phone call did set me to thinking about all the colorful names that have been given to the towns and communities scattered across our state, and the origins of the names.

I've traveled all across this great state of ours on numerous occasions. I have been, as the saying goes, from Rabun Gap to Tybee Light and all points in between. I have a particular penchant for wandering off the main roads and exploring the lesser known highways—the little lines on our state road map. It's a good way to meet folks. During my travels I've found myself in some very interesting places with equally interesting names.

For instance, last spring I visited a community in northwest Georgia called Plum Nelly, because it is "plum" out of Tennessee and "nelly" out of Georgia. In the opposite corner of the state is a town called Fargo, because it is as far as one can go and still be in Georgia.

In northern Fulton County there is a community called Shake Rag. It got its name from the early days of railroad travel. If there was a need for the train to stop as it passed, so the story goes, someone would stand by the tracks and shake a rag to signal the engineer. When Eugene Talmadge was the scourge of Georgia politics he would often monitor election returns and one of his favorite expressions was, "Well, we've heard from the Shake Rag district. Now we can all go to bed."

If you take a trip down US Highway 25 through Bulloch County, in southeastern Georgia, you'll run smack dab into a place called Hopeulikit. This town got its name because the US postal authorities rejected several previous name proposals.

One of my favorite stories regarding the naming of a town

is the one about Resaca, in northwest Georgia. In reality, this town was given its name by Mexican War veterans in honor of a great victory at Resaca de la Palma. The legend is much better. According to the story, a farmer had a quite homely daughter who couldn't seem to attract a beau. The old man offered a substantial dowry and finally got someone to take him up on his offer. To make sure the arranged wedding went off as planned, the man placed a bag over his daughter's head before escorting her down the aisle. The preacher preformed the ceremony and then the old farmer lifted the bag off his daughter's face to allow the groom to kiss his bride. According to the story, the groom took one look at the girl and screamed, "Re-sack her," thus giving a new name to the farming community.

We have some pretty unusual towns with some interesting stories of their own in our part of the state. There's a community called Between over in Walton County, so named because it is between Monroe and Loganville.

Also in Walton County is the town of Social Circle. Social Circle supposedly got its name because a group of settlers, tired out from spending the day digging a town well, sat down to rest and began to pass around a jug. As the jug got emptier the men got rowdier. One man's wife, sent to check on the progress of the digging, is said to have remarked quite sarcastically, "Isn't this a social circle!"

Fire water is also said to have played a part in the naming of a town ten miles down the road from Social Circle. Again, according to legend, town organizers agreed to name the town after the man who stayed sober the longest at the celebration for settlement. The only teetotaler in the bunch, Mr. Mansfield, supposedly had the town named in his honor.

With all these unusual place names dotting the Georgia map, Conyers and Rockdale County seem downright boring. Conyers, of course, was named for Dr. Conyers, a Covington banker who bought the land for the railroad station and right of way. Our county was named for the Rockdale Baptist Church, so called because of the subterranean granite with which we're blessed.

I'm sorry to report that I could not accommodate Miss Bobo's request to come to Ty Ty and talk about Sherman. I'm already booked that day—at the Methodist Church in Splitsilk.

How 'Bout a Pork Pig Sandwich?

I can think of nothing more Southern than barbecue. Dozens of people called me after this column first appeared in print telling me where to go to get the best barbecue. I say the same thing to readers of this book that I said to them: "Don't tell me about good barbecue--take me to it."

A man stepped out of a pickup truck the other day and handed me a brown paper bag. "Got a little something for you," he told me.

You need to be careful when a man gets out of a pickup truck and hands you a brown paper bag. There's a real good chance the contents could be illegal, immoral, or intoxicating. I very carefully opened my gift and discovered, to my delight, that the content was none of the above. What it was was a T-shirt, from one of my favorite establishments—Sprayberry's Barbecue in Newnan.

The gesture was so thoughtful that I couldn't bring myself to complain that there wasn't a pork pig sandwich in the bag somewhere. Just seeing the shirt made my mouth water and my taste buds scream for some of the succulent hickory-smoked meat, drenched with the red nectar some people call barbecue sauce, and served with white bread and slaw. It's so good it would make a dog jump off a meat wagon, and you can quote me on that.

If you aren't from around here, you may not realize that discussing barbecue can be a dangerous proposition. Folks will get into a cuss fight quicker over barbecue than just about anything I can think of. In fact, barbecue ranks right up there with politics and religion when it comes to controversial discussion topics. Not only is it hard to reach a consensus as to where the best barbecue is served, there is no clear agreement as to what does and does not constitute or deserve to be called barbecue in the first place.

For instance, a very nice friend of ours, who can't really help being from Pittsburgh, recently invited my family over for a "barbecue." I was pleasantly surprised and couldn't wait to tie on the feed bag at my friend's house. Imagine my disappointment when I arrived in her back yard to find her husband roasting hotdogs and grilling hamburgers on a gas grill. Let's get one thing perfectly clear. Wienies ain't barbecue.

Neither, for that matter, is beef. My mother-in-law is a dear lady and affords me much better treatment than I deserve, but she has an unnatural aversion to pork. She won't eat it. I think it has something to do with the Yankee blood flowing through her veins. (Her mother was from Wisconsin, of all places.)

Anyway, my mother-in-law eats beef soaked in spicy red sauce and thinks she's eating barbecue. As long as we're setting things straight, let me make one thing perfectly clear. If it doesn't involve the north end of a south bound hog, slow cooked over hardwood coals for close to a day, it just ain't barbecue. If you don't believe me, look it up. It's in the Bible. I think it's in the 35th chapter of Deuteronomy.

Eating beef and calling it barbecue originated in Texas, I believe. You can't really hold it against them. Folks have to make do. I've been told that goat is the meat of choice at some Texas hoedowns. Please know that I have nothing against goats, but I won't knowingly go somewhere to eat one.

Memphis, Tennessee is famous for barbecued pork ribs. These do, of course, come from a pig, and I've been known to eat far more than my share of this delicacy. However, I've never been more disappointed than the time I went to the world famous Rendezvous Restaurant in Elvis's hometown. The ribs were rubbed with all sorts of seasonings and served dry. If I don't have to wash my face after eating ribs I might as well have eaten a hotdog, in Pittsburgh.

OK. Is everybody clear, now? Barbecue is pork, slow

cooked over hot coals, and dripping with sauce. By the way, it should be pulled from the bone or chopped on a wooden board with a cleaver. Sliced doesn't count. I'm not completely inflexible, however. The sauce can be vinegar or tomato based.

Now that we've decided what barbecue is, let's talk about where to eat it. There are thousands of places across the South that serve a more than passable pork plate. A good rule of thumb for selecting a barbecue joint is to check the parking lot. If there is an equal number of pickup trucks and luxury cars out front, it's a good sign. Harold's Barbecue, out by the Federal Pen, is a good example of such an establishment.

Avoid places that are too fancy or seem to put an unusual amount of stock in how well dressed the servers are. Having old men with crewcuts and tattoos behind the counter is a definite plus. If fried shrimp or pasta is on the menu, leave immediately.

I've eaten barbecued pork pig sandwiches from Tuscaloosa to Hahira and all points in between. My personal favorites are the previously mentioned Sprayberry's and the Fresh Air Barbecue in Jackson. It's a toss up. I don't know which I'd choose at gunpoint. I do know that I've got to stop writing now and go get something to eat.

If you think all this discussion of barbecue has made me hungry, just wait until I write about catfish!

Just a Little Slice of 'Catfish Heaven'

If there is anything that can raise a Southerner's ire quicker than the Great Barbecue Debate, it's a discussion about who serves the best catfish. I maintain the same policy for catfish as I do for barbecue. Don't tell me about better catfish--take me there and buy me some. Until someone does, Henderson's Restaurant is still 'Catfish Heaven' to me.

Let's talk about catfish. If you are a regular reader of this column you know that I am engaged in a never ending quest to stay in touch with my Southerness. You can't get more Southern than catfish. If sweet tea is the "Champagne of the South," as it has been called, then catfish, dredged in cornmeal and fried up until it is crisp on the outside, its sweet white meat tender and moist on the inside, is truly the "Nectar of the Southern Gods."

Catfish and me go back a long ways. My family used to have fish fries quite frequently. I remember watching the menfolk cook fish in a black cooker over a wood fire. Catfish was always the entree of choice. My mother's friend, Gladys Rogers, made a dish to go with catfish called "Hell-in-the-bowl." It consisted of diced tomatoes, finely chopped Vidalia onions, hot peppers, with the emphasis on hot (thus the name), and vinegar. It would make a puppy pull a freight train.

As I grew older I discovered restaurants and have spent the better part of the past three decades roaming the South in search of Catfish Heaven. Now, if you aren't from around here, let me fill you in on some particulars about finding a good place to eat catfish. To begin with, forget chain restaurants. Catfish needs to be eaten at a family-owned restaurant where the same person has been cooking the fish and dropping the hushpuppies forever. Pride is one of the main ingredients when you're cooking catfish and it's hard to obtain pride when you work by the hour for a national franchise.

There are a few other rules to go by. Check the parking lot. It should be about fifty-fifty with local cars and those from surrounding counties. You may certainly try a place with a paved parking lot, but gravel is much preferable.

Avoid places that are too fancy. Folks who spend time and energy trying to make a restaurant cute don't have time to do justice to the fish they are cooking. It's OK for a catfish place to have curtains on the windows, but not a necessity. By no means should they match the tablecloths. Not having tablecloths is a plus. The decor should be limited to framed slogans, plaques of appreciation from local athletic teams, and pictures of the owners' grandchildren.

If you walk into a catfish place and are not greeted with a friendly smile, leave immediately.   Look around the room.   If conversations are going on between tables, that's a good sign. If the waitresses call customers by name, that's even better. Don't be offended, or even surprised, if your hostess asks if you need to see a menu. Most patrons are probably regulars and know it by heart.

About the menu. It can have items besides catfish, just not too many of them. Shrimp, steaks, cheeseburgers, even bar-becue, are all acceptable. But the main feature needs to be cat-fish. All-you-can-eat should be an option. The catfish should be served with slaw, French fries, and, of course, hushpuppies. If you're below the gnat line, cheese grits and slices of onions will come on the side. If it's your first time in the place, order the catfish, with sweet tea to drink.

I've eaten catfish at scores of establishments across the South, including several in the immediate area. The best catfish in the free world are served at Henderson's on Highway 36, just south of Covington. It meets all the criteria listed above, and then some.

I've been eating with the Henderson family for most of my forty-some-odd years. When I say family, I mean family. Mr. Clarence Henderson, who started the business, passed away a few years back, but in my mind's eye I still see him, every time I walk into the place. He's still walking among his guests, which is how he truly treated his customers—as guests—in his white apron, a pitcher of tea in one hand, a coffee pot in the other, a smile on his face, and beads of sweat on his bald forehead.

Mrs. Henderson has been standing behind the cash regis-ter for as long as I can remember. She hasn't aged a day in over thirty years. Son Clarence is still back in the kitchen, up to his elbows in cornmeal, frying the most delicious catfish this side of heaven. Sometimes he's joined by his brother David. Practicing law in town during the day doesn't stop him from cooking fish at night, just as teaching at Eastside High doesn't stop sister Clarice from being everywhere at once—taking orders, bussing tables, and passing out plates heaped high with hot food, which is consistently good, night after night, year after year.

I'm sure many of you have your favorite places to eat fish and I'm glad some of you settle for fish not cooked by Clarence Henderson. It's hard enough to get seated, as it is. But if you've never had catfish in a down home atmosphere—you ain't been in Dixie, yet. And if you know a place that serves better fish—take me to it. I'll have to taste it to believe it.

Flag Flap Decisions Should be Left to Southerners

I know this is a tough issue. We all think that we need to rally 'round the flag to show our loyalty to the South and her heroes, not to mention our Southern pride and heritage. But it just ain't so.

I 'spect I'll make just about everybody mad today. I'm fixin' to talk about the flag. Not the one we pledge allegiance to each day with it's fifty stars and thirteen stripes. That would be Old Glory. Washington carried it across the Delaware. Marines raised it on Iwo Jima. Neil Armstrong placed it on the moon. Car dealers fly it all day and all night. I'm not talking about that flag. I'm talking about the Georgia flag, which has come under fire recently because of the St. Andrews cross that adorns a full two-thirds of the banner.

Before I begin my comments on the flag, let me take you on a virtual tour of my living room. It has a fireplace against one wall with an oak mantle above it that my daddy-in-law made. A hand carved bald eagle adorns one side of the mantle. A bronze sculpture of Robert E. Lee and Stonewall Jackson, mounted on horseback and meeting for the last time in a glade at

Chancellorsville is on the opposite end.

On the wall above the roll top desk my mother bought for me when I got married is a print of a guy about my age leaning against the Vietnam Wall in Washington D.C. My Eagle Scout Award and some Bert Adams camp patches I designed are in frames next to it.

One entire wall is a bookcase, filled with hundreds of books. Many are about American history, a subject I've studied all my life and taught for a great part of it.

There are other prints on the walls. One shows General Lee meeting the remnants of Pickett's division returning from a failed charge up Cemetery Ridge at Gettysburg. Another shows Lee and Jackson in church, heads bowed, tears rolling down their cheeks. There is a print of the Stone Mountain carving and other prints of Lee and Jackson individually.

The lump under the quilt in the corner, playing a video game, is my ten year old son. His name is Jackson Lee Huckaby. I think you get the picture.

I am an American. I am a Southerner. I am a historian.

I understand the events that led up to the War Between the States. I never refer to it as the Civil War; there was nothing civil about it. I understand the motives of the political leaders and I understand the motivation of the men who fought, on both sides. I also understand the motives of the men who added the Confederate battle emblem to the Georgia flag in 1956.

Please know where I'm coming from when I say that Georgia really does need to change her flag.

I know that many, many people want to keep the flag the way it is. Trust me. I truly understand how they feel. No one is more proud of being Southern than I am.

I know that Robert E. Lee, who served valiantly in the United States Army and turned down full command of that same body, fought not to preserve slavery but to defend his homeland. I am fully aware that the vast majority of Confederate soldiers believed that they were fighting for personal liberty and independence, not so their rich neighbors could continue to own slaves.

I know that most of the Georgians who favor keeping the flag believe it does represent their Southern heritage and not racism. Unfortunately, these well intentioned people are not aware of the flag's history, or, if they are, allow emotion to overcome logic when they make their arguments for keeping the flag.

The Georgia flag was changed to send a message to the Supreme Court that our state would defy its integration order. That's the end of the story. That's a fact, no matter how hard we wish it were otherwise. The Georgia General Assembly turned the Confederate flag into a racial symbol when they did that. The battle flag actually replaced three bars that were added to the flag by a state legislature full of Confederate veterans. They were representative of the Stars and Bars, the official Confederate flag, and were put there to honor Confederate soldiers. The 1956 lawmakers took away that heritage and replaced it with their symbol of hate and defiance. Those are the indisputable facts. A flag should represent all the people of a state, and a flag designed to promote a segregated society can never represent all our people. Think about it.

Now, having said that, let me say this. Last week this newspaper ran a column by someone named Lars-Erik Nelson. Nelson works for the New York Daily News. He called the Confederate flag a flag for "losers" and his column was full of disparaging remarks about Southerners who fought under the flag and those who honor it today. His column showed that he is completely ignorant of the facts surrounding our country's greatest tragedy and has no understanding, whatsoever, of the Southern psyche. Of course he calls for us to stop displaying all Confederate flags immediately.

I've got a message for Mr. Lars-Erik Nelson. We will change our flag in our own due time as soon as a majority of Georgians think through the issues and realize why it is the right thing to do. In the meantime, inflammatory remarks from his kind will only make people more determined not to change it. We don't need any hyphenated-named Yankee from New York tending to our business, and as for me, Lars-Erik Nelson can just kiss my rebel ass.

It's Time to Take a Stand . . . for Sweet Iced Tea

This column, to my surprise, drew more comment, from a wider area, than just about any other. Everything is changing in the South, and much of the change is not for the better. Some things we just need to hold onto, and sweet iced tea is one of those things.

It disturbs me greatly to address this topic, but never let it be said that I shirk my responsibility. It has come to my attention that we in the South have a drinking problem. I'm not talking about booze, although I'm sure the consumption of wine, beer, and government whiskey has increased exponentially since moonshining went out of style. Our problem is worse than that.

We are losing the fine art of making sweet iced tea, and are allowing many establishments to get by without serving it at all. This is not a trivial matter, y'all. Drinking sweet iced tea is a part of our culture and has been for generations. Losing our penchant for making and enjoying the drink that has been called the "Champagne of the South" is just one more step toward losing our distinctiveness. Pretty soon one won't be able to distinguish Conyers from Omaha.

I was eighteen years old before I learned that every family in America doesn't drink sweet tea at every meal. My mama made it the same way every night, forever. She would boil water in a copper kettle and then pour it over a large tea bag into a Corningware pitcher. After the tea steeped a while she would add sugar, not quite a whole scoop, while the tea was still hot. It was perfect, night after night, year after year. Of course I didn't appreciate it, just like I didn't appreciate country fried steak one night a week, fried chicken at Sunday dinner, and either biscuits or cornbread every night.

When I ate supper with my friends their mama's served sweet iced tea, too, and it always tasted pretty much like the tea at our house. No one asked me what I wanted to drink. They just filled up the glasses, that had once been jelly jars, with ice and poured the tea.

When I was eighteen my mama and daddy and I took an improbable trip to New York City. We got in our 1968 Buick and headed north. Twenty hours and two breakdowns later, we found ourselves on the outskirts of Manhattan Island. We got a room at the Holiday Inn in Jersey City. After freshening up from our long ride, we went down to the hotel restaurant to get a bite to eat. When the waiter asked for our drink orders, I naturally said I'd have iced tea.

The rather stuffy server informed me that they didn't serve iced tea. He acted a little bit like I had ordered a glass of curdled milk.

My daddy asked him if they served hot tea. The guy said that they certainly served hot tea. He then admitted, under great duress, that they had ice on the premises. Daddy ordered a pot of hot tea and three glasses of ice. He steeped the tea, added several packages of sugar, and poured it over the glasses of ice the waiter had reluctantly brought. Porterdale had come to town, and so had sweet iced tea.

When I went away to college my horizons were expanded somewhat. I began to accept the fact that if I traveled above the Mason-Dixon line and ordered tea to drink with my meal it would not be a satisfying experience. The tea would come unsweetened. Everyone knows that no amount of sugar in the world will adequately sweeten a glass of cold tea. Almost as bad, the tea will have only one or two ice cubes floating on top. Everyone also knows that the glass should be plumb full of ice before the tea is poured into it. Otherwise it gets too watery.

Everyone also knows, or should know, that when you order iced tea in a restaurant, refills are free. I almost started the War Between the States all over again at a Lum's in Washington D.C. one night when my waiter, a bowlegged fellow who spoke with a lisp, tried to charge me eleven dollars and a quarter for the seven glasses of tea I had consumed with my meal. The matter was eventually resolved, but even if I'm elected President of the

United States, I won't be able to eat supper at the Lum's down near the White House.

Well, folks up north can drink what they want with their meals. Far be it from me to tell them how to live. If my whole world was covered by snow six months out of the year, I probably wouldn't want ice in my drink, either. But when their customs concerning the South's standard drink infiltrate down here, we need to do something.

For years I have noticed that we are having a little bit of a problem concerning our tea consumption. More and more frequently I've been invited to people's homes where sweet tea is not served. I somehow manage to grimace and bear it. (I can't quite grin at no sweet tea.) I've ordered tea at local dining establishments only to be told that sweet tea was not served. No problem. I just don't go back to those places. I've learned to automatically order an extra glass of ice with my tea to combat the one floating ice cube practice. I've learned to cope.

But Sunday I had an experience that blew me away and brought the iced tea problem to a head. I was at a place I had never eaten. I was told that they did, indeed, serve sweet iced tea. When mine arrived it contained half a cube of ice and half a lemon and, worst of all, was full of shrubbery. My wife insisted it was mint, but I think the waitress plucked it right out of one of the potted plants hanging from the ceiling. The tea tasted like it came right out of a can. If it was sweet or freshly brewed, I'm a midget Russian astronaut.

Enough is enough. Sons and daughters of the South unite. Stand up for your heritage. Demand that sweet iced tea be served at all places, public and private, the way God and your mamas intended.

The next thing you know, we'll be drinking Perriere with moon pies instead of RC Colas.

2

No Matter Where the Road Leads . . . Georgia's always on my mind

No Matter Where the Road Leads . . . Georgia's always on my mind

I love to travel. Always have. My earliest travel experiences came in the back seats of several secondhand Buicks. My family usually went on vacation once a year and the destination was almost always Jacksonville Beach, Florida.

What great times those were! There were no interstates and, of course, no air conditioning--at least not in any of the cars we owned. To combat the heat, and to save on a night's lodging, we would set out for Florida in the wee small hours of the morning. I would sleep for a great portion of each journey.

We weren't as safety conscious in those days. There were no seat belts, of course, and I often slept on the back deck while my sister stretched out across the back seat. I can remember looking up through the glass behind me at the night sky, trying as hard as I could to spot the Big Dipper. Eventually the hum of the tires on the rough Georgia pavement would serenade me to sleep. Occasionally, I would be startled awake, or even thrown from my perch, when my daddy had to slam on brakes for an unexpected stop sign or to avoid hitting a possum.

My parents had a great time on vacation. They would sing the miles away and the fact that neither could carry a tune in a bucket did nothing to diminish their enthusiasm or their enjoyment. It was enough for them that they were on the road, traveling side by side, toward some hard earned and well deserved rest and relaxation. In fact, "Side by Side" was one of the songs they most frequently butchered.

Since our cars were usually old and not in particularly good shape, occasional breakdowns were part of the adventure. Usually the problem was no more severe than an overheated engine or a broken fan belt, but my daddy, who, like me, never met a stranger, spent the down time getting to know the locals who hung out at the service station in whatever town we happened to be in.

As I have grown older, I've had opportunities to travel across a great portion of our great country. Some people carry pictures of their children with them when they travel. We carry our children. There is no better education than traveling the highways and byways of America, seeing the sights and talking to the people, up close and personal, if you will.

Wherever I go, I take my Southerness with me. Honesty compels me to admit that it usually shows, too. I'm certainly thankful for that. I wouldn't want anyone to think that this old mill village boy would try to put on airs when he got a few miles out of town.

When I get ready for a trip outside the South, I often think of the late Dean William Tate of the University of Georgia. Dean Tate thought that the world began and ended at the Georgia state line. He considered Florida the tropics and Alabama the far west. One day he was visiting with us in the lobby of Russell Hall and, for some reason, was all riled up and talking about how bad things were "up north."

I finally got up the nerve to ask him how much time he had spent up north. He looked at me with righteous indignation and replied, "Why son, I spent a week in Nashville one time."

I know just how he felt. Although I was born with a touch of wanderlust and love to travel whenever possible, the best part is always coming home.

This chapter is about experiences I've had away from home. I hope you enjoy.

Thanks for the Memories

*It's one thing to tell someone about history. It's quite
another to show them. For years I had studied the events
that led to the founding of our country. Finally I was able
to travel to New England and see the birthplace of liberty
for myself. I was lucky enough to get to share the experience with some eighth graders who will, I hope, remember
it as long as I will.*

     My colleagues at Edwards Middle School and I took about
three dozen of our students on a field trip last weekend. We went
to Boston. Not the Boston in south Georgia, between Morven and
Thomasville. The one in Massachusetts. The Boston of Paul
Revere and Fenway Park and JFK. The Boston that's covered
with snow on the Ides of March. The Boston that had northeast
winds ripping through the clothing of our Southern bred children
like they weren't wearing any. That Boston. Hey—it was warm
last August when we planned the trip.

     It was really a great trip. We saw more in three days than
some natives see in a year, and being in the cold and snow was an
adventure for our students. But as our plane landed at Hartsfield
International Sunday night, I couldn't help but think about how
field trips have changed. When I was in school our field trips
didn't involved airports. I recall going to the sewage treatment
plant once. In the second grade we packed a picnic lunch, boarded
a yellow school bus, and visited the Grant Park Zoo. We also got
to see the Cyclorama. My girlfriend accidentally dropped a candy
apple over the railing onto the head of one of the soldiers in the
diorama. Fortunately, it was a Yankee soldier. I took the blame
and for punishment had to sit on the bus while the other children
stopped at Tastee Freeze for ice cream on the way home. Ain't
love grand?

     My mother used to tell me a story about her class trip in
high school. She was a child of the Depression and of a single

mother with four children to raise and no work. Her class at Social Circle High went to Jacksonville Beach, courtesy of some businessmen in town who believed that, even in hard times, young people should be rewarded for hard work. According to the story I've heard since birth, my mother's class stayed in a rented house. The chaperones did the cooking and the students—all twenty-one of them—played on the beach all day. As they were leaving for the trip my grandmother gave my mother all the money she had in the world to take on the trip for spending money. I believe it was a dime.

On their last night at the beach, the Social Circle Class of 1941 got to go to the boardwalk. My mama still had her dime. She spent a nickel for cotton candy and with the other nickel rode the Ferris Wheel and has testified many times that she had never seen a prettier sight than the reflection of the full moon on the ocean, as viewed from the top of the Ferris Wheel. She also recalls that she had never tasted cotton candy before and in her words it was "the best stuff I'd ever put in my mouth."

My grandmother never had much material wealth to share with her children, but with her last dime she bought my mother a million dollars worth of memories that have lasted a lifetime.

Our trip to Boston was a bit more extravagant than my mother's trip to the beach on the eve of World War II. It was certainly more educational than a trip to the sewage plant and more eventful than visiting the Cyclorama. We walked the Freedom Trail and reenacted the Boston Tea Party. We ate clam chowder and baked cod and toured the USS Constitution. We were very proud to discover that *Old Ironsides* earned her nickname because she was built from sturdy Live Oak, harvested on Georgia sea islands. We relived the Camelot years at the Kennedy Library and the witchcraft hysteria at Salem. We retraced the path of Paul Revere and stood by the rude bridge at Concord which bore witness to the *shot heard round the world*. But throughout the entire trip I couldn't help but wonder if our students' parents were buying them a lifetime of memories. I hoped so, because they had spent considerably more than a dime.

On the village green in Lexington we did an impromptu reenactment of the skirmish there between the Minutemen and the British Regulars. As I was explaining how the drama had unfolded, some 224 years earlier, I repeated the words of Captain Jonas Parker, first American to die in the Revolution. "Don't fire unless fired upon, but if they mean to have a war, let it begin here!"

I don't know who threw the snowball at that precise moment. But the ensuing snowball fight was probably the greatest battle to take place in Lexington since Paul Revere left town. As I sought cover and watched the faces of our students, glowing with excitement, I knew. They were making memories. They were learning, but they were also making memories—and memories last a lifetime.

Jekyll in Spring—A Little Slice of Heaven

The most relaxing week of my year is spent camping and riding bicycles on Jekyll Island. Once a playground for the filthy rich, now it is a treasure that we all can enjoy.

Jekyll Island—Even as you read this I'm enjoying a restful week at one of my favorite places on earth. Spring Break at Daytona or Ft. Lauderdale? Been there. Done that. Panama City? They don't call it the "Redneck Riviera" for nothing. Walt Disney World? At this time of year? No thanks. I'll keep visiting the quiet little island that was once the playground of millionaires.

My wife's family has been camping on Jekyll Island during spring break forever. It's one of many wonderful traditions I married into. Another is hauling hay when it's 103 in the shade, but you have to take the rough with the smooth. Right?

The week we spend camping at Jekyll is the most relaxing week of my year. My family travels a lot. After most of our vacations we need a week off to rest and recuperate. But not this one.

There are accommodations to fit every life-style and budget on this tiny little hideaway. We camp. In fact, we've pitched our tents on the same campsite each of the past eighteen years, except one. In 1992 we had a different priority. Now we celebrate a birthday at Jekyll each year.

Always an early riser, I get up most mornings and take a bike ride down to the beach to watch the sun slowly climb out of the Atlantic Ocean, signaling the beginning of another day in Paradise, Georgia style. The beach is isolated at that time of day. I'm alone with the sun and the water and a few gulls or pelicans. When I return to the campsite the coffee is ready and the campfire from the night before has been rekindled. At no other time or place is reading the morning paper so pleasurable. The others accuse me of riding to see the sunrise every morning just so I won't have to brew the coffee or build the morning fire, but that's not really true.

Our morning activities usually include a long bike ride. There are bike paths everywhere. Some go through the salt marsh on the northern end of the island. Others take the adventurous rider in front of the cottages once owned by the Rockefellers and the Carnegies and their like, through the woods past an alligator pond, or out to a state park on the secluded south beach. Spring comes early to this part of Georgia and azaleas and dogwoods abound. My favorite trail winds in and out of Live Oak trees that are hundreds of years old. Spanish moss hangs over the path and Cherokee Roses grow alongside. Deer, raccoons, rabbits and wild turkeys are common sights. The path winds along the bank of the Jekyll River and Sidney Lanier's Marshes of Glenn form a watery plain of a thousand shades of green on the other side. When the wind is right, we ride on the beach, reveling in the feeling of the salt spray on our faces.

Our bike rides are magical. We stop each day at the little

airstrip and if we're lucky get to watch a small plane take off or land. It's fun to stroll along the docks at the marina and talk to the yachters about their adventures and various ports of call. We almost always walk out on the pier to see if the fish are biting and sometimes, if the water's warm enough, people are pulling a shrimp net in the sound. Stopping at the island's only drug store for an icecream cone makes the morning complete.

There are dozens of things to do in the afternoon. Sitting around camp reading paperback novels is high on the list. So is playing on the beach or digging for sand dollars at the ocean's edge. There are also kites to fly, frisbees and baseballs to throw, sand castles to build, and birds to watch. Beginning to get the picture?

Some people come to Jekyll to play tennis and golf. I got in eighteen holes myself Monday, but only because my son wanted to play. I have to admit I played well. Two over par! I would have shot better if it hadn't been for that blasted windmill hole.

Suppertime is the best part of the day. A couple of times a week we might venture out to a seafood restaurant, but nothing beats the smell of steaks sizzling on the grill or the sound of fish frying in deep oil or the taste of fresh boiled shrimp served up with corn on the cob and eaten outside as the sun begins to settle over the marsh.

Evenings are exciting, too. That is, if you call sitting around the campfire, reliving the days activities with people you love, exciting. Sometimes we sit and look at the embers and talk and sometimes we just sit and look at the embers. Finally we retire to the cozy warmth of our sleeping bags, happy and content as humans have the right to be.

The best part of Jekyll Island is the slow pace and the absence of the throngs of people that crowd other spring break destinations. I pray it stays that way. So if learning what a wonderful place it is has made you want to visit Jekyll in the spring, I have a suggestion. Get on I-75, and drive north!

A Postcard From the Beach

I fell in love with Myrtle Beach the first time my wife Lisa and I visited there. Now I go back every chance I get. I've made good friends there, like Dick Timmerman and his family. Playing in the surf and eating fresh seafood every night makes the Grand Strand a true vacation paradise.

North Myrtle Beach, South Carolina. As I write this, I am sitting on a balcony watching the eastern sky begin to turn red and gold as the sun climbs slowly out of the Atlantic Ocean. Yes. A cup of steaming hot coffee sits on the table beside me. What's the expression? Nobody said life is fair. This week, I get the bear. Normally, the bear gets me.

I have a confession to make. They say it is good for the soul. I am a two-timer. Everyone who knows me knows of my love for the red clay hills of the Georgia Piedmont. Alas, I have a second love. The low country of South Carolina. So far my love affair with the Grand Strand has been limited to short lived trysts— temporary flings, if you will. However, if any place on earth could tempt me to permanently leave my native Georgia, it would be this part of the world.

As long as I'm confessing, I'll make another. For a long time, I avoided going to Myrtle Beach. I had no interest in the place. I decided I didn't like it without even going there. I think it was because of the name.

Myrtle. It reminded me of a girl I went to grammar school with. Her name was Myrtle and I didn't like her. She was the one who always volunteered to take names when the teacher left the room. She wrote my name down in the third grade because I read a word aloud in my reading book while Miss Elizabeth Willis stepped down the hall to take a dip of snuff. Miss Elizabeth Willis paddled my backside when she got back to the room. Because of that I never liked Myrtle and never wanted to visit a beach that shared her name.

My wife, Lisa, had grown up camping at Myrtle Beach

and tried to talk me into going there on vacation the summer after we were married. I was adamant. I wasn't going. What would we do all day? Sit around on the beach waiting for someone to tell on me for reading out loud? For all I knew Miss Elizabeth Willis might have retired to Myrtle Beach. I could just see her there, in one of those old fashioned bathing suits with long pantalets and a skirt, lurking behind a beach umbrella, waiting to pounce out and paddle me. Nothing doing.

We went to the Outer Banks of North Carolina, instead. We had a wonderful time, too, until a hurricane decided to visit at the same time we were there. We were among thousands of people who were evacuated off the north end of the island. Since we had three days of vacation left, I consented to stop at Myrtle Beach. It was love at first sight!

That was seventeen years ago. Lisa and I have made over twenty-five trips back to the Myrtle Beach area since the first one. It's like a second home. We have stayed at places from Little River to Pauley's Island and all points in between, and haven't found an area of the beach we don't like. We've camped at state parks and private campgrounds, stayed at small mom and pop hotels and luxury condos. Every visit has been a little slice of heaven.

We've watched the area grow from a rather cozy resort area to a sprawling and seemingly endless stretch of All-You-Can-Eat seafood restaurants, beach shops, miniature golf courses, amusement parks, and high rise hotels, not to mention enough country music shows to make Branson and Nashville envious. Naturally there is shopping galore.

But the main attraction, for us, is the ocean. Fresh local seafood is a close second. I love the ocean and could sit and watch it all day long. That is, I could sit and watch it all day if I didn't enjoy getting in it so much. The thing I like best about Myrtle Beach is the fact that the ocean has waves. Great big waves that allow one to raise body surfing to a high art.

The other people here can have the golf courses, of which there must be a hundred. They can shop 'til they drop at Barefoot

Landing and Broadway at the Beach and the factory outlets. They can ride the rides at the Pavilion and dance the shag or visit the Bowery where the band Alabama, country music legends, got their start. I'm going to sit on the beach and read a book and play in the ocean. All day. All week. I might come off the beach in time to drive up to Calabash to eat some fish and shrimp and scallops. If I feel real energetic I might throw the frisbee with my ten year old son, or build a sand castle with my seven year old daughter. I might even walk up the beach with my wife and teenaged daughter, if I won't embarrass them too much.

Hey! Being at the beach is a tough job, but somebody has to do it.

Having a wonderful time. Wish y'all were here!

Life on the Road a Mixed Blessing

I guess you can have too much of a good thing, after all. As much as I enjoy travelling, I got a bit more than I bargained for on this improbable trip through our country's Eastern corridor.

Somewhere on the East Coast—As you read this my family and I are loaded into our Dodge Caravan, headed up the east coast. Taking a tip from Dinah Shore, we are trying to see the USA, albeit not in a Chevrolet. We are in the early stages of an extended camping trip during which we hope to watch whales off the coast of Maine and eat fresh lobsters from roadside pots, view the majesty of Niagara Falls, fulfill a lifetime dream, of mine at least, by taking in the Baseball Hall of Fame at Cooperstown, New York, tour the Amish country of Pennsylvania and relive Picket's ill-fated charge on the battlefield at Gettysburg. We haven't decided what to do the second week.

My family has been fortunate enough to travel quite a bit together. Traveling with kids is a bit of a mixed blessing. Former Alabama governor George Wallace once defined a mixed blessing as having your daughter come home at three in the morning, carrying a Gideon Bible. So it is with traveling with kids—you have to be prepared to take the rough with the smooth.

I've learned certain truths by seeing the country with my family. For instance, there is an unwritten law that makes it impossible for any two children or a wife to be hungry or need to use the rest room at anywhere near the same time. I've also discovered that to obtain the number of minutes a child can sit in the back of a car without asking "are we there yet" one must take the square root of the child's age divided by the number of hours sleep the driver—always me in our case—was able to obtain the night before, and then subtract the number of days you've been on the road. As you can deduct, the number grows infinitely small, in direct proportion to the driver's PQ—patience quotient.

Nonetheless, the open road has quite an allure for me and I love visiting new places and creating new memories. My wife says that I never meet a stranger, and I love the people we encounter on our journeys. Also, so many memorable things happen when you travel. We are only two days into our current trip and my diary is getting quite full. For instance, we stopped at the South Carolina Welcome Center early one morning. We were too early, in fact. The place didn't open for another hour and a half.

As I approached the locked door of the office, before I realized that it was still closed, I noticed a rather threadbare gentleman get out of a fairly ragged old car. He shook the door of the building a couple of times then put his head against the glass and peered inside. Trying to be helpful, I told him that I believed they had not opened yet.

"I need a map," was his quite matter-of-fact reply.

"I believe they'll be open in an hour and a half," I countered, pointing at the sign on the door.

"Guess I'll wait," he responded. "They want a durned fortune for a map in a fillin' station these days."

I used the facilities, which weren't closed, and backed out of my parking space. My new friend was sitting patiently on a bench beside the door, waiting for 9 o'clock and a free map. I couldn't help but wonder which of us had our priorities in order.

I noticed two other trends during our first day on the road. For one thing, Conyers is not anonymous anymore. I try to talk to everyone I meet. Whenever you get in a conversation with a new friend—remember, I never meet a stranger—one of the first and safest questions is, "Where are you from?" I never say Atlanta. I always, in fact, say Porterdale, if my wife, Lisa, isn't in earshot. When she is, she makes me admit that we live in Conyers. Everyone has heard of Conyers, Georgia these days. The name seems to be burned into the collective minds of the nation.

The second thing I've learned is that it doesn't take long to leave home. On our very first evening we ate at a restaurant somewhere along I-95. I'm not sure of the town. I'm not even real certain of the state. It could have been Virginia or Maryland or Delaware. But I'm certain that they didn't serve sweet tea, and they thought that one cube of ice was enough for a whole glass. The waitress at the place we ate breakfast the next morning didn't even bother replying when I asked if they served grits. She just looked at me like I had two heads and walked away.

I'm not worried about starving while we're gone, however. We're cooking most of our own food and I smuggled a couple of cans of Spam into the food box. I'll survive, unless Lisa finds the Spam.

Keep watching this space to find out what life is really like above the Mason-Dixon Line.

Even in Maine—Georgia is On My Mind

For most of my life I had dreamed of vacationing along the rugged coast of Maine. It took nearly fifty years, but I finally made it. It was everything I had imagined, and more. The view from Cadillac Mountain is truly awe inspiring, but I don't think I'd choose it over my daily red clay sunrise.

Bar Harbor, ME—I'm not exactly sure how far it is from Conyers to Maine, but however far it normally is, it's twice that when you drive here with a wife and three kids. No matter how great the distance, it's well worth the trip.

I don't want to sound like I'm auditioning for one of those twelve dollar travel guides, but the only word that can adequately describe the rugged beauty of Maine's coast is spectacular. For over a hundred miles steep cliffs plunge downward toward rocky beaches that are washed with the deep blue water of the north Atlantic—the cold north Atlantic. I tried to go swimming at one of the few sandy beaches on Mt. Dessert Island, which is where Bar Harbor is located. I lasted about thirty-five seconds in water up to my ankles. My feet turned blue and shrunk from a ten-and-a-half to a seven. I was, however, smart enough to get out of the water, which is more than I can say for some Yankee Americans who were swimming around in the frigid bay like they were at Daytona Beach on the 4th of July.

When my family and I pulled into Bar Harbor I thought we were up north. It certainly looked that way on my map. Turns out we are actually "down east," according to Maine residents who are here on vacation. Of course, according to the folks who have driven up from Boston for the weekend, we are not in Bar Harbor at all. We are in "Bah Hahbah." These are the same people, by the way, who "pahk" their "cahs" in the "gahrahge." And they think I talk funny.

One thing they have here in Maine is the lobster pound. All along the highways there are little roadside stands serving lobsters. Pick out the ones you want and they drop 'em in boiling seawater for 20 minutes, then you're good to go. They sell lobsters up here like we sell boiled peanuts at home, and for about the same price. It pains mc to admit it, but they are one up on us. Lobsters are way better than boiled peanuts.

The only thing more plentiful than lobsters in Bar Harbor are rude New Yorkers. I ran into a couple at a lobster pound. I saw them eyeballing my license plate as they pulled up behind me and got out of their shiny new Lincoln Continental. Now understand, these lobster pounds are casual. I was overdressed in my T-shirt and shorts. I mean at these places—no shirt, no shoes—no problem. These guys were in white oxford button-down shirts with power ties. They looked as out of place as a Baptist deacon at a liquor store.

Taking one more look at my car tag they ambled up behind me in line, grinning like a couple of mules eating briars. In a mock Southern accent, taken directly from a bad TV movie, one of them said, "Well shut my mouth. I believe you all is from Georgia, isn't you?"

I looked around rather pointedly and responded, "Well, there's only one of me here, but yes, I'm from Georgia."

Mr. Intelligent then asked, "Does you all have lobsters down in Georgia?"

At that moment my twenty-three years in the classroom served me well. I fixed him with my best teacher stare and after a long pause replied, "No, we don't. But we do have enough manners not to make fun of visitors."

The guy reacted like a sixth grader caught on the eighth grade hall with bubble gum and a water pistol. He fell all over himself apologizing. Trying to make amends, he asked me what I did "down in Georgia."

I told him I was Lieutenant Governor. I didn't think Mr. Taylor would mind and think of the story the guy had to tell his wife when he got home.

One of the best things we did here, other than eat lobsters and torment New Yorkers, was to go whale watching. We got on a boat and went thirty miles out to sea. Magnificent creatures, eighty feet long, swam alongside and under our vessel. We saw them leap into the air and dive majestically, their tails slowly disappearing beneath the surface. It was truly an awesome experience.

I was standing along the railing of the boat when I felt a strong hand on my shoulder and someone shouted into my ear, "How 'Bout Them Dawgs!" I quickly remembered that I was wearing a UGA baseball cap, turned backward against the wind. A fellow member of the Bulldog nation had found me on a boat, thirty miles off the coast of Maine.

Turns out that I was talking to a doctor from Columbus who had sat in the same seat in Sanford Stadium for the past thirty-eight years. Talk quickly turned to football and the good doctor reminded me that the beginning of fall practice was only two weeks away. I suddenly felt an urgent need to get off that boat and head south. Maine is a beautiful state, but it ain't where I want to be during football season.

Y'all watch for us. The "Lieutenant Governor" will be home soon.

3

There's No Place Like Home . . . where dull moments never exist

There's No Place Like Home . . .
where dull moments never exist

The person who coined the phrase, "There's never a dull moment," must have had a home very much like ours. Imagine a family composed of two parents with two or three jobs each, three children, all three years apart and all involved in a wide array of school, church, and social activities, add an assortment of pets and friends, plus a dash or two of misadventure and you'll get a pretty accurate picture of the Huckaby household.

Sometimes life seems to revolve around soccer and basketball, other times around the crises of the week, and, at still other times, school activities and the social calendar. One thing is crystal clear--it always does revolve, and at a dizzying pace.

If you will indulge me, I'll introduce my family. My wife, Lisa Potts Huckaby, is a lifetime resident of Rockdale County. A graduate of Valdosta State College, now University, she worked 14 years as an obstetrics nurse before going back to school to become a nurse-midwife. She is my rudder and keeps me sailing a semi-straight course.

Our first child, Jamie Leigh, was born in 1985. She looks exactly like her mother and is intelligent and articulate. She sings and dances and spends hours on the internet.

Our son, Jackson Lee, was born in 1989. He is a typical boy and likes sports and outdoor activities and avoids baths like the plague.

Our baby, Jenna Elizabeth, is the wild one of the bunch. She came along in 1992 and seems determined to make us old before our time.

This chapter deals with our desperate attempts to be a typical family, whatever that may be.

Is Atlanta Night Life
Gone With the Wind?

I learned my lesson. Lisa and I have gone back to spending our Friday nights in front of the fireplace with our glasses of prune juice and a couple of good books.

It seemed like a good idea when I planned it. An evening in Atlanta with my lovely wife, Lisa. It had been a long time since we'd enjoyed a night out on the town. With all our kids and all our jobs, a big night for us is pizza in front of the fireplace and a rented movie not produced by Disney.

I'd planned this night for months. *Miss Saigon* was coming to the Civic Center. We'd seen it once, but from the balcony, a hundred thousand miles from the stage—or so it had seemed. This time, the very day tickets went on sale I started calling the box office. I wore out the speed dial on three phones, but finally got through and secured choice seats. They weren't an arm and a leg, either. They were an arm and two legs, but you only live once. Right?

As our big night approached I could hardly wait. Lisa would wear a black velvet skirt with sequins. We'd have an intimate candle lit dinner. It would be like the old days. We'd sit with our faces close together—laughing, talking, enjoying a romantic Italian dinner. Then we'd take a stroll in the night air, enjoy the play, and maybe even go to an out of way bistro afterward for coffee and something sweet. The night would be ours and pure magic.

She wore denim. But, of course, she looks lovely in denim. The first seven restaurants we tried in Buckhead had three hour waits. The eighth seated us right away. Our server had long purple hair, three earrings in each ear and wore too much makeup. He was a nice enough guy, but he wore too much makeup. We did sit with our faces close together. We had to. Punk rock music was blaring at decibels that would rival a shuttle lift-off.

The menu wasn't exactly Italian, but we did recognize a couple of entrees. We placed our orders and waited patiently, hoping for the best and wishing we had an interpreter for the music. After thirty minutes, our server, who had now dyed his hair orange and added a fourth earring, informed us that the chef had taken ill and our meals would be delayed indefinitely. We opted for a different restaurant. The service at *The Varsity* wasn't bad, for a Friday night. The grease from the onion rings hardly stained Lisa's jeans at all.

After dinner we still had time to kill and decided to visit *Underground Atlanta* for a nostalgic trip back in time. *Underground* was a happening place in Atlanta back in the '70s. Blind Willie, the Ruby Red Warehouse Band, and a dozen other entertainers kept the streets rocking until the wee hours and the place was alive with college students, suburbanites out on the town, and conventioneers from Cleveland and Des Moines and hundreds of other cities. Last Friday night *Underground Atlanta* was a perfect example of what Atlanta must have been the day after Sherman left. After ten minutes, spent nervously strolling up and down the practically deserted streets, we decided to head for the Civic Center while we were still able.

The Atlanta Civic Center. There's another Atlanta icon left over from the days when the Regency Hyatt's twenty-two stories towered above the city. It was something to behold in its day, but is now a little like a once glamorous movie star trying to look her best in a thirty year old gown that no longer fits. It's tattered and frayed around the edges and the once luxurious seats are a little rickety and threadbare. But our location was excellent! We took our places and eagerly awaited the first act of *Miss Saigon*.

Just before curtain time a couple came in and filled the seats in front of us, the only vacant seats in our section of the auditorium. She was a pleasant looking lady with a hairdo large enough to make an Alabama beauty queen jealous. He was six-six with the widest head I've ever seen on a human being. And they were so in love! They sat with their heads together all night long.

The play sounded great. If I could have seen any of it, I'm sure I would have thought the acting superb as well. In case you're wondering, we skipped the dessert and coffee. Next Friday night we'll be back to double pepperoni and extra cheese. I hope all the copies of *Old Yeller* aren't checked out.

Child's Play Can Bring Unexpected Joy

Just in case you wonder--Jackson took a season off from soccer to give baseball a try. He played the outfield and got to chase two balls all season. He is now solidly back in the soccer fold. Jamie had a wonderful dance experience and has given up her dream of becoming a pediatrician to pursue a career as a Radio City Music Hall Rockette.

As a father of three, who knew everything there was to know about parenting, right up until my first child was born, I share this advice. Don't ever boast about what your children will never do, because as sure as grits is groceries—they are certain to someday do whatever it is that you say they won't.

Case in point. Soccer. There was a time when I looked upon the sport of soccer with total disdain. Those of my generation considered it a communist sport. We thought those who played it were renegades whose mothers probably dressed them funny. No way a child of mine would ever get near a soccer ball, much less play on an organized team.

I have a confession about soccer. The first soccer game I ever saw, I was the coach. I didn't know a cross from a corner kick, but the principal at Clarkston High School needed someone to coach the girls' varsity soccer team and I needed the money. We played the first half of our first game with twelve players on the field. My players tried to tell me I was in err, but I shushed them. At halftime the boys' coach came down and pointed out my mistake. How was I to know the goalkeeper counted as a player? She didn't even have the same color jersey as the rest of the team.

That first season was a bit rocky. The officials kept putting colorful cards in front of my face. They insisted that I shouldn't yell at them like I did in football and basketball. I didn't think that a game in which a coach couldn't yell at a referee was much of a game. My first soccer team won 8 games, lost none, and tied 2, in spite of me. I coached varsity soccer for six years and, having learned to appreciate the game, was thrilled when my son wanted to play. Now my family joins the rest of Conyers at the RYSA fields every Saturday. The first time my son scored a goal I couldn't have been more proud if he had hit a grand slam in the seventh game of the World Series. So much for my kid never playing soccer.

Case in point number two. Dance Team. From the time my daughter was born I insisted she would never be a cheerleader or dancer or drill teamer or baton twirler or anything else than dressed up in shiny costumes and performed on the sidelines. I coached girls' basketball forever, and while I have never had anything against cheerleaders or dancers or the like—I was determined that my child would never be one. Like every other girls' coach, I secretly dreamed she would become an All-State player, average thirty points a game, and win at least one State Championship for her old man.

About a month ago, my seventh grade daughter, who has never shown an interest in playing basketball, broke the news to me that she was trying out for the school dance team. My worst nightmare was becoming a reality!

Edwards Middle School has an outstanding dance team. They perform at all of our school's football and basketball games and their coach, Donna McCullough, keeps her charges in line better than the toughest drill sergeant. She makes them work hard and keeps them out of trouble. Her program is such a success that over a hundred girls try out each spring for the 18 spots available. Dance team is a big deal, but I wasn't sure it was the right big deal for my daughter.

First I was afraid she'd make the dance team and then I was afraid she wouldn't. For weeks I went to sleep each night with the sound of music seeping through the walls and the floor jarring above me as my once little girl worked on learning intricate dance steps far into the night. During the week of tryouts the tension in our house was thick enough to cut. The most offhanded remark caused anxious eyes to fill with tears. By Friday, the actual day the squad would be selected, the entire family's nerves were on edge.

Tryouts were a three hour ordeal after school. Each girl had to dance a routine in front of a panel of judges. Some were asked to come back and dance a second time. Then everyone was sent home to wait for the phone to ring. A call from Mrs. McCullough meant that you had earned a spot on the squad and thus a chance to attend summer camp, purchase an expensive uniform and accessories, and practice ten hours a week throughout the rest of this millennium and well into the next. And I'd never seen my daughter work so hard or want something so badly in her life.

Thirty minutes after arriving home from tryouts—an eternity in middle school years—the phone rang. At least it tried to. My daughter picked it up before the ring actually escaped. I heard the scream, signifying that she had indeed made the squad. Immediately the tears started flowing. Tears of joy and thanksgiving. And when I went in to give Jamie a congratulatory hug, I noticed that her eyes were a little misty, too.

Huckaby Menagerie Gets a New Edition

*As this book went to press, Ally McCat had completely
taken over our house and Miss Kitty, aka Shortlife, seems
destined to outlive me.*

There is a new baby in the Huckaby family. No, not a
human baby. There hasn't been an especially bright star in the
east, has there?

Our new addition is a four-legged creature. We have a
baby kitten.

That may not seem so remarkable, but you must under-
stand--I am not an animal person. At all. In the least. I never had
pets as a child and have always been uncomfortable around cats
and scared to death of dogs. I didn't even like going to the zoo as
a child, to see Willie B. When my wife, Lisa, and I got married, I
was adamant that there would be no pets in our house. I should
have made her sign a prenuptial agreement to that effect.

My no-pet rule lasted longer than I thought it would, actually. About seven years into our marriage, Lisa came home from
work with a kitten. I insisted that she take it back where it came
from. She asked me how I felt about separate bedrooms. I decided having a kitten wouldn't be so bad. I was wrong.

Having a kitten was worse than having a baby. There was
no way to control it. It made noise all night and was always un-
derfoot. If it wasn't, then evidence of it was. I nicknamed our
kitten Shortlife, because that's what I predicted it would have
around our house. I threatened to give it away and tried to get my
friend, David Hays, to put it in a bag and toss it in the river.

When we'd had Shortlife about three weeks we were getting ready to go away for a weekend. Shortlife, or Miss Kitty, as
the rest of the family called her, decided to pick that morning to
climb her first tree--a rather tall oak beside our back deck. My
family decided that we couldn't go out of town and leave the kitten in the tree, and no amount of coaxing would get her to come

down, nor would saucers of milk or offerings of cat food. I tried to convince Lisa and the kids that the cat would come down on her own. After all, I've never seen a cat skeleton in a tree.

It was no use. I had to climb the oak tree and "rescue" the cat. Of course, every time I got close to her she would climb higher. There I was, risking life and limb, 40 feet high in an oak tree, trying to get my hands on a cat that didn't want to come out of the tree in the first place. When I finally caught her, she showed her appreciation by scratching my arms to pieces.

That was 10 years ago. Shortlife is still with us, and we have reached an understanding. Whenever she wants in, I let her in. Whenever she wants out, I let her out. I feed her when she's hungry and give her water when she's thirsty. Otherwise I leave her alone, and she does as she pleases. She sleeps wherever and whenever she chooses. I should have such a life.

In addition to Shortlife, we have a pen full of rabbits with names like Georgia and Dixie and Savannah. They belong to my daughter, Jamie. She takes care of the rabbits. I don't bother them, and they don't bother me. At least they have nice Southern names. Who says children can't be brainwashed.

We had a dog for a while. His name was Midnight. He was a big, playful Lab. Purebred. He was as black as midnight, thus the name. Honesty compels me to admit that I came to love Midnight. I've never known such a loving creature as that dog. We were blessed with his presence on our farm for two years and saw him grow from a tiny puppy to a giant of an animal. He roamed the fields and pastures and swam in the lake. Occasionally he went visiting around the neighborhood, but the good people at the pound always called us to come and get him—for a fee. Midnight was like folks. He disappeared on Thanksgiving weekend two years ago, along with eight other large purebred dogs from our neighborhood. What a coincidence. We may get another dog when we get over the heartbreak of losing Midnight. Another 10 or 20 years might do it.

But now we have a baby kitten. A tiny, scrawny, black little thing with white boots and inquisitive eyes. My wife and daughter conspired against me. They told me they were going to the store to get something for me and came home with a new pet. They didn't lie. They did go to the store, to buy food for me to feed the kitten.

What's a guy to do? Miss Kitty, aka Shortlife, doesn't seem to mind, so why should I? The new kitten's name is Ally, after Ally McBeal. Ally Cat. Cute.

I tell you one thing, though. I'm too old and fat to climb trees anymore. If Ally Cat climbs up in the oak tree, she's on her own.

Yeah, right. I've said that before.

It could be worse. None of my kids have mentioned wanting a pet boa constrictor. Not yet, anyway. I'll keep you posted.

Time Flies When You're Having Fun

Jamie Leigh Huckaby arrived, finally, on October 3, 1985, weighing in at 10 pounds and 3 ounces. The first child only comes once, and I am exceedingly thankful for that.

Y'all will have to excuse me if I act a bit strange for the next few weeks. I had a very traumatic experience last weekend and it has really effected me. I went to bed last Saturday feeling perfectly normal. When I awakened last Sunday, October 3, I realized that at around 12:30 that afternoon my daughter, Jamie Leigh Huckaby, would be 14 years old.

14. A one and a four. A ten and four ones. Two times seven. Almost a decade and a half. 365 days away from being eligible to drive a car, for goodness sake. How in the world could that possibly be?

It was just last week that my wife, Lisa, told me we were expecting our first child. I was a young guy with a much flatter stomach, a lot of hair on my head and none on my face. I was thrilled to learn that I would be a father. I just assumed our first child would be a boy and began making all sorts of plans for his arrival.

Those of you who are parents remember all the activity that surrounds the announcement that a new addition to the family is on the way. The first thing we had to do was remodel our small ranch house. We had to make room for more stuff. We enlisted my father-in-law, who can build anything, to build a storage house at the back of our lot so we could move some of our stuff outside in order to make room for the new baby's stuff. Didn't help. We still needed more room and enclosed the garage. Raise you're hand if you've been there and done that.

About six or seven months into our pregnancy we had something called a sonogram done. I thought a sonogram had something to do with submarines, but they did it right there in the doctor's office. He assured us that our new baby would, indeed, be a boy. I believe my reaction to this news was very typical. I sent Lisa home to paint the nursery blue while I went shopping. I bought an electric train, a basketball, a football, two baseballs, a bat, a glove, an autographed poster of Mickey Mantle, a 1985 boxed set of Topps baseball cards and a pair of Converse All Stars. Got to make sure kids get off to a good start.

When I got home from my shopping spree, Lisa was eating a hot fudge sundae, with taco chips and salsa. She sent me back out—for Varsity onion rings. She told me to hurry because I had to come home and paint the nursery blue.

The last two months of the pregnancy were a flurry of activity. Lisa spent her time cross stitching neat things for the nursery wall, which by now was blue, with rocking horse wall paper. Most of her decorations had Jamison, the name we'd picked out for our son, sewn into them.

Our first baby did not come on time. Do they ever? We looked for our new arrival throughout the month of September.

This was back in the old days, when only doctors and drug dealers were allowed to carry things like beepers and cell phones, so I had to stay near a phone at all times. This created a huge dilemma when Georgia played Alabama in the football season opener.

Lisa was very understanding about my desire to see the game. She gave me a choice. I could go to the game, or I could continue to live. David Hays, who had been best man at our wedding three years earlier, stayed home and watched with me on television. Talk about a friend! We were both miffed when we didn't have to dash to the hospital during halftime. We were more miffed when Alabama won the game.

After a month of waiting and several false alarms, we checked into the hospital to have labor induced. I wasn't sure what that meant. I found out that it meant I got to sit in a chair and watch television for 26 hours while Lisa breathed funny, sweated, and screamed a lot. After more than a day of all that, some nurse came in and gave me a yellow paper gown and a white mask and made me scrub my hands with yucky red stuff. They wheeled Lisa into the operating room and I got to watch them deliver our first child by Caesarean section. I did fine, too. I didn't faint or barf—until later.

The baby was big, and wrinkled, and messy, and to everyone's surprise—a girl!

I knew we should have had that test done in a submarine.

As soon as I knew everyone was OK, I ran out and bought a pink shirt for myself, some pink roses for my wife, and a Mary Lou Retton outfit for my daughter.

We left the nursery blue, but I don't think it had a bad affect on Jamie. She has been the joy of my life and has turned into a very typical teenaged girl. We may have to have the telephone surgically removed from her ear, but other that that, she's pretty much a keeper.

If the next 14 years fly by as quickly as the last 14, next week's column will be about my grandchildren—graduating from high school.

'For Better or For Worse'—She Wasn't Just Funnin'

I'm sure Lisa Carol Potts didn't know what she was in for when she traded her middle name for my last name. We've had lots of ups and downs, beginning with our very un-usual honeymoon. I keep telling her, however, to be patient, because God isn't quite finished with me. I'm sure she wishes He would hurry.

Today is my anniversary. Well, it's not just mine. I share it with my wife, Lisa. On this very day, also a Saturday, seventeen years ago, I stood at the alter at Rockdale Baptist Church, nervously waiting for my bride to walk down the aisle and join me. The cotton farmer who was serving as my best man gave me two-to-one odds that she would be a no show. If she had known what was in store for her, she might have made a prophet of him.

Our marriage went very smoothly for the first ninety minutes. Then the honeymoon started. We had, I guess you could say, a Charles Dickens honeymoon. "It was the best of times, it was the worst of times."

We decided to honeymoon in New Orleans, because Scarlett and Rhett had. We departed the church at about 9 PM in our midnight blue Chevrolet Monte Carlo. I wanted to take the T-tops off. Lisa, then, as now, the pragmatic partner in our marriage, pointed out that the temperature was in the thirties. I left them on and we drove west.

Our first stop was at a 7-11 in Auburn, Alabama. Lisa had contracted a cold during the week leading up to our wedding and sent me in to buy Tylenol. The foreign guy behind the counter looked out at our car with "Just Married" emblazoned on the back windshield, looked down at the Tylenol on the counter, and sadly shook his head.

"Headache, already," he said with a thick accent. "Not a good thing."

I could "Amen" that.

Round about midnight we reached our destination for the evening—Montgomery, Alabama. It ain't exactly Maui, but it suited us. We checked into the nicest hotel in town, the Holiday Inn. When the guy at the front desk found out we were on our honeymoon, he gave us the George Wallace suite, complete with complimentary cigars. Lisa wouldn't smoke hers.

We checked in and Lisa went into the powder room to do whatever brides do in the powder room on their wedding night. I did what men do while brides are in the powder room—I turned on the television and found a football game.

A commercial came on. Bear Bryant, Alabama's legendary football coach, was sitting beside a table, staring at an old black and white photo. A phone was on the table beside him. Bear looked into the camera and mumbled, "Have you called your mama lately?" He paused for a moment and then added, "I sure wish I could call mine."

When Lisa came out of the powder room I had a heck of a time explaining why I was on the phone with my mother.

New Orleans was wonderful. For several days we enjoyed breakfast on our balcony, strolled through the French Quarter, took in the night clubs and fancy restaurants, rode a riverboat on the Mississippi River, and did all the other things honeymooners do. (Lisa's headache cleared up. Unfortunately, they still return intermittently.)

On the fourth night of our stay in the "City that C.A.R.E. forgot" I started getting a stomach ache. I assumed it had something to do with the 48 raw oysters I had consumed at the Acme Oyster Bar on Bourbon Street that afternoon. We tried to go about our business, but I spent the entire night in pain. The next morning, while Lisa toured the Louisiana Superdome, I toured the Superdome bathrooms. After our visit to the Dome, we took in the horse races. I was literally prostrate with pain by now, but it was Lisa's first trip to the track and she was winning. She told me to hurt in silence so she could concentrate on her race card.

To make a long story short, five o'clock found my 21 year old bride of five days weaving her way in and out of rush hour traffic, trying to find a hospital so that she could avoid becoming a 21 year old widow. She finally made it to the emergency room of the Hotel Dieu, which was not a hotel at all, but a very fine hospital.

The doctors there said that I had a bowel obstruction and needed immediate surgery. I refused. It was the day before Christmas Eve and I wasn't spending our first Christmas in a New Orleans hospital.

Lisa lied to the hospital staff and told them she was a registered nurse. It was just a little lie. She was a nursing student, six months away from graduation. The doctors shot me full of morphine, bumped two poor souls off a flight to Atlanta, and sent us home.

Within hours of landing in Atlanta I had been operated on by Rockdale's finest. We spent the rest of our honeymoon, Christmas, and New Years in the hospital. Lisa slept on a cot at the foot of the bed. I knew then that I had a keeper.

And indeed I do. For seventeen years I've been way more trouble than I'm worth, but my bride has always stayed beside me, just like she did on our ill fated honeymoon. When she said, "For better or for worse," she meant it, and I thank God for that. I couldn't exist without her.

Thanks, my love, and Happy Anniversary.

1999—It's Been a Very Good Year

As time continues to fly by, the years seem to get shorter and shorter. Pretty soon, January will be followed by December and everything else will simply run together. It's good to pause for reflection. 1999 was in some ways the best of times, but in other ways, well . . .

They tell me there are three days left in the Millennium. I'm not sure I believe that. After all, in two thousand years I bet somebody lost track of a day or two here and there. Don't look for a recap of the millennium here. The most talented writers couldn't recount all the great events of a thousand years in the space I'm allocated, so I won't even try.

Are we really leaving the 20th Century behind at midnight on Friday? Was the first year of this century 1900 or 1901? Technically, aren't we about a year away from the 21st century? I know you can't tell it by all the lists the magazines and television shows are coming out with. I don't agree with most of them.

Until that discrepancy is cleared up, I'm not writing an end of the century column, either. I also don't feel compelled to say good-bye to the '90s, even though I'm pretty sure we counted those days right. It's hard for me to get excited about a decade during most of which Bill Clinton was President.

Still, it doesn't seem right to end my first year as a columnist without some sort of nostalgic look back, so if you'll bear with me, I'll make note of some of my personal highlights from 1999, which was a pretty good year for the Huckaby clan.

We were blessed to be able to do a lot of traveling this year, which is one of my passions. We visited over twenty states, spent close to fifty days on the road, and made memories that will last a lifetime—and beyond. Some were as simple as relaxing under the stars in a hot tub on a mountain side overlooking Gatlinburg. That won't make my wife's list. She doesn't think outdoor hot tubs and twenty degree temperatures go together, but the other three kids in our family and I thought it was great.

I'll also never forget the thrill of being able to teach forty eighth grade history students about the Battle of Lexington and Concord by staging a giant snowball fight on the Lexington Village Green. I'll treasure the memory of jumping on a bike and, along with my kids, riding around Jekyll Island every evening "chasing the sundown." If you haven't seen the sun set over the Marshes of Glynn County in Coastal Georgia, you've missed some of God's most magnificent handiwork.

We were fortunate enough this year to spend a week on one of South Carolina's beaches. I could ride the waves of the Atlantic Ocean all day, everyday, without becoming bored, and there are enough great seafood restaurants along the Grand Strand to visit a different one every night for a year.

We spent one of the longest days of my life driving our van from Fayetteville, NC to Portsmouth, NH. I don't recommend it, but if were necessary in order to see the majesty of the Maine Coast, eat fresh lobster from roadside stands, and watch whales dive out of the blue north Atlantic and slowly submerge, waving their great tails at our boat as they disappeared beneath the surface, I'd do it again tomorrow.

I took my ten year old boy to the Baseball Hall of Fame in Cooperstown, NY, and I don't care what the women in the crowd thought about the tears in my eyes as I reached up and touched the plaques of legends like Ty Cobb, Lou Gehrig, and Mickey Mantle. The thousands of men in the place all understood.

We rode the Maid of the Mist right up to the the very edge of Niagara Falls and saw the spectacular beauty of the Horseshoe Falls from the Canadian side. One night later we discovered that John Denver was right when he claimed that West Virginia was almost heaven. We also had the opportunity to enjoy the beauty of our own state, from the pristine Blue Ridge Mountains to the cobblestone streets of Savannah.

As great as our experiences on the road were, my best memories during 1999 didn't involve traveling. They involved people. I have had the opportunity to enjoy working with some of the best kids and most dedicated educators in the world, at Edwards Middle School and Heritage High School. As always, I've learned much more than those I have tried to teach.

I've also had the opportunity to read my very own column in this newspaper twice a week, which is truly a dream come true and I've had the opportunity to meet hundreds of wonderful people and make many new friends. Even the sadness of having to say good-bye to one of the dearest people in my life was tempered by the graciousness of friends and family.

I don't think 2000 can top 1999 for me. 1999 was truly a great year, but no matter what that little bug does Friday at midnight, I think my resolution for the new year, the new decade, the new century, and the new millennium, will be to continue to see as much of the world as I can, and to treat other people as well as they have treated me this year.

Happy New Year.

Friday Nights are Frightful When Spent in the ER

Jackson Lee Huckaby is a skinny little boy who needs to take a few assatall pills, which are special pills for those people who have no ass a'tal. As often as he visits the Emergency Room, pretty soon he'll qualify for a frequent faller discount.

OK. In the words of the immortal Larry Munson, "Get the picture." It was last Friday afternoon. It wasn't the thirteenth, but it should have been. Fridays, as you know, are sacred. Last Friday was particularly precious because my basketball team had been eliminated from the region tournament the previous Tuesday and for the first time in three months I was looking forward to having a Friday evening off.

All day long I allowed myself to dream of a nice quiet evening, relaxing in front of the television. I was certain that my wife, Lisa, would be waiting for me when I got home with my slippers and a light snack to tide me over until the delicious dinner she would prepare was ready. For the past twelve Fridays our evening meal had been super sized and served with fries. I couldn't wait to get home.

It was not to be.

I knew something was amiss when I pulled into the driveway and my son, Jackson, didn't run out to greet me, demanding that we feed the cows, play basketball, rent a movie, and all the other things ten year old boys want to do when their daddies come home. Instead, I found Jackson sitting in the easy chair that I had been coveting. There was a frown on his face, tears in his eyes, and an icebag on his arm. I knew immediately that it was broken.

It was the third time Jackson has broken his arm. At least this time he had done it at school so I wouldn't get accused of child abuse like I had the other two times. Jackson, you see, is skinny. He's a skin-and-bones kind of kid who has to dance around in the shower to get wet. He doesn't have a lot of padding on his bones and when he falls on them, they break.

Jackson suffered his first broken arm one Thanksgiving. We had seen the movie "Aladdin" the day before. Jackson had been impressed with the flying carpet and was certain that if he sat on a rug on his top bunk and had his sister, Jamie, push him off, he would fly, too.

He was only four.

The mishap occurred right in the middle of the Auburn-Alabama game. The score was tied and I had Bama and the points. Lisa was at work at the hospital and I called her and told her to meet me in the ER when the game was over. She was completely unreasonable and made me come right then. I couldn't even wait until half time.

Jackson's second fracture came a couple of years later. Of course it happened, again, while Lisa was at work and I was watching the kids. This one was the baby sitter's fault. She had let them watch "Live Atlanta Wrestling" the previous night while Lisa and I were at prayer meeting. This time his baby sister, Jenna, put him in an airplane spin and threw him off the bed. (I told you Jackson's skinny.) His wrist didn't have a chance. When he hit the floor it snapped like a green twig.

They really gave me the third degree at the Emergency Room. They were convinced I was manhandling my son. They sat me in a straight chair and aimed a flashlight in my face for hours, but I never wavered from my story. Luckily the kids told the same one.

As soon as I looked at my boy's arm last Friday I knew there would be no quiet evening at home. We were headed to the emergency room. If you've ever been to an emergency room—any emergency room—on a Friday night, you know they are anything but relaxing.

One Friday evening, while I was living in exile in south Georgia, I began having sharp pains, from indigestion, as it turned out. At the time I was certain it was a heart attack. My friend had to carry me to the ER of a local hospital. What an experience! Death would have been preferable.

We were met at the entrance by a ward clerk that I'm sure served in Hitler's Gestapo. She left no stone unturned in her mission to discover my entire medical history, all the way back to conception, and before. She got particularly upset when she couldn't force me to admit that I knew what had killed my paternal great-grandfather who died twenty-seven years before I was born.

Even worse than the ward clerk was the head nurse, Freida Von Armtwister, who made certain that I didn't see anyone who could do me any good until she had verified that my insurance company's assets were greater than the gross national product. She also made my friend verify his coverage, just to be on the safe side and made us sign oaths of allegiance to the United States and swear that neither we nor any of our ancestors had ever plotted to overthrow the government. Confederate veterans didn't count. By the time I saw a doctor, I didn't hurt anymore.

Luckily, we didn't have quite that type of ordeal last Friday. In fact, the service was relatively speedy. We were in and out in under four hours.

For the record, the cast is blue and stays on for six weeks. I don't know what Jackson saw on television last Thursday night. He says he fell down on his own, but his cousin insists he was pushed—by a girl.

I told you, he's skinny.

Birthday Outing
Helps Span Generation Gap

More evidence that the more things change the more they stay the same. And by the way, after a slow start, the Globetrotters won the game.

My boy, Jackson Lee Huckaby, has a birthday today. He turns 11, which is a shame in a way because ten year old boys are just about dead solid perfect and 11 year old boys turn into middle schoolers. Ugh!

We got Jackson the same day we got a new bull, Curly. Curly was a lot less trouble, but Jackson has been a lot more fun.

I wanted to do something special for Jackson's birthday so I told him he could invite four of his buddies to go to Atlanta last Sunday to watch the Harlem Globetrotters play in the new Phillips Arena. They were all excited about the trip but they all asked the same question when invited. "Who are the Harlem Globetrotters?"

I couldn't believe my ears. Has society gotten so sophisticated that we are raising a generation of children who have never been exposed to the greatest collection of clown-athletes ever to don a pair of high cut sneakers? I told the kids they were a basketball team and let it go at that.

The group met at our house Sunday afternoon for the

obligatory pizza, cake, and ice cream. I drafted my buddy, Gary, to go with us to help with crowd control and we headed off to Atlanta around 2 PM. That was, perhaps, our first mistake of the day. There was another basketball game in town Sunday, the SEC Championship, and also an auto show at the World Congress Center. To say that parking was at a premium is an understatement. We had to pay for a parking space approximately what the British paid for Manhattan Island, but we finally found one. Gary and I hurried our covey of youngsters down the windblown street and into the arena. We found our seats just as the Globetrotter's mascot came out to warm up the crowd.

I thought the same thing you did. The Globetrotters got a mascot? I guess it's a sign of the times. The mascot was an acrobatic little creature with a giant globe for a head, thus the name "Globie." After a few minutes of his antics the visiting team was introduced. To our surprise, the Trotters weren't playing the Washington Generals. This day's opposition would be provided by a group of green clad giants known as the New York Nationals. They were introduced to a polite smattering of applause and then the house lights were dimmed and anticipation grew as we waited for the stars of the day to be introduced. My mind began to wander back in time and for a few moments I was ten again, too.

I remember my first introduction to basketball as played by the Harlem Globetrotters. We were spending a rainy Sunday at home and the phone rang. It was my cousin, Buck. He was all excited about this crazy group of guys who were playing basketball and told my daddy to turn on the television. He did, and there they were, in living black and white. It took us a while to figure out that they hadn't escaped from a local funny farm, but were, in fact, incredible showmen, not to mention pretty fair country ball players. I became an instant fan and looked forward to their annual appearance on television.

You remember the Globetrotters of those days, I'm sure. Meadowlark Lemon was the undisputed "Clown Prince of Basketball." He would play gags on the official, pull an assortment of trick balls out of a bag on the sideline and make hook shot after hook shot from half court.   Curly Neal was a teammate of Mead-owlark. He was the greatest dribbler in the history of the world. As we sat in the darkened arena, I resigned myself to the fact that the guys we were about to watch couldn't compare with the guys of my memory.

Finally the spotlights brightened and there they were, the year 2000 version of the Harlem Globetrotters, wearing the same baggy red and white striped shorts as their predecessors. *Sweet Georgia Brown* erupted from the speaker system as they formed their famous "Magic Circle" and started passing the ball behind their back, through their legs, and around their bodies at impossible angles and at a blinding rate of speed.

For the next two hours the boys in our charge were glued to their seats, mesmerized by the action on the floor. They never once asked to go to the restroom or to get snacks. In this age of high tech entertainment and short attention spans it was heart warming to know that the same tricks and stunts that brought me so much pleasure over the years could also entertain my son's generation. I think I had as much fun watching Jackson and his pals as I did the show on the floor. They smiled and giggled and laughed out loud throughout the performance.

The behind the back passes, between the leg dribbles, and slam dunks didn't captivate as they once did. They've become pretty common place. But the tricks and stunts and constant patter played just as well in 2000 as they did in 1960. It was still funny when a player teased the referee and everyone still ducked when a player tossed a "water bucket" full of confetti into the crowd. The reigning Clown Prince, Showtime Gaffney, wasn't Meadowlark Lemon. He lacked the great elastic face of the former and he missed all three of his half court hook shots, and there was no one who could dribble like Curly Neal, but it didn't matter. It was still a great show.

What a great day! Some things really do transcend generations. Thanks, Jackson, for showing your old man the time of his life. Happy Birthday.

4

Precious Memories . . . how they do linger

Precious Memories . . .
how they do linger

Some people are born into our lives. Just as blood is thicker than water, we accept these people for what they are and love them--warts and all. We laugh and cry with them. Sometimes we fuss and fight with them and sometimes we hurt with them, but we love them--whether because of or in spite of what they are--we love them instantaneously, because they are family.

Other people sort of ease their way into our lives and become a part of us gradually, over time, until we love them like family and can't really remember a time when they weren't a part of our lives.

Unfortunately, life is fleeting. We often don't appreciate the best moments of our lives until it's too late. As people come into our lives, they also go away--sometimes suddenly and unexpectedly.

Nothing is constant. Life, by its very nature, is all about change. Today's joy will be tomorrow's memories, but thank goodness for the memories. Where would we be without the memories?

They are indeed precious and, thankfully, they do linger.

Profile in True Courage

Becky Hutchins Digby loved life as much as any person I've ever known. Her's was filled with so much pain and suffering that it would have been easy for her to have become bitter. She never did. She taught everyone she touched something about living. Those of us who knew her and loved her continue to miss her, but we also are better people for having known her.

Today's my birthday. I was born on March 10, 1952. Truman was president. For you history impaired youngsters out there, that's Harry Truman, not the guy from last summer's movie. Last week was my friend's birthday. She was 45 on March 1. This column is about Becky.

When I was very young I read a book by President John F. Kennedy called *Profiles in Courage*. He told stories about people who had overcome various obstacles in life to achieve fame and fortune and great accomplishments. One of the people he wrote about was Mickey Mantle. I forget the rest. But I do know that all of the people in President Kennedy's book were yellow livered cowards compared to my friend Becky.

I first met Becky when I was in the ninth grade. Thanks to the luck of an alphabetical seating chart I became good friends with her brother, Jimmy. I met Becky when I visited their house to spend the night. I'll never forget being in their house for the first time. I was 14 and had never seen wall to wall carpeting or an upstairs or light switches on the wall.

Jimmy and I would remain great friends throughout high school and become roommates in college. I could write a book about our exploits. In fact, I already did. Becky wasn't in it. I swear. Becky started out being Jimmy's kid sister, but the two of us became close friends as time went by. She got me through two years of French in high school when I didn't know a parlez vous from a Frances. She played a piano better than . . . well, not being very cultured, I don't know who to say—but better than anyone I ever heard.

Becky had a disease called Lupus. I don't know much about Lupus, but it's one sorry and sinister illness. During the ice storm of '73, while we were both at UGA, Becky was fighting for her life at Piedmont Hospital. She was there for months. I don't remember all the particulars and they aren't important, but I do know that several highly educated doctors indicated that there was little hope for recovery. That wouldn't be the first time Becky would prove doctors wrong. She would leave Piedmont Hospital and return to school and graduate from college.

Becky was lucky, in many ways. She had a loving mother and brother and a saint for a father. For years she went through dialysis on an almost daily basis. She suffered through the agony and disappointment of two kidney transplants that failed. But here's where the courageous part comes in. Becky never let her illness get the best of her. Never. She absolutely refused to allow the dreaded disease to curtail her zest for living. She continued to live, every day of her life.

Twelve years ago I spent the longest week of my life in the intensive care waiting room at Crawford Long Hospital, waiting for my daddy to die. He finally did, on a Saturday. When I got home, totally despondent, I pushed the message button on my answering machine and there was Becky's always cheerful voice, telling me about the new kidney transplant she had gotten that seemed to be working. Just like Becky. She brought joy and happiness to the saddest day of my life.

About eight or nine years ago Becky played the piano at an anniversary party for my wife, Lisa, and me. She seemed happier than I had ever seen her. As I walked her to her car she shared a confidence. She was seeing someone and it was serious. A few months later she married Dan. Everyone who knew Becky rejoiced in their happiness.

I only saw Becky occasionally over the past few years. You know how things go. We get busy with our own lives. But every time I did run into her, she was the same Becky. Smiling, laughing, worrying about her big brother and never complaining about her numerous health complications. She never let her health shut down her life, or dim her positive outlook.

As I said, today's my birthday. I don't think there will be a celebration. My wife's not big into those kinds of things. But, boy, was there a celebration for Becky last Saturday! It was at the Baptist Church in Covington. Becky's friend, Bill Callaway, performed on the grand piano. He's the second best pianist I've ever heard. Marshall Edwards, one of the greatest preachers I've ever heard and one of Becky's truest friends, came to speak on her behalf. He was wonderful. Beyond eloquent. Hundreds were there to show how much they loved Becky. I just hope that before she passed away last week she somehow knew how much we all loved her, because I don't think I ever got around to telling her.

Her husband, Dan, hugged my neck as we were leaving the church. Southern men hug one another's necks at funerals. Through our tears he told me, "We lost a great American girl."

You got that right, Dan. You got that right.

Yes, Conyers, There Is a Santa Claus

Bernie Bourdon lived three months after this column first appeared. He was able to return home and spend time with the people he loved. He was fully aware of what faced him and did not fear death. Fittingly, his legacy is not in the way he died, however, but in the way he lived. And make no mistake, he did live!

I know it is almost Easter and not Christmas. Give me a little credit. Nonetheless, I'm writing about Santa Claus this week. You need to know about him. Trust me.

About a hundred years ago, in the *New York Sun*, Frances Church wrote a now famous response to a little girl named Virginia who had written the newspaper asking if there really were a Santa Claus. Church, of course, answered in the affirmative, but in the answer spoke of intangible qualities such as "love, generosity, and devotion." Church went on to say that just because no one had ever seen Santa Claus didn't mean he wasn't real.

I've seen Santa Claus. He is very, very real. He has lived and worked among us here in Rockdale County for the past thirteen years. He moved here, fittingly enough, on Christmas Eve in 1986. With his jolly smile, ample belly, snow white beard, and twinkling eyes, he looks just like the jolly elf Clement Moore described in his classic poem, *The Night Before Christmas*. He doesn't go by Kris Kringle or St. Nicholas or any of those other names though. To us, he is just Bernie. Bernie Bourdon.

Most of us know Bernie, but few know about him. Bernie was an executive for a telecommunications company in Canada for thirty-seven years. (That is close to the North Pole.) He retired to Florida to live the good life in a nine room house complete with swimming pool, country club membership and all the other amenities one earns through a lifetime of hard work and professional excellence. Three years into retirement Bernie's wife died of cancer and the lives of unknown thousands would change.

Bernie left the comfort of Clearwater to come to Conyers and the Monastery of the Holy Spirit. He was determined to devote himself to God's service. After spending 60 days with the other monks, his spiritual advisor in the order urged Bernie to devote himself to doing God's work among God's people. No one ever did more.

Bernie plays Santa Claus in dozens of places every Christmas. Those of us who know him best know he's not playing. Any money he ever gets for his appearances goes to his ministries. He never sets a fee. He always says the same thing when asked about compensation. "Anything you give me is more than I had before."

For the past twelve years Bernie has completely given himself to the people of our area. Sure, he has gladdened the hearts of countless children while bouncing them on his knee and inquiring about Christmas dreams and wishes. But this Santa Claus does so much more. He used his skills to begin a nonprofit organization called Techable. His company adapts computers and fits them with keyboards that can be used by those with physical challenges that make it impossible to use a standard machine. There is never a charge for the service. Techable also adapts toys so children with physically disabilities can know the joy of play. Who but Santa Claus would think of that?

Bernie also started a Meals on Wheels ministry twelve years ago and now over one hundred people a week in Conyers, Covington, and Lithonia depend on Bernie and his volunteers to bring them a warm meal and a warmer smile. But for the past few weeks, these people have been missing out. Bernie is in an Augusta Hospital, fighting for his life. One of those routine surgeries, the kind other people have, didn't go so well. I know Bernie very well. He would really covet your prayers. His very life may depend on your prayers. If you can't pray for Santa Claus, who can you pray for? I know he would want me to ask you for your prayers. He would also ask for prayers for his son Steven, who keeps lonely vigil at his father's bedside.

Bernie will also need money. As much as he'd want me to ask for your prayers, he'd hate for me to ask you for money, but he's given all of his away. He also doesn't get help from the government because he's not a citizen. Not a citizen. That's a laugh. I don't know how you can help financially, but Jessie Walker of the Conyers Kiwanis Club does. The number's listed.

Over a hundred years ago a writer for the *New York Sun* answered in the affirmative a letter from a little girl named Virginia who had written inquiring if there was, indeed, really a Santa Claus. The writer mentioned words like love, generousity, and devotion. The Sun was describing Bernie Bourdon without knowing it. The writer also mentioned that no had ever seen Santa Claus.

Well, I have. If you've met Bernie Bourdon, so have you. May God bless him.

Unexpected Treasure Found at Cooperstown

Will Rogers never met a man he didn't like. I never met a man that didn't like Jeff Autry. He was one of a kind. I loved him with all my heart and I miss him, hard, every single day of my life.

The highway sign read, "Cooperstown—Next Exit." I could hardly believe that after 40 years of hoping, wishing, dreaming, and scheming, I was within 15 miles of the Baseball Hall of Fame.

My love affair with baseball began at an early age. My bonds of affection with our National Pastime have been strained from time to time, but never broken. The Hall of Fame has been the epitome of everything baseball, at least in my mind, since I was six years old and my daddy bought me a book full of punch out baseball cards depicting all its members.

I looked at those pictures of Ruth, Gehrig, Cobb, and the others over and over, handling the flimsy pasteboard until the edges were rounded and dog eared. I memorized the statistics on back and am more familiar with the accomplishments of the big leaguers of a bygone era than I am with today's overpaid stars.

Like most boys of my generation, I lived baseball. Mantle and Mays and Koufax are as much a part of my childhood as skinned knees and the Mickey Mouse Club. I devoured every word written about the history of the game and its great players, and every book and article I read made Cooperstown seem like the Holy Grail. I could only dream of visiting there. For a boy growing up in Porterdale, it might as well have been on Mars as in upper state New York.

But there I was, less than 15 minutes from the front door. Like a child at Christmas I watched each mile roll off the odometer, thinking we'd never get there. My family thought I had taken complete leave of my senses. There is no description for how I felt as I finally handed my ticket to the red jacketed usher and walked through the turnstile into the Mecca of baseball.

It was everything I had envisioned, and more. Life size statues of Babe Ruth and Ted Williams greeted us in the museum lobby. The great hall itself was right before me with bronze plaques honoring all the legends. I went from one to another, becoming more excited with each discovery. Joe Dimaggio. Cy Young. Honus Wagner. Stan Musial. Yogi Berra. There wasn't one for Pete Rose.

For hours we explored the exhibits. The amount of memorabilia was overwhelming. Uniforms, bats, balls, gloves. I was in baseball heaven. Then I found a giant exhibit devoted completely to Babe Ruth. In awe I stood and gazed at the great man's uniform and spikes and glove and a world of other items. Then I spotted it. It was about the size of a silver dollar. Stump's Babe Ruth medallion!

Let me tell you about Stump. His real name was Jeff Autry, but everyone called him Stump because he resembled one. People also called him the "Sausage Man" because he made his living delivering his family's Holifield Farm sausage to area restaurants and grocery stores. Jeff Autry never met a stranger or had an enemy. Not a single one of either.

I met him when I coached his son, Greg. Greg was a really small kid when he first went out for my football team and I tried my best to run him off. Impossible. Since I couldn't make him quit, I made him my quarterback. He played football and basketball for me for four years. I have never coached a greater competitor.

Over the years that Greg was in my program, his family and I adopted one another. Who can say how those things happen? All I know is that for almost twenty years Jeff Autry was the greatest friend I ever had. We enjoyed life together. He was always there to pick me up when I was down or take me down a peg when I got too full of myself. He was friend, brother, and father rolled into one. Words can't describe how close we were.

Jeff was raised in an orphanage, the Jolly Home, which brings me to the Babe Ruth display in the Hall of Fame. Babe

Ruth, of course, was also an orphan. Jeff used to tell his wife, Margaret, and me about how Babe Ruth's widow would send silver medallions to the Jolly Home for the boys there to sell on the street corners of Atlanta. We always laughed at his story and pretended not to believe him. In fact, we teased him about his Babe Ruth medallions unmercifully. Of course he couldn't produce one.

Jeff—Stump—was taken from us, suddenly and unexpectedly, six years ago. He was stricken by a heart attack in the middle of the night, on Labor Day weekend. I never got to say goodbye and I've missed him hard every day since. A dozen times a day there has been something I wanted to share with him—a story, a joke, a dream for the future. The grief passes slowly, you know.

And there I was in the Baseball Hall of Fame and right there in the Babe Ruth exhibit was one of the medallions that Jeff Autry had sold, as a boy, on the streets of Atlanta. My wife and kids already thought I was crazy for the way I was reacting to my trip to Cooperstown. Now everyone else did, too, as I stood in front of the display case laughing hysterically while huge tears rolled down my cheeks.

Jeff, if the Rockdale Citizen is circulated in heaven, I saw your medallion. It was a thing of beauty—just like you were.

Did She Ever Know That She's My Hero?

My mama died in her sleep at 4 AM on December 15, 1999, four days after this column appeared. My prayer is that she died knowing how much she was loved.

It's been a tough week. My mama's sick. Not just a little sick; the kind of sick that you don't get better from. The kind of sick where the nieces and nephews come by the hospital and the children take turns sitting in a chair in the corner of the hospital room, pretending to try and sleep, while a flood of memories runs through the brain, like a cerebral version of the old television series—*This is Your Life*.

Hospital rooms have always been depressing to me. None more so than the one I sat in the other night. The white lights from the Christmas tree outside on the lawn were visible through the window, but somehow they didn't bring much cheer.

My mother has always been my hero. What's that old song? Is it something about the wind beneath my wings? She has certainly been mine. No one has ever loved two children more than my mother has loved my sister and me. Any shortcomings we have are not her fault. The only shortcoming she might have had as a mother was loving us so much that she overindulged her children on rare occasions.

It's amazing how such a strong woman, one who worked so hard all her life, can be left so weak and defenseless, ravaged by disease, beyond the help of the great body of medical knowledge we have at our disposal.

My mother was raised by a single mother during the Great Depression. She probably had as little as anybody ever has, but I never heard her complain about what she did without while growing up. I never heard her complain about anything she didn't have as an adult either.

She worked hard in the cotton mill most of her life. She was a weaver, and was thankful for the opportunity to go to work each day and earn a better living for her family than her mother had been able to earn. She worshipped my father. No man ever had a more loyal wife.

It's funny what a person thinks about. As I sat in the darkened corner of the hospital room the other night, listening to the noises in the hall, watching the clock on the wall advance, minute by minute—visions of my childhood came to me.

I remembered my mother making cornbread in the same black pan, meal after meal, year after year. I've had her show me how dozens of times. I can use the exact ingredients and cook it the exact same amount of time at the exact temperature. Mine never tastes as good as hers. Not even close.

As I studied her wrinkled face, I could see the beautiful, clear skinned lady who used to sit in the floor and play jack stones with me and let me lick the bowl when she made cakes. I wonder if kids still want to lick the bowl. I doubt it. Pretty unsanitary, I guess.

As I looked at the gray hair framing my mother's face I suddenly thought of the permanent parties the ladies on our street used to have. They would gather at our house and give one another permanents. I swear, the smell of Tony Home Permanent permeated the hospital room.

Most of my memories of my mother revolve around some form of work, for she was never an idle person. I remember counting the minutes until the 3 o'clock whistle blew at the mill. She would get home at twelve after three. We lived close to the mill. I guess everybody in Porterdale lived close to the mill. She would always come in and we would share "a bite to eat." A tomato sandwich, in season. Maybe some fried peas with a slice of onion. Only recently did I realize that she came home from working eight hours in the mill and ate a snack because she had not had lunch at work.

At six she would have supper on the table and it was always a full meal and always delicious. After the supper dishes were done she might sit down and watch television, but not without clothes to fold or sewing in her lap.

She made sure that my homework was done. She made sure that I had enough hugs and enough switchings. She listened to me say my prayers at night and woke me up in the morning. Heaven only knows what she did in between. She laughed at my jokes, bragged on my accomplishments, and traveled across the state to watch my basketball games.

She has never quit worrying about me or my sister. The few words she's been able to speak this week have been to assure us that she's all right and not to worry about her, but to take care of what we need to do.

What we need to do. We all feel like we need to do so

much, don't we? We need to work. We need to play. We need to be here. We need to be there. We need to do a million things.

We need to pay more attention to the treasures in our lives, while we still have them, because all of a sudden, your greatest treasure is lying in a hospital room and all you can do is sit in a chair in a corner of a dark room and watch her while the light from the world's saddest Christmas tree shines through the window and makes shadows on the wall beside her bed.

Sorting Through a Lifetime of Memories Can be a Tough Job

Dealing with the death of a loved one is tough in a lot of ways. My Christian faith sustained me as I watched my mother die because I knew she would soon be in a better place. There were hundreds of relatives and friends around during her visitation and funeral They helped sustain my sister and me. Going through a lifetime of memories as we prepared to sell the house in which we spent our childhood was tough and lonely and something I never want to repeat.

I drew tough duty last weekend. I'm not referring to chores created by the winter weather. Surviving the ice storm on Sunday was a piece of cake compared to what I went through Saturday, which was, fittingly, a cold, gray day in its own right. That was the day that we had to clean out my mother's house and get it ready for a new occupant.

My mother passed away in December. She had lived in Porterdale for my entire life and most of her own. You accumulate a lot of stuff over sixty or seventy years. Children of the

Depression, my parents, like many of their generation, held on to most of what they had. My daddy, in particular, was reluctant to throw away something just because it was old, broken, or used up. He used to warn us that "hard times" might come back. I hope times never get any harder than they were Saturday as I, along with my wife, Lisa, and my sister and her husband sorted through a collection of lifetime treasures and old junk, and tried to decide which was which.

I started in my old bedroom. I knew we were in for a long day when I opened the first dresser drawer and found it full of trivial things that had once belonged to me. There were old report cards, pictures, high school newspapers and a plethora of other memories, precious to me, but meaningless to everyone else.

There was a campaign poster promoting "Maddox Without a Runoff," which hearkened back to the "Guvnah's" unsuccessful reelection campaign in 1974. That is an election night that I will never forget. Neither will former cotton farmer, David Hays. I'm not telling what happened and I hope he's not, either.

In the same drawer there was a simulated straw skimmer from Ruby Red's Warehouse, a good time emporium in the old Underground Atlanta. The hat was a souvenir from a night on the town with my college roommate, Jimmy Hutchins, and his sister Becky, who was taken from us last March.

I also found a picture of a skinny little Boy Scout on his way to Bert Adams for his first summer camp. I got homesick just looking at the picture. My first week at camp was the loneliest of my life. I don't care if I was only twelve miles from home and with all my best friends. My mama wasn't there and that was the first time I had been separated from her. The man in the picture with me was Aubrey Barnes, Porterdale Scoutmaster for I don't know how many years. We called him Boony and never appreciated the time he spent with us until it was too late to tell him. There was another picture of Boony Barnes. He was pinning an Eagle Scout award onto a strong and clear eyed fifteen year old. What a difference four years can make.

I spent thirty minutes in one dresser drawer before Lisa,

the pragmatic one in our family, took over. She sent me to another part of the house, promising to put all my precious possessions in a box and take them home to a place of honor in our attic.

I went back to the den and proceeded to go through the family desk. There were just as many treasures there. I found a Bibb Manufacturing Company pay stub from 1963. The week John F. Kennedy was killed my mother worked 56 hours in a cotton mill and brought home 112 hard earned dollars. And I complain about what teachers make.

There was a ticket from the Georgia-Alabama game in 1946 and a World War II ration booklet with three stamps left unused. There were also a box of letters addressed to Myron Ellis, my mother's maiden name. The return address indicated that they were from Homer Huckaby, my father. I couldn't bring myself to read them. Maybe on another day.

I don't know how long I sifted through the treasures in the old desk before Lisa came in and shooed me out of that room, too. I do know that there are now a lot more boxes in our attic than there were before last Saturday.

After being exiled from the den, I joined my sister in the kitchen. My mother spent the greater part of her last twelve years on earth sitting in her kitchen, leaning on the table that had been her mother's. The television and the phone were her companions. She enjoyed baseball during the summer. She was a huge Cubs fan, because their games came on before her bedtime. She watched game shows and old movies the rest of the year.

I found my sister sitting in a chair, boxing up kitchen items to give away. She picked up a heart shaped pan that was black from use. I think it was intended to be a cake pan, but my mama made cornbread in it on special occasions. For the first time that day, I cried.

We didn't exactly finish cleaning out my mother's house last Saturday, which is a bit of a problem, because we sold it last Friday. Some things just can't be done in one day. There's always next weekend. Besides, we've packed up the love letters and the cornbread pan. The rest should be a piece of cake.

5

Life Is Not a Ball game . . . ain't that a shame?

Life is not a ball game . . .
ain't that a shame?

Sports has always been a big part of my life. My earliest sports memory occurred when I was four years old. I wanted to stay under the house and dig for doodle bugs with my playmate, Linda King. My daddy made me come inside and watch a baseball game with him. I was four. I didn't understand baseball, but I remember being mad as I sat on the linoleum floor of the living room watching shadowy images on our little black and white television set.

The only thing I remember, other than the fact that my doodle bug hunt was interrupted, was my daddy screaming "He did it! He did it!" over and over and a man on the television jumping into the arms of another man, which seemed strange, even to a four year old. My daddy had the foresight to make me watch the only perfect game in World Series history.

Naturally, I didn't appreciate the significance of what I had seen until many years later, but the image of Yogi Berra jumping into Don Larson's arms has stayed in my mind across the decades, along with thousands of other indelible memories of events I have experienced, or seen in person, or through the miracle of television.

Baseball was the first sport I loved. Dizzy Dean and Pee Wee Reese brought the New York Yankees of Berra, Mickey Mantle, and Whitey Ford into our living room almost every Saturday and Sunday throughout those endless summers of my boyhood. I read every book I could get my hands on about the Bronx Bombers--Ruth, Gehrig, Dimaggio--they were like the knights of King Arthur's Round Table to me.

College football, University of Georgia style, would soon rival the Yankees for my affection and attention. Red and black blood still flows through my veins and the names of Buck Belue, Bill Stanfill, and, of course, Herschel Walker, mean as much to me as the names of Charlie Trippi and Frank Sinkwich meant to my father.

Three years after Don Larson's perfect game, a man named Ronald Bradley moved to Newton County, where I lived, and created a basketball fever in the community that would infect me, perhaps as deeply as anyone. Terry Rutledge, Tim Christian, and the other Newton County Rams were as much heroes to me as the professional players I watched on television. I grew up to become a Newton County Ram and being even a small part of that outstanding program dramatically changed my life.

Basketball helped me have the opportunity to get a college education and has opened up a world of opportunity to me over the course of my lifetime. It has helped me make a living and allowed me to meet some of the most wonderful people in the world.

My mother used to get a bit put out with me over what she saw as my obsession with sports. I remember her admonishing me over and over that "life ain't a ball game." She was right, you know. It really isn't.

Ain't that a shame?

Shirt Fits to a Tee

*I freely admit that I've never been much of a pro football
fan, at least not since the days of Tarkenton, Unitas, and
Lombardi. When the Atlanta Falcons actually made it to
the Super Bowl, I had to jump on the band wagon.*

All of a sudden I just had to have one. I had resisted for
weeks. The tension mounted and the bandwagon filled and I resisted jumping on board. But it was Friday morning and the Super Bowl was two days away and the whole school was decked
out in Dirty Bird attire and there I was in my standard khakis and
oxford button down. I couldn't stand it any longer. I persuaded a
friend to go out amongst the madness and find me the perfect
shirt to commemorate the historic cultural event we were about to
experience.

Don't misunderstand. I'm not anti-Falcons. I took more
than a passing interest in the franchise when it began. After all,
the NFL was still the NFL back then. Those were the days of
Johnny Unitas and Paul Hornung and Sam Huff. Joe Willie Namath
was a brash upstart and Vince Lombardi was master of all he sur-
veyed. There's no need to rehash the Falcons' dismal history. It's
been done to death over the past two weeks and besides, their
ineptitude really had nothing to do with my disinterest in them.
The Braves were just as dismal as the Falcons for years and I
spent night after night watching the Superstation, listening to Pete
and Ernie. occasionally venturing down to the Stadium and hoping for the miracle that finally came.

No, it hasn't been futility that has kept me from being a
Falcon fan. There's just not that much of me to go around. In the
fall I give my heart and soul to the Georgia Bulldogs. I was Bull-
dog born and Bulldog bred and when I die I'll be Bulldog dead.
There just isn't enough of me left after a Saturday afternoon in
Athens to offer true allegiance to another team on Sunday. It would
be almost like having two wives. Heaven knows, one's plenty.
So over the years I've paid less and less attention to professional

football. I've always disparaged people who become rabid fans when a team hits a hot streak and then crawls back into the woodwork when times get bad. When Georgia won the National Championship in 1980 I saw people wearing red and black that couldn't spell Dawg. And ever since the Braves went from worst to first, good seats at a baseball game have been scarcer than hen's teeth. I was determined not to become a nouveau Dirty Birder. When they beat the Vikings in overtime I was picnicking beside a river in the great Smoky Mountains—oblivious to the game or its outcome.

But last Friday, I reiterate, I could stand it no longer. I had to have a T-shirt and a good friend went out in search of one. Came back with a dandy, too! It was black with the traditional Falcon emblem. It also made reference to the Dirty Bird dance craze and had a Super Bowl XXXIII logo. A perfect collectible, which is what it has now become. I wore it twice. All day on Friday, while hope still sprang eternal, and then again on Sunday, while the Broncos brought the Atlanta faithful back to reality. Nothing to do after Sunday but add my Falcons shirt to my collection of shirts that I just had to have at the time.

I have to keep those shirts in a secret place so my wife, Lisa, won't make dust rags of my cherished memories. It was fun going through the stack of old shirts Sunday night. (Why waste time?) Right there on top was my 1980 National Championship T-shirt. It's mostly threads. I wore it slap to death. I once threatened to wear it to every game until we won another championship. Ray Goff caused me to rethink that vow.

Of course I came across a T-shirt from the Braves first trip to the World Series. It had caricatures of all the players. Whatever became of Lonnie Smith, anyway? I found a shirt I bought in Gettysburg, Pennsylvania commemorating the 125th anniversary of the great battle there. Being from Americus, Georgia perhaps Dan Reeves can take some solace in knowing that at least General Lee knows how he feels.

I was confused about the logo on one particular shirt. I couldn't figure out what the slogan meant. It said, "S A W B."

Then I remembered. It was a holdover from the days when Andrew Young was mayor of Atlanta and complained that the whole state was run by "smart aleck white boys." I think he said smart "aleck." There was also a 30 year old shirt with a picture of former governor Lester Maddox riding his bicycle. Backwards of course. The words emblazoned under Lester's picture summed up my feelings toward the outcome of Sunday's game. It read, "Phooey!"

The last shirt I looked at had a picture of the late Atlanta Constitution columnist, Lewis Grizzard and his dog Catfish. I was inspired! I decided I had to know what Lewis thought about Sunday's game. I put away my T-shirt collection and called The Physic Hotline. I hooked up with a soothesayer named Madame Darla. She assured me she could put through a call to heaven—for a fee. I agreed and she got right through to St. Peter. Unfortunately, Lewis wasn't there. Seems that when he found out the Falcons were in the Super Bowl he and Catfish asked for a two week pass to go and visit Satan—and get in a little ice skating.

Dream Team Caps Dream Season

I "retired" from coaching basketball in 1992. After a six year hiatus Dr. Wayne Watts persuaded me to "come out of retirement" to coach the girls' team at Edwards Middle School. I will always be thankful to Wayne Watts for that favor. He gave me back a great part of my life.

Perfection. It's the dream of every person who has ever participated in athletics. Some admit it. Some don't. I do. I want to win every time they turn the scoreboard on. I have been a player, manager and coach in Little League, Middle School, High School, and college. I've coached over fifty high school and middle school seasons in football, basketball, soccer, softball, and track. I've had very good teams—and some not so good. My teams have won championships and played in state tournaments and traveled as far as the Big Island of Hawaii, just to play basketball. But the perfect season always eluded me.

My high school team played East Rome for the state championship in 1970 at Georgia Tech. We stayed at a hotel directly across the expressway from "The Dome" and walked over for the game. I found a ten dollar bill on the ground as we entered the building. I was sure this would be our lucky night. It wasn't. The walk back across the bridge that night was a hundred miles long.

I was a manager and trainer at the University of Georgia back in the days when everyone in the Southeastern Conference that didn't play their home games in Lexington, Kentucky thought all field goals counted three points. Football was number one in Athens. Spring football was second. Basketball was an afterthought. In our first game my freshman year we lost to Rollins College. No one on our team could even locate Rollins College. The best thing that ever happened to one of our Georgia teams was getting snowed in at a tournament in Charlotte. We got to see the Jackson Five when Michael was a small black boy.

I entered Georgia as a journalism major but switched to education so I could coach basketball. I wanted to be my high school coach. I didn't want to be like him—I wanted to be him. It took me almost twenty years, but I finally realized that no one could be him. I found coaching terribly frustrating. By most yardsticks I was a successful coach, but not by the standard I set for myself. Winning never felt as good as losing hurt. I gave up coaching basketball for five years.

Two falls ago I agreed to coach the girls' team at Edwards Middle School. I told myself there would be no pressure to win. I would just teach fundamentals, help the girls learn the game, and not worry about winning and losing. I lied. I continued to live and die with every bounce of the ball. When my team lost in the semifinals of the league championship tournament last year it felt like the world had stopped turning. I wondered why anyone would ever want to coach—especially me.

And then came this year. I realized very early that this team would be special. I had a point guard who was fast as lightning released from an August storm cloud. She handled the ball like it was extension of herself.

I had wings who could handle the ball, drive to the basket, and play string music on the nets from 15 feet. I had post players who could score and rebound and play defense. I had a long bench full of substitutes who could be ready to perform at a moments notice, and often had to do just that.

More importantly, I had a group of girls who were willing to put teamwork ahead of personal glory. They were willing to practice hard and be pushed without pouting. I had a group of girls who showed up day after day, week after week; always eager to learn from their mistakes; always willing to pay the price; always willing to strive for perfection.

This team stormed through the regular season, winning all twelve games without being seriously challenged. Their average margin of victory was 30 points. They maintained their focus through the first three rounds of our league championship tournament and arrived at the championship game against Rising Starr Middle School with a perfect 15-0 record. But Rising Starr was also 15-0 and the game was at the Rising Starr gym, in Fayetteville. We had already made that long trip twice last week and had to get up Saturday morning and do it one more time. No one could have faulted these girls if they had lost, especially me. But these girls weren't about coming close. They had set a goal of perfection and meant to obtain it. It wasn't easy. They fought to a 28-24 halftime lead and then put the home team away in the second half for a 46-31 win. 16-0. League Champions. Perfect season.

Elise, Vicki, Rachel, Courtney, Jasmine, Sandriel, Stephanie, Alison, Jennifer, Michelle, Christie, Melanie, Lauren, Tiffany, Katie, Joy and Jackson. The Dream Team. A little slice of heaven and a dream come true for an over the hill, middle aged coach. Thanks ladies. You're simply the best.

A Yellow Jacket That
Even a Bulldog Can Love

Those who know me best know it takes a special person indeed to make me praise a Yellow Jacket. Wayne Kerr qualifies. (But to hell with Tech!)

It's a week until football season. Beginning next Saturday I will join 80,000 or so of my closest friends for weekly prayer meetings in Athens, or places like Knoxville, Jacksonville, and Oxford, Mississippi. We may start a new millennium here in four months but on January 1 in Oxford, Mississippi it will still be 1968.

After spending ten or eleven weeks in warm-up games, my Bulldogs will travel to Atlanta's North Avenue for our annual bloodletting against the Trade School. Of course I mean Georgia Tech. To all true Bulldogs, they are "The Enemy."

Now understand one thing. I didn't become a Georgia Bulldog, I was born a Bulldog. I was raised on stories about Frankie Sinkwich and Charlie Trippi and the glory days when Wally Butts, Georgia's "Little Round Man," paced the sidelines of Sanford Stadium. During my formative years Georgia Tech beat Georgia almost annually, including one stretch of seven straight years. Even after Theron Sapp broke the drought, Bobby Dodd's boys seemed to have the upper hand, until Joel Eaves hired Vince Dooley to come to Athens and restore order to the world of college football. Georgia Tech was a hated word in my household. In fact, I learned to say "To Hell With Tech" before I learned the Pledge of Allegiance.

Of course, now, the worm has turned. During the past three decades Georgia has beaten Tech on such a regular basis that the rivalry has lost a bit of its edge. Some of my Bulldog brethren actually view Florida or Tennessee as bigger rivals. But not me. I don't like Georgia Tech. I didn't like them when Lenny Snow used to hurdle the line of scrimmage and I didn't like them when scholar athlete Eddie Lee Ivory gained 300 plus yards on some frozen field somewhere. I didn't like Georgia Tech when Eddie McShan refused to play one Saturday because he got his feelings hurt and I didn't like Georgia Tech when Bill Curry accused everyone but Tech of cheating to win. I certainly didn't like Tech last year when, thanks to two horrible calls in the second half, they finally broke our winning streak.

I used to tell people that I wouldn't pull for Tech with two engines out on the team plane. I still wouldn't. I used to tell people, "I don't like Georgia Tech, or anybody that does." Then I met Wayne Kerr.

I'll tell you two things right now that you can put in the bank. One—You can't be more Georgia Tech than Wayne Kerr, Class of 1973. He was a cheerleader at Tech, for goodness sakes. He married a Tech graduate who was the daughter of a Tech graduate. He has three beautiful and brilliant daughters. One, Shana, is already a Tech freshman and will spend this fall dressed in white and gold and screaming ugly things about my Alma Mater. I'm sure the other two will soon follow. All of that, and I still like Wayne Kerr, which brings me to my second point.

It's impossible for a person, in good conscious, not to like Wayne Kerr. He's what God had in mind for Adam, back before Eve turned his head. He is a genuinely nice guy who, despite what Leo Durocher said, will never finish last. He's so gracious during football season that he almost takes the fun out of beating Tech. He actually congratulates me after every Georgia win.

For those of you who may not know, or know of Wayne, let me tell you about him. Wayne Kerr. 48 years old. A dentist. Well over six feet tall and thin as a rail. He can still wear his college cheerleader sweater, and does. He has sandy blonde hair, blonde eyebrows, a perpetual impish grin, and wears a Mickey Mouse watch so he'll remember not to take himself too seriously.

I met Dr. Kerr at my church, Ebenezer United Methodist, where he has served in a variety of leadership roles, including Lay Leader and Chairman of the Administrative Board. But he does so much more for our church than fill a spot on the duty roster. If we need someone to make a serious speech to the congregation, Wayne is our man, but he's also our man if we need someone to dress up as a Blues Brother and dance the Funky Chicken. (See above reference to Mickey Mouse watch.)

Wayne Kerr's civic service doesn't end at the church door. He is a Partner in Education with many local schools and bestows the Kerr Cup, named after his father, a long time Florida juvenile court judge, to outstanding student citizens at several schools. His list of Civic Awards and memberships is longer than five miles of bad Alabama road. The Kiwanis Club, the Jaycees, this newspaper, and a dozen other organizations have had the good sense to honor him for his contributions to society in general and Rockdale County in particular.

Perhaps his greatest contribution has been to those who are least able to express their appreciation, which is just as Wayne would have it. When his dental office was condemned because the government wanted to build a road through it, he donated the building to charity and had it moved to the northwest corner of our county. Thanks to him, and others, there is now a free clinic offering dental and medical services to people in our community who would otherwise have nowhere to turn.

I could go on and on and on, but I think I can sum up my opinion of Dr. Wayne Kerr by using an oft repeated phrase of the late Lewis Grizzard. He is truly a great American. I can give no higher praise.

But I'm going to make myself hate him for three hours on November 27.

Memory Lane Winds Through Homer Sharp Stadium

High School. What precious memories were created during that awful, scary, wonderful time. Would I really relive those four years? In a New York minute!

My wife and I took a trip Friday evening. We traveled ten miles, and twenty-five years, back in time. For the first time in forever I attended a football game at Homer Sharp Field in Covington. I think it is now called Sharp Stadium. You know how things change. But some things do stay the same.

I'm a native of Newton County and Sharp Field was a big part of my childhood, my youth, and my early adulthood. My first trips there were to watch the Newton Rams play teams like Morgan County, Henry County, and the dreaded Gainesville Red Elephants. My cousin, Jerry Bouchillon, was on the football team when I was just a toddler and we would sit in the stands on Friday nights and watch him play. That was well over forty years ago. That Latin guy was right. Time does fly. It was at Sharp Field that my cousin Buck, Jerry's older brother, taught me to stand up when the band played Dixie.

When I got a little older, my neighbor Larry King's presence on the team was enough to require my attendance at all the games. By then I was at the stage of being more interested in playing two hand touch behind the end zone than watching the game. We wadded together paper cups for a football.

One of the true highlights of my humble athletic career occurred on Sharp Field when I was in the fifth grade. I won the local Punt, Pass, and Kick Competition when Corky Ballard shanked a punt. My prize was an honest to goodness Baltimore Colts football jacket, with genuine Naugahyde sleeves. I don't know how many naugas had to die to make my jacket, but I am eternally grateful to each and every one of them. I wore that sucker year round until it wore slap out.

My only experience as an actual player on Sharp Field came in the eighth grade when I was a part of a program called the Baby Rams, a precursor to the Middle School football programs we have today. I was a very bad fullback and even worse quarterback, but was on the field enough to remember the smell of the mud, the taste of the turf, and how much an underweight thirteen year old can be hurt, physically and emotionally, when he doesn't compete well on a football field.

I didn't play football in high school, but there was never a contest played at Sharp Field without me present. Honesty compels me to admit that, though a true fan of our school's football team, I was even more a fan of the Blue Rambler Band. If I were really being honest I would go a step further and admit that I was a fan of one of the band's majorettes. Whatever, if the lights came on, I was in the stadium.

After I graduated from college I came back to Covington to teach and coach. One of my responsibilities was to coach the football team at Cousins Middle School. Thankfully, I was a much better eighth grade coach than I was an eighth grade player, and some of the happiest and most satisfying moments of my life were spent on the sidelines of Sharp Field. It was there that I learned firsthand that I could make a difference in the life of young people, and that what goes on on the football field goes way beyond blocking and tackling and scoring touchdowns. My Cousin players and I had a bond that few groups have ever known, and for one wonderful night in November we were kings of our admittedly limited domain as we defeated Fayette County 45-6 to win our league championship. Championships in football on any level had not been a Newton County staple and it seemed that the whole county came out to help us rejoice.

I also coached football at Newton High and my last game at Sharp Field was also my last visit, until Friday night. The gap, I believe, was twenty years. Some things were very different from the Sharp Field of my childhood. For one, I was now a visitor. My school, Heritage, had come to do battle with Newton County's Eastside High. In addition to the aforementioned name upgrade, the stadium's sides had been switched. What once had been the home grandstand had been relegated to the visitors, and it seemed to have shrunk considerably. The home side had been moved across the field and was absolutely huge. It sported a large and modern press box and the lighting system was much improved over the old wooden post lamps that used to illuminate the center of the field and leave the endzones in semidarkness.

There wasn't a rickety wooden grandstand in sight, the home team wore green instead of blue and white, and the band didn't play Dixie. Come to think of it, they didn't have any majorettes, either. I guess baton twirling is a lost art.

But some things were the same. The smell of mud and popcorn and hot chocolate still permeated the air. When I walked around to the home side at half time to watch the magnificent Heritage band, I saw scores of the same people I sat in Sharp Field with during high school. They were watching their children play.

On the field, nothing had changed. The cheerleaders, although a bit more athletic than those of my youth, were still pretty and cheered their hearts out for their respective teams. The coaches still paced the sidelines, exhorting their charges to do their best. The players still blocked and tackled and ran and passed and played their hearts out, as if no moment in time would be more important than the 48 minutes of competition on this warm September night.

You know, they may have been right. They just may have been right.

New Georgia Coach is a Man With a Plan

As this book went to press what started as a promising season for Jim Harrick's Bulldogs had gone somewhat sour. But Rome wasn't built in a day, you know, and at least we beat Georgia Tech.

We're deep into football season and the Braves are gasping for breath in the fall classic which television has pushed so close to winter you can smell hickory logs burning in the fireplace—so, naturally, I'm writing today about a basketball coach. If pumpkins are for sale on the side of the road it must be close to round ball season.

Last Saturday I had an opportunity to spend a few minutes with Georgia's newest basketball coach. His name is Jim Harrick and, truth be known, the announcement of his hiring wasn't met with overwhelming joy across the Bulldog nation, for a couple of reasons. One, I guess, is that he isn't from around here. Georgia folks, for some reason, seem more trusting of people who grew up putting grits on their breakfast plates. For another, he took the road to the Final Four at UCLA, won the whole thing, and wasn't asked to stay. That raised some eyebrows in some quarters.

Coach Harrick is replacing Ron Jirsa, one of the nicest guys in the world. Some say that Jirsa was too nice, and lacked the ability to make his players toe the line. I don't know about that. I do know that his back to back winning seasons would have been deemed highly successful ones at the University of Georgia during most of its basketball history. For years, those who follow college sports will remember, basketball was the third favorite sport at every Southeastern Conference school not named Kentucky, right behind football and spring football.

Jirsa, however, followed Orlanda "Tubby" Smith, who may be the best there is in the country at what he does. He blew into Athens on a west wind from Tulsa, immediately carried Georgia hoops to a level of excellence never known in the Classic City, then departed for greener pastures. Actually, he departed for bluer pastures—those of Lexington, Kentucky, where he promptly won a National Championship, which is the expectation when you play in an arena haunted by Adolph Rupp's ghost. After two seasons the powers to be at Georgia decided that Jirsa wasn't the man. He was released and Harrick was hired. It may have been Vince Dooley's best decision since "give the ball to Herschel."

Harrick is all basketball. Trust me. I've been around enough basketball coaches to know the real deal, and Harrick is the real deal.

I spent maybe twenty minutes talking to him last Saturday morning. I've seldom seen the animation and enthusiasm Coach Harrick demonstrated when talking about the team he inherited. I felt like he was coaching me.

He talked about the players—the ones who were busting their fannies and the ones who needed a fire lit under them. I believe those players will soon find out where Coach Harrick keeps his matches. He talked about playing defense and rebounding and running and putting pressure on the opponents. He mentioned the need for all players to know humility and called the bench a coach's greatest ally. I liked that! But none of those things are what impressed me most about Jim Harrick. The fact that he was headed for a football game on the coldest day of the season wearing short sleeves wasn't what impressed me, either.

The reason I believe Jim Harrick will be a winner at the University of Georgia is that he made it known to me, an insignificant stranger, that he was here to teach the Georgia players how to play basketball. His intention is not to recruit and administrate. He intends to be on the floor, bouncing around, directing traffic, putting his hands on his players, getting inside their heads, and showing them how it's done.

All the great coaches are teachers first. More than offensive sets and transition patterns, Coach Harrick talked about the importance of discipline and fundamentals. Discipline and fundamentals. Those are the keys to success in middle school, high school, college, the pros, and in any endeavor in life.

As I was visiting with Coach Harrick I couldn't help but wish that my players could be exposed to him and his enthusiasm for the game. He almost made me want to skip the football game and go back home to open the gym for practice. Almost. Not quite.

Jim Harrick will be in Conyers next Tuesday, speaking to the members of the Rockdale County Bulldog Club. I haven't asked, but I'm sure that Vince Evans at Evans Pharmacy in Olde Town can tell you how to reserve a spot to hear him. You'd be doing yourself a favor if you made a reservation. You don't even have to be a basketball fan or a Bulldog. Coach Harrick is so enthusiastic and inspiring that he will make your blood flow a little faster no matter what your station in life.

Tubby Smith might find himself looking over his shoulder a bit up in the Kentucky penthouse. And Georgia Tech coaching genius Bobby Cremins had better watch out! There's a new guy in town—and he's bad to the bone. Now if we can just teach him to eat grits.

Same Loving Feeling
in a Brand New Gym

*If ever anyone deserved to have a basketball facility
named in his honor, it's Ronald Bradley. He was the best
there was at what he did--which was not to coach basketball, but to teach young people. There can be
no higher calling.*

The old gym was a big brick cube, with wooden bleachers on
either side, topped by two rows of small square windows. The
floor was solid and as polished as the most precious stone. Heaven
help you if you ever strayed upon it wearing street shoes. There
were dressing rooms downstairs, under the bleachers. They resembled dungeons, especially on the visitors side, which was il-
luminated by one bare light bulb, hanging from a cord in the center of the room. The roof leaked. Buckets were hung from the
rafters to collect the rainwater. Birds roosted in those same rafters.

In summer the gym was hot. In winter, it was even hotter,
especially on the nights the home team played basketball. The
heater and the body heat of the three thousand fans who wedged
their way into the 1800 available seats, made the gym stifling,
especially to the opponents who had to face the Newton County
Rams on the hardwood during the 17 years Ronald Bradley
coached basketball at Newton High.

I quit telling people about Newton County basketball long
ago, for two reasons. For one thing, people who didn't experience Ram basketball firsthand just couldn't understand. Secondly,
people didn't believe the things I was telling them. I get accused
of lying often enough when I deserve to be. I didn't like being
accused of lying when I was telling the truth.

From 1958 until 1967, the Newton County Rams won
129 straight basketball games at home. I know that for a fact. I
was there for most of them. No team, high school, college, or

professional, ever won more. As amazing as the streak was, the sheer number of victories is not the story. The story is the reaction of the people of Newton County to "The Streak," and more specifically to the players and the coach who forged it.

Every game played at the old Newton High gym was a sellout for close to ten years. Every game. Every year. Standing room only and people turned away. When the Tuckers and the Griffins and the Hart Counties of the basketball world came to town, people would line up seven and eight hours ahead of time, just to get inside the building. Every seat would be filled and people would be standing and squatting four deep around the floor. There were times when it was hard to see the boundary lines because of the spectators. I've seen grown men stand on ladders twenty feet off the ground to look through the windows.

I was describing the crowds to a college chum one day and he asked about the fire marshal. I assured him that the fire marshal was at every game. So was the sheriff, Henry Odum, Jr., who loved every kid who ever called Newton County home, but especially loved the boys with crew cuts and blue blazers who sat in one corner of the gym, watching the girls play, awaiting their turn. Those were, you see, the Newton Rams. Never very big, nor particularly athletic, they were, year in and year out, the most disciplined and most dedicated and most fundamentally sound school boys to lace on a pair of Converse All-Stars.

You could count on two interruptions in every girls' game. The first would come when the boys in blue blazers stood up to walk to their dressing room. The roar of the crowd would become so loud that the girls' players couldn't hear the officials' whistles. When the visitors stood up to go to their dungeon to dress, the chant of "Ram Bait, Ram Bait," had the same effect.

The gym was nicknamed "Death Valley" and for good reason. Most teams who came to Covington to play were out of contention by halftime. The few times teams got close, the intimidation of the crowd and the skill of the Ram players turned dreams of upset into bitter disappointment by the fourth quarter. When the game was well in hand, the Newton students would unroll a giant banner, proclaiming to the world that the old gym was, indeed, "Death Valley." There was always a postscript scrawled under the Death Valley sign that read "We Love Bradley."

They did, too, because Ronald Bradley, the coach and architect of the Ram dynasty, brought glory and honor to an entire county, but more importantly, he taught his students lessons far more important than how to dribble or shoot or play defense. He taught them lessons about effort, and pride, and courtesy, and respect, that would last a lifetime and help them become successful people long after their basketball days were over. I know. I was one of the people.

Sunday they dedicated a new gym in Newton County. It is beautiful and modern without a single bucket hanging from the rafters. They named the new facility the Ronald M. Bradley gymnasium, not because of the winning streak he put together or the championships he won, but because of the good solid citizens he helped to build; the doctors, lawyers, businessmen, school teachers, and all the rest. They named the building for him because he touched the people of Newton County in such a way that they will never outlive his influence.

The people, fittingly, came back, to replay the old games, hug one another's necks, and remember the way it was. As I watched the people and listened to the testimonials one thing was obvious—they still love Bradley.

Know what? So do I. So do I.

It Wasn't Supposed to End This Way

A couple of weeks after this column appeared Laney Harris was named First Team All-State.

Her name is Laney Harris. I first knew her when she was seven years old. What a great kid! I can still see her in my mind's eye. She was tall and skinny and her hair was long and straight and almost platinum in color. She wore a perpetual grin as she bounced around her grandfather's car dealership. She seemed to always have a cast on her arm.

I remember taking her to Athens to watch the Lady Dogs play basketball. Most kids tire easily at a college game and their attention wanders to the people in the stands, the cheerleaders, the giant mascots, and the concession stand. Not Laney Harris. She sat on the edge of her seat, her eyes riveted on the action for the entire game. There was a spark in her eye. Even at seven there was a passion for the game.

I suppose Laney Harris came by her love of the game honestly. Her mother, Donna, was an outstanding player at Cherokee County. The ageless Ron Ely was Donna's coach. He believed that girls could and should work as hard as boys long before Congress tried to legislate such matters through Title IX.

Laney's father was an All-State player at Newton County during the Bradley days, when Ram basketball was synonymous with excellence throughout Georgia and beyond. He went on to star at Truett-McConnell and North Georgia College and coached at North Georgia and Gainesville Junior College before returning to Covington to devote his energies to raising a family.

Laney's uncle, Stan Harris, played on the 1964 state championship team at Newton County and her cousin Trudy, Stan's daughter, also played there. She was good enough to be invited to travel with an All Star team to the big island of Hawaii to shoot the rock. She could shoot it, too. I know. I was the coach.

As I said, Laney Harris came by her love of basketball honestly and has a very good bloodline.

Laney's no longer a skinny seven year old with a cast on her arm. She has grown into a beautiful young lady. She is six feet tall and slender. Her hair is still long and still very blond. She could easily be a fashion model, gracing the cover of Mademoiselle. I believe she would prefer to be featured on Sports Illustrated. She still loves basketball and has developed into an outstanding player.

Laney grew up shooting hoops with her dad in the driveway. She first played competitively when she was seven, in a ten and under boys' league. She was the best player. Although she was also a ranked tennis player, her passion lie in the roundball game, and as she became old enough for school ball, she dropped out of competitive tennis to concentrate on her basketball skills.

As she entered the ninth grade her family moved to Loganville. For the past four years she has helped the Lady Red Devils become one of the best teams in the state. Last year she led her team to the Final Four and this year's squad was ranked number one in Georgia for most of the year.

Laney is an incredible player. She has supreme court awareness and plays tenacious defense. She is an excellent ball handler and passer and deadly shooter. She averaged over 17 points a game this year. Her high was 34. She made 9 three pointers in one game and 8 in another. Her coach, Bill Bradley, who is the son of her father's coach, Ronald Bradley, insists Laney was just as valuable off the court as on.

According to Bradley, Laney infected his other players with her love of the game. She led them on a mission, to compete for the state championship. It was because of Laney, according to him, that the players worked so willingly in the weight room and the gym during the off season. They wanted to be the best and Laney made them believe they could be.

I sat and watched Loganville's last victory of the season Friday night. Sadly, so did Laney Harris. She was sidelined, her foot in a cast from a stress fracture that got continually worse instead of better. The cast was red, to match her team's uniforms.

Although she couldn't play, Laney did everything she

could to help her teammates. She walked out on crutches to help form the run through line during the introductions. She sat and fidgeted on the bench, yelling encouragement to the girls on the floor. She hobbled out to meet the team during time-outs, offering water and encouragement. At one point, when her team's lead was cut to six in the fourth quarter, she helped the cheerleaders start a chant of "Defense...Defense."

When her team won, she helped them celebrate.

Loganville will not play for the state championship this weekend. They lost on Saturday night to a stronger team. Laney Harris, again, did everything she could to help her team, and she was just as crushed as the rest when their efforts fell short. This was supposed to be their year—her year. The season wasn't supposed to end like this, nursing an injury. It was supposed to end in the winner's circle. Now she and her team and the community will have to live the rest of their days with "what if . . .?"

But after the hurt and disappointment fade, Laney and her teammates will be left with the pride of knowing that they gave everything they had to be the best that they could be. There are few that can honestly claim that. And there is lots more basketball in Laney's life. Next year she will play for Furman University.

Her foot will heal, stronger than new, and with her long blond hair, she'll look great in purple.

6

What Have We Done to Our Young?

What Have We Done to our Young?

I guess every generation is convinced that young people are going to hell in a hand basket. I remember that when I was a little boy I used Bosco, (yes, the chocolate syrup) to paint side-burns on my face so I would look like Elvis Presley. I realize I should be embarrassed by that admission, but I'm not. Everyone remembers, of course, that he couldn't be shown on the Ed Sullivan Show from the waist down because of his "vulgar" gyrations.

I wish Ed Sullivan could have lived to see MTV. He would be done forgave Elvis. Elvis might have shook his pelvis, but he never showed it to anybody on live television.

After Elvis, came the Beatles, and then the hippies, and then the war protesters. And now, all of the children of the '60s are grown up and have teenagers of their own. Many people insist that our current generation of young people are irretrievably lost.

Those folks just haven't been around the right teenagers. Sure, society and parents who have abdicated their duties as parents have created far too many mixed up kids who are searching for attention in misguided and dangerous ways. But the large majority of teens are just normal kids, trying to fit in--just like the teens of every other generation. Others are simply golden.

Parents and teachers and all other manner of adults need to remember--Raising kids is like raising a garden. We reap what we sow. We really do.

Another American Tragedy

Columbine. We'll always remember that name.

We'd reached the end of another school day. When you teach eighth graders and you're down to the final stretch, reaching the end of another school day is cause for celebration. If you've been able to overcome raging hormones complicated by spring fever and actually taught your students something, that's a bonus.

The afternoon announcements had been made and we were waiting for the buses. I turned on the television in my room, hoping to get news of the situation in Kosovo from CNN. Just as I expected, we saw more violence. Shooting, bombing, senseless killing, random death, destruction, blood, heartache, tragedy. All the things associated with war. But the scenes being shown were not from the killing fields of eastern Europe. They were from a modern high school in Colorado, located in an upscale suburb of Denver.

Students were killing students. Young people killing other young people. Again.

It's happened several times over the past three years. One time is too many. Someone walks into a school with weapons and begins creating a horror story more terrible than anything Hollywood could imagine. More terrible because it is real. Real people die. They stay dead.

As soon as my students were dismissed Tuesday I hurried home. I couldn't wait to be with my family. Safely inside our own four walls, I stayed glued to the television, as, I'm sure, millions of others did across the land. The images I saw will never leave me.

SWAT teams were everywhere. SWAT teams and schools should never be mentioned in the same sentence. There were also helicopters and a camouflaged vehicle that looked like some sort of a tank. Yellow school buses belong at schools. Tanks don't. Let me say it again. Tanks and SWAT teams don't belong at schools.

For three hours relieved students continued to run from the building in small groups, with their hands behind their heads. Parents waited at a nearby elementary school, praying that their child would be the next one transported to safety.

Dazed students frantically searched for friends and loved ones. Some cried.

Some trembled.

All were terrified.

TV reporters interviewed several students. They were all intelligent and well spoken. They looked exactly like the students in my suburban school. That's because they are. The scene could have been played out at any local school. That's the insanity of it all. Our society has come to this because we're overly permissive and have a whole generation of parents who fear being parents. We call ourselves enlightened and ridicule people who stand-up for the values our country was built upon. Heaven forbid we tread on a child's self-esteem by disciplining them when they do wrong or forcing them to conform to standards of common decency.

Something has to change in our culture. The madness has to stop. If our children are not safe in school, they are not safe anywhere. The sad thing is, the scary thing is, the absolutely terrifying thing is: There's not one thing that anyone at that school could have done to prevent Tuesday's atrocity.

What to do? Like everyone else, I wish I knew.

I do know this. We can't just wring our hands and do nothing.

Abraham Lincoln once said something to the effect that no army in the world could, by force, so much as "take one drink from the Ohio River or make one footprint on the Blue Ridge." He went on to say that if America were to die, it would be suicide; we would fall from within. Watching Tuesday's tragedy unfold, I couldn't help but think that our pulse is weakening. I don't know if the fabric of our culture is about to completely unravel, but the gruesome scene in Colorado is enough to warn us that we need to check our seams.

And Now the Monster is Here

*In my wildest dreams I never imagined that I would ham-
mer out this column exactly one month after the one on
Columbine. I pray I never have to write about such a
subject again.*

Damn!

I know this is a family newspaper. Damn, anyway.

One month ago I wrote about the horror of watching a
school massacre in Littleton, Colorado. It was terrible. It was
tragic. It was scary. It was community just like ours. It was 1,500
miles away.

This morning it wasn't 1,500 miles way. It was here. Right
here.

We were looking forward to a great day at Edwards Middle
School. The school-wide honors program was to take place.
Hundreds of students were to be honored for outstanding achievement. They were dressed in their Sunday best, eagerly awaiting
the arrival of their mamas and daddies, shortly after lunch.

Their parents came, in droves. But they came early. They
came running. They came crying. They came in a panic. They
didn't come to see their children march to the front of the gym and
receive a certificate. They came to see them -- to hold them, to
take them home and cherish them. They came just to be sure they
were alive.

Once again, the monster that has become American society reared its ugly head. This time the monster wasn't in Colorado, or Arkansas, or any other distant place. It was here. Our
eighth grade students will attend Heritage High School next year.
Their older siblings go there now. I will teach at Heritage next
fall.

The same old story. A student-turned-gunman walks into
a school commons area at the most crowded time of day and begins firing randomly. Once again the nation's attention is focused
on a school tragedy. But this time it is different.

The children who were shot were friends and neighbors. One of them I taught in Sunday School.

The snatches of conversation and rumors and names of victims were all familiar to us.

The sobbing students who were worried about their friends and family members were in my class.

The frantic parents were flooding into my school.

They were people I live with and play with and go to church with, and they were frantic because a gunman had opened fire in our school.

I walked outside to help direct parents to their children. Helicopters were circling overhead. Helicopters were circling above our school.

Students began arriving from the high school, looking for parents and younger siblings. One young man told me he heard shots and saw smoke. Saw smoke coming out of a gun in OUR school.

The bright young students being interviewed on television were all people we know.

The president of the United States was on television expressing regret over another incident of school violence in our school.

A former student came up to me looking for a hug -- from anyone. She described how she had scrambled under a bench when the shooting started. I remember telling her and her classmates, just one year ago, all the things they would need to do to survive in high school. Scrambling under a desk to avoid gunfire was not one of the things I discussed.

I said in my Littleton column that it could happen anywhere. And now it has.

Dozens of people have asked me already this morning, "How did we come to this?"

Of course I don't know exactly how. But I do know we didn't get here overnight. We got here little by little. Little by little we have become too permissive. Little by little we have given our children too much of what they wanted and too little of what they needed. Little by little we have listened to those who would tell us that firm discipline would harm our children. Little by little we've given our children more and more things and less and less attention. We are reaping what we have sown.

What will have to happen before we decide that enough is enough?

I didn't know the answer to the problem a month ago. I don't know the answer now. But I do know we better start looking harder for the answers, because the monster isn't in Colorado anymore. It's here.

Damn!

A Terrible Reason for a Very Nice Visit

In the introduction to this chapter I said that some of today's teens are golden. Brittany and Cary are golden.

Visiting. We don't do it enough anymore, do we? When I was little, visiting was something to look forward to. Folks would sit and talk for hours. They didn't need an excuse, or a television set for background noise. They actually talked to one another about whatever was on their minds—or hearts.

I had visitors the other day. Two Heritage High School students, their mothers, and one little sister. We sat in my living room and talked. Mostly they talked. I tried to listen. They shared with me what was on their minds—and hearts. They told me about visitors *they* had last week. Their visitors came all the way from Colorado. They flew all the way to Georgia to talk about what was on their minds—and hearts.

My visitors were named Cary and Brittany. They are both intelligent, articulate, and sensitive young ladies. They are both involved in church and school activities as well as athletics. "All American Girl" would be an appropriate label for either of them.

Brittany and Cary told me that their guests last week, though visiting from clear across the country, were much like them. They, too, were intelligent and articulate and sensitive. They, too, were active in school and church and sports. They had so much in common. In fact, they had too much in common.

As you have probably guessed by now, the Colorado teens were from Columbine High School in Littleton, Colorado. Columbine and Heritage. Littleton and Conyers. Six weeks ago, few, if any, students from either school had heard of the other. Certainly these two schools and these two communities were unknown across most of the nation and content with their obscurity. Now that has changed forever.

What a great idea. Students, teachers, and parents from an upper middle class town twenty-five miles from Denver can visit students, teachers, and parents from an upper middle class town twenty-five miles from Atlanta. Rocky Mountains meets Deep South. The kids could hang out and listen to music. Maybe they could take in the laser show at Stone Mountain.

The idea was great. The reason for the visit was tragic.

The Columbine students were here to share their experiences, to support the Heritage students, to find solace for themselves by talking to other kids who had suffered the trauma of having their innocence and safety shattered, suddenly and unexpectedly, and permanently. They came to look for reasons and to try and figure out how to prevent the terrible thing they had experienced from reoccurring in some other anonymous high school in some other anonymous suburb.

Hearing the stories, even second hand, of the Columbine students was fascinating. According to my visitors, the Columbine students were just happy to be able to talk about their experience to a group who cared, and would not try to sensationalize their stories on the six o'clock news. The saddest part of the discussions was the idea that the Heritage and Columbine kids could form a joint support group for the next place it happened. Dear God, don't let there be a next place. Please.

I've never spent an hour with two more impressive teens than Cary and Brittany. Both had been greatly moved by their experience. One had carried images of Columbine in her subconscious for a month and wondered if it could happen here. One had dismissed the thought of ever experiencing such a thing first hand. Both had been exposed to the terrible truth that it could happen here. Both had compassion for the young man who shot up their school. Both had searched their minds for reasons and had come up empty, but both were more than willing to continue to search for a way to make things better. They wanted to reach out to those outside their group and to make them feel wanted and loved.

As the students' mothers entered the conversation, we batted around all sorts of theories and ideas. There have been many theories and ideas batted around lately. We didn't come up with any easy answers or quick solutions. Easy answers and quick solutions seldom solve anything, do they?

Brittany and Cary had one other thing in common. They had caring parents who were willing to be parents and not buddies, who were willing to take the time to know where their children were, who they were with, and what they were doing. They were willing to set limitations and expectations for their children. If all children could be so fortunate as to have such parents, I could go back to writing about eating turnip greens and cornbread and making fun of transplanted Northern Americans.

"If You Can Read This, Thank a Teacher"

I've often said that my timing is terrible. I was a student when the teacher was always right and a teacher when the student is always right. My teachers were wonderful. They had to be to put up with me.

I love bumper stickers, although I must admit many are offensive and can't be quoted in this medium. I saw one last week that read, "Clean up the South—Put a Yankee on a bus." It was meant in good fun, I'm sure. I saw another that said, "All dirt roads lead to Clemson." I know several Clemson fans who would be deeply offended by that message, if someone were to read it to them.

Many years ago, while a student at UGA, I was driving down the narrow streets of Athens behind a vintage Volkswagen Beetle. While the car was stopped at a traffic light, I noticed a bumper sticker--"Honk if you love Jesus." It was a beautiful spring day and I was feeling particularly jovial, so I gave my horn a spirited honk. The person in the Volkswagen, a very large middle aged lady, stuck her head out of the window and screamed back at me, "Can't you see the *blankety-blank* light's red?" So much for Christian charity.

One of my favorite bumper stickers of all time is the classic: "If you can read this, thank a teacher." Since schools all around the area are starting back this week, I find that message particularly appropriate. Thank a teacher. What a novel idea. I wish I could go back and thank all of mine.

I can remember my first day of school as if it were yesterday. Well, maybe day before yesterday. It was, after all, 1958. I marched into Porterdale School wearing overalls, brogan shoes, and a black eye patch, the result of a summer accident that almost cost me my sight. My teacher was Miss Ruby Jordan and if I live to be a hundred, I'll never forget her. She took me on the most marvelous journeys, introduced me to the most remarkable people, and provided the most exciting adventures any six year old boy has ever experienced. She did all this without ever leaving her classroom. She did it through the magic of reading.

In my mind's eye I can still see Miss Jordan, sitting in her straight back chair, surrounded by little "lint heads" like me, clutching a book in her worn hands. Her arms were covered with age spots. Her hair was gray and her features were stern, but the brown eyes behind her wire rim glasses held a special twinkle. She would read to us, wonderful stories of *Mrs. Minerva and William Green Hill* and the *Tales of Uncle Remus*; columns from the Atlanta Constitution and stories from (gasp!) the *Bible*. Little by little she transferred this wonderful ability to us, her students.

She clearly loved books and taught her students, at least this one, to love and cherish books, too. She also took us on walks and taught us how to hold a baseball bat, this in the days before World Series trips for four year old T-leaguers. She wiped our noses when we had colds and scolded us when we were bad. She made us popcorn balls on special days and when my class finished first grade she postponed her retirement plans and taught an extra year so she could be our second grade teacher.

Miss Ruby Jordan didn't just teach us—she loved us, and she taught us to love learning. It's been forty years since I've seen Miss Jordan. In fact, she died many years ago. But rarely does a day go by that I don't think of her and her mannerisms and little sayings. A day never goes by that I am not touched by her influence. And, of course, she went to her final reward without my ever telling her how special she was to me. I hope she somehow knew.

I was fortunate enough to have many wonderful teachers. Betty Robertson was my fourth grade teacher. No one ever made learning more fun. Mrs. Carter Robinson was the toughest teacher I ever had. We were convinced that she knew so much about Georgia history because she had experienced most of it, but she instilled a love of history in me that made me want to share it with other generations.

Mr. J.T. McKay was among the most unorthodox teachers I ever had—and one of the most effective. I can still recite poems he encouraged me to learn several decades ago. My high school civics and PE teacher, and basketball coach, Ronald Bradley, taught me that if I reached for the stars, even if I fell short, I just might land on a cloud. He continues to inspire me to this very day.

I don't remember beans about biology, but much of what I know about listening to and caring about students was derived from my biology teacher, Lee Aldridge, aka Mrs. A. Joe Croom was probably the best teacher in the history of the world, and one of the best people. Like so many of the others, he left us without my ever telling him what an impact he had on my life.

I could go on and on. Every teacher I ever had impacted my life in some way, but I think you get the point.

School is back in session and our children are, once again, in the hands of their teachers. Those teachers aren't perfect, but they sure do try hard. Take it from a little old mill village child— They don't just touch the future, they mold it. If you were able to read this, tell one, "Thanks." You can't imagine how much it would mean to them.

Lost Kids Are a Tragedy . . . Not a Majority

As this book went to press, PBS was still showing this documentary and the great majority of kids in Rockdale County were still A-OK.

What an absolutely magnificent autumn weekend! Cool and crisp and dry. Recent rains have washed away some of the smog in our air, and as I walk up my driveway each morning to retrieve the newspaper, I can actually see stars sparkling in the night sky. Yes, I'm an early riser.

There are so many things I'd like to write about today, like the simple pleasure of sitting by a fire, drinking coffee, devouring the Saturday morning paper word by word.

I'd like to write about the World Series which we will be hosting for the fifth time in nine years. The Yankees are coming! Atlanta against New York. New South against Metropolis. We took care of their junior varsity last week. Now we have to face the A team.

I'd like to write about the glory of college football in the South on days just like today. Georgia will be trying to stop the Kentucky Air Force this afternoon. I sat in the broadcast booth with a genuine living legend at the last home game. What a story that would make.

There are a hundreds of things I'd rather write about than the topic that I feel compelled to discuss. I need to write about what a national documentary called the lost children of our community. Lost children. I can't think of a tougher subject. Children shouldn't be lost.

Everyone in our community, and a great number of people across the nation, have heard about the *Frontline* documentary about the "Lost Children of Rockdale County." Most of us saw portions of it between innings Tuesday. Many probably saw the replay Thursday night. It was horrifying. It was tragic. It was distressing. It is hard to imagine that many children in our community whose parents have no idea who they are are what they are doing.

I suspect the *Frontline* crew could go into almost any suburban community and find the same number of children who suffer from having parents who have abdicated their responsibilities as parents. We happened to be the community that suffered a syphilis epidemic, so here came the cameras.

When I was in junior high we had a lice infestation in our school and our school nurse, Annie Lee Day, had to pick through everybody's hair. Some kids had to wear salve on their head under one of their mother's stockings for a few days. I'm glad Miss Annie Day didn't live long enough to have to treat the children in the *Frontline* program.

Again I say, the program was distressing. Children shouldn't be having sex. Children shouldn't be having group sex. Children shouldn't be getting drunk and staying out at night and hanging around parking lots and smoking cigarettes. Children shouldn't have to try and find their own way in today's troubled society. They should be led firmly by parents who love them enough to set limits to their behavior and enforce those limits. But all of that is not what I feel like I need to say.

This is.

The PBS documentary gave the impression that a majority of teens in the Rockdale community were as lost and misguided as the few they so vividly portrayed. It's just not so. The program gave a few minutes of footage to kids who are pursuing whole-some activities instead of drugs and sex, but it made them look like they were outside the mainstream. They are not.

I am so sick of the media glamorizing the worst of our society. I wish, just once, I could see a network give coverage to some of the positive things teens do. Every afternoon there are thousands of teens who don't go to one another's houses to get drunk and experiment with sexual deviance.

They practice softball, for instance, until they are good enough at what they do to spend a whole weekend battling against the best teams in Georgia before losing the State Championship game in eleven innings.

They march and play music, until they are good enough at what they do to go to competition after competition and come home time after time with ratings of superior.

They stay in a teacher's room, who is giving freely of his own time, and play trivia games and seek knowledge, and learn for the simple joy of learning. Then they go off to other schools and bring home trophies for knowing more than anyone else.

They roll out mats and do cartwheels and flips and stunts that you would have had to go to the circus to see twenty years ago.

They play football and basketball and baseball and soc-cer; they wrestle and swim and run for the joy of running. They sing and dance and perform. They visit nursing homes and go on church mission trips. They hold down jobs and do chores at home. Sometimes they simply go home and do homework or watch tele-vision or go to the movies or talk on the phone. They are good kids. There are thousands of them

Sadly, there are children in Rockdale County who are lost, mainly because their parents didn't take the time or effort to help them map out a path. It's tragic and I feel for them. But there are a hell of a lot more kids who are not doing bad things.

I wish, just once, somebody would stick a camera in one of their faces.

Quick School Fix—Chapel Programs

This column is dedicated to the memory of Mr. Joe Croom,
who is probably in heaven right now explaining to Mr.
Homer Sharp that the chapel program the Key Club
actually put on, on Friday, was not the one he approved on
Thursday night.

Everybody and his brother seem to be concerned about the state of the public school in today's society. People say that schools are not safe and that learning is not taking place. They usually point to standardized tests, such as the Iowa Test to back up their claims. I think that's a rather unfair gauge. Most of my students have never even been to Iowa.

President Clinton is certain that adding 100,000 new teachers, at the expense of the Federal government, will solve the problem. Bill Clinton is from Arkansas. Isn't that where Lil' Abner was from? Check the performance of the students at the Dogpatch Public Schools to see how effective Slick Willie's education programs have been.

Roy Barnes thinks that holding teachers and administrators accountable for poor test performance will whip our schools into shape. Right. We're not really trying now. If Governor Barnes wants to hold somebody accountable, he needs to convince parents that students should be sent to school with the expectation of learning and behaving themselves.

I don't claim to be as smart as the president or the governor, but I have an idea for improving schools. More chapel programs. That's right. Chapel programs.

When I was in high school, back in the dark ages, before PCs, MTV, and ITBS, we had chapel every Friday morning. It was the highlight of the week. It shortened the school day, gave us something to look forward to, and introduced us to a wide variety of cultural interests.

We filed into the auditorium right after homeroom and

began our program by saying the Pledge of Allegiance. After that, someone would read a short verse from the Bible and say a prayer. We weren't aware that our First Amendment rights were being trampled upon because we were exposed to the Bible and a prayer.

After our rights had been abused by our school's failure to separate church and state, we would have a program. Sometimes students would perform, sometimes people from the community would speak, and sometimes we would have an expert come and share with us. An expert, of course, is someone who doesn't know any more about a subject than a local, but is farther away from home.

I liked it when Basil Rigney's Blue Rambler Band played for chapel. Basil Rigney was a stern taskmaster who coached the band the way Vince Lombardi coached the Green Bay Packers, with similar results. Basil Rigney would probably be arrested for child abuse today for bruising the feelings of the musicians in his charge. Back then he was teaching them music, and discipline, and doing a heck of a job at both. The Blue Rambler Band closed every performance by playing *Dixie*, giving everybody an excuse to stand and cheer, right there in the auditorium, a cardinal sin under other circumstances. We didn't know we were racists and bigots. We just liked the song.

At one chapel program a year, our school counselor, Eddie Najjar would perform a hilarious skit about getting peanut butter off the roof of your mouth. Mr. Najjar must have weighed 350 pounds, but he seemed light as a feather when he danced across the stage to do his skit. I will always remember his advice for doing well on the SAT. "Get a good night's sleep and select a good set of parents." Parents again. I don't think Eddie Najjar and Roy Barnes would have gotten along.

One year, two of our students dropped out of school and joined the army. They soon wound up in Vietnam. Every week, our principal, Mr. Homer Sharp, would read letters from these two former students in which they described the horrors of war and admitted that sitting through World History was preferable to walking through a booby trapped jungle looking for Viet Cong.

Both guys, by the way, made it home and returned to school to graduate.

My favorite chapel program of all time was when Linda Faye, Atlanta's first weather girl, came to Newton County High School to talk to the student body about meteorology. Before Linda Faye, Guy Sharpe was cock of the walk in Atlanta weather forecasting. Linda Faye didn't have more accurate weather forecasts than Guy, but she had much nicer legs, which she showed off by coming to our school wearing the first miniskirt I had ever seen. When she walked across that stage I was very glad that I had been made to sit on the front row because I had smuggled a piece of chewing gum into homeroom. It was Juicy Fruit. The aroma gave me away.

When I looked up and saw Linda Faye standing right above me in that miniskirt I thought I had died and gone to heaven. Future cotton farmer turned land developer, David Hays, was sitting right beside me. He looked like he had been caught between a warm front and a high pressure area.

Mr. Sharp was quick to realize that none of the boys in the auditorium were likely to learn anything about weather forecasting as long as our guest stood at the front of that stage. He politely interrupted her and escorted her down off the stage and had her present her program from floor level.

Linda Faye is exhibit A in my case for more chapel programs. I don't remember the formula for finding the area of a trapezoid and I'm not sure how many elements there are in the Periodic Table, but I'll never forget the day the weather girl came to Newton High.

Roy Barnes Barking Up the Wrong Educational Tree

Governor Barnes, naturally, had the political clout to get his reform bill passed, almost intact. It is the law of our state and we educators will be charged with making it work. For the sake of our students, I hope we are up to the task.

I see in the news that Governor Roy Barnes has a grand plan to reform education. Doesn't everyone?

Somebody always wants to revamp the way schools are run. All too often it's politicians that haven't spent time in the trenches, eight hours a day, 180 days a year. They usually have a knee jerk reaction and implement a new program that has had supposedly positive results in a study done by people who turned to educational research because they found out they couldn't teach. The problem with these programs is that we often find ourselves fixing things that aren't broken, throwing the baby out with the bath water, and any number of other cliches that shouldn't appear in a ninth grade English paper, much less this column.

I've attended school for 41 of my 47 years, as either a student or a teacher. I think I am qualified to write about schools and trends in education. I've seen some real doozies, too. When I was a student at the University of Georgia I had several education classes taught by professors who hadn't been inside a real classroom in decades.

They were big on teaching about discipline in those days. Now it's called classroom management. Our professors taught us that when we became teachers we should reward good behavior and ignore bad. They said that all acting up was caused by kids craving attention and that if they could get that attention by solving an equation or answering a question about the Bill of Rights, they wouldn't stick the pigtail of the girl in front of them in the ink well, figuratively speaking.

The problem with that theory was that it was a bunch of

malarkey. It was wrong, in other words. A dude, or dudette for that matter, that wants attention and doesn't get it will not stop acting out, the dude or dudette will simply resort to more outrageous behavior. "Not going to notice me sticking the girls' pigtails in the ink well, huh? Let me see you ignore my setting her hair ribbons on fire!"

Get my drift?

Another thing wrong with the above theory is that it completely disregards the fact that some kids are just mean, and that others haven't been taught to behave at home.

There was another big movement afoot in the education world when I was getting started in the profession. "Open classrooms." No longer would we squelch the creativity and imagination of our students by confining them to desks and restraining them within four walls. For an entire year I taught science in a building that had no inside walls. As I taught I could see no less than five other classes. So could my students. It's hard enough to compete for attention with twenty-five other students. Throw five other teachers and roughly 120 students into the mix and you will soon see why that particular school built walls around their previously open classrooms.

IGE was another big educational deal when I first started teaching, back in the previous century. Individually Guided Education. Every child learns in a different way and at a different rate of speed. Armed with large packets of worksheets and other printed materials, the teacher was supposed to facilitate learning by monitoring the progress of thirty self motivated students who would all love working their way through the materials. Thirty students working on thirty different lessons at the same time? No problem. Teachers, we were told, could do the job by being energetic and motivated. Right. And I'm a midget Russian astronaut.

Don't even get me started on whole language.

Now Roy Barnes says that education in Georgia is the pits and the blame falls upon the classroom teacher and the school administration. He's going to whip us all into shape. We have to shape up or ship out! He's going to improve the quality of teaching by taking away our job security. He's going to improve morale and performance by giving brand new teachers $6000 signing bonuses while veteran teachers haven't received a pay scale increase in five years because it tops out at twenty years of service. If schools don't raise performance, which Roy Barnes equates with standardized test scores, then the state will take over the schools, or allow all the students to transfer elsewhere. All that would do is lower some other school's test scores.

I have a news flash for Roy Barnes. He's wrong.

Most teachers that I've known are competent and dedicated and try their hardest to help children learn, even when the children themselves have no motivation to do so and even when there is no support whatsoever from the parents. They work longer and harder than ever before. No politician could be more disappointed than teachers when students don't learn. Threats and intimidation are not going to turn teachers into magicians. The root of the problems in education extends far beyond the classroom. In fact, it runs all the way back to the students' homes.

Roy Barnes needs to quit bad mouthing and threatening the school teachers he has and figure out a positive way to offer them help. He might discover that they aren't as easy to replace as he thinks they'll be. Throwing money at a problem doesn't always fix it.

I think most teachers feel like me. Last spring a friend said to me, "I wouldn't do your job for a million dollars."

"Neither would I," I replied. "Neither would I."

7

Holidays...
the best times
of our lives.

Holidays . . .
the best times of our lives

Time. We measure it in hours and minutes, days and weeks, and months and years. We begin, and end, each year with a holiday. Pretty good plan, eh?

Holidays. The special days we set aside to remember and celebrate. Christmas, Easter, Thanksgiving, the Fourth of July-- all have their own special charm. All, of course, have become too commercial and overblown and, naturally, we have all lost the true meanings of all the holidays and none are as special as they once were--back when we were kids.

Or are they? Only time will tell. I often wonder if our childhood holidays were as idyllic as we remember them. Perhaps our minds have selectively discarded certain memories, the way we sort through junk in our closets, throwing aside some memories and tucking others away for safe keeping. Time after time we pull these treasures out of the recesses of our minds and turn them over and over, examining them and embellishing them until our memories of reality replace reality itself.

Deep thoughts to introduce such a happy chapter in this book. The last thing I want to do is make someone think--particularly on a holiday. So Merry Christmas and Happy New Year. Sit back with a cold turkey sandwich or a glass of eggnog and enjoy reliving the best days of our lives.

Indelible Memories of
Childhood's Christmas

*This column appeared as a feature on the front page of the
Rockdale Citizen on Christmas Day in 1998. My weekly
columns began the next week, proving that Christmas
miracles still happen.*

So it's the week of Christmas and school is out. I can't
help but wonder if today's young people are as glad to be out of
school and as full of anticipation over Christmas as we Baby
Boomers were back in the '50s. Somehow I doubt it.

I was talking about Christmas with my mother last week
and the subject of money came up. My mother was quick to
remind me that Christmas is not about money. As usual, Mama
was absolutely right. I began thinking about the Christmases of
my childhood.

I was raised in Porterdale, a child of the mill village. I
have wonderful memories of Christmas and very few, if any, have
anything to do with money or material things.

Instead, I remember the feelings of the season and things
that money really doesn't buy. My greatest fear as a parent is that
I'm not providing my children the same legacy of memories and
values that my hard-working and loving parents bestowed upon
me.

Christmas in Porterdale was certainly different than
Christmas in Suburbia, circa 1998. For one thing, it didn't begin
at Labor Day, or Halloween, or even Thanksgiving. It began on
the day school let out for the holidays with a community Christmas program in the Porterdale Gymnasium, a mammoth building
by the standards of that day. The entire village turned out for a
program put on by the children of Porterdale School. The show
was heavy on scripture, prayer and Christmas hymns. The fact
that leaders in Porterdale paid no attention to Supreme Court rulings concerning prayer in school didn't seem to hurt any of us.

The highlight of Christmas was seeing the giant Porterdale Christmas tree in all its lighted splendor. It always touched
the ceiling of the gym, which had to be at least 40 feet tall. Neither
Rockefeller Center nor Rich's department store had anything on
Porterdale. B.C. Crowell would read the Christmas story, straight
from the King James version of the Bible. His voice was what
Luke must have had in mind when he wrote it.

After the program the students lined up and walked down
to the gym floor to receive their "Christmas Boxes" from Mr. B.B.
Snow, superintendent of the Bibb Mills. The boxes were brightly
colored cardboard, bigger than a shoe box. The contents never
varied. There were two red apples, two oranges, and two tanger-
ines. Also two boxes of raisins, a bag of hard candy, a giant peppermint stick, and bag of mixed nuts containing pecans, English
walnuts and what I've grown to learn were Brazil nuts. We children of Porterdale lived to get that box of goodies. I could make
the peppermint stick last a week.

The program would last until twilight. The air always felt
the same as we left the gym to walk home, our treasure box
clutched under our arm. It was clear and crisp and full of magic.
The town Christmas decorations would have been turned on during the program. There were giant Christmas trees in all the parks,
a family of snowmen, a choir of carolers and a life-sized nativity
scene. But the main attraction, without which it wouldn't have
been Christmas in Porterdale, was the star on the water tower. My
kids have seen light displays at Callaway Gardens and Lake Lanier
and our very own horse park. Each boasts millions of lights. But
I'm absolutely certain they've never been as impressed as I was
with that simple five-pointed star. It didn't blink or dance or change
colors. It just sat there, towering over our village throughout the
Christmas season, reminding us of another star, 2000 years earlier.

Of course we had television specials in those days, but
they were not on videotape at our instant disposal and they didn't
include characters like Arnold Swartz-can't-spell-his-name fighting over a motorized toy. They were strictly black and white with

heroes like Bing Crosby. Santa Claus wasn't in every store or on every street corner. We wrote letters to him and made list after list after list of our dreams and wishes, taken straight from the pages of the Sears-Roebuck Catalog. Of course we understood that Santa would pick one or, in a good year, two things from the list to actually bring, but it was sure fun making the list. One year I got an electric train. I ran it around that oval track for a million hours. I still remember exactly what it sounded and smelled like. Christmas trees were an important part of Christmas at our little house. Ours was never very grand and if one bulb went out the whole tree was dark, but it was decorated with love (and lots of icicles).

The week before Christmas used to last two eternities. Now it's over in a nanosecond. But I can close my eyes and be 9 again. The magic of Christmas can carry me back to the unheated bedroom of my childhood. I can feel the weight of three or four handmade quilts and the coldness of the window pane against my nose as I would peer into the dark sky, hoping against hope to catch a glimpse of Santa and his reindeer against the star-filled night sky. I remember very few of the presents I actually received, but I hope I never lose the memory of that delicious feeling of anticipation that made Christmas Eve the most magical night of year.

My life has certainly changed. I live 8 miles and a million light years from the Porterdale of my youth. I don't think my kids are spoiled, but I don't think they'd ever get excited over a shoe box full of fruit, either. There's no Sear-Roebuck catalog anymore. I can't help but wonder if my three will one day wax nostalgic over gazing for hours at an Internet toy site. Their lives are saturated with all the glamour and glimmer of what passes for Christmas these day. I don't think it's possible to find any toy that would capture their hearts like an electric train. In fact, I bought myself--I mean, my son--one a few years back. It traveled far less than a million trips around its multilevel track system before the thrill was gone. I fear that my kids are far too sophisticated to fall asleep with their noses against a cold window pane.

So, what's the answer? How can I instill in them a sense

of the magic of Christmas? I was looking through a book the other day, and I think I found a constant. The book was written by a physician. His name was Luke. The passage was familiar and still reads the same as it did when I was 9. The miracle of Bethlehem is as significant today as it was 50 years ago--or 2,000 years ago--and will be 2,000 years from now. Peace, love, hope, and joy make Christmas memories--not money. I can make sure my kids have those things. We all can.

Merry Christmas to all--"and on earth, peace, goodwill toward men."

If Not the Dreamer, Honor the Dream

There was a time in my life that I couldn't conceive of writing a positive column about a holiday in honor of MLK, Jr., which just goes to show that times, and people, do change.

Monday off. Cool. Who'd argue with Monday--any Monday--off?

Well, for a long time a great many people argued against this particular Monday off, because this Monday is the day we set aside to honor the memory of Dr. Martin Luther King Jr., civil rights leader, Nobel Peace Prize winner--and dreamer. You remember the arguments.

"Why have a holiday in his honor when we don't have one for other great Americans like George Washington and Abraham Lincoln?"

"He caused more harm than good! The FBI said he was subversive!"

"Just one more thing crammed down our throats!"

"They can't make me pay honor to him. I don't care what they close down."

I heard them all, and many others that were even more mean-spirited. I probably even made some of the same arguments. I was raised, after all, in a different world and my vision was admittedly colored by the times. I lived through the turmoil of the '60s. Huntley and Brinkley brought the Selma and Montgomery race riots right into my living room. Martin Luther King Jr. wasn't widely supported in Porterdale. When Bull Conner turned fire hoses and dogs on marchers in Birmingham, most people I knew pulled for the dogs. I saw state troopers surround my high school in riot gear while the student body from my county's black high school marched in protest of school desegregation policies. I saw National Guardsmen and policemen with trained dogs patrolling the streets of Atlanta, "The City Too Busy to Hate," on the night of Dr. King's death. I lived through the days of the civil rights movement without understanding anything about it.

But since those turbulent days I've been forced to study the '60s with an objective eye, in order to teach it to a generation not yet born when that fateful event occurred in Memphis. Looking at who we were during those days is not always easy and raises hard questions. Was my generation of Southerners really raised in a world where people couldn't eat in a restaurant or drink from a water fountain or sit on a bus or in a movie theater because of their skin color? Did we really hate people we didn't even know for wanting what we all wanted? Did we really curse and spit on and even kill children because they wanted to go to school and learn and be somebody? Was that really us? Sadly and shockingly, it really was.

But one man had a dream. He dreamed of freedom and justice and equality for his people and for all people. He dreamed of a country that lived up to the promises made by our Founding Fathers in documents such as the Declaration of Independence and the Constitution. He dreamed of a country united in brotherhood, a nation of individuals working together for the common good.

And he didn't just dream. He was willing to work to make his dream a reality. He marched. He made speeches. His stirring words spoke to our collective conscience. He made it impossible for fair-minded and good people to ignore the wrongs of our society any longer. He went to jail for his dream. He subjected himself to hatred and mockery and persecution for his dream. And three decades ago he gave his life for his dream.

Now we have a Monday off, and there are still those who argue that we should not honor one man, particularly this man, in such a singular fashion. Perhaps we should and perhaps we shouldn't. But even those who just can't bring themselves to honor the man should be able to honor the dream. After all, isn't the dream of liberty, justice and equality the American dream? Absolutely. Long live the dream.

Help wanted for
the Valentine Impaired

The week after this column appeared, strangers stopped me on the street to ask what I finally bought my wife for Valentine's Day. I told them I bought her an iron. I really bought diamond earrings, and I didn't have to sleep on the couch.

I need help! Valentine's Day is only four days away and I haven't a clue what sweet, thoughtful, original and—above all —romantic, gift I can give to Lisa, my wife of 16 years, mother of my children and eternal sweetheart. She already has a really nice iron and I gave her an electric can opener for Christmas. I didn't skimp either. I got the deluxe model, complete with built in knife sharpener.

Back when we were dating it was easy to pick out the

perfect gift. No matter what I chose, she at least pretended that it was exactly what she wanted. Flowers, candy, dinner in a nice restaurant with candle light and soft music. In other words - the usual stuff. Early in our marriage (translation - before kids) having a romantic day together was pretty easy, too. Especially if Cupid's holiday fell on a weekend, as is the case this year. We could sleep in. I could serve breakfast in bed and perhaps draw her up a nice warm bubble bath.

Even after our first child came along we could manage to find a baby sitter and have a nice dinner and take in a movie. I did learn that a romantic comedy works best for Valentine's Day. One year I took her to see that Freddy Kruger guy and wound up sleeping on the couch - alone.

Now we have three kids. Every baby sitter in the metro area has blocked our number.

If we can't go out, I need to at least come up with a special gift. But after 16 years together, I've exhausted all ideas. She has forbidden me to send her flowers because she always gets stuck paying the bill. She doesn't like getting the candy that comes in those red, heart-shaped boxes. The kids get to it first and poke their fingers in it, looking for the right type of center. The little pieces of brown paper get scattered all over the house. What the kids don't destroy is left sitting around until it's hard as a rock. We throw it out just in time to make room for chocolate Easter bunnies.

When I was much younger (and much dumber) I thought lingerie was the perfect Valentine's gift. After all, it came in red and was lacy and frilly - and *I* liked it. A few years ago I realized that all the lingerie I brought home either wound up in a box in the attic (next to my discarded T-shirts) or was taken back to the store and exchanged for something long and warm in a really nice flannel.

One year I decided that it was truly the thought that counts and made my wife a really special handmade card. I cut out the hearts myself. I sacrificed, too. I had waited until the last minute and couldn't find any red construction paper around the house, so

I actually cut up one of my vintage Georgia Bulldog Schedule Calendars. She didn't seem to appreciate the significance of that gesture. I wrote a nice poem to go on the card.

"Roses are red, concrete is gray.

I love you, on Valentine's Day."

At first she laughed and seemed impressed. Then she started looking around for the real gift. When she realized that my handmade card was it, her whole demeanor changed. The couch was especially uncomfortable that year.

I've tried taking her away on trips, too. One year I rented a nice little cabin in the mountains. How was I to know that there was a Hare Krishna convention booked there the same weekend? At least we collected a lot of flowers and reading material and the tambourines died out about 3 a.m. The next time I book a cabin I'm making sure it has a couch. That floor was hard. Cold, too!

I considered jewelry but decided against. I'm afraid I'm a little taste impaired when it comes to picking out jewelry. An old high school girlfriend once accused me of putting the tack in tacky. Besides, jewelry stores make me nervous. I went into one once. Next thing I knew I was dressed in a tuxedo, standing in front of a Baptist preacher in a church so full of flowers that it smelled like a funeral home.

As you can see, I'm in a real dilemma here and would appreciate any suggestions that you think will keep me off the couch this weekend. And just in case I flub up again - Lisa, if you read this column... no matter what inappropriate present I come up with, please know I love you. I will always love you.

Hallmark Can't Quite Say It

This column was the last Mother's Day present I was ever able to give my mother. Call your mama. I wish I could call mine.

It was my wedding night. One week before Christmas. The early part of the bowl season. Georgia vs. Penn State in the Sugar Bowl was coming up, but on this night Auburn was playing some nondescript team in the Bluebonnet Bowl. We were on our way to New Orleans for our honeymoon and stopped to spend our first night as husband and wife in Montgomery, AL. Yeah, I know.

Lisa, my bride, was in the powder room of the honeymoon suite (Yes, there was a hotel in Montgomery, with a honeymoon suite) doing whatever it is brides do to get ready to come to bed on their wedding nights. I did what grooms do on their wedding nights while brides are getting ready. I turned on the television to watch a few minutes of the football game.

A commercial was playing. Isn't there always? Bear Bryant, the legendary Alabama football coach, was in the commercial. Bear Bryant is the only football coach in America to have an animal named after him.

His face looked like it was carved out of granite. He was sitting in a chair, gazing at a black and white photograph. On the table beside the picture was a rotary telephone. After a few moments the Bear's gaze lifted from the picture and he stared right into that Montgomery hotel room The camera zoomed in on coach Bryant's face and there was a tear in the corner of his eye. Then he spoke, and his voice sounded like he had a throat full of gravel. He said, "Have you called your mama lately?" I felt like he was talking directly to me. Then he looked back down at the photograph for few more seconds and mumbled, "I sure wish I could call mine."

That had to be one of the great commercials in television history, but when Lisa came out of the powder room dressed in her lovely white satin and lace ensemble, I had a heck of a time explaining to her why I was on the phone, long-distance, talking to my mama.

Fortunately, I can still call my mama, but I don't do it often enough. Sunday is Mother's Day, the day we set aside to honor those who brought us into this world. How on earth do we do that? How can we possibly show our mothers how much we appreciate all they have done for us? No card or basket of flowers or gift could ever convey how much my mother has given me.

My mother was not a soccer mom or flower of society or business professional. She was much more. She was a mama. She worked in a cotton mill 8 hours a day then came home and cooked dinner every night. She kept our house clean, and my sister and me in clothes. She also found time to make sure our school work was done. She knew who our friends were and what we were up to.

My mother loved me enough to teach me right from wrong. She loved me enough to give me everything I needed and also loved me enough not to give me everything I wanted. She gave more hugs that switchings, but enough of the latter to keep me in line. She protected me from harm, but allowed me to try things and fail or succeed on my own. She did not meddle in my life but made sure I knew that she was, and is, always available when I need her. She did without so that I could have. She and my father made sure I knew the importance of education, and that gift has taken me places I've never dreamed of and opened doors that I never imagined would be opened to me.

Hallmark can't cover all of that in a greeting card.

Whatever way I find to try and say thank you on Sunday won't be adequate. I think what my mother would really want is what she's given me all these years.

Love. Unconditional love. As long as my mama is alive, I'll know there is one person who loves me, no matter what.

Have you called your mama lately? It think I'm fixin' to call mine.

Trick or Treat . . .
It's Goblin Time Again

My children will soon have outgrown Halloween. How in the world will I get my annual fix of candy corn and Tootsie Rolls?

Rush to the store and stock up on candy. String orange lights across your yard and rig up your boom box to play spooky music. Tape plastic witches to your front door. It's Halloween.

Halloween, has changed drastically since I was a child. What hasn't? It amazes me to ride around our community and see all the lawn ornaments and decorations that pop up before the first leaf has changed. The stores have aisles and aisles of candy, fancy decorations, and, of course, costumes. Heaven forbid a child of the nineties be forced to go out into the night and beg for candy without a designer costume and a sculptured mask.

Halloween in Porterdale had little to do with stores and spending money. Good thing. The holiday was all about kids and creativity and imagination. We got to draw Halloween pictures at school, depicting the scariest night of the year. I drew the same picture for six years, of a gray two story house with a picket fence. The fence always had a jack-o-lantern on one gate post and a black cat on the other. There were orange and yellow leaves on the trees, ghosts hovering around the house's chimney, and the silhouette of a witch flying across a full moon. Talk about imagery.

The night before Halloween was a big one at our house. My mother and I would make my all time favorite, popcorn balls. Cut-rite wax paper and Karo syrup are as much a part of my Halloween memories as the pumpkins we carved. Occasionally Mama would bake sugar cookies from dough colored with orange food coloring and my sister and I would use raisins to make faces on the cookies, which I never ate, because I hate raisins. Once or twice we made caramel apples.

I guess we weren't too worried about communicable diseases in our little school because we still did things like bob for apples. It makes me cringe to think about all those dirty little faces submerged in the same washtub full of water, trying to bite the same apples. To my knowledge, no one ever caught anything, so I guess it wasn't the worst thing in the world.

The main event, of course, was Trick-or-Treat. We children would talk about what we were going to "be" for weeks and weeks and change our minds more often than we changed underwear. We had seen store-bought costumes in the Sears-Roebuck catalog, but I can't recall anyone ever wearing one. We made our own. There were lots of hoboes wandering the streets of Porterdale on Halloween night. Just blacken your face, put on your daddy's old hat, and sew patches to your clothes. You were a hobo. Gypsies were popular for girls. A colorful blouse, your mama's skirt, a scarf, heavy makeup and a dangly earring. Viola!

There were, of course, pirates, cowboys, witches, scarecrows, and dozens of ghosts. One of the worst whippings I ever got was when I cut eye holes in one of my mama's best sheets so that I didn't have to be a hobo for the third straight Halloween.

As soon as night fell the children of Porterdale would take over the village. We had free reign. There were over 500 houses in Porterdale and we made it a point of pride to visit every single one. There was no need for parents to accompany kids. Older siblings took care of the young ones. Every house in Porterdale was a safe house. The only thing to fear was the "Soap Sally" who might come out from under the bridge as you were crossing the river. She liked to catch little children and put them in her big black pot and make soap out of them. Luckily, I survived hundreds of trips across the Yellow River bridge without encountering her.

The treats were often homemade, which we didn't appreciate at the time. There was also bubble gum, hard candy, candy corn, suckers, and a few miniature candy bars. On one Halloween, a family on Elm Street invited everyone to come in and watch the first color television set in Porterdale for five minutes. It was better than a popcorn ball.

Children actually knocked on doors in those days and

asked, "Trick or treat?" as a question. The only trick we were allowed to do was scatter acorns across the porch of the person who stiffed us on candy, and heaven help us if we forgot to thank our benefactor for a treat, even if it was an apple dropped carelessly into our bag, smashing our homemade cookies.

While we fashioned our own costumes from materials on hand, we did get to buy an occasional mask at the dime store. They were stiff pieces of plastic with an elastic band which always broke. We called them "door faces." One year, about a week after Halloween, a lady from our church, infamous for being the homeliest person in three counties, came for a visit. My sister, Myron, walked into the living room where my mother was chatting with our guest and asked, "Mama, when is she going to take her door face off?"

I'm not sure how my sister survived that incident, but she did.

Sadly, our kids can't be allowed on the streets alone, and it would destroy their self esteem if we had them make their own costumes. Heaven forbid they walk into someone's house and watch television as a treat. But, hopefully, they will make some fond memories of their own this weekend to share with another generation who just won't understand how it was in the "good ol' days."

Happy Halloween and safe trick-or-treating. But watch out for Soap Sally. She may still be out there somewhere.

Taking Time Out To Count a Long List of Blessings

God continues to bless me and my family far beyond what we could ever deserve. The fact that you're reading this book is proof positive of that. Praise God from whom, indeed, all blessings do flow.

Thanksgiving. What a wonderful holiday and what a

wonderful concept--pausing to give thanks.

My thanksgiving memories are of a warm and cozy home, the Macy's parade with giant balloons, the Radio City Music Hall Rockettes, and, of course, Santa Claus. I don't remember ever sitting around the table with a multigenerational family while my father carved a turkey, ala Norman Rockwell. My mother thought turkey was too dry and was more partial to chicken, but her dressing was unsurpassed and I loved to smell the sage and black pepper in it, before she put it in the oven

My favorite part of Thanksgiving was, and still is, reading Furman Bisher's column in the Atlanta Journal-Constitution every year. We were a Constitution family and Bisher writes for the Journal, but the issues were always combined for the holidays. I hope Mr. Bisher won't mind, but I am going to be bold enough to share some of the things I'm thankful for this year. They say that imitation is the most sincere form of flattery. Consider yourself flattered, Furman.

I'm thankful, for one thing, that my family had the newspaper delivered to our doorstep every morning, even when we had little else, and I'm thankful that we had the Encyclopedia Britannica and other books, even when we had to go outside to find our bathroom. Reading changed my life.

While I'm being thankful for my childhood, I'll go ahead and say that I'm thankful for being raised in Porterdale, during a time when entire towns really did help raise children, and for the Bibb, who provided more than everything we needed.

I'm thankful that I don't still have to go out on the back porch to use the bathroom, but also thankful that I am isolated enough from my neighbors that I can if I want to. I'm thankful my wife doesn't edit my column, or my last blessing wouldn't have been counted, at least not in this public forum.

I'm thankful for young people who say "sir" and for signs on restaurant doors that say "Thank you for not smoking."

I'm thankful that Larry Munson tells me about the Georgia games I can't see in person, and I hope he lives forever, because Georgia football wouldn't be the same without him. While we're on sports, I, for one, am thankful for the thrills the Braves have given us in the '90s, because I remember all too well the '60s, '70s, and '80s.

I'm thankful that I don't live in Buffalo, or Pittsburgh, either, for that matter, and I'm thankful that an entire continent separates me from California.

I'm thankful that my sister and brother-in-law are spending this Thanksgiving in a brand new home.

I'm thankful for stadium seating in theaters, because no matter how tall the person in front of me is, I can still see.

I'm thankful for the onions in Waffle House Hashbrowns, the butter, salt and pepper in grits, and Tabasco and shredded cheese in chili. I'm thankful for fried catfish, any time, anywhere, but especially at Clarence Henderson's on a Saturday night. I'm thankful for the person behind the counter at the Varsity that will still scream at me, "What'll ya have?" instead of saying, "May I help you?" I'm also thankful that more restaurants seem to be willing to prepare my salad for me, instead of sending me to a bar to make my own.

I'm thankful for the headlights of my wife's car coming down the driveway in the middle of the night, after she's been called in to deliver a baby. Time and the stork wait for no man!

I'm thankful that my middle-school-aged daughter is at the school every afternoon after school, practicing with the dance team, instead of the places some children find to go. I'm also thankful that my ten year old son wants to go to the gym with me and that my second grader loves to read as much as I did. And I'm thankful for the smell of Crayola crayons.

I'm thankful when, at church, we sing a song I know by heart, if for no other reason than I don't have to put on my glasses to read the words in the hymnal. And I'm thankful when the speaker, any speaker, says, "In conclusion . . ." (especially if he or she means it.)

I'm thankful for long walks in the woods and that I live in a place where an inch of snow can create a 24 hour holiday.

I'm thankful for the doctors and nurses at Newton General Hospital who have taken such good care of my mama this week, and although I won't get to eat her dressing tomorrow, I'm thankful for the previous 47 Thanksgivings in which I did.

I'm especially thankful that the little lady from Montezuma has given me the privilege of sharing my thoughts, opinions, and general foolishness with the readers of this newspaper for the past eleven months, and hope I can to continue for a long, long time. And I'm thankful for the readers who tell me how much they enjoy my column, even when it's not as good as it should be.

Happy Thanksgiving, and may God bless you all.

'Tis the Season to Shop 'til You Drop

A wonderful thing happened shortly after this column appeared. Someone stole my wife's credit card. I let them keep it. They spend way less than she does.

It became official, I believe, as soon as the funny looking guy with the beard hit the high note Thursday night and the Rich's Christmas tree exploded into light. The Christmas shopping season is here. Beware of women searching for gifts!

Yesterday, of course, was the biggest shopping day of the year. Stores opened before the sun even thought about coming up and offered all sorts of enticements to draw customers. One department store chain offered color televisions at about a third of their normal price. The ad said limit of two. Most people thought that meant two per customer. They really meant two per store. Sure, the chain lost money on each set they sold, but they made up for it by selling chocolate covered cherries and Grill-o-matics at huge markups. It's a great country, isn't it? All kinds of ways to make money—all you have to do is figure out what they are.

My wife and teenage daughter like to sleep. It's their passion. 364 days a year I have to hire the Third Army Band to wake them up. OK. So, I really use a tape of the Third Army Band. You get the point. They are bad about wanting to sleep all day. But not the day after Thanksgiving! They are up before dawn and ready to shop until they drop. Literally.

They had plotted all day on Thursday with the other female members of the family. While we men were sitting around the living room, belching, watching football on television, and eating one more piece of pecan pie, the women turned the kitchen into a war room. Maps of the metro area were taped to the wall with malls, shopping centers, and free standing stores highlighted with color coded markers. Ads from the morning newspaper, which had to be brought in with a wheel barrow, by the way, were spread out all over the table and counters. The place looked like Eisenhower's bunker on the eve of D-Day.

This massive planning strategy began shortly after lunch at one family member's home and continued through turkey sandwiches and more dessert at a second person's house. Finally, the battle plans were laid. The lists were compiled, the check books and charge cards were inspected and pronounced ready, and the cell phones, vital for communication about unannounced sales, were charged and ready to go. An eerie silence fell over our house as the females in my family put out their clothes for easy access and went to bed.

Now I know what you're thinking. You're thinking, "What does this male chauvinist pig know about shopping? He probably walks into a mall, goes directly to what he wants, buys it, and leaves the store."

You're exactly right. But I do know what I'm talking about when I describe shopping on the day after Thanksgiving. I once accompanied my mother on such a trip. We went to Belvedere Mall and every car in Atlanta was there. Those of you who are natives to the area will know how long ago that was. The rest of you will have no knowledge of anyone having ever shopped at Belvedere Mall. We drove around in the parking lot for over an hour before giving up and leaving. The day was not a total loss, however. We bought a pair of roller states at the hardware store on Candler Road. That reminds me. Anybody know where I can find a skate key?

I also ventured out on a shopping expedition as an adult on the morning after Thanksgiving—once! I was looking for a Cabbage Patch Doll. You remember the craze, I'm sure. I wanted to "adopt" one for my newborn daughter, a real one; one that had a cloth face and Xavier Robert's autograph on it's bottom. I stood in line at a Toys-R-Us along with several thousand females in track shoes and warm-up suits. The smell of cologne hung over the air like napalm. Finally, the junior assistant store manager approached the front door carrying a big ring of keys. He wore a frightened look, like a deer caught in headlights. When he swung the door open the women stampeded. I'm not sure what happened to the door opener. One moment he was there and the next he was gone. I hope he didn't leave small children behind.

I didn't get a Cabbage Patch Doll that day, but luckily, my wife's aunt, a battle hardened veteran of dozens of one day sales, did, so Jamie didn't have to suffer through life as the only child in her generation to have to grow up without a doll with an autographed butt.

Yesterday seemed to go well for Lisa and Jamie. I was a bit concerned, I must admit, when American Express sent a complimentary limo to drive them to the mall, but when they returned late last night they looked content and the garage held most of what they bought. Besides, they explained, "Christmas only comes once a year."

Thank goodness for that.

And in case you're wondering, my Christmas shopping is already done, too. I'm giving everyone on my list cookbooks called "Dinner on the Grounds." If you haven't gotten yours, there are only 27 shopping days left until Christmas.

O' Christmas Tree, O' Christmas Tree

In case you're wondering, this year's tree was the best yet.
But, then again, aren't they all?

This weekend will be the biggest of the year for the purchase of Christmas trees, which has become a giant industry in this country. What hasn't?

Christmas trees have always held a special place in my heart. Nothing is more magical than a Christmas tree, with sparkling lights, brightly colored ornaments, and tinsel.

When I was a child my daddy always bought our family Christmas tree at the local Big Apple. The truth be known, my daddy didn't believe in spending more than one or two of his hard earned dollars on a tree that would be tossed in a few days, so most of our trees were of the Charlie Brown variety. Still, decorating that tree was one of the highlights of the year. We only had a couple of strands of lights and they were the kind that if one went out they all went out.   By most standards, our trees were pretty barren, but not to us. My mama always said, "It will look just fine when we get the icicles on," and it always did

Ideals Magazine changed my opinion of Christmas trees. Ideals was a beautiful magazine, full of beautiful pictures, stories, and poems. In fact, a local lady, Mrs. Mamie Ozburn Odum, often contributed her poetry to the publication. The *Ideals Magazine* always had pictures of elegant Christmas trees, beautifully decorated, with hundreds of lights. I got spoiled by looking at those pictures and dreamed of having such trees.

My mother, always willing to help our dreams come true, took over the Christmas tree buying duty and would hoard her extra change to be able to afford a nicer tree at Christmas. The only thing she ever hid from my father was how much she paid for our Christmas trees.

We were traditionalists. We used multicolored lights that didn't twinkle, even when white lights became the rage. We never went to the small bulbs and never used bubble lights or any of the other fads. Mama always put the lights on the tree, then we would get to help hang the ornaments, including a very special string of little glass beads, shaped like Christmas bells. The icicles went on last and we had a constant battle as to whether they should be hung separately and delicately or tossed in the air and allowed to fall where they would. Families have broken up because of the great icicle debate.

During the '60s someone came up with an aluminum Christmas tree. If you remember where you were when JFK was killed, you remember aluminum Christmas trees. You didn't put lights on them, just glass balls, all of the same color. My sister had to have one. The ornaments on ours were red, but the Christmas my brother-in-law was in Vietnam we changed to blue. We had a big color wheel to shine on the tree, which would change from red, to blue, to green, to orange, as the wheel rotated. We set the aluminum tree up in the front room and kept our real tree in the living room.

I never got over my love affair with Christmas trees and when Lisa and I were married, I vowed to have the biggest Christmas tree our dwelling would hold, regardless of costs. The first year of our marriage we began a tradition that has lasted 17 years. All year, we empty our pockets of change, every day, into a big jar. On Thanksgiving night we wrap and count our coins and use the money to buy our tree and new decorations. You'd be amazed at how the money adds up each year and we don't have to feel guilty about spending too much for our tree.

Of course we buy a real tree. I'd move to New Jersey before I'd put up an artificial tree. We usually drive to the State Farmer's Market to choose our tree. People buy houses with less time and effort.

I usually lose my religion, not to mention the Christmas spirit, when we get the tree home and I have to get the tree to stand up straight. I wish one of those NASA rocket scientists would do something really useful, like design a Christmas tree stand.

I send everyone out of the house for several hours while I put the lights—multicolored, of course, on the tree. Last year there were 2000. *Ideals Magazine* doesn't have anything on me anymore. Putting two thousand lights on a twelve foot tree can be very frustrating and sometimes I say words little kids shouldn't hear.

After the lights are in place and my family returns from exile, we eat supper—boiled shrimp and oyster stew—and then we trim the tree with the hundreds of ornaments we've collected over the years. Some are homemade and some are Hallmark's best, but all have a special place in our heart, and on our tree.

We've had our share of Christmas tree disasters through the years. We can tell the same stories as everyone else—of every needle falling off and trees having to be replaced on Christmas Eve—of trees crashing to the floor in the middle of the night—of lights going out all at once—but when I see the magic in the eyes of my children as they sit in front of the fire and stare at our tree, night after night, I believe that all the trouble we go through in our quest for the perfect tree is worth it, and I have yet another blessing to count.

By the way, I'm putting the lights on our tree tomorrow afternoon. If you're anywhere in the vicinity of Ebenezer Road—cover your ears.

"This is a Christmas to Remember"

This column was written and submitted to the Rockdale Citizen by my daughter, Jamie, as a Christmas surprise for me. It was one of the best Christmas presents I've ever received.

"Setting our hopes on a big snow tonight

We'll wake up to a world of white,
It's gonna be a Christmas to remember.
Light up the fire with Nat King Cole,
Always sentimental and don't you know that
It's gonna be a Christmas to remember."

The chorus of Amy Grant's "A Christmas to Remember" just about sums it all up. Think back. Go ahead--it's not that hard. Go back in your mind to all the Christmases in the past. Christmases filled with holly, trees, carols, and Santa Claus.

Maybe you remember when the Rich's tree was still on top of the Rich's bridge and maybe you used to ride the "Pink Pig." Remember the Christmases when you used to buy cute little Richie bears that wore sweaters and hats.

If you think back really hard you may even remember a Christmas when it snowed. You might remember when aluminum Christmas trees and big colorful lights were the decor of most houses in America or when Jimmy Carter thought that if we didn't use Christmas lights we could conserve energy.

When you were little, did you go to Christmas Eve services at church and then maybe even go look at all the Christmas lights? You probably couldn't sleep at night because you were so excited about what you might find under your tree the next morning--and heaven forbid--you might have even peeked--trying to get at least a glimpse of Jolly Old Saint Nick. I've been told that Santa used to only make wooden toys. Maybe your best memories are trying to find the perfect gift for your parents and loved ones.

Those are great memories that we all have and you probably have your own collection of memories to add to my list. But a lot has changed. We still fill the holidays with wreaths, carols, trees, cookies, and Santa. Rich's still has a giant tree--but it's no longer on top of the bridge. It still lights up on the high note of "O Holy Night." The pink pig no longer exists and I know few people who even remember ever riding it--all who haven't are very deprived. Richie Bear is no longer wearing a cute little sweater with Christmas trees but this year he's wearing a tux with "2000" written on it. I wouldn't call it cute, either. The clerk asked me if I would like to buy one but I told her that I would prefer Macy's adorable Millennium Snoopy. And have you noticed that most things aren't focused on Christmas this year as much as the New Year?

I don't even remember the last time it snowed. I've never seen an aluminum tree--well, take that back--I think that's what Lucy wanted on *It's Christmas Charlie Brown!* Now we cover our houses with white icicle lights. And we don't even give a thought to saving electricity. Santa must not even know the meaning of wooden toys--now children's gifts are video and computer games.

Christmas Eve services are still held and people still drive around just to look at Christmas lights. Children can't sleep on Christmas Eve and never will, and Santa better be careful at night, because we still peek. And we still look for the perfect presents for those we love so much. Daddy--this is for you.

But let's concentrate on THIS year. Let's make memories this year. I've already started. I made very bad sugar cookies. I mixed up two recipes. I guess Rachel (character on *Friends*) is not the only klutz when it comes to the kitchen.

> *"Time doesn't stand still*
> *Many things change*
> *But some things never will*
> *The memories we share*
> *The songs we always sing"*

So join me and let this Christmas truly be " A Christmas to Remember."

Jamie Huckaby

Christmas—A Time for Sharing

Many people wrote me after this column appeared and said that it inspired them to do something extra for others during the Christmas season. I couldn't ask for a greater compliment.

Christmas is only three days away? How did it get here so fast? Remember the expression, "slow as Christmas?" It's obsolete, for me at least. I think I still have boxes in the basement from last Christmas.

Christmas is a time for memories. I'm pretty big into memories. My friends are often amazed that I remember details of our shared past that they just can't quite recall. My wife, Lisa, has a ready explanation for that. She says that I remember things that never happened.

During this time of year radio stations and newspapers and school teachers who are desperate to keep their students busy, and quiet, for a few moments solicit Christmas memories from their listeners, readers, and rowdy students, respectively. In fact, this column began on Christmas Day, one year ago, when I took time to write about my memories of Christmas in Porterdale, during my childhood.

Just last week, I was thrilled to see that my daughter, Jamie, had written an article for this paper about her Christmas memories. I was a bit apprehensive about what kind of memories I might have helped make for her. My biggest concern as a parent is that I will raise spoiled children who value the material things in life over the things that are really important.

I was very pleased as I read Jamie's piece. She wrote about the anticipation leading up to Christmas morning and of trying to stay awake to catch a peek of Santa doing his work, but didn't mention one present or gift.

Mostly, Jamie remembered the sights and sounds and feelings of Christmas. She remembered many of the same things I treasure so much. The joy of decorating the tree, the wonderful music of Christmas, the lights and decorations, and, more than anything, the feeling of peace and love and happiness that comes from having one's family and loved ones gathered together for a celebration of love.

During this time of year, however, I always feel a twinge of sadness, and perhaps guilt, because I and my family have been so blessed and because there are so many children in the world who will not have the opportunity to experience the kinds of Christmases that my children experience. I'm not referring to the Christmas morning memories when my children rub sleep from their eyes and come down the stairs to explore the myriad of gifts Santa has strewn across our living room floor. I'm talking about the other side of Christmas. The important side.

There are children in Rockdale County who have never even witnessed a church play at Christmas, much less had the opportunity to don a halo or bathrobe and play the part of an angel or a shepherd. They've never been inside a church, followed their mothers fingers along a hymnal, or heard the beautiful story from Dr. Luke's book about a baby King who was born in a stable and rested upon sweet-smelling hay in a far away manger.

There are children who are growing up without traditions of any kind. That is so sad to me. Building family traditions doesn't have to cost. Every Christmas Eve, just before bedtime, I don a silly looking Santa Claus hat and my family joins me on the hearth for the reading of "A Night Before Christmas," followed by the real Christmas story from the Bible. There are so many children who have never even sat down for a meal with all of their family present.

There are many children who have never known the joy of wishing for a special gift and then finding it under the tree or in a brightly wrapped present on Christmas day. That is sad. But it's not as sad as knowing that there are children who have never known the joy of giving to someone else.

My very favorite Christmas memory came when I was about seven years old. My daddy had been given the task, by his Sunday school class, of taking "Christmas" to a family who otherwise would have none. We filled up the trunk of his old Buick with things for the family, who lived out in the country in a small, unpainted house.

We drove up into their yard on the afternoon of Christmas Eve. A worn out looking lady in a faded house dress answered my daddy's knock on the door. Dirty faced children seemed to be everywhere. They watched in amazement as we brought in a tiny little tree, a string of colored lights, a few ornaments, and a box of icicles. The mother put her brood to work decorating the tree while we brought in the rest of the stuff.

There was a hot meal and groceries and Bibb Christmas boxes, which contained fruit, candy, and nuts. There was also a set of clothes for every child, a wrapped present for each, and a bag of toys for the mother to distribute after the children had gone to sleep. The children were beside themselves with excitement. I don't know the mother's name, but even though it has been forty years, not a Christmas goes by that I don't see her face in my mind's eye, with tears rolling down her cheeks as she watched her children celebrate Christmas. I think I remember tears in my daddy's eyes, too.

I wish the whole world could know the feeling I had that Christmas. I'm sure there are families in our community who are doing without this year, too. Three days left until Christmas. Maybe it's not too late to find them.

Christmas Greetings to Those at Work

This column remains dedicated to the public servants who sacrifice their time and energy for the rest of us--even when it means working on Christmas Day.

It's Christmas Day. The most special day of the year. If you have kids, as we do, you've been up since very early this morning. In fact, it might seem as if you've hardly slept at all, what with waiting up for Santa and all.

Christmas Day is, of course, a day for traditions. Maybe yours is to have a big breakfast, before opening mountains of gifts. Maybe your family gathers for a huge Christmas dinner, which is in the middle of the day, by the way. The meal in the evening is supper. Whatever your traditions, I hope you've been able, as I have, to spend your Christmas day in the comfort of a nice warm home, surrounded by people you love.

Some folks don't get to do that, you know. Some folks have to work, even on Christmas Day. I'd like to salute them. They are the people who give us Aunt Sally's phone number in Detroit when we decide we want to wish her a Merry Christmas and can't find her number to save ourselves. They are the people at the Waffle House who feed us if we have to be on the road, speaking of which, they are also the people who work at the ho-tels, motels, and inns across the nation. I seem to remember an innkeeper who played an important part in the first Christmas.

They are the people who work at convenience stores so that we can run out and buy batteries that didn't quite make it down the chimney and the folks who make it possible for us to rent tapes and video games, or go to a movie. I feel especially sorry for those people. I assume they aren't working by choice, but because of someone else's greed. Heaven forbid, we miss a chance to make an extra nickel, even on Christmas Day. If Ebenezer Scrooge were alive today, Bob Cratchit wouldn't even get the one day a year off.

Many people are at work right now because we just can't get along without them. For them there are no silent nights, no matter what date appears on the calendar. Take the firefighters for instance. We don't think about them unless we knock over a heater or an electric wire short circuits and we find our house ablaze.

The police officers are working, too. It would be nice if we could get the criminals to promise and take Christmas off, but anyone who has seen "Home Alone" knows that criminals just can't be trusted. Someone has to monitor the jails today and someone has to patrol the highways. Someone has to insure our safety while we are enjoying our holiday at home.

The EMT's in our community are on duty, too. Just in case, you know. And the men and women of the Armed Forces are spending Christmas far from home, helping fulfill the long ago promise of "peace on earth."

Don't forget the doctors and nurses. Please don't forget the doctors and nurses. My wife was a nurse for fifteen years. She spent her share of Christmases away from the family celebration. I'll not pretend that I was ever happy about her absences. This year she's at home, but if she weren't, I know I'd be much more understanding.

I've had the opportunity to observe doctors and nurses up close and personal over the past month. I now understand why nurses have been called angels of mercy. I knows the ones who cared for my mother throughout the seemingly endless nights would rather have been home with their families, but you would never have known it. I'm sure many of her care givers are at work right now, taking care of people who need taking care of.

My wife is now a nurse-midwife. That means she goes to the hospital and births babies. Babies don't pay much attention to the clock or the calendar, either. They may come at any time— night or day—even on Christmas. When the phone rings, off she has to go, into the night. Perhaps there are doctors and midwives delivering babies and taking care of mothers at this very instant, while we're having another piece of pecan pie or taking a nap in our new recliner.

Two thousand years ago there was a young couple traveling far from home. The woman was pregnant, and sometime during the night, her time came. She was probably scared to death, being in a strange city and far from home. Someone probably went for a midwife, who had to leave the warmth of her own home to go out into the night to deliver a baby and take care of a new mother—a stranger.

I'm glad she did, because we're having a pretty nice birthday celebration at our house for the child she delivered. I wonder if the midwife's family minded that she went to work in the middle of the night. I wonder if anybody thanked her. I wonder what would have happened if she hadn't gone when the call went out.

I wish I could take a piece of sweet potato pie or a cup of hot cider or some form of Christmas cheer to all the public servants who are spending Christmas Day working on our behalf. I can't. But I can say thank you, and I will. Thank you, and if I may paraphrase the words of Dickens's Tiny Tim, may God bless you, every one. Merry Christmas.

Long List of "Bodacious" Resolutions

As this book went to press I had not broken every single resolution, but it was very close.

Happy New Year, y'all. If you are reading this I guess it's safe to assume that the world didn't come to an end on the stroke of midnight. If you're reading it inside, using electric lights, then the Y2K bug wasn't the monster it was supposed to be. If someone is having to read this to you, you're either too young to understand much about this column, or you partied last night like it was 1999. Whatever the case, Happy New Year, y'all.

This is the day, of course, to make resolutions—to pledge to do things differently in the year 2000. The year 2000? It's really here, isn't it? Hard to believe. I remember sitting around with my friends in high school, talking about the dawn of the new millennium and trying to figure out if we'd still be here to see it. Sadly, some of us aren't. Things like car wrecks, cancer, and the Vietnam War kept many of my high school classmates from the big party last night.

I actually made it, and 47 isn't nearly as old as it looked in 1970 when I graduated. Funny thing. I spent New Year's eve sitting in front of the television watching Dick Clark host the countdown at Time's Square. I did the same thing 30 years ago. I got older. He didn't. But I digress. Then again, don't I always?

Resolutions. Usually I resolve not to make any because most of them are broken by the time the last college bowl game kicks off, anyway. But this year, I do have a long list of resolutions. Something about starting a new century seems to make New Year's resolutions almost mandatory. However, my resolutions won't be of the usual eat less, exercise more, spend less variety. No, indeed. If I'm going to publish a list of resolutions, I'm going whole hog. I'm going to allow myself to be a little bit bodacious.

For starters, I'm not going to promise to eat less. In fact, I'm determined to eat more. My wife and Dr. Atkins have turned me into skin and bones over the past two months. My pants are falling off and I've taken up my belt as many notches as I can, so I'm going to go back to eating more—especially catfish. I wonder if Henderson's Restaurant is open tonight? I'm going to eat more grits, too. After all, grits is groceries. And I'm going to have cornbread at least twice a week and fry chicken at home once a month. There. It's in writing! Ask me in March how this resolution is going.

I'm also going to work less and play more. I recently discovered that the world would not stop turning on its axis if I wasn't busily engaged around the clock. I'm going to make more time for my family and myself. I was recently reminded that none of us will live forever.

I also resolve to take long walks in the woods, read Uncle Remus stories to my kids, even when they are not interested in hearing them, and turn off the television, especially when it's just on for background noise. I'm going to play more board games, tell more stories, and make someone laugh, every single day.

In the year 2000 I'm going to turn back the clock and write letters to my friends—the kind with paper, pen, envelopes, and stamps. If you don't get yours soon, let me know. I'm going to smile more and worry less. I'm going to try and be a little more Southern. I've noticed lately that I've started speaking faster and have all but stopped slurring my R's. I've got to watch that.

I would resolve to clean out the basement and laundry room, but that would take until the next century and prevent me from fulfilling all my other resolutions.

I'm going to spend less time on the freeway and drive the back roads more. I'm going to forgo franchise fast food joints and eat at family owned restaurants every chance I get.

I'm going to take my boy fishing more than twice this year.

I might clean out the gutters and replant the tulip bed, but don't hold me to those.

I am, however, going to do the crossword puzzle, if not every day, at least once a week.

I'm going to try and be a little more obnoxious when it comes to college football. I've tempered my emotions a bit over the past few years. I've actually tried to be gracious toward opponents, whether Georgia wins or loses. I don't really like being that way. I'm going back to gloating over victories and being sullen when we lose.

I'm going to get all of my columns in early and actually meet the publication deadlines for all of the books I have in the works.

Above all, I'm going to give thanks for every new day, because each day is a gift not promised us. And I'm going to try my very best to live, every day of my life, in 2000 and beyond. I hope you do, too.

Happy New Year, y'all.

Mardi Gras or Not, New Orleans is Hot

My most eye-opening New Orleans experience occurred over 25 years ago. My buddy made me promise never to reveal his identity. So far, I haven't, but there's a chance I could be bought--cheap.

Today is just another Wednesday for most of us. We went to bed last night right on schedule and grumbled a little this morning when the alarm clock went off, but eventually crawled out of bed and stumbled to the kitchen for that first cup of coffee—the one that turns us from groggy zombies into normal human beings.

About 500 miles west of here, however, today is anything but normal. It's the day after Fat Tuesday, which is the culmination of the carnival period known as Mardi Gras. Way down yonder in New Orleans they have been celebrating the survival of another winter with parties and parades and a general spirit of debauchery. Last night, on the eve of the Christian season of lent, was the big blowout. There ain't enough aspirin in the world to cure the headache hanging over the Crescent City today.

I've been to New Orleans on a number of occasions, the first when I was 16 and passing through with a group of Boy Scouts. Our leaders walked us through the French Quarter at 7 o'clock on a Sunday morning. Even then we saw things our tender eyes would never forget.

My wife, Lisa, and I honeymooned in New Orleans, just like Scarlett and Rhett. We'd been on Bourbon Street for maybe five minutes when I was approached by a skinny little street urchin, who looked to be about twelve, but who was wise beyond his years. He walked right up to me and said, "Hey, mister. I bet you ten dollars I can tell you where you got your shoes."

I was thirty at the time. He was, as I said, about twelve. He was way smarter than me. I thought about his proposition for a moment and then decided to teach him a lesson. I knew he had no way of knowing that I had gotten my shoes at White's Department store in Covington, GA. I agreed to the bet. He made me promise not to squelch and then handed a ten spot to Lisa to hold. I did likewise and then asked, "OK, where did I buy my shoes?"

He grinned up at me and responded, "Hey, man! How do I know where you bought your shoes. I don't even know you. I said I could tell you where you *got* your shoes and you got your shoes on your feet, on Bourbon Street, in Orleans parish in New Orleans, Louisiana, in the US of A. Pay up!"

I'd been had, but it was ten dollars well spent. I've gotten way more than ten dollars worth of enjoyment from telling the story.

I was in New Orleans during Mardi Gras one time. It was in the late '70s and the policemen were on strike. As soon as I arrived in the city I made the same mistake thousands of others did and parked in a no parking zone on Canal Street. When I came back to my car, three hours later, there was a ticket on the windshield, along with a note explaining that while the policemen might be on strike, the members of the Louisiana National Guard were not. Another expensive lesson in the city that C.A.R.E. forgot.

I can't say that I really took part in Mardi Gras. I was more like an observer and spent most of my time standing around with my mouth open, staring in disbelief. It's amazing what alcohol can do to people's inhibitions. It's also amazing what otherwise normal and rational human beings will do for a string of plastic beads thrown from a Mardi Gras float. I won't go into the details, but if you know someone who has been to Mardi Gras and comes home with an inordinate number of beads, you can bet that person won't tell his or her mama too many details about the trip. The city claimed they were going to crack down on flashing this year. I heard they made 400 arrests. That's like filling up a mayonnaise jar with water in hopes of draining the ocean.

A college buddy and I stopped off in New Orleans on our way back from the Cotton Bowl in Dallas one year. For some inexplicable reason, we signed up for a night life tour, the kind usually reserved for blue haired ladies from Des Moines and their husbands. Sure enough, we were the only two people on the bus younger than 70, but we had a great time. One stop we made was at the 500 Club, where we saw an exotic dancer named Sandra Sexton. My friend got a much closer look at the feature attraction than I did. He was invited up on stage to be a part of the act. The dancer rewarded him afterward with a great big kiss and an autographed photo.

He was the envy of the entire bus. Retired salesmen from

Toledo and Topeka slapped him on his back and congratulated him on his good fortune as we made our way to the Cafe du Monde for beignets and cafe au lait. He was so pleased with himself that he carried his souvenir picture into the restaurant.

We were laughing and talking and replaying the events of the evening. My buddy had just taken a big bite of his powdered donut and a big sip of coffee to wash it down when a waiter, noticing the picture of Sandra Sexton, said to us, "I see you've been down to the 500 Club. You know, Sandra Sexton used to be a guy."

My buddy sprayed powdered sugar and coffee all over the folks at our table. He had assisted, and kissed, New Orleans's first sex change stripper.

I don't know what kind of stories people will bring back from Mardi Gras this week, but if they can top mine, I'd sure like to hear them.

8

"There's a Sweet, Sweet Spirit in This Place . . ."

"There's a Sweet, Sweet Spirit in this Place . . ."

The Bible tells us that if we raise up a child in the ways of the Lord, he will not stray from that path when he grows older. That's not an exact quote, of course, but I believe I got the general gist of the passage right.

I was, indeed, raised up in the ways of the Lord, in the Julia A. Porter Methodist Church in Porterdale. What a great congregation of believers they were! My father taught the Gleaner Sunday school class in that church for many years. He was a student of the Bible and taught me to be, also.

I'll not claim for one moment that I have always lived according to the lessons of life I learned so well at the Methodist Church in Porterdale, but I do know that I've never fallen beyond the help of the Lord's grace, and that is a comforting thought. To paraphrase one of the old standards from the Cokesbury Hymnal, the way of the cross most certainly does lead home.

Thankfully, I've found a church home for my family and myself at the Ebenezer United Methodist Church, about a stone's throw from my mailbox. We don't use the Cokesbury Hymnal any more, but we still pay lots of attention to the red words in the scriptures--the ones Jesus spoke.

This chapter is dedicated to all the wonderful saints who helped teach this little ol' linthead boy that Jesus loves even me.

I Could Almost See the Scars

It's easy to know what Jesus would have us do in a given situation. Actually doing it can be a whole 'nother matter.

It was July hot in August. I don't know exactly what that means, but I heard it in a song once and liked the way it sounded. Taking my wife and three small children to Washington D.C. for summer vacation sounded like a good idea when we planned the trip—in February. After five days in our nation's capitol, we had had about all the fun we could stand for one week. It was the last morning of our trip and we were eating breakfast in the Union Station Food Court.

If you haven't been to Washington, you should. It's a national treasure. Sadly, it is overrun with homeless people, con artists, and panhandlers. Sometimes it is hard to tell them apart. During our week in Washington we had heard every conceivable story known to man in an effort to pry money away from the tourists. I had become very adept at ignoring pleading eyes and outstretched hands.

Back to Union Station. My wife had secured a table amidst the throng of people. I was trying to juggle two trays laden with biscuits, eggs, hashbrowns, coffee, orange juice, and the like— typical fast food breakfast fare. A young man in a green fatigue jacket came up to me. He had long hair, a three day old beard, and carried a backpack. I made a point not to look into his eyes as he approached me and asked for a handout. I didn't even pay attention to his words. I just gave him the brush off and began to sort out my family's food items.

The young man then did a strange thing. He thanked me, even though I hadn't given him anything, including one moment's attention.

I watched him as he walked up to a well dressed man at the next table. This was obviously a businessman, on his way to work. He was dressed in an expensive looking blue suit, a briefcase was at his feet, and he was reading the paper. This time I did listen to the young man, even though he wasn't talking to me. "Might I have a bit of breakfast?" he asked the fellow at the neighboring table.

The man looked up from his paper into the youngster's dark brown eyes. Without saying a word, the businessman tore in half the Styrofoam plate that held his breakfast and raked half of it onto the portion of the tray he had torn off. He handed this to the young beggar, along with an unopened carton of milk.

The young man thanked his benefactor, carried his breakfast over to a counter, then bowed his head and said grace before he began to eat.

I felt like two cents as those words from Matthew that I learned as a child and have taught my children echoed in my brain. "That which you do for the least of my kingdom, you also do to me."

I watched the stranger with new eyes as he picked up his food and began to eat. I could almost see the nail scars in the young man's hand.

What Would Jesus Do?
Rest When He Was Tired for One Thing

I hope reading this column does for you what writing it did for me. It reminded me that God made the seventh day for rest because He knew that we all needed to, probably much more often than we do.

"In the beginning was the Word, and the Word was with God, and the Word was God. . . And the Word became flesh and dwelt among us." I didn't write that. John did. A long time ago.

Pretty neat story, huh? What a concept. God came to

earth and lived among the people. Not only did he live with us, he was one of us. The Bible tells us that while he was a man on earth Jesus *was* a man on earth. He lived with his family, ate food, drank wine, worked in his daddy's carpenter shop, went fishing with the boys, and did what people do. He knew temptation and fear, minded his mama, and even cried when his friend died.

He spent three years as an itinerate preacher. Did real well, too. It's been two thousand years and folks are still talking about his sermons. He walked all over his part of the world, never had a parsonage to call his own, cared for the sick, fed the hungry, and taught the people. Of course he had to attend numerous committee meetings with his disciples. With a schedule like that it stands to reason that Jesus, having become a man, would get tired. When he got tired, he withdrew from his work and rested. Says so right there in the Bible, in several places.

Jesus came to earth, of course, to die for our sins. I'm no theologian, but I also believe he came to show us how we should live our lives. Even Jesus rested when he was tired, and he knew that he couldn't really rest in the midst of all the hubbub and confusion he lived and worked in. Time after time scripture tells us Jesus went off alone to rest and pray, to commune with his Father.

Jesus was showing us what we should do. In today's world we move in dozens of directions at the same time. We work too much so that we can buy things and store up riches on earth. We drive our kids around at a dizzying pace, trying to keep them in every activity imaginable. The busier we are, the more we seem to take on. I'm more guilty than anybody. Sometimes we need to do what Jesus did when he got tired. We need to find a place of solitude. We need to rest. We need to talk to God. We need to listen for His reply.

My family and I did that over a recent weekend. We found a marvelous place called Covecrest Christian Retreat and Conference Center, in the north Georgia mountains. We rented a little cabin. It had a kitchen and a front porch with rocking chairs, but didn't have a television or telephone or any other electronic device. My kids didn't know how they would survive.

They survived by fishing in the pond, walking in the creek, climbing nearby mountains, and standing under an icy cold waterfall. We even sat on the front porch and read books and pulled out a dusty Cokesbury hymnal and sang camp meeting songs.

Jesus knew what he was doing when he went off alone to rest. We should try it more often. It makes life better. I wonder how many other good examples he set for us.

Saying goodbye isn't easy . . . Even for us Methodists

As this book went to press, David Hancock was alive and well at Oak Grove UMC, and Bob Winstead has fit right in at Ebenezer, proving once again that "all things work together for good for those who love the Lord."

I've been a Methodist all my life. In fact, my mother claims I was a Methodist for nine months before I was born. The first trip I took, other than home from the Porterdale Hospital, was to the Julia A. Porter Methodist Church on the first Sunday of my life. The Cradle Roll in that church was one of the first places the name Darrell Huckaby was ever recorded. You get the picture. I am a lifetime Methodist.

The history teacher in me won't allow me to write about being a Methodist without recognizing the fact that John Wesley began the Methodist Church along the Georgia coast shortly after James Oglethorpe founded the colony. Near Christ Church on St. Simons Island stands the Wesley Oak under which Wesley is purported to have preached. It has been said that Wesley was "set on fire with the Holy Spirit and people came from miles around to watch him burn."

Shortly after Wesley's methodical manner of worship had became a new Christian denomination, itinerant preachers, called circuit riders, began to travel across Georgia and the south on horse-back, spreading the gospel and ministering to backwoods populations. As Methodism grew and evolved, the idea of the itinerant preacher remained. Every Methodist preacher is an itinerant preacher. There are no permanent appointments in the Methodist Church. When a minister arrives to pastor a church, it is understood that it is just a matter of time until he or she will be leaving.

I told you that to tell you this: Having been a Methodist for 47 years, I have seen a lot of preachers come and go. All have brought great joy, some upon coming and others upon leaving. I'll never forget the preachers of my youth. One of my favorites was A.J. Bruyere. His father had played for the original Green Bay Packers, the ones sponsored by the meat packing plant, and he had a scale model of Lambeau Field, complete with handcarved players, in his office. On Sundays when the Falcons were in town, you could rest assured that the sermon would be very short. Preacher Bruyere, on those Sundays, would be halfway out of his robe before the benediction was pronounced.

When I was about 12 or 13, Preacher Bruyere went on a Sabbatical to the Holy Land. His interim was Dr. Dallas Tarkenton, father of UGA and NFL legend Fran Tarkenton. Every teenaged boy in the church came every Sunday while Dr. Tarkenton was with us in hopes that his famous son would show up. One Sunday he did, and played touch football on the lawn after the service. It was the greatest day in church since Pentecost, or at least we boys thought so.

During my high school days a saint of a man named Harold Lyda was pastor at Porterdale. Preacher Lyda was tall and thin and one of the most humble and sincere people I've ever met. About the same time the Reverend Lyda was with us, Bill Cosby had out a hugely successful comedy album in which he talked about his boyhood friend, Old Weird Harold. I wish I could say that the youth of the church never used that nickname for our pastor, but I can't. I can say, however, it was never meant to be mean spirited or disrespectful. In fact, Harold Lyda had a positive impact on my life that, I fear, he'll never know about.

I have known dozens and dozens of other Methodist ministers. Some, of course, I've known better than others. Although I've known many and respected most, I love at least one--David Hancock. David Hancock came to my church, Ebenezer United Methodist, five and a half years ago, along with his wife Cheryl and their children, Whitney and Andrew. Our church needed something special at the time, and something special is exactly what we got. Ebenezer means rock, and David Hancock has been a rock for our church when we most needed a rock. He has ministered to our church and to our community.

I'm sure that as David reads his name in this column, he trembles with fear about what I might write. You see, David has become one of my favorite targets for practical jokes. He is probably scared to death that I might share one or more of the better ones with the world. But, not to worry, David, I'll not publish what happened when you left your seat at the Braves game, or your response when you got a call from the Rockdale County "Building Authority" concerning preschool improvements. I won't even tell folks how you got out of speaking to the "Young Atlanta Christian Businessmen's Luncheon" so that you could go to Opening Day at Turner Field on April 1.

I won't even harass you about being a Tech fan, because I know you secretly like Georgia and just pull for Georgia Tech to make your daddy mad.

I will say this, however. We hate to see you go. I'm speaking now for the congregation you helped double in size during your short tenure, and the Rockdale community. We understand the nature of the Methodist beast, and will love and support your successor, but we hate to see you go.

I'll also remind you, that on the darkest day of your life, there will be a light shining for you in Conyers--the one you and Cheryl lit in our hearts when you came here. Go in peace, and don't forget the way back. And to Whitney and Andrew, don't forget. You owe me a dollar.

Sweet Salem Spirit
Spans the Generations

Change, someone once said, is the only constant in life. One thing I hope never changes is the spirit that prevails every August when folks return to Salem Campground to worship, fellowship, and remember.

Hot! Lord, it was hot! It had been over 100 degrees during the day. The setting of the sun had dropped the temperature a degree or two, but not much more than that.

I was sitting on a hard wooden bench. My shoes had been long discarded and my toes were digging into the wooden shavings beneath them. Sweat was pouring from my brow and running down my face and into my eyes. My ankles were even sweating. To tell the truth, I was just about miserable from the heat --but there's not a place in the world that I would have rather been last Friday night than at Salem Campground for the start of the 171st Salem Camp Meeting. Folks have been gathering across the road from the Salem spring every August since 1828. The great hand-hewn tabernacle was built a decade before Sherman passed through. Electricity was added while FDR was president. For almost 200 summers, good people have worshiped and fellowshipped here, sang gospel songs, prayed, and listened to hundreds of preachers.

Camp meetings originated in Kentucky, but were quickly adopted by the rest of the rural South. They provided a chance for farmers and their families to gather with others, once the summer crops were laid by, for fellowship and worship. Most of the annual camp meetings have long since disappeared, giving way to "progress" and more sophisticated worship services. But to experience a part of the South's heritage, not to mention a taste of the old time religion, come to the open arbor on Salem Road around 7:45 any night this week.

If you take me up on my offer, be sure to dress comfortably. Don't fret if you have small children. They can play in the shavings on the floor. They've been doing it forever. Several years ago one of the Salem preachers, a big time evangelist from California, took exception to the large number of children in the service. He gave the program director an ultimatum--"Get the children out of the tabernacle, or I'm headed back to Hollywood." It was amazing how quickly he was offered a ride to the airport. He decided to stay. Many of the children who were playing in the sawdust that week still come to Salem. Their children are now playing in the shavings, but if that bothers either of this year's preachers, they have not mentioned it.

Salem offers a unique cultural experience. Large crowds of people come from all walks of life, but it's much more than a cultural or social event. Many have found it life changing. Friendships and romances have begun here and countless souls have been saved and redirected. Be forewarned, you'll be hot, but the homemade ice cream served afterward will make up for the heat. Come prepared to be moved spiritually, and plan to come back, year after year, because that's when you really come to understand why Salem is such a special experience.

My mama first brought me to camp meeting while I was still in diapers. I married into a family that tents at Salem and have been fortunate enough to spend the entire week of camp meeting here each of the past 20 years. I see the same families year after year and have watched folks grow up, get married, and bring children of their own here. Of course, every year, there are familiar faces who are no longer with us, and we are reminded that death, too, is a part of life.

One of the faces I've missed this year is that of Mrs. Mary Sue Ramsey. Last year she attended her 100th camp meeting at Salem. That's right! One a year for 100 years. She used to tell me stories about coming to Salem on her daddy's wagon, back before the Wright brothers had first flown an airplane. Mrs. Ramsey, as recently as last August, sat behind me at every service, singing hymns, from memory, with great gusto. She passed away last March.

Last Friday night as we opened camp meeting with our theme song, "Sweet Sweet Spirit," I couldn't help but look over my shoulder, back across the campus toward Mrs. Ramsey's tent, remembering how she used to slowly make her way down the hill. Of course, Mrs. Ramsey wasn't coming down the hill Friday evening, but her grandson was. Joe Cook and his wife, Monica, were pushing a stroller. Riding in the stroller was their 7 month old daughter. Fittingly, her name is Ramsey.

That's why Salem is so special. I have no doubt that in the year 2099, Ramsey Cook and her descendants will be joining my descendants and others on hot August nights to sing the old songs and hear the gospel. As they sit and fan themselves and smile through the heat, they will be encompassed by the same sweet spirit that engulfs those of us who gather now for the last camp meeting of the 20th century.

But I bet they're not as hot as we've been this week.

No Spot Is So Dear

"There's a church in the valley
by the wildwood,
No lovelier spot in the dale;
No place is so dear to my childhood,
As the little brown church in the vale."

That song is by Dr. William Pitts. I used to sing it from the old Cokesbury Hymnal. You remember. The one with the brown cover. I always thought about my church as I sang that song, even though the Julia A. Porter United Methodist Church was not brown, but of red brick and was on a hill instead of in a vale. Of course, when I first started singing that song I didn't know what a vale was.

This weekend I needed to have my picture made for a book I've written that will be released, finally, in a few weeks. It's publication is only two years late, but that's another story. I decided to have the picture made in front of the Methodist Church in

Porterdale.

One might think that having a picture made for a book cover is quite a complex process. I suppose that for some it is, but not for me. I put film in the camera, hand it to my wife, Lisa, and ask her to take my picture. We had a grand old time Sunday afternoon in front of my childhood church. Our photo shoot probably lasted ten or fifteen minutes. We would have finished much sooner but after I had posed for 15 or 20 shots, Lisa realized there was no film in the camera. Once we overcame that obstacle, the wind refused to cooperate. Every time Lisa got ready to snap a picture, the wind would begin to blow what little bit of hair I have left in every direction. We finally got what we hope will be a suitable shot.

We were about to get in our car and leave when I realized that I had not been inside the church in close to twenty years. How could that be? Where does the time go? We decided to go in, but the doors were locked. Hoping I wasn't being a bother, I knocked on the door of the parsonage, which is right beside the church. A gentleman wearing a white dress shirt and tie answered the door. I knew I had the preacher. Nobody else in Porterdale would have on a white shirt and tie at three in the afternoon.

He was very gracious and volunteered to let us in the church before I even asked. He seemed genuinely glad to do it, too. Reverend Davis, which I learned was his name, escorted us around to the side door of the church, the one I was carried through when I was just a few days old to be placed on the Cradle Roll, as the list of Methodist babies was called in Porterdale.

The first thing I spotted was the water fountain. Surely it couldn't have been the same one my daddy held me up to when I was a toddler. I couldn't resist having a drink. The water tasted just the same, cold and pure.

As we walked into the sanctuary I felt at home. Time had gone backward. I looked up at the beautiful vaulted ceiling and remembered all the times when I, as a boy, had tried, unsuccessfully, to count the boards that line the ceiling. I took in the beauty of the arched windows, with the sun shining through the frosted glass. I admired the glorious stained glass window behind the balcony. I sat in one of the pews for a moment.

To my wife and children, and Reverend Davis, the church was empty. But not to me. All around me, on the seemingly empty pews, were the folk I grew up amongst. I could see each one, in their special places.

Marion Johnson was playing the organ. Neil Wheeler was leading the singing. Mrs. Annie Lee Day was in her spot in the choir loft and Red Few was in his. Someone once said that we always had a large and enthusiastic choir at Porterdale. Mrs. Annie was large and Red was enthusiastic.

Mrs. Estelle Allen was right down near the front, on the right side of the church. She may have been the sweetest woman I ever knew. I don't think she ever missed a funeral at our church. I could see Spunk Ivey and his wife Dora in my mind's eye, too. Mr. Ivey was Mayor of Porterdale forever and went over fifty years without missing a Sunday at church. Mrs. Ivey taught me Sunday School and prayed openly that I would make a preacher. I guess she'd be disappointed at how I turned out.

There were so many special people whose presence I felt in that empty church. They were mill people, for the most part, simple and honest and hard working. They came to church and gave their offerings and gave their time, lots of it, to children like me. They helped teach us right from wrong. They taught us important lessons like to turn to the middle of the Bible to find the Psalms, and to close our eyes when we prayed, and that we really needed to pay attention to the red words because they were the ones Jesus spoke. More importantly, they taught us that we were somebody and that we were loved.

I didn't want to take up too much of the preacher's afternoon, so we left before I was really ready to go. As we were leaving, though, I could make out the hymn that the angel choir was singing in my mind. It was Precious Memories. How they linger. How they do linger.

9

Everything's Not Pickrick . . . but it still ain't bad.

Everything's not Pickrick . . .
but it Still Ain't Bad.

Politics, along with religion, are two things that can't bear much discussion without angering people. Therefore, the smart thing, of course, would be to avoid discussing religion and politics. Usually, I do. Usually, but not always.

I've always had a keen interest in politics, even before I understood much about them. My father used to tell stories about Eugene Talmadge and his son, Herman, and Richard B. Russell, that Georgia giant of the U.S. Senate. Later I had the privilege of meeting many of our state leaders in person. I've never been invited to dinner at the White House, but I once road down Peachtree Street with Lester Maddox in a Model A Ford on the Fourth of July. It's hard to top an experience like that.

I've found myself on the unpopular side of many political fences, but never let it be said that I have ever been a mugwump, which is a gutless creature that sits on a fence with its mug on one side and its wump on the other. I have always been one to take a stand for things I believe to be right.

My daddy was a yellow dog Democrat. He would vote for a yellow dog if it were running on a Democratic ticket. I'm not and I wouldn't. I'm not sure I'm a Republican, either, although I'm a lot closer to Ronald Reagan than Bill Clinton.

Whatever I am, I am not afraid to express my opinion, so hold onto your hat and proceed with caution.

We Baby Boomers Have Arrived

If you are a fan of Bill Clinton's, you should probably just move on to the next selection. Of course, if you're a fan of Bill Clinton's, you probably stopped reading this book a long time ago, if you ever started at all.

I was in Athens recently at a social studies conference. A bad day in Athens is better than a good day most other places. The keynote speaker at my conference had a world of charts and statistics about the demographics of America's population. I was startled to realize that my generation-- the Baby Boomers--is now firmly ensconced in middle age. I'm older that my father used to be. I'll never play center field for the Yankees. My generation in middle age! How did we ever get there?

The startling realization that my bald spot is growing proportionately to my belt size started me to thinking about comparisons between my generation and that of our parents. Our mamas and daddies were heroes. They lived through a depression and fought Hitler. Beat him, too.

They ate buttermilk and cornbread and cooked at home. They saved their money and paid cash. They placed a value on truth and honor. They promised a brighter future for their children--and delivered.

I began to consider the common experiences that make my generation unique. We were the first to grow up with television. Captain Kangaroo and Howdy Doody were our childhood friends.

We stood in line at the school cafeteria to eat a sugar cube so we wouldn't get polio. Doctors came to our house and gave us penicillin shots when we took sick. We watched Mickey Mantle and Willie Mays and Johnny Unitas. We cherished their performances on the field and didn't care what they did when the game was over.

My generation was scared to death by the threat of nuclear

war. We saw Nikita Khrushchev pound a table and promise to bury us. We knew people who had fallout shelters. We lived through the Cuban Missile Crisis. In the fifth grade, during the height of the Cuban scare, we had a nuclear attack drill during school every day for weeks. Miss Mary Tripp made us sit under our desks and cover our heads. Miss Mary Tripp was one of the best teachers at Porterdale School but she obviously didn't know beans about nuclear bombs.

We, the Baby Boomers, watched transfixed as John Glenn orbited the earth. We saw the world stop for three days when a president was killed. We were the generation which realized that there were inequalities in our society that couldn't be tolerated and did something about it. We realized that the earth had a finite amount of natural resources and began to try and conserve them. We protested a war that we didn't believe in. We turned up our noses at cornbread and buttermilk and started drinking bottled water.

For years we were told by our teachers that we would be the leaders of tomorrow. Wouldn't you know it? Our teachers were right. Tomorrow is here and we are the leaders.

We are movers and shakers. We are surgeons and firemen and Baptist deacons. We are teachers and school board members and CEOs. And for the first time, the leader of the free world is one of us. And he's now standing trial for perjury and obstruction of justice. He has been impeached. Everyone agrees he did what he's accused of and are now merely haggling over a fitting punishment.

Doesn't that make a person stop to think? Is our president, with his apparent lack of moral judgement and penchant for disregarding the truth, reflective of our whole generation?

I have a friend from Harlan, Ky. Harlan is in the coal mining region of Appalachia. People there, by necessity, are cut from a different bolt of cloth. One day I was returning from St. Simons Island and stopped to buy gas at a station on the expressway. As I was filling my tank I noticed a Kentucky tag on the car beside mine. Just to be neighborly I tried to strike up a conversation with the owner of the Kentucky car. "I see you're from Kentucky," I said. "I have a good friend from Harlan, Kentucky."

The stranger looked at me with ice cold eyes and said, "Don't judge the whole state of Kentucky by a man from Harlan." He screwed on his gas cap and went inside to pay.

That applies here. Don't judge an entire generation by one president from Arkansas. The Baby Boomers aren't all like him. Are we?

Everything Was Pickrick Under the Gold Dome

Lester Maddox is, without a doubt, one of the most contro-versial politicians in our state's history. He is also one of the most honest. With Lester Maddox, what you see is what you get. He is, truly, one of a kind. I'm proud to count him as a friend.

There we were under the great gold dome. The whole Huckaby clan was gathered beneath the rotunda, inside the Geor-gia State Capitol in Atlanta. We were there by special invitation from the State Department of Transportation. I have to admit, I was a bit nervous when I got a letter in the mail from the DOT. I was afraid they had found out I was with the guys that stole that stop sign from Dixie Road in 1968.

They hadn't. We were invited to a special ceremony dedi-cating the Lester and Virginia Maddox Bridge, which spans the Chattahoochee River on I-75. What a great location. That bridge separates Cobb and Fulton Counties. Half the people in America cross that bridge on their way to Disney World. The other half cross it to come into Atlanta to work every day. The sign on the bridge will be seen, understand. No one deserves the honor more than our former governor and his lovely first lady. I mean that.

I know that Lester Maddox was a segregationist past the

time it was fashionable. George Washington owned slaves but I haven't noticed anybody refusing to spend dollar bills with his picture on them. Let me go ahead and say what many of the self righteous among us are thinking. How could they honor such a man by naming a bridge after him? I know he closed his Pickrick Restaurant rather than integrate it, depriving all of us, by the way, of some of the best fried chicken in the world. I know about the axe handles, too, except they were pick handles. Unfortunately, that is all most people know about Lester Maddox. They know the Lester Maddox portrayed by the media, and that's all. Most don't know the man, or his true record.

I first met Lester Maddox in 1968. He walked into my American History class, unannounced, and told all of us what a great country we lived in. He also told us to behave ourselves and mind our teacher and try to learn. Now I teach American History. Lord, I wish the governor would walk into my classroom and tell my students to behave themselves and mind me. Over the years I was fortunate enough to become good friends with this man and have learned an awful lot about him. Much of it is public record, much is not.

When Lester Maddox was chosen to be governor by the General Assembly of Georgia, many people openly feared that he would embarrass himself and his state. Nothing could have been further from the truth. The only people he embarrassed were the folks who had to take their hand out of the public till and the people who could no longer dictate state policy. Lester Maddox ran the most open and honest administration in the history of this state. You can look it up.

One day a week he opened his office to anyone who wanted to come in and talk. Have you tried walking into the governor's office and having a chat lately? He reformed our prisons and did away with the chain gang. He gave teachers, among the most poorly paid in the nation at that time, a 25% pay raise over his four year tenure and the so called racist appointed more black Georgians to state positions, including white collar jobs, than all governors before him combined. I'm not politicking. I don't think Lester Maddox is running again. I'm just stating facts.

The special day last week was not for dredging up the past. It was meant to honor the accomplishments of a truly good man and to honor the memory of his partner of "61 years, one month, fourteen days, fifteen hours, and 40 minutes"—this according to the governor himself. There were dignitaries galore. Guy Sharpe was there and so was the Reverend Norman Price. Commissioner of Agriculture and former Maddox campaign manager, Tommy Irving, spoke. So did Lt. Governor Mark Taylor. There's a lot of him to speak. Others made speeches, too. Roy Barnes sent a letter. All the people who spoke used words like character and honesty and decency. Those words don't ring true with enough of today's politicians.

The day clearly belonged to Lester Maddox and he was bouncing around the capitol in his seersucker suit as if it were 1966 and he was about to roam the state nailing Maddox Country signs to south Georgia pine trees. His energy and enthusiasm belied his 82 years and his six bouts with cancer. It was vintage Maddox, a reminder of a bygone day in Georgia politics.

Bubba McDonald closed the festivities by singing *God Bless America*, at Governor Maddox's request. That ol' boy can sing. We all joined in on the chorus, and for a few minutes, at least, believed that America would, indeed, be blessed.

By the way. Hosea Williams was in attendance, along with his driver, I hope. Somewhere along the line he and Lester Maddox took time to know one another and found out they had much more in common than they had differences. They are very close friends. Imagine that. I guess a bridge is a pretty good symbol with which to honor Lester Maddox, after all. He built a lot of them. More than most people will ever take time to know.

Controversy or Not—Here I Come

*Nothing has changed concerning this topic since this
column was first published, including my opinion.*

This is a mistake. I know it's a mistake. I know I should
not delve into this topic. Subjects such as who serves the best
barbecue and which state university has bribed the best teenaged
athletes to play football cause enough controversy. I know I will
offend some people. Others will not be able to see my position to
save their collective lives. Some will call me names and demand
my head on a platter.

Having said all that, let me say this. I don't care. This is
an opinion column and I have a right to express mine, even if it is
not politically correct and even if some don't agree with me. It
won't be the first time that's happened.

Thursday afternoon President Michael Adams of the
University of Georgia announced that, despite court rulings against
the practice, the University of Georgia would continue to use race
as a criteria for acceptance to my beloved Alma Mater. I think he
was wrong.

Let the onslaught begin. But before you call me a racist
and a demagogue and accuse me of being a member of the Ku
Klux Klan, at least hear me out.

First of all, let me say that I am not against any qualified
person attending the University of Georgia. Even as I type these
words—by the way—do we still type, even if we don't use a typewriter? Probably not. Sorry. Got sidetracked. Even as I process
these words I know some will say, "That racist so and so doesn't
want African American students at the University of Georgia. That
just isn't so, and just because I disagree with President Adams's
decision doesn't mean that I am against people of any ethnic background being admitted to our state's flagship university. I just
don't want them to get preferential treatment.

I was born during the time of a segregated South. As I
grew up, so did the region. I lived through the integration of

schools, restaurants, and society in general. I have been able to see, as I've grown older and hopefully wiser, that many people I still respect and admire were on the wrong side of that issue. I've spent time on the wrong side of it myself. I don't believe for one minute that I'm wrong now.

I lived through a day when many people, including some of our highest elected officials, insisted that black students were intellectually inferior to white students. The first time I had a black classmate was in the ninth grade. Due to the luck of an alphabetical seating chart a girl named Sandra Hollingsworth, a recent transfer from the all black R.L. Cousins High School, sat right in front of me. It took about one test for Sandra to blow the theory of intellectual inferiority right out of the water. She was way smarter than me. She's a doctor now, by the way, if you need more evidence than one Algebra test.

I know what the black students went through who integrated our schools. They were looked upon as trouble makers. They were mocked and ridiculed and worse. Looking back on those days, they were some of the bravest people I have ever known. They were pioneers. They were hand chosen, during the days of separate but equal, to prove that they and theirs deserved to be treated as equals. Even during those misguided days of my youth I believed that. I still do. That is why I am against Dr. Adams's decision.

I believe that he is demeaning the African American students in Georgia's schools. I believe that he is saying to them, "We realize that you can't produce on the same level as students of other ethnic backgrounds, so we don't expect as much out of you."

What kind of message does that send? Where is the justice in telling one student who has an A average and an SAT score of a thousand points, "Sorry, you don't qualify. Of course the person in the seat beside you who has a lower score and lower GPA does qualify because, well, their skin tone is different, and their people haven't had the cultural advantages your people have had."

Dress it up any way you want to, that's what Dr. Adams is saying.

We've spent too long telling children and young people that they aren't capable. We've lowered standards; we've lowered expectations; we've made allowances—for people of all colors. When you expect less and accept less, you'd better believe you get less.

It's time we judge people on their ability. It's time we expect the best of all people. It's time we raise our expectations and reward those who achieve regardless of race or gender. It's time we judge people "not by the color of their skin, but by the content of their character." Didn't Dr. King say that? Didn't he die for promoting that opinion. Doesn't it apply to everyone?

Sorry if I offended anyone, but that's my opinion, and I'm sticking to it.

Flag Flap Decisions Should be Left to Southerners

I know, y'all. I know. But we really do need to change it.

I 'spect I'll make just about everybody mad today. I'm fixin' to talk about the flag. Not the one we pledge allegiance to each day with it's fifty stars and thirteen stripes. That would be Old Glory. Washington carried it across the Delaware. Marines raised it on Iwo Jima. Neil Armstrong placed it on the moon. Car dealers fly it all day and all night. I'm not talking about that flag. I'm talking about the Georgia flag, which has come under fire recently because of the St. Andrews cross that adorns a full two-thirds of the banner.

Before I begin my comments on the flag, let me take you on a virtual tour of my living room. It has a fireplace against one wall with an oak mantle above it that my daddy-in-law made. A hand carved bald eagle adorns one side of the mantle. A bronze sculpture of Robert E. Lee and Stonewall Jackson, mounted on horseback and meeting for the last time in a glade at Chancellorsville, is on the opposite end.

On the wall above the roll top desk my mother bought for me when I got married is a print of a guy about my age leaning against the Vietnam Wall in Washington D.C. My Eagle Scout Award and some Bert Adams camp patches I designed are in frames next to it.

One entire wall is a bookcase, filled with hundreds of books. Many are about American history, a subject I've studied all my life and taught for a great part of it.

There are other prints on the walls. One shows General Lee meeting the remnants of Pickett's division returning from a failed charge up Cemetery Ridge at Gettysburg. Another shows Lee and Jackson in church, heads bowed, tears rolling down their cheeks. There is a print of the Stone Mountain carving and other prints of Lee and Jackson individually.

The lump under the quilt in the corner, playing a video game, is my ten year old son. His name is Jackson Lee Huckaby. I think you get the picture.

I am an American. I am a Southerner. I am a historian.

I understand the events that led up to the War Between the States. I never refer to it as the Civil War; there was nothing civil about it. I understand the motives of the political leaders and I understand the motivation of the men who fought, on both sides. I also understand the motives of the men who added the Confederate battle emblem to the Georgia flag in 1956.

Please know where I'm coming from when I say that Georgia really does need to change her flag.

I know that many, many people want to keep the flag the way it is. Trust me. I truly understand how they feel. No one is more proud of being Southern than I am.

I know that Robert E. Lee, who served valiantly in the United States Army and turned down full command of that same body, fought not to preserve slavery but to defend his homeland. I am fully aware that the vast majority of Confederate soldiers believed that they were fighting for personal liberty and independence, not so their rich neighbors could continue to own slaves.

I know that most of the Georgians who favor keeping the flag, believe it does represent their Southern heritage and not racism. Unfortunately, these well intentioned people are not aware of the flag's history, or, if they are, allow emotion to overcome logic when they make their arguments for keeping the flag.

The Georgia flag was changed to send a message to the Supreme Court that our state would defy its integration order. That's the end of the story. That's a fact, no matter how hard we wish it were otherwise. The Georgia General Assembly turned the Confederate flag into a racial symbol when they did that. The battle flag actually replaced three bars that were added to the flag by a state legislature full of Confederate veterans. They were representative of the Stars and Bars, the official Confederate flag, and were put there to honor Confederate soldiers. The 1956 lawmakers took away that heritage and replaced it with their symbol of hate and defiance. Those are the indisputable facts. A flag should represent all the people of a state, and a flag designed to promote a segregated society can never represent all our people. Think about it.

Now, having said that, let me say this. Last week this newspaper ran a column by someone named Lars-Erik Nelson. Nelson works for the New York Daily News. He called the Confederate flag a flag for "losers" and his column was full of disparaging remarks about Southerners who fought under the flag and those who honor it today. His column showed that he is completely ignorant of the facts surrounding our country's greatest tragedy and has no understanding, whatsoever, of the Southern psyche. Of course he calls for us to stop displaying all Confederate flags immediately.

I've got a message for Mr. Lars-Erik Nelson. We will change our flag in our own due time as soon as a majority of Georgians think through the issues and realize why it is the right thing to do. In the meantime, inflammatory remarks from his kind will only make people more determined not to change it. We don't need any hyphenated-named Yankee from New York tending to our business, and as for me, Lars-Erik Nelson can just kiss my rebel ass.

An Eye Opening Experience Under the Gold Dome

I'm glad I didn't spend too much time at the state capitol on this visit. After seeing the legislation passed by this year's General Assembly, I have decided that I was in a scarier place that I had realized.

I took a trip to the Gold Dome the other morning. I was interested in talking first hand to some of our esteemed state legislators about the governor's education reform bill. I'm all for any measure that will improve education in Georgia, or anywhere else for that matter. I just wanted to hear for myself that our current crop of lawmakers didn't intend to throw the baby out with the bath water in what seems like the inevitable passage of the governor's much discussed overhauling of our public schools.

I was reminded as I observed our General Assembly in action of the old adage that if a fellow ever watches laws or sausage being made, he'll never care for either again. I can say a hearty "amen" to that. I couldn't believe the way those folks were wandering around, reading the newspaper, and carrying on conversations, seemingly oblivious to people who were making speeches on important issues. If my civics class acted like those legislators, I'd have them all in detention. It wasn't long before I had seen enough and decided to take a walk and admire the newly refurbished building.

Although I have made many trips to the capitol I am always impressed by the history that permeates the building, although I've heard it said that at one time, more legislation was passed in the smoke filled rooms of the old Henry Grady Hotel than on the floor of the legislature. I enjoyed my little tour of the building, although I missed being able to see the two headed calf that once graced the museum on the top level.

I couldn't help but pause and admire the bust of James Edward Oglethorpe, who founded Georgia nearly three centuries ago. His original idea was to form a colony for debtors between the Savannah and Altamaha rivers. If everybody that lives between those rivers today spends money like my wife, I'd say that General Oglethorpe pretty much got his wish. Somebody stole her charge card last summer. I didn't report it for three months because the person that stole it spent way less than she did.

I also spent some time in front of the portrait of former governor Lester Maddox. There he was in his seersucker suit with a portrait of his beloved wife Virginia in a frame on the desk he was standing beside. I couldn't help but grin, again, at the large mullet in the picture, wrapped securely in the Atlanta Constitution, which the governor often proclaimed was only fit for wrapping fish. He should see it now.

There were several Confederate battle flags in display cases in the capitol. Real ones that had been carried into battle by real men, many of whom left home never to return, and many of whom returned to the burned out remnants of what had once been home. I couldn't help but wonder how they would feel about the furor being caused by their once proud flag.

It was such a beautiful day that I decided to walk outside and admire the grounds of our statehouse. No one had told the flowers or the trees that it was almost spring, but it was nice to be outside, anyway. I took time to examine many of the statues that surround the building. I paid homage to Governor Joseph Brown and his wife, General John B. Gordon, and, of course, Tom Watson. Jimmy Carter was in a place of honor, wearing a work shirt with the sleeves rolled up, which is somehow appropriate for the peanut farmer who would be president.

I finally got around to the southeast corner of the grounds. There stood my very favorite sculpture—former governor Eugene Talmadge, feet braced, finger pointing, shock of hair falling down over his forehead, and, naturally, coat thrown back to reveal his trademark red suspenders.

I stared into the bronze face of that great populist politician and then read the inscription on the base of the monument. It was a quote from Gene's own lips. "I may surprise you, but I'll never deceive you."

They don't make politicians like Gene Talmadge anymore. He was a champion of the little man, especially the little man who lived in rural Georgia. During the days of the county--unit system, in which a vote in Taliaferro County was worth ten or twenty in Fulton, he made no secret of the fact that he didn't care if he ever got a vote in a district that had street car tracks.

He was elected governor four times, the first on the promise of a three dollar automobile tag, which would have been a boon to poor Georgia cotton farmers during the height of the depression. When the state legislature refused to go along with the new governor's proposal, he found an obscure state statute that gave the governor the right to suspend any part of any tax during a state of emergency. It didn't take Ol' Gene long to create an emergency and suspend all tax on car tags—except three dollars.

The poor dirt farmers who gave him his political base believed him when he said, "You only have three friends in this world you can trust—God, Sears-Roebuck, and Gene Talmadge."

My daddy used to enjoy telling the story of the time he informed an old clod buster at a country store over in Arnoldsville that the state was going to move Stone Mountain.

"Ain't no way in tarnation they could move that big old rock," said the farmer.

"Gene Talmadge said they were," responded my daddy.

"Reckon where they're gonna put it?" was the old man's reply.

No. They don't make politicians like that anymore. I started to go back inside the capitol after my visit with Eugene Talmadge's statue, but decided against it. I had seen enough for one day.

By the way, I don't plan on taking any field trips to the sausage factory anytime soon. I decided after watching our legislature in session that there are some things we're better off not knowing.

10

Were the Good Old Days as Good as We Remember?

Were the Good Old Days as Good as We Remember?

Those were the days, weren't they? How many times have we all said that? For me, the good old days took place in a four room house in the mill village of Porterdale. We had linoleum floors and no closets. A space heater in the living room provided heat for that room and the kitchen. Layers of hand sewn quilts provided heat for the bedroom, as long as you stayed under them.

The bathroom was outside. A bare bulb hanging down from the ceiling in each room provided light. Their was no such thing as air conditioning, at least not as far as we knew. The television was black and white and could pick up three channels. The radio was AM and the telephone was a party line.

The car was second hand. The city limits of Porterdale was our entire world most of the time. A trip to town was a big deal. Movies were a dime and Cokes were a nickel. They came in little green bottles.

Eating out was unheard of. Home cooked meals were a given--every night. We could, and did, play all over the village and only had to report in at meal times and at dark. Nobody worried about where we were or what we were doing, nor did they need to. Our schools were friendly and safe. Our teachers always had the last say and paddled our bottoms when they needed paddling.

Were the good old days really that good? Yeah. I believe they were. Come now, with me, and lets play "remember when . . .?"

Clothes Make the Person? . . .
Lord I Hope Not!

Fashion, if anything, has taken a turn for the worse since this was published.

I'm fixin' to do something my mama told me never to do. (If I were from a more sophisticated region of our great nation I would say, "I'm about to go against the lifetime advice of my mother." But, since I'm a proud son of the South, I'm fixin' to do something my mama told me never to do.) I'm gonna talk about people's clothes.

My mama was a child of the Depression. She was one of four children being raised by a single mom before it became fashionable. Her dresses were homemade hand-me-downs which she felt fortunate to have. She constantly reminded me that whatever a person wore was probably the best they had, and if she ever caught me making fun of someone's clothes she'd send me out to cut a switch.

Despite that long-standing warning, I'm still fixin' to make fun of folks' clothes because today's teen fashions are, well, funny. At least to me. Have you been to a mall or other teen hangout lately? The platform shoes girls wear should come with a parachute so if they fall off their shoes they'll at least have a chance at survival. My 13-year-old daughter has footwear so ugly they'd make bowling shoes look stylish.

Teenage girls are also heavy into skintight polyester pants with flared bottoms. They come in purple and orange and neon green and are worn with tops two sizes too small and bare midriffs. The midriffs are bare to accentuate the belly button rings. If anyone can explain to me why someone would poke a hole through a perfectly intact navel, I'm willing to listen.

As bad as teen girl fashions are, boys' styles may be worse. I've gotten used to baseball caps being turned around backward. If everyone wants to go around looking like Yogi Berra, so be it.

But I'll never get used to guys wearing blue jeans with legs big enough for a family of four. And these elephant-sized pants are worn so low they defy gravity. The inseam winds up at the knees. I understand that's called "bustin' slack." For those teenagers who think they invented the style, I was bustin' slack 40 years ago, but not on purpose.

I was in the third-grade and had outgrown the one pair of overalls I wore to school every day. Mama told me to stop by the store and get a new pair on the way to school. The dry goods store in Porterdale opened at 7 a.m. so people on the third shift at the mill could shop on their way home. In our wonderful little town a 9-year-old could shop on his own and sign the ticket. But there was a problem this particular morning. The only overalls available were three sizes too large. The sales clerk, who I'm sure worked on commission, insisted they were perfect.

Promising me that I'd grow into them, he rolled up the cuffs and sent me off to school. Everyone else at Porterdale School had mamas who wore hand-me-downs during the Depression, too. Nobody mentioned my pants and all was well until recess. We had a giant sliding board on our playground and the real fun of the sliding board was to wait until the teacher wasn't looking and then to slide down one of the long poles that held it up--fireman style. I climbed the steps of the slide and waited until my teacher was watching the girls on the jungle gym. I climbed out on the support pole and slid. The excessive material of my pants got caught on a bolt. I wound up on the ground in my step-ins and my overalls were still at the top of the slide. Naturally every child on the playground had chosen that precise moment to turn their collective attention to the sliding board. I started running and didn't stop until I was safely inside my mama's kitchen.

I begged my parents to move to a new town, but they wouldn't.

A word of advice to today's teenage boys. Wear what you want, but don't go near the sliding board.

By the way, after reading the first draft of this article, my daughter, Jamie, rummaged through some boxes in the attic and came up with a picture of me taken in 1971. I believe I was on my way to a Three Dog Night concert. I was nattily attired in bright orange-and-white-striped polyester pants, bell bottoms, of course. The skintight shirt perfectly matched my 3 inch platform shoes and my sideburns would have made Elvis envious.

Hmmmmmm. I think I'll go hang out at the mall. These new fashions are pretty cool.

Longing for Just One Snow Day

Two winters have passed since this column was published. We've had half a dozen close calls and two ice storms . . . but no snow.

It's just not fair. Like every January, thousands across the metro area have listened to and watched every weather forecast, hoping against hope for that rare Georgia snowfall that would close schools and give everyone an unplanned holiday from math and science classes, homework, pop quizzes and school food.

And those are just the teachers. The kids would probably enjoy a snow day, too.

Every week the weather guys (and girls) tease us with the "S" word in their trailers. Then they make us stay tuned for further details. We sit and watch the news all through the dinner hour to learn that Tennessee and North Carolina and Minnesota will get snow.

The north Georgia mountains will get a dusting. Metro Atlanta? A possible trace with no accumulation. Where's the justice in that?

Don't get me wrong. I'm not demanding or even hoping for a blizzard. I know when I've got it good. I thank the Lord every night I wasn't born in Buffalo or Cleveland or anywhere else in the frozen tundra north of Nashville. But every couple of years a nice blanket of white would be nice. Just enough to create a siege mentality, sending everybody to Kroger for bread and milk and closing everything down for a day or two. Who can forget the joy of an unexpected snowstorm?

Back before we had 3-D weather and satellites and all the modern equipment that enables our meteorologists to track the first trace of frozen precipitation from its conception, snow would sneak up on us every now and again. Wasn't it wonderful? You go to sleep--nothing. Wake up. It looks like a Christmas card outside. Everyone sits by the radio straining to hear their school system listed among the closings.

As soon as you heard that school had been cancelled you put on every piece of warm clothing you owned and headed out to make snow angels, build snowmen, seek out opponents for snowball fights and find a hill to slide down.

Of course we knew what to do in the snow. We'd all seen it on TV and in books. But we in the South had to make some concessions to the fact that snow was such a rarity. For instance, there were no mittens or gloves in my whole town. We wore socks on our hands to protect them from the cold. It took about two snowballs for them to be soaking wet and colder than bare hands.

Naturally there were no sleds in Porterdale, but cardboard was a passable substitute. We never seemed to have the right kind of snow for making snowmen, which was just as well because we wouldn't have had top hats or scarves to decorate them with any way. But we would stay outside all day, never thinking about complaining of being cold or wet. Surprise snowstorms were one of the jewels that made childhood such a precious treasure and, unfortunately, seem to have gone the way of Guy Sharpe and record players.

OK. No more surprise winter storms for the metro area. We'll take a planned one. Let all the television and radio stations tell us about it days in advance. Let them all claim to have been the first with the forecast and the most accurate. Just let it snow.

It used to snow. Remember Snowjam? I want to see big flakes falling out of the sky. I want to watch the ground get covered. I want to build a giant fire and cook a pot of chili all day. I want the pleasure of waking my kids with the news, "It's snow-ing!" and then watch the excitement on their faces as they scurry around to put on all the warm clothes they can find. I won't even complain when they come in and out of the house a dozen times, strewing water and wet clothes.

I'll tell you how badly I want snow. I won't even mind hearing all the Yankee-Americans who have infiltrated our part of the world laugh at how excited we get over winter weather, and I'll only get a little mad when they continue to harp at us about not being able to drive on icy roads.

Which reminds me. I was watching the weather last night and schools were closed in Buffalo--because of snow. I also saw footage of lots of snow-related car wrecks in Illinois and Michigan. I guess Southern drivers went up there and caused them.

Meanwhile--think snow and happy sledding!

An Evening at the Movies . . . '90s Style

The features keep getting worse and prices keep getting higher. On our last foray to the movies we took the kids and spent $57.50 for tickets, Cokes, and popcorn for five. That's more than twice what the British paid for New York. Come to think of it, maybe we got a better deal, after all.

My wife decided that we would go to the movies the other day. That's not something we do often. The last time we went to the movies, in fact, the film was in black and white and didn't involve talking. Well, maybe it hasn't been that long, but you get the point.

When I was growing up in Porterdale, you had to go to town if you wanted to go to "the Show," as we called it. Going to town meant going to Covington to the Strand Theater. Now that was a movie house!

I think it cost a quarter. If you said "please" and "thank you," when you bought your ticket, Mrs. Brownie Osborne, the owner of the theater and ticket seller, would often give you a free pass. Mrs. Brownie Osborne appreciated politeness.

Usually I had money for popcorn and a Coke. You didn't get free popcorn for saying "please" and "thank you," but we all did it anyway, because we were brought up right. I can't remember the exact cost of the refreshments, but I'm pretty sure 15 cents covered both items.

The Strand Theater had a special section of seats in back where couples could sit. It was dark as a dungeon in that area, and I'm not sure what went on because I never had the nerve to sit there. I was scared enough that Foy Harper would shine his flashlight on me and tell me to "shush" while sitting in the relative safety of the regular seats. That was Foy's job. He was the usher. He would tear your tickets as you came in and then patrol the aisles during the movie. Heaven forbid anyone talk during the feature presentation. If one did, that person had to deal with Foy, who weighed all of 100 pounds, but ruled the aisles of the Strand Theater with an iron fist--or--flashlight, as the case may be.

I saw some great movies at the Strand Theater in Covington, and they were all preceded by a cartoon and one or two previews. There was only one movie per week. The movies weren't rated, but they didn't need to be. The most violence I ever saw was John Wayne shooting Indians and bad guys. The most titillating thing was Annette Funicello in a two-piece swim suit.

I don't remember all the movies I saw at the Strand, but many do stand out. I remember seeing "The Blob" and being scared to death for months that a great glob of gunk would roll right over Porterdale and take away every person and house. I saw Elvis movies at the Strand and Walt Disney classics like "Peter Pan" and "Bambi" and "Toby Tyler Joins the Circus".

I even saw *Gone With the Wind* at the Strand Theater. I was the ninth grade and had finally gotten up enough nerve to ask a girl to meet me at the movie. The young lady, who shall remain nameless, was from Covington, and was developed far beyond her years. I'm not talking intellect, either. I showed up on Friday night to view Margaret Mitchell's classic tale of the Old South convinced that I would receive an education, in more ways than one.

Sure enough, no sooner had Scarlett said "yes" to her first husband than the young lady I was sitting with was holding my hand. By the time Rhett danced with Scarlett at the bazaar, she was snuggled against my shoulder. Wouldn't you know it! An emergency had arisen at home. My sister had decided to go to South Carolina and get married to my brother-in-law, who was being sent to Vietnam in 36 hours. My mother had come, in person, to the Strand Theater to fetch me home. Just as I was about to put my arm around my companion's shoulder, which would have been a first for me, the powerful beam of Foy Harper's flashlight landed right on me. Sometimes at night I can still hear Foy's voice saying, "Here he is, Mrs. Huckaby. I found him. He's down here with a girl."

Drat my luck. By the time I got up enough nerve to ask another girl to meet me at the show, the Strand Theater was a mere memory.

I did indeed take my wife to the movies. We drove 30 miles to a giant theater with stadium seating and surround sound. It cost more than a quarter to get in. I said "please" and "thank you." The ticket seller called me a wise guy and didn't mention a free pass. I could feed my family for a week on what they wanted for Coke and popcorn. Thank goodness the concession stand took credit cards.

There were 16 movies to choose from. The Strand didn't show 16 movies in four months. They were rated everything from G to can't-say-in-a-family-newspaper. We saw Notting Hill. There was no cartoon, but they did show 37 previews. The movie was semi-funny. Julia Roberts was the star. She was pretty to look at, but she didn't have a thing on Annette, and Annette never talked ugly.

All in all, we had a good time and may even go back sometime, if we win the lottery.

Today's Society Needs More Mama-isms

Like all good Southern boys, I was raised up doing what my mama said. My mama, like most I suppose, had a few things she told me over and over and over. Her mama probably told them to her. I call them mama-isms. I'm not sure they are in such wide spread use today. I never hear my wife use any of them with our kids.

I wonder when American mothers turned away from mama-isms. I bet it was about the same time they started putting the Andy Griffith Show on in color and tried to replace the irreplaceable Barney Fife with Warren. Remember Warren? He came in about the same time the designated hitter did, and did about as much for the Mayberry police force as the DH did for the American League.

I believe we'd be better off if we brought back some mama-isms, and made our kids pay attention to them. Like, "Being nice don't cost a thing and is worth a fortune," or "Please and thank you will take you further than a Cadillac, for a lot less money."

I was told every day, "You say 'Yes, Ma'am' and 'No Ma'am.' I don't want folks thinking you're a Yankee child."

Did you ever hear, "Don't run with a sharp stick. You'll put your eye out?" That was one of my favorites. I have scoured newspapers nearly every day of my life looking for one mention of an incident in which a kid actually put his eye out by running with a sharp stick. I've yet to find one, but it still sounds like something good to tell kids not to do.

One that my mother said to me every time I ever left home in my whole life was, "You better behave yourself. You never know who might be watching you." You know, my mama was absolutely right about that. No matter how far I travel, I always run into someone I know. Whenever I do, my first thought is, "I hope I was behaving myself when they saw me. I'd hate for word to get back to my mama that I wasn't."

Another mama-ism from my youth was, "walking ain't

crowded." This was one she used when I would ask her to take me somewhere that was within easy walking distance—say, six or seven miles.

If I ever indicated that I was afraid to stay by myself at night her advice would be to "strike a match" if anyone bothered me. I think the implication was that my ugliness would scare anyone away who intended to do me bodily harm. This included the boogy man and the Soap Sally. It was before the days of home intrusions, but come to think of it, I've never been accosted in a dark room. This mama-ism was a direct contradiction of another favorite, "Act as good as you look and you'll do fine."

"You're old enough for your wants not to hurt you," indicated that no matter what movie star or athlete endorsed an item that I didn't need, I wasn't getting it.

Of course, one mama-ism used by mothers everywhere was "always wear clean underwear in case you're in a wreck." I was, in fact, in a wreck once. The condition of my underwear didn't cross my mind and none of the doctors or nurses mentioned it, in a positive or negative way. Speaking of clean underwear reminds me of a mama-ism my grandmother used to use. I guess that would make it a grandma-ism. She always assured us that whatever we were scared of, be it snake, spider, or barking dog was always more afraid of us than we were of it.

I was staying with my grandmama one summer. We were having a drought and the well was dry so she sent me to the creek to get a bucket of drinking water. When I got to the creek, a big ol' snake was sunning itself, right where I needed to fill up my bucket. Needless to say, I returned to the house with an empty bucket.

My grandmother, naturally, wanted to know why I didn't get the water.

I said, "Granny, I couldn't get any water. There was a big ol' snake down at the creek and I was scared of it.

She replied, using her favorite mama-ism, "That snake is as scared of you as you are of it."

I assured her that if that were the case, that water wouldn't be fit to drink anyway.

If my mama finds out I told that story she will probably use another favorite. "I'm gonna wear you out when I get you home."

Lord, she would, too.

I'm not sure what mama-isms today's soccer moms use to make sure their children grow up to be decent, respectful folks. I hope one that never goes out of style is the one that none of us can hear too often. "I love you, son. You know I love you."

Thankfully, I always did know that—and still do.

Take Your Shoes Off . . . If You Dare

I got thank-you notes from several drug stores after this column appeared. It seems that Band-aid and methylate sales skyrocketed in the area.

Whatever happened to going barefoot? I went out to Porterdale to visit my mother last weekend and she reminded me that it was May 1, which was always the magic day for being allowed to go without shoes. It didn't matter if it were 97 degrees on April 30, those shoes better be on your feet when you walked out the door. By contrast, On May 1, be it a hundred degrees or be it 48 degrees, as it was last Saturday, bare feet were fine.

Looking back on my childhood, it's hard to remember

why going without my shoes was something I wanted to do so badly. It might have been that we only got one pair of shoes per school year. Mine were always of the brown brogan variety. We bought them at the beginning of school and they lasted until summer, no matter how many sizes my feet grew. It might have been just getting relief for my toes that made being without footwear so appealing. Porterdale was the sandspur capitol of the world in those days. It was impossible to wander the village without getting one's feet stuck a hundred times. Usually the more agile among us could stand on one foot and pick the sandspurs out of the other. If you happened to get them in both feet at the same time you just balanced on the edge of one foot. You knew you had a bad case of the stickers if you ever had to sit down to pick your feet. Sitting, of course, created the possibility of getting sandspurs in your bottom. You'd find out who your real friends were when you got a backside full of sandspurs and needed help removing them.

During the summer months, the washing of feet, removal of imbedded stickers, and swabbing of said feet with hydrogen peroxide was an evening ritual performed all over our little mill village. A kid might go several days between tub baths, but no child in Porterdale ever went to bed with dirty feet.

Sandspurs weren't the only affliction awaiting the barefoot children of Porterdale. We also had to worry about the dreaded stubbed toe. I'm not sure today's children even know what a stubbed toe is. I'm not talking about a little garden variety, "Oh, I stubbed my toe." That doesn't even qualify. I'm talking about a running full speed, didn't pick my foot up high enough over the curb, black and blue, nearly broken, blood everywhere, red medicine and six Band-Aids, stubbed toe. If you've never had one, you wouldn't understand. It's impossible to put into words how painful they were. About one a week was my summertime average.

In addition to sandspurs and stubbed toes barefoot children had to deal with hot pavement, stepping on an occasional piece of glass, or a serious burn from some inconsiderate person who threw a cigarette down without crushing it under the heel of his or her shoe. The fact that Porterdale had a large population of stray dogs added a whole different risk to summertime.

We live on a farm and there are no sandspurs that I'm aware of. Neither are there curbs, broken glass, cigarette butts, or hot pavement, but my kids still don't go outside barefoot. One reason is that they have so many pairs of shoes, it would be a shame not to wear them as much as possible. Today's kids have shoes for school, shoes for church, shoes for playing in mud, and shoes for playing on sunny days; not to mention soccer shoes, basketball shoes, ballet shoes, clogs, flip-flops, and water shoes.

Of course, there is a shoe monster that lives in our house and invariably picks on the youngest child, who may not go outside barefoot, but never wears shoes in the house. And it never fails that when we are ready to go somewhere the little one can only find one shoe. Tolstoy could have written War and Peace in the time I've spent looking for one shoe. There are two rules concerning shoe searches. Rule number one. The time it takes to find the shoe is directly and inversely related to the amount of time you have to get where you are going. The later you are and the more important the engagement the longer it will take to find the shoe. I had to petition my church to start Sunday School twenty minutes later because I could never find my child's shoe.

The other rule is that the shoe will invariably turn up in the most illogical place it could possibly be and the child will never have had anything to do with its disappearance.

If my reminiscing about the good old days has made you nostalgic, go ahead and take your shoes off and go outside. My mama says it's all right. But be careful where you step and don't stub your toe. Band-Aids and peroxide are more expensive than they used to be.

It's Summer—At Last

*We survived the summer of '99, but barely. After travelling
to Maine, Niagara Falls, Myrtle Beach, and the north
Georgia mountains, not to mention keeping up with our
kids' activities, we were all ready for school to start back.
We needed the rest.*

Just two more days and sounds of jubilation will ring out
across Rockdale County. From Milstead to Magnet and all points
in between, teachers will shout for joy. Students might celebrate,
too.

I once was accused of going into teaching just so I would
have the summers off. Not true. There were many reasons I became an educator. June, July, and August were just three of them.
Of course, these days you can scratch August from your list of
benefits. I must admit, I do enjoy summer. But not as much as I
used to when I was growing up in Porterdale.

Summers then, of course, began around Memorial Day
and ended after Labor Day. They seemed eternal. My kids have so
many activities that my family can hardly squeeze in a week at the
beach or a camping trip. Heaven forbid we miss something. Especially not a camp.

My kids go to church camp, Cub Scout camp, cheerleading
camp, basketball camp, dance camp, academic camp, music
camp—you name it, there is a camp for it. Of course, few, if any,
involve a tent or staying overnight. I don't know when our society became so dependent on camps for our kids, but I think it was
somewhere between Mickey Mantle and Dennis Rodman.

Every activity my kids are involved in this summer requires three things. One is a registration form. It was easier to
register for the draft than Cheerleader Camp. For Vacation Bible
School, which isn't called camp, yet, but I'm sure one day will be,
we had to register three months in advance. Dance camp registration required a signature in blood.

The second thing about each activity is they all cost money.

A great deal of money, actually. I'm glad my parents didn't have to pay for me to become enriched and entertained all summer. If they had, I would have been out of luck. The combined fees we are paying for all our kids' camps is more than the gross national product of several small countries. Combined!

The third thing about these activities is that adults are 100% in charge of organizing and administering them. Sometimes it's hard to tell if the activity is meant to benefit the child or the adults.

Of course, all of the activities require that children be dropped off and picked up in automobiles. I think it's a law that if a family has more than one child, at least two children must be involved in activities which begin and end at the exact same time, in diametrically opposite ends of the county.

Oh, for the good old days when I was a poor little disadvantaged mill child. We had activities, too. Whatever we got together and decided to do was our activity.

We played baseball during the mornings. No uniforms. No coaches. No helmets or dugouts or pitching machines or fences with advertising. We just played. For hours. Sometimes it was only five to a side. Hit it to right field, you're out. If there weren't enough for a game we played roller bat or push up or flies and grounders. Every kid got a hundred times at bat a day.

The pool opened at one. All afternoon we swam. A dime to get in. If you didn't have a dime, B. C. Crowell would let you in, anyway. We'd play Marco Polo, sharks and minnows, and dive from the high board. We'd come out at supper time looking like prunes.

In the evening we'd get together and play chase, tag out of jail, freeze tag, or just catch lightning bugs. Sometime during the week we'd try to collect enough Coca Cola bottles to trade in for movie money for Saturday.

We walked everywhere we went and every adult in our community watched out for every child. Slip off to the river to go fishing and your mama would know about it before you got home.

The only activity involving grown-ups was Vacation Bible

School. They provided the glue and construction paper and popsickle sticks and read us the red words out of the Bible. You didn't register. You just showed up. If they ran out of cookies or Kool Aid, they would just make more.

We didn't stay inside and watch television and we didn't have Nintendo or Gameboys or the internet. Gee. Aren't we all glad our children won't be as deprived this summer as we once were?

Too Much Television for Kids is Not a New Concept

Shortly after this column was published we invested in a new satellite dish system. Now we have over 200 channels to choose from. Of course, according to my wife and kids, there is still nothing on.

There was much to do in all the newspapers recently concerning a study that claims children watch four and a half hours of television a day. At first I was aghast. "How terrible," I thought. I did what every respectable parent would do—I overreacted.

"Turn that mindless drivel off," I said to Jenna, my rising second grader, who was perched in her customary spot in the middle of the living room floor, eyes glued to a cartoon.

"What's drivel?" she responded.

"Never mind, " I said. "Turn off the television and go outside and play.

"It's still dark," she responded, "and pouring down rain." (We are early risers in the Huckaby household.)

I was not to be deterred from saving my child from the vast cultural wasteland. "Well turn off the television, anyway," I demanded.

Being the obedient child that she is, she turned off the television. An hour later I went looking for her and found her sitting at the computer. She was on the internet, in a "Kids Only" chatroom, talking to a third grader from Rochester, Minnesota with the screen name Spike.

"Come on Jenna," I said. "Rug Rats cartoons are just starting. Make yourself at home in front of the television set and I'll fix some popcorn."

Do kids watch too much TV? Probably. But face it. Who can blame them? They have giant screens with surround sound and a hundred stations to choose from! My generation grew up with a small screen and the picture was, of course, black and white. We had three channels to choose from—2, 5, and 11-- and we were glued to the screen, too. We would sit and stare at a test pattern. If you're under the age of 47, go ask someone what a test pattern was.

Sociologists say our children are adversely affected by all the television they are watching, but I don't believe it makes as much of an impression on my kids as it did on me. Forty years from now, I bet they won't be able to name complete network lineups. I don't think they can name what they saw last week. But I remember almost every show, including the day of the week, time it came on and channel.

There were some great shows for kids. Remember Captain Kangaroo and Mr. Greenjeans? How about Buffalo Bob Smith and Howdy Doody? Every Atlantan of my generation, and that includes those of us in the Newton and Rockdale County hinterlands, grew up watching Officer Don and the Popeye Club. Anyone remember the contents of the goody bags in the treacherous game, ooey-gooey? Remember learning to count backward from 5 because that's how Officer Don started the cartoons? I ate tons of canned spinach, even though I hated the stuff, but never developed bulging biceps.

In addition to the Popeye Club, there was a kids show featuring a witch named Miss Boo, the Friday Night Shocker with Bestoink Dooley, and of course the Mickey Mouse Club. It was a must-sec. The best part was the serials. Most of my buddies were partial to the Hardy Boys, but I liked Spin and Marty. I must admit, I probably watched the Mickey Mouse Club a while longer than most because I had begun to admire the way Annette Funicello filled out her Mousecateer sweater.

Saturday was great for television. Cartoons came on first, of course, and then a Tarzan movie, although when they showed one with someone other than Johnny Weismiller as Tarzan, I lost interest.

Roy Rogers, King of the Cowboys, came on on Saturdays. Roy had a sidekick named Pat Brady, who had a Jeep named Nellibelle. Pat Brady was always saying "mustard and custard!" when his Jeep wouldn't crank, which is as close as people came to cussin' on television in those days. When Trigger, Roy's Golden Palomino, died, Roy had him stuffed and he did the same to his dog, Bullet. I guess Roy's wife, Dale Evans, was a bit relieved that Roy went before she did.

Other Saturday favorites were Sky King ("Penny to Songbird, Penny to Songbird") and Fury—"The story of a horse, and the boy who loved him." They ended just in time to watch Dizzy Dean and Pee Wee Reese broadcast the Baseball Game of the Week, which happened to be between the New York Yankees and whoever they were playing. The game was never boring. The Falstaff Brewing Corporation was the sponsor of the Game of the Week and I do believe Dizzy Dean sampled the product as the game progressed. His commentary grew more and more colorful with every passing inning.

I'd say television made quite an impact on me. I could go on forever about the programs I watched on that old black and white set. In fact, I'd like to discuss the prime time schedule, but I don't have time. I've got to get on AOL and do a little research on a guy named Spike.

There She Was . . . Miss America

I felt certain I would get a call from the new Miss America after this column appeared asking to tell her side of the pageant story. I was ready to allow her to reveal all--but the call never came. Drats!

I confess. I watched the Miss America Pageant Saturday night. I didn't watch the Florida—Tennessee game because both of them couldn't lose. Besides, watching Miss America is a happy link to my childhood.

We always watched Miss America. It was one of the highlights of the television season, ranking right up there with the Bob Hope Christmas Show. Live from Atlantic City—The Miss America Pageant.

I'm sure those of you who are Baby Boomers and older did the same thing, even if you won't admit it. We'd sit and watch the parade of states. Each contestant walked across the stage wearing a ribbon with her state name, sashayed up to the microphone, and announced her name and the state she represented. "I'm Wendy Wellbuilt and I'm Miss North Dakota!" It was a great geography lesson. Hard evidence that there really is a North Dakota.

Burt Parks, who became associated with the pageant about the time Arizona became a state, was always on hand. His wisecracks and small talk were intended to entertain the audience while the girls changed clothes back stage. My daddy's favorite part of the pageant was the swimsuit competition. I was about thirteen before I realized why, which means that my son, Jackson, can watch the show two more times. After that he stays upstairs and watches Florida beat Tennessee.

My sister liked the evening gown competition and my mother leaned toward the talent portion of the show. Her comments never varied from year to year.

"That Miss Mississippi sure can tap dance."

"I believe this year's Miss Texas can twirl a baton a whole lot better than last year's."

"Miss New York sure does look natural with that dummy. I can hardly see her mouth move."

I don't remember what other talents the contestants demonstrated back in the '50s, but I do recall that that the arts of ventriloquism, tap dancing, and baton twirling were always represented. I'm pretty sure I left the room when the ballerinas, classical pianists, and opera singers did their things.

After two or three hours, the accounting firm of Priceless and Icehouse would narrow the field and those whose beehives had not yet fallen would answer some antiseptic questions about whether women should be required to wear high heels and beads while they cooked supper and waited for Ward, Wally, and the Beaver. Finally, they would announce the winner. She would be given a crown, roses, and a fur coat. She always cried buckets as she paraded down the runway while Burt Parks sang "There she is, Miss America." I never understood why she was crying. Burt Parks didn't sing that bad. After her tearful walk, she was escorted to a big throne at the top of the stage. My whole family would always insist, for whatever reason, that the ugliest girl won and vow not to watch the next year. But we always did. So did the rest of the country. It was irresistible Americana.

The Miss America Pageant has gone through some rough times over the years. I think their troubles started when they dumped Burt Parks as a host because he was so old and hired Tarzan (actor Ron Ely) to take his place. They lost a lot of credibility with that move, as well as a lot of viewers who sat in on the show for purely nostalgic reasons.

They refused to pay royalties to the guy who wrote their theme song and for a couple of years weren't even allowed to have someone sing "There she is," even though there she was.

Vanessa Williams broke the color barrier, becoming the first African American Miss America, but had to give up her crown because Playboy Magazine revealed that she had had considerably more exposure than the pageant could bare, so to speak.

Other beauty pageants have stolen a little of Miss America's thunder. The Miss USA pageant, for instance, doesn't pretend to be about anything but flesh and beauty. That show is heavy into bikini swimsuits and there's not a tap dancer or baton twirler in sight.

A few years ago a debate came up as to whether to continue the swimsuit competition in the Miss America pageant. The pageant decided to let the people of America vote. Duh! The men voted that the swimsuits stayed by an overwhelming margin. That was like letting second graders vote on whether to have recess.

The swimsuit competition is still a bone of contention. This year's finalists were asked if they thought it was demeaning to women. Nine out of ten said that it was a great display of physical fitness. Right. I was watching that part of the program thinking, "I bet Miss South Carolina has a great resting heart rate." And Georgia Tech recruited Joe Hamilton because of his potential in calculus.

Now the pageant leadership is considering allowing divorced contestants as well as those who admit to having had an abortion. They would still ban contestants with children. What a concept. It's acceptable to have killed an unborn child but not to be a mother. "There she is ... our ideal?"

The times they are a changing. I wish we could change them back—to the days of Burt Parks and baton twirlers.

Old Man Winter Ain't What He Used to Be

The temperature dipped below freezing 17 straight days after this column appeared and we endured ice storms on successive weekends. I had to holler "calf-rope" and admit that Old Man Winter still had a frosty bite.

Is it just me, or is Old Man Winter losing a bit of his bite? Let's face it. Winter just ain't what it used to be. I don't pretend to be a scientist. I can't explain and do not fully understand the green house effect or the diminishing ozone layer or other factors that some say are causing global warming. I do, however, know this. It ain't as cold as it once was.

Winters were tough when I was a little boy. No, I'm not going to talk about how I walked four miles through the snow to get to school every day. It hardly ever snowed in Porterdale when I was little, and when it did, they closed school so we could stay outside and play in it. But I did walk to school, as did most of the other children in our town. It was only about a mile, not four. But I remember that being one cold mile in winter time.

The worst part of the walk to school was crossing the bridge over the Yellow River. I know why they have those signs, "Bridges ice before roadways." It was cold as a well diggers bottom going across that bridge in January and February. I still remember bundling myself up in my coat and hat. Remember those old leather caps, lined with fur? They had a little bitty bill and flaps that you could pull down over your ears. We did too, because if you didn't, your ears would feel like ice cubes and Nippy Harcrowe would sit behind you in class and thump them all morning. Nippy Harcrowe took great pleasure in thumping ears that had turned red from being ice cold.

I would start out every winter with a pair of gloves. The first one was always gone after about two days. That wasn't so bad because I could carry my books with one hand and put the other in my coat pocket. By the second week of winter, both gloves were long gone, which meant that by the time I got to school my hands were as red and frozen as my ears were when I couldn't find my cap.

Getting to school wasn't the only hardship created by the harsh winters I remember from my childhood. Bedtime created a set of problems all its own. Our four room mill house didn't have central heat. We had a gas space heater in the living room which kept that room and the kitchen fairly comfortable. There was no heat in the bedrooms. Of course, we never spent any time in the bedroom until it was time to go to bed. Then we crawled under several layers of homemade quilts and went to sleep, or tried to.

Sometimes it would be so cold that you'd resort to sleeping in a stocking cap, or "sock hat" as we called it. The problem with that was that the darn thing itched so much, you couldn't stand to wear it. The windows would frost completely over and sometimes there would be a thin layer of ice on the inside.

Heaven help you if you needed to go to the bathroom during the night. It was outside, on the back porch. Nothing in the whole world could possibly be colder than bare feet on a linoleum rug. You don't know cold if you haven't crawled out from under a nest of quilts and stepped barefoot onto cold linoleum.

I think winters were colder in general back in those days, but occasionally we'd get a real cold snap and the temperature would hover around zero degrees for a few days. That would create real problems, because most of the houses, which were built on brick pillars about four feet off the ground, were not underpinned. The cold air whipping under the houses would cause the pipes to freeze and we'd be without water until the temperatures began to rise. Of course, when they did begin to rise it created a whole new problem. Frozen pipes usually burst. When the water began to flow again it would flood the kitchen, causing my Daddy to cuss and giving Oscar Harold Jackson, who was the plumber in town, a lot of overtime.

To try and avoid frozen pipes, anytime Guy Sharpe predicted that the Siberian Express, which is what he called a cold front coming down from Canada, was on it's way, we would wrap our pipes with newspaper and masking tape, catch up buckets of water, and leave the faucet in the sink dripping, which was supposed to prevent the water in the pipes from freezing.

I don't know how often these cold snaps came through, but I do remember that the river froze solid a couple of times when I was little and having a wind burned face and chapped lips was as much a part of life as stumped toes and bee stings were in the summer.

Now, of course, we have it made. Our floors are carpeted and warm and our pipes don't freeze. My kids hardly ever wear a jacket because they never have to be outside long. The farthest they have to go is a few feet, from the car to the house. I'm not sure they even make those leather caps with the ear flaps any-more, and if they did, I know I couldn't make my boy wear one.

Be it global warming or changing life styles or whatever, winter isn't nearly as bad as it used to be. Most people are prob-ably glad, but I sort of miss the cold weather. I think I'm going to watch the weather channel, and the next time the jet streams comes down toward us from over the North Pole, I'm going to leave my water dripping, just for old times sake.

My Apologies to Old Man Winter

The apology worked. We had an early spring.

A couple of weeks back I wrote what I intended to be a nostalgic and somewhat amusing look at the way winters used to be. In the column I suggested—all right—I came right out and said that Old Man Winter had lost a little bit of his bite. I be-moaned the fact that we hadn't had frozen precipitation in our little corner of the Southern world in a few years and even men-tioned those two catch phrases "global warming" and "depletion of the ozone layer."

Well, a world wide conference on Global Warming was canceled in Washington D.C. this week—because of ice and cold weather. You know, of course, what the past two weekends have brought us, weather wise. But honest, it wasn't my fault!

It's amazing where people will place blame. I got dirty looks everywhere I went this week. I'm used to being abused and ignored by my wife and kids. I'm a husband and a father. It comes with the territory. But this week, total strangers have fixed me with stares icier than the pine trees that crashed onto the power lines last Sunday.

I went to a store the other morning to stock up on supplies. I made the mistake of listening to the television weather guy who was predicting about a hundred inches of snow, followed by thirty more inches of sleet, topped off with freezing rain that would keep us inside until Easter. I searched high and low for stocking caps and gloves. Jenna Huckaby intended to build a snowman, don't you know, and I couldn't let her little hands get cold, could I?

I couldn't find any caps or gloves. I finally asked a supposedly helpful sales associate in a bright red smock if she could help me locate the items I needed. She looked at me like I had the plague. "We're sold out," she finally responded. Under her breath I heard her mutter, "Thanks to your stupid column."

Needless to say, I was perplexed, and had no idea what the lady meant by her statement.

That same morning, one of my co-workers came by my room. Her normally fluffy hair was stuck to the sides of her head, as if it hadn't been shampooed in a few days. Her response to my good morning greeting was to make a face at me and bark, "It might be if I hadn't been without power for the past three days." Under her breath I heard her mutter, "Thanks to your stupid column."

Later that afternoon I sat down at the lunch table, in my usual spot. Two people got up and moved to a different table.

"What's wrong with them?" I inquired of the only person who chose to stay and have lunch with me.

"They are cold!" she replied, and then added, "Thanks to your stupid column."

Before I could remark, another lady approached us and said, "My husband said to tell you not to write any more columns about how mild the winters have become. He said you jinxed the weather."

I couldn't believe what I was hearing. All these people were blaming my column for the winter weather we've been having. As if I had any influence over anything. I can't even get our cat to go outside to use the litter box or my wife to make a sweet potato pie. I sure can't control the weather.

I wish I could influence world events by what I write. That would be better than having Aladin's lamp. All I'd have to do is write something and the opposite would happen. The first thing I'd write about is what a great recruiting class Georgia Tech is going to sign next week. Then I could just sit back and watch all those giant linemen and stud hoss defensive backs defect to other schools.

I think my next column would be about how money is the root of all evil and how glad I am that I'm not burdened with having any. Think how the green stuff would roll in if I wrote that!

This is kind of fun. It makes me dizzy thinking about all the things I could say! I could write about how glad I am the Braves haven't been able to win the World Series the last few years. I could write about how much I enjoy sitting in traffic on 138. I could even write about how glad I am we have smoking sections in restaurants, so I get the advantage of breathing polluted, cancerous air without having to buy cigarettes myself.

Get it? All the opposite things would happen and we'd have more World Championships, less traffic, and smoke free restaurants.

Trust me readers. My column has nothing to do with our recent blasts of winter weather. Just to prove it, I'm going to give you a preview of next week's column.

Say, you remember how it used to be back in the 1970's? Every now and then we'd have trees and even whole houses flattened by tornadoes. Wonder why we never have tornadoes anymore?

Just kidding. I wouldn't really do that. And just in case Old Man Winter really does subscribe to the Citizen— "Calf- rope! We give up! Go back to Buffalo—pretty please?"

High Prices at the Pump
are Giving Me Gas

As this book went to press, gasoline prices had continued to climb. They had gotten so high, in fact, that I was considering parking my car and trying to get a good price on a horse.

It's finally time to talk about gas. Not the kind you get at the all-you-can-stand-to-eat Mexican buffet, but the kind we were paying about 78 cents a gallon for last year which now is going for $1.39.

The joy of buying gas has been on the decline for years. I'm sure most of you remember the good old days when service stations—"fillin' stations" in Porterdale terminology—really offered service. I'm fully convinced that future historians will write that the decline of Western civilization started with self-service gasoline pumps.

We went from being met at the car with offers to "fill 'er up?" and "check that oil for ya?" to getting out of the car and doing it ourselves, but at least we got to go inside the store and pay a human being. Now we don't even get to do that. We just swipe a piece of plastic through a magnetic gizmo and pump away. (Am I the only one who has trouble figuring out which way the card should face?)

Last summer I drove from Conyers to Maine and back— nearly 3000 miles. I bought over 200 gallons of gasoline and never handed my money, or my credit card, to a human being. I did go inside one establishment to ask for directions. It was a waste of time. The guy behind the counter didn't speak English. Even if he had, something tells me he wouldn't have been able to distinguish Bar Harbor from a bar of soap. I wasn't from around there but he was from a whole lot farther away than I was.

Y'all remember how it used to be. You'd drive up to a gasoline pump and a guy with his name sewn across his pocket in cursive letters and a rag hanging from his belt would greet you at your car window. "Reg'lar or ethyl?" he might ask.

My daddy used to tell a story about a guy who was real cheap but wanted people to think he was a big spender. He'd always tell the attendant to fill it up with hi-test while holding one finger outside the car window, indicating he wanted a dollar's worth.

Besides pumping your gas for you, the friendly fillin' station attendant would check your oil, wash your windshield, tug on your fan belt to make sure it wasn't about to snap, check the air pressure in your tires, and change the baby's diaper. He did all this while you sat right there in your car, if you so chose. If you wanted to stretch your legs, you could get out and buy a pack of peanuts and a bottled Coke. Everyone knows, of course, that a true Southerner poured the peanuts into the Coke before consuming them.

You got all of this service and then you paid about a quarter a gallon for your gas.

Sometimes stations would declare "Gas Wars." Ask a young person of today about a gas war and they are likely to recall Desert Storm. These weren't that kind of war. The way it worked was that one station decided it could get a few more customers if it sold gas for, say 28.9 instead of 29.9. Pretty soon the station on the other corner would drop down to 27.9 and so forth. Before you knew it, stations were practically giving gas away. Of course, with those big ol' 440 cubic inch gas guzzling engines we had back then, we wasted lots more money riding around town looking for the cheapest gas than we actually saved by buying it.

When folks had dropped prices as low as they possibly could, they started using other gimmicks to entice you to fill up at their place. One station gave away dishes. They were supposed to be something called Melmac, which isn't exactly fine China, but still sounds better than plastic, which is what they really were. Another gave away "Tenna Toppers," which were orange Styrofoam balls. The idea was to place them on top of your radio antenna, making it easier to locate your car in a parking lot. The problem was, this turned out to be a very successful promotion and it was almost impossible to find your car because everybody had a 'Tenna Topper.

My favorite gimmick was at the Gulf Station. They rigged up a hose which, when you drove over it, would trigger a big clock on the front of the station. The clock had a sweep hand with a little Gulf man on the end of it. It took ten seconds for the little Gulf man to travel around the face of the clock. If you weren't met by a smiling Gulf attendant by the time the Gulf man made it around the clock, your fill-up was free.

Every Friday and Saturday night my buddies and I, while cruising around town, would drive over to the Gulf station every fifteen or twenty minutes. We'd pull up to the pump, triggering the Gulf man on the clock and forcing Shorty Simpson, who was as wide as he was tall, to put down his Playboy magazine, tug on his pants, and run out toward the pumps. Shorty would arrive, out of breath, at our car window at about the same time the man on the clock reached 10. Naturally, we would drive away.

Eventually Shorty would say to heck with it and just sit there when we drove up, drooling over Miss May. Then, of course, we would sit there. What a great trick. We got free gas and got to hear Shorty cuss. Shorty knew more cuss words than anyone else in town.

Like so many other things, gas wars are probably gone for good. It's just as well. If we started saving too much money on gas the government would probably just confiscate it. Besides, who needs a 'Tenna Topper, anyway?

What We All Need is More Time on the Front Porch

I still haven't been back to sit on my friends' front porch, but it's still on my list of things to do.

I had to visit some folks the other day to pick up something I needed. Actually, we didn't get to visit. Nobody visits anymore. We're much too busy. I just dashed in and dashed out.

I wish I could have stayed, because they had a great front porch. It was big enough for five rocking chairs, arranged in a semicircle so folks could actually look at one another while they talked. It faced the east so if people had been sitting and rocking and conversing, they would have been warmed by the morning sun. It was also covered, to provide shade during the heat of the day.

What I wouldn't have given to have been able to sit a spell, rocking and talking and enjoying the fine spring day. But I had deadlines to meet and places to be. I was much too busy to waste time sitting on a front porch.

Isn't that a pity?

We have all gotten too busy to sit on the front porch. Most new houses don't even have one. We have a small one and even have a couple of rocking chairs on it, but about the only time I ever actually sit and rock is in the summer months when I carry my coffee and my newspaper out there and enjoy a few moments solitude.

The house I grew up in, in Porterdale, had a great front porch. It went all the way across the front of the house. Half of it was "screened in" and half wasn't. It had a swing big enough for three people and several rocking chairs.

We spent a lot of time on our front porch. In the fifties and early sixties Highway 81, through Porterdale, was one of the busiest in the state, especially at shift changing time. I used to sit on the front porch swing, watching cars go by for hours at a time. My sister and I would play a little game. We'd each pick a color and get points for each car that passed that was the color we had picked. She always won, but I didn't care. It was something to do.

During the hot summer months we'd sit on the porch in the evening, when the air had begun to cool just a bit, and shell peas and butter beans and pull the husks off fresh corn. My mama would fill two freezers with fresh garden vegetables every summer, all of which were either shelled or shucked on the front porch. They would last almost all winter, too. When I'd get tired of shelling or shucking, mama would tell me to take a break and chase the lightning bugs that always flittered around the bushes in front of the porch.

Porterdale had sidewalks. That's another thing we don't have enough of these days. People used to walk up and down them, too, giving other folks a chance to invite them up to sit and talk. And folks did. Sitting on a front porch talking to people is a whole lot better way to spend an evening than sitting in front of a television set watching someone try to win a million dollars.

When I got a little older, I would sit on the front porch late at night, watching for my daddy to come home from the second shift at the mill. I could tell his headlights from all the other cars in town and as soon as I saw them come up the hill toward our house I'd hurry through the house to meet him. A thirty minute talk before bedtime was better than not seeing him at all.

When I became a high school front porch sitter I quit noticing the colors of the cars that passed our house and started noticing the drivers, especially when they were young and female. When I was in the ninth grade, Sheila Bates, who was homecoming queen and captain of the varsity cheerleaders, rode by our house in a convertible with the top down. She saw me sitting on the porch and honked her horn and waved at me. I sat there for hours watching for her to come back by, but she never did.

Not too many years later I learned that there were better things to do while sitting on a front porch swing on a hot August night than shell peas. My daughter will be in high school soon. Maybe it's a good thing our porch isn't big enough for a swing, after all.

When I went away to college, one of the things I missed most, other than my mama's cornbread and fried chicken, was the time we used to spend on the front porch. The person who coined the phrase "quality time" probably had front porch sitting in mind.

The day of my daddy's funeral, twelve years ago, I sat in that same front porch swing and wondered if life would ever be the same again. A cotton farmer from Mansfield sat beside me, saying nothing. I doubt if I ever told him how much having him there helped that day.

My mama died last December and we sold her house. I rode by it the other day and there were kids' toys all over the front porch. That made me smile. I hope they find as much happiness on that front porch as I did.

I think I'm going to spend more time on my own front porch this spring. Who knows. Maybe I'll even go back to the house I visited the other day and invite myself to sit in the shade with the people who live there while we rock and solve the problems of the world.

Well, I might.

11

It's a Grand old Flag...
and long may it wave!

It's a Grand Old Flag . . .
and long may it wave!

Patriotism. Now there's a word that seems to have gone out of style.

In my opinion, which is the only one I ever express, we don't do a good enough job impressing upon our children the importance of those who have fought and died to make our country the greatest on earth, which I am fully convinced it is.

The flag has become more of a decoration than a symbol of freedom and the *Star Spangled Banner* is something we sing before ball games.

Our country was founded by honorable men who believed in an ideal and were willing to risk their lives so that other people could live in a land of liberty. Down through the generations, others have had to leave home and take up the cause of Freedom around the globe.

These people were special. We owe them much more than a short chapter in this book. For now, at least, a short chapter in this book is all I can offer. That and a word of thanks for protecting our grand old flag and a prayer that it may forever wave over "the land of the free and the home of the brave."

Remembering the Regular Guys

This column first appeared in the Atlanta Journal-Constitution on Memorial Day in 1997. Tony Piper's name is still on that black marble wall.

My daughter, Jamie Leigh, is going to Washington this week with her fifth-grade class from Sims Elementary School in Conyers. I hope her teachers don't mind, but I asked my daughter to look up an old high school buddy for me while she's there. I showed her his picture in my class yearbook and told her where to find him.

My buddy's name is Tony Piper. I haven't seen him since the night in early June when we graduated from Newton County High School. That was 27 years ago. It seems like a week. Tony and I weren't the best of friends. We didn't really run together, But we were pals. We had classes together and cut up together. In P.E. one day, my elbow caught his mouth. His tooth was chipped and his mouth bled right through English and world history. For two years, he good-naturedly threatened to get me back.

Tony wasn't an honor graduate. He wasn't on any athletic teams or in the band. He was just a regular guy. He was a little shorter than average and well put together, with curly black hair, bright brown eyes and a swarthy complexion. He would have made a great pirate.

The last time I saw Tony, he was loading a cooler of beer into the trunk of a friend's Camaro. He and about half of our newly graduated class were heading to Daytona Beach. We shook hands and slapped each other on the back. I warned him about what not to do at the beach. He grinned and promised that he'd try his darndest to do all the things I had warned him against.

I've never forgotten Tony's grin. He had never bothered to have the tooth repaired that I chipped. We promised to get together over the summer and keep in touch, and all those other things graduating seniors promise each other, but we never did.

That fall, I left my home in Porterdale to begin my education at the University of Georgia. Tony got drafted and began his education at Fort Benning.

As I said, I never saw Tony after we graduated, but I'm having my daughter look him up, just like I do whenever I'm in Washington. He's easy to find. He's just a little northeast of the Lincoln Memorial. He's Section 3 West, Line 119 on a black marble wall.

He shares that wall with almost 60,000 other regular guys who were asked to do something for their country. Tony's war wasn't one of your popular wars—like World War II or Desert Storm. His war was politically incorrect. But I had Civics and U.S. Government with Tony—trust me, he wasn't aware of the politics. He swore an oath to defend the United States of America and I'm sure he felt that if his fighting in the jungles of Southeast Asia wasn't necessary to the defense of his country, his leaders wouldn't have sent him there.

As a history teacher, I struggle each day with finding ways to help young people realize that the freedom they take so much for granted was not free, but was purchased at a terrible cost. About a million and a half regular guys, like Tony Piper, have paid the ultimate price. Tony paid it on July 31, 1971. Fourteen months after Daytona Beach.

Memorial Day is supposed to be the day we say thanks to those who have made that supreme sacrifice. I hope we can pause long enough today--during our cookouts and fish fries and pool parties—to remember why we're having a holiday.

And I hope that an 11-year-old girl can rub her fingers across a name on a wall and understand—just a little— what her daddy's old friend was asked to give on her behalf. I hope we all can.

Conceived in Blood . . . Born of Words
Happy Birthday USA

I respectfully dedicate this column to all the brave men and women who have served in the Armed Forces of our country. Thanks.

It was early summer in Philadelphia, PA. Trust me. Georgia ain't got nothing on Philadelphia when it comes to heat in July. The day I was there was the hottest in the history of the weather bureau. You can look it up. 105 degrees in the shade, if there had been any shade. I was there with my wife, Lisa, and our daughter Jamie, who was still in a stroller. We were waiting in a long, long line to get inside Independence Hall and see where the Declaration of Independence had been signed. A kid came by with a cooler on a little red wagon, selling Cokes for two dollars a piece. It was the best money I spent on the trip. We finally got inside to view the place where the world had been changed in 1776. It was worth the wait.

Here's why we stood in the heat for two hours to see inside an old building. England had set up about a dozen colonies in what they called the "New World" in order to help the British economy. You know—raise raw materials themselves. Buy low. Sell high. Not much different than today. The system worked out pretty well, too. They had a good thing going. Then old King George III got greedy.

One thing led to another—unfair taxes, high tariffs, unrealistic trade restrictions. The colonists soon realized that they didn't even have the rights that their fellow Englishmen across the pond enjoyed. A few radicals like Thomas Payne, John Hancock, Patrick Henry, and Samuel Adams began stirring up the masses. More stuff happened. The Boston Tea Party. More harsh laws. More strong words.

Words. The revolution began with words. Words put together in such a way as to cause people to think about the human condition. Words spoken with eloquence and passion that stirred the emotions of a people and drove them beyond words and ideals. Words which caused people to decide that principles such as liberty and freedom were more important than security and safety.

"Give me liberty or give me death." Seven words.

"Taxation without representation." Three words.

"If they mean to have a war, let it begin here." Eleven words.

Words turned to action. On a cold April morning a group of farmers stood on a village green and faced the strongest army in the world. The British regulars fired into the crowd of farmers and the farmers fled. Seven miles down the road they would not flee, however. They would return fire upon the British, time and time again, chasing the invaders all the way back to Boston town.

Twelve months later, the finest this new land had to offer met right there in Philadelphia, in the building we waited in the heat to see. The birthplace of our country. These weren't poor, downtrodden citizens who had nothing to lose. These were the most successful men in the colonies. They had prospered under British rule. They met throughout the long hot summer of '76 and debated principles with little or no thought of their own best interests. I wonder if the world ever witnessed such a gathering of wisdom and honor in one place, before or since.

Red haired Thomas Jefferson, who would pen the document that they finally agreed to sign. Benjamin Franklin, author, inventor, and entrepreneur, whose wit and wisdom held the convention together more than once.

"We must all hang together, or surely we shall all hang separately." Twelve words.

John Hancock, who signed the document in letters so big that King George III could read it without his spectacles. Georgia's own Button Gwinnett, who would die in a duel of honor before a year passed. Richard Henry Lee, whose grandson would fight on a far different field of honor. Samuel Adams. John Adams. Fifty-seven men in all pledged their lives, fortunes, and sacred honor to an idea; an idea based on a basic statement of human rights.

"We hold these truths to be self-evident: that all men are

created equal, that they are endowed by their Creator with certain unalienable rights, that among these are life, liberty, and the pursuit of happiness." Thirty-five words.

By signing the Declaration of Independence, these men were signing a death warrant, if their revolution failed. It did not. Many of the signers did lose their lives. Many lost their fortunes, but not one lost the honor which they saw as sacred.

Thus on July 4, 1776, our country, the United States of America, which had been conceived in the blood of Lexington and Concord, was born. Born with words as her midwife. Words, yes. But words backed up by a noble people who have paid a tremendous price to see that the honor of our founding fathers has been upheld throughout the generations.

Celebrate this weekend. Enjoy barbecues and fish frys and family gatherings. Visit the lake or the pool or the beach or the mountains or the neighbor's back yard. Watch the parade or run in the Peachtree Roadrace or do any of the things Americans do to celebrate our birthday. But remember. Please take time to remember. Our freedom has never been free and never will be. We've been given a wonderful legacy. We must all be ever-vigilant if we want to pass it on to the next generation.

Happy Birthday, USA.

We Run into Heroes in the
Most Unlikely Places

I am glad that I inherited the trait from my father of never meeting a stranger. I was particularly glad on this occasion when I was able to add Mr. Pinkerton's name to my ever growing list of friends.

An old man sat in front of me at last week's high school football game. I'm a sucker for old men, especially when they wear houndstooth hats. My daddy used to be an old man and often wore a houndstooth hat. I hope the gentleman who sat in front of me doesn't mind being called old, but he is. He told me so himself. He is 83. That's pretty old.

Personally, I've never understood why people object to being old. It sure beats the alternative.

But back to the gentleman who sat in front of me at the game. He and his family had been sitting right behind the student cheering section. When they realized that the students were not just standing for the kickoff, but rather the whole game, my new friend and his family began to search for higher ground. They wound up in front of me.

I watched my new friend throughout the first half. He sat beside his wife and, I learned, his daughter. He leaned on a beautiful hand carved cane and didn't say much. He paid closer attention to the band at halftime than he had to the game. During the second half he turned around and made a comment to me about the Braves jacket I was wearing. It was finally football weather last Friday night.

Seeing my jacket inspired him to relate an interesting tidbit about his past. When he was in the army, back in '44, he had a driver for his jeep. Turns out his driver would go on to play baseball in the big leagues and would eventually wind up as a coach for the Braves. I guess the connection was that my new friend's jeep driver wore a coat like mine to work.

I had an option here. I could nod politely and say "uh

huh," or I could reply with a question or comment of my own. In addition to being a sucker for old men, I'm also a sucker for men who served in the armed forces during the '40s. The army was pretty busy back then, you know. I asked him if he had served overseas. That was all I needed to say. He was off and running.

I learned that the gentleman in the hound's tooth hat had, indeed, served overseas. He was in North Africa first. Later he was sent to fight his way across Italy. He was part of the largest invasion in the history of the world and landed in France around the first of August in 1944. That's three weeks after D-Day. He fought his way across France and had made it all the way to the Rhine River by the time Germany surrendered. Upon his return to the States after WW II he joined the Alabama National Guard. Wouldn't you know it? They were Federalized and he got another all expense paid trip overseas. This time he went to Korea. Korea was just as unpleasant a place to visit in the early '50s as France had been in the '40s.

I learned a lot more about Mr. Pinkerton, which is my new friend's name. I learned that he graduated from the University of Alabama and also attended Auburn and UGA. I learned that he had been a teacher and a school principal and I learned that I had, in fact, taught his granddaughter. She was part of the Heritage band's flag corps, thus the rapt attention to the halftime show.

I was very glad that I had worn my Braves jacket to the game, thus giving Mr. Pinkerton a reason to strike up a conversation with me. I was reminded, once again, that a huge number of the old men we run into and take for granted every day are not just old men. They are heroes. They left the safety and security of this country, said goodbye to mamas and daddies and wives and children and friends and sweethearts and left home for the duration. They fought Hitler and Tojo and won. They saved the world. They really did. They saved the world.

Then they returned home and helped build this country into the greatest industrial power in the history of the world. They made sure that their children were the best educated generation with the most opportunity in the history of our republic.

Look around you. Those old men you see in fast food restaurants and stand behind in line at Wal Mart are not just old men. Take time to talk to them. Find out their stories. Tell them thank you. We're about to head into a new century and pretty soon all the heroes that preserved our society will be gone. Then we won't be able to thank them, or hear their stories. Or learn from them.

During our conversation Mr. Pinkerton expressed dismay that November 11, Veteran's Day, is all but ignored in this country. I agree. We should pay more attention to that day. But I also don't think we should wait until Veterans Day to thank the Mr. Pinkerton's of the world. They deserve our gratitude every day and for some of them November 11 might be too late. As for me, five weeks before Veterans Day, I'd like to say, "God bless all the Mr. Pinkertons, and God bless America."

12
Just Stuff

Just Stuff

Everywhere I go these days, I seem to run into people who read my column, and they all seem to have questions. The most often asked question, other than, "How much do you get payed?" is "How long does it take you to write your column ?"

That, of course, varies from day to day.

The next most popular question is, "Where do you get all your ideas for columns?"

That is a good question. A lot of my column ideas come from my memory, of course. I often write about my childhood in Porterdale. Sometimes I write about my family and other times about the people I meet at work or at play.

Sometimes, I must admit, I really struggle for a topic. I often sit down at my desk and place my fingers on the keyboard of my word processor without a clue as to what my subject will turn out to be. So far I've been lucky. I've never drawn a complete blank.

The columns in this chapter didn't seem to fit into any neat little category. They are a hodge podge on a wide variety of subjects. Some of them, however, are among my favorites. I hope you'll like them, too.

The Times They Are a'changin' at UGA

The young lady about whom this column was written is still a student at UGA. I'm not sure if that's because of my help or in spite of it. Whichever the case, she's still one of Georgia's finest, and one of my all-time favorite people.

There are a thousand better things to do on a Sunday afternoon in spring than sit inside writing a paper for English 101. But I've known Stephanie since she was in diapers and she is so sweet and has those beautiful brown eyes and besides that, her uncle was best man at my wedding, so how could I say no?

It was really sort of fun. I got to help write about Mickey Mantle. I'm sure this precious child wasn't born the last time Mantle homered in Yankee Stadium, but she wrote about him, nonetheless. After we'd finished the assignment, she questioned me about the "good old days" at UGA—back when her uncle and I were freshmen. She was wondering if things had changed much. I believe they have.

For one thing, it takes about a 1200 on the SAT to qualify for admission. Two of us used to get in for that. For another thing, the Fifth Quarter is long gone and so is Bob Poss' Restaurant. What I wouldn't give for one of his barbecued pork pig sandwiches—or a BP special, which was a chargrilled hamburger steak with melted cheese and grilled onions on top. It was served with hush puppies by a lady with a gold tooth who was at least a hundred years old.

And Dean Tate doesn't stand outside the coliseum in his red baseball cap holding a bullhorn to direct registration. Students register over the internet now, from the comfort of their own homes. What sissies! How will they learn toughness if they never have to figure out how to sneak into registration early or push and shove to get the last class card for the only easy professor in the biology department. Dean Tate would roll over in his grave if he knew about electronic registration.

I believe the students are much more sophisticated than

we were thirty years ago. Thirty years? How could it be possible? That Latin guy who said "Time flies" was right on the
money. It was almost three decades ago when I entered the great
and wonderful University of Georgia. I can't remember what I
had for lunch yesterday, but every moment of my first week in
Athens is crystal clear. I must have walked a hundred miles because I wasn't sure which bus to ride. It was 102 degrees every
day, but I sweltered in long sleeve button down shirts because I
wanted to impress the coeds by looking collegiate.

I know I was the most naive of my five thousand classmates, and the most homesick. Oz wasn't nearly as different
from Kansas as UGA was from Porterdale. I lived in a dorm with
more Yankees than Sherman brought with him. Talk about culture shock! They could have been from Mars and Neptune instead of Pittsburgh and Brooklyn. I was the only freshman on my
hall and the upper classmen all made fun of the way I looked and
the way I dressed and, especially, the way I talked. They also sent
me out after curfew every night on Waffle House runs. I never got
caught, but I gained twenty-five pounds my first quarter.

I didn't tell Stephanie much about what her uncle and I
did in college. The statute of limitations hasn't expired on some
of the stuff and some of it was just too stupid to admit, but there
were a few moments worth savoring, which I shared with my
tutoree.

I told her about her uncle's roommate stealing a hat right
off a policemen's head the night before the 1972 Auburn game.
He snatched it and ran like the wind. The policeman was Kent
Lawrence who, at that time, was probably the fastest man who
had ever played football at UGA. Our buddy was caught, tackled,
and headed for jail after three steps. Kent Lawrence was not just
a good cop, he was a good guy. After our friend had been bailed
out, his arresting officer came by the dorm to make sure he was
all right and stayed long into the night. Auburn and Pat Sullivan
won the game the next day.

I also told her about the Streaking Phenomena. During
one unbelievable week there were people all over campus run-

ning, walking, being pushed in wheelchairs, riding horseback, ala Lady Godiva, and even jumping out of airplanes—all naked as jay birds. One night over 1200 students disrobed and walked a mile across campus, filing two by two into Sanford Stadium in an attempt to break the "world streaking record." She really wanted to know if her uncle and I participated, but I refused to answer. Our Founding Fathers didn't think up the fifth amendment for nothing.

I could have reminisced forever, but there was work to be done. Maybe she'll come back one day soon.

One thing hasn't changed at UGA. The Freshman English teachers are still brutal graders. We only got a B on our Mickey Mantle paper. Next time I'll tell Stephanie we should write about Herschel Walker.

Wedding Bells Are Ringing

I finally was able to retire from the wedding photography business. Now the only time I cry on Saturday afternoons is when my wife hands me the list of chores she has lined up for me to do.

It's spring. The dogwoods have bloomed, pollen has turned our entire city yellow, Freaknik has come and, thankfully, gone, and wedding bells are ringing. Young men's thoughts may turn to baseball in the spring, but young women's thoughts turn to marriage.

I didn't know what true happiness was until I got married. Of course, by then it was too late. (Just kidding. Honest!)

I go to a lot of weddings. Twenty-five or thirty a year. Over two hundred in the '90s. Before you ask, no, I'm not a glutton for punishment, nor do I have an unusual addiction to dry cake and punch. I get paid to go to weddings. At least I get paid to photograph weddings.

I became a wedding photographer quite by accident. Someone was getting married at the last minute and needed pictures. I had a camera. One thing led to another. Now I spend over half the Saturdays in the year saying, "Big smile! Don't blink!" I've yet to ask someone to say cheese.

Unusual things happen at weddings. Some are downright funny, or would be if the participants weren't so stressed out. A person's wedding day should be the happiest day of his or her life, but few people allow themselves to enjoy it. Most are too busy worrying that their perfect day will lack perfection.

I once photographed a wedding involving a four year old child. He was the ring bearer. He had trouble standing still at the alter. Imagine that. You dress a four year old boy up in a tuxedo, give him a white satin pillow to hold, ask him to pose patiently for pictures and be kissed on the cheek by a four year old flower girl, and then expect him to stand still for thirty minutes on a Saturday afternoon in front of two hundred people. How thoughtless of him not to cooperate.

The groom was disturbed by the child's behavior at the alter and as he and his bride were making their way up the aisle, after the ceremony, he began to complain. By the time the newly-weds got outside the church they were shouting at one another. The groom got into his rented convertible and drove away in a huff, leaving the bride to attend the reception alone. Luckily, I got paid in advance.

I was shooting a wedding, in another state, which involved a groom who was a Marine Corps pilot. The night before the wedding he and his buddies went out on the town for a final fling. I'm not sure, but I think they visited establishments that featured adult entertainment. I'm fairly certain alcoholic beverages were involved. The Marines got into an argument, which turned into a brawl. I don't know what the other guys looked like, but the groom could only have one side of his face photographed. The bride was not amused. Just a guess, but I'd be willing to bet the honeymoon was less pleasant for the groom than it might have been.

One nervous young groom arrived at the church without the wedding ring. By the time he discovered his mistake he didn't have time to send for it. I loaned him mine for the service. He wore it on his honeymoon and lost it in the ocean. Or so he said. My wife was about as amused as the bride of the Marine.

One bride got cold feet and canceled on the very morning of the wedding. I did photograph a wedding for her, exactly 52 Saturdays later. The groom was different. Even though I've only been in business ten years, I've had several repeat customers. One person claimed the trifecta and has booked me for all three of her weddings. Nothing like satisfied customers.

I've seen wedding cakes collapse, attendants faint, and one poor bride dropped lipstick on the front of her dress, leaving a red streak six inches long. I learned from that experience that hairspray, nail polish remover, and Clorox are worthless at getting lipstick out of white satin. Whiteout and spray paint don't do much for fabric, either.

Most weddings are in the afternoon or evenings which always reminds me of a quote by Joe Willie Namath. He once advised, "Never get married in the morning. You don't know who you might meet that afternoon."

However, I'm a romantic at heart and despite the divorce rate and the odds against long unions, I always get sentimental when I watch the newlyweds exchange vows. I find myself hoping that all couples will feel like Mr. T. K. Adams. Mr. Adams was band director at Cousins Middle School when I was a rookie teacher and he took me under his wing. He remains one of the wisest men I've ever known. He told me many times, "The only regret I have about marriage is that I wasn't born married."

Me too. And to all the spring couples—Happy Honeymoon.

Driving a Stick Shift Isn't All it's Cracked Up to Be

As this book went to press my oldest child, Jamie, was only half a year away from being old enough for a learner's permit. I wonder if buying her a straight shift car would deter her from driving?

While driving through Olde Town the other morning, I encountered a traffic jam. As I approached Milstead Avenue, I saw what I assumed was the reason, and it was a peculiar sight. A gray haired man in a business suit was standing in the middle of the road, seemingly carrying on a conversation with a black Jeep Wrangler. I must admit that my first reaction was, "What a place to carry on a conversation!" As my lane began to move and I got closer to the situation I couldn't help but laugh.

Behind the wheel of the Wrangler was a teenaged girl who was obviously having her first intimate encounter with a straight shift and a hill. The gray haired gentleman was trying to explain the finer points of the brake, the accelerator, and the clutch. I'm sure the young lady was wondering why automakers would place three pedals in a car to be used by a person with only two feet. She was also thinking, I bet, that driving a straight shift wasn't nearly as much fun as it looked.

As I passed the unfortunate driver, a long line of very patient motorists had formed behind her. She was alternately lurching forward a few inches, choking down, cranking her car, and lurching forward a few more inches. Tears of frustration were running down her cheeks. As the late Tennessee Ernie Ford would have said, "Bless her little pea pickin' heart."

While I completed my errands, my mind began to wander. For a brief while I was sixteen again, driving to a Braves' game in an Opal Kadet with four on the floor. That car was a cruel trick foreign automakers played on General Motors. I was, for the first time, venturing outside the borders of Newton County behind the wheel of that car. As if that weren't adventure enough,

I was with a date. Amazingly, I arrived at the Atlanta Stadium parking lot without incident. It was leaving the game when my problems started.

All 40,000 spectators were trying to leave the parking lot at the same time by way of the same exit. I headed, instinctively, for low ground and the back of the parking lot. The policeman directing traffic turned me around and made me follow the crowd, right toward a very steep hill. Thinking back on the incident, I'm certain he knew I was in a car I couldn't drive and with a girl I wanted desperately to impress. As fate would have it, the line of traffic came to a complete standstill just as I reached the steepest part of the hill. Naturally, as I tried to let out the clutch, very carefully, so as not to run into the car in front of me, I choked down.

No problem. Could happen to anybody.

I cranked the car and tried again. Same results.

Over and over and over. We cranked. We lurched. We choked down.

By now sweat is pouring from my body. I am beyond embarrassed. To make matters worse, the people leaving the ball game were not nearly as patient as those folks in Conyers last week. They began to blow their horns and scream at me. The sadistic cop who had sent me up the hill in the first place added insult to injury by shouting at me to get my junk heap out of the way.

My date, to her credit, didn't laugh or make fun of me— at least not then. In fact, she offered to help by mashing the gas while I controlled the brake and the clutch. Her efforts were futile and having her leg on my side of the console made me even more nervous than trying to drive the car.

Finally, in desperation, I inched my way into a U-Turn, in direct violation of Officer Sadist, and headed toward the back of the parking lot. Downhill I could do. We were going in the wrong direction, but at least we were going.

We drove in slow circles around the Atlanta Stadium parking lot until all the cars had departed the scene. Then we eased our way up the dreaded hill, out of the parking lot and onto Capitol Avenue, where we promptly missed the turn which would have put us on I-20, headed home.

When I realized I had missed my turn I did what any another mortified 16 year-old would have done. I panicked and took the first available road. We were on I-85 South, headed toward the Atlanta Airport. We passed several exit ramps but I was afraid to get off on any of them because they were all so steep.

Thank heaven, we finally ran across I-285. Naturally we got on 285 headed in the wrong direction, but, "Hey. It's round." We finally got back to my date's house, a mere two hours after the baseball game had ended. Her father actually believed our story about why it took us two hours to make a thirty minute trip. I guess he had driven a stickshift, too, once upon a time.

To the young lady in the black Jeep Wrangler. Don't feel bad. We've all been there. Just remember, in the words of Billy Bob Fraley, first inductee into the Shade Tree Mechanic Hall of Fame, "If you can't find them, grind them." And trust me, driving a stick shift won't be the last thing you do that looks like more fun than it really is.

Buckle Up—It's Time for Class

I teach Social Studies now. It's not nearly so dangerous.

While sitting in traffic on 138 last week, I realized I was beside a Driver's Education car. Even before I saw the magnetic sign on top of the car I noticed the white knuckles and terrified expression of the person beside me. The driver looked a little nervous, too.

As traffic cleared I proceeded and soon left the student driver behind, but my thoughts turned to other days when I might have been the uneasy instructor. I taught Driver's Education for a number of years in a variety of settings. It's not the most soothing way to make a living. In fact, I had more than my share of Maalox moments.

When I was in my mid-twenties I took temporary leave of my senses and accepted a teaching job in south Georgia. Trust me. Life is different below the gnat line. The people are among the nicest in the world, but the pace of life was not exactly Buckhead. I'm sure the slower tempo would appeal to me now, but was a tough adjustment for a single guy in the '70s.

One of my duties was to teach Driver's Education one period a day. The headmaster of the school assured me that it would be the easiest part of my schedule because all the kids in that rural community had grown up driving tractors and farm vehicles. Together the students and I learned that driving a car on city streets was much different than driving a tractor across a plowed field.

I should have known what to expect when on the first day of school one of my students-to-be, a senior cheerleader who had a driver's license and was taking the course to improve her insurance rates, drove her mother's car into a ditch on the way to school. Her father happened to be one of my best friends in the community and her mother was in the habit of feeding me fried chicken after church on Sunday. I helped the young lady out of the ditch. She was grateful, but the subsequent teasing at the hands of her family was unmerciful.

Anyone familiar with Driver's Ed knows that a certain number of hours are devoted to class discussion, book work, and the ever present videos that are designed to scare the dickens out of anyone who sees them. During one of my scintillating lectures about pedestrian safety I mentioned that in our urban communities a person gets hit by a car every 30 minutes. One overgrown boy in the back of the class, who might have been the only person still awake, slowly raised his hand.

Impressed that he wanted to respond, I called on him. "Coach Huckaby," he said in a slow South Georgia drawl, "Somebody ought to tell that fool to stay on the sidewalk."

The same student was driving the Driver's Ed car through the streets of beautiful downtown Pelham one morning. I gave him instructions to turn right at the next traffic light, which happened to be green. He dutifully turned on his blinker and made a perfect stop at the green light.

"Go ahead," I encouraged him. "Make your turn."

He turned and smiled at me and said, in that same slow drawl, "You can't fool me, Coach Huckaby. The sign says 'turn right on red.'"

To my amazement, he sat there and waited until the light turned red, then looked both ways and made his turn. The young man drove with me the whole year without ever understanding about turning right on green as well as red. But he didn't run over any pedestrians, on or off the sidewalk. I'm not sure exactly what became of that student, but I'm fairly certain he's not in aerospace engineering.

My students and I had all sorts of adventures during the two years I spent in south Georgia. I enjoyed the excitement so much that I continued to teach the course when I returned to the Atlanta area. Driving with inexperienced teenagers on a country road is one thing. Driving on 285 is quite another.

I didn't know what life in the fast lane was all about until I let a group of students talk me into driving from College Park to the Varsity for lunch. Surprisingly, we negotiated the traffic and got there without incident. The problem came when it was time to leave the Varsity. If you've ever tried to cross three lanes of traffic and make a left turn onto North Avenue at noon on a given Friday, you understand what the fifteen year old girl whose turn it was to drive was going through. She finally picked what she thought was an opportune time and hit the gas. I guess she just assumed all the taxis heading toward her would stop. I've never heard so many screeching tires in my life. Nor have I been cursed in so many languages at once. I didn't understand what any of the drivers were saying, but the sign language was quite clear. Miraculously, everyone survived her takeoff unscathed, but that was our first and last trip to the Greasy V.

I taught Driver's Ed for several years after that and am firmly convinced that I'd have lots more hair and less gray in my beard if I had stuck to the academics. I haven't driven with a student in years and I'm very glad of that. In fact, any time I get disillusioned with my English classes, I can be very thankful that reading Shakespeare doesn't require a seat belt.

It's Diet Time Again

I actually did find a diet that worked and lost 35 pounds in less than two months. Then Christmas came . . . and the rest is history.

OK. This is it. This time I'm really going to do it. Yours truly is about to embark upon a very stringent diet—again. This time the weight is going to go away—and stay gone. Nothing to it. I'll burn more calories than I consume and in no time at all I'll be as slim and trim as I was back before my first child was born.

At the time my wife, Lisa, became pregnant for the first time I weighed about 160 pounds, compared to the 214 pounds I currently carry around with me. In the ensuing nine months we both gained fifty pounds. Hey, I wanted to be supportive! She ate for two—I ate for two. She wanted hot fudge cake at midnight. What kind of husband would let her eat alone? When she had cravings, I shared them. When she didn't have cravings, I had them for her. She got larger and so did I. She replaced her wardrobe with maternity clothes. I let my belt out another notch and started wearing my pants below my belly instead of around it.

She left most of her extra weight in the delivery room, except for the 10 pounds we brought home with us, wrapped in a pink blanket. I'm still trying to lose mine. Actually, I've been at it for quite a while. Our oldest child will be 14 in a month. I have tried dozens of times to lose weight with varying degrees of success. There are several reasons I have such a hard time with dieting.

One problem is, I have an image to maintain. Everybody who knows me knows that I pride myself on being a Southerner, and that the Southern male is expected to consume large quantities of fried chicken, ham, sausage, bacon, buttermilk biscuits, fried catfish, and, of course, barbecued pork and Brunswick stew. We have a heritage to maintain and never let it be said that I haven't done my part.

Another problem is that the calendar works against me when I try to lose weight. For instance, Jamie, the child with whom I got so large in the first place, was born in October. The first month of her life I couldn't really be expected to fall off any. Snacks and late night feedings go hand in hand and with friends and neighbors bringing food over and such, I actually put on another pound or two. But as soon as that month was over I was determined to start dropping pounds.

Wouldn't you know it? Right at the end of October— Halloween. Not wanting to disappoint the small ones in the neighborhood, I bought a large supply of Trick or Treat candy. It rained that year on Halloween. Somebody had to eat all those leftover Snickers and Butterfingers, and so it goes, year after year. Get the Halloween candy cleaned up and it is Thanksgiving. The very holiday developed around food. Thanksgiving leads right into December and the whole month is just one big Christmas party after another.

January is good for New Year's resolutions about weight loss, but realistically it just isn't feasible. You're expected to eat ham hocks and black eyed peas and cornbread on the first day of the year in order to assure good luck. By thirty minutes past noon my resolution to cut back on my eating is already shot.

Now television begins to work against me. The weather is too bad in January and February to do anything but sit inside and watch the tube. Do you have any idea how many college basketball games are televised during January and February? Eating just goes with watching college basketball on television. Carrot and celery sticks don't exactly do justice to the game, either. We're talking chips and dip. Lots of chips and dip.

Start my diet in March? Forget it. The Road to the Final Four is paved with chicken wings and salsa.

Easter comes in April. No use starting a diet and having to break it on Easter Sunday. Might as well wait until after Spring Break. Isn't that when the Girl Scout cookies are delivered?

Now every May, I do make progress. I'm thinking about going to the beach and putting on a bathing suit, so I eat pretzels and watch the Braves. I even start walking a mile or two every day.

But May is followed by June and July and summer is such a great time for cookouts. Hard to lose weight on a diet of t-bone steak and ribs, not to mention hamburgers and barbecued chicken. We certainly travel during those months, and nobody diets on vacation. August is Camp Meeting month, which means hearty meals and homemade ice cream every night. It's a wonder I don't weigh more than I do.

But this time I'm serious. I've carried this weight around for 14 years, and when I sit down to my Thanksgiving dinner, I intend to be thankful that there is at least thirty pounds less of me to feed. Starting today, September 1, I am on a strict diet. I'll keep you posted concerning my progress.

Of course, Saturday is Georgia's home opener and there are several tail gate parties I'm expected to attend. Monday is Labor Day. No school. We will probably have a fish fry in the noon hour and a barbecue Monday evening.

Well, next Tuesday, I'm going on a diet. And this time I really mean it!

Is There a Lawyer in the House?

*After this article appeared, the paper got a letter from an
irate reader who insisted that Ben Matlock wore seersucker suits. After weeks of investigation I finally drove to
the Andy Griffith museum in Mt. Airy, NC where they have
one of the Matlock suits on display. I must admit, it may
not be linen, but that sucker definitely ain't seersucker.*

I've been wondering lately why lawyers get such a bad
rap. People snicker when you mention the word attorney. The
internet has entire web sites devoted to lawyer jokes. Oglethorpe
wrote in the original Georgia charter that they should be permanently banned from the colony. If you believe everything you
read, lawyers are the personification of evil.

They couldn't be all that bad, could they? Luckily, I've
not been involved in many legal entanglements but I do know
several members of the bar and they seem like regular folks. The
ones I know have wives and go to baseball and soccer games on
Saturday, just like the rest of us.

I'm sure some of them even go to church on Sunday. In
fact, two members of my Sunday School class are lawyers. I've
never seen them steal from the offering plate and when fellow
class members ask for prayers because they've been in a car wreck
or something, I've never seen either of them hand out a business
card, at least not inside the church.

My first cousin is an attorney in Covington and he's not
so bad. In fact, I was called to sit on a jury for one of his cases and
he told the judge right away that we were kin. Of course, he was
under oath.

My wife's cousin married a lady lawyer and she asked
me to photograph the wedding. She bought lots of pictures and
never once mentioned suing me because one of her bridesmaid
was overexposed in a few shots.

So where do all the complaints about lawyers come from?

Can't blame it on a right wing conspiracy. Someone else already has that excuse.

Maybe it's because attorneys, by the very nature of their business, spend a lot of time with criminals. What's that old saying about guilt by association? " If you lie down with dogs, you get up with fleas?"

It couldn't be John Grisham novels. Lawyers already had a bad reputation before *The Firm* became popular.

I guess that leaves television to blame. Maybe people have a negative image of lawyers because so many are portrayed as unscrupulous and a bit greedy on television shows. I don't know a habeus from a corpus but I have to admit that there are a few shows about the law profession that I enjoy watching on TV.

One of my favorite shows, in fact, is Ally McBeal. She is a skinny little thing who wears real short skirts and works in a Boston law firm, along with several very weird characters, including her ex-lover and his current wife. Her roommate works for the DA's office and usually winds up facing her in court. Her firm's office is right over a nightclub, which is convenient, because everyone winds up there drinking and dancing after every case.

The most unusual feature of the office is the unisex bathroom where all sorts of drama takes place, but not before everyone gets down on the floor to check under the stalls for eavesdroppers. The show is a bit off the wall and I'm not sure why I like it so much. My wife insists it's because the star's skirts are so short, but there must be a deeper meaning. If the practice of law was as much fun as Ally McBeal makes it seem, I'd sue somebody every week.

I know one thing. Ally McBeal could never work for Perry Mason. Remember him? He defended a murder case every week. It's a wonder there was anyone left in Los Angeles to kill by the time O.J. came along. Perry had a loyal secretary named Della Street, but they were never, to my knowledge, alone in the same bathroom. Paul Drake was Mason's private detective and always got sent away to places like Las Vegas to track down the real killer while Perry Mason stayed around to argue with Lt. Tragg of homicide.

Not only did Perry Mason always get his client off the hook, he always shamed or tricked the real murderer into admitting his or her guilt by blurting a confession with five minutes left in the show, which gave Perry, Paul, and Della, just enough time to go back to his office for a cigarette. Guess he never thought of renting space over a nightclub.

My favorite television attorney of all time, though, would have to be Ben Matlock. For those of you who may not know it, after Opie was grown, his daddy moved from Mayberry to Atlanta, changed his name to Matlock and hung out his shingle. He was like a down-home Perry Mason. He had a closet full of identical white linen suits and celebrated all his victories by eating two hotdogs with everything. That's healthier than smoking, but not as much fun as dancing.

So what's the truth about lawyers and the practice of law? Are most lawyers as upright and boring as the ones I know, or as glamorous and daring as the ones on television? My guess is that, like everyone else, they're somewhere in between. And if I've slandered or libeled anyone with this column—I plead the Fifth.

Floyd—An Ill Wind that Blew Little Good

Floyd wasn't nearly as bad as advertised, at least not for the Georgia coast. But if we believe the people who are supposed to know about those things, it's only a matter of time until "the big one" blows in.

We saw it first on the six o'clock news. Or was it the five o'clock news? It's hard to keep track these days. Way out in the

Atlantic, not far from the southern coast of Africa, was a tropical wave. We, my kids and I, noticed because none of us had heard of a tropical wave.

By the time the eleven o'clock news came on, (and I'm real sure it was eleven because that's ninety minutes past my bedtime) the tropical wave had become a tropical depression, with a name. It was called Floyd, just like the barber on the Andy Griffith Show. This Floyd was no mild mannered fuddy duddy though.

I'm not sure if it was the next morning or two mornings before Floyd turned into a full blown hurricane, but I know it was soon enough. There it was, circling counter clockwise around its evil eye, growing almost exponentially, its sustained winds reaching 150 mph. It was a category 4. Stronger than Hugo. Twice the size of Andrew. It was larger, in fact, than New England. It packed more potential devastation than Camille. And when we went to bed Tuesday night, it had a bulls eye bead on Savannah, Georgia's charming mother city.

Hurricanes have always fascinated me. I love the ocean. My wife, Lisa, and I made a vow long ago that within 24 hours of our youngest child graduating from high school we would move to an oceanfront cottage to spend our remaining days. Hurricanes do strange and terrible things to oceanfront cottages, but the lure of the sea is so strong for me that I'm willing to suffer through one every couple of years.

But back to Savannah. Savannah is one of my favorite places on earth. I haven't had a good year if I don't get there several times. I love walking along River Street, watching, with equal fascination the boats churning up the broad Savannah River and the people, mostly tourists, who duck in and out of the candy stores, bars, and gift shops. Every time we go there I make my kids suffer through impromptu history lessons as we look for the star embedded in the sidewalk that marks, supposedly, the exact spot upon which James Edward Oglethorpe first stepped when he brought the original colonists to Georgia. By the way, none of that first boatload were actually debtors, but many Georgians have tried to live up to the term debtor's colony since. I know I've done my part.

We always find that spot and then head down the street, me chomping on a praline, that wonderful Southern concoction of crystallized sugar, pecans, and a million fat grams. The rest of my family leans toward chocolate and caramel turtles. Our River Street strolls end, invariably, with a photo session at the Waving Girl statue.

Of course there's much more to Savannah than River Street. Practically the entire city is a museum with all the old buildings and beautiful squares. It's a walker's paradise. One can't talk about Savannah without mentioning the wonderful seafood restaurants, the coastal fishing villages, and Tybee Island, with its historic lighthouse.

And there was Floyd, supposedly heading right toward Savannah.

The danger seemed so imminent that mandatory evacuations were ordered for all of Georgia's coastal counties. You saw the footage on the news, just like I did. Interstate 16 became a one way exodus. Bumper to bumper the huge caravan came, filling all lanes on both sides of the expressway. They came with whatever possessions they could pack up in short notice, many with no idea of where they would find a place to stay and none knowing what they would find upon their return. Two of that great exodus were dear friends of mine, George and Lorraine Simpson. They left behind a lifetime of memories and possessions and, in a kennel far from harm's way, their blind dog named Pug.

We all know now that sometime Tuesday night upper level winds and steering currents and other factors I don't pretend to understand turned the massive storm to the north. Savannah was spared. For a while it looked like Charleston would be hit, and then Myrtle Beach. By the time Floyd actually came ashore it had miraculously lost much of its punch. It brought torrential rain to the east coast, but spared us the devastation we had feared.

After the fact, many outspoken people with 20-20 hindsight have criticized the powers to be that ordered the largest evacuation in our country's history. Officials have been accused of overreacting and crying "wolf." I don't agree.

I think it's way better to be safe than sorry. I'm very glad that I'll be able to eat pralines again on River Street. I'm very glad the Simpsons found their house in one piece when they got home. I'm very glad the only pier left on North Myrtle Beach did not wash away. But sixteen people did not survive Floyd. It could have been much worse.

When the next hurricane threatens, which may be next week, err on the side of safety. Buildings can be rebuilt. Things can be replaced. Even the Waving Girl can be recast if necessary. Lives can't be. So to the people blessed with homes on the coast. When the next one blows, y'all come—inland.

Of Blind Dates and Other Matters of the Heart

This piece is dedicated to James T. (Jay) Milligan, one of the funniest human beings I know, and the one person in the world who told more people about my date with "Aunt Bea" than I did.

I was standing around in a parking lot the other night. When you have three kids with half a dozen activities each, you spend a lot of time standing around in parking lots. This happened to be the church parking lot on a Sunday night.

Several of us parent/chauffeur types were waiting on MYF to be over and the conversation turned to points of origin. (We got to talking about where we were raised.) Naturally a chorus of "Did you know so and so?" began. One person in the crowd happened to mention having had a blind date with a girl someone else knew. We were off, full throttle, down memory lane. Each person had a better blind date story than the last.

I said nothing. Most of my blind date experiences were too painful to recount, even in the church parking lot.

Upon returning home, however, I started thinking about some of them. Honesty compels me to admit that there were many, as I was almost thirty before I met my wife, Lisa. Our meeting, courtship, and subsequent marriage, of course, put an end to all of my dating, blind or otherwise.

I don't think I ever had a blind date in high school, but I did get "fixed up" a few times in college. On a couple of those occasions I wound up wishing that I were blind. Ever the gentleman, I never let on that I was disappointed. Besides, I was smart enough to know that my companion of the evening never opened her door and felt like she had won the lottery, either.

I don't mean to sound insensitive here. I know that beauty is only skin deep, but as any college aged male will tell you, ugly goes all the way to the bone. One date in particular stands out in my mind. She was the only true two-bagger I've ever met. You've heard, I'm sure, the old colloquialism about a date being so homely you'd need to put a bag over her head to take her out in public. With a two bagger, you put a bag over your head, too, just in case hers falls off. This was that girl. It was the only time in my life that I just bolted and ran.

Now I know what some of you are thinking, and no, I don't judge books by their covers. I know that looks aren't what is important. I also know that while a car runs on gas, it takes a spark to get it started.

Some of the blind dates I had in college turned out to be very pretty, but dumb as a box of rocks. I took a history major from a large Southern university to Stone Mountain and she wanted to know who those guys on horses were, carved into the side of the rock. Another sweet young thing, from deep south Georgia, was confused when we went to see a movie starring Robert Redford because she was certain she had seen him killed in Butch Cassidy and the Sundance Kid, back at the drive-in in Cuthbert.

Once I graduated from college, blind dates became even more frequent. People just seemed to worry about a guy in his twenties who was not married. I went out with cousins, sisters, aunts, school teachers—all of whom were billed as sweet, fun to be with, and having great personalities. The results were never good, but for some reason, I kept getting fixed up. Until I met Aunt Bea.

I was living in a trailer in a pecan grove in Meigs, Georgia. It's 7 miles north of Ochlocknee and 12 miles southwest of Cotton. A friend from Covington was also serving time in South Georgia and living in Albany. His wife, knowing I was a stranger in a strange land, called one evening. She had the perfect person for me to meet. I should have known better, but being alone in Meigs, Georgia does strange things to a young man's mind.

I called this perfect person on the phone. She sounded nice enough and we made a date for dinner and a movie. I drove the thirty miles to her apartment, found her unit, and knocked on the door.

The person who answered my knock was the spitting image of Aunt Bea, from the Andy Griffith Show. She had the same face, the same frumpy house dress, and the same hairdo. I was in a state of shock, but running was not an option.

We drove around Albany until I found a restaurant that looked deserted. She ordered liver and onions. We then went to the worst movie house in the city to see the worst movie. She grabbed my hand as soon as the house lights went down and refused to let go. The feature lasted three hours. It seemed like twelve. As we finally left the show my worst fears were realized. Two teachers from my school were in the lobby. I had to acknowledge them. To their credit, they smiled and said nothing more than hello.

That is, until the next day. When I arrived at school the next morning they were both in my room to greet me. "We have only one question," they said. "Who baby-sat Opie last night?"

I was cured. I never went on another blind date. In fact, I met Lisa shortly after that. She looks nothing like Aunt Bea, so when she asked me out I quickly said, "yes." We've been together ever since.

But if you're ever in Albany and see a nice lady with a beehive hairdo, eating liver and onions in a nice restaurant—tell her Gomer says "Hey!"

Is Walt's Wonderful World About to Be Gone With the Ratings Wind?

As this book went to press, Tinkerbell was still lighting up Cinderella's castle every Sunday night. The world of Disney on television was still wonderful and the powers to be at Disney still hadn't found a girl actress who could hold a candle to Annette.

You can't believe everything you read in the newspapers. This may come as a shock to some of you, but just because it's in the newspapers doesn't mean that it's the gospel truth. I'm not talking about this newspaper, of course. I'm referring to all those other newspapers out there.

We all remember seeing the picture of Harry Truman holding up the front page of the Chicago Daily Tribune with big headlines saying, "Dewey Wins." Problem was, all the votes hadn't been counted. Dewey didn't win.

Last week I read in the AJC that Georgia was going to upset Tennessee. Believe me. Dewey did much better against Truman than Georgia did against Tennessee.

Newspapers are full of stories that might or might not be true. I hope the story I read last week is not. According to the headline, ABC is contemplating taking the *Wonderful World of Disney* off the air after the current season. Say it ain't so!

Those Sunday night shows are one of the last remaining ties to my childhood. Everything else seems to have gone the way of the hula hoop and Coca Cola in little green bottles. Sears-Roebuck doesn't even have a Christmas Wish Book anymore. And now we may lose Walt Disney on Sunday nights.

My whole family used to gather in front of the television on Sunday nights, anxious to discover what wonders Mr. Disney had in store for us. He would always appear, you remember, at the beginning of the program to introduce the show. He would be in a room full of books in front of a giant world globe. When I was a child I remember thinking it would be like dying and going to heaven to have a room like that.

Walt Disney would chat for a while and then walk over and take a book off the shelf. He would open it up and a story would magically come to life. Sometimes Jiminy Crickett, with a top hat and umbrella, would pop out of the book. Sometimes it would be cartoon features with Mickey Mouse, Donald, Pluto, Goofy, and the gang. Disney presented nature studies long before Marlin Perkins. Sometimes he would choose a history book from the shelf. Those were my favorite shows. I believe that my love for history is due, at least in part, to the shows Walt Disney presented on Sunday night.

The stories might not have been historically accurate, but they aroused my interest, and made me want to learn more. Johnny Tremain taught me how the American Revolution began. The Swamp Fox showed me how the war was fought in our part of the world.

I didn't like watching the Civil War shows, *The Great Locomotive Chase* and the *Drummer Boy of Shiloh*. The wrong side always won. Without a doubt, my favorite Sunday night Disney Serial was *Davy Crockett, King of the Wild Frontier*. Week after week I followed Davy and Georgie Russell from the hills of Tennessee all the way to the Alamo. I still can't walk into one of those gift shops in the mountains without trying on one of the fake coonskin caps and begging my wife to take my picture.

Of course, the same actors played all the characters. Fess Parker was the Swamp Fox and Davy Crockett. He even played the Yankee spy in the Great Locomotive Chase. Took me years to forgive him for that. Tim Consodine was a regular and so was Kevin Cochran, who played a little boy named Moochie. Don't even start me thinking about Annette.

Some weeks the show would feature Disneyland, in California. Central Florida was still swamp land and orange groves at this time. I remember staring in amazement at all the rides and attractions. I never in a million years dreamed that I would be able to actually see such a place.

At some point the show changed its name to *Walt Disney's Wonderful World of Color*. Tinkerbell, Peter Pan's fairy friend, would fly over Cinderella's castle and wave her magic wand. At that point the screen would, supposedly, turn into a world of color. It stayed the same on our set. By the time we had a color television I had found other things to do on Sunday night and left Walt Disney to others. I rediscovered the show when I had kids of my own.

We're not as faithful to the current show as my family was. Let's face it. We have a hundred channels now instead of three and Michael Eisenwhoever is no Walt Disney. The bill of fare is wholesome family movies these days, and who wants to watch wholesome family movies when there's so much trash available? I think Whoopie Goldberg has taken Annette's job.

Although the Walt Disney Corporation is a giant conglomerate with making money it's prime objective, it still creates magnificent family entertainment and gives my kids a chance to laugh at the same things I did. If it disappears from television another part of what was good about my generation's childhood will go with it.

I hope ABC changes it's mind. I like watching the show, especially the beginning. Tinkerbell still waves her wand over the castle and now I have a color television.

"Pork Skin Diet"
Ends on Thanksgiving Day

The Atkins Diet worked wonders. I lost 35 pounds eating bacon, eggs, steak--and pork skins. I went off the diet on Thanksgiving. By Ground Hogs Day I had gained 40 pounds back.

A couple of months ago I boldly announced that I was going on a strict diet. I had good intentions of doing just that, too. Of course we all know that good intentions pave the path to you know where.

I tried. I really did. But there was just too much good stuff out there to eat. I live in a house with three kids who are junk food addicts and a wife who could eat Hosea William's entire "Feed the Hungry" larder and not gain an ounce. By the time September turned to October I had gained three more pounds and David Hays, cotton farmer turned land developer, was openly making fun of my protruding belly.

On October 16, fate intervened in the ongoing battle of the Huckaby bulge. Lisa and I hosted a Sunday school party at our house. The entertainment for the evening was provided by the football teams from the state universities of Georgia and Tennessee. For the hundredth straight year the orange team volunteered to kick my team all the way back to Athens. It was a great night if "Rocky Top" is your favorite song.

However, the night was not a total loss. While I was stuffing my face with chicken wings, salsa, potato chips and onion dip, several rather svelte members of my class were telling me about an amazing new diet they had discovered. It was actually an old diet that had been reintroduced by a doctor somewhere named Atkins. My friends explained to me that the diet was an all protein, no carbohydrate thing in which you can eat all the bacon, cheese, and t-bone steaks you can force down your gullet, but no ice cream, pasta, or refined sugar.

It sounded too good to be true. I filled a tortilla chip with bean dip and asked about snacks. "Cheese," was the first response from my new found weight loss gurus. Not too appetizing for me.

Then someone said that I could eat all the peanuts I wanted. Someone else added, "and pork rinds." I think they meant the last remark as a joke. It was actually the selling point. My wife hasn't let me have a pork skin in the 17 years we've been married.

"It's a done deal!" I promised, "as soon as I finish that coconut pie I have out in the refrigerator."

The next day we began. I say we because my lovely wife Lisa, who has to run around in the shower to get wet, was as enthusiastic about the possibilities of my losing weight as David Hays and my Sunday school class. She went out and bought me the "Dr. Atkins Diet Revolution" book, three dozen eggs, ten pounds of bacon, a dozen ribeye steaks, and 32 cans of dry roasted peanuts. I was ready to go.

The first three days on my pork rind diet went well. I ate huge amounts of bacon, eggs, cheese, and hamburger steak, without the slightest twinge of guilt. Amazingly enough, I actually lost two pounds. After four days my body began to tremble a little bit, so Lisa brought home a car load of vitamins to replace the nutrients I wasn't getting. The trembling stopped.

For a week or so, the diet was fun. What a novelty! I could turn the prescribed food pyramid upside down and eat like a pig, as long as I stayed away from anything healthy. After the first week, although the pounds were falling off, I started having nearly uncontrollable cravings for mashed potatoes and rice. It was of little consolation that I could eat all the butter and mayonnaise I wanted, because there was absolutely nothing to put them on. I did discover, however, that French onion dip goes real well with pork skins. At night I began to dream about white bread and sweet iced tea.

When my friends were singing the praises of all the wonderful things I could have, they never mentioned all the things I wouldn't be able to eat. Some things you don't appreciate until you can't have them.

Like orange juice. Who would ever think orange juice

would be banned from a diet, along with toast, grapefruit, apples, oranges, and bananas? Forget about a bowl of cereal in the morning. Milk either, for that matter. Pretend grits do not exist.

Lunch is a salad. That's it. But with all the Italian dressing you can pour on that sucker.

Dinner is any type of meat and some cabbage. No corn bread, black eyed peas, potatoes, rice, pasta, rolls, sweet tea, or anything else that wasn't available to cave men. I wonder why Fred Flintstone wasn't as skinny as a rail.

I vowed to stay on the diet until Thanksgiving. So far I have. At the five week mark I have lost 25 pounds, from 215 to 190, and taken my belt up two notches. I've even gotten compliments on how much better I look. The jury is still out as to whether it has been worth it. I do feel better and haven't dreamed about white bread in a couple of weeks.

But let me tell you this. I'm going back to the real world of sugars and starches on Thanksgiving Day. When they put my mama's dressing and sweet potato pie on the table, everybody had better stand back. What's left of me could hurt somebody!

E-Mail Address Opens New Can of Worms

After this column appeared I was besieged by even more e-mail. I'd like to hear from you, too, but don't send anything after 9:30 at night. I go to bed early.

My column has appeared in this space for over a year now. During that time I have developed a very good working relation with the paper's editor, Alice Queen. The relationship works like this: She tells me what to do and I do it. It was easy for me to get in the swing of things here at the newspaper. That's the exact same arrangement I have with my wife, Lisa.

A few weeks ago, Alice and I had a discussion about whether I should add an e-mail address to the bottom of my column. I discovered the internet, quite by accident, two summers ago and found out that while it may be as addictive as heroin it is cheap and nonfattening, so it's one of the few vices Lisa allows me to enjoy.

My discussion with Alice over adding my address to my column went something like this:

Alice: "I want you to start putting your e-mail address at the end of your column so we don't have to keep spending money forwarding all your mail to your house. It cost the paper 33 cents last month!

Me: "Yes ma'am."

So now I have an e-mail address at the end of my column and all the people who are too lazy or too cheap or too illiterate to send me a real letter can just log on to the old internet and fire away. Boy, they have, too. I thought it might be fun to share some of the more interesting comments.

One thing I have noticed is that people have some really strange screen names. I state my opinions week after week in this forum. Not only my name but also my picture accompanies my opinion. I'm not afraid to take a stand on such controversial issues as barbecue and catfish and the Confederate flag. I state my case and let the chips fall where they may. These people who e-mail me use names like Bubbasbuddy006 and Bigmamagal807. It's easy to be brave under a pseudonym like IAMClassless417.

Many of my critics have rather long memories, too, because I have gotten response this week concerning columns that ran months ago. Talk about carrying a grudge. I haven't had a chance to respond personally to my e-mails so, if you will indulge me, I'll just answer in this space.

From JoiseyGal911: Dear Mr. Huckaby. I resemble your remarks about Yankees moving to the South. If you had to listen to New Jersey accents twelve months a year, you'd come south, too.

Dear JoiseyGal. I don't mind your coming here. It's the staying that bothers me.

From ImaHogg: Dear Dummy. How can you say that Sprayberry's has the best barbecue. I'm an expert on pork and I can tell you about a dozen places better than Sprayberry's.

Dear Ima. I'll tell you the same thing I told the woman who said she knew of better catfish than Henderson's. Don't tell me—take me. I'm like Delta. I'm ready when you are.

From RollTide006. Huckaby. iffen you thinks all the teachers in ga is so great, how come is it that my boy Cecil done had to spend three years in the same grade when we get him to school at least twict a week.

Dear Roll: I can't understand it either. That's a real mystery to me.

From JohnnyReb1861: Dear Mr. Huckaby. How can you write that the Confederate battle flag should be taken off our state banner. You are just an ignorant, liberal, Yankee-loving traitor to the South. How can you live with yourself after writing rubbish like that?

Dear Johnny. Sometimes I do get really sad. When I do, I either go outside and kick our cat, Sherman-Grant, or I sit by the fire and read the obituaries from the New York Times.

From JRocker 49. Dear Mr. Huckaby. I read your very patriotic Veteran's Day column about all the men who died pro-tecting our Constitution and Bill of Rights. Could you go over that part about Free Speech and Freedom of Expression one more time?

Dear John. Certainly. As soon as I get through explain-ing to PRose14 why doing drugs a gazillion times is not as bad as gambling.

From PattyPrude111. Dear Mr. Huckaby. I was appalled

that you would tell someone to "kiss your rebel rump." You should be ashamed of yourself. How could you use a word like rump in this newspaper?

Dear Patty. Actually I didn't use the word rump. The editor did. I used a much more descriptive word, which reminds me of a story I once heard about President Harry Truman. His press secretary approached his wife one day and implored, "Mrs. Truman, can't you please get the president to stop using the word manure in his speeches?"

The First Lady replied, "Sir, you don't understand. It's taken me fifteen years to get the President *to* use the word manure."

From Blindandcrookedref666. I told you Georgia was gonna lose to Tech.

Dear Blind and crooked. I don't want to talk about it. (But he didn't fumble.)

From Flirtyone: I really like the picture of you on the front of the paper, but doesn't your wife complain about your beard tickling her face when you kiss.

Dear Flirty. It's really never come up. I've only had my beard six years.

I think that just about catches me up on this week's correspondence. Y'all keep those e-mails coming.

Darrell Huckaby
DHuck08@aol.com

Need Two

(304 pages, hardcover) 18.95

Need Two tells the story of two college kids on a road trip to New Orleans to watch Georgia play Notre Dame in the 1981 Sugar Bowl. The two guys have no money, no car, and no tickets, but four days before the big game decide they can't live if they aren't in New Orleans to watch Herschel Walker and the Georgia Bulldogs compete for the National Championship. In his inimitable style, Huckaby spins a great yarn as he reveals who they blackmail to get a car, who they lie to to get tickets, and all the trouble this unlikely pair get into--and out of--along the way. It is a *Must-read*, even for Georgia Tech fans!

Dinner on the Grounds

(192 pages, softcover) 15.00

Dinner on the Grounds contains recipes and heart warming stories from old fashioned church dinners. The recipes are of the old-fashioned-made-from-scratch-mixed-with-love variety. The stories are Darrell Huckaby at his best. This book was released in December, 1999 and has proven popular across the South. Some Yankee-Americans have even reported enjoying this unique offering.

**Darrell Huckaby can be read online at
www.rockdalecitizen.com**

Order Form

To order additional copies of *Grits is Groceries* or Darrell Huckaby's other books, copy or clip this order form and mail to:

Darrell Huckaby,
2755 Ebenezer Rd.
Conyers, GA 30094

Name _____

Address _____

_____

Please rush me:

_____ copies of Need Two ($18.95)   _____

_____ copies of Dinner on the Grounds ($15)   _____

_____ copies of Grits is Groceries ($20)   _____

Plus $3.00 PER ORDER   _____3.00___

TOTAL   _____

Personalize Books to:_____

_____

_____

Make checks payable to Darrell Huckaby.

PERSONAL
AND SOCIAL
DEVELOPMENT
The Psychology of Effective Behavior

PERSONAL
AND SOCIAL
DEVELOPMENT

THE PSYCHOLOGY OF EFFECTIVE BEHAVIOR

Louis S. Levine
SAN FRANCISCO STATE COLLEGE

*Holt, Rinehart
and Winston, Inc.*

New York · Chicago · San Francisco · Toronto · London

September, 1963
Copyright © 1963 by Holt, Rinehart and Winston, Inc.
Library of Congress Catalog Card Number: 63–8494
25236–0113
Printed in the United States of America

for . . .
    Jo Ann
    Linda
    Alene

Preface

Students in "Personal Development," "Mental Hygiene," and similar classes bring with them high hopes that these courses will be relevant to their lives. Along with their enthusiasms these students generally have had only a modicum of previous experience with formal course work in psychology. The instructor who is sensitive to the student's expectancies and to his psychological innocence is confronted with the problem of how to speak to the student's interests without doing violence to psychological data and theory.

In order to deal with this problem, I have modified the content and approach of these courses for more than a dozen years. This text is built upon that experience. It assumes that the objective of extending the student's range of cognitive categories pertaining to the complex process of personality development constitutes a worthy, though difficult, academic undertaking. It further assumes that the student's interests are best served if the course content is organized within a systematic frame of reference (in this case a rudimentary theory of personality) that accommodates to the sequences set by the life cycle.

This book includes topics that compel attention, topics such as love, loneliness, death, marriage, and work—topics that as far as present knowledge is concerned require psychological treatment that is tentative, sometimes speculative, and at points provocative. Although intensive treatment is afforded these fundamental issues of life itself, the book is not a substitute for psychotherapy or general psychology; it makes no attempt to prescribe the unprescribable. The text strives only to provide a frame of reference and a set of concepts useful to the student as he surveys, selects, and orders his perceptions of himself and his world.

In the synthesis of a cognitive frame of reference with the student's interests and experience the special excitement of learning can be felt keenly. It is my hope that this text may make a contribution toward this end.

This book has been greatly improved as a result of the experience and wisdom of the publisher's advisory editor, Theodore Newcomb, whose talent and patience are reflected on every page. I also am indebted to Jack Black, Barbara Cannell, Anne Carlsen, Nancy Cozzens, Morton Keston, Marilyn Heilfrom, and Donald Strong, who contributed generously of their time and knowledge in their helpful criticism of the manuscript. Without the assistance of Page Davis, Patricia Givens, Josephine Harrison, Henriette Lahaderne, and Millicent Lesser, this book would still be in draft form. I am especially grateful to the artistry of Wayne Miller, who provided most of the photographs. San Francisco State College has afforded the students, the academic freedom, and the spirit of educational adventure that have motivated this effort.

L.S.L.

San Francisco
November 1962

Contents

PART ONE

Understanding Human Behavior

THIS BOOK treats man's development from birth to death; it attempts to relate the private images he has of himself and his values and beliefs to the complex interplay of physical and social forces that motivate him and to the psychological processes that provide direction to his actions.

In this first section, the scene is set; the ideas and information essential before the individual can take the stage, as he does in Part Two, are specified. Psychological terms and concepts are presented to provide not only a language for discourse but also a framework into which data pertaining to man's development can be fitted.

1.

Behavior, Science, and Values

    Man's complexity has always intrigued, puzzled, challenged, and frightened him. He has pondered his fate and wondered whether he controlled his destiny. He has taken pride in his ability to reason and has been ashamed of his capacity to destroy. And throughout time man has sought to understand how he becomes what he is. All men, scholars and laborers, artists and craftsmen, seek to extend their understanding of themselves and of others. Even the private unspoken questions of, "Why did I do that?" or "I wonder if anyone else has ever felt as I do?" represent the need and the wish to understand more fully the meaning and roots of behavior.

    By extending his knowledge man can enhance his effectiveness and develop the talents and skills required to meet the demands of his environment. He becomes better able to anticipate the consequences of his own behavior and he improves his chances of living peacefully and productively with himself and with others. From the individual's standpoint such understanding assures more effective utilization of his intelligence and potentialities in meeting the requirements of his environment and in predicting the behavior of his associates. Having knowledge of himself and of others, he can achieve a greater degree of control over his world than would otherwise be possible. Thus, he can increase the opportunities for health, safety, security, and satisfaction for himself, his family, and his associates. To the extent that he understands human behavior, he can act to correct conditions of illness, insanity, poverty, and delinquency. Through knowledge and action based on that knowledge, man might reduce the fears, prejudices, and hatred arising from his ignorance of himself and redirect his energies and resources to issues of

3

human welfare. As the individual's knowledge of human behavior can contribute to his own effectiveness, satisfaction, and dignity, such knowledge, if achieved by all men, might ensure human survival.

The Purpose of This Book

Much of the information that follows is drawn from the body of knowledge known as psychology, but this book does not set out to be a comprehensive introduction to that science.[1] Rather, it is a book about people, their feelings and thoughts, their relationships with others, and the uses they make of their abilities. It describes the forces that shape the individual's development, and it specifies the characteristics of effective psychological functioning.

This book provides information that will be helpful to the person who is interested in human behavior and who is thinking about himself, his personal relationships, and the utilization of his resources. As such, it provides a guide for part of the journey toward the reader's fullest self-development, toward his clearer understanding of how he can contribute to the development of others. But it does not provide a set of short cuts to the attainment of emotional maturity or psychological effectiveness; no book can substitute for the experiences or the relationships necessary for maximal self-development. While these vital learning processes are continuing, however, the outline provided can have personal as well as academic significance to the reader.

This first chapter has three main parts: first, a general statement about the nature of behavior is followed by a review of some familiar attitudes toward it and a discussion of the factors that complicate its understanding. Then the scientist's and the layman's approaches to behavior are contrasted; and finally attention is given to certain aspects of scientific theory and the relation of values to science.

Human Behavior

"Human behavior" covers a multitude of acts. Some are so clearly demonstrable that observers can agree on what an individual is doing: he is eating, conversing, driving, painting, writing, listening. We call these acts "overt." At the same time there is a whole complex of "inner" activities, such as thinking, feeling, and imagining, frequently called "covert." This pair of opposites—"overt–covert"—does not, however, designate inherent properties of behaviors, but rather the extent

[1] The student interested in extending his knowledge of psychology as a science should consult the texts on general psychology listed at the end of this chapter.

to which the behaviors are directly apparent to observers who agree on what they are seeing. Inner behaviors that are inferred from outer behaviors—for example, anger from tense facial muscles and clenched fists—are considered covert, and usually observers will be in less agreement in identifying covert behaviors than they will be in naming overt behaviors.

Behavior is the manifestation of life. Each individual's work, play, and social life represent continuing sequences of his overt and covert behaviors, interacting with those of other people in his environment. It is from these interactions that he acquires knowledge of the attitudes, behaviors, and ideas which bring pleasant or unpleasant consequences, of behaviors that are acceptable or unacceptable to the group, and of the adequacy or inadequacy of his own actions.

If a student is to understand how behaviors of one person influence —and are influenced by—those of another, or how patterns of events contribute to the individual's development, he must be able to observe, report, and interpret with a minimum of error. This is not a simple matter, however, because of the limitations of man's sensory apparatus, the multiplicity of relevant observations, the complexity of human experience, and the problems involved in tying together these observations, impressions, and interpretations.

What a person sees and hears of the behavior of others constitutes only one aspect of his experience. He also experiences pressure, pain, cold, warmth, and is able to smell and to taste. All these sensations provide data about the events in his environment. But the response he makes will not always be predictable merely from knowledge of the stimuli—that is, from the nature of the events initiating the response. For example, two persons who are exposed to the same visual stimulus, such as an ink blot, may offer widely differing reports of what they "see" (2).[2]

The human being is limited in his ability to observe. There is only so much of what goes on about him that he can see, feel, hear, or smell. Because of these limitations, he may observe some significant aspects of a situation and not others, or he may observe all the essential aspects, yet in his interpretation give undue emphasis to some elements of the situation and insufficient emphasis to others.

For example, persons who are shown candid camera pictures will identify the emotions depicted with a high order of accuracy when they can infer from the picture what is going on in the situation. If the picture includes only the person's face, the judgment is apt to be less correct (4). Similarly, if one lacks knowledge of the events that signifi-

[2] Numbers in parentheses refer to the lists of references at the end of each chapter.

cantly influenced an individual's response, one may find it difficult to describe accurately the relationship between the overt behavior and the stimuli that evoked it.

The complex nature of human experience is such that the meanings of behavior learned at one time and place may then be incorrectly applied to a different, though superficially similar, situation. For example, highly inconsistent parental responses may lead the child to expect the behavior of other persons to be similarly inconsistent. If this expectation persists, he may habitually misperceive and misinterpret the actions of those around him.

Two other aspects of "human nature" interfere with our understanding of behavior. The emotional components of our "state of mind," of which we may be only partially aware, may influence both what we "see" in a given situation and how we interpret it. The enthusiastic rooter is more likely to "see" the fouls being committed against members of his own team than is a neutral observer. Our physical state also may influence the way we interpret events. The person who has not eaten for four hours is more apt to "see" shadowy figures on a screen as edible objects than is the person who has just eaten (3).

To make the extension from observations to their interpretation, the student requires some systematic means of "tying them together." Such "tying together" is accomplished through the use of ideas about how the events are related to each other. We will consider this in more detail later; the point to be noted here is that the understanding of behavior requires ideas about how the pieces fit together, and that difficulties in understanding behavior can sometimes be traced to the absence or oversimplification of these ideas.

The Individual and the Understanding of Behavior

Since most persons spend a good part of their lives in the presence of others, it is not surprising that expressions of confidence in one's own ability to understand and evaluate behavior are frequently encountered. Often the individual who takes for granted his own competence as a judge of people is relying on such time-worn—but widely held—folk sayings as "people with red hair are hot tempered," "a shifty-eyed person cannot be trusted," or "persons with high foreheads are intelligent." Regardless of the extent to which they use such widely held myths as a basis for their opinions, people often take their expert knowledge of others for granted.

Considering how much one does know about people, we can see why a person might assume his own "expertness" in this area. He knows what behaviors are appropriate to different situations and the extent to which he can act in the manner expected of him. He has learned to recognize the behaviors that go with his place in the family, in school, or at work. He has acquired some knowledge of what is legally or socially required and forbidden. He can readily recognize actions of others that are contrary to what is appropriate in a given situation.

Yet people are complex organisms, and one often finds it hard to understand why they behave as they do. Sometimes their actions may be surprising, disappointing, shocking. Even one's close associates may respond quite differently from what is anticipated. A friend may act in a manner quite inconsistent with his stated self-interests. The student who wishes to be admitted to a professional graduate program may not study hard enough to earn the grades required for admission. One may observe more dramatic instances, in which a person knows that overeating or excessive smoking is injurious to his health but refuses to abandon the habit.

Science and the Understanding of Behavior

The difficulties complicating man's effort to understand human behavior also are encountered whenever he tries to relate natural events to one another. His limited observational capacities, his inability to give accurate emphasis to all aspects of the problem before him, the influence of his emotions, and the difficulty of inferring meaning from his observations, all handicap him in his efforts to understand any aspect of his world. Through the years, man's awareness of these obstacles to knowledge has led to his developing methods for evaluating evidence and for systematically relating observations to one another, and procedures for testing assumptions about these relationships. These methods and procedures have contributed significantly to extending man's knowledge in all spheres, including the study of man himself, and while they will not be precisely the same for all problems, they have a common origin in what Dewey describes (1) as the "scientific attitude":

> In short, the scientific attitude as here conceived is a quality that is manifested in any walk of life. What, then, is it? On its negative side, it is freedom from control by routine, prejudice, dogma, unexamined tradition, sheer self-interest. Positively, it is the will to inquire, to examine, to discriminate, to draw conclusions only on the basis of evidence, of taking pains to gather all available evidence. It is the intention to reach beliefs, and to test those that are entertained, on the basis of observed fact, recognizing also that facts are without meaning save as they point to ideas. It is, in turn, the experimental attitude which recognizes that while ideas are

necessary to deal with facts, yet they are working hypotheses to be tested by the consequences they produce.[3]

Dewey's statement makes it clear that the possession of a scientific attitude is not limited to professional scientists. All men may share the scientist's desire to predict accurately the outcomes of specific situations or to modify conditions to achieve a particular result. But all men do not value the scientific attitude equally, and relatively few are skilled in the methods and techniques utilized in any one of the scientific disciplines.

However, these different methods and techniques are merely specific ways of applying the same principle. Regardless of the phenomena being considered the scientific acquisition of knowledge involves: (a) stating a research problem by asking a clear and answerable question; (b) formulating a hypothesis; (c) defining all terms and methods used; (d) collecting and analyzing the data; and (e) verifying the conclusion by repeating the study. Thus, all terms, procedures, and methods must be explicitly specified so that other investigators can corroborate or reject the findings. The body of knowledge arrived at by these five steps is what we know as science.

Science provides a means for evaluating the adequacy of beliefs concerning natural events and phenomena, but those pertaining to events or conditions outside the scope of objective human experience are scientifically untestable. The proposition that there is a life after death must be accepted or rejected on other than scientific grounds. Beliefs that cannot be communicated to others or cast in forms suitable for investigation also are outside the realm of science. The assertion that the poetry of Keats is superior to that of Shelley may be debated, but it cannot be evaluated scientifically until the definition of "superior" is agreed upon.

A person having a scientific attitude is willing to examine the evidence for his beliefs. Clinging to absolute convictions about natural events without considering the evidence is inconsistent with a scientific attitude, for science deals in tentative, not final, truths. In the kingdom of science, beliefs are always open to examination no matter how strongly held or imposingly supported.

Although the specific procedures employed by different sciences vary, they have in common the goal of accumulating and evaluating evidence. All sciences provide for careful observation, and many of the devices popularly associated with the scientist have been developed to extend

---

[3] John Dewey, Unity of science as a social problem. *International Encyclopedia of Unified Science,* Vol. I, No. 1–5. Copyright 1955 by the University of Chicago. Reprinted by permission.

the scope and power of his senses. The astronomer's telescope and the biologist's microscope enable the observer to see stars and cells that are invisible to the naked eye. In addition, the scientist deliberately and explicitly attempts to classify his observations. Such classification is helpful as he tries to understand how events and their antecedents and consequences are related. Classification also assists him in communicating his procedures and results to his colleagues, so that they can duplicate the investigation and verify his reported findings.

One of the scientist's most important and useful methods is the experiment. An experiment enables the investigator to study the relationship between events. In the simplest experiment, the scientist observes any changes occurring in the relationship between two variables as he alters one of them. For example, if the experimenter were interested in the relationship between the intensity of light and the size of the pupil of the eye, he would increase and decrease the intensity of the light and observe the subsequent contraction and expansion of the pupil. The variable altered by the experimenter—in this case, the intensity of light—is termed the *independent variable*; that which is changed as a result of its relationship to the independent variable is the *dependent variable*. It might, for example, be observed that when the independent variable, the intensity of light, is increased, the dependent variable, the pupillary diameter, decreases. In psychological experiments, independent variables often include conditions within the physical and social environment, while dependent variables include the sensations, behaviors, or decisions attributable to changes in the environmental (experimental) conditions.

When an experiment is performed, the scientist will attempt to prevent any variable other than the two being studied from entering into the experiment. Excluding the variables that might influence the relationship between the independent and dependent variables is called "controlling" the conditions of the experiment. Such control is best accomplished by maintaining all possible conditions at a constant level throughout the experiment—in other words, by eliminating them as variables.

In scientific studies conducted within the laboratory, control over the conditions that might influence the relationship between the independent and dependent variables is often more readily achieved than in studies conducted outside of it. When psychological studies are undertaken in actual life situations it is, of course, not possible to control all the features of the environment to which the persons being studied will be exposed. Yet it is still essential that conditions which could alter the relationship of the independent and dependent variables in some way be taken into account and excluded in the analysis of the findings. In the life situations in which persons are studied through interviews, individual case histories, performances in specially created situations, and responses to psychological tests, the scientist will utilize a "control" group in his efforts to identify as clearly as possible the specific relationship between independent and dependent variables. A control group is used as a basis for comparison to the group studied, and in every significant respect it is similar to the studied group except that it is not exposed to the independent variable of the experiment. For example, we might wish to study the effectiveness of a course entitled "How to Learn" in improving the achievement of eighth grade students. Two groups of students would be selected, one to be taught the course and the other—the control group—to go without it. Both groups would be as nearly identical as possible in achievement levels, intelligence, sex, reading ability, and family background. Following the course, the achievement levels of the two groups would be compared. If the performance of the experimental group were sufficiently higher than that of the control group, we could assume that the difference was due to the beneficial effect of the course.[4]

THE HYPOTHESIS: A PREDICTION OF
A FUTURE EVENT

Scientific research is often undertaken to test a specific prediction or assumption that appears reasonable in terms of the available evidence. This prediction or assumption is termed a hypothesis. In some respects, the scientist's hypothesis corresponds to the nonscientist's informed guess, in which he uses his experience of the past to formulate his expectations of the future.

Consider the case of the employee who decides to wait until after lunch to ask his boss for an extra week's vacation. His experience tells him that in the mornings his employer is preoccupied with the details of his business and is quite unapproachable. After lunch, he usually appears to be less harassed. The employee assumes that his request will have the best chance of being granted if it is presented under the most favorable conditions. His data indicate that the period after lunch satisfies these conditions, and he acts accordingly.

In deriving a prediction from certain assumptions and designing a test of the prediction, the employee's approach parallels that of the scientist's in formulating and testing a hypothesis, but in some respects

---

[4] Statistical procedures are available to assist the scientist in determining how great the differences between the groups must be before he can discard the possibility that they were the result of chance.

the two differ. The nonscientist's prediction is quite private; he does not reveal his assumptions or his hypothesis, while the scientist is expected to state explicitly his hypothesis, the assumptions on which it rests, and the procedures to be followed in subjecting it to test. The scientist tries to state his hypothesis in such a way that the data provided by testing it can lead either to its acceptance or to its rejection. In scientific studies, findings that do not uphold the hypothesis may stimulate the investigator to check his assumptions and the reasoning that lead from them to his hypothesis. He also may check his experimental procedures to be certain that all relevant factors were controlled, and that the research plan afforded an adequate test of the hypothesis.

FRAMES OF REFERENCE

The series of ideas into which scientists and laymen fit discrete observations and facts is known as a frame of reference. As the term implies, a frame of reference provides a skeleton or structure to which one can refer when an idea or observation is communicated. To the extent that persons share common frames of reference, they will literally talk the same language, for language itself provides one frame of reference. Yet within the same language there will be many possible frames of reference, since ideas concerning different types of events will require special systems.

The statements comprising the frame of reference are expressed in a special vocabulary because people with the same frame of reference usually use similar words. For example, religious people use such concepts as "sin," "guilt," "salvation," "God." Economists speak of "profit motive," "laborers and capitalists," and "markets." Freudian psychologists talk about "id," "ego," and "superego." Scientists speak of "hypotheses," "laws," "probability," and "empirical." These words are concepts that enable people to *explain* what they observe and to an extent they determine *what will be observed*. The frame of reference of the baseball fan, for example, is of such a specialized nature that the statement, "In the last half of the ninth, Jones died with the winning run on third," can communicate a considerable amount of information to another baseball fan, but the person unfamiliar with the special frame of reference might believe that some profound misfortune had brought an end to Jones' life. What is communicated, of course, is the way the inning ended: Jones had no opportunity to win the game because the final out occurred.

The frame of reference we employ will determine what inferences to related events we make from a specific communication of an event. A mother says to her small child, "You are a naughty boy." Hearing only this, one can make a number of different inferences as to how the boy's actions may have displeased his mother, depending upon one's frame of reference. A frame of reference also provides a pattern to fit together the pieces of information available. Having some idea of what the picture may resemble when the jigsaw puzzle is completed makes the task more manageable.

Persons studying similar problems and using similar methods and procedures usually employ a common technical language and the same general frame of reference. In psychology, for example, the general frame of reference used in studies of behavior is probably shared by most psychologists. Within this general frame of reference, however, psychologists will utilize many specialized frames of reference, depending on the problems investigated and the methods employed, and this is true of all areas of knowledge that have become highly specialized.

THEORY AS A FRAME OF REFERENCE

When a frame of reference possesses certain characteristics, it may be termed a scientific theory. In a scientific theory, the assumptions that are systematically related are called constructs. These constructs are not "real" in the sense that they are directly observable. Rather, they are tools that help us in thinking about natural phenomena; they stand for particular events or relationships among events. In the same way that the word "chair" is an idea symbolizing an object to sit on and is not the object itself, so constructs such as "electricity," "atoms," or "gravity" should not be confused with the processes to which they refer. Constructs enable the student to summarize and name events and processes of considerable complexity. Through the use of constructs, he can refer to conditions that he believes explain his observations. From sets of constructs that are systematically related he can make predictions and formulate testable hypotheses.

Since theories provide a means of organizing facts, observations, and ideas about natural events, they provide a basis for explanations of "how" observed events developed. From interpretations afforded by scientific theory, hypotheses may be formulated and tested. As bases for explanations and as sources for hypotheses, theories serve as springboards to new ideas and knowledge.

The scientist will clearly and publicly specify his theory and the hypotheses derived from it. He will evaluate his theories by the extent to which they fulfill their functions; therefore the accuracy of the predictions made from the theory and the amount of new knowledge to which the theory leads serve as two measures of its adequacy. In addition, "good" theories can account for the observations, events, and knowledge of the field they cover, and they are systematic; their parts or constructs fit together logically. Finally, an adequate scientific theory constitutes what is termed an "open system," in that it can always be modified as new evidence becomes available.

Although theories are often considered academic and of little value to practical men, many successful men owe their success to the quality of their theories and their ability to use them to predict future events with accuracy. The practical man may be unable to describe his theory or specify the constructs that comprise it; nevertheless, he relies heavily on it as he attempts to make predictions. "Nothing is so practical as a good theory."

Both scientists and laymen seek to acquire knowledge, though their procedures may differ. Each may desire such knowledge as a basis for action or as an end in itself. Men may study the problem of delinquency, for example, in order to learn more about its causes. Since delinquency is a part of human behavior, such knowledge may be sought for the purpose of adding to the storehouse of psychological information. On the other hand, the problem which the criminal presents to society necessitates study of the most effective methods of treating him, so knowledge of the causes of delinquency also may be pursued for its practical applications.

Values and the Understanding of Behavior

Whether knowledge is sought for its own sake or as a basis for action, the values held by scientists and nonscientists play an important part in motivating the search and in determining the problems to be investigated.

Many aspects of human behavior that interest both the scientist and the citizen are of such a nature that it is difficult to separate the value aspects from the scientific. Consider the following statement of fact: in its efforts to protect itself and at the same time to care for the mentally ill, the feebleminded, and the delinquent, society confines large numbers of such persons to institutions. During the course of a year, more persons spend some time in these institutions than reside in cities such as Cleveland, New Orleans, or San Francisco, or in the states of Alaska, Delaware, and Vermont combined (5).

Both scientists and nonscientists may be impressed by the number of inmates of institutions. They may consider the seriousness of the problem not only in terms of the cost of caring for these people, but also in terms of the loss to society of their creative potentials. They may think of institutionalization in terms of a profound personal problem for the individuals and their families. Emphasis on the tragedy, unhappiness, and waste represented by the lives of these institutionalized persons understandably can lead to judgments that the causes of institutionalization *should be* identified and eliminated; that the reduction in numbers of persons confined in such settings is *desirable* and that the objective of improving the productivity and satisfactions of these persons is *worthy* and *good*. By definition, holding some objective to be desirable and good constitutes a value judgment. These judgments, depending on their relation to the individual's self-concept, will vary in the degree and quality of emotional response associated with them. Values that are central to the person's self-concept—for example, honesty and integrity—will have greater potential than values held by the individual that are peripheral to his self-concept. A person may value punctuality yet become less emotional if he is kept waiting by a close friend than would be the case if the friend deceived him.

Frequently the same question is posed by the scientist and the non-scientist: How can the number of persons institutionalized each year be reduced? Both may have equally strong feelings about the value of this objective. The emotional reactions associated with this judgment may interfere with an objective appraisal of the problem and the means for finding a solution. The scientist insulates his biases and emotions from his efforts to seek an answer by using the safeguards inherent in his methods of collecting and evaluating evidence. The scientist is not without feelings and the value judgments regarding what is "good" and "bad" that are associated with these feelings. He does, however, have a method that prevents these value orientations from interfering with his search for appropriate solutions to his problems.

Finally, whether or not individuals defend and apply their findings will depend upon their values. Some scientists investigate phenomena only for the sake of knowledge and have little emotional interest in the application of their findings; others feel an emotional commitment to action and attempt to institute changes based upon the knowledge they have accumulated. An individual who is a citizen *as well as* a scientist may, therefore, make two types of statements in appearances before the public. In his role as *citizen* he is entitled, in a democracy, to indicate what he feels *should be* the state of affairs; for example, a reduction in institutional commitments. In his role as *scientist* he can offer the results of his investigations as evidence on *how* to achieve this end. His first statement is a judgment and there is no reason why it should be considered of greater value than the judgments of other citizens. His second statement is a scientific conclusion that says, "*If* institutionalization is to be reduced, *then* the actions proposed will achieve this end, according to my research." The reason for the existence of science and its methodology is that at present it is the best way man has for learning how to obtain whatever objectives his values led him to desire, but no scientific method has been developed to establish what values we should—or should not—cherish.

Judgments of desirability will often have an emotional response associated with them. One may be shocked by newspaper accounts of violence and brutality, or of the misconduct of persons in the public eye. The strong emotional reactions to such incidents may interfere with the objective appraisal of the people and the behaviors involved; such reactions can be obstacles to understanding, and in some instances may prevent a person from acting in his own best interests. To ensure that our biases and emotions do not impede efforts to extend our knowledge of behavior, the attitudes of the scientist and the care he takes in evaluating evidence may well be emulated. Further, because of the relationship between the values one holds and the emotions associated with them, the student of behavior should consider his own value orientations and the parts they play in the judgments he makes.

Since value judgments, according to this text, cannot be separated completely from the study of human behavior, the value orientations implicit throughout this book should be stated.

The Value Orientations of This Text

THE PURSUIT OF KNOWLEDGE

Activities and conditions that contribute to the acquisition of knowledge are considered valuable and worthwhile. Freedom to inquire into man's relationship to the physical and social world is basic to the acquisition of knowledge. In addition to such freedom, the accumulation of knowledge depends on attitudes that respect the pursuit of truth as a valuable human endeavor, whether it be through a laboratory experiment, a work of literature, or the study of one's self. This value does not in itself provide a basis for judging the desirability of the uses to which the knowledge is put. Such applications of knowledge are evaluated in terms of the following value orientation.

HUMAN DEVELOPMENT

Activities contributing to the fullest development of man's capacities, talents, and skills are regarded as desirable. The extension of his awareness of the natural world and the world of people, of himself and of his own capacities to react and to reason is part of the human developmental process and is considered natural and "good." Activities that enhance the individual's psychological, intellectual, physical, and social development as expressed in all aspects of his life are regarded as constructive and desirable. An individual may undertake these activities —and thus demonstrate this value—either on behalf of his own development or for the sake of the development of other persons. Behavior, activities, and conditions that impede the fullest realization of any individual's potentialities are regarded as undesirable.

The value orientation indicated above differs from religious beliefs about desirable behavior that spring from the acceptance of an authority external to man. The value orientation of this book is limited to man and his relationships to his fellows. As the subject matter of this book is restricted to human behavior, so the information upon which its value orientation is based is limited to the behavior of man. Thus the pursuit of knowledge and activities on behalf of man's development are considered to be valuable human endeavors in their own rights.

This is not to say that there must be conflict between values derived from a consideration of human relationships and those which are in accord with standards derived from authority external to man. In fact, values arising from a humanistic position, from a study of man, may be identical or overlap appreciably with those values arising from religious or philosophic beliefs. The following quotations afford examples of the way the value orientation of this text may resemble orientations relying on external authority:

> Hatred is not diminished by hatred at any time. Hatred is diminished by love; this is the eternal law. (Buddhism)
> Therefore, all things whatsoever ye would that men should do to you, do ye even so to them. (Christianity)
> Confucius was asked: "Is there one word that sums up the basis of all good conduct?" And he replied, "Is not reciprocity that word? What you yourself do not desire, do not put before others." (Confucianism)
> No one is a true believer until he loves for his brother what he loves for himself. (Islam)
> Do not unto others that which is hateful to you. (Judaism)[5]

Although it is interesting to note that each statement drawn from a different religion pertains to the same theme, the significant point is that the theme itself readily follows from the belief that behaviors which contribute to the development of other persons are desirable.

Since this is a book about personal and social development, characteristics of optimal development will be listed at points in the following chapters. By their very nature, such lists will reflect the text's value

[5] Cited in Lyle Tussing, *Psychology for Better Living*. New York: Wiley, 1959, p. 24.

orientation and constitute value judgments. But the reader should not be misled by this emphasis on values, since they are not presented for the purpose of indoctrinating him. Rather, these values are made explicit to help him to understand human behavior. To succeed in this task, he will require knowledge of his own value orientations, the way they influence what he observes, and the manner in which they affect the inferences he draws from his observations. He will also require an example of how a value orientation emphasizing a deep regard for both the scientific approach to the evaluation of evidence and the individual's fullest development can be utilized without doing violence to either emphasis. This text attempts to provide such an example.

Summary

While man may sometimes assume his expertness in understanding behavior, the inconsistencies he observes, his inadequate explanations of important incidents, and the incorrect predictions he often finds himself making have stimulated his desire to extend his knowledge and to seek more effective ways of organizing it. To the degree that he is able to understand himself and predict the behavior of others, he can increase his control over his environment and the opportunities for satisfaction and security for others, as well as for himself.

However, many barriers impede his progress toward these objectives. His senses are limited, and it is difficult for him to be aware of all the events in his environment and to integrate and weigh their relative importance. The emotional components of behavior influence both his observations and the interpretations drawn from them.

The scientist who studies the physical world encounters similar problems, however, and through the years he has developed increasingly effective procedures for observation and for testing his interpretations in the light of available evidence. Such methods are applicable to the study of human behavior and can be employed effectively when dealing with problems about which evidence can be secured, but those outside the realm of objective human experience are also beyond the reach of scientific procedures.

To enhance communication, persons studying similar problems and using similar methods are likely to employ a common frame of reference. And when the assumptions within a frame of reference are systematically related and pertain to natural events the resulting theory will permit the scientist to organize his facts and observations in such a way that he can make predictions and formulate testable hypotheses.

Both scientists and nonscientists may desire knowledge either as an end in itself or as a means of attaining other ends. In either case, it is

important that they recognize the ways in which their values and
emotions will influence their choice of problems to study, the methods
they employ, and their interpretation of the findings.

References

1. Dewey, J.   Unity of science as a social problem; in *The International Encyclopedia of Unified Science*, Chicago: University of Chicago Press, 1955.
2. Frank, L. K.   Projective method for study of personality. *J. Psychol.*,
1939, *8*, 389–413.
3. McClelland, D. C., and Atkinson, J. W.   The projective expression of needs:
I. The effect of different intensities of the hunger drive on perception.
J. Psychol., 1948, *25*, 205–22.
4. Munn, N. L.   The effect of knowledge of the situation upon judgment of
emotion from facial expressions. *J. abnorm. soc. Psychol.*, 1940, *35*,
324–338.
5. U.S. Bureau of Census.   *Statistical Abstract of the United States: 1960*.
Washington, D.C.: Government Printing Office.

Selected Readings

These texts provide an introduction to the areas of knowledge contained within the science of psychology.

Crutchfield, Richard S., and Krech, D.   *Elements of Psychology*. New York:
Knopf, 1958.
Hebb, D. O.   *A Textbook of Psychology*. Philadelphia: Saunders, 1958.
Hilgard, E. R.   *Introduction to Psychology* (ed. 3). New York: Harcourt, 1962.
Morgan, C. T.   *Introduction to Psychology*. New York: McGraw-Hill, 1961.
Munn, Norman L.   *Psychology: The Fundamentals of Human Adjustment*.
Boston: Houghton Mifflin, 1961.
Smith, K. U., and Smith, W. M.   *The Behavior of Man*. New York: Holt, 1958.

2.

The Nature of Man
and the Developmental Process

Man is a complex creature. He builds and destroys, loves and hates, cares for and kills. He has feelings, ideas, and passions. He goes to the opera and to baseball games; he has infinitely varied languages, customs, and ceremonies. Men are different and they are similar. Some fly jet planes; others pound their clothes clean along river banks. Man is our object of study; the study is of ourselves, for whatever man is, that is what we are.

Man is first of all an animal and whatever else he becomes he remains part animal (3). He eats, sleeps, breathes, and reproduces. He possesses a physical structure and a sensory apparatus that require exercise and activity. He seeks the company of others of his species and from such contact acquires behaviors that are similar to theirs. He strives to survive, adapting his behaviors to environmental conditions in ways that will bring him the most comfort, gratification, and safety.

Although one man shares much with others of his species, there are marked differences among men, just as there are marked differences among animals of the same species. From his ancestors he acquires the constellation of muscle, bone, tissue, organs, and cells that identify him as a human being and as a particular human being. From his experiences with other men he learns the expectations, values, responses, and attitudes that contribute also to his uniqueness.

Man differs from other animals in that he can more rapidly co-ordinate a wide range of information from outside and inside his body, information drawn from the past as well as the present and integrated with reference to the future. Such integration involves the coordination of stimuli acting upon his sensory apparatus and the triggering of responses related to survival and gratification from the body's various systems and organs.

Man's coordination is mediated by his complex brain and nervous system. The human being has "extraordinary sensitivity of some cells (the receptors) to environmental events . . . and an equally extraordinary speed and precision of movement in others (the muscles)" (8). Hebb notes that the nervous system accounts for the integration of the various parts of the body as well as for their timing, so that the appropriate system and organs of the body are active at the proper times and in the proper relationships.

By virtue of these abilities, man has distinct advantages over other animals. His more complex nervous system allows him a greater capacity to utilize symbols that represent past and future experiences. Thus, he can think of himself, his situation, his relationships to others about him; he can learn to meet new and immediate problems by applying pertinent knowledge communicated by others or acquired from his own experiences. (What is called forth will, of course, always include the emotional components of the symbols, and the fact that these emotions may sometimes lead us to inappropriate actions will be the subject of further discussion in Chapter 4.)

Man's existence as a biological being in a world of people has not been overlooked by those seeking to explain why he behaves as he does. Some investigators have given primary emphasis to the nature of his physical endowment, arguing that just as he inherits physical characteristics so he may receive and pass on psychological traits such as intelligence, diligence, responsibility, or aggressiveness, attributing these to inherited physical structures, to instincts, or "human nature." Some have proposed that only environmental experiences determine man's behavior. Others explain his actions in terms of some concept of normality. After mention has been made of several of these approaches, the developmental view of man will be presented as one that provides a more meaningful frame of reference for the study of human behavior.

Heredity and Environment

A number of remnants from folklore reflect the considerable popularity that heredity has enjoyed as an explanation of human behavior. The adage "Like father, like son" and such false beliefs as that of attributing a child's attitudes and interests to the mother's experiences during pregnancy or his special skills and talents to his parents' genes, persist as satisfying explanations for some persons as they attempt to account for their observations.

In addition to these broad misconceptions about the process of heredity, there is confusion about that which is properly identified as hereditary. Some persons assume that conditions existing at birth are attributable solely to heredity and all that occurs following birth is due to the environment. This, however, is an oversimplification. A variety of conditions, such as radiation or some viral diseases, can influence the development of the child before birth. On the other hand, examples can be cited of individuals who have shown no sign of developmental disorder at birth and through their early adulthood but who subsequently demonstrate the symptoms of Huntington's chorea, an inherited defect in which progressive deterioration of certain brain cells occurs, but which is not evident until the later adult years. Animal experiments have shown that the genes themselves can be modified by the environmental stimuli of x-rays, temperature changes, or chemicals. This further illustrates the difficulty of clearly demarcating the hereditary and the environmental.

Although the distinction between the two is difficult to define, evidence is available that a genetic factor is responsible in some cases for specific physical structures which account for developmental disorders. Examples are tuberous sclerosis and neurofibromatosis, disorders characterized by unusual growth in the brain and nerve fibers that markedly affects the individual's physical and intellectual development, and phenylketonuria, a disorder of protein metabolism, which is responsible for about 1 percent of those institutionalized as mentally defective.

The genetic inheritance—the chemical substances contributed by the parents to the cell from which the fetus develops—of patients with these conditions includes recessive genes that account for abnormal physical structures. It is important to note that only organic substances that affect the structural characteristics of the body are transmitted from one generation to the next; there can be no direct transmission of behaviors, interests, or talents as such.

Another point of view is that physical structures and biochemical characteristics may be inherited that "predispose" an individual to certain behaviors associated with developmental disturbance. In research on schizophrenia, Kallman found that if one identical twin had been diagnosed as schizophrenic, then in 86 percent of the cases the other was also schizophrenic. The comparable figures for full siblings were 14 percent and for step-siblings, 1.8 percent. Kallman concluded that an hereditary defect, possibly producing a metabolic disorder, predisposed the individual to schizophrenia. The disease would become manifest if other contributing factors were added (9).

Although geneticists are able to account for the hereditary transmission of certain physical characteristics, such as eye color or the ability to taste a particular chemical, and for some highly specific developmental disorders, few of them would subscribe to an "either-heredity-or-environment" position in explaining complex behavior. The majority of scientists prefer to view behavior as the result of the interaction of both these factors. Many persons continue to uphold the extreme positions, however, and scientists in the past have presented evidence favoring one or the other in explaining behavior. Because the several approaches taken to the problem are matters of methodological and historical interest, some brief mention will be made of them.

HEREDITY

Statements such as, "Well, his achievements, after all, are to be expected since he comes from good stock," or, "Considering his blood, it's not surprising he got into trouble," represent the common tendency to account for a person's behavior in terms of his inheritance. The older studies will be cited that attempted to evaluate this role of inheritance. They utilized the family pedigree method, which seeks to establish the frequency of occurrence of particular behaviors or characteristics among the ancestors or descendants of an individual or among his relatives.

In a study on the inheritance of feeblemindedness, published in 1912, Goddard (6) described 480 descendants of a Revolutionary War soldier—who was given the pseudonym of Martin Kallikak—and a mentally defective barmaid. Of these, 143 were mental defectives, 33 were prostitutes, 24 were alcoholics, 3 epileptics, 3 criminals, and only 46 were considered unquestionably of average or above-average intelligence. The same soldier later married a woman of superior intelligence. In the same number of generations, only 4 of his descendants were reported as defective or delinquent.

In an earlier work, published in 1869, Sir Francis Galton (4) described his use of the pedigree method in his studies of genius. He reported that 997 men, identified as eminent, had 332 close relatives who also were eminent, a number that was more than twelve hundred times larger than would have been anticipated on the basis of chance.

Although pedigree studies such as these demonstrate convincingly that intellectual and social competence is higher in some families than in others, the interpretation that only hereditary factors are responsible for the uniformity of family achievement is vulnerable to attack. To test hypotheses about the effects of heredity it must be assumed that the environmental influences are constant, or that they are operating in a random or chance manner. In the pedigree studies, neither of these assumptions can be met. The effects of "good" environmental conditions in the Galton studies of genius and of "poor" environmental influences in the Goddard study could have influenced the results markedly. In addition, the tendency of persons to "mate selectively," that is, to marry individuals who resemble themselves with respect to ethnic, economic, and intellectual characteristics, complicates the interpretation of the results.

To offset some of the difficulties encountered when the pedigree method is applied to human beings, selectively bred animals have been studied under controlled environmental conditions. In one well-known study, Tryon interbred rats who performed well on learning a maze (17). He also interbred a "stupid" group of rats, who made many errors while learning the maze. From each of eighteen successive generations, the rats whose maze performances were the best for the "bright" group were interbred; similarly, the poorest performers for each generation in the "stupid" group were interbred. By the seventh generation there was almost no overlap in the distributions of error scores; that is, the performances of the poorest rats in the "bright" group were better than the performances of the most skillful rats in the "stupid" group.

Although subsequent research (14) has suggested that the differences between the two groups might be more readily attributable to differences in emotional and motivational factors than in learning abilities, the hypothesis of a relationship between the behavior and the genetic history of the animals was given support.

Interest in the genetic components of the crucial physical differences between animals who perform well and those who do not continues to be a matter of scientific interest. Such research is presently being conducted with lower forms of animal life, notably with the fruit fly, *Drosophila,* since the time interval between generations is short and a large number of offspring is available for study. In the Tryon study, for example, eleven years were required to carry out the successive breedings.

Since only animals can be bred selectively and subjected to a controlled environment, present investigators rarely resort to human pedigree studies of the Galton and Goddard variety. The lower animals' inability to engage in abstract thinking and to use language imposes restrictions upon the interpretation of the results obtained in animal studies, so proponents of the nurture or environmental position look to research on human behavior for support for their contention that it is primarily modified by the individual's environment experiences.

The genetic influences operating in the development and character of certain physical structures have led to a common misconception of

the role of heredity in accounting for the relationship between physical
structure and psychological characteristics. The tendency to assume a
causal relationship between conditions existing concurrently is evidenced
in the comment, "John inherited his father's temper." Such a case may
very well be an example of imitation, and research has given no support
to the belief in the hereditary transmission of most psychological traits.

A different issue, though one frequently perceived as the same,
arises from the question of whether specific bodily characteristics are
associated with specific psychological characteristics. Even if such an
association were to be clearly established, which has not yet been done,
the source of the psychological characteristics would still be unidentified.
The fat person may respond to the social expectation that he be jolly,
and the short man may behave aggressively to offset his feelings of inferiority about his physique.

In recent years, the relationship between body build and psychological characteristics has been investigated by Sheldon at Harvard. He
devised an elaborate scheme for describing both body build and
psychological temperament and studied the correlation between the two
extensively (15). The results of these investigations have been interpreted
in various ways; since the design of the studies is vulnerable to some
criticism, other investigators must duplicate Sheldon's findings before
they can be accepted as demonstrating a causal relationship between
physique and psychological characteristics.

The effort to establish such a causal relationship is not new. In
Julius Caesar, for example, Shakespeare commented:

> Let me have men about me that are fat;
> Sleek-headed men, and such as sleep o'nights.
> Yond Cassius has a lean and hungry look;
> He thinks too much; such men are dangerous.

In 1895, Lombroso, an Italian anthropologist, offered a theory
ascribing the characteristics of the genius to various physical and
emotional deficiencies. In other studies he attempted to relate criminal
tendencies to specific physical features.

Almost a hundred years before Lombroso, Gall, an anatomist, put
forth the view that psychological, temperamental, and moral traits were
related to the shape of the skull. This theory, called phrenology, was
based upon the assumption that the shape of the brain corresponds to
the shape of the skull, that the "mind" can be analyzed into a number
of separate functions, and that these functions are localized in specific
areas of the brain (2). Although science has failed to find support for
these three assumptions or for the major hypothesis that specific human

characteristics are associated with head shape, supporters of phrenology still exist. Even today naive individuals are cheated by "experts" who offer advice to a client on the basis of the shape of his head and face.

Studies of the relationship between physique and psychological traits, such as those conducted by Sheldon, do not settle the issue of the relationships between behavior and man's inheritance. In one study, for example, a correlation between body build and delinquency was found (5). On this basis, one might conclude that there is an hereditary tendency for the athletically built young male to become delinquent. Another interpretation would suggest that while very few individuals possessing this particular build become delinquent, in areas where delinquency rates are high the stronger and more active individuals are more likely to become leaders because they fulfill the requirements imposed by the role. Hence it seems that the thesis that certain types of roles in certain environments impose more or less specific physical requirements provides a more complete explanation of such behavior than does the genetic one.

In later sections of this book, the relationship between physique and behavior and between the individual's body and his attitudes toward his physical appearance and prowess will be considered. However, since attitudes toward self are derived from social and psychological experience and are not transmitted genetically, we will not go into the matter in this section, which deals only with the relationship between heredity and behavior.

ENVIRONMENT

In contrast to the hereditarian, who emphasizes the individual's native endowments, his inherited physical structure, and the specific biochemical and neural characteristics acquired from his ancestors, the environmentalist accounts for men's character and behavioral differences in terms of differences in patterns of experience, in reactions to the requirements and expectations of the environment. Those holding extreme hereditary and extreme environmentalistic positions have very different concepts of the degree to which human behavior is modifiable, as indicated by the following well-known quotation of Watson (18):

Give me a dozen healthy infants, well formed, and my own specified world to bring them up in and I'll guarantee to take any one at random and train him to become any type of specialist you might select—doctor, lawyer, artist, merchant-chief, and yes, even beggar and thief, regardless of his talents, penchants, tendencies, abilities, vocations and race of his ancestors.

Though less extreme than Watson, other environmentalists have presented studies in which the influence of environment on social and intellectual development was emphasized (13). On these studies statistics were offered to demonstrate the relationship of low income level, poor housing, and unemployment to delinquency, crime, and psychological instability, and to support the position that environmental influences are of primary significance in accounting for human behavior.

Though the nature and nurture conflict subsided for a time, with the advent of quantitative measures of intelligence the proponents of the two views found a new field for controversy. Whether intelligent behavior could be explained primarily in terms of inheritance or environment was a question of considerable practical importance. If intellectual abilities were determined by inherited characteristics, then intellectual level should be identified as early as possible and the appropriate training should then be instituted. According to this view, planning of education and career would be undertaken in light of the individual's intellectual abilities, and any efforts to change the level of his intelligence by manipulation of his environment should be considered useless.

On the other hand, the environmentalist, believing that intelligence resulted from the experiences confronting the person during his early years, would focus his attention on the home and school situation in order to provide as desirable an environment as possible. He would perceive intelligence as a variable responsive to changes in the environment and therefore capable of improvement with the individual's exposure to favorable circumstances.

Psychologists have attempted to determine the relative influence of heredity and environment on intelligence by comparing the intelligence test scores (see page 200) of children reared in various settings. True siblings, children placed in foster homes, and institutionalized children have been studied.

In general, the greatest similarity between intelligence test scores occurs for identical twins[1] in the same environment. Fraternal twins living together are only slightly more similar than regular siblings under the same conditions. The intelligence test scores of siblings are about as similar as those of parent and child.

In an interesting study of the nature-nurture problem, a geneticist, a psychologist, and a statistician—Newman, Freeman, and Holzinger—compared nineteen pairs of identical twins who had been separated

---

[1] Identical twins develop from the same fertilized ovum and have the same chromosomes; fraternal twins develop from separate ova, so their hereditary similarity is only of the same order as that of siblings born of the same parents at different times.

during their early years (13). The identical twins reared in separate homes had intelligence quotients that were less similar than those of identical twins reared together, but more similar than fraternal twins in the same household. It was also noted that the more marked the environmental and educational differences, the greater the differences in the intelligence test scores of the identical twins reared apart.

In studies of young children the similarity of the intelligence scores of parents and their children reared at home was found to be greater than those of foster parents and their foster children. Though a relationship between the intelligences of children at home with those of their real parents was established, it was not close enough to ensure the absence of environmental factors.

The proponents of both views, the hereditarian and the environmental, have mainly demonstrated that all behavior appears to be a complex composite of biological and environmental, especially social, forces. The physical endowments of the individual set the limits of his possible performance, but his actual performance within these limits seems attributable to the experience he has acquired—particularly the social components of his experience.

In closing this section on the hereditary and environmental views of the primary influences on man's behavior, a final point of emphasis is important. Although it is the popular tendency to assume that hereditary conditions are unchangeable and environmentally determined ones are modifiable, this assumption does not hold in practice. Alteration of genetic structure by radiation, for example, and the dietary treatment of the child who has phenylketonuria represent the modification of conditions imposed by heredity. On the other hand, there is considerable evidence to indicate that it is erroneous to assume that prejudices, fears, or entrenched habits are readily changeable because they are not genetically determined.

Human Nature and Instincts

Other theories that attempt to account for behavior in terms of man's inherited physical constitution include those that use the terms "human nature" and "instincts." Statements such as "It's human nature for men to fight with one another" imply that such inclinations are innate, unlearned, universal among all men, and are unlikely to be modified by environmental influences.

The issue of what constitutes native or inborn behaviors was the subject of considerable investigation during the period just preceding and following the First World War. Much attention was given to classifying instincts, and lists were compiled that included such complex behavioral patterns as the "herd instinct," and the instincts of "self-assertiveness," "self-abasement," and "female coyness."

Scientists observed that animals whose nervous systems are less complex than man's manifested certain behaviors instinctively as un-learned reflex patterns. The mother rat feeding and protecting her young was demonstrating the maternal instinct. Since human mothers also act in specific ("maternal") ways, it is not surprising that even the com-plicated process of caring for the human infant was presumed to be unlearned.

Incidents of desertion, neglect, and infanticide raised some doubts about the instinct theory, but it was not until additional researches by anthropologists were published that the popularity of the theory waned. In some cultures, for example, it is customary to give away one's children; in others, mothers put some of their infants to death to equalize the sex ratio in the family (11). The complicated techniques of caring for the human infant, as well as the desire to fulfill the responsibilities of motherhood occur, then, not as a series of reflex acts, but as the result of learning what is expected.

Aggressive behavior also has been considered a constitutional, in-born characteristic of all men, and such an explanation was supported by history and the Biblical prediction that wars would persist until the end of time. Studies of various societies in which people do not engage in warfare or compete aggressively with one another, however, revealed contrary evidence (11).

Psychological and economic processes were linked in the early 1600's when political philosophers such as Hobbes and Smith developed the concept of the "economic man." In their views, and in the writings of more recent philosophers such as Marx, the acquisition of personal possessions, goods, and material objects was considered the expression of a fundamental, inborn, unlearned human characteristic. Though data exist indicating that animals may demonstrate unlearned acquisitive be-haviors such as the hoarding of food, the assertion that man by his nature is acquisitive is not supported by cultural studies. In societies such as ours where material possessions are highly valued, the quest for such possessions may reflect a desire to enhance one's status, or to be admired by others, and the acquisitive behaviors are a product of the desire for social prestige.

"Self-assertiveness" was another of the so-called instincts identified. Again, the studies of other cultures revealed that competitive behavior and striving for personal recognition, which is taken for granted in our society, is not always evident in others. Hopi children, for example, do

not compete with one another either in school or in their games
(11, p. 115).

In recent years psychologists have tended to discard the term
instinct; they have retained the idea, however, that complex patterns of
behavior that are unlearned, but whose appearance may depend upon
patterns of previous learnings as well as the genetic inheritance, and
which are characteristic of a species, are properly termed *instinctive.*
According to the present view of instinctive behavior, although the
complex pattern of activity is often quite variable, the end state to
which it is directed is quite specific. As Hebb (8) notes:

> Man everywhere has a fondness for the sound of his own voice,
> singing and listening to songs, telling elaborate tales for their own
> sake (some of them being true), or talking when there is no need of
> communication. Man everywhere uses tools, organizes social groups,
> avoids darkness in strange places. All cultures are said to have
> developed string games, related to the childhood game of cat's
> cradle. The taboos of incest or of food use, the belief in spirits good
> or evil, the tendency to ornament the body in particular ways and
> to impose strong sanctions against ornamenting it in other ways—
> all these things which, in detail, are subject to the influence of
> special learning but which in one form or another spring up in
> every society of which we have knowledge. In detail, therefore, they
> are not species-predictable; but in a larger sense they are very much
> so.[2]

In current psychological thought, instinctive behaviors and learned
behaviors are seen as shading one into the other. It is no longer acceptable to consider complicated patterns of action, such as engaging in
combat, as manifestations of an "aggressive instinct." Rather, the aggressive act is viewed as the product of biological inheritance and learning;
man acquires genetically the physical structure required for effective
assault (his arms and fists) and he learns the motive to defend himself
and his loved ones and how and when to anticipate danger. The
difficulty—and even the impossibility—of clearly identifying behaviors
that are free of either instinctive or learned aspects is underscored.

In this text aspects of man's behavior that are modified as a result
of his developmental experiences are given emphasis and their instinctive
origin, derived from his species membership, is assumed. Consider, for
example, this text's position that a person learns to distinguish the
behaviors which bring reward and pleasure from those which bring him

[2] Reprinted by permission from D. O. Hebb, *A Textbook of Psychology,* p. 126.
Copyright, 1958, by W. B. Saunders Company.

pain and punishment. He learns how to communicate, to provide pleasure to others, to protect himself. He learns what details of social behavior are appropriate at home, at school, and at church. He learns what it is to be a boy or a girl and what is expected of him because of his sex. He learns how to behave toward members of the opposite sex, how to conduct his courtship, and how to fulfill the responsibilities of marriage and parenthood. All such learnings derive from man's potentialities for behavior that are determined by his membership in the species.

Thus the view that man's behavior is attributable not to instinct *alone* but to the development through his experience of his genetically determined potentials forms the basis of the belief that action can be taken to direct or improve undesirable social behaviors. It suggests that the understanding of behavior is not provided by a few simple formulations, but necessitates a careful study of the social world and man's place in it.

Normality

The abandonment of the theory that instincts could provide a basis for a total understanding of human conduct posed many difficult questions. If "instincts" or "human nature" could not account for the behavior of human beings, then other explanations were necessary. One attractive alternative to the discarded theories was that individuals share many traits and characteristics with others in their culture because of similar experiences, as well as because of similar bodies.

It has therefore become fashionable to characterize individuals as "normal" or "abnormal," not only as a method of describing them, but in a way that suggests that these terms explain behavior. Although it is no longer the vogue to account for a person's behavior as the manifestation of human nature or of a particular instinct, the term "normal" is often used in its place. When this is done, the meaning and usefulness of the term "normality" must be questioned.

Since neither of the definitions of normality to be discussed below has more than descriptive value, its usefulness is quite limited in providing a frame of reference for an understanding of behavior. A sophomore girl in college who does not use lipstick may be behaving in a way that will be labeled "abnormal" by her classmates, and though this may describe the behavior, it does not explain it. The widespread use of the terms, however, the value attributed to the "normal" label in our culture, and the confusions arising from the varied meanings attached to it necessitate giving attention to its several usages.

THE STATISTICAL CONCEPT OF NORMALITY

According to the statistical concept, normality is defined as the correspondence of the individual's behaviors and characteristics to those that most persons manifest. The typical or average set of behaviors is considered normal and the assessment of normality consists of determining the degree to which the individual conforms to the average; the degree to which he is above or below average determines the extent of his abnormality.

This view accepts the behavior of the group as its standard for reference. Since cultures and societies vary, the particular group used will account for the specific behaviors identified as normal. For example, aggression and competition characterize the behavior of the Mundugamor of New Guinea, whereas the Arapesh—also of New Guinea —are described as passive, docile people (12). If the Mundugamor were used as the standard for comparison, the quiet, unassertive, and non-competitive person would be considered deviant, but in comparison with the Arapesh he would be normal.

In the statistical determination of normality, the ethical character of the group's behavior and any special circumstances affecting the individual's ability to provide an average response are not considered. For example, persons in Germany during the period of Hitler's power who denounced religious persecution would be classified as abnormal.

According to this conception, critical factors in the life of an individual that may have influenced his attitudes, behaviors, and self-perceptions are irrelevant. Although for other purposes consideration might be given to the reasons for an individual's being deviant, the mere existence of his deviancy constitutes the single basis upon which the determination of abnormality is made.

Since the positive values are associated with the terms "normal," "typical," and "healthy" in our culture—they are "good"—and negative values are attached to "abnormal," "atypical," and "ill," it is necessary to note that statistical information in itself does not provide a basis for value determinations, for judgments of right and wrong, good or bad. According to this view, if intelligence is the characteristic upon which the determination is based, the genius with an intelligence quotient of 170 is as deviant as the idiot with a quotient of 30.[3] It is customary in our society to value normality, although such valuation is not derived from the statistical information upon which the determination is based, but from philosophic, religious, or moral beliefs.

[3] A discussion of intelligence quotients is provided in Chapter 7.

In a study of the sexual behavior of men, for example, Kinsey reports that nearly three fourths of boys between the ages of sixteen and twenty have had heterosexual experience (10). In an investigation of character, Hartshorne and May found that a large percentage of grade school students cheated if they were given the opportunity (7). According to the statistical conception of normality, the sexually abstinent adolescent boy and the honest student would be considered deviant.

It is apparent that a judgment about the desirability of specific behavior requires more than a statement of what most people do. As the statistical definition of normality fails to provide a basis for its valuation, so it also fails to explain behavior. To say that a person acts in a bizarre manner *because* he is abnormal, or to account for a child's boisterous play by saying he is a normal six-year-old, sounds like an explanation of the behavior, yet does not provide it and represents an interesting example of circular reasoning.

THE ARBITRARY CONCEPT OF NORMALITY

The statistical concept of normality considers the behavior of the group as the criterion, and does not in itself constitute a basis for valuation. Many persons who might be asked to define normality, however, would provide definitions independent of the group's behaviors, such as

"To be normal is to be physically and morally clean."

"If you avoid the use of artificial stimulants such as liquor or nicotine, you are normal."

"It is normal to be able to control yourself at all times. The person who is emotional is not normal."

The use of the term normal as an arbitrary standard comes closest to its original usage, since it derives from the Latin word *norma,* meaning standard or carpenter's square. Definitions of this type are based not on the behavior of most people, but on some set of explicit statements concerning desirable behavior or on concepts of right or wrong drawn from philosophic, religious, or moral beliefs.

When the arbitrary approach is adopted the criteria for the assessment can be explicitly stated, and in this respect it is similar to the statistical approach. The two differ significantly, however, in that the latter relies on the knowledge of the behavior characteristics of a group of persons, whereas such knowledge is not relevant to the arbitrary determination of normality. That over 40 percent of the adult population in the United States drinks alcoholic beverages may be quite irrelevant to the person who believes that the use of alcohol in any form constitutes a destructive and perverse act.

To those whose standards of normality emanate from fixed and arbitrary values, then, the behavior of the population is not a significant fact in the assessment of normality. They might assess the behaviors of large segments of people in foreign cultures as abnormal, applying the same standards or criteria to all people irrespective of cultural influence.

Different interpretations of man's behavior underlie the two approaches to the determination of normality. The statistical concept, which places its major emphasis on the behavior of the social group of which the individual is a part, is associated with values that attach great significance to the degree to which man adapts, adjusts, or conforms to those about him. According to this view, man is seen as an organism primarily responsive to the demands of his physical environment and social experience, and his uniqueness as an individual is not given especial emphasis. This approach is also apt to support the view that change in man's behavior is most readily accomplished through change in his social and physical environment.

By its presentation of specific behavioral statements constituting the criteria for normality, the arbitrary approach gives emphasis to the view of man as an actor upon his environment. In this approach, man is perceived as possessing a high order of self-determination; he can make choices involving his future activity; he can behave in accord with rational principles, disregarding or little influenced by social conditions and the behavior of those around him.

Both approaches make it possible to state explicitly what is meant by the term *normal*. In the statistical concept, the group can be indicated along with the behaviors and characteristics being used as the basis for the determination of normality; in the arbitrary approach, the standards that must be met to qualify as normal can be specified. Though they are not particularly helpful in explaining behavior, both views do offer a limited means of categorizing and describing persons.

In view of the limitations of these concepts of normality, however, neither is recommended to the reader interested in assessing and understanding behavior. Neither provides a statement sufficiently detailed to serve as a helpful frame of reference for ideas, observations, and evidence pertaining to behavior. To replace these concepts of normality, the reader is offered a view of man as not only an adaptor to or an actor upon his environment, but as a developing, vital, and unique individual who is himself and whose behavior is a product of his native endowment and his social experience. This is the developmental view of man.

The Developmental View of Man

The developmental view does not provide for simple categories. It recognizes that an individual may be described in terms of his personal feelings, attitudes, values, and aspirations; the nature and quality of his social relationships; the work he performs and the satisfaction he receives from it.

A high level of psychological and social development is indicated when the individual is functioning effectively with respect to his intrapersonal (within-self) behavior, his interpersonal (with-other-persons) behavior, and the use of his abilities in satisfying and productive work. Although the indices of "effective behaviors" will be specified in detail in later chapters, the following general statement describes persons whose behavior reflects a high level of psychological and social development:

> Such a person is comfortable with himself; he feels he is a worthy and acceptable person. He is free of internal conflict and is able to set goals for himself that are consistent with his capabilities. He is able to maintain satisfying relationships with other people without having to sacrifice his integrity through total capitulation to the wishes or attitudes of others. He is able to respect the needs, feelings, and rights of others. Such a person is able to enter into mutual love relationships. He is able to direct his aptitudes, talents, and intelligence toward worthwhile personal and social objectives.

The above statement describes a peak of personal and social development that for most persons represents an ideal goal. It identifies three areas of psychological and social development: the intrapersonal, the interpersonal, and the application of one's abilities in work. Each of these areas is emphasized in this book. Each is presented in sufficient detail to provide not only a frame of reference, a descriptive statement of the individual, but also a tentative basis to approach an understanding of behavior. Indices of effective psychological functioning that relate to man's development and to the text's value orientation are provided. These indices pertain primarily to adults and are outlined in the final section of the text.

CHARACTERISTICS OF THE DEVELOPMENTAL PROCESS

Life is an active process; stimuli impinge upon the human being's sensory receptors and throughout his nervous system networks of cells are activated, patterns of electrochemical interactions take place, and the internal events that follow lead to his muscular responses, to the statements he makes, and to the ideas he entertains. And when this moment passes, he no longer is quite the same. In the fleeting interval of time, he has become a new person. Sometimes the pattern of events results in dramatic changes, as when the child speaks his first word or takes his first step. Sometimes responses are followed by satisfying consequences that increase the likelihood of similar responses to similar situations. Responses that bring such satisfactions may have occurred by intent, by reasoned forethought, or by luck, but whatever their bases, after such responses the individual is no longer quite the same. When viewed as a continuous pattern of events and experiences, the changes that take place within the individual as part of life activity constitute the developmental process.

The processes of psychological and social development are related to those of physical growth and the development of physical capacities and skills. This relationship is dramatically evident in such instances as that of a child's learning to walk. During the first four years his size, strength, skills, and comprehension and awareness of himself in relation to others have all developed rapidly. He makes his transition from crawling to walking behavior, not as a result of his experience, training, or practice, but because he is sufficiently developed physically, because his bones, muscles, nerves, brain, and balance mechanisms have reached a certain point in their structural development. The physical process, independent of experience, that accounts for new behavior is termed "maturation." Once maturation sufficient for walking has been reached, however, his proficiency in walking and his confidence in climbing and jumping are determined by his training, experience, and the requirements of his situation. And just as the physical abilities an individual possesses contribute to the range of experience available to him, so such experience can contribute to the extension of his physical skills and abilities.

It must not be assumed that because of this close relationship, particularly during the early years, there is complete correspondence between physical growth and psychological and social development throughout the person's life. On the contrary, though these processes interact, they do not proceed at the same rate, and in the adult years when the person's vision, hearing, and motor skills are declining, he may be continuing to develop psychologically and socially, undergoing major changes in attitude, behaviors, and feelings. The decline in strength and physical skill and the illnesses associated with aging constitute new experiences and necessitate psychological measures directed toward the maintenance and protection of personality. These measures represent in themselves a facet of the developmental processes that continue despite the decline of physical functioning.

One view of psychological development is that it represents the individual's continuing effort to bring all the facets of his life together in a harmonious relationship; that such integration has more than a maintenance function and is directed toward realizing all his potentialities. Thus, there is no point where one arrives, and a person never reaches a stage in his life where his development ceases. As Allport has expressed it, the person is always in the state of "becoming" (1).

In addition to the interactions between the physical and the social and psychological, the developmental process has several other features. That it is continuous and characterized by change has already been mentioned, but it is also a cumulative process.

The term *cumulative* refers to the succession of events and experiences that have an effect on the individual. Each specific effect may be of considerable or of relatively little consequence, but represented in the individual's approach to the events and experiences he confronts are the cumulative effects of all his previous reactions. An understanding of the individual thus necessitates knowledge of the pattern, the relationships of the series of experiences that have constituted his life; it implies that a search for the single event or experience that is "the" explanation of a facet of his personality is apt to be unfruitful.

William Stern, a psychologist who studied the process of psychological development as it was reflected in the behavior of children, observed that "there is indeed nothing in the development of only momentary value, everything keeps on working, even if only as a tool for other efforts, everything heaps up powers, makes reserves, opens roads that determine future life" (16).

The cumulative building of successive experience upon experience occurs as an additive process. There is no reversing of the direction of the process, even though at times of stress an individual's behavior may resemble that of a younger person or in later life physical decline may be accompanied by social and psychological disorganization. Even in these instances, or when mistakes are corrected, the cumulative effects of experience are being expressed behaviorally; they are not "undoings" or turnings back of the "psychological clock."

The continuous and cumulative nature of the developmental process suggests also that the psychological status of a person is never fixed at one point. This view is in opposition to the belief that the individual's basic emotional and psychological characteristics are completely established prior to his entry into elementary school and that subsequent experience merely results in the extension of established characteristics and tendencies.

If we say that the adolescent or adult can change as a result of his experiences we do not thereby picture him as totally responsive to each situation, in the manner of a chameleon whose skin color adapts to its surroundings. The identity the individual acquires during the early years is of significance in determining what he will be like as an adult, but the experiences of the adolescent period and adult life also play an important role in influencing psychological development.

Each of the stages of life—infancy, childhood, adolescence, the early, middle, and later adult years—will provide its special stimulus to the individual's thoughts and daydreams and to his actions and achievements, for within each culture the group's expectations of what is proper, permissible, and desirable for the different roles of those stages are made clear to him and he internalizes them. These expectations and untested abilities, together with the desire for new experiences and for approval from those he loves or esteems, combine to account for the new behaviors that are evidence of development. Man's impetus to change and to develop therefore stems from many sources, outside as well as within him: from the culture, friends, parents, teachers; from his own need to satisfy himself more effectively and easily; and from his reactions to his changing physical potentialities.

Impetus to change, to extend one's range of behavior, by abandoning outmoded habits and acquiring new skills may come from many quarters, but its most characteristic feature is the individual's sense of a degree of dissatisfaction with accustomed modes of response. Such dissatisfaction is not necessarily the result of a conscious analysis; it may be represented in states of physical tension, as in the activity of the infant whose maturing body demands movements and exercise that previously were not required.

One of the conditions accounting for inadequate development, a state referred to as "fixation," springs from the complete gratification (or overgratification) of the individual's needs by those close to him. The excessively indulgent mother who accurately anticipates her child's every wish may cause his inadequate psychological and social development by depriving him of these experiences of dissatisfaction. However, the reader should realize that excessive deprivation of the infant's and young child's needs also can result in the condition where there is little impetus to change.

In the developmental approach, the behaviors of the individual are considered in the light of his particular physical condition, his abilities and experiences, and the demands and expectations of his society. According to this view, the significance of a behavioral act cannot be evaluated without this consideration, and the assessment of behavior in terms of this approach is made only in relative, not absolute, terms.

THE DEVELOPMENTAL APPROACH
AND MENTAL HEALTH

From the point of view of this text, an individual enjoys "mental health" if he develops and functions effectually in the areas of intrapersonal, interpersonal, and work activity. Conversely, "mental illness" describes a low level of effectiveness in these three areas. The terms "mental illness" and "mental health" are not employed, however, since they emphasize the concept of illness or its absence. The reader will note that the conditions described in this text relate to a large extent to learned behaviors attributable to the individual's specific psychological and social development even when they result in low levels of effective functioning. Hence, even though "mental illness" and "mental health" may be useful shorthand terms that call forth an image having some meaning to the public, they are put aside in favor of the concepts of development and effectiveness.

Summary

Although he shares many characteristics with the other animals, man possesses two unique abilities: he can utilize symbols to represent events and experiences and he can communicate his observations and impressions to others. Man is able to think about himself and his relationship to the physical and social world. His complex nervous system both accounts for his superior achievements and rules out simple explanations of his behavior.

Human nature and instincts have been offered as explanations of human behavior. Although in vogue for some time, the instinct theory is now viewed as explaining more adequately the actions of lower animals than man's more complex behaviors. Evidence that "instincts" such as aggressiveness, self-assertiveness, or maternal behaviors are learned has been acquired through comparative cultural studies, and instincts are now generally considered as only the substratum of unlearned reflex responses to simple stimuli that are probably universal in the species.

The developmental view of man is offered as a means of evaluating and understanding people. It holds that the individual may be described in terms of his personal feelings, attitudes, and values; in terms of the nature and quality of his social relationships; and in terms of the work he performs and the satisfaction he derives from it. In his search for gratification of his needs, man is continually confronted with new situations that demand some modification of his behavior. These continuous changes make up the process of social and psychological development, and while they are related to—and interact with—physical development, there is not complete correspondence between the two.

Man's impetus to develop socially and psychologically has various sources: physical changes, relationships with parents, friends, and teachers, dissatisfaction with his present situation or with his ability to manipulate it effectively. Thus, the developmental approach to understanding behavior requires consideration of the individual's physical history as well as his psychological and social experience of the culture of which he is a part. The concept of developmental status affords an alternative approach to issues frequently considered under the heading of "mental health."

References

1. Allport, G. W. *Becoming: Basic Considerations for a Psychology of Personality*. New Haven: Yale University Press, 1955.
2. Boring, E. G. *A History of Experimental Psychology* (ed. 2). New York Appleton, 1960.
3. Diamond, S. *Personality and Temperament*. New York: Harper, 1957.
4. Galton, F. *Hereditary Genius*. New York: Macmillan, 1869.
5. Glueck, S., and Glueck, E. T. *Unraveling Juvenile Delinquency*. New York: Commonwealth Fund, 1950.
6. Goddard, H. H. *The Kallikak Family*. New York: Macmillan, 1912.
7. Hartshorne, H., and May, M. A. *Studies in Deceit*. New York: Macmillan, 1928.
8. Hebb, D. O. *A Textbook of Psychology*. Philadelphia: Saunders, 1958.
9. Kallman, F. J. *Heredity in Health and Mental Disorder: Principles of Psychiatric Genetics in the Light of Comparative Twin Studies*. New York: Norton, 1953.
10. Kinsey, A. C., Pomeroy, W. B., and Martin, C. E. *Sexual Behavior in the Human Male*. Philadelphia: Saunders, 1948.
11. Klineberg, O. *Social Psychology*. New York: Holt, 1954.
12. Mead, M. *Sex and Temperament in Three Primitive Societies*. London: Routledge, 1935.
13. Newman, H. H., Freeman, F. N., and Holzinger, K. J. *Twins*. Chicago: University of Chicago Press, 1937.
14. Searle, L. V. The organization of hereditary maze-brightness and maze-dullness. *Genet. Psychol. Monogr.*, 1940, *39*, 279–325.
15. Sheldon, W. H. (with the collaboration of S. S. Stevens). *The Varieties of Temperament: A Psychology of Constitutional Difference*. New York: Harper, 1942.
16. Stern, W. *Psychology of Early Childhood up to the Sixth Year of Age*. New York: Holt, 1924.
17. Tryon, R. C. Genetic differences in maze learning ability in rats. *Yearb. Nat. Soc. Stud. Educ.*, 1940, I: 111–119.

18. Watson, J. B. *Behaviorism* (rev. ed.). Chicago: The University of Chicago Press, 1930.

Selected Readings

Anastasi, A. *Differential Psychology*. New York: Macmillan, 1958.

Diamond, S. *Personality and Temperament*. New York: Harper, 1957.

Harris, D. B. (ed.). *The Concept of Development*. Minneapolis: University of Minnesota Press, 1957.

Klineberg, O. *Social Psychology*. New York: Holt, 1954.

Newcomb, T. *Social Psychology*. New York: Holt, 1950.

Tinbergen, N. *The Study of Instinct*. New York: Oxford University Press, 1951.

3.

Personality: Component Selves and Processes

To obtain a full record of an individual's development, it would, as we have seen, be necessary to include all the information about his genetic and constitutional inheritance, as well as the experiences affecting his physical development. Geographic, situational, and interpersonal conditions that he has encountered, and even his prenatal environment, would be an additional part of this record.

It would incorporate a complete description of the culture in which the individual has moved: his language, values, and religion, and his national, local, and family affiliations. Even more significantly, it would provide a record of the vast number of interactions between biological and social influences as they occurred within him and as they accounted for his behaviors.

Such a record would provide a basis not only for understanding the characteristics, attitudes, and behaviors shared by the individual with all men of his culture, but also for understanding the combination of events and experiences that have contributed to his uniqueness, to his individuality as a human being.

Since it is impossible simultaneously to consider all the information pertinent to human development, the student of behavior must choose those aspects on which he can focus. Thus the sociologist may focus on the social components of behavior, the physiologist on the interrelationships and functions of the various systems of the body. This text will

41

focus on man's psychological development and on the examination of the components of what is termed "personality"; this is the starting point of our study.

In everyday usage, "She has a nice personality" implies that the girl is an attractive and pleasant person, and "He has a tremendous personality" may suggest that the young man is impressive, outgoing, and persuasive. This use of the term relates to the appearance, manner, and impression the person provides for his associates. Although the meanings assigned to it in popular usage are consistent with its Latin source, *persona,* meaning mask, psychologists interpret the term differently. To them, "personality" includes not only the individual's manner and appearance, the mask, but also the motives, feelings, wishes, and self-impressions of the person, which are less readily apparent than the "face" he shows publicly.

What is found behind the mask? There are the private and personal beliefs and feelings that the individual carries with him but does not share even with his closest associates; there are positive beliefs about one's self in which the individual may think of his talents and abilities as outstanding though undiscovered, as well as negative feelings of being weak, lacking in special capacities, undisciplined, and at times unworthy; there are the person's ideals, particularly those concerned with what he would like to be or do.

Behind the mask are the reasons for a person's adopting different appearances for different occasions and different individuals or groups. These reasons may be quite outside the range of his conscious awareness, and he may don masks appropriate to the occasion without particular attention to his reasons for doing so. But if the psychological meaning is to be considered, then the reasons are of interest to us.

When attitudes, interests, or traits are utilized to characterize a person and to provide a basis for prediction about his future behavior, they become a part of the psychological meaning of personality. Thus, "personality" is used to refer to characteristics that are relatively stable. Even though the term "personality" is not used, an example of such usage is provided by the following excerpt from a questionnaire sent to a teacher who is endorsing a former student for admission to college:

From the questionnaire:	*The teacher's response:*
Describe the applicant's character and integrity.	The applicant is honest, trustworthy, conscientious, and reliable. He has high standards of personal integrity and a keen ethical sense.

| Describe the applicant's scholarship and intellectual ability. | The applicant is thorough and attends to detail, he is intellectually curious and independently pursues the investigation of issues that excite his interests. Although he is not a brilliant student, his intellectual ability is of a high order. |
| Describe the applicant's manner in his relationships with (1) other students and (2) the faculty. | The applicant is friendly, though not expansive in his relationships with students and faculty. His manner is quiet and self-contained. He is somewhat less communicative in his contacts with the faculty than with students, and is generally reserved and dignified. |

In their attempts to predict whether the student will succeed in his program, the college authorities will relate the endorser's statements to other available information about the applicant. They will assume that the basic personality thus revealed will not change appreciably and will therefore use it for assessing the student's probable success in college.

Considering the ways it is utilized, we can conclude that "personality" refers to some constellation of factors within the person; that it is the product of all previous experiences; and that while it is not identical to behavior, its components are inferred from behavior.

An individual's behavior is partially determined by the immediate situation, the events to which he attaches meaning or to which he is in some way responsive. Behavior also results from the expectations, needs, experiences, and capabilities that the person brings to the situation. Thus, in the statement, "Behavior is the result of the interaction of the personality and the situation," the significance of personality to the situation (how personal factors influence what is perceived, responded to, and acted upon) and the significance of the situation to the personality (how environmental factors influence what is perceived) are given due consideration; one cannot understand and predict behaviors without a thorough knowledge of both.

Although important aspects of the situation may change, as when an individual goes from high school to college, it is assumed that there is sufficient similarity between the circumstances and sufficient stability of personality to predict that a person will behave in a new situation as he did in the old. This assumption must be made cautiously, however, and the significance of his perception of the environment as well as of its objective features must not be overlooked. The student who perceives the freedom of the college dormitory as a release from strict parental supervision, for example, will probably behave in a fashion quite different from the way he did at home.

A Definition of Personality

Many definitions of personality are available, but Allport's (1) statement is perhaps the best known: "Personality is the dynamic *organization* within the individual of those psychophysical systems that determine his unique adjustments to the environment."

The term "dynamic" in the definition calls attention to the ongoing nature of the developmental process and to the continual interaction of the components of personality. Emphasis on the organizational aspects recognizes the patterned nature of these components. This pattern accounts for the individual's essentially similar approaches to different environmental situations and also to his specific individuality.

In other definitions of personality, these ingredients have been considered as "predispositions to behavior." They include the individual's perceptions of himself, other persons, and his environment, and the activities within the individual that account for the manner in which he perceives and interprets events. The nature of the activities that are organized includes an individual's thoughts, feelings, and wishes. The range of such patterned activities is suggested by one statement that defines personality as "that which predicts behavior given the situation" (3). The term "psychophysical systems" in Allport's definition calls attention to the unity of the physical and psychological processes and specifically rejects the common tendency to think of "mind" and "body" as separate entities.

In our consideration of personality, we will utilize two fundamental sets of interrelated constructs: the self, its component selves; and the intrapsychic processes. These concepts or constructs will be defined and described in the present chapter and will be elaborated and utilized to clarify the material that follows.

The Self

Of the concepts that relate to personality, the self is most easily understood, for everyone possesses an image or idea of what he is like. He may see himself in the mirror of his "mind's eye" in terms of physical appearance and manner and in terms of traits, habits, abilities, and attitudes. In addition to being able to think of himself as if he were looking from a distance, he can experience his own physical being—the sensations of his body surfaces as they touch external objects, the sensation of touching or seeing himself, the feelings of movement of his body and limbs in space. Thus the self is an organizing set of responses, reactions, and experiences that together with the intrapsychic processes provides the individual with the feeling of being the same person from one day to the next, or from one experience to the next.

The self is the person as he is known to that person; it is that part of his own personality of which the individual is aware through his knowledge, beliefs, impressions, and sensations; it is his image of himself as a physical and social being, what he believes he wants to be seen as by other persons, and what he believes he should be like. This image is so highly valued that in some instances survival itself is valued less than the maintenance of a self-concept that has honor, family, or national pride as an important part.

Challenge of a man's honesty is likely to call forth a more hostile response from him than criticism of his choice of neckties, but as reasonable as it might seem, this comment requires the qualification, "depending on the person's self-concept." Since individuals differ in the images they have of themselves and in their bases for valuing themselves, detailed knowledge of the person's self-concept is necessary in order to predict responses and reactions accurately.

The self includes not only the person's beliefs about his own characteristics but also what he wishes to represent of himself to others and what he believes he should be. These interrelated subselves will hereafter be referred to as the personal self, the social self, and the ideal self.

THE PERSONAL SELF

As the infant gradually becomes able to recognize the existence of a world distinct from himself, the personal self develops. This aspect of the self is the image the person possesses of himself as a physical and social entity, and it becomes, as a result of the individual's developmental experiences, a highly organized system of attitudes, beliefs, impressions, habits, and values. From its primitive beginning, as a vague and imperfect awareness that the source of food, the breast or bottle, is part of the outside world and not part of one's own body, the personal self develops to such a degree that the adult is able to think of himself as a specific person, one whose particular combination of experiences makes him unique, in some ways different from all other persons. He feels that he is an entity, a unity, a being with an identity that is shared with no one else. Yet this identity, which only he knows and which constitutes the personal self, will differ in some respects and in varying degrees from the impression that other persons have of him.

If this is the case, the question "Which identity is correct?" is an important one, since it is essential for the student to understand at the beginning of the study of personality that a person's perception of himself may be inaccurate (in the sense that his associates would not agree with it) and still possess as much significance as it would if it were "accurate"—in some cases even more. Both sets of information are important, as is the correspondence or lack of correspondence between the sets. In reference to the personal self, however, the essential information has to do with the content of the self-concept and the development of this concept. The factors that influence the individual in deceiving himself or that account for his lack of awareness of certain of his own characteristics will be treated in later chapters.

That the individual's self-image does not necessarily correspond to the image others have assigned him does not mean his self-image will not be of considerable significance in understanding his behavior. If one knows, for example, that an individual believes he is the general of a great army, one would expect him to issue orders, insist on respect, and evidence an air of authority; to talk in the language of military men and make comments about strategies and tactics. If the individual really is a general, these predictions would hardly seem surprising, but if he is not, these predictions made on the basis of knowledge about his personal self would be more accurate than if he had been expected to behave as an ordinary citizen.

THE SOCIAL SELF

Even before he is aware that he exists separately from those who attend his physical needs, the infant begins without consciousness on his part to react to certain stimuli, such as crying when he is hungry, wet, or cold. The alleviation of discomfort states by the attentions of others leads to an awareness that his behaviors may produce certain consequences and that such consequences will depend on the responses of others to him and to his behaviors.

As the image of himself gradually becomes clarified and organized, his recognition of the relationship of his reactions to the behavior of those about him is also clarified and refined. He becomes more sensitive to the nature of the "stimulus value" that he has for other persons; he perceives more clearly that he evokes reactions in others. The nature of these reactions depends on several sets of conditions that operate in conjunction with the actual behaviors he manifests. For the individual, however, much learning of the expectations others hold for him has occurred even before he goes to school. Not all these expectations are directed exclusively to him as a specific person; many are part of the culture and are expressed in terms of "proper behaviors," such as: "Children are to be seen and not heard," or "A child should respect his elders," or "One should always tell the truth." Yet in addition to learning the proper social behaviors or rituals, the child will also acquire a gradually increasing awareness that to attain his own ends and objectives, some of his behaviors will be more effective than others.

The attitudes, experiences, and feelings that underlie the individual's social behavior—the behavior that relates to other persons, whether or not they are present—comprise the social self. That aspect of the self which the person presents publicly results from his image of himself as a social being and from his intentions, objectives, and wishes for himself as they involve the responses of others. The social self thus includes the image that he wants to create in his contacts with others, as well as that which he believes he does create; it has to do in part with what he wants from other persons and what he hopes to achieve or maintain in his relationships with them.

The social self is not identical with either the social stimulus value which a person possesses or the sum total of his social skills; rather, it represents his perception, his attitudes, and his feelings about himself in relation to other persons. The image which others have of him may differ markedly from that which he has of himself, as is the case with the personal self. A person may think he was the life of last night's party; he may distinctly recall his brilliant conversation and sparkling humor. Others at the party may have seen him as a bore who monopolized the conversation and who tried too hard and without success to be funny. Although it is important in understanding the individual to know how the group actually responded to him, it is basic to such understanding that one knows how the individual saw himself, how he believed he was functioning, and what it was that he was trying to accomplish. It must be remembered that though inferences as to the nature of the individual's social self are made from his actions with other persons and his attitudes toward them, behavior is a function of the total personality and the total situation.

THE IDEAL SELF

As the personal and social selves are developing during the formative years, the image the person has of what he wishes to be is also assuming a definite character. This image, the ideal self, will represent in part the ideals of the culture, which include such virtues as loyalty, honesty, and truthfulness, impressed upon the child as desirable by the parents. It also represents that which is specifically valued by the

child's parents, so that wishes to be highly successful or wealthy or to
have great status and prestige may represent part of the ideal self.

The ideal self will include an image of masculinity or femininity,
an image influenced by the individual's experiences with his parents, as
well as those provided in the culture. For some persons the ideal self
includes a concept of masculinity that emphasizes physical strength and
action as depicted in the TV westerns, or of femininity reflecting the
Hollywood version of the glamorized and sultry movie star.

Since the ideal self is the image of the person he wishes he *could* be,
one aspect of it is the person he believes he *should* be. The loss of self-
esteem that persons experience when they feel guilty can sometimes be
attributed to the conscious recognition of having failed to live up to
valued standards of conduct. These standards often have their origin
in those valued by their parents, and sometimes the adult who knowingly
behaves in ways which would have brought parental disapproval will
feel guilty. In these instances the values have become a part of the ideal
self and sometimes, particularly, in periods such as adolescence, there is
conflict among the standards acquired from parents, those originating
in the peer group, and those that the person develops on the basis of
his own thinking. Not all feelings of guilt can be traced directly to the
degree to which the image of the ideal self fail to coincide with that of
the personal self, for the self-images are conscious and the individual can
identify them, whereas feelings of guilt can stem also from processes
occurring within the individual of which he is unaware.

Most persons wish to improve in some respects or to possess characteristics they are now lacking, so the ideal self differs to some extent from
the personal self. Psychologists are interested in these differences when
they are large, because such discrepancies represent one means of measuring self-esteem. The individual who feels that he is actually very different
from what he would like to be values himself less than if his wished-for
image essentially coincided with his self-impressions, and it is sometimes
considered a sign of improvement in his psychological condition when
the difference between the two selves is reduced. Sometimes particular
sets of life experiences results in a narrowing of the gap; sometimes
special assistance such as psychological counseling is needed.

Although people are aware of their wishes of what they would like
to be, they are not apt to share all the details of these wishes with others.
Some aspects of the ideal self are retained as private, as are some aspects
of the personal self. When the individual feels a glow of satisfaction with
himself for an accomplishment, even though it may go unrecognized by
others; when he experiences a feeling of virtue for having refrained from
"wrong" or "bad" actions; such feelings of self-esteem involve the ideal
self.

The personal, social, and ideal selves represent man's images of himself. He can describe some aspects of his self-images and consider even those details that he does not discuss. His self-concepts are consciously available to him, though his ideas about himself may not be accepted by his associates. His self-concepts include those he can readily put into words. He may or may not communicate these impressions of himself to others, but he can do so if he chooses. Other self-concepts are less readily verbalized, they consist of the images in his "mind's eye" of the feelings and sensations that he has of his own body and of himself as a physical entity. Though conscious, these images are not easily described. Knowledge of the person's conscious pictures of himself, what he wants to represent to others, and the wishes he holds for himself enables us to make many inferences about him and can offer a basis for predicting his future actions. Yet the accuracy of such predictions is increased when it is based also on the detailed statement of personality, that is, when it includes the frame of reference supplied by the intrapsychic processes.

Knowledge of these processes enables the student to deal with psychological events and experiences outside the range of conscious awareness —whether or not they have at one time been within the individual's awareness. The intrapsychic processes provide a framework that makes it possible to relate the selves to each other and to account for their development. These processes are drawn from a theory of personality known as psychoanalysis, which was developed by Sigmund Freud and his followers.

Freud's Major Contributions

Sigmund Freud, who lived from 1856 to 1939, was a psychiatrist who originated the theory and techniques of psychoanalysis. There is considerable controversy over certain aspects of his theories, but although the following basic contributions of his theories were keenly debated when he first presented them, they are now widely accepted and are utilized by almost all workers in the fields of psychiatry, clinical psychology, and social work.

1. *Early childhood experiences influence psychological development.* Freud pointed out that the experiences of the child during infancy and early childhood have a significant effect upon psychological development, and he provided a technique whereby experiences of the early years, which seemingly have been forgotten, can be recalled. Today widespread attention is given to the psychological atmosphere in which the young child is reared, and the influence of psychoanalytic theory on modern education is increasing.

2. *Human behavior is influenced by irrational as well as rational*

motives. In his presentation of the intrapsychic processes, Freud took issue with the commonly accepted view of his day, that man was a totally rational creature. The psychoanalytic position held that there are impulsive and irrational aspects of man's behavior. And though, according to Freud, those aspects of behavior become to a large extent controlled and inhibited in the course of man's social development, they play a more significant role in influencing behavior than is generally supposed.

3. *Behavior is multidetermined.* In psychoanalytic theory, the multiplicity of determinants of behavior is fully recognized. This implies that any specific behavior may be explained by a number of different combinations of motives and causes. It follows that similar sets of motives and causes may result in different behaviors for different individuals.

4. *There are different levels of conscious awareness.* Freud also pointed out that people may be quite unaware of the origins of their behavior. He introduced the term "unconscious" to account for our lack of awareness—our forgetting of experiences that may continue to have effects upon our behaviors.

5. *Psychological equilibrium is maintained through the use of the "mechanisms of defense."* In its efforts to maintain a state of minimal conflict among its components and to minimize the anxiety it experiences, the personality employs certain protective and defensive techniques. These techniques are utilized by all people and have a significant influence on perception and behavior; they will be discussed in detail in Chapter 5. Such terms as *rationalization, projection,* and *sublimation* have come to have wide usage in our everyday language.

Freud's theories underwent many changes during his long and highly productive life, and his followers have introduced many further modifications. These theories have not yet been scientifically verified, but considerable research and experimental evidence support many of the basic ideas. The five points noted are accepted within the fields of psychiatry and psychology with a minimum of controversy, and the concepts of id, ego, and superego are generally recognized as having value in describing complex psychological processes. Freud's great influence on our culture may be seen in fields of literature and art as well as in the social sciences.

In Part Two of this text, attention will be centered on the developmental experiences and their effect upon the individual's personality. In this discussion, the arational, as well as the rational and irrational, aspects of behavior will become evident as the multiplicity and complexity of human motivation are described. In tracing the individual's life from birth to death, we will give consideration to both unconscious motives as determinants of behavior and characteristic behaviors that he may utilize in maintaining a favorable and harmonious balance among the components of his personality. This text will therefore rely heavily upon the contributions of Freud. Although the statement of personality development that is presented is influenced by, and in some important respects follows, Freud, it should not be considered a statement of Freudian theory. For an introduction to the important and very complex theories of psychoanalysis, the student should consult the readings recommended at the end of the chapter.

The Intrapsychic Processes

ID PROCESSES

The first of the intrapsychic processes of value in describing complex psychological processes are those of the id. These involve primitive and basic biological impulses and, as Fenichel describes them, are "a dynamic driving chaos of forces which strive for discharge and nothing else, but which constantly receive new stimulations from external as well as internal perceptions" (4, p. 16). Brown has noted that "if the strivings originating in the id were not controlled by reality and society we should become neither adults nor civilized but rather live in a timeless world of immediate sensory gratification and discomfort" (2, p. 163). Although these primitive and innate tension states and the impulses to which they give rise are often labeled "the id," this practice encourages the tendency to conceptualize human personality in terms of separate and distinct parts. A more useful and probably more justifiable formulation describes personality as resulting from many interrelated processes that influence each other, that change in intensity and in their patterns of relationships. We shall therefore speak of id *processes* as aspects of the personality.

The id processes have their origins in tension states or states of physical excitation, which may be internally activated, as in the case of hunger, or may be reactions to externally imposed conditions, such as physical restraint. It is believed that these basic impulses and elemental biological urges underlie all human activity.

Id processes probably can be observed most clearly during infancy. The inability to tolerate delayed gratification, the immediate response to physical discomfort, and the apparent striving for an optimally pleasurable state are most evident in the infant who has not yet developed an awareness of the world and the fact that it is external to himself. Even after the infant grows to adulthood, id activities continue, though they are now usually directed and controlled by other aspects of the personality. They are most clearly observed in the behaviors of adults who are not concerned with the world about them. Such persons may be unable to recognize society's taboos against wanton destruction or violence. They may be uncomprehending and unperceptive of the attitudes of others toward unrestrained gratification of sexual and other physical needs. Pleasure-seeking behaviors that have an unprincipled and unbridled character and that are engaged in without thought or concern for one's own long-term welfare or the welfare of others, also are examples of the operation of id processes. When gratification is sought in light of the conditions of the external world or of one's own best interests, however, other processes of the personality are joining with those that spring from the id in mediating behavior.

The student will immediately be aware that a great deal of channeling and directing of id impulses must occur if man's constructive, creative, intellectual potentialities are to be realized. These complex activities are very different from those which would follow from completely uninhibited satisfaction of natural id impulses. Although intellectual and creative activities may be initiated by the impulses of the id, their origin may not be at all apparent in controlled, purposeful, adult behaviors.

EGO PROCESSES

The gap between physical impulses seeking immediate gratification and organized, controlled, intellectual, and rational behavior is bridged by the activity of the ego processes. To the extent that it is possible, the ego processes accomplish the gratification of the pleasure wishes in the light of existing realities. The ego is that aspect of the personality which is more or less aware of the world and of the conditions which may bring pleasure or pose a threat to the personality.

When perception and thought are purposeful and self-protective, when activities have the objective of enabling the individual to satisfy safely his primitive and biological urges, then they are mediated by the ego processes.

Such processes enable the individual to communicate with the "outside" world and are directed toward enhancing the realistic opportunities for pleasurable experience. They are involved in the many choices, discriminations, and decisions that are made consciously or that underlie planful, self-interested behaviors. Thus, the activity of the individual, though initiated by the id, is channeled and directed by ego processes that have as their objective not only the satisfaction of id demands but also the individual's safety and welfare.

In addition to mediating between id impulses and the realities of the external world, the ego also mediates between the needs of the id and those of the third aspect of the psychological self, the superego, in an attempt to effect maximal satisfaction for both of them. As will be evident from the later discussion of the superego, this function is a difficult one since id impulses are often incompatible with superego demands. The effectiveness of ego processes in minimizing the effects of id-superego conflict will determine in part the degree to which the individual is able to function effectively.

The three-year-old child is far less able to think in terms of tomorrow than is the seven-year-old child. The ability to control needs for immediate gratification is a characteristic of developing ego processes. The infant may be considered "egoless," for the processes which we associate with adult activity—perceiving, thinking, controlling one's impulses—are not present in the infant, who lacks the physical capacities and the experiences involved in ego development.

As the infant becomes more capable physically, he is able to touch, taste, hear, see, and smell the objects and people that comprise his world. He becomes aware that objects and people can sometimes be manipulated so that they contribute to his pleasure. He also learns that certain behaviors are to be avoided because they result in pain rather than pleasure. These learnings, which relate to the gratification of wishes or to the avoidance of discomfort or pain, are considered part of the activity of the developing ego. Through the functions of memory and imagery, ego processes make possible the retention of associations between events, experiences, situations, and behaviors and the pleasure or pain linked to them.

Purposeful thought is an important ego activity that consists of a weighing of various alternatives before the adoption of overt behavior. Thought carries an essential function for the person who must choose one of several possible lines of action in his attempt to gratify primitive impulses or the wishes related to these impulses. The interrelationship between the impulses of the id and the thinking and directing activity of the ego are illustrated in the following incident involving a college freshman.

For several weeks Paul has been sitting opposite the same pretty girl in his English class. Although he has never spoken to her, he finds himself preoccupied with his thoughts of her. He has had fleeting daydreams in which he has swept her off her feet, and at night he has dreamed about her. Paul has pondered his approach for a long time. He has wondered whether she might become aware of the intensity of his feelings if he talked to her casually. He feels so strongly about her that he is afraid to take the risk of making a poor impression. It is as if one part of his personality keeps pushing him toward her, saying to him, "Go ahead; talk to her; you want to talk to her; don't be a coward; you like her." At the same time another aspect of his personality keeps saying to him, "Take it easy; don't rush her; get more information about her; don't be too eager; don't jump in until you know what you are doing."

In this situation, Paul's wishes are very clear. He feels very much attracted to this girl and would like her to feel the same way about him. His wishes, however, are controlled and directed by ego processes which compel him to consider the circumstances, and to take time to choose the action most likely to bring desired results. He carefully thinks through and weighs the value of each alternative. Paul's ego is functioning in such a way that it restrains him from acting in an impulsive fashion. Ego activity is also evident in his attempts to learn as much as he can about the young lady. He carefully observes who talks to her in the college cafeteria. He notes whether she comes to class by herself or with other young men and whether it is the same one every day. He is aware of the way she responds to the instructor's comments, and he manages to find out where she lives and the program in which she is enrolled.

In this case, Paul's ego is working to ensure the best chance of gratifying his wishes. His thoughts, plans, and restraint are mediated by ego processes. How well Paul will succeed in his efforts to win the girl's affection will depend in large part on his ability to act in terms of the realities in the situation. The more effective Paul's ego, the more capable he will be of gratifying his wishes within the limits imposed by reality and the less will be the likelihood that he will behave in ways which would threaten his self-esteem or jeopardize his self-interests.

The interrelationship between the id and the ego must be clear if the student is going to understand the material that follows. Id processes are those that energize an individual in his quest for the gratification of basic biological needs or of wishes associated with those needs. The term "ego" relates to those processes that provide direction for and control over the impulsive inclinations of the id. The ego, then, attempts to provide maximal gratification for the pleasure-seeking impulses within the limitations and conditions imposed by reality.

For example, a four-year-old child is hungry and spies the opened cookie jar her mother has left on the table. She remembers that her mother has just gone outside to talk to one of the neighbors and reflects that there is little chance that she would be caught in the act of taking a cookie. She knows that she is not supposed to take cookies without asking her mother, but she is hungry and, since her mother is not on the scene, feels that she can take one safely. The same child might have acted quite differently if she had known that her mother was in the next room. In either case, the consideration of possible punishment and of the likelihood of successfully gratifying the wish for the cookie would be considered quickly and almost automatically by the ego. The child made her decision in terms of her own wishes and the anticipated consequences of her behavior and was not influenced by moral considerations or by questions of right or wrong.

In the incident just cited, the child was hungry. She desired immediate relief from these feelings of discomfort. She was aware of her feelings of hunger, and at the same time she was aware of the opportunities for satisfying her appetite. She saw the cookie jar on the table, and she knew from her previous experience that cookies were tasty and satisfy the type of craving which she was presently feeling.

As that aspect of the self which accumulates memories of previous experience and translates that experience into implications for present and future behavior, the ego also was responsible for the child's concern as to the whereabouts of her mother. One of the realities with which she had to cope was her mother's disapproval of her eating cookies without permission. When she had been caught taking cookies before, she had been spanked. Thus, in this situation, her perception of reality (Mother was next door and would not be back right away) was such that she felt she could act on the basis of her wish without incurring punishment.

In this example, the ego processes determine how and under what conditions the wishes of the id can be fulfilled. The ego also allows the child to proceed with minimal delay in gratification. In many instances, however, the ego may carry out the function of restraining, redirecting, or delaying the immediate gratification of the wish.

In part, the ego processes involves what the individual expects of himself and those about him. These expectations are the result of his *perceptions* and *interpretations* of the experiences he has had in his efforts to gratify the wishes of the id in his contacts with the world of other human beings and non-human objects. It is the ego which comes to know that certain behaviors bring parental displeasure or punishment. It is the ego which mediates between the internal wishes and the external world. In the sense that it is used here, the development of a strong and healthy ego is essential to personal and social effectiveness. Such an ego is reflected in purposeful planning, in accurate assessment of one's own resources, and in the correct identification of the crucial characteristics of the situations with which one is confronted. Strong ego processes enable an individual to delay immediate gratifications and to work toward long-term objectives. The abilities to profit from experience and to acquire the knowledge and skills required for survival and satisfaction are characteristic of strong ego processes.

THE SUPEREGO

The development of the superego depends upon the development of those aspects of the ego that enable an individual to distinguish among the responses of others toward himself and to link such responses to accompanying behaviors. Superego processes occur as a result of the individual's acquisition of the values held by his parents and by society. His attitudes and his judgmental evaluations of what is proper or improper guide his behaviors and restrict the free expression of his impulses. Though these superego processes may reflect the standards of the society, they are more accurately described as personal standards that an individual has taken within himself.[1] As a consequence, his emotional assessment of himself may reflect standards that differ from those of his group, either in their content or in the intensity of his reactions to their transgression.

The superego processes are not a consciously recognized list of approved and disapproved behaviors and attitudes. Rather, these processes operate for the most part below conscious awareness and they have an emotional force that opposes expression of impulses not compatible with superego standards. The emotional aspects of superego processes is illustrated in the conflict an individual experiences when he is exposed to temptation, or the guilt and unworthiness he feels upon even thinking about an unacceptable act or impulse.

The child's personal standards and values grow out of a variety of experiences with his parents, other adults, and his playmates. He learns what types of behavior bring approval or disapproval by others. The judgments of others gradually become less significant than the approval or disapproval he directs toward himself. His interpretation of the attitudes of others provides the basis from which he derives his own concepts of right and wrong (his "conscience"). From this process comes the feelings of punishment experienced by the person who responds to an impulse or wish and then feels guilty for having transgressed.

CONSCIOUS AWARENESS AND THE
INTRAPSYCHIC PROCESSES AND SELVES

The interrelationships among the id, ego, and superego processes are rarely clear to the person himself. When the person is not aware of his wishes, the factors affecting his perception of the situation,

[1] Various terms, such as "internalization," "incorporation," and "introjection," have been used to designate the process whereby the standards, values, and attitudes of others are "taken within oneself."

or the internalized moral codes that account for his behavior, the interaction of the components of personality are said to take place within the unconscious. Thus, the interplay of id, ego, and superego processes may occur at the level of our conscious awareness or at an unconscious level.

The three processes of the psychological self interact in such ways that we are often not aware of all of the reasons underlying our behavior. That experiences, seemingly long since forgotten, might have certain meanings for us, meanings which are not easily understood, attests to the existence of several levels of awareness.

That level at which we are immediately cognizant and aware of what is going on about us has been termed "consciousness." A different level is indicated by the term "unconscious." At this level, memories of experiences and events are not immediately available to us. The idea, the events, the situations of the past have seemingly become lost. Some people have difficulty in recalling the events of their childhood, yet after specialized inquiry into these apparently forgotten experiences they are able to recapture the feelings as well as the ideas that accompanied the experiences.

As the personality develops throughout the individual's life span, it becomes increasingly complex. The term "differentiated" is utilized to characterize the increasing number of more or less distinctive facets of the personality and their refinement. In contrast to the infant's limited awareness of the world around him, the adult's psychological life contains a great multiplicity of associations and meanings. New experiences and learnings give rise to new meanings that continually increase the complexity of the personality.

Man's behavior may be interpreted as being directed toward the achievement of a state of maximal balance among the intrapsychic processes of the personality. Thus, the person who is not at peace within himself may yet be functioning psychologically in such a way as to maintain the best possible balance among the intrapsychic processes. His behaviors may reveal the possibility of considerable internal turmoil. In such a case they may be, from a statistical point of view, very deviant. An extreme example is that of the person who has unshakable beliefs that he is all-powerful, a great general, a king, or the president. His resulting actions form the reason for removing him from his home and usual environment and placing him in an institution. For this type of person, gross behavioral derangement may represent a means of maintaining his internal psychological processes in as favorable a state of balance or integration as is possible for him.

Finally, it must be noted that the selves result from the interaction of the intrapsychic processes, and the perception of self, along with the activities related to thinking about oneself, represents an aspect of ego activity. Although the images of the self are within conscious awareness, an individual may not consciously recognize the degree of inaccuracy of these self-perceptions nor realize the existence of self-deceptive activities that are directed to maintaining a favorable balance among the intrapsychic processes. The next chapter will provide a detailed statement of how self-deception may occur as a result of the personality's need to maintain and protect itself.

Summary

The constructs of the selves and intrapsychic processes comprise the personality, a term designating the patterns of motives, feelings, and attitudes that, given the situation, account for behavior.

Although the acts of perceiving and thinking of oneself are performed by the ego, the individual's self-concept, a set of conscious images utilized in thinking of his own body, abilities, weaknesses, and aspirations, is the result of the interaction of the intrapsychic processes. Thus, the individual is aware of himself even though he may not be conscious of the interaction among the processes accounting for his self-concept.

The personality processes function to maintain as integrated and harmonious a balance among its components as is possible in the light of the individual's developmental history. When this balance is accomplished through self-deception, however, the impression that an individual's associates have of him may differ considerably from his self-concept. Maximal understanding of the individual and his behavior is achieved through knowledge of his personal aspirations, his self-perceptions, and his feelings about the ways in which others perceive him, as well as through information about the intrapsychic processes which account for these self-images.

References

1. Allport, G. W. *Personality: A Psychological Interpretation.* New York: Holt, 1937.
2. Brown, J. F. *The Psychodynamics of Abnormal Behavior.* New York: McGraw-Hill, 1940.
3. Cattell, R. B. *Description and Measurement of Personality.* New York: Harcourt, 1946.
4. Fenichel, O. *The Psychoanalytic Theory of Neurosis.* New York: Norton, 1945.

Selected Readings

Hall, C. S. *A Primer of Freudian Psychology*. Cleveland: World Publishing, 1954.

Hall, C. S., and Lindzey, G. *Theories of Personality*. New York: Wiley, 1957.

Harsh, C. M., and Schrickel, H. G. *Personality Development and Assessment* (ed. 2). New York: Ronald, 1959.

Wylie, R. C. *The Self Concept*. Lincoln: University of Nebraska Press, 1961.

4.

Psychological States:
Needs, Conflict, and Anxiety

In Chapter 3 the over-all concept of a basic structure of personality was outlined. The subordinate concepts of the self and the intrapsychic processes will be elaborated in this chapter and the next, in order to afford a sufficiently detailed foundation for the study of personal and social development.

The processes and conditions discussed in the next two chapters are often utilized by psychologists to explain behavior, but they are inferred rather than observed directly. In the experimental situation these inferences evolve through the study of the relationship between independent and dependent variables, or in the life situation through an analysis of a situation and the person's response to it. The inferences specifically pertain to hypothesized variables that intervene and account for the relationship between the independent and dependent variables, between the stimulus and response, or between the situation and the reactions it elicits. These inferred variables (hypothetical constructs), such as needs and anxiety, have a place in the theory of personality being developed in this text. Theory serves the student of behavior as a bridge; it enables him to make the passage from events presently observed to events predicted in the future, and it also provides a means of "explaining" present observations on the basis of previous events.

Needs

An example of how *need,* one particular hypothetical construct, is used to explain a simple behavioral sequence is provided by observation of an office worker. After sitting at his desk for several hours, he walks to the water fountain, takes a drink, and returns to his desk. The observer explains this sequence of events by saying, "He needed a drink." Possibly the worker "needed" the exercise or some relief from monotony, or possibly he "needed" the water, a "break," and the exercise. Though we do not know the need or needs operating in this example, our observer noted a sequence of events and was willing to explain the behaviors in terms of an inferred state of fluid deprivation. In this type of inferential process the need is often named in terms of the objective, goal, or end state which terminates the action sequence and satisfies the organism's requirement.

Many specific actions may reach the same satisfying end state. The man in need of food may seek a grocery store, a restaurant, a handout, or his own dining room; he may partake of various foods, and he may engage in various dining rituals. A need is thus defined as the action tendencies implementing a specific end state (12). Biological needs are those physical requirements essential to survival, and they are named in terms of such end states as food, fluid, oxygen, elimination, and activity.

When the individual is stimulated either externally or internally and such stimulation persists and evokes sustained activity, the term *drive* is employed. Often the deprivation of a need is followed by a drive state specific to that need. The need for fluid is accompanied by a dryness of the mouth and throat, and the individual engages in sustained effort to locate something to drink.

Although the discussion so far has been confined to the biological needs, the definitions of drive states and needs are also applicable to psychological needs. Psychological needs relate to the requirements of the personality and they are learned, in contrast to biological needs, which are unlearned. Even with these distinctions, it is often difficult, in practice, to separate the physical from the psychological. As the infant develops into the adult, his behaviors grow increasingly complex and the extent to which biological needs account for the person's actions decreases.

During the development of personality, many needs come into play. For each person, these needs have an order of increasing significance, and it has been proposed that those which are "basic" must be at least partially gratified before the "higher" needs can become operative. Though this text uses need categories that are somewhat different from those suggested by Maslow, the concept of "hierarchy" which he proposed (10) is relevant to this presentation. As the concept will be employed here, however, each person is considered to have his own hierarchy of psychological needs. In the relationship between psychological needs and physical needs, the hierarchical principle is reflected in the following quotation (10):

> For our chronically and extremely hungry man, Utopia can be defined simply as a place where there is plenty of food. He tends to think that, if only he is guaranteed food for the rest of his life, he will be perfectly happy and will never want anything more. Life itself tends to be defined in terms of eating. Anything else will be defined as unimportant. Freedom, love, community feeling, respect, philosophy may all be waved aside as fripperies that are useless, since they fail to fill the stomach. . . . When there is plenty of bread . . . higher needs emerge and these, rather than physiological hungers, dominate the organism.

Although the quotation suggests that physical needs take precedence over psychological needs, that satisfaction of physical needs will be sought before the psychological needs become operative, it is necessary to qualify the idea of a fixed hierarchy. Not only do many behavior sequences reflect the combined operation of physical and psychological needs, but psychological needs will predominate over physical needs in given situations for limited time intervals. A sleepy student remains awake in class, for example, or a hungry salesman completes his last call of the day before going to dinner.

In considering psychological needs it is helpful to keep the relationship between personality and behavior in mind. Although in the course of his development unlearned and reflexive behaviors decrease in their significance to him, the individual's behavior is a product of the interaction of the situation and the personality. Needs have been partially defined as action tendencies, but when considering psychological needs it is necessary to note that action tendencies refer to the dynamic interplay of selves and intrapsychic processes and to their behavioral manifestations. In the discussion of psychological needs the custom of identifying the needs in terms of the end state is also observed.

Because many different behavioral patterns can lead to the same end state, knowledge of an individual's psychological needs will have little predictive value without knowledge of his developmental history. With this added information we can eliminate many of the possible courses of action that our subject might initiate. The following excerpt from a college counselor's report of a series of interviews with a sophomore whose grades were poor and who was facing final examinations, illustrates the point.

> At this point the student has needs to maintain his image of himself as a competent and capable individual and as a person wiser and more experienced than his years would suggest. In view

of his history, it therefore seems doubtful that he is going to be able to apply himself effectively to the studying necessary to pass the final examinations in all his subjects. It is possible that he will adopt an attitude of being above it all and make a display of his casualness and his indifference to the examinations. Not expending the energy in trying to pass protects him psychologically, in a peculiar way, from experiencing a sense of failure, though realistically his behavior will result in not passing his examinations. This rather paradoxical situation results from the fact that the student would only experience a sense of failure if he actually committed his energies to an effort to pass; by not doing so, he is able to maintain his self image. Since it is likely that his behavior will result in his dismissal from school, a contingency that is also inconsistent with his self image, it may be anticipated that he will voluntarily withdraw in order "to accept" employment.

In this example, the inference is made that the student has a strong need to maintain and protect a particular image of himself. Three behavioral patterns that could enable him to satisfy this need are considered and the one that is most likely in view of his history is predicted.

Since any list or definition of psychological needs depends on the theory of personality from which it derives, there is no one list or set that can be offered as "true." Needs are hypothetical constructs; their usefulness depends on the help they provide in conceptualizing psychological activity and the degree to which they contribute to the prediction of behavior.

For purposes of simplification, the theory of personality outlined in this general introduction to personal and social development employs only three need categories, which are overlapping and not distinctly separate from each other.

THE RELATEDNESS NEED

The relatedness need refers to the requirement of feeling in communion with other persons. Details of its development from the basic conditions for the infant's survival will be described later, but it can be noted here that this is the first psychological need to become manifest in the life of the individual and that it serves as a basis from which other psychological needs are differentiated. The behaviors of the small child who does not want his bedroom door closed and of the adult who joins various clubs and associations provide a basis for inferring that the relatedness need's end state, the feeling of communion with others, is being sought.

The distinction between the desire to feel in communion with others and the desire to be in the actual physical presence of others should be noted, however. The *affiliative need* has as its end state being in the presence of others, and though this may arise from action patterns also utilized in the effort to satisfy the relatedness need, the two are not identical. One may feel lonely and isolated not only in large groups, for example, but in the presence of one's family and friends as well.

The end state of the relatedness need is the feeling that one is in a state of communion with other persons. The work of a research scientist, a writer, or an artist may be solitary, yet it represents for these individuals their means of attaining a feeling of communion.

The uneasiness and, in some instances, the desperation evoked when one feels isolated and out of touch with others represents a reaction to marked failure to gratify the relatedness need. This need can never be *fully* and permanently gratified. Its character is apparent in many of the wishes people hold and in many of their behaviors.

The imposed isolation of the prisoner in solitary confinement is considered among the most severe of punishments meted out in prisons today. Interference with the individual's customary means of maintaining his feeling of communion with others, through isolation imposed by prison, illness, or loss of the senses upon which persons rely in maintaining their feelings of communion, may result in considerable distress and personality disruption.

The affiliative need, the need for actual contact with other persons, has been shown to be quite specific, in that persons desire to be in the presence of others who are confronting situations similar to theirs. When persons are under stress or feel anxious, this need seems to grow in intensity (16).

THE SELF-MAINTENANCE AND
PROTECTIVE NEEDS

The needs in these two related categories have as their end states the preservation of the self-image. Since these needs operate not only in connection with the self, but also in connection with the maintenance of balance among the intrapsychic processes, they are apparent in the activity of the total personality.

When a person risks his life in "daredevil" behavior, when in time of war he would rather die than let down those who are counting upon him, when his honor "requires" that he commit hara-kiri, his needs to maintain a self-image are stronger than his wishes to survive. These examples reflect the strength and force of the psychological need to maintain and protect the personality.

Such needs lie also behind the many undramatic and routine action patterns comprising everyday life: the work that is performed, the hobbies that are pursued, and the relationships in which persons engage can have as significant features their contributions toward the preservation of valued self-images.

The maintenance and protective needs are closely related to the intrapsychic processes as the latter influence each other in attaining their most harmonious balance. As a result of the intraction of the intrapsychic processes, the personality functions at the highest level of efficiency that is possible for it at a given time and under given conditions. Valued self-images are preserved to various degrees depending on the degree of balance achieved among intrapsychic processes. The external conditions or internal impulses that would tend to disrupt the intrapsychic balance or necessitate the revision of the self-concept are guarded against through the use of behavioral patterns known as mechanisms of defense (see Chapter 5).

The maintenance and protective needs may be clearly evident when persons are under stress, have been threatened, or are feeling unsure of themselves. Shakespeare's line: "The lady doth protest too much, methinks," is the comment of an astute observer who notes the overreaction of a person attempting to protect herself.

Empirical evidence suggests that individuals will attempt to maintain the self-images which they created when at the highest level of their personality integration and development. Such efforts will be apparent even in the face of changed environmental and social circumstances. Knowledge of the person's present or "reality" situation may therefore be less helpful in understanding what images are being maintained than knowledge of the images that were associated with an earlier period. The older citizen, retired and dependent on others, may still be endeavoring to maintain the self-image of a valued and contributing member of society, and an understanding of his behavior or that of any person whose circumstances have undergone marked change must be achieved through the study of the self-image that he strives to maintain.

ENHANCEMENT NEEDS

When man's physical, relatedness, maintenance, and protective needs have in large part been fulfilled, the need to extend his potential for self-development—or as it has sometimes been called, for self-actualization—becomes apparent. The enhancement needs cover the personality's requirements that man's resources, talents, aptitudes, and capacity for experience be cultivated and given opportunity for expression. These needs go beyond the preservation of the self as it is: they influence the total personality in the direction of further development.

In addition to the constructive and creative achievements that may be realized by persons endeavoring to satisfy their enhancement needs, another aspect of these needs requires emphasis. This is the action patterns that are directed toward the end state of becoming one's ideal self and that may include thoughtful and contemplative behaviors, solitary avocational activity, or single-minded devotion to one's work.

If the individual is to have the best chance to gratify these needs, he requires a special environment, an environment in which the person as such is valued and his worth is not measured solely in terms of his material possessions. He is viewed instead as a complex being of many facets with a unique combination of talents and aptitudes. In such an environment his right to pursue interests that have appeal to him and that do not hurt others is taken for granted.

Conflict and Need Frustration

In the process of growing up, every child experiences frustrating events that can spur him to try out new ways of attaining his goals and to learn new skills and new symbols. Such obstacles and privations may be relatively mild and transitory or they may be crushing in their effects, but they are inevitable.

Every maturing individual also finds himself in many situations in which he has needs or desires that are mutually incompatible and cannot be satisfied simultaneously. No matter what objective he attains, he is left with some feeling of dissatisfaction. In fact, the developmental sequence itself necessitates a certain amount of mutually conflicting activity on the part of the constituents of the personality.

Some attention will now be given to need frustration, various reactions to frustrating events, and the development of frustration tolerance. Types of conflict situations will be discussed and the distinction between these and intrapsychic conflict will be emphasized.

The developmental process should not be thought of as a succession of gratifying experiences. It is probably more accurately viewed as a fairly orderly series of events that become progressively more demanding, more complicated, and, in a sense, more frustrating of immediate needs. While the opportunities for immediate impulse gratification become increasingly restricted, the individual grows physically and his image of himself becomes more and more complex. It not only has more facets, but the qualities and characteristics that combine to make him the unique person that he is become increasingly definite and refined.

As the personality develops and differentiates, the needs that must be satisfied proliferate. Although the opportunities for securing need satisfactions multiply as the child becomes increasingly able to master his environment, it is inevitable that he will be exposed to situations in which his own skills, resources, strengths, or talents will not be adequate to obtain certain need satisfactions. It is further inevitable that the individual will confront external obstacles that prevent the attainment of desired objectives. Such external and internal states of conditions, which are in fact—or are perceived as—thwarting activities essential to the enhancement, maintenance, or protection of the psychological self, are considered frustrating events. Simply stated, a frustrating event occurs when the person perceives that his progress toward a desired goal or objective is impeded by a barrier or a limitation.

A frustrating event resulting from an *internal* limitation was observed in the case of a college freshman. After achieving an outstanding academic record in a small rural high school, she entered a large state college located in a metropolitan center. Away from home and her mother's assistance, and despite an extremely conscientious approach to her schoolwork, she could achieve only a "C' average. While for many students this would represent a satisfactory record, for her it represented a frustrating event because the need to maintain and protect the well-established image of herself as an "A" student was not satisfied.

A frustrating event resulting from an *externally* imposed limitation is seen in the case of the boy who had been counting on the use of his father's car on the night of the big dance. An unavoidable change in his father's plans resulted in the car's being unavailable. If the boy's self-image had not included a need to be perceived as an independent, sophisticated young man, the maintenance and protective needs would not have been frustrated. But the use of the family car was seen as a means of satisfying the need; not attaining it was a frustrating event because he believed his date would not think well of him if he could not take her to the dance in his "own" car.

Frustration results also from the simultaneous presence of conflicting needs. The section pertaining to conflict (pp. 73–79) is devoted to a presentation of perceived situational conditions and relationships of the intrapsychic processes especially conducive to frustration.

SOME REACTIONS TO FRUSTRATING EVENTS

When an event is accompanied by an increase in an individual's physical tension level, then it can be said that he is experiencing frustration. Faced by this frustrating event, the individual may exhibit increased activity directed toward the goal or substitute goals, or an intensified emotional reaction, or both. The more closely an individual's self-esteem is dependent upon the attainment of his objectives, the greater his sense of frustration when his goals are blocked or thwarted.

Consider the individual whose ideal self-image includes the picture of himself in the years ahead as a distinguished surgeon. His self-esteem is closely related to his progress toward that goal. He has directed his efforts toward gaining admission to medical school, and if he fails he may experience intense frustration because he has placed a high value on admission. His failure to win a varsity letter or to be valedictorian of his class also may engender frustration, but these failures do not have the meaning for him that a failure to obtain entry to medical school has, since his own worth and value are not so closely tied to these goals. If the student believes that the failure to gain admission to the medical school of his choice will not prevent his being admitted to another school which in his eyes is almost as good, then failure will bring less frustration than it would if he believes that his rejection bars him from the medical profession. If he has an opportunity for an alternative professional career—such as the law—which he values as much, or almost as much, then his frustration will be less than if he has tied his hopes to the single objective.

CONSTRUCTIVE REACTIONS

Frustration may cause an individual to act constructively, to learn new skills, to try out new methods, to combine habitual acts into new patterns. In the absence of frustration as it is defined here, there would be little motivation for a person to extend the range of his knowledge or to develop the talents required in his interactions with the world. In conditions of prompt need gratification, he would fail to progress along the developmental scale. Such failure has been termed "fixation." However, just as excessive need gratification may result in developmental arrest, so may excessive frustration (5). In instances of prolonged and consistent frustration, developmental disturbance is due to failure to achieve the gratifications accompanying goal attainment. In the absence of such essential reinforcement, activity remains aimless and the opportunity to find relief (and the accompanying reinforcement) in drive reduction is limited.

The developmental process is helped by the challenge to learn new skills, to try new problem solutions, and to combine previously learned behaviors into new combinations and patterns, so long as the efforts meet with occasional success. With the successful try, reinforcement of the specific behavior pattern that accomplishes the objective occurs and the individual is more likely to expend efforts in seeking alternative approaches to other desired goals whose attainment is frustrated. Moderate frustration is thus viewed as an incentive to actions that otherwise would not be tried. Actions leading to the acquisition of skills and knowledge that increase the person's control over his environment are viewed as constructive reactions to frustration. The beneficial results of frustrating events are most likely to occur when the ego processes have been sufficiently established to allow the individual to perceive the frustrating event clearly and in all its aspects. Only under such circumstances can the individual consider alternative goals and only then has he a reasonable opportunity to acquire the skills necessary to the attainment of these goals.

Not all reactions to frustration can be considered constructive. Some reactions that are not consonant with purposeful effort and that may even interfere with constructive acts will be discussed in the next section.

FIXATION AND REGRESSION

The developmental progression through the various life stages has been compared to an army advancing through enemy territory. At various important points the army leaves part of its troops behind. The more men left behind the weaker the advancing force and the more likely to retreat in the face of strong opposition. This simile suggests that during the developmental progression not all aspects of the personality develop at the same rate. The term *fixation* is employed to describe the "leaving behind" of those aspects of personality whose development is arrested. Fixation occurs as a result of either excessive gratification or excessive deprivation of the person's various needs. In excessive frustration behavioral patterns do not lead to goal attainment. Hence no reinforcement of any behavioral patterns occurs nor are the gratifications associated with drive reduction available. In excessive frustration the activity level of the infant or child is at first unusually high. This state of excitation is possibly in itself uncomfortable and the child learns that a lethargic reaction is more comfortable. In the following chapters concerned with development, attention will be given to the various relationships and factors conducive to personality development and to those that tend toward developmental fixation. There is a close relationship between the amount of troop strength the army leaves behind and its likelihood of retreating to these positions of strength behind the lines. Whereas fixation in the simile pertains to the troops left behind, regression is analogous to the process of retreat.

Regressive reactions to frustration are encountered frequently, although they are among the least constructive human behaviors. In psychological literature, there are two meanings given to the term *regression*. One denotes a return to an earlier stage of development. An individual who "regresses" adopts specific attitudes and behaviors that characterized some earlier period of his development. If he sucked his thumb for solace in his childhood, he might in his regressed adult state put his thumb in his mouth when he experiences frustration. Or an adult who engaged in temper tantrums in his childhood might exhibit similar behavior in a frustrating situation. This use of the term sometimes refers also to the reactions of individuals with serious behavioral disorders. As applied to a schizophrenic person, whose postures and behaviors may resemble those of an infant, the term refers to a general return to an earlier developmental stage.

A more general meaning of the term regression, and the one adopted in this text, refers to the exhibition of primitive behavior in response to frustration. In such instances, relative to his general capabilities, the person displays behaviors that are unorganized, gross, and ineffective. Regression in this sense does not imply the return to a specific behavior characteristic of an earlier period but rather implies a return to earlier and often less complex stages of behavioral organization. Regressive behaviors of this type are not enduring. A person may be petulant, childish, tearful, or ineffectual for a period, but with attainment of his objective (or its substitute), a decrease in the need for the objective, or diversion of his attention, he again exhibits the purposeful, organized activity of which he is capable. "Primitive behavior" refers to previously learned actions that are less refined, less differentiated, and less effective than later learned behaviors.

The observation that behavior becomes more primitive under conditions of frustration is consistent with the results of research by Barker, Dembo, and Lewin (2). They studied two- to five-year-old children in a situation designed to evoke frustration. After an initial play period that enabled the investigators to rate the quality and complexity of the children's activities, the children were allowed to play with toys that were more fascinating and desirable than the first set. Frustration was induced by requiring the children to return to the first toys, while they were able to see—but not to reach—the more attractive toys through a wire screen. Since the earlier play had precipitated a state of aroused desire for the unattainable toys, the situation satisfied the formal definition of frustration. The level of play that followed the frustrating episode was about one-and-one-half years below the level that the children had demonstrated in the first play period. As a result of frustration, the play became less complex, less constructive, and less well organized, and these regressive reactions were accompanied by a number of instances of aggressive behaviors.

AGGRESSIVE REACTIONS

Aggressive behaviors are those that are direct attacks, or that represent attacks, usually on another person or persons. Such behaviors are accompanied by anger and destructiveness and may be directed toward a specific individual, one who is seen as blameworthy. In other instances the targets of aggressive behaviors may be merely convenient or accessible objects, bearing little relation to the provoking agent. An aggressive reaction may be covertly expressed via words, gestures, or manner. A diffuse aggressive reaction was evidenced by a seven-year-old boy who had been refused a second dish of dessert. His reactions included pounding on the table, breaking a dish, striking his mother and younger sister, slamming the screen doors, kicking the cat, pulling the covers off his bed, shouting, and finally throwing himself on the floor and banging his feet against the wall.

According to one point of view, all aggressive behavior results from the frustration that follows interference in goal-directed activity (4). In addition to their interest in the conditions that evoke aggressive reactions, psychologists have studied the content of the aggression and the direction of the reaction. For example, in his research into responses to frustrating events, Rosenzweig (15) noted that some persons characteristically tend to direct their aggressive and hostile behaviors outwardly toward persons or objects that are blamed, abused, threatened, punished, or attacked. The opposite direction of the aggressive reaction is noted in behaviors in which the individual turns his irritation upon himself instead of upon others; he is the recipient of his own anger and feels that the conditions evoking frustration could have been averted or circumvented had he been more efficient and more capable. In a third pattern of response to frustration, the aggressive content is minimized; the conditions that cause the frustration are responded to as if they were of no consequence, and no one is blamed.

These three categories of reaction to frustration are termed the extropunitive, intropunitive, and the impunitive and can be illustrated in the reaction of the person in a restaurant who has a plate of soup spilled on him. In the extropunitive reaction, the waiter is the object of wrath, "Why don't you watch out, you clumsy oaf!" The reaction takes a different direction in the intropunitive response of, "It's all my fault; I shouldn't have been sitting here." In the impunitive situation, the person might say, "Well, that's life, and I was going to get the suit cleaned anyway."

FRUSTRATION TOLERANCE

The ability to tolerate an increase in the tension resulting from a frustrating event is termed *frustration tolerance*. Individuals differ with respect to the degree of frustration tolerance they possess. Such differences were observed in a study of hospitalized patients (7). A series of simple tasks requiring concerted effort was administered and scored. The patients were then asked to perform tasks they did not know were unsolvable. When patients "failed" to complete these tasks the examiner showed mild disappointment and then asked the patients to perform solvable tasks similar to the first series. Performances before and after the frustrating series of tasks were compared, and the ability to tolerate the frustration evoked by failure was found to be reflected in levels of performance essentially the same at the end of the experiment and at the beginning. Lower levels of frustration tolerance were reflected in reduced levels of performance on the tests in the final part of the study. It was found that patients diagnosed as neurotic and alcoholic exhibited lower levels of frustration tolerance than did patients with no emotional problems.

A considerable amount of learning must occur in the development of frustration tolerance. For example, the individual learns that immediate gratifications can be delayed, that long-term goals are sometimes best served not only by delaying immediate satisfaction but also by avoiding overt behavioral expression of the frustration. Since internal deficiencies and external obstacles make it inevitable that every person must forego some of his goals and objectives, development of a capacity to tolerate frustration is a necessary part of the attainment of personal and social effectiveness. The ability to tolerate frustration does not mean that one pushes out of his conscious awareness all thoughts associated with unconscious impulses. It involves, instead, the conscious recognition of the desired objectives and the reasons for their being desired, and an evaluation of how they might be achieved, replaced by substitutes, held in abeyance, or even abandoned.

This part of the individual's ego processes requires an optimal set of conditions for its development. Excessive immediate gratification of an individual's needs fails to provide the conditions for his development of frustration tolerance, just as excessive frustration of his needs results in such prolonged tension and emotional disruption that the learnings upon which frustration tolerance is built cannot occur. As the term is defined and utilized in this book, some frustration is not only an inevitable part of life, but also results in much constructive and creative activity, for it stimulates efforts to find alternative methods of achieving goals. It necessitates reappraisal of aims and techniques, and it causes the limits of knowledge to be extended.

Conflict

Frustration occurs not only when progress toward a specific goal is blocked, but also as one of the important by-products of psychological conflict. Conflict is defined as the simultaneous presence of contradictory impulses, desires, needs, or processes. Expanding this definition, we can say that the conflict situation is one in which the person experiences alternative wishes or desires which can only be partially fulfilled, since the satisfaction of one set of desires precludes the attainment of the other set or sets of desires.

Before intrapsychic conflicts are considered in detail, however, graphic representation of various types of perceived conflict situations may help in understanding the implications of this definition. Four types of conflict situations can be characterized, each involving the person's perception of himself in relation to his own goals, objectives, and situation.

APPROACH–APPROACH CONFLICT SITUATION

One type of conflict situation has been termed the approach–approach conflict. In it, a person is confronted simultaneously with two or more divergent lines of activity, all leading to desired goals. Behavior that will achieve one goal rules out the attainment of the others. In the simplest approach–approach conflict situations an individual may choose between two equally desirable alternatives. He may, for example, go with his friends to the beach, or he may stay home and play tennis. There are few disruptive consequences to this type of choice, provided that whatever decision is reached leads to satisfaction.

In this simple, perceived conflict situation the alternate choices and the individual's position with respect to them may be depicted in the following manner:

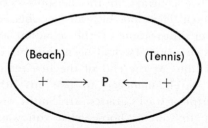

The diagram depicts what has been termed by Kurt Lewin (8) the *life space,* the psychological situation as it is perceived and experienced. The arrows represent the strength of the respective forces that are converging upon the person (*P*). In this case both alternatives are positive, and the decision depends upon the relative attractiveness of the alternatives; the closer the alternatives approach each other in attractiveness, the greater the conflict.

AVOIDANT–AVOIDANT CONFLICT SITUATION

In the avoidant–avoidant conflict situation, a person is confronted with the necessity of making a choice among two or more alternatives, all of which he perceives as undesirable. It is an hour after Jimmy's usual bedtime when his father angrily announces, "Jimmy, you will either go to bed immediately or I will spank you." Both choices confronting Jimmy, of going to bed or receiving a spanking, are undesirable. The situation would be depicted in this way:

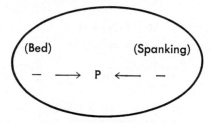

This representation of Jimmy's life space, or of his perception of the situation, indicates that both the alternatives have negative values for him. In this situation the equality of the negative values attached to his perceived alternatives suggests that the conflict situation will not be resolved easily for either Jimmy or his father. It is difficult to predict from this diagram how Jimmy will react to these undesirable alternatives.

The avoidant–avoidant conflict situation contains greater potential for precipitating frustration than does the approach–approach conflict, since both choices are contrary to the person's desires. For example, Jimmy desires to watch television; he wants neither to go to bed nor to be spanked. Another illustration of the avoidant–avoidant conflict is seen in Carl Smith's situation. He had been enjoying college life and the freedom it afforded him. At the end of the first semester he failed one major subject and barely managed to pass his other courses. Upon receiving the transcript of Carl's grades, Mr. Smith wrote his son a letter that read, "It is up to you to choose what you want to do. You can either apply yourself to your school work next semester or return home and go to work. I will not pay your college expenses next year unless your grades improve substantially." Carl knew that his father meant exactly what his letter had said, and neither of the alternatives presented appealed to him.

APPROACH–AVOIDANT CONFLICT SITUATION

The approach–avoidant conflict situation is characterized by a single goal or objective that is perceived as having both positive and negative aspects.

For as long as John could remember he had wanted to be a lawyer, but now that he was halfway through his pre-law courses, he was beset with uncertainties. The field still interested him, but the long period of training ahead presented many problems. There was not only the question of financing it, but also the objections raised by his fiancee. Ann hoped that they would be married shortly after his graduation and that he would accept her father's offer to work in his firm. She was very definite that she did not want him to be a lawyer. For John, the goal of being a lawyer had positive aspects, but to go ahead in this direction would mean displeasing Ann as well as having to find a means of defraying the cost of his education.

The conflict situation which John was experiencing could be characterized as an example of the approach–avoidant situation and would be represented in this way:

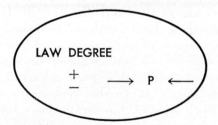

DOUBLE APPROACH–AVOIDANT CONFLICT SITUATION

Some conflict situations are perceived by the person as involving two alternatives, each of which has positive and negative features. In this complex situation the individual is both attracted and repelled by different aspects of each alternative. The employee who considers playing golf instead of going to work confronts a double approach–avoidant conflict situation. To play golf would be enjoyable, but he would have to go to considerable trouble to make the necessary arrangements. By going to work, the employee believes, he would be able to take care of several important matters that require attention, but by doing so he would be confined to his office for the day and unable to take advantage of the pleasant weather and his need for exercise.

The double approach–avoidant conflict situation is illustrated below:

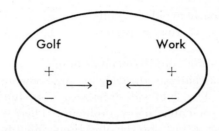

The four types of perceived conflict situations are adapted from the work of Kurt Lewin, who developed a theory of behavior emphasizing the necessity of understanding the person's "life space," the person's perception of himself in relation to his perceived environment (9).

In research studies, psychologists have created situations in which an experimental subject, animal or human, experiences simultaneous conflicting desires, and in which the subject's reactions to the conflict can be accurately observed and measured. The conditions of the experiment can be controlled; that is, the factors that might influence the subject's reactions or the outcome of the experiment can be held constant, and irrelevant influences can be almost entirely eliminated.

In a well-known series of experiments, for example, Masserman conditioned cats to respond to a light or buzzer as a signal of food in the food box. They were then trained to press a lever that turned on the light or sounded the buzzer. When they had been conditioned to this second phase, a conflict situation was created by subjecting the animal to a blast of air when the lever was pressed. In this situation the cats manifested approach reactions to the lever as a means of securing the food, together with avoidance reactions to the possibility of an air blast. In general, the results of Masserman's studies indicated the presence of physiological components of emotion in the cats exposed to these conflict experiences. Although the behavior of individual cats varied, it usually included changes in respiration, pupillary reflex, and heartbeat (11).

In a study utilizing human beings as subjects, college students were required to select the brighter of a pair of lights. When they failed to do so, they received a mild electric shock. When the conflict was increased by the experimenter's bringing the two lights to almost the same brightness, the students demonstrated physical reactions associated with heightened emotion (6).

DEALING WITH CONFLICT SITUATIONS

Experimental findings based on animal and human subjects support the view that conflict situations can evoke both emotional and behavioral responses that are nonadaptive.

Since the meaning a conflict situation has for any specific person is dependent on his psychological structure, reactions to conflict situations are highly varied. This means that the major focus in a study of conflict must be on the factors that determine the individual's *perception* of his situation. Each of the four types of conflict has been described in terms of situations as they were perceived by particular individuals.

Conflict situations that evoke minimal anxiety and present the person with clearly defined and consciously recognizable alternatives are frequently encountered by everyone. In such instances, the resolution of the conflict may be facilitated by taking the following steps:

1. carefully defining the goals and alternatives;
2. obtaining all available essential information pertaining to the goals and alternatives;
3. listing the respective advantages and disadvantages under each goal or objective;
4. eliminating from the list certain advantages or disadvantages that appear insignificant after being spelled out on paper;
5. further clarifying the situation by discussion with a respected adviser;
6. adhering to a time limit or deadline for reaching a decision;
7. accepting the decision reached as the best possible one in light of the situation and the presently available information.

Unfortunately, many conflict situations are not so simple that they can be resolved by taking these steps. The psychological process that produces anxiety and that may prevent the clear perception of alternatives must be considered in the resolution of intrapsychic conflict.

INTRAPSYCHIC CONFLICT

The contradictory goals, wishes, and impulses that make up the intrapsychic components of a conflict situation stem from the different functions of id, ego, and superego processes and from their interaction in the maintenance and preservation of the personality.

According to this view, contradictory personal goals result from the interaction of the intrapsychic processes. Goals related to the immediate gratification of sexual needs may be inimicable to the achievement of long-range goals. Id activity impels an unmarried person to seek gratification of sexual impulses, for example, but ego processes may compel restraint in the light of reality factors such as the consequences of disclosure or the possibilities of pregnancy. Id processes can conflict with both ego and superego processes, as in the case of the unmarried person who restrains his impulse to seek sexual gratification not only because of the reality factors, but also because his superego processes bring the values and moral standards acquired from his parents and the culture to bear on the issue.

An individual sometimes wishes to strike out against someone who threatens his self-esteem or frustrates him by limiting his behavior. These aggressive feelings may be evoked by the parent or teacher who criticizes him or the employer who denies him something he desires. Though the wish to aggress may frequently be evoked by the conditions of everyday life, ego processes weigh the consequences and operate to restrain overaggressive behavior.

At times ego and superego conflict may occur. An example of such conflict would be the case of the person who is aware that if he acts in accordance with his religious or ethical beliefs, his behavior will be unacceptable to his friends and to most people with whom he has contact. The person whose moral convictions prevent his pledging allegiance to the flag, registering for the draft, or signing loyalty oaths may also want to retain the goodwill of his friends and neighbors. Acting in accordance with his moral convictions may cause him to lose friends and possibly his job. Consideration of the consequences to himself and to his family of following his moral convictions may engender a state of intrapsychic conflict. His ego processes impel him in the direction of compliance, while superego processes impel him to take an opposite course of action.

Intrapsychic conflicts that involve only the ego and superego processes may exist only in theory, since in most cases all three components of the self are probably involved in varying degrees. Id–superego conflict influences ego function, for example. Although the effect of this conflict on ego function will depend on the nature of the conflict and the experiences that have been formative in the individual's psychological development, one general point is worth emphasis: the ego processes will function in whatever ways are essential to minimize anxiety and to preserve the concepts of himself that the individual values.

An individual in a conflict situation may waver between the alternate goals. Because the alternatives have about equal attractions for him, some indecision is bound to occur. The feeling of wanting to go both in the direction of a particular objective and away from it has been termed ambivalence. The same term is applied to the contradictory feelings, wishes, or attitudes that one may feel toward a person, group, or institution.

The complex process of psychological development engenders many ambivalences. For example, the parent who is loved as the source of comfort and protection may also be feared and hated as the punisher and depriver. The individual reacts positively to persons or agencies that will take care of him and make his decisions for him, but he may also hate them for depriving him of his freedom of action.

One of the most difficult, and most important, ideas a student of psychology has to understand is that he may simultaneously like and dislike the same person, that he may have feelings of both love and aggression toward the same individual. Ambivalent reactions occur frequently in conflicting situations and in intrapsychic conflict.

Emotion

Although reference has been made to emotional reactions such as affection, anger, rage, fear, and elation, a discussion of emotion has been reserved for this point in the text since it is an essential aspect of frustration and conflict and provides a link between the material on the development of the personality and that in the next chapter on its maintenance and protection.

Emotional reactions involve a complex interplay of all the physical systems of the body: the central nervous, endocrine, muscular, and skeletal systems. Events in the environment may result in increased heart rate, perspiration, and in changes in blood pressure, muscle tension, and gastrointestinal activity. These physical changes are usually accompanied by pleasant or unpleasant feelings and are expressed in changes in the general activity level of the individual. If the stimulus event is perceived as being consistent with the enhancement or maintenance of the individual's self-concept and if it contributes to the satisfaction of his relatedness need, the emotional reaction is experienced as positive and desirable. If the stimulus event is inconsistent with the maintenance or enhancement of self-esteem or presents some threat to the individual's relatedness need, the resulting emotion has the quality of a negative or undesirable state. The attainment of desired goals, such as securing a coveted position, negotiating a successful business transaction, or discovering another person whose company is pleasurable, have accompanying emotional reactions of a positive character. Reactions to losing loved ones and to being treated unfairly have negative emotional connotations.

During the first months following birth, infants have been observed to exhibit three clearly discernible patterns of emotional reactions: first, excitement, later, distress and delight. In the two-year-old child, these early patterns have developed into a number of fairly discrete emotions, among which fear, disgust, anger, jealousy, joy, elation, and affection can be distinguished (3).

As the child matures physically and as his social experiences accumulate, his emotional reactions become both more specific and more varied, and he begins to learn the gestures, facial expressions, and sounds denoting specific emotions that are fairly consistent with a given culture. Even so, it has been demonstrated that the accurate identification of emotions from photographs is improved when the judge is provided with pictures showing the subjects' activities and surroundings in addition to their facial expressions. The more information a judge has about the preceding events, the more likely it is that his judgment of the emotional reaction will be correct (13).

The physical reactions associated with emotion are not easily differentiated into separate patterns for the different emotions. In a study of physiological responses to anger- and fear-provoking situations, fourteen measures of physical functioning were simultaneously recorded for all subjects. These included pulse rate, heart stroke, breathing, face temperature, hand temperature, galvanic skin response, and muscle action currents. Half the indices showed no substantial differences between the fear and anger reactions (1).

Several of these measurements (pulse rate, blood pressure, breathing, and galvanic skin response) are used in the well-known "lie detector." After an individual's reactions to neutral questions or terms have been measured, he is given another series that contains references to the "crime." Regardless of his attempts to conceal the truth, the detector will note physical reactions to the key stimulus words or questions. Although the technique is not infallible in determining guilt or innocence, it vividly illustrates the involuntary physical reactions occurring with emotion.

In a famous study of the connection between emotional and physical reactions, investigators observed the activity within the stomach of a man who had a surgically constructed passageway that allowed food to be placed directly in his stomach and that permitted direct recording of changes associated with emotional fluctuations. It was noted that events precipitating emotional reactions were accompanied by changes in the gastric fluids and in the color and texture of the stomach lining. These changes were similar to those that precede the appearance of peptic ulcers (17).

The study of specific emotional patterns and their antecedent or subsequent physical states is the subject of a medical specialty termed psychosomatics. It appears that chronic and intense emotional activity increases the likelihood of certain disease processes, particularly those of the gastrointestinal system, such as ulcers. Probably it is also related to some disorders of the circulatory system, such as high blood pressure and heart trouble.

The relationship of specific disease processes to psychological characteristics is investigated in researches such as one in which peptic-ulcer patients in a hospital were compared to nonpeptic-ulcer patients in their approaches to a pin-ball game. They were required to indicate the scores they hoped to attain, and it was found that the patients with peptic ulcers tended to set unrealistically high goals for themselves. They were therefore unable to do as well as they wished, and even superior performances did not satisfy them (14).

ANXIETY

Among the emotions are the so-called anxiety reactions, and these have considerable significance in the individual's physical health and psychological effectiveness. Anxiety is a complex emotional state, with both physical and psychological aspects. Under certain conditions, it is one of the concomitants of intrapsychic conflict. Although moderate anxiety has been shown to be a motivating force that may impel an individual to seek and try out alternate actions, intense or prolonged anxiety is detrimental to health and to effective psychological functioning.

The physical aspect of the anxiety reaction is similar to that occurring when a state of fear is stimulated by overt danger. When life or safety is endangered, the bodily systems react appropriately through acceleration of heart action, increased secretion of adrenalin, inhibition of digestive function, and heightened muscle tone. Physical reactions that occur in a state of fear are generally appropriate, for they help the individual either to defend himself or to escape from the danger. In states of fear, the stimulus evoking the reaction is specific and identifiable; in everyday language, the person knows "what he is afraid of." In anxiety states, however, the physical reactions are often elicited under conditions in which the stimulus is vague or unknown. In some instances, the stimulus may be clear but anxiety is aroused by the unpredictable and uncertain implications of the situation. When a person receives a summons to appear in court to answer a charge of reckless driving, for example, the stimulus is specific, but the outcome is uncertain. Anxiety reactions include feelings of general uneasiness, muscular tension, tightening in the stomach, and moistening of the palms. A person may say, "I feel as if something dreadful is going to happen," or, "I'm all keyed up and on edge, and I don't know why."

Anxiety may be thought of as the reaction to the *expectation* of danger, which involves the possibility of being hurt either physically or psychologically. A person may perceive that a situation can cause him to lose self-esteem or to behave in ways that would be contrary to his own self-interests. This perception may not be within his conscious awareness; he may be quite unaware of what he is reacting to as dangerous. He may react to external stimuli or cues outside himself, to internal stimuli or his own impulses and feelings, as indicating danger. When a person responds to the expectation of danger, we say that he feels threatened. In essence then, anxiety is response to threat, and feelings of threat may be activated by a person's perception of certain aspects or conditions of the external environment; they may also be experienced as reactions to his own impulses.

Although it is not precisely correct to say that the cause of anxiety *is* intrapsychic conflict, the concomitance of anxiety and intrapsychic conflict has a special significance for the assessment of intrapersonal adjustment. Of particular interest are the techniques adopted by a person in attempts to ward off anxiety reactions. These techniques also enable him to deal with intrapsychic conflicts so that he can maintain his self-esteem. The complex interrelationship between anxiety and conflict is illustrated by the following conversation between Susan, a college sophomore, and her counselor.

> *Susan:* Everything is all mixed up.
> *Counselor:* It's hard to know what to do.
> *Susan:* Yes, that's it exactly. I just don't know what to do. I want to be popular and go out a lot, but everytime I have a date I go through the same old business.
> *Counselor:* You wonder if it's worth it.
> *Susan:* Yes, I know that boys can't understand why I can't be affectionate. In fact, I can't understand it myself, except I guess I was brought up to believe that you don't even let a boy kiss you goodnight until you have gone out with him quite a few times and really know him well. But the boys here expect you to kiss them the first time you go out with them and if you don't, they won't ask you out again.
> *Counselor:* You want to go out, but don't feel that you can go along with what they expect.

Susan: Well, that's partly it, but it's really that I get very upset when I am out. I keep worrying about whether I'm saying the right things and whether I'm making a good impression. Then if the boy seems to like me, I start worrying if he will try to kiss me and if he does, whether I'll go all to pieces. This thing has reached the point that the whole day before a date I worry about it, and I can't study or concentrate. In fact, I'm so on edge that I can't eat anything before I go out and I'm so keyed up that if we go someplace to eat, I can never touch anything on my plate.

At the time of this interview it was evident to the counselor that Susan was experiencing rather intense anxiety reactions and that these were related to intrapsychic conflicts evoked by the dating situations. It was not until many sessions later, however, that the counselor and Susan were able to achieve an understanding of the origins of the conflict. During her sessions it became clear that her wishes to be loved physically were very strong, although they were opposed by intense superego forces. She felt that these impulses were evil and unnatural and that they would bring destruction if expressed.

The origin of superego attitudes such as these is to be found in the relationship between a child and his parents. The child who has learned that it is "bad" to express any kind of strong emotional reaction and that such expressions bring parental displeasure or punishment, comes to react anxiously whenever a situation evokes either positive or negative impulses. An irrational association between forbidden impulses and feelings of impending disaster sets off an anxiety reaction. The anxiety sequence begins with a stimulus that evokes an urge or impulse for which gratification is desired. Superego and ego processes, which are mobilized to oppose the impulse, result in the person's reacting *as if* the expression of the urge would place him in jeopardy.

As has been noted earlier, the physical reactions associated with anxiety closely resemble those that occur when a person is exposed to physical danger. In the anxiety sequence, the specific danger is often not consciously recognized by the person, though the situation evoking the reaction may be easily identified, as in the case of Susan; the threat of danger is to the personality. This threat may be acutely experienced when forbidden impulses and urges are evoked, but it is not a conscious, logical, or rational assessment; it is a rapid ego and superego reaction to the impulse, which has been taught by the person's previous experiences. Although he reacts physically as if his life were threatened, the conditions that precipitate the anxiety reaction may hold no threat of physical danger. The significant point is that they *do* threaten the person's self-esteem or enhancement and maintenance of the personality.

Anxiety may occur almost simultaneously with the arousal of impulses whose expression would bring social disapproval or censure. The person whose superego processes compel him to feel uneasy about his own honesty or capability, for example, will be extremely vulnerable in any situation that he sees as threatening his self-esteem. Charges of dishonesty or of ineptness may provoke feelings of anxiety and anger and behaviors directed toward self-protection; he will quickly perceive threat in any situation and will experience anxiety reactions as the result of such perceptions. The person whose id–superego conflicts are less intense or different in form may well react to a similar situation without feeling any challenge to his self-esteem.

The origins of anxiety thus lie in either internal or external stimuli which initiate a feeling or a perception that the unity and integrity of the personality are threatened. The readiness to perceive threat to one's reputation, honesty, or integrity reflects intrapsychic conflict; the over-readiness to respond to threat represents the effort to hold anxiety to a minimum. The efforts to minimize anxiety involve behavioral patterns that have been termed "defense mechanisms" because they function to protect the unity of the personality. The more inclusive term, "mechanisms of adaptation," adopted in this text to describe both these behavioral patterns and those that maintain and contribute to the development of the personality through mastery experiences will be discussed in detail in the next chapter.

Summary

The psychological activity of the personality may be viewed as directed toward its maintenance, protection, and development. In addition to these needs, the need to feel in communion with others is also considered a basic motivation of human behavior.

Although it is an inevitable characteristic of life and an essential contribution to human development, the thwarting of needs and wishes results in an increase in muscular tension and in feelings of frustration. Closely associated with frustration is the conflict situation, which results from an individual's holding simultaneous wishes, objectives, or inclinations wherein the satisfaction of one set precludes the satisfaction of the other. In addition to these perceived situational conflicts, the intrapsychic processes may impel the individual toward mutually contradictory goals, and the processes themselves can be in conflict.

Anxiety, a complex emotional reaction having psychological and physical properties, occurs when the individual experiences threat. Anxiety differs from fear in that the conditions which precipitate it are often unclear, the actions to be taken are equivocal, and the outcome uncertain. In fear situations the danger is identifiable and the physical responses are adaptive to the extent that they contribute to the person's effectiveness in combating the threat or in escaping from it.

References

1. Ax, A. F. The physiological differentiation between fear and anger in humans. *Psychosom. Med.,* 1953, *15,* 433–42.

2. Barker, R. G., Dembo, T., and Lewin, K. Frustration and regression: an experiment with young children. *Univ. Ia. Stud. Child Welf.,* 1941, *18,* No. 386.

3. Bridges, K. M. B. Emotional development in early infancy. *Child Develpm.,* 1932, *3,* 324–41.

4. Dollard, J., Doob, L. W., Miller, N. E., Mowrer, O. H., and Sears, R. R. *Frustration and Aggression.* New Haven: Yale University Press, 1939.

5. Fenichel, O. *The Psychoanalytic Theory of Neurosis.* New York: Norton, 1945.

6. Freeman, G. L. A method of inducing frustration in human subjects and its influence upon palmar skin resistance. *Amer. J. Psychol.,* 1940, *53,* 117–120.

7. Hybl, A. R., and Stagner, R. Frustration tolerance in relation to diagnosis and therapy. *J. consult. Psychol.,* 1952, *16,* 163–170.

8. Lewin, K. *A Dynamic Theory of Personality.* New York: McGraw-Hill, 1935.

9. Lewin, K. Behavior and development as a function of the total situation; in L. Carmichael (ed.), *Manual of Child Psychology* (ed. 2). New York: Wiley, 1954.

10. Maslow, A. H. *Motivation and Personality.* New York: Harper, 1954.

11. Masserman, J. H. *Behavior and Neurosis.* Chicago: University of Chicago Press, 1943.

12. Miller, D. R., and Swanson, G. E. *Inner Conflict and Defense.* New York: Holt, 1960.

13. Munn, N. L. The effect of knowledge of the situation upon judgment of emotion from facial expressions. *J. abnorm. soc. Psychol.,* 1940, *35,* 324–38.

14. Raifman, I. Level of aspiration in a group of peptic ulcer patients. *J. consult. Psychol.,* 1957, *21,* 229–231.

15. Rosenzweig, S. The picture-association method and its application in a study of reaction to frustration. *J. Pers.,* 1945, *14,* 3–23.

16. Schachter, S. *The Psychology of Affiliation.* Stanford: Stanford University Press, 1959.

17. Wolf, S., and Wolff, H. G. *Human Gastric Function: An Experimental Study of a Man and His Stomach* (ed. 2). New York: Oxford University Press, 1947.

Selected Readings

Carlson, A. J., and Johnson, V. *The Machinery of the Body* (ed. 4). Chicago: University of Chicago Press, 1954.

Dollard, J., Doob, L. W., Miller, N. E., Mowrer, O. H., and Sears, R. R. *Frustration and Aggression.* New Haven: Yale University Press, 1939.

Dunbar, F. *Mind and Body: Psychosomatic Medicine.* New York: Random, 1947.

Lewin, K. *A Dynamic Theory of Personality.* New York: McGraw-Hill, 1935.

Masserman, J. H. *Behavior and Neurosis.* Chicago: University of Chicago Press, 1943.

May, R. *The Meaning of Anxiety.* New York: Ronald, 1950.

Rosenzweig, S. An outline of frustration theory; in J. McV. Hunt, *Personality and the Behavior Disorders.* New York: Ronald, 1944, 1: 379–388.

5.

Learning and Adaptive Processes

Personal and social development consists in acquiring new behaviors and refining those already established. In the course of development the personality becomes increasingly complex and the component selves and processes become differentiated; the self-images become sharper, the individual perceives himself and his relationships to those about him in more clearly defined terms; he becomes more aware of the controls he must maintain over his own impulses in order to abide by social conventions and to avoid hurting other persons or himself. He acquires techniques, patterns of actions or of action tendencies that serve to gratify physical and psychological needs. He learns how to deal with life's inevitable frustrations and resolve situational and intrapsychic conflict. He acquires the means of protecting himself against the disruptive effects of anxiety and he adopts and utilizes the behaviors, skills, and knowledge necessary to cope with and master his environment.

To the extent that these behaviors, action tendencies, and patterns of action are acquired as the result of the person's experience and not from changes in his physical structure, it may be said that they are learned. The individual learns what he represents to himself and to others, what is permitted and what is required. People learn to love and hate. Some learnings have a strong "affective" or emotional aspect: the child learns to fear the dark; people recoil at the sight of a snake. Emotional reactions of anxiety are learned even though what it is that has been learned may be unclear; the individual cannot account for his reactions or does not understand what in the immediate situation has triggered his response.

The term "learning" also includes the child's growing awareness of signs of parental pleasure and displeasure and understanding of the consequences of parental reactions. He learns which behaviors result in gratification and which result in pain or discomfort.

Learning is also of the type that occurs in school, through the study of books or through being told of someone else's experience. Such learning is accomplished through the use of signs and sounds that represent events, meanings, or relationships between events and meanings. These events or facts may be far removed from the person's immediate experience, as in the study of history or geography.

Although "learning" is considered by the typical person to be restricted to the learning of symbols, all behavioral changes resulting from experience must be regarded as learned phenomena and requiring explanation. At this time the factual information covering the various types of learning is not readily accounted for by any single theory.

Learning is one of the major areas of research in psychology. The student should note that the following discussion represents a minimal presentation of several of the key ideas suggested by learning theorists; it is not presented as a summary of the vast number of research projects undertaken, nor does it attempt to include the whole range of theoretical interpretations of the ways in which individuals learn. The reader who is interested in obtaining more information on the learning process, particularly as it has been studied in the laboratory, should consult the readings cited at the end of the chapter.

Conditioning

In the course of specifying the details of how one stimulus event becomes associated with another and providing an objective means for measuring the response evoked by the association, Pavlov developed a method of approaching a number of puzzling issues. Conditioning principles, for example, can be applied to the learning of unreasonable fears; to the development of associations between logically unrelated events; and to learning that takes place without the subject being aware of it. Pavlov made careful observations of the amount of saliva his experimental dogs secreted when presented with food. He developed techniques for accurately measuring the flow from the salivary glands and he was interested in the conditions that caused this secretion. In his studies, food was utilized as a stimulus and the flow of saliva as the response, a response that could be objectively measured in terms of the amount of secretion within a given period of time.

Pavlov found that he could establish new associations between stimuli and responses. For example, after a sufficient number of trials in which a tone was sounded during the presentation of food, the tone itself, unaccompanied by food, was sufficient to elicit the salivary response. Thus, the initial association of food (unconditioned stimulus) with salivation (unconditioned response) was followed by an association between the tone (conditioned stimulus) and the salivary response (conditioned response).

The conditioning sequence in which a stimulus, having no "natural" or logical relationship to the elicited response, becomes associated with it may be illustrated as follows:

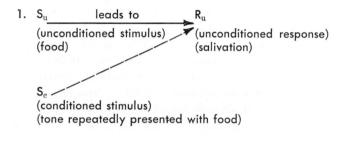

1. S_u ———— leads to ————→ R_u
    (unconditioned stimulus) (unconditioned response)
    (food) (salivation)

    S_c
    (conditioned stimulus)
    (tone repeatedly presented with food)

2. S_c ———— leads to ————→ R_c
    (conditioned stimulus) (conditioned response)
    (tone) (salivation)

A characteristic of this type of conditioning procedure is that the subject is presented with a stimulus (S_c) in addition to the stimulus (S_u) which regularly produces the desired result (R_u) (6).

GENERALIZATION, DISCRIMINATION, AND EXTINCTION

Watson's classical experiments with an eleven-month-old child (13) are of special interest in the study of conditioning. He demonstrated that a fear response could be associated with a stimulus which originally did not elicit this response.

The child, Albert, was placed in a play situation that included blocks, a number of furry objects, and a white rat. He showed no fear reactions until a loud crashing noise was sounded shortly after the introduction of the rat. The noise (unconditioned stimulus) evoked crying behavior (unconditioned response). In this phase of the experiment, the sequence "introduction of rat ———→ loud crashing noise" was repeated until the association between the two was well established.

In the next phase of the experiment, Albert was permitted to play with the blocks and then was exposed to the furry objects. Prior to his being conditioned to fear the rat, Albert reacted normally to both the blocks and the furry objects. Following the conditioning, the blocks still evoked no unusual response, but crying behavior occurred in the presence of the furry objects.

The second phase of this experiment demonstrates two additional principles derived from studies of conditioning. The first is that a response associated with one stimulus may be elicited by other stimuli that are perceived as being similar to the original. This is the phenomenon of "generalization" and it serves the useful function of enabling us to respond to stimuli without having to develop new associations for each new stimulus situation. A child soon learns to distinguish all animals from all people, even though he is unacquainted with the particular individuals or animals. However, generalization may also account for behaviors that are inconsistent with the individual's best interests if he generalizes to situations in which the response is inappropriate. A child may call all four-legged animals dogs without taking into account other identifying characteristics. In Albert's case, not only was a fear reaction evoked by a harmless stimulus (the rat), but the fear reaction was then generalized to include a whole class of stimuli, furry objects, which were not dangerous.

Generalization is complemented by another conditioning principle known as "discrimination." Although generalization may allow two different stimuli to elicit the same response, the response to one of these stimuli will cease if it is not periodically reinforced by presenting the unconditioned stimulus with the conditioned stimulus; the organism has learned to discriminate between the two stimuli. Failure to elicit a response or the weakening of an established response by lack of reinforcement is termed "extinction."

Reinforcement

The principle of reinforcement occupies a central position in a number of learning theories. It is utilized to account for the strengthening of the association between a stimulus and a response. Such strengthening occurs in the classical conditioning situation when the unconditioned stimulus is paired with the conditioned stimulus; thus, the presentation of the food along with the bell in Pavlov's experiment served to strengthen the association between the bell and the animal's salivation.

In the life situation events resulting in tension reduction or in the completion of motivated activity are termed reinforcers. The reinforced response provided in a given situation will be more likely to be repeated than responses that are not reinforced. When the reinforcer is pleasant (positive) it is also termed a reward; when unpleasant (negative) it is termed punishment.

The child who brings his father's newspaper to him at the end of the day is apt to repeat this performance if he receives an affectionate and approving response from the father. If the child's performance is ignored, then he is less likely to repeat this behavior on subsequent occasions. The association between the desired response and the conditions preceding it are more likely to be strengthened when reinforcement follows quickly after the response and when it is consistent and regular than when it is delayed, inconsistent, or irregular. For reinforcement to strengthen an association between a stimulus and response, or to increase the likelihood that a situation will evoke a particular reaction, it is not essential that the individual be aware that his responses are being reinforced.

It is possible to condition a person without his knowledge to utilize some words more frequently than others. In studies of verbal conditioning the psychologist accomplishes this result by responding according to a prearranged program with a nod or approving comment whenever the speaker provides the word or words to be reinforced. In such studies the use of gestures or brief comments such as "good" or even sounds that communicate approval have been shown to be effective reinforcers.

SECONDARY REINFORCEMENT

The parent or teacher interested in strengthening the associations between a child's responses and the conditions preceding them will reinforce the "correct" responses when they occur. Such reinforcement may be merely a nod of approval, a smile, or a sound that indicates that the performance was noted. The operation of approval, attention, or recognition as a reinforcer is due to a feature of the conditioning process known as secondary reinforcement.

Secondary reinforcement operates in the formation of new associations between stimuli and responses. It is accomplished by pairing a well-established conditioned stimulus with a new stimulus, as is shown in the diagram.

1. $S_1 \longrightarrow R_1$

2. $\left.\begin{array}{c} S_1 \\ S_2 \end{array}\right\} \longrightarrow R_1$

3. $S_2 \longrightarrow R_1$

In the diagram above, S_1 and S_2 represent the conditioned stimuli, and R_1 the conditioned response. If S_1 is a tone and R_1 is salivation, then the first step represents an association developed by the regular classical conditioning procedure, described in the Pavlov experiment in which food reinforces the association. If S_2 is a light that is paired with the tone (the second step in the diagram), an association is established between the light and the salivary response. Secondary reinforcement has been demonstrated (the third step in the diagram), for it has not been necessary to present the unconditioned stimulus (food) in order to establish the association between the light and salivation.

In Pavlov's classical conditioning experiment, the simultaneous presentation of unconditioned stimulus and conditioned stimulus is the crucial factor in accounting for the learning that has taken place when a previously neutral stimulus elicits a conditioned response. Conditioning learning based on this principle of contiguity—the concurrent presentation of unconditioned and conditioned stimuli—has been extended and modified by a number of theorists. In one current theory offered by Dollard and Miller (3), the roles of response and reinforcement are crucial. They describe the learning sequence in terms of drive, cue, response, and reinforcement.

The relation between drive, the first of the conditions, and the psychological needs described in the previous chapter is of interest at this point. It will be recalled that "psychological needs" refer to the requirements of the personality, while the term "drive" refers to any strong stimulus, either external or internal, that impels to action. Thus it is possible to view the behavioral expression of psychological needs as responses to drives. The precise statement of how the psychological need is transformed into physical action is not yet available. The proponents of the learning sequence now being described offer considerable evidence that "secondary" or acquired drives (which could be classified as psychological and learned) develop from, and are related to, the innate, unlearned "primary" drives consisting of conditions such as hunger, thirst, and pain.

While the drive impels the individual to action, it is the *cue* that accounts for the direction and characteristics of the response. A motorist, for example, brings his car to a halt when he sees a stop sign (a cue) and continues his driving when he sees a green light. The cue is also a stimulus—in this case, a member of a special class of stimuli having directional value. Stimuli may have both drive and cue characteristics. The air raid siren not only impels the individual to act, it also signals to him to seek a bomb shelter.

Dollard and Miller note that before any response can be rewarded and learned, it must occur. They go on to point out that in many different types of teaching or training situations, the instructor attempts to arrange the environment so that the behavior to be learned can occur. In situations where the response is likely to occur frequently, obviously the instructor has less difficulty than in those in which learning involves responses that occur rarely.

The likelihood of a particular cue's eliciting a specific response depends on the individual's previous learning. A cue can evoke a number of different responses and these can be ordered from the most probable to the least probable. When a response at the top of the order (sometimes termed a hierarchy) is emitted and is not rewarded, its dominant position is weakened and on a subsequent occasion it may be replaced by the next response in the order.

According to this view of learning, the crucial factor in strengthening the association between the stimulus condition and any specific response is the nature and amount of reinforcement. Thus rewards and punishments following immediately upon responses that are provided to cues will tend to strengthen the association between cue and response. Reinforcement is not limited merely to the events and conditions that would be included as rewards and punishments: "prompt reduction in the strength of a strong drive stimulus acts as a reinforcement" (3). Thus, acts that are performed under a high state of drive will tend to become associated with the cue stimulus when there is a prompt or sharp reduction in the drive. If an acquired drive to attract attention is operative, for example, and an individual whose response hierarchy has clowning behavior at the top is given cues evoking that behavior, to the extent that he receives the approval of the group, the likelihood increases that he will act like a clown on subsequent social occasions—on subsequent occasions when he wishes to attract attention.

The complex behaviors characteristic of human activity consist in large part of learned drives and learned (secondary) reinforcements, and these behaviors can be modified if previously neutral stimuli acquire reinforcing properties. This is illustrated in an interesting experiment in which hungry chimpanzees were trained to use poker chips as "money." By placing a chip in a vending machine, the chimpanzee received a grape. After the chip-in-the-machine-to-receive-a-grape behavior was well established, the chimpanzees were trained to "work" for poker chips. Their work consisted of pulling a heavy lever in order to receive their "wages" in the form of poker chips. They worked for the chips, which could be converted into food, in a manner indicating that these neutral-toned stimuli had acquired reinforcing properties, and that the acquisition of such properties constituted an important aspect of learning (14).

OPERANT CONDITIONING

In a learning sequence that has become known as operant conditioning and that has been the subject of vigorous investigations by B. F. Skinner and his associates, the subject is rewarded when it provides the particular response which is to be associated with a particular stimulus. To strengthen the association between a lever in an animal cage (the stimulus) and the pushing of that lever (the response), for example, food (the reinforcing stimulus) is given to the animal when it presses the lever.

Since human behavior frequently serves the function of operating on the environment in order to elicit something from it, there is an interesting parallel between the format of the operant conditioning experiment and certain aspects of human learning. In a study of the conditioning of verbal behavior, the experimenter reinforced all statements of opinion without the subject's being aware of it. The reinforcement consisted of indications of agreement with the opinions. The results showed a marked increase in the tendency to offer opinion statements when they were reinforced, as compared to their frequency under conditions of no reinforcement (12).

Since the learnings that account for psychological development are unintentional, in large part, and often occur without awareness, it is expected that operant conditioning studies may eventually provide more explicit and precise statements than are presently available of the conditions whereby the individual learns who he is and what he represents to others and to himself.

The principles derived from operant conditioning have been utilized in the development of the various devices, including teaching machines, that are grouped under the heading of "automatic teaching techniques" (10). These devices utilize the principle of reinforcing the correct response by directly or indirectly indicating the correctness of the response and permitting the students to proceed to the next "frame." A frame consists of the unit to be learned; ordinarily this is a limited amount of information or a limited number of relationships. Mastery of the new learning must occur before the student proceeds. Repetition of previously learned material is frequent in order to allow for additional reinforcement.

Although they are presently used most frequently in industrial or military training for highly specific skills, it is anticipated that learning machines will eventually become a part of the public school program in subjects such as language and mathematics.

Cognitive Learning

In the conditioning theory of learning, which gives prominence to the role of reinforcement, what is learned is usually considered to be a series of specific muscular reactions that are associated with specific cues. Other theories of learning have accounted for behavioral change by stressing the individual's cognitive and purposive activity and his perception of the relationship between his own needs and the conditions or events that would lead to their gratification.

In one such theory, Tolman gives emphasis to the goal-directed activity of the individual. In this approach, it is of central interest to study the nature of the "signs" the environment presents to the subject; he is thought of as seeking to reach goals in ways that require the expenditure of the least amounts of effort. In Tolman's "sign-learning" theory the actor's perception—how the individual sees himself and his situation—has an important bearing on his behavior and on what he learns. The learning process consists not of the association of response to stimulus but rather of the learning of a path to a goal, which is marked for the individual by signs; he is "learning not movements, but meanings" (5).

Of considerable importance in this approach to learning are the expectancies the individual holds that relate to or serve as the goals to which his behavior is directed. In a classic experiment that demonstrated the operation of such a goal expectation, monkeys were taught to look under a particular box in order to find a banana. When lettuce leaves, a food that they liked less than bananas, were found under the box, they continued their search for the bananas. Their continued effort supports the view that what had been learned was an expectation specific to the banana and not fulfilled by the lettuce. According to this theory, when the expectation is fulfilled it is said to be confirmed, and learning depends not on reinforcement but on the confirmation of expectations (11).

As would be expected from the variety of learnings that theories must explain and the gaps in our knowledge of the nature of learning, no one theory fully covers the range of data subsumed under the term. It has been suggested that "trial and error learning"—the learning occurring as a result of the identification of an effective response in a random series of possible solutions to the problem at hand—is most readily explained on the basis of reinforcement-conditioning theory. "Insight learning," in which the principle manifested by a problem must be identified in order to reach a solution, sometimes in only one trial, may be most readily dealt with by cognitive-expectancy theories (4).

The reader should note that all the patterns of behavior referred to as mechanisms in the next section of this chapter constitute learned responses having an adaptive character. In the second part of the text, beginning with Chapter 6, the situations confronted by persons at various stages of their development are considered: in these situations the individual learns who he is, how he can maintain himself, and how he can function within himself and in relation to other persons.

The Adaptive Mechanisms

Most of man's covert and observable behavior may be thought of as being learned and adaptive to the circumstances that surround him. Not only do his thoughts, his work, and his goal-directed pursuits fit into adaptive patterns, but so do his recreational activities and even those behaviors that seem to be aimless, purposeless, or even nonadaptive.

In the following discussion of adaptation, the emphasis is on those patterns that represent the personality's activity in maintaining, protecting, and enhancing itself. This discussion of the patterns of perceiving, interpreting, and responding to stimuli in terms of the requirements of the personality will focus on intrapersonal activity. We must understand these patterns of activity before going on to consider the two additional factors in the evaluation of an individual's psychological development. These are the behaviors manifested in relationships with other people (interpersonal development) and the degree to which individuals utilize their abilities and talents in productive and satisfying work.

A study of the psychologically adaptive processes and their behavioral representations, termed "mechanisms," provides clues to the explanation of behaviors that are seemingly unrelated to the maintenance of life. Some human effort goes far beyond that required for physical survival. In time of war, maintenance of the self-image requires actions that are almost certain to bring injury or death. Feelings of loyalty to comrades or of responsibility for the group may impel a soldier to behave in ways that lead to his own destruction. The Japanese practice of hari-kari, in which personal honor is considered of more importance than physical survival, becomes understandable when it is viewed as a way of maintaining a valued self-concept.

The mechanisms with which we are concerned are arbitrarily divided into those that serve the maintenance and protective functions (defense mechanisms), and those that contribute to the enhancement functions (mastery mechanisms). The mechanisms of adaptation operate to maintain a state of maximal balance among the intrapsychic processes and the selves. It is important to understand that this balance is always maximal for an individual, given his particular conflicts and his particular resources for dealing with these conflicts, but that this maximal balance is not the same as a high level of intrapersonal development. The attainment by an individual of the greatest possible degree of intrapersonal harmony does not insure his meeting the standards for maximal development.

The mechanisms of defense, concerned with the maintenance and protection of the personality, accomplish the best possible balance of the intrapsychic processes and the selves by controlling or circumventing anxiety stemming from internal conflict. The mastery mechanisms, which contribute significantly to self-esteem, function to decrease the numbers and kinds of situations that can arouse anxiety. In the assessment of development, both the amount or level of anxiety and the means the individual utilizes in protecting against its disruptive effects are of importance.

Mechanisms of Defense

The conditions of psychological development and the related conditions imposed by living within a society result in the individual's developing an awareness of the signals that represent danger for him. He learns that unrestrained expression of his sexual or aggressive inclinations is unsafe, that action without consideration and forethought may bring undesirable consequences, and that the number, complexity, and confusions of the "do's" and "don'ts" of the world are obstacles to the provision of the protection and gratifications he desires. He also becomes aware that transgressions against his own standards bring feelings of guilt and depression. Because of these learnings and many others, most men have experienced anxiety reactions. Thoreau's statement that "the mass of men lead lives of quiet desperation," may not be literally true, but if it is interpreted to mean that most men experience anxiety in varying degrees, it can be accepted as psychologically sound. As frustration must be considered an inevitable product of the experience of living, so one must consider that anxiety itself will be unavoidable for most people; therefore the *presence* of anxiety is not as significant in the assessment of intrapersonal adjustment as are the *effects* of anxiety in interfering with the individual's psychological and physiological functioning.

Just as the presence of anxiety per se is not indicative of disturbed development, so the utilization of the mechanisms of defense does not in itself have special significance in the assessment of development. Probably each of the patterns of perceiving, interpreting, and responding to be described is relied upon by everyone at some time. Though they are given separate names, such as repression, projection, or displacement, these patterns are used in combination. The effectiveness of the defensive processes depends upon the severity of intrapsychic conflict, the stresses in the external situation, and the combination of defenses the individual employs, as well as upon the opportunities available to him for resolving the conflict.

Although the defenses function to maintain the personality by protecting the person from experiencing disruptive anxiety, under certain conditions they may handicap his efforts to cope with his environment. When intrapsychic conflicts are so pronounced that most of an individual's energy must be mobilized against the ensuing anxiety, then there is little left for the business of living, and the individual's effectiveness is diminished. In addition, the defenses erected against anxiety can result in distorted perceptions and interpretations of the external world or in inappropriate behaviors.

REPRESSION

Repression is one of the major defense mechanisms and is the one mentioned most frequently by authors of books on mental hygiene and adjustment. The term *repression* refers to the exclusion of thoughts, feelings, and wishes from conscious awareness. It has some similarity to the process usually termed "forgetting," and a superficial analysis might easily confuse the two.

In the usual course of living, an individual has a vast number of both pleasant and unpleasant experiences, some of which touch him deeply. For many of these experiences there are corresponding visual images or perceptions. These impressions or recollections grow dim with the passage of time and with the intervention of more recent experiences —the experiences are forgotten. If the occasion demands it, the individual may try to remember them, and in some cases he succeeds; in other cases, his failure to remember may be caused by events that have intervened between the time of the experience and the attempt at its recall. This has been termed "retroactive inhibition." For example, it is known that less forgetting occurs during an interval of sleep than during an equal number of hours spent in the usual activities of daily life. When the experience cannot be recalled, it is as if something written on a blackboard has been erased. Though this analogy is not an accurate statement of the forgetting process, it is the way that many people think of forgetting.

Repression also accounts for the failure to remember, but it is a process different from that just described. Repression may be compared not to an erasure, but to the concealing or blocking from view of something written on a blackboard. Under certain conditions, the experience may still be made available to view, or more correctly, remembered.

Men who were exposed to severe stress during battle conditions sometimes experienced acute reactions of anxiety and emotional disturbance. During World War I such reactions were termed "shell shock," but on the basis of greater knowledge of the condition they are now termed "traumatic neuroses." "Traumatic" refers to a condition of trauma or wound, and when it is paired with the noun "neurosis," it refers to a psychological disturbance created by an unusually upsetting experience. It was frequently observed that in traumatic neurosis there was loss of memory for events that had occurred during the period of acute stress, even though the patient was still disturbed by these events. The memory loss, or amnesia, was often so complete that nothing could be recalled of events that had extended over several days. Under the influence of relaxant drugs or hypnosis, however, the individual was able to describe things that he could not recall while conscious. Cases such as those illustrate the influence of the mechanisms of repression, not of simple forgetting.

The loss of memory for certain events was less dramatically demonstrated by a study in which students rated the experiences that had occurred during their Christmas holidays as pleasant, unpleasant, or indifferent. A month and a half later the students were asked again to list their experiences, and it was found that a higher percentage of pleasant experiences were remembered than of those rated as unpleasant (8). The mechanisms of repression can account for the differences in the memory of unpleasant and pleasant events.

In studies of the influence of failure experiences on learning and retention, it has been found that more items were forgotten when persons had learned them in failure situations than in nonfailure situations. It was observed that when threats to self-esteem were removed by explaining the nature of the failures, there was some recovery of memory for the items which had been "lost" to awareness (1).

The complex interrelationship of repression, anxiety, and conflict will be described in the following pages, and as a starting point, the ability of intrapsychic conflict to evoke anxiety when aspects of the conflict signify threat will be recalled. Thus, an impulse that had been punished when it was expressed behaviorally may be opposed by ego processes and hence inhibited when it occurs again. The contradictory wishes for immediate impulse gratification and for safety constitute conflict, and the possibility of the impulse's effecting a break through into behavior constitutes a threat that arouses anxiety. Even though it is opposed, the presence of the impulse creates an anxiety-provoking state that is unsatisfying and unpleasant. Repression serves the function of protecting against the admission of anxiety-provoking wishes, thoughts, or feelings into awareness; thus, a previously painful experience will not be recalled, or an impulse to aggress may be unrecognized. Repression neither resolves the conflict nor dispenses with the anxiety associated with it; to a degree, it merely protects one from consciously confronting the wish, thought, or feeling that has the potential for evoking anxiety. As will subsequently be noted, the person may not recognize the source, but he still experiences, directly or in disguised form, anxiety reactions or their equivalents.

Before an illustration of the mechanism of repression can have meaning it is necessary to indicate that an event is experienced in bodily movements and in the awareness of oneself, one's emotions, and the situation. Visual images and other sensations comprise the content of what the person is aware of while experiencing an event. Following the event, to an extent he can re-experience the state in the sense that movements, emotions, images, and sensations similar to those which occurred previously are again evoked. He remembers the event when he recalls the visual images and the sensations associated with the event. An experienced event may be represented symbolically through a specific image or thought that constitutes only a fragment of the total experience. Such a symbolic representation can remain in one's conscious awareness, or may be seemingly lost to awareness, or the symbolic representation of a previous event may be responded to when confronted in a different context and at a time far removed from the original experience. The images and symbols representing an experience are not necessarily easily understood as direct and logical products of the experienced event. And finally, the images and symbols associated with an experienced event can be "split off" from the sensations and emotions that constituted the original experience, and while the emotional state associated with the symbolic representation of the experience can be active, the images and symbols essential to memory of the event can be repressed.

A young woman who was receiving intensive counseling related that she was seized with acute anxiety whenever she had to wait. During the period of waiting she would experience a feeling of impending disaster, and she would perspire, tremble, and become nauseous. The most acute reaction she had ever experienced was while waiting for a parade celebrating the Chinese New Year. She became so tense that she had to return to her home.

It was not until several days later, while she discussed the incident with her counselor, that the associations between her emotional reactions, the parade, and the waiting situation became at all clear to her. She described a number of less intense reactions to other situations in which she had been kept waiting, and then she recalled her mother's impatience with her whenever she failed to be prompt. She recalled the punishment she received on these occasions and the unpleasantness associated with them. One particular memory stood out, which she had not thought of for years. At the age of five or six, after she had put on her best dress in preparation for a party, her mother placed her in a room that was usually closed and instructed her to sit still until she was called. After waiting alone for what seemed to her to be a very long time, she became restless and impatient. She began whirling about the room with her arms outstretched. This playful interlude came to an abrupt halt when she brushed against her mother's most prized possession, a Chinese vase. The vase fell, and the aftermath was severely disturbing. Her mother screamed at her, spanked her, and then went off to the party, taking her sister but leaving her home.

This incident suggests that the associative process between the symbolic representation and the affect (emotion) may not be logical; there was no reasonable connection between the general act of waiting and the general reaction of anxiety. The relationship becomes clear only when its meaning to the individual in terms of his experience is considered. If an emotional reaction "does not make sense" one cannot infer that there are no relationships which account for it; one can only conclude that they are difficult to identify. The associative process is not obvious and clear-cut. Episodes or fragments of experience may be found to relate to other fragments of experience with which they seemingly have little in common.

In the example, waiting was associated with anxiety reactions. The fact that the incident had a Chinese theme aroused far stronger reactions of anxiety than had been evoked by any previous waiting incident. It was as if the fears and pain experienced when the vase was broken were again brought into play by the episode of waiting for the Chinese New Year's parade to begin. However, although this report illustrates the associative process, the information is too limited to provide a clear statement of the nature of the conflict situation to which the anxiety reaction was related.

At this point several hypotheses might be formulated concerning the nature of the girl's intrapsychic conflict and its relationship to the anxiety she experienced in any waiting situation. One would be that the conflict among id, ego, and superego processes developed out of the experiences this girl had had with her parents and sister over many years. The incident in which she was punished for breaking the vase was not the sole cause of the conflict state, it was only one of many incidents that had influenced her psychological development. Like many of the other significant experiences in this girl's life, this incident contributed to her feeling that disobeying her mother was unforgivable and that the only proper behavior was complete compliance with her mother's expectations. Aligned with the judgmental component of the personality was the ego process, which was influenced by the fact that she was punished in one way or another when she disobeyed and that the consequences of displeasing her mother were serious and painful.

At the same time, the ego processes were developed while she received minimal affection from her highly critical mother. This frustration of her desires for affection created profound wishes to aggress against the mother as well as the sister, who was perceived as being the favored child. But to strike back at her mother would cause the loss of whatever minimal affection was available and also occasion the painful experience of punishment. And, of course, the deep belief that the expression of aggressive or emotional impulses, or even their contemplation, was sinful also conflicted with the wish to express them. Thus, the wish to aggress, to strike back at the mother, evoked oppositional reactions from the ego and the superego processes, with the resulting repression of the aggressive wish.

The anxiety experienced by this girl as an adult was related to intrapsychic conflicts that began in the developmental experiences of her childhood. The conflicts and their potentials for initiating the anxiety sequences had persisted over many years, even though the memory of incidents such as that described had not been consciously retained. Many explanations are available to account for the removal of symbolic representations of experiences or memories from consciousness. When this occurs the memory is seemingly completely lost. Yet under certain circumstances—and frequently to the individual's surprise —he finds that the memory returns.

Although the occurrence of repression is acknowledged by most psychologists, different explanations are offered for its growth and function. All of these, in our present stage of knowledge, must be tentative.

One suggestion is that it is an active, though involuntary and unconscious, process blocking from awareness those symbols which are linked to unpleasant conflict. Such blocking may apply not only to symbols specifically associated with the conflict, but may generalize to include broad segments of experience that seemingly have little relation either to earlier events or to events in the immediate situation. There was little obvious "cause" for the girl in the example to become acutely anxious, since her immediate situation (waiting for the parade to begin) contained no overt danger.

The involuntary process differs from the deliberate shift in attention that occurs when one decides to put aside a difficult question or problem. When a person says to himself, "I won't think about that any more," or, "I will put that out of my mind for the time being," he is utilizing a process that is termed "suppression." Suppressed material can be reintroduced to consciousness by the deliberate decision to do so; repressed material is ordinarily unavailable to consciousness, since it operates expressly to prevent the awareness of forbidden or dangerous impulses or wishes. The act of repressing is involuntary; we do not know that unacceptable wishes and impulses and the ideas associated with them are denied access to consciousness.

It is essential to understand that repression does not resolve conflict; it partially insulates the person from experiencing the anxiety reactions associated with conflict. Its effectiveness in protecting against anxiety depends upon the strength of the conflicting wishes, thoughts, or feelings and the strength of the counterforces of the personality acting to prevent their behavioral expression. The intensity of the intrapsychic conflict, as well as the nature of the situation external to the individual, will determine, in part, how effectively repressed defenses accomplish their functions. To some extent, everyone must utilize repression to prevent the memories of relatively minor physical and psychological hurts accrued in the process of developing from entering awareness and monopolizing consciousness.

As a defense, however, repression has a number of features that limit its usefulness to the individual. Although repression of large segments of previous experience serves an internally adaptive and protective purpose, it may reduce a person's social effectiveness and decrease his ability to pursue valued objectives. "Forgetfulness" of the details of the experiences accounting for his anxiety, guilt, or anger deters him from "profiting from experience." In addition, it prevents him from knowing what parts of his present situation have anxiety-arousing potentials. He is forced to deal with the total experience as if it were responsible for his uneasiness. As a result, he may be so strongly impelled to avoid similar situations that his social effectiveness becomes even more curtailed. A solitary, friendless person may describe his feelings accurately when he says, "I become quite tense and uncomfortable when I have to be around people." But he may be quite in error in attributing his reactions to his current total situation. Heavy reliance on repressive defenses often results in unwitting self-deception, and under such conditions there is little opportunity for corrective action in the form of mastery of the conflict.

Aside from its adequacy as a defense and from its influence on personal effectiveness, massive repression may restrict an individual's ability to experience and demonstrate mirth, sorrow, compassion, affection, or anger except in blunted or disguised form. When such blunting occurs, much of the richness, intensity, and vitality of life become unavailable to him. The complexities and subtleties of life can be appreciated and reacted to only through direct access to one's own experience; repression disrupts within-self communication.

REPRESSION AND DENIAL AS "BLOCKING" DEFENSES

Closely related to the repressive type of defense is "denial." In this case, the individual rejects the stimuli that impinge upon him; he does not see those which have special threat for him. In denial, the person fails to "see" and hence to recognize and think about the anxiety-arousing stimuli, with the result that his perceptions of himself, for example, may be at marked variance with others' perceptions of him. In understanding their reactions to him, he may be at a considerable disadvantage and may be unable to take action that would improve his self-understanding. In repression, wishes, thoughts, and feelings associated with pain and unpleasantness are excluded from awareness. In denial, an experience is excluded from consciousness through a seeming failure to "see" (perceive) the significant elements of the event and thus to respond to their presence. A person with a profound physical disability, for example, may refuse to admit that he is impaired. All contrary evidence and argument will be vehemently rejected or dismissed. The denial process operates in part on the basis of selective perception, since the person perceives stimuli that are acceptable to him and fails to respond to stimuli that lack meaning for him or that posses anxiety-provoking potentials.

Since they prevent the conscious recognition of forbidden impulses or the perception of stimuli that are related to forbidden impulses, repression and denial defenses may be considered "blocking defenses." Their use makes it very difficult for a person to perceive accurately or clearly the nature of the conflicts that give rise to his anxiety. The person who relies heavily on repression and denial may be acutely aware of his feelings of anxiety and of their inappropriateness, but he is quite unable to account for their origins. This is not surprising since the defense itself renders useless the very means required for such comprehension—the conscious awareness of the experience associated with anxiety and conflict.

The mechanism of repression does not itself account for behaviors in which an individual may appear to be emotionally unexpressive or unable to modify his usual activity pattern. In these cases he is sometimes evidencing the psychological immobility that results from intrapsychic conflict. The impulse to act initiates a feeling of threat; the expression is therefore opposed by ego or superego processes, and action appropriate to the impulse is inhibited. When intrapsychic conflict is sufficiently intense, there may be considerable reliance on the mechanisms of defense, but behavioral inhibition is correctly considered a result of conflict itself and not of the defenses necessary to protect against the anxiety aroused by the conflict.

The difficulty of distinguishing between repression and inhibition is illustrated by the results of an experiment in which persons were required to read words flashed on a screen. Comparisons were made between the lengths of time required to read words considered anxiety-arousing and to read words considered neutral. Changes in the electrical conductivity of the skin were used to measure emotional reactions to the words. The actual reading involved both the perception of the word and the response of uttering it. Results indicated that anxiety-provoking words were capable of evoking emotional responses even though the subject did not report seeing the word (7). Failure to report seeing the word could be due to the blocking action of the denial defense that prevented the word's entry into awareness or to inhibition of the overt response because such response (expression) seemed unsafe. When one is attempting to account for the absence of behavior, it is difficult to know whether an impulse or reaction fails to become overt because the wish has been repressed or because its motor expression has been inhibited. In practice, therefore, repression, denial, and inhibition are often assumed to be closely linked processes operating together.

In repression and denial the impulses and symbols which if admitted to consciousness would be anxiety-provoking are blocked out; in other defenses these impulses or symbols are transformed into impulses and symbols that can safely be given entry to awareness. Often the blocking and transforming defenses are utilized simultaneously to prevent awareness of an anxiety-laden impulse or the symbols associated with it. In such instances elements of the unacceptable impulses, wish, or thought will be repressed while other elements of it will be transformed, and having been divested of their anxiety-provoking potential will appear in consciousness in disguised form.

PROJECTION

John was known to his fraternity brothers as a suspicious individual with whom it was difficult to get along. He talked very little and never provided any information about himself. He was aloof and had no close friends. He ungraciously rejected all invitations to participate in dances and other social affairs. In view of his behavior, his fraternity brothers were surprised and angry when they learned how he had described them to a college newspaper reporter. Asked for a "confidential" statement on fraternity life, John criticized his fraternity brothers vehemently. He said they were unfriendly, snobbish, and distrustful of one another. When word about his comments reached the house, his roommate exclaimed, "Imagine John's saying that! Why, all he did was describe himself and the way he acts. It's like the pot calling the kettle black."

In effect, John's roommate provided a concise comment on "projection," a major transforming mechanism. This defense process protects against anxiety by preventing symbols, words, images, and ideas from gaining entry into the individual's awareness in their original form. In addition to repression of the intrapsychic conflict with which the symbols are associated, the distinguishing feature of the mechanism of projection is the assignment to others of qualities, characteristics, and motives that actually relate to oneself. When attributed to someone else, such qualities are less anxiety-provoking than they would be if they were identified as one's own. Instead of thinking, "I want to hurt him," the person believes, "He wants to hurt me." When asked why he did something naughty, a small child will frequently point to a brother or sister and say, "He made me do it."

Although the militant fanatic who crusades violently against some special form of "sinfulness" seems to be motivated by his own impulses to engage in the behaviors against which he crusades, his platform must be judged on the basis of its own merits, not on the personal motivations of its protagonist. Similarly, the case for or against capital punishment, changes in procedures for treating criminals and delinquents, and the modification of laws protecting persons accused of subversion must be evaluated on the basis of argument and evidence that pertains to the issue. This caution is necessary since stands on either side of such issues can be attributed to psychological motivation to protect against anxieties associated with the expression of unacceptable impulses. The person who projects his own intense aggressive impulses to others believes that the only effective deterrent to homicide is the execution of convicted murderers. Even though such an analysis explains why some persons argue with great vehemence in favor of capital punishment, the validity of the argument must be established or refuted apart from the motivations of its critics or proponents.

In an interesting study of the processes of projection, members of a fraternity were asked to rate both themselves and the other members on stinginess, obstinacy, disorderliness, and bashfulness. Each student's ratings of himself were compared to his ratings of others and with the averaged ratings assigned to him by the group. It was found that the students who tended to rate others as possessing specific undesirable characteristics and themselves as acceptable in the same characteristics were actually rated by the group as possessing the particular undesirable traits to a high degree. For example, the persons who scored themselves as being generous, but who were evaluated by the group as being stingy, tended to judge the other members of the fraternity as being stingy. Such conclusions applied only to those students whose self-ratings deviated markedly from the ratings assigned to them by others (9).

The use of projection to ward off anxiety accompanying guilt reactions is suggested by the results of a study of eight-year-old children (15). After each child had been given a desirable toy and one that was less desirable, they were divided into two groups. Each child in one group was then asked to give one of the toys to another child. The children in both groups were then asked which toy another child would have given him. The children who had been asked to give up a toy indicated more frequently than did the others that their friends would have given the less preferred toys. Actually having to give up the toy initiated a sequence of reactions that included conflict between the desire to be greedy and the wish to be good, guilt over retaining the favored toy, anxiety aroused by the "bad" feeling of greediness, and defense against the anxiety by imputing stinginess or greed to the friend.

Although it has an internally adaptive and protective function, extreme reliance on projection may result in behaviors that are obviously characteristic of inadequate psychological development. For example, the projective mechanism is observed in the delusions of very disturbed persons, who may be terrified by what they "see" or "hear," who may be impelled into violence to "protect" themselves, or who may carry out "messages" to inflict harm on others.

DISPLACEMENT

Displacement is another major transforming defense mechanism that protects against the conscious recognition of anxiety-provoking impulses or wishes. This protection is achieved by channeling an impulse or wish toward persons or objects other than those toward whom it was initially directed.

The displacement process has been illustrated in various cartoon sequences, such as the one that begins with a husband's meekly accepting his wife's abuse at home. The scene then shifts to the husband's office, where he is shown as a raging tyrant, shouting orders and frightening his employees. The implication is that since he was unable to express hostility toward his wife, he redirected his pent-up feelings toward his subordinates.

Displacement is illustrated by an event that occurred in an English literature class. The morning had been an extremely trying one for Carol, who had received a phone call from her mother before she left the dormitory. Phone calls from home were always difficult. Her mother usually gave her a little lecture and although Carol did not know why, the trivial suggestions her mother made during these discussions upset her. Today's call was even more trying than usual. Not only did her mother make suggestions as to how she might rearrange her room in the dormitory and what she should wear at the formal, she also told Carol that her plan to spend Easter vacation with her roommate was unacceptable. Since she saw her parents frequently, she couldn't see the point to her mother's insistence that they would miss her if she didn't come home. Carol recalled that it had always been like this; whenever she wanted very much to do something, her mother always managed to overrule her. She disliked herself for always giving in so meekly and decided that someday she would really be able to handle the situation without having to comply with her mother's wishes.

Carol's thoughts about vacation were interrupted by Professor Jones' remarks about the poor work turned in by the students on his last examination. He said that some members of the class with unusual ability were doing work that was far beneath their capabilities. Carol felt that he was looking at her when he made this remark, and she felt guilty. She wondered why everyone had to pick on her. At the end of the hour, the professor asked her to remain. "Here it comes," she said to herself and suddenly, without further thought, she began accusing the professor of being the poorest teacher she had ever heard of. Through her tears and temper, she went on to shout many insults at him. After she had calmed down, she realized that Professor Jones had only asked her to remain for a few minutes, that he had said nothing else to her. And the strange thing about it was that she really liked him.

The process of displacement is usually not so obvious as it is in this example. The transforming of impulses or wishes occurs without our knowledge, although, in retrospect, we well might wonder how such strong feelings came to be elicited by the particular situation.

When anxiety is evoked by the impulse to express positive feelings, they also may be displaced. If their expression would be threatening, strong feelings of affection for one person might be redirected more "safely" toward a different person or, as is sometimes the case, toward animals, or into activities that bring some gratification without involving a risk of provoking anxiety.

COMPENSATION

The mechanism of compensation resembles that of displacement, for it directs the individual's energy and effort toward objectives different from those with which they were originally associated. Not only does compensation transform the symbol that represents the impulse, but it is accomplished through activity that is different in form and character from the initiating impulse. For example, aggressive impulses come to have neither an aggressive form nor an aggressive meaning as far as the individual is concerned.

Impulses or wishes that cannot be directed toward their original objectives are provided with compensatory gratifications via substitute outlets. The original and popular meaning of compensation differs from that presented above. Alfred Adler originated the term "compensation" and used it in conjunction with his theory that man's activities are directed toward overcoming real or imagined inferiorities (2). He described it as the process of mastering a limitation or handicap by developing supplemental strengths and skills, and it is in this sense that the term is popularly used. Demosthenes is said to have compensated for a childhood speech impediment by becoming a great orator. Many oversimplified psychological explanations of the behavior of famous figures, such as Napoleon and Franklin D. Roosevelt, have been presented in terms of the compensatory process. Although Napoleon's small stature may have played some part in his ambitions, an explanation of his behavior based solely on the idea that he was compensating for his lack of height fails to do justice to the complexity of the psychological processes that motivate men.

Compensation can be viewed as one of the defenses protecting the individual from anxiety. Activities that would evoke anxiety by forcing conscious recognition of impulses, wishes, or thoughts are put aside in favor of activities that enable the individual to express his impulses in disguised form. When such compensatory activities contribute to enhanced self-esteem while they assist in the reduction of anxiety, they resemble the mastery mechanisms described later in this chapter.

REACTION FORMATION

In reaction formation the anxiety-evoking symbols, impulses, or wishes are transformed into their opposites. An individual may even resort to activities that bring him into contact with his most severe conflicts. Thus, the person who defies death in aerial acrobatics may actually be motivated by his own anxieties related to death.

Through the use of reaction formation, the individual may develop characteristics or traits that are directly opposite to those he cannot accept in himself. The "brave" acrobat refuses to admit, even to himself, that the thought of death evokes unusual anxieties. The individual who cannot express intense hostility directly may defend himself against anxiety by transforming his hostility into lavish affection. In like manner, a person who is threatened by his affection for another may be critical of and hostile to that person. The "virtuous" person who is "shocked" by stories of immorality may be transforming his sexual pleasure or curiosity into disdain in order to protect himself from the anxiety that would ensue if he became aware of his own impulses. Many prize-fighters are said to be worried about their masculinity.

Reaction formation may be particularly evident during adolescence. Many of the acts of bravado, defiance, and self-assertion that characterize this period may actually represent reaction formation to impulses and wishes which are thought to be cowardly or childlike. If an adolescent admitted his fear or his dependency, he would become anxious and his self-esteem would suffer.

RATIONALIZATION

The defense mechanism known as rationalization affords protection against anxiety by the unconscious provision of acceptable reasons or excuses for the impulses or motives that actually impelled the person to action. In this, the most apparent of the defense mechanisms, the observer may note inconsistencies and faulty thinking as the person attempts to justify his behavior. Thus, the teacher who "explains" his severe and punitive attitudes toward his students by insisting that such treatment helps them build "character" may be known to his associates as being indifferent to his pupils' well-being. By rationalizing, a person is able to avoid the anxiety and guilt he would feel if he admitted impulses or wishes that are inconsistent with his self concept. Although rationalization may enable a person temporarily to maintain his self-respect, such respect is achieved by self-deception and its value is limited. If the rationalizer does not continually enlarge his self-justifying explanations, he will eventually be trapped into acknowledging the inadequacies of his own beliefs about himself. The value of the defense is further limited, for it prevents the person from appraising his own efforts and performance accurately. The rationalizer may fail to learn from experience and is often inclined to extend his rationalizations rather than to alter his behavior.

The rationalization process allows a person to present reasons for his attitudes or behaviors that are acceptable to himself and that are usually socially desirable or logical. The reasons offered are the result of the defensive process, however, and they are not those that actually account for the behavior in question.

Two manifestations of the rationalization process have been termed the "sour grape" and the "sweet lemon" techniques. The "sour grape" mechanism derives its name from the legend of the fox who, when he found that he was unable to jump high enough to reach a bunch of grapes, decided that they were sour and undesirable. Similarly, an individual may defend himself against loss of self-esteem by convincing himself that his goals are really not desirable. The "sweet lemon" technique allows a person to defend himself against anxiety and loss of self-esteem by seeing the "bright" side or the advantages of his situation. This "Pollyanna" technique may be used to excuse himself for giving up or for not trying. In discussing the fact that he had not learned to read, an adolescent boy of average intelligence said, "Actually, it's a good thing I never learned to read, since this way I won't have trouble with my eyes."

INTELLECTUALIZATION

Intellectualization could be classified either as a defense mechanism or as a mastery mechanism, for it may function to maintain the personality or to enhance it. Projection, displacement, compensation, and rationalization all involve some transformation or disguising of the symbols associated with unacceptable impulses or wishes before they are permitted entry into awareness. This is not necessarily the case with the process of intellectualization. Symbols associated with the conflict area or experience may be admitted into awareness, *but* they have become isolated from the impulses with which they were initially associated, impulses involved in intrapersonal conflict and invested with emotion.

In the process of intellectualization, threatening impulses or wishes are isolated from the ideas, visual images, or memories that symbolize them. The symbols themselves may appear directly in consciousness and be the subject of the thoughts, preoccupations, and philosophizing of the individual, or they may be partially modified and disguised. The prolonged discussions of the adolescent about sex, or the preoccupation of many adults with horror stories or with sadistic sexual detective stories, may represent attempts to deal with unresolved conflict areas.

Highly abstract and philosophic discussions of love, religion, and the meaning of human existence also may represent, in part, the process of intellectualization, even though academic and theoretical issues may seem far removed from specific concerns about sex, morality, or death. Such concerns may provide the impetus for highly abstract speculations and in this way an individual may be able to make a preliminary approach to issues that arouse anxiety. By isolating the impulse from its intellectual content (symbol), the individual may be able to confront issues that trouble him, to talk, to think, and to read about them and even to share his thoughts with others. Thus, under certain circum stances, the conditions that provoke anxiety in these areas for him may decrease. With increased knowledge and with the feeling that others share his concerns, the emotional charge of the impulse is lessened and to that extent, the process has a mastery as well as a defensive character.

Depending upon the function that intellectualization serves for a given person, whether that of defense, mastery, or both, reliance upon this mechanism may result in the acquisition of knowledge, in the development of abstract academic, scientific, or esthetic interests, and in skills in the communication of such interests. Intellectualization may account for the scientist's objectivity in research or the surgeon's dispassionate attitude during an operation.

Mechanisms of Mastery

Defensive patterns of behavior are neither discrete nor distinct; they merge into one another, and in practice it may be difficult to discriminate among them. Not only are the boundaries that separate one mechanism from another arbitrarily determined, but in reality the list may be longer or shorter than the one presented here. Many of the texts recommended at the end of this chapter catalog the mechanisms somewhat differently; but however they are catalogued they have a common function, that of defending against the disruptive effects of anxiety, and a common aim, that of maintaining and protecting the personality. Each of them is to some extent self-deceptive, and to this extent, each reduces the individual's opportunity for achieving adequate relationships with others or for realizing his full potential.

It has been noted that these internally adaptive patterns of behavior are universally employed and that their use by an individual is not in itself a significant indicator of maladjustment. Furthermore, the mechanisms of defense supplement those of mastery in a positive manner. Distinctions between the defense and the mastery mechanisms rest not on the forms of the behavioral patterns, but on the functions they serve. Those patterns that contribute to self-esteem and that reduce anxiety by decreasing the intensity of intrapsychic conflict are termed *mastery mechanisms*. As the discussion of intellectualization indicated, a particular behavioral pattern may serve both adaptive functions: defense and mastery.

In the mastery mechanism the significance of the environment as an influence on self-perception is directly acknowledged. Although it cannot be assumed that success in mastering his environment is an accurate measure of an individual's psychological development, it similarly cannot be assumed that psychological development is completely independent of the successes achieved in coping with the challenges that living entails. The reactions of others, particularly parents, friends, and teachers, to the individual's behaviors, to behaviors that are judged good and bad or that are evaluated as successes and failures, are reinforcing. From the reactions of others to his efforts the individual's self-concept is reinforced, modified, or in some instances threatened.

The relation between psychological development and achievement (defined as the acquisition of prestige, power, or wealth) cannot be detailed in any general statement. The significance of attainment to the individual depends on the motives underlying the achievement, the needs satisfied by such attainment, and the sources of self-esteem available to the person. The significance to the individual of his achievements depends also on the extent of his intrapsychic conflict and the pattern of his defenses. Yet from what we have said of the basis for judging psychological development it is clear that the inclusion of the use of the individual's abilities in satisfying and productive activity—where the defining criteria of *productive* is the degree to which the activity contributes to the development of others—necessitates a consideration of the individual's social and occupational performance. The mastery mechanisms and behaviors relate the possible effects of such performance to the personality, particularly of those aspects of social performance that most clearly express the personality in its interaction with the environment.

At times, a defense mechanism may pave the way for eventual mastery of problems involved in intrapsychic conflict: defensive behavior may provide an individual with the time he needs to master a conflict and may afford him the protection he requires before he can approach his conflict areas.

Consider the situation of a secretary whose difficulties in relating to her male employers were at least partially reflective of unresolved intrapsychic conflict that began in early experiences with her father. Her feelings of hostility toward male authority, her belief that such feelings were morally wrong, and her desire to please others in order to be liked, all combined to evoke intense anxiety. Without the protection afforded by her defenses, she would have been unable to function in a work situation with a male employer. As it was, the emotional force of her long-standing conflict was sufficiently separated from its content to allow her to perform her duties satisfactorily and to maintain adequate, if not perfect, relationships with her employer and with her office associates. Not only was she able to redirect the aggression she felt toward her employer, but she felt less compelled to produce superior work at any cost than would have been the case had she not been protected against the anxieties precipitated in this area. By enabling her to remain in the situation, her defenses permitted her to have new experiences in which she could evaluate and appraise her own reactions. Given sufficient time, she began to understand that the feelings which may have been appropriate in her relationship with her father were inappropriate in her relationship to her employer, who literally was not her father and who was unlike him.

This insight was followed by increasing awareness of her own feelings. As it became possible for her to enjoy a comfortable and pleasant working relationship with her employer, the general anxieties precipitated by male authority figures lessened. Eventually the intensity of her hostility toward males and her tendency to express such hostility diminished, along with her feelings of unworthiness and guilt when she was criticized. Finally, she was able to recall early painful experiences with her own father, and with such recall there was some change in the emotional reactions aroused by him (and others "like him").

This illustration demonstrates the reduction in intrapsychic tensions that may result from the combined operation of mastery and defense mechanisms. If his conflicts are not severely disabling initially, this type of experience may enable a resourceful person with adequate defenses to substitute new reactions for his habitual inappropriate feelings. The example indicates the intimate relationship between the two types of adaptive mechanisms. It also demonstrates the way in which mastery mechanisms may effect a reduction in intrapsychic conflict, but it should not be interpreted to suggest that such conflict is easily resolvable by following a prescribed formula.

The mastery of conflict and of the anxiety associated with it is achieved in different ways by different persons. These patterns of mastery have some attributes that resemble those of the defense mechanisms, but they are less specific and consequently more difficult to catalog. For example, although identification will be discussed as a mastery mechanism, under certain conditions it might be included in a list of defense mechanisms.

IDENTIFICATION

Identification involves the adoption of values and attitudes that significantly influence how the individual thinks of himself and how he wants to be seen by others. If projection is thought of as a process that provides a person with a psychological means for ridding himself of unacceptable impulses, then identification may be thought of as its opposite. Through identification with persons who have exercised a significant influence on his development, an individual takes to himself the attributes, standards, and characteristics that are valued by them.

The identification mechanism may be operative in the behavior of the small girl who plays house or in the boy whose idol is a popular sports figure. Although identification may be self-deceptive, enabling a person to think of himself as possessing qualities that are not actually his, the identification process may serve more than a protective function. By taking as his own the standards and qualities he considers admirable in another person, an individual's actions may be influenced, even though he does not consciously or specifically acknowledge their source. Identification results in acquiring behaviors, thoughts, and values in some degree similar to those of a "model," but this process is different from frank imitation and more complex. A person's imitative behavior may be considered identification if he believes that he really does possess the attributes of the model. The person who identifies with another may acquire not only definite behavioral attributes but also certain feelings of conviction or of power that are in a sense "borrowed."

Identification plays an important role in defining the qualities for which an individual will esteem himself. Although the possession of certain values does not insure their expression in behavior, when valued behaviors do occur, they are reinforced by the person himself, and thus they are likely to be repeated and extended. Such repetition and generalization enhance self-esteem and also delimit the area of activities, symbols, and impulses associated with intrapsychic conflict. The process of identification probably plays an important role in accounting for the acquisition of societal values and in the learnings that preserve the cultural heritage.

MASTERY BEHAVIORS

In learning to master themselves and their environments, individuals may exhibit many behaviors or patterns of behavior that are too variable to be classified as mechanisms; nevertheless, they are of great significance in the assessment of psychological development.

The process of psychological development consists essentially of the individual's gradual acquisition of the skills and knowledge he requires to meet the demands of both his environment and his impulses, and to mediate between them. All specific knowledge and skills are potential mastery behaviors, but their actual contribution at any specific time to enhanced self-esteem and to the reduction of intrapsychic conflict depends on many factors involving the environmental situation, the individual's

Challenge and response!

The world is comprised of all kinds of challenges—some small, some significant. Some baffle, intrigue, and gratify, some bring defeat and despair. Challenge represents the opportunity for social progress and, for the individual, provides his chance to master his environment and to increase his knowledge and extend his skills. In rising to the challenge the person focuses his attention and mobilizes his energies; previous learnings are applied, adapted, and combined and, when the challenge is met, the person's response repertoire has been increased and his self-satisfaction enhanced.

The child is curious and responsive to the mysteries of his environment; he has great potential to learn—and he *will* learn if his efforts to do so are encouraged, if there is meaning for him in the challenge, and if those who are responsible for his learning value learning and value him.

Wayne Miller—Magnum

capacity, the nature of his conflicts, and his ability to utilize his personal resources.

Although it would be erroneous to believe that every person's psychological development is directly related to the extent of his knowledge and skill, there is an important relationship between the two. The term *knowledge* is a broad one and includes understanding of the physical world, of self, of people, of their history, and of the factors related to their behavior. The level of development achieved by any individual can often be raised by his acquisition of new knowledge and skills, which can contribute to enhanced self-esteem, to a reduction of anxiety, and to the more effective use of his talents and abilities.

It will be recalled that secondary reinforcement can extend the range of stimuli which evoke a conditioned fear reaction, so that previously neutral situations become stimulating. Stimuli which arouse feelings of threat may bear little resemblance to those initially associated with the conflict. The less knowledge a person has of the relationships between himself and events in his external world, the greater is the likelihood of this kind of generalization among very dissimilar stimuli. In contrast, the more knowledge a person possesses, the more opportunity he has for making appropriate discriminations between those situations that actually possess the potential to hurt him and those that are harmless.

Possession of information may not be sufficient to counteract long-standing anxieties, those incurred under severe stress, or those associated with intrapsychic conflict of moderate to severe intensity. Under such circumstances, mastery behavior requires not only knowledge but also the experience of re-encountering the anxiety-provoking stimuli under new and less stressful circumstances. Such experience may be achieved by some persons in the normal courses of their lives, but others may benefit from the services of professional persons in specialized situations who can help to provide the experience necessary for mastery over intrapsychic conflicts.

Mastery mechanisms, those processes that contribute to self-esteem and to the reduction of intrapsychic conflict, play an important role in human development. The behaviors associated with these processes are of interest to society, for it is through them that a person not only approaches his own potential but also becomes able to contribute to the development of others. It is through such behaviors that human beings are able to exercise their faculties and to be more than passive organisms, blindly and mechanically responding to the forces that impinge upon them or to their own impulses. Further, it is through mastery behaviors that individuals demonstrate the constructive, integrative, and creative qualities that are among the essential characteristics of the life process.

Summary

In the complicated process of growing up in a confusing, competitive world, the individual comes to realize that society fails to provide the protections he desires; that it imposes many restrictions upon his behaviors, thwarting his attempts to satisfy his increasingly complex physical and psychological needs. Early in his life he experiences the unpleasant by-products of conflict and frustration, and he begins the long and difficult process of learning to avoid them, minimize them, or deal with them constructively.

The process of personal and social development thus consists of the individual's acquiring new behaviors and refining old ones, or adapting and utilizing techniques, skills, and knowledge designed to satisfy his needs. And to the extent that all that all these changes in behavior result from experience and not from physical growth changes, they are said to be learned.

Learning is such a complex process that it is probable that no one theory can explain it. It has been suggested, however, that "operant conditioning" might offer the most explicit, precise statements available about unintentional learning, that "trial and error" learning might best be explained by reinforcement-conditioning theories, and that "insight" learning is more completely accounted for by cognitive-expectancy theories.

The operation of many of these principles is apparent in the learning of adaptive patterns of behavior. These adaptive patterns may serve protective functions, in which the disruptive effects of anxiety are guarded against, as well as mastery functions, in which self-esteem is enhanced and intrapsychic conflict is reduced.

The combined operation of mastery and defense behaviors in reducing intrapsychic tension can enable individuals to be more than passive organisms, blindly and mechanically responding to forces impinging upon them. The more knowledge a person has of himself and of the relationships between himself and the events in the external world, the more likely he is to make appropriate generalizations and discriminations, the more able he is to counteract anxiety effectively and to demonstrate his constructive and creative qualities.

References

1. Aborn, M., The influence of experimentally induced failure on the retention of material acquired through set and incidental learning. *J. exp. Psychol.*, 1953, *45,* 225–231.

2. Adler, A. *Study of Organ Inferiority and Its Psychical Compensation.* Washington: Nervous and Mental Disease Publishing Company, 1917.
3. Dollard, J., and Miller, N. E. *Personality and Psychotherapy.* New York: McGraw-Hill, 1950.
4. Hilgard, E. R. *Introduction to Psychology* (ed. 2). New York: Harcourt, 1957.
5. Hilgard, E. R. *Theories of Learning* (ed. 2). New York: Appleton, 1960.
6. Hilgard, E. R., and Marquis, D. G. *Conditioning and Learning.* New York: Appleton, 1940.
7. McGinnies, E. M. Emotionality and perceptual defense. *Psychol. Rev.,* 1949, *56,* 244–251.
8. Meltzer, H. Individual differences in forgetting pleasant and unpleasant experiences. *J. ed. Psych.,* 1930, *21,* 399–409.
9. Sears, R. R. Experimental studies of projection: I. Attribution of traits. *J. soc. Psychol.,* 1936, *7,* 151–163.
10. Skinner, B. F. Teaching machines. *Science,* 1958, *128,* 269–977.
11. Tinklepaugh, O. L. An experimental study of representative factors in monkeys. *J. comp. physiol. Psychol.,* 1928, *8,* 197–236.
12. Verplanck, W. S. The control of the content of conversation: Reinforcement of statements of opinion. *J. abnorm. soc. Psychol.,* 1955, *51,* 668–676.
13. Watson, J. B., and Rayner, R. Conditioned emotional reactions. *J. exp. Psychol.,* 1920, *3,* 1–14.
14. Wolfe, J. B. Effectiveness of token-rewards for chimpanzees. *Comp. Psychol. Monogr.,* 1936, *12,* No. 60.
15. Wright, B. A. Altruism in children and the perceived conduct of others. *J. abnorm. soc. Psychol.,* 1942, *37,* 218–233.

Selected Readings

Bruner, J. S. *The Process of Education.* Cambridge, Mass.: Harvard University Press, 1960.
Hebb, D. O. *The Organization of Behavior.* New York: Wiley, 1949.
Hilgard, E. R. *Theories of Learning.* New York: Appleton, 1948.
Mowrer, O. H. *Learning Theory and Behavior.* New York: Wiley, 1960.
Osgood, C. E. *Method and Theory in Experimental Psychology.* New York: Oxford University Press, 1953 (Part III, "Learning").
Woodworth, R. S. *Dynamics of Behavior.* New York: Holt, 1958.

PART TWO

Personality Development and the Life Cycle

FROM BIRTH to death, life is a continuing succession of events and experiences, complexly interrelated and ever changing. The task of understanding a person and his life is both difficult and challenging. It is a task with which novelists and scientists and, in a way, nearly all persons are occupied. To understand another person—or oneself—is clearly a valued goal, but the pathways to such knowledge are numerous; they lead in different directions, they are sometimes indistinct and may even be indiscernible. In an attempt to map these pathways, a frame of reference for categorizing behaviors, events, and experiences was presented in the previous chapters.

Now this frame of reference will be fitted into a mold set by the life span, one that accommodates development from birth and infancy through adolescence and the early adult years to the middle and later adult years and death. These periods overlap and merge into each other; in each it is possible to note some of the physical, social, and psychological events affecting the individual and his development, events commonly confronted by persons within the same phase of the life cycle, but to which they respond uniquely and in terms of their own previous experiences and present expectations.

6.

Infancy and Early Childhood

This chapter is concerned with the first five years of the child's life, a period during which dramatic changes occur in his appearance, size, skills, and ability to communicate. Infancy, the period from birth to the child's second year, and early childhood, extending to his fifth year, cover the span through which he progresses from the helpless state of the baby to the remarkably self-reliant youngster who can be away from home for considerable intervals of time every day, can feed and dress himself, and is ready to associate with strangers, both children and adults.

In the past, depending upon the times, the culture, and the disciplines to which they were committed, writers have presented many different views of childhood. Early Greek and Roman writers were concerned about the child only as a future citizen. During the eighteenth century, the moral nature of the child was debated by philosophers and theologians; by some he was seen as "innately depraved," born in sin, and by others as possessing inherent goodness. To Locke, the baby's mind was a "tabula rasa," a blank sheet, and Rousseau, a French philosopher and teacher, believed the child possessed an innate moral sense and should be permitted freedom to develop his potentialities without the corrupting restraints imposed by society.

Many regarded the child as a miniature adult, and consequently they had little understanding of his developmental status or the nature of his psychological and social growth. Until recently, within the last eighty years, the prevalent viewpoints were those mentioned above. The scientific collection of data pertaining to children's behavior and growth did not begin until the 1880's with the work of Preyer, who presented methodical observations of young children in the form of "baby biographies." Since that time, persons trained in such field as psychology, sociology, anthropology, and psychiatry have systematically observed children and have related these observations to theories of child development. The material that follows is drawn primarily from the data of these investigators, whose work lies within a specialized field of knowledge, child psychology.

Physical Development

INFANCY

At birth, the infant (or neonate) is a dependent and helpless creature with a vast capacity for physical growth and development. He possesses the potential to see, to hear, to differentiate people and things, to manage his own movements, and to fend for himself, though of course he now can do none of these things. In his development he will share with others of his age group some observable characteristics of growth and increasing physical proficiency, characteristics that are independent of his culture or his learning opportunities.

At birth, he possesses the essential systems of the body and is able to register all kinds of sensations, though perhaps not acutely; he can make many complex sensory and motor responses, though they are largely reflexive. For example, the infant reacts to light almost immediately after birth, and although his pupil will dilate or contract reflexively, depending on the amount of light to which it is exposed, he is not able to focus on near or distant objects because the requisite nerves and muscles have not yet developed. When the optic nerve and ciliary muscles of the eye have matured sufficiently (during the two to three weeks following the child's birth), he is able to accommodate to near and distant objects and to follow their movements across his field of vision. Similarly, though the potential is present at birth, the infant requires a period of weeks to months before he can distinguish colors and coordinate his hand and eye movements.

The ability to taste and smell appears very soon after birth. After the first two or three months the infant can detect changes in his formula; moreover, although he may be deaf for a brief period because of mucus in the ear canal, he soon responds to sounds. In addition to his responses to these stimuli and to temperature, pain, and kinesthetic stimuli, the neonate is able to perform such complex activities as sucking, swallowing, crying, hiccoughing, shuddering, and stretching.

Growth, Maturation, and Learning

During the first years, the infant's quantitative change in bodily dimensions, or his *growth*, and his qualitative changes in complexity of structure, or his *maturation*, occur at a rapid rate that slows down as he enters early and middle childhood. This development follows an orderly sequence; it has a definite pattern, in which areas of the body adjacent to the spinal cord develop at a more rapid pace than those which are distant from it, and in which the development of the head proceeds at a more rapid rate than areas of the body farthest from the head. Such growth makes it possible for the infant to acquire the skills of movement. No attempt will be made here to give a detailed description of the gradual development from fairly simple head and arm movements to the more complicated ones involved in walking, writing, and speaking. The important point is that their development results from the interaction of physical growth, maturation, and learning, and parents who attempt to teach skills before the child attains the degree of growth and maturation necessary will meet with little success.

When accounting for the acquisition of new behavioral patterns, it is often difficult to identify and distinguish the contributions of maturational and environmental factors. Studies seeking to make such an identification have attempted to minimize the subjects' opportunities for practice and learning or have provided training while making allowance for the individual's maturational level. For example, Hopi children, who except for short periods of freedom are confined to cradle boards during their first months of life, were studied by Dennis to determine the effects of this restriction (10). The findings indicated that cradle-board children walked at about the same age as those whose movements were not restricted. In other studies, children's performance levels in activities such as stair climbing, typing, and memorizing digits were noted and the amount of training at various maturational levels was varied, depending upon the specific experimental conditions. Identical twins were often utilized, so that the performance level of the child who received training in the activity could be compared to his twin who did not.

In general, the findings indicate that little is gained by training a child in complex motor skills before he has achieved the maturational level that will enable him to profit from such instruction. A mother, for example, would do well to postpone her attempts to train her child to control his bowel movements until he is approximately eighteen months old. By this time, the development of the neural tracts essential for voluntary control of the muscles involved in defecation is complete, and the infant can learn to empty his bowels voluntarily.

What does the future hold for this new arrival?

From the warmth and safety of his intrauterine environment he has emerged into a world that will no longer respond automatically to his needs; a world that requires him to breathe and digest his own food; a world of whose definition and meaning he will only gradually become aware; a world that, as his sensory organs and muscles develop, slowly becomes recognizable and manageable.

From his biological beginnings the qualities of humanism can flower. Whether the infant's potential humanity will become fully realized depends on many factors—time, learning, and environmental circumstances. With good fortune he will think, reason, and respond to beauty, he will become an individual with his own identity and conscience, he will care for himself and for others— and eventually, he will transmit his genetic and cultural inheritance.

Irrespective of where or to whom he is born the appearance of the new arrival renews the cycle of man—he is the future.

Wayne Miller—Magnum

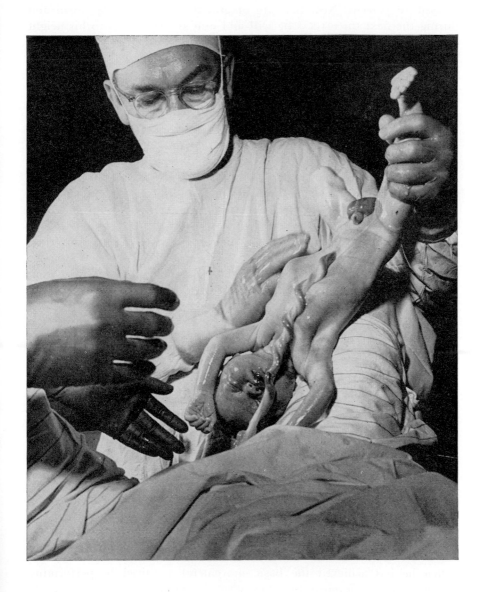

THE YOUNG CHILD

During the transition from the dependency of infancy to the activity of early childhood, many changes occur. The two-year-old has grown in size; since birth his weight has tripled and his height has increased 70 percent. Now his rate of growth begins to slow down and during the next three years he will add nine or ten inches to his height and will gain about fifteen pounds.

Complex Motor Skills

As his legs grow faster than the rest of him, his general body proportions have become much more adultlike and he begins to lose his "top-heavy" look. The babyish cast of his face is disappearing, and his features are becoming more individualized and definitive. Accompanying these alterations in bodily proportions is the impressive development of the skeletal, muscular, and nervous systems that account for the preschool child's increased endurance and proficiency in motor skills. Instead of the awkward, rather poorly coordinated, gross movements of the young infant, the child from two to five displays increasingly adept, fluid, and controlled movements. Much research has been concerned with this development, and studies have been made of the development of the specific motor skills that together account for the increasing physical facility the child demonstrates as he grows older. It has been noted, for example, that while some children are proficient in skills such as climbing, skipping, throwing a ball, or tricycling before three, the majority of children show a degree of skill in these activities by the age of six.

One developmental study of this type (22) utilized teachers' observations of over 2000 four-, five-, and six-year-olds. These observations supported the view that between the stage during which the child makes no attempt to perform a task and that at which he attains a high order of proficiency in it, he will progress through two intervening steps. One involves the development of the required skills. In these he may demonstrate various levels:

> Attempts activity but seeks help or support;
> Tries even when not helped or supported, but is inept;
> Is progressing but is still using unnecessary movements;
> Is practicing basic movements;
> Is refining movements.

When he has achieved the basic movements required in performing specific activities, levels of proficiency within the next step are noted. He may show:

Coordinated movements;
Easy performance with display of satisfaction;
Evidence of accuracy, poise, and grace.

Gutteridge notes that following this period, the final stage in the developmental sequence involves the adroit execution of the skill with variations in its use (22).

As in the period of infancy, learning and maturational factors combine to provide the development of motor skills. Although specific skills such as shooting marbles, writing, talking, and buttoning clothes require practice and imitation, the fact that certain skills develop in most children at certain ages indicates the significance of maturational factors. Other complex skills, such as ball throwing, seem to improve not with specific but with general practice of other activities, so long as these activities utilize some of the coordinated movements necessary in the complex skill. Research suggests that although the infant performs about equally well on all motor skill tests, his proficiency in the various skills will tend to vary as he grows into the early childhood period. Thus, he may throw a ball in a clumsy manner, yet ride a tricycle very well (7).

Sensory Judgments

Closely related to the young child's development in motor skill is his increasing ability to make sensory judgments. Much human behavior involves reactions to objects in the environment and to the individual as an object. During early childhood his accurate perceptions of such objects increase as the cerebral cortex and frontal lobes of the brain develop and enable him to take advantage of his additional experience. With increased physical capacity and experience, his ability to blend the sensations of hearing, sight, taste, smell, and touch improves. He not only can associate one sensory experience with another but now can name these sensations and perceptions. And in developing the ability to judge size and shape, distance and space, speed and direction of movement, and time intervals, the image he acquires of himself as a physical entity becomes more sharply defined.

The development of motor skills and his increased adeptness in making sensory judgments contribute to the child's ability to identify himself in relation to other persons; through the use of his fine muscles, his skill in manipulating objects and in moving himself about, and his eventual use of language, the child gradually becomes aware of the degree to which he can control and manipulate his environment to decrease its threatening aspects and increase its gratifying ones. These abilities gradually appear and improve during the first several years of the child's life. Since they are based upon maturation, they are observable in almost all children, but this does not mean that every child will have the same psychological experiences associated with their development. Physical, social, and cultural factors of the environment interact with the effects of the maturational forces within the child to produce the unique individual.

Genetic Inheritance

The social and cultural forces that impinge upon the developing child blend to produce conditions never exactly duplicated in the developmental pattern of any other person. But before leaving the topic of physical development, it must again be emphasized that man's limits, as well as his potentialities, are set by his genetic inheritance. Diamond (11) states that, "individuality is no more than the quantitative variation in characteristics which are shared by all the members of a species. It is the species, not the individual, which determines the important dimensions of variation."

In addition to considering the maturational and environmental influences which account for the acquisition and demonstration of behaviors, Diamond's statement suggests that the emergence of some behaviors and the nonemergence of others are attributable to the characteristics of the species. Such a view is supported by the work of comparative psychologists, who endeavor to extend our knowledge of human behavior by studying phases of development shared with other species. In one interesting study by the Kelloggs (31), the motor and social development of an infant and a young chimpanzee were compared directly. When the study began, the infant, Donald, was two and a half months older than Gua, a seven-and-half-month-old chimpanzee. For nine months, the chimpanzee and the child lived in the same household and shared the experiences of being cared for, dressed, and fed; they had in common the parents' efforts to teach them the skills expected of the young child.

Gua seemed to learn some of the motor skills, such as holding a cup or using a spoon, more rapidly than Donald, possibly because the maturational levels required to perform these tasks are reached sooner in chimpanzees than in man. On child development tests that evaluated performance on tasks involving motor skills, the performance levels of Donald and Gua were comparable, and in many of their reactions to persons the similarities were striking. At the conclusion of the nine months, however, it seemed clear to the Kelloggs that Gua would not achieve the pattern of behavior expected of human beings. For example, they note that Gua:

. . . possessed fewer inhibitory responses than the human subject. She was thus a creature of more violent appetites and emotions, which swayed her this way and that, seemingly without consideration of the consequences. . . . She seemed to follow her ruling impulses with little permanent regard for restraining circumstances. In this respect she was coarser than the child and more elemental in her motives (31).

These conclusions could be interpreted to mean that Gua lacked some of the characteristics associated with ego processes. These processes control and direct the skills essential in achieving gratification of one's needs in the light of prevalent environmental conditions, and they necessitate both inhibitory responses and the anticipation of the consequences of one's behavior. As will be noted later in this chapter, the ego processes begin to emerge gradually in the human being and by his sixth month the beginnings of these processes are evident.

Genetically determined limits and potentialities of the species do not exclude the highly significant differences existing among human beings. Since these differences and the conditions accounting for them are of major concern in this text, attention is now directed to the crucial importance of social and cultural influences on the development of personality during infancy and early childhood.

Personality and Society

GENETIC AND ENVIRONMENTAL INFLUENCES

Within the range of his limits and potentialities as a member of the species of man, the individual's psychological development corresponds to the development of those reared in the same society and the same family. At the same time, each individual's development varies sufficiently from those of others to challenge the student of human behavior to account for human individuality.

Like all living organisms, the human being is responsive to his environment and requires from it the essentials for sustenance and survival. In the transactions between the individual and his surroundings, the direction as well as the detail of human development takes shape. Although environmental conditions operating prior to a child's birth markedly influence the direction of his development, it is in most societies only infrequently that the effects of a vitamin deficiency, an infection, or the action of x-rays sufficiently disturb the environment provided by the mother to contribute to developmental disorder.

Following birth, the child's environment changes significantly. No longer are all his needs satisfied by his immediate surroundings. The environment is now more complex; the stimuli that impinge upon him are more varied and elicit a wider range of responses than those of his uterine existence. The infant's immediate surroundings following birth include other persons of whom he only gradually becomes aware but who nevertheless play a significant part in his development. These persons constitute a segment of the society into which the child is born. Their personalities incorporate the heritage of the past: the values, customs, and beliefs acquired from previous members of the society. These learnings, which represent the content of the civilization, are termed the *culture* and are transmitted indirectly to the child through his relationships and contacts with the persons who care for him. Thus the culture may provide the *content* of what the child learns; it may also influence *how* the parent perceives his responsibility to the child as well as his beliefs about appropriate child-rearing practices.

Anthropologists, sociologists, and psychologists, who are interested in the relationship between culture and personality and in the way in which society's beliefs, customs, and values become a part of the self of each individual, have studied child-rearing practices of many societies, some familiar, some distant and little known.

An example of the latter is found in the work of Dubois among the people of Alor, an island in the Dutch East Indies (13). The adult Alorese were characterized as suspicious, distrustful, anxious, and given to sporadic outbursts of aggression. Dubois attributes these personality characteristics to infant and childhood experiences that are severely frustrating. These begin as early as the child's second week of life, when the mother leaves him for the entire day in the casual care of older children or whomever else is available to feed him occasionally. This pattern of rejection and hostility continues as the child grows older.

Feeding frustrations increase as the child grows. Weaning may be hastened by the mother's second pregnancy. She weans the child by pushing him away or slapping him. The mother will sometimes deliberately stimulate jealousy in a child by taking another infant to feed. . . . After the child is three [he] spends the day playing near the house under the casual supervision of an older sibling or an aged adult. Under these conditions, the mother being absent from eight in the morning until five in the afternoon, feeding is sporadic. During the day the child shifts for himself. He gets scraps from other children.

Children's sleep is much disturbed: a good deal of activity goes on at night, dancing, wandering in the village, narrating dreams and eating. Many of the dances last all night, at which children of

five are often present. Children take cat naps when they can, on
the verandah or leaning against an adult. In other words, the sleep
and rest of the child is a matter of small concern to the parents.

Children are sent on errands very early, and are sent off in a
peremptory manner. There is no permissive, encouraging, nor even
deliberate training; they learn by restrictive injunctions, shame,
ridicule and intimidation. They are not taught many avoidances or
taboos. A boy often has . . . fingers and arrows poked into his
distended abdomen; if the child is irritated by this he is greeted by
cries: "Hit him. Kill him." The children do not have open fights,
but slyly pinch and run. Frightening children and threatening to
cut off hands or ears are common, but never for sexual misdeeds.
However, the severity of discipline or fright is not as decisive a
factor as the fact that the child may be punished on one occasion
and consoled on another for the same offense, and consequently he
can form no consistent picture of what adults expect of him.[1]

In contrast to the Alorese, the Japanese, according to Gorer, a
British anthropologist (20), emphasize indulgence with regard to infant
feeding. The Japanese baby is offered the breast before hunger signs
appear, and weaning takes place gradually. Gorer believes that these
infant experiences lead to a minimum of hunger anxiety, for Japanese
adults are typically indifferent to meal schedules. In regard to toilet
training, however, Gorer reported (though his observation has been
questioned) that in earlier times the Japanese placed considerable
emphasis upon regularity, with schedule lapses harshly punished. To
this early childhood training, he attributes the distaste of dirt and
emphasis upon rituals of neatness and tidiness of the adult Japanese.

Margaret Mead (35) describes the Arapesh of New Guinea as a
society in which cooperation toward a common goal is maintained
through person-to-person ties rather than through clique rivalries, and
she traces this pattern to the earliest experiences of the Arapesh infant.
The newborn child is fed and cared for continuously by both the mother
and the father. Breast feeding is permitted all day and is an experience
in which both mother and child delight. Children are handed from
relative to relative for care, learning early that security and affection
accompany each interpersonal relationship. The infant is encouraged to
play near the mother while she works and is warned never to venture
far from the familiar. Early experiences thus tend to reinforce the child's
belief that many sets of kind parents exist in the Arapesh community.

Evidence secured by anthropological studies of the type cited indicates that infant-rearing practices vary extensively from culture to

---

[1] Reprinted by permission from Cora Dubois, *The People of Alor*. Minneapolis,
University of Minnesota Press. Copyright, 1944, by the University of Minnesota.

culture and even within the same country. On the basis of sociological research conducted in the United States, Davis has suggested that child-rearing practices typical of middle-class families are not representative of lower-class families. The specific findings have been questioned by more recent investigators, but the general conclusion must be that the influence of the subcultures, centering about different ethnic, racial, or economic backgrounds within one country, is important in personality development. Davis' study emphasizes the fact that common citizenship among peoples of a country does not ensure a common culture. The subcultures in a society as complex as ours permit widely different patterns of child-rearing practices.

Although research has not resulted in the formulation of precise relationships between infant-rearing practices and personality traits or characteristics, there is support for the position that the infant's psychological development is affected by his early experiences with the persons responsible for his care. Such experiences involve a great deal more than the specific techniques of child care. In the study of relationships between physical needs and psychological development, careful consideration must be given to the quality of the relationship between the infant and those who care for him, the "climate" in which he is reared. What is the quality of the parent-child relationship? Do the parents value their children as children? Do they accept demands, noise, and various childlike behaviors as part of the developmental process? Are they able to limit the child's activity or direct the child without feeling guilty? Are they able to provide the child with a sense of stability and support?

These questions cannot always be answered by direct observation of the behavior of parents and children. Erikson describes an observer of American Indians who noted that Sioux parents and children who had been separated for long periods of time did not kiss each other publicly upon being reunited. The observer concluded that the Sioux parent has little regard for his child. However, Erikson describes the Sioux culture as one in which the child is actually highly valued and indulged. The Sioux adult, on the other hand, has concluded that the white man must hate his children, for he may physically strike them as well as scold and criticize them.

THE FAMILY AS A UNIT

Although its structure may vary from one culture to the next, the family, a group of individuals related to one another by blood and marriage and sharing a continuing relationship, constitutes the agency most directly responsible for the transmission of the cultural content of the society to the growing child. Sometimes, in addition to the care of the young, the family unit also assumes the responsibility for the protection and care of the aged and infirm. In American culture, these functions are now shared by other agencies.

The nature of the family unit depends partially upon the form of the marriage relationship. Although the focus in this text is on the monogamous marriage, it is not to be assumed that this marital arrangement, in which a man and a woman enter into a legally sanctioned and recognized continuing relationship with one another, is universal. In one tabulation of the marital relationships sanctioned by a large number of societies (32), monogamy was found to be practiced in only 66. There were 378 societies having a marital form known as polygyny, in which the husband is permitted more than one wife, and in 31 societies, the wife was permitted more than one husband.

In addition to the influence of the husband and wife relationship, economic considerations and customs also determine who is included within the familial arrangement. It may be extended beyond the husband and wife and their children to include many other relatives. It may also include individuals who live within the family and acquire the status of a relative even though no blood or marital ties exist.

The significance of the family—of the totality of relationships among its members—in the development of personality, is illustrated by several studies. In one study which compared the achievement of the children of immigrant parents from two different ethnic groups (50), it was noted that the pattern of family relationships in the two groups contrasted markedly. In the high achievement group, the mother was the dominant parent, but decisions regarding family issues were discussed and considered openly by all the members, among whom there was an appreciable closeness. In the low achievement group, family relationships formed a pattern centering about a dominant, authoritarian father and a passive, submissive mother. In this group the father was not particularly approachable, and he often made the decisions for the entire family without consulting the other members.

The significant effect of the total pattern of family relationships on the direction of an individual's development is shown also in a study conducted by Stolz and her associates of children born during wartime (49). The effect of the absence of the father during the first year of the child's life was considered. In comparing children whose fathers had been absent to children whose fathers stayed with the family, it appeared that the absence of the father had detrimental effects on the children's socialization and adjustment. They were more anxious, less socially mature, more dependent upon their mothers, and less able to benefit from their opportunities to learn than were the children whose fathers were present. In any interpretation of these findings, it is important to note that the re-entry of the father, a father whom the child had never known, caused a distinct change in the pattern of the relationship between the mother and the child. The effects of so abrupt a change in the total familial situation are highly significant, and were not due solely to the father's prior absence, but also to the shifts in the familial roles and responsibilities that occurred at the time of his departure and again upon his return.

After categorizing relationships within families, Baldwin (1) reported that children reared in families characterized by a warm, permissive, democratic atmosphere were inclined to be sociable, competitive, and active. Children from homes where more rigid restrictions were common tended to show little aggression, disobedience, initiative, or tenacity. Strict, authoritarian homes, according to a similar study by Radke (36), were apt to include children who showed little curiosity, originality, and spontaneous expression. Similar predictions might be made about the development of aggressiveness, passivity, and dependence. Several studies (28, 45) support the hypothesis that, in general, a child learns to be aggressive or passive or dependent when such behavior is reinforced through reward or special attention by parents. This reinforcement is not necessarily provided by parents consciously, nor is its rewarding aspect necessarily perceived consciously by the child. He may respond to more subtle cues, such as his mother's frown when he snatches a toy from his baby brother or his father's smile when he shows an interest in the football he was given for his birthday. However, our knowledge of the operation of secondary reinforcers and the reinforcing aspects of drive reduction indicates that the influence of parental behaviors on child behavior is a technical and complex subject. The reader is cautioned against the temptation to oversimplify and is advised to consult the references at the end of this chapter.

That the total pattern of familial relationships must be considered in identifying the developmental influences impinging upon the individual cannot be emphasized too strongly. An accurate picture of the family's influence on the individual requires the understanding of a complex pattern of interlocking relationships. This pattern is difficult to identify and understand without first considering the relationship of the members of the family to each other. The following discussion of the child's early relationships with his mother and father and siblings is only the starting point in understanding the family unit as such.

THE MATERNAL RELATIONSHIP

Through the hundreds of contacts that the helpless infant has with his mother as she tends to his needs for food, liquids, and warmth, he becomes a social being, one who is perceptive of others and their significance for him, who can fend for himself, and who eventually can care for others. The way he functions as a social being and the way he perceives himself and responds to others have their beginnings in these contacts. Experiences of which he is probably unaware and later will not remember, and that may occur prior to his knowing there is a world outside himself, are crucial to his social and psychological development. Such contacts follow a brief though frequently repeated sequence: physical need, heightened motor activity, and muscular tension; satisfaction of need, reduced motor activity, and lessening of muscular tension.

Within this sequence there are many possibilities for variation in the mother's approach to the child. To what needs does the mother immediately respond? How does she handle the infant? Is she comforting or scolding? Relaxed or tense? Happy or angry? Is she physically capable of caring for the child? Is there help available to her? How many other children or adults must she care for? The variations in mother-child relationships account, in part, for the differences in adult personalities, as well as for differences in adults' perceptions of themselves and their behaviors in interpersonal relationships.

Although complete details of the mother-child relationship and its subsequent influence on adult personality cannot be specified at this point, and available research results are by no means similarly interpreted by all students of personality development, it is generally agreed that the character of the mother's relationship with the child is of great significance to his psychological and social development. Illustrations of the research supporting such a conclusion follow in this section and in the material pertaining to intrapsychic processes beginning on page 154.

Studies by Sears *et al.,* Levy, Coleman *et al.,* and Zemlick and Watson (44, 34, 9, 55) have attempted to measure the subtle communications of the mother's feeling toward the child, and their results lend support to the hypothesis of the importance of prenatal attitudes on child-care practices. Whether the pregnancy was planned or accidental, whether it came early or late in marriage, whether it was normal or difficult, all these conditions tend to affect the mother's feelings of acceptance or rejection of the child. On the basis of reports from 100 women, Wallin and Riley related the mother's attitudes toward her pregnancy to subsequent infant adjustment. For mothers of two or more children, nausea, vomiting, and discomfort during pregnancy (symptoms often associated with dissatisfaction and resentment toward pregnancy) were found to be related to infant feeding and elimination difficulties and to excessive crying and the need to be held.

Studies by Goldfarb (18), Escolona (14), and Brody (5) indicate that the mother's negative feelings and the degree of sensitivity she possessed in handling the infant's needs, her consistency, and her freedom from anxiety had measurable effects upon the child's inner tension and subsequent development and behavior. Sears, Maccoby, and Levin (44) produced evidence that maternal coldness was associated with the later development of feeding problems, persistent enuresis, and aggressive behavior.

These investigations of the effects of the mother's feelings on the child's development employed objective measures of maternal attitudes and characteristics and used statistical methods of relating the data to indices of infant development. Another source of information concerning the mother-infant relationship is reports of observers working with children in hospitals and clinical settings.

One such observer, Margaret Ribble, studied more than 600 infants (37). She found that in instances in which the mother spent considerable time in playing with the baby, in rocking, petting, and otherwise "mothering" him, the infant was likely to experience good gastrointestinal functioning. The infant deprived of such mothering, she reported, was more likely to be prone to various physical ills.

The Infant's Well-Being and "Mothering"

Ribble's description of "mothering" is of particular interest, since it clearly delineates the feelings and emotions as well as the actual behaviors involved in the mothering process. These feelings and emotions are important components of the psychological "climate."

> The newborn baby still needs to be carried about at regular intervals until he can move and coordinate his own body. This helps to strengthen his sense of equilibrium and to give him a feeling of security. Also, he must have frequent periods of actual contact with the mother because the warmth and the holding give him reassurance. Contact takes the place of the physical connection before birth when the child was like an organ of the mother's body. In addition, mothering includes the whole gamut of small acts by means of which an emotionally healthy mother consistently shows her love for her child. . . . Obviously, feeding, bathing, and all the details of physical care come in, but in addition to these duties, which can easily become routine and perfunctory, we mean all of the small evidences of tender feeling—fondling, caressing, rocking, and singing or speaking to the baby. These activities have a deep significance.[2]

[2] Reprinted by permission from M. Ribble, *The Rights of Infants*. New York, Columbia University Press, 1943. Copyright 1943 by Columbia University Press.

In another investigation of the relationship between infant experience and physical and psychological development, Spitz studied infants reared in institutions (47, 48) One group had contact with their mothers, and a comparable group of infants was cared for by nurses who attended to their physical needs with a minimum of contact. The infants whose mothers had free access to them and who were played with, caressed, and fondled were more alert mentally and more capable physically. Spitz concluded that lack of contact with the mother had a significant effect upon the health and behavior of the child, quite apart from the adequacy with which the infant's physical needs were met.

Anna Freud and Burlingham (15) studied children who were removed from English cities during World War II. Although necessary for the protection of the children, this program often resulted in the child's separation from his mother. These investigators noted that children thus separated often had temper tantrums, various fears and sleeping difficulties, and eating disorders.

Since clinical observations such as those of Ribble, or clinical research studies such as those of Porter, Goldfarb, and Spitz, necessarily lack the specificity and the controls that are possible in laboratory studies, the results frequently must be considered as provisional until additional supporting data become available. Because of the range of observations included in such clinical studies, however, they may provide unusually productive areas for subsequent investigation and may lead to varied and fruitful hypotheses.

Hypotheses based upon the studies cited and those contained in the recommended texts at the end of this chapter postulate that the quality of the relationship between mother and infant is a significant factor in the child's development, that it is not merely the physical care which the mother provides for her child, but also her caressing, loving, playing, and talking which affect development.

It is also hypothesized that the child's basic perception of himself depends upon the nature of the relationship he enjoyed with his mother. His earliest feelings of being valued, of being wanted, or being the object of love and affection are the foundations for the feelings he will have as a child and as an adult about himself and about others. It is within this relationship that an individual first learns that all his demands cannot be met and that his wishes and desires are not always respected. The child who is secure in his relationship with his mother slowly becomes able to accept most frustrations, for he views them not as indications of any lack in himself, but as reflections of the objective external world. Thus, the mother is the mediator of the infant's environment, an agent of reality for the child as well as his major source of self-esteem. She can communicate through her behaviors the implicit rules, regulations, and demands that characterize the greater society. If she is indulgent, constantly acquiescent to her child's demands, and unable to say "No," she may actually restrain him from developing his own potentialities and resources. Such an overindulgent mother not only fails to represent reality, but may unconsciously use her relationship with her child to gratify her own needs.

Physical Contact in the Mother-Child Relationship

Psychologists have been interested in the general nature of the mother-child relationship, and also in the specific details of the way in which the child acquires particular patterns of response to the mother, patterns that are later employed in perceiving and responding to persons other than the mother. In many of these studies, the mother has been thought of as the source of food and hence as a reinforcer of those behaviors leading to drive reduction. Although this "explanation" is widely accepted (granting its oversimplification), some research psychologists have investigated other significant factors in the formation of the special attachment of the child to the mother.

One recent series of studies has aroused considerable interest (24). Harlow used infant macaque monkeys in his investigations of the infant-maternal relationship, and in an introductory statement to his report he expresses doubts that affection deriving from the infant's relationship to its mother has its origin in the specific activities associated with nursing and feeding.

> It is entirely reasonable to believe that the mother through association with food may become a secondary-reinforcing agent, but this is an inadequate mechanism to account for the persistence of the infant-maternal ties. There is a spate of researches on the formation of secondary reinforcers to hunger and thirst reduction. There can be no question that almost any external stimulus can become a secondary reinforcer if properly associated with tissue-need reduction, but the fact remains that this redundant literature demonstrates unequivocally that such derived drives suffer relatively rapid experimental extinction. Contrariwise, human affection does not extinguish when the mother ceases to have intimate association with the drives in question. Instead, the affectional ties to the mother show a lifelong, unrelenting persistence and, even more surprising, widely expanding generality.[3]

In a test of the relative importance of nursing and of "contact-comfort" (the satisfactions derived from intimate physical contact),

[3] Reprinted by permission from H. F. Harlow, "The Nature of Love." *Amer. Psychol.*, 1958, *13*, 673–685. Copyright, 1958, by the American Psychological Association.

Harlow constructed two mother-substitutes, one "made from a block of wood, covered with sponge rubber, and sheathed in tan cotton terry cloth," the other made from a wire mesh cylinder with a block of wood for her head. A light bulb behind each radiated heat. The mother-substitutes were made with a single breast from which the infant received its supply of milk. The pictures on page 143 show the cloth and the wire mother-substitutes. During the 165 days of the study both groups of infants had access to both the cloth and wire mothers. One group was fed by the "wire" mother, the other group by the "cloth" mother. According to the need-reduction hypothesis, the monkeys would spend more time with the mother-substitute that nursed them. Yet, contrary to the prediction, both groups of infants spent a far greater percentage of time on the cloth mother. Harlow states:

> We were not surprised to discover that contact-comfort was an important basic affectional or love variable, but we did not expect it to overshadow so completely the variable of nursing; indeed, the disparity is so great as to suggest that the primary function of nursing as an affectional variable is that of insuring frequent and intimate body contact of the infant with the mother.

In subsequent investigations of the strength of the affectional bond, Harlow recorded the infant's responses when confronted with fear-evoking stimuli. Here again, irrespective of the infant's source of milk—the wire or the cloth mother—the infants would cling to the cloth mother when frightened (see page 143). Even when the infant was prevented by a Plexiglas cover from having direct contact with the cloth mother, her presence in new situations reduced the number of fear reactions.

Harlow's studies thus present evidence that the physical contact of the infant with a mother whose "skin" is comforting to him adds to the effects of postural support and nursing in contributing to the significance the mother assumes for the child. Such significance is observed in the amount of contact with the mother initiated by the infant and by the degree to which her presence contributes to reducing his fear reactions. From Harlow's studies one could hypothesize that the relatedness need in human beings, the need to feel in communion with others, may partially have its origin in the contact-comforts the infant receives from his mother. This work adds to the specificity of the explanations for the development of the relatedness need, a need which is evident in the affectional reactions of the child to his mother and which also operates in the love the mother shows for her child.

To both daughters and sons the mother (or mother-substitute) represents also femininity and womanliness. Her attitudes toward household duties and care of her children and her attitudes and feelings about

How reassuring to cling to mother!

The danger is less frightening and there is comfort and security in holding tight to mother or being held by her. Every mother who has comforted her
infant by cuddling and caressing him knows that positive responses are evoked
by such bodily contact. But the question that intrigues the psychologist is why
the infant responds positively. Is the mother's meaning to the child derived primarily from her role as the gratifier of the infant's "oral" needs? Or does
the infant have a need for bodily contact with the mother that is independent
of the infant's other needs? In his efforts to answer questions such as these,
Professor Harlow studied the behavior of infant monkeys who were separated
from their real mother and were fed warm milk by artificial mothers. By providing one with a terry cloth skin and by controlling various conditions, including the amount of milk each would provide, he was able to compare the
relative significance of nursing and skin contact in infant behavior. This research revealed the considerable significance that skin contact plays in the
mother-child relationship.

However, additional findings, other than those related to the primary purpose of the study, were reported several years after the results of the initial
investigations had been made public. These later findings indicated that the
infants "raised" with artificial mothers were themselves unable to fulfill satisfactorily the mother's role. Their maternal inadequacies, impotence, impatience, and disinterest in their offspring underscore the significance of the
mother in the emotional development of the infant.

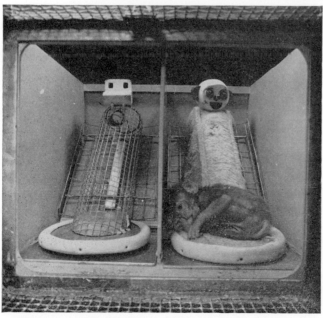

herself as a wife affect the child's earliest concepts of the woman, wife, and mother. The desirability attached by a girl to being a woman and the satisfactions she later achieves in taking her place in her family and her society are acquired in large measure through her relationship with her mother. A son, too, gains from his mother his first and probably most lasting impression of the worth and status of womanhood. And from the relationship between the parents, both son and daughter develop concepts and attitudes about the nature of the marriage relationship.

THE PATERNAL RELATIONSHIP

The classic concept of the family unit prevalent at the turn of the century, and still present in nonurban areas of this country and Europe, assigns to the father certain specific expectations and assumes that he is the strong, dominant parent who takes responsibility for earning the family livelihood and whose word is law; matters of dispute and discipline and decisions of importance are considered to be within his domain. Under such circumstances it is probable that a considerable "psychological distance" separates the father from his children, especially when the relationship is compared to that involved in present expectations of the father. He may be aloof and inaccessible to them except in matters of discipline and decision, and they may hesitate to approach him for help or understanding.

The Father and the Child's Perception of the Outside World

Although the father's role in American culture today can hardly be described in this way, studies indicate that some of the elements contained in the description are still valid. In oversimplified terms, it can be said that if the mother is the major source of attention and affection for her child, the father is probably the major source of his child's impressions of strength and of the outside world. Such impressions are often determined, in part, by the father's activities as provider and disciplinarian. This dichotomy of roles between mother and father does not apply to all families, however, since the roles are not this precise. Mothers and fathers often share responsibilities for handling finances, for management and care of the household, and for rearing the children. The picture of the mother as a passive, compliant person and the father as an assertive and dominant figure within the household represents also an oversimplification or a distorted generalization of the most usual relationship between parents in our society. Included within this oversimplified generalization of the usual relationship between parents in our society is the impression that the father is the sole contributor to the economic support of the family. That the mother shares the responsibilities of the "provider" is indicated by statistics regarding the approximately twelve million wives in the labor force in the United States. The periods during which they work seem to be related to their ages and the ages of their children. As Glick (17) notes:

> During the first year after marriage about 40 percent of the wives have jobs away from home. During the second or third year, many drop out of economic activity to have children and the proportion of working wives falls to about 30 percent. For the period when women have children of preschool age (under 6 years old), only about 15 percent are labor force participants. After all of the children have reached school age, nearly one-third of the wives are in the labor force.[4]

The Father and the Child's Perception of Authority

Within the relationship of the child (boy or girl) to the father may be found the beginnings of adult attitudes toward authority. The father's relationship to his children usually constitutes their first and most impressive experience with authority. An individual's attitude toward his employer or toward his employees, his acceptance of "experts," and his respect for leaders of government, industry, or labor often reflect the nature of his relationship with his father during his developmental period. Experiences with a father who is strong, supportive, emotionally responsive, and consistent allow an individual to develop attitudes toward authority that are quite different from those that develop when the father is fearful, critical, inhibited, and inconsistent.

Persons who are afraid of authority figures may exhibit two very different patterns of behavior. Some may conform to every anticipated wish of the authority figure. They are complying, subservient, and ingratiating, even though underlying these behaviors, often outside of awareness, there may be considerable hostility that cannot be expressed directly. Another pattern of response to authority is sometimes observed in those fearful persons who resist all rules, regulations, supervision, and control. They may respond too intensely and too quickly to whatever is perceived as the unjust imposition of authority.

Depending upon the strength of his role in the family, the father reinforces, extends, and refines the child's concepts of good and bad. The child takes within himself paternal attitudes that become a part of his

---

[4] Reprinted by permission from P. C. Glick, "The Life-Cycle of the Family." *Marriage and Family Living*, February 1955, p. 9. Copyright, 1955, by National Council on Family Relations.

superego processes. Although the mother may play a more dominant role in some cases, it is usually as if the father's voice scolds when ethical standards are violated and praises when worthwhile goals are reached.

Actually the "pure case" of the succorant mother and the dominant father is found only rarely in contemporary society. The mother who works and the father who shares the shopping, does the laundry, and cares for the child are not uncommon. Thus, the roles of mother and father, though clear-cut in the preceding discussion and in popular belief, in practice are defined for the child by the actual behaviors of the parents. In his relationship to his child the parent may come close to filling the social expectation of his role or he may not. In either case he may feel that he is or is not treating his child as he should. The complex nature of parent-child relationships is suggested by the comments calling attention to the significance of the behaviors of the parent toward the child, the importance of social beliefs as to the parent's role, the parent's expectations of himself, and how he perceives himself and his child.

SIBLING RELATIONSHIPS

The term *siblings* refers to children of the same parents, irrespective of sex. Although family size in itself has no predictable influence on the child, the presence of brothers and sisters within the family unit affects the child's psychological development, either in terms of the influence of the siblings on the relationship between him and his parents, or in terms of the direct interaction between him and his siblings. In either case, siblings are important forces in his social and psychological environment.

Children reared together are compelled to interact cooperatively or competitively. Conditions often arise in which cooperative activity can benefit several of the children. Although the periods when the children's objectives coincide may be infrequent, particularly in the estimation of parents, opportunities are afforded for experiences not directly available to an only child. More obvious to the observer are the expressions of competitive activity, which may have their origins in the quest for parental approval and affection. Even within the sibling group there are many opportunities to learn the techniques and the ethics of competition. The advantages of cooperative activity and the necessary rules of competition can both be learned somewhat more readily by the child who is reared with siblings than by the singleton (only child).

On the other hand, it should be pointed out that there is little evidence to support the popular notion that the "only" child has more problems or is less stable than his peers. Some studies suggest that he is less popular with his age group and more inclined to such disturbances as temper tantrums, fears, and enuresis (40). But others have found him to be more cooperative, dependable, and popular than his peers (21). The conflicting results suggest that the only child's development is more a reflection of the way in which his parents view him and have attempted to assist him in learning to live cooperatively than of his status as a singleton.

The concept of sibling rivalry has been given considerable attention by child psychologists and other professional persons interested in the child's psychological development. With the arrival of the new sibling, the psychological and social environments of the older child or children change. Studies of the effects of such changes show that they may range from favorable and constructive to traumatic or even devastating.

The degree to which the older child feels displaced or rejected because of the arrival of the infant depends largely on the strength and adequacy of the parental relationship he has previously enjoyed. His age at the time of his sibling's birth determines the degree to which his physical demands on his mother will be interfered with by those of the new arrival. The child's expectations of what the situation will be with a new brother or sister in the house also influence his reactions to the sibling. The hostility sometimes expressed by a child toward an infant can be upsetting to the parents. A mother reported that George, her four-year-old, had seemed pleased with his new brother, and also very concerned and protective. He would ask such questions as, "Would it hurt the baby if you dropped him on his head?" The mother was inclined to interpret this concern somewhat differently after she noted that whenever he could do so unobtrusively, George would enter the nursery and pinch the baby until he screamed.

Most children do not express the hostility they feel toward the new sibling as directly as did George, but the expression of the older child's hostility is frequent enough to constitute a problem for many parents. Often the parents are unaware that their child resents his sibling as an intruder who has deprived him of his position as the center of his parents' attention and affection. The feelings of being rejected may be reinforced and intensified by behaviors of the parents in taking care of the infant or in displaying him to relatives and friends, by criticism or punishment for waking baby up or for any expression of resentment toward the baby. Unfavorable comparisons, the use of one child as a model for other children, or the lavish praise or reward of one child in the family all tend to perpetuate and to enhance feelings of hostility and bitterness between siblings.

At a more subtle level are parental reactions to the illness of a child, particularly when it is prolonged or when it results in chronic disability. In such instances, the attention and concern of the parents may be resented by the other children even though they hide or inhibit their feelings. Even when expressed, these feelings of resentment may through the superego process evoke strong guilt reactions on the part of the child. Parents who are sensitive to the child's feelings of displacement and who can accept the child's expression of hostility toward the infant are able to create conditions that minimize hostility between the siblings.

The Influence of Birth Order

Circumstances that result in the death of a parent or that require older children to care for younger siblings also will influence the pattern of interrelationships among the members of a family. The psychological place of each child in a family is often related to his *ordinal birth position* among his siblings. Certain differences exist in the psychological and social structure of the family for the first child compared to those for the second or last.

For example, the first born has the unique experience of having an unchallenged claim to his parents' attention; consequently, the impact of a sibling will be different for him than for the second or third child. Because of his physical development, the first born will be given priority over younger brothers and sisters in matters involving responsibility and self-determination. The second child is weaker and less capable physically than his older sibling. He has a less exclusive claim to the parents' attentions and grows up in an environment that includes close contact with another child as well as with adults.

The differences in responsibilities associated with birth order and the expectations held for children by other members of the family because they are the oldest or youngest emphasize the point made earlier that the psychological influence of the child's familial environment is best understood when the interactions of all its members are considered in toto. The influence of ordinal position may begin to operate even prior to the child's birth. Sears and his associates (44) found that the percentages of mothers and fathers who stated they were "delighted" with the prospect of the child's birth were greatest for the oldest child, next highest for the middle, and least for the youngest child.

The effects of the parents' inexperience are evident in the greater inconsistency of their dealings with the first child than with later children. Whereas first-born children are apt to be given freedom to be noisy and aggressive, they are also more likely to receive fairly severe discipline. In contrast, later born children may have less freedom and less severe discipline. In addition to experiencing inconsistency in treatment, the first child also may experience the effects of parental anxiety and over-protection, and the loss of his favored position when displaced by the arrival of younger siblings. Thus, it is not surprising that in studies of behavioral reactions to fear-evoking situations, first-born children are reported to demonstrate greater anxiety and need for association with other persons. Schachter found (42) that when college students who were first-borns were frightened by the prospect of physical pain, they tended to seek the company of others to a greater extent than those who were later in the ordinal sequence. Citing other data consistent with his findings, Schachter notes that effectiveness of combat fighter pilots is lower among first-borns, and that nursery school children who are first-borns tend to show more dependent behaviors than do later born children.

While they should be interpreted cautiously, results of other studies agree that older children appear to be less aggressive than their peers but to exhibit more behavior problems (8, 43). The youngest children tend to be more self-confident, ambitious, and persistent than their siblings, and research involving middle children lends some support to the belief that they are more gregarious, affectionate, and easily led (4, 21, 38).

The relationship that an individual has had with his siblings during childhood is reflected in later attitudes and behaviors toward the persons with whom he must cooperate or compete. A person who has unsatisfactory relationships with his parents and siblings may develop self-perceptions that cause him to feel hopeless about having his talents recognized or to feel that he will never be treated fairly by persons in authority, or that all efforts to compete with associates will fail. On the other hand, the person who can enjoy his associates, who can respect authority without fear, and who believes, unless he has reasonable evidence to the contrary, that his efforts will be evaluated justly has probably enjoyed relatively satisfying relationships with parents and siblings.

Relationships with siblings provide experiences that contribute to the development of ego and superego processes. The ability to evaluate the attitudes, behaviors, and needs of others and to utilize these evaluations in ways best suited to the gratification of basic desires is strengthened by experiences with brothers and sisters, and the ethics of behaviors toward other persons also emerge in part from relationships with siblings.

In the preceding paragraphs some maternal, paternal, and sibling relationships have been described and some of their implications for the infant and young child have been mentioned. Before proceeding with a more detailed statement of the factors influencing personality development during the early years, the possibility that persons living within the family—relatives, boarders, or servants—may also exercise an influence within the family circle, and hence on the personality development of the child, cannot be overlooked. The aunt or nurse who is at home to take care of the infant or young child fulfills the functions of the mother and thus is significant to the child; in similar fashion, the grandparents, uncles, or "honorary" relatives should be considered as parts of the family unit. Their specific influence depends upon the nature of their contacts with the child and their position and status within the family.

During the first several years of the child's life, his world consists of the people who comprise the family unit, and it is not until he approaches the period designated as childhood (that is, until he approaches his fourth and fifth year) that he is likely to have sufficient contact with "outsiders," playmates, and nursery school teachers for their influence to become significant. When he does venture outside the family, the previously acquired patterns of responding to other persons will be relied upon; moreover, the requirements made of him in his experiences outside the home provide opportunities for generalizing his adaptive behaviors and for the abandonment of infantile and dependent behaviors. But this takes us ahead too rapidly; first it is necessary to consider how the actors we have placed upon the family stage, the mother, father, and siblings, interact with the infant and young child as he proceeds through his first five years and how such interactions influence his personality development.

Personality Development

The process of growing up psychologically consists in part of learning what the world is like. Knowledge of what he can expect of others and of himself in a variety of situations enables a person to react emotionally and behaviorally in ways that are appropriate to his situation and to his own self-interest. This knowledge is acquired throughout a lifetime, but the very early years are the time of most rapid learning.

THE BEGINNINGS OF SELF-IDENTITY

The learning of self-identity begins with the gradually sharpening awareness that the world exists apart from one's own body. The infant, with his limited visual and neural development and his limited experience, is at first not only the center of his universe; he *is* his universe. Although he is aware of sensations of discomfort, pain, satiation, or satisfaction, this is not a conscious, thoughtful awareness, but is rather an unthinking responsiveness to his own bodily needs and to those events that lead to their satisfaction. When the infant is hungry, cold, constipated, or tired, a state of physical (muscular) tension ensues. In addition, certain physiological processes occur that correspond to those observed and recorded in frightened or anxious adults. These include accelerated heartbeat, increased flow of adrenalin into the blood stream, and inhibition of digestive processes. Frequently the infant's cries are a signal for the mother to feed him, change him, or in some other way take care of his immediate need; and with satisfaction of the need the tension subsides, allowing bodily processes to function again at the usual level.

As his sensory and neural organ systems develop and his experiences with sights, sounds, and people become more extensive, he is able to recognize differences between himself and the world outside himself. Sensations that were at first internal visual and auditory images are now gradually perceived as being qualities of external objects, of people and things apart from himself. The ability to make this distinction is a primary characteristic of psychological development beyond the infantile stage. This infantile period contains the beginnings of the psychological processes that have been included under the term "ego." The ego, which mediates between the individual's impulsive physical inclinations and the external world, begins to function as the infant gradually develops an awareness of the distinction between that which is body and that which is nonbody. Separation of the physical self from the external physical environment is an ego function and the ego is influenced in the discriminations it makes by the experiences it has during its development.

It is also apparent that the infant's survival, as well as the quality of that survival, depends upon the accessibility of other persons and the adequacy of their efforts to satisfy his needs. As the previous discussion pointed out, it is through the pattern of experiences that follows an aroused need—tension state, appearance of the helping person, reduction of tension state with satisfaction of the need—that the need to feel in communion with other people gradually develops as a psychological need apart from the physical needs with which it was initially associated. As the personality develops, psychological needs proliferate and become more complex, and it is more difficult to establish their relationship to physical needs.

The Child's Mastery Experiences

Particularly important to ego development are mastery experiences. By mastery experiences are meant those episodes in which the child achieves, through his own efforts, previously unattainable objectives. Even though the child may experience considerable frustration, his attempts to master elements of his environment and of his own body in order to achieve difficult objectives are part and parcel of growing up. These mastery activities, learned through seeing, hearing, smelling, tasting, touching, manipulating, and experimenting, are all involved in ego development.

During the second, third, and fourth years of the child's life he acquires physical mastery over many aspects of his environment and himself. He can move about on his own accord, feed himself, and control his bowel and bladder. He has acquired the ability to communicate lucidly with others; many symbols now have meanings for him and provide a basis for his expectations of this world. The child's concept of himself, although not inflexibly defined, has become clarified and refined, for by the fifth and sixth years he has many impressions of what is expected of him. These impressions remain with him, although they may be modified by subsequent experience. If the child's impressions conform with reality and provide him with a sound basis for mediating between his internal impulses and the external world, his ego can be described as strong. If his impressions of what is expected of him are inaccurate and he has no sound basis for mediating between inner impulses and the external world, his ego can be described as being weak.

EMOTIONAL DEVELOPMENT

In this learning process involving both satisfactions and frustrations, the development of emotional responses is of interest. Because of his limited experiences and the inadequate development of his cortex, the outer layer of the cerebral hemispheres of the brain, it is unlikely that the infant experiences emotions as they are known to adults. His emotional responses probably stem from inner tensions and they are diffuse, generalized, primitive, gross. Many studies have attempted to differentiate the infant's emotional responses. He cries, grimaces, withdraws, smiles. But judges seldom agree either upon the stimulus or upon the emotion expressed.

As he grows older, the child begins to react more to external stimuli than to internal cues within his body. To varying degrees, he learns controls and modes of expression that are appropriate responses to cultural symbols. The importance of learning in the development of emotional expression is illustrated by many studies. The reader will recall, for example, Watson's experiment involving Albert and his fear of furry objects. In an ambitious study by Goodenough (19), the mothers of fifty children kept for an extended period daily records of incidents of anger.

In general, it was found that with age there was a gradual decline in random, undirected outbursts of anger and an increase in anger overtly directed toward the source, whether it was a person or an object.

The modes of expressing anger also showed a change: crying and kicking decreased, whereas verbal responses, striking, and stamping the feet increased. Girls expressed anger less frequently than boys and for both sexes the frequency of anger-producing situations decreased. No difference was noted in the duration of anger expression, suggesting that perhaps longer outbursts were less tolerated as the child became older. Anger arising out of problems in social relationships increased with age, whereas conflicts related to certain routine habits within the home and to authority tended to decline. It is, however, important to realize that certain conditions affect a child's frustration tolerance. Thus, the hungry, tired, or ill child may respond angrily under these circumstances and not under others.

There is much evidence to suggest that many fears are learned. Hagman (23), in a study of the relationship between the fears of children and of their mothers, questioned the mothers of thirty girls and forty boys, ranging in age from seventy months to twenty-three years, about their children's fears and how they were handled. The children tended to express the same fears as the mothers, particularly those involving storms, dogs, and insects.

Jersild and Holmes (29) offered support to the hypothesis that fears of tangible, specific objects (noises, falling, animals, strange places) decrease with age, whereas fears of symbolic ones increase. They also found a correlation between fear and intelligence, the brighter child tending to perceive threat more quickly than others and thus to be more fearful. However, by the age of five all the children in their study responded to the fear-evoking situations regardless of intelligence. It can be predicted that given a wide range of fear-evoking situations at all age levels the brighter child will respond more rapidly to threat. Whether the response is expressed as fear or as some behavior to deal with the fear situation or as a response that conceals his fear from others depends on what the child anticipates as a consequence of the expression of fear. Girls learn that it is acceptable for them to express their fears, boys learn that to do so is "unmanly." In the study cited, a significant difference was found between the fear reactions of boys and girls, with girls expressing more than boys, but here again, wide individual differences were noted.

Before concluding that fears tend to decrease with age, it should be remembered that one cannot assume that fears are nonexistent merely because they are not expressed. Since our culture exerts considerable pressure against overt fear reactions, it is quite possible that children learn to disguise their real feelings; moreover, the increasing incidence of anger reactions as children grow older suggests that the child may convert his fear responses to anger since society permits more open expression in this realm.

Since many preschool children are confronted with the arrival of a baby brother or sister who presents a threat to their secure position in the family, study of the complex emotion of jealousy is particularly important. The jealous preschool child may react aggressively, he may regress or withdraw, or he may repress his feelings completely, depending upon how his parents handle the problem.

Not all emotions expressed at this age are disruptive ones, although perhaps research has tended to center on them. While the causes of smiling and laughter as social gestures are difficult to determine, among preschool children laughter often accompanies physical activity, and it most often occurs in social situations. Blatz and his colleagues (3) suggest that it occurs when a conflict has been resolved, and Justin (30) found sources of laughter in situations involving suspense, superiority and incongruity, and relief from strain.

EGO DEVELOPMENT

The child reared in a family where displays of both affection and hostility are frowned upon may learn to behave in a seemingly unemotional manner. His natural, impulsive expressions of love or hate are controlled by ego processes developed when the expression of feeling brought parental displeasure. Such ego controls may continue to operate long after childhood, so that the adult may fear his own positive and negative feelings to such an extent that he can neither love adequately nor express any observable hostile reaction. This id–ego conflict, which has persisted from childhood into adult life, may affect the way such a person thinks of himself and may markedly influence the kind of relationships he has with other people. His inability to make close friends and his need to be pleasant and agreeable may be traced to a lack of inner peace attributable to conflict between the id and ego processes.

As the child grows he encounters situations that involve other persons and that increasingly necessitate his learning to mediate between his own impulses and the demands of reality. These situations in themselves represent developmental phases that provide the context or the problem conditions in which child and parents react to each other. In this parent-child interplay, the child deals with parent and problem in terms of his previous experiences as well as his current perceptions and reactions. His ego processes (his abilities to perceive the world, to formulate appropriate expectations, and to behave in ways that provide maximum internal balance) will develop from his relationships with the significant people in his life. The crucial effect of any of these relationships depends, in part, upon the developmental point at which it occurs.

The total experiences of early childhood strongly influence self-perception, for they provide the child with feelings pertaining to his value as an individual. After recognizing his own existence as a separate being, he may come to feel that he is a person who is valued by his parents either for what he does or for what he is. If he feels valued for his achievements and accomplishments, or for his self-control, or for his compliance, then he will have to achieve, inhibit, or comply in order to feel that he is a person of worth. If he is accepted by his parents as a child, and if his actions are understood and responded to without tension, then there will be little emphasis on achievement or compliance per se, and the child will perceive himself as a member of the family who is valued for what he is rather than for what he does.

Establishing Oneself in the Context of the Feeding Situation

Of particular significance in the infant's personality development are his early feeding experiences, the degree of satisfaction or frustration he experiences, and his parents' handling of the weaning process. Intrinsic to the feeding process is the use of the oral apparatus, the mouth, tongue, and lips, the most highly sensitized and responsive area of the infant's body. Feeding is the most important event in the infant's daily schedule. His tendency to put "everything" into his mouth is his way of learning what things are like. This habit of oral contact is one of the most important influences in establishing both his sense of being separate from the rest of the world and his fundamental psychological need to feel related to and be in contact and in communion with other people.

Numerous books on specific child-care practices began to appear in the early years of this century. Many were written by physicians as well as psychologists, and it is interesting and sometimes amusing to note the radical changes that have taken place in the advice given. At one extreme the rigid, disciplined feeding schedule, with little regard for the infant's hunger needs, was proposed; at the other extreme was a complete "demand" schedule that contributed to the child's domination over the household. The relative merits of breast and bottle feeding were continually argued and even today the issue is not settled.

From anthropology have come various studies involving cultural and class differences in child-rearing practices, particularly with reference to feeding, weaning, and toilet training. The Davis and Havinghurst study, mentioned previously, revealed that middle class parents tended at that time to be more rigid and punitive than low or working class parents. Subsequent research by Whiting and Child (53), however, does not support this difference in all areas. Perhaps in the intervening ten years, education about relaxed child-rearing practices had its effect.

According to theories advanced by Sigmund Freud, experiences during the oral period are of considerable importance for the child's later personality development. If the infant's needs are severely frustrated, his development is fixated, and characteristics of the earlier level persist. One need not accept this part of Freudian theory, however, in order to appreciate the importance of oral experiences and their association with much of the child's earliest social learning.

Weaning: Developmental Crisis or Mastery Experience

During the later stages of infancy another point is reached that has special significance in the child's psychological development. The shift from breast or bottle to a cup represents a major developmental accomplishment. As Sears, Maccoby, and Levin (44) point out:

> The child must learn not to want to get his food by sucking. He must learn to like to drink the same food he formerly got by sucking. He must learn to want solid foods. He must learn the manipulative skills required for eating them—biting, chewing, and the use of fingers and utensils, as well as drinking from a cup. He must learn to do without being held while he is eating.[5]

The weaning process, then, has considerable psychological significance; depending again on the mother's own feelings about herself and her child, the child may come to make increasingly fine differentiations between that which is his own body and that which is not. The transition is important also because the mastery of an activity so directly related to his own gratification contributes to the child's developing ego processes. He begins to learn self-control and acquires a more detailed knowledge of what is expected of him by others and what he can expect of them. Weaning that occurs under conditions of duress or tension may also affect ego development significantly, for the child may learn to expect others to frustrate his wishes and to be unreliable and depriving.

Because some investigators related it to early or severe weaning, others to bottle versus breast feeding, or perceived it as evidence in support of Freudian theory, and because the dental profession condemned it as being responsible for malocclusion, the widespread habit

[5] Reprinted by permission from R. R. Sears *et al., Patterns of Child Rearing.* New York, Harper, 1957. Copyright, 1957, by Harper & Row, Publishers, Incorporated.

of thumbsucking has been the subject of much attention and research for a considerable period of time. Results of various studies of thumbsucking have supported the hypothesis of the significance of the oral zone. For example, physicians have reported fingersucking in newborn babies (16). Levy, along with Roberts, Ross, and Yarrow, found some relationship between thumbsucking and oral deprivation, and many have interpreted their findings as supporting the Freudian theory that sucking is a need or drive, a source of erotic pleasure, not merely a reflex action related to the hunger drive (33, 39, 41, 54).

On the other hand, Sears has hypothesized that sucking is a learned secondary drive developing strength from its association with a primary drive which is rewarded by feeding. Studies do, in fact, demonstrate that sucking becomes more persistent if it is rewarded through the feeding process. Although such studies give support to the learning concept, they do not invalidate the Freudian theory, since a direct test of whether the oral drive is actually primary is not possible.

Freud postulated also that adults whose oral needs during infancy had been either deprived or excessively gratified often remain fixated at this level of development, and as adults can be characterized by certain habits, such as excessive smoking or drinking, and traits such as dependency and pessimism. The oral character has also been described as a "parasite," because he values the dependency relationship and makes excessive demands for protection, sympathy, and support. The contention that there is a simple one-to-one relationship between adult personality characteristics and specific feeding practices has not been given much research support, however. It is probable that a relationship exists, but that it is a much more complex one than that postulated by Freud.

Control of Bladder and Bowels

Between the ages of two and three years most children in our culture become able to control their excretory functions. Neural mechanisms have developed sufficiently to allow voluntary control of urination and defecation, but physical control does not automatically enable the child to respond with the bathroom behavior desired by his parents. He must learn to coordinate his physical functions with parental expectations. The child learns that wetting his pants not only causes him to feel physically uncomfortable but also brings parental disapproval. Scoldings, punishment, or parental pleadings contribute to the child's awareness that it is desirable to control excretory functions and to use toilet facilities.

Generally, the acts of urination and defecation are in themselves pleasurable to the child; the physical discomfort due to distension of the bladder or colon is relieved. When such relief occurs along with approval, as when the child urinates or defecates while seated on the toilet, physical gratifications are reinforced by the reward of the parent, who smiles or indicates in other ways his satisfaction with the child's behavior. The feeling of pleasure associated with control of the physical self is reinforced by the bestowal of parental approval.

The mastery of these excretory functions may have other psychological significances as well. The child may become aware that his excretory activities are very important to his parents. Just how overtly important it is to parents that a child be "trained" and how much pressure they will apply to achieve the objective depends on many aspects of the family situation, including the parents' own toilet-training experiences and attitudes.

When parents are unusually apprehensive that their child may never become adequately toilet trained the child is apt to have feelings and beliefs reinforced that one must give something to parents in order to warrant their approval. In such instances the child's potential to control and manipulate his parents is considerable. He can please them and gain their approval by controlling his bowels, or he can accentuate their anxiety and concern by soiling himself. Although it should not be assumed that the child of an anxious parent always consciously decides to soil himself to intensify parental concerns, the toilet-training situation does afford the child with a means of rewarding or punishing the parent. And it is within the parental-child relationship during the toilet training period that the child's awareness of himself as a being who can act upon and to an extent control his environment is greatly extended.

Dollard and Miller (12) found that excessive timidity and over-conformity tended to result from severe toilet training practices. A child cannot differentiate at this early age between his parents' reactions to cleanliness and to him as a person, and he may interpret their reactions as disapproval of him, thus perceiving himself as being unworthy and insignificant. He may also tend to build negative or fearful attitudes toward his sexual and excretory organs.

Many adults recall vividly the keen feelings of shame they experienced as children when their lack of control was ridiculed or scolded by their parents. Some persons carry into their adult lives childish fears that partially stem from their toilet training experiences. The adult who fears he will lose control of himself, who is made anxious by disorder and who fears losing the good will of his associates unless he provides them with gifts or in other ways ingratiates himself to them, may be reflecting the effects of severe or possibly inconsistent reactions from parents to his toileting. The adult may also carry with him from his experience during this period feelings that in order to protect himself he must withhold himself, and that he should be very careful and controlled if he is to get people to do what he wants.

It has been suggested that the origin of attitudes such as these may be found in the experiences of children who learned means of effectively controlling their parents' behaviors. The child who demanded a reward or bribe to move his bowels or who learned that his parents' concerns for him were most evident at the times when he was constipated discovered a powerful technique for manipulating his parents. The technique of withholding one's self and of giving for personal gain are utilized in varying degrees by many adults whose ego processes still bear the marks of the experiences of early childhood.

During this period the child learns very rapidly what the world is like. The conditions that govern his relationships with others during this period will markedly influence the ego process of perception. In other words, if the anxieties or hostilities of the parent during the toilet training period cause the child to feel that he must always comply or buy approval or that he must withhold himself in order to cope with adults, then these feelings will markedly influence what he does in his later relationships with people. If his ego has developed adequately, he will be more reality-oriented than if his ego processes have been adversely influenced by the events of early childhood, including the activities associated with toilet training. For example, several studies have established some association between severity of toilet training and children's later aggressive behavior. An investigation by Bernstein (2) produced a significant relationship between severe training and negativism, immaturity, and lack of communication. On the basis of mothers' reports, Sears (44) found evidence that emotional disturbance was most prevalent when bowel training was started when children were very young (less than five months old) and when the training was severe, less when it began when the child was from five to fourteen months old and was less rigid. When the child was older than nineteen months at the institution of bowel training, a greater degree of emotional disturbance was reported than for the five- to fourteen-month-old group.

Although the theories of Freud hypothesize quite specific relationships between the experiences occurring during the "oral" and "anal" periods of the child's life and the development of later behavioral patterns, this text does not view activities such as weaning and toilet training as leading to specific personality characteristics, though it regards them as having considerable psychological significance. These experiences are important because they provide a context through which the actions and attitudes of the mother and father contribute to the child's perception of himself in relation to other persons. Such patterns become the modes—the characteristic ways of perceiving and responding to other persons—that the individual develops in attempting to satisfy his need for relatedness and his needs to maintain and protect himself—or, more specifically, the psychological part of himself, his personality.

The Early Use of Symbols

Purposeful thought and language are important ego activities. The young child who has learned to recognize his separateness from the rest of the world is able to distinguish among the people and among the various aspects of the world that impinge upon him. He comes to recognize that a sound or an expression or particular sequence of events may symbolize something else. But until considerable experience is acquired, his associations between the symbol and the "something else" it represents are highly personal. The association may be incorrect, illogical, and irrational and it may make little sense to the adult observer. The basis for such personal associations has been illustrated in the case of Albert (p. 89), in which furriness came to be associated with a fear-producing situation. Many similar connections are far more obscure in origin, especially to the casual observer. Such thinking is technically referred to as autistic and is characterized by the fact that the connections between stimuli and the responses evoked are highly personalized and are not logical, predictable, or reality oriented, but are the "accidental" products of the conditioning process. The infant, for example, may come to recognize that crying behavior brings mother to the crib and that mother at the crib means a diaper change, food, fondling, or cooing noises.

Thus, during the child's earliest years, when thought is autistic and does not follow a logical pattern and the ego processes are only beginning to develop, emotional reactions may be conditioned to particular experiences. These experiences establish associations between symbols and internal physical states of relaxation or tension. Although the precise details of how such emotional learning occurs have not yet been established, the research previously cited lends support to the view that it is attributable to the emotional attitudes of the person who cares for the infant. A tense, anxious, hostile, or fearful mother may go through the motions of doing all the things indicated in books on child-rearing practices and yet find that her baby is not eating, sleeping, and reacting as he is supposed to.

The emotional reactions and sensitivities acquired from the emotional and psychological characteristics of the parents may have a profound effect upon the development of the child's concept of himself as well as of what can be expected from all adults. While the child's basic attitudes develop following the gross recognition that he is separate from the world, his continuing experiences enable him to make increasingly detailed differentiations among people, events, and symbols, and this continuing refinement is influenced and shaped by his emotional experiences.

Rational Thought and Gratification

Although the child's thinking is still not the logical, rational, and orderly activity that it may become in later life, it has advanced so rapidly that symbols now evoke specific ideas and emotional reactions. These symbols sometimes retain their original meanings for the adult long after he has begun to think in logical terms. The developing abilities of the child to perceive his world, to think symbolically, and to do things that bring him what he desires depend upon the processes we have identified with the ego. The refinement and development of ego processes enable the child to obtain maximum gratification with the least risk. The young child has become so aware of his world that he can react in terms of what he has learned from previous attempts to secure satisfaction of his wishes and impulsive inclinations. Reactions that are influenced and affected by previous experiences are reflective of a higher developmental stage than those which were in evidence during infancy.

During infancy, the id processes were dominant. The infant's behaviors and psychological activities were unrestrained and unreflective expressions of desire, uninfluenced by reality considerations. With the emergence of discrimination, thought, and language, there is increasing ability to secure gratification of desires. Knowledge of the environmental situation, parental attitudes, and the many unspecified rules and regulations that govern his world enables the child to attempt to gratify his wishes in terms of the existing conditions. At times his knowledge of the situation may provide him with expectations that impel him to restrain his impulsive inclinations.

The type of conflict situation in which the impulses of the id are opposed by ego processes is termed id–ego conflict. Ego activity directed toward the protection of the self and avoidance of pain may involve restraint, redirection, or control of those id activities that experience has learned to be dangerous. The child learns that his impulsive behaviors bring certain consequences. When they bring pain, discomfort, or parental disapproval, associations are formed or reinforced between the behavior and the pain. Eventually, even the impulse, though unexpressed behaviorally, may be sufficient to engender the feeling of internal conflict. The intrapersonal (the within-self) conflict is initiated by an impulse or wish to act. The wish evokes the feeling of threat and an almost simultaneous protective reaction causing the impulse to be held in check or to be expressed indirectly.

Language

As the present chapter has indicated, from the time the child is one and a half to two years old until he enters first grade, his rate of intellectual and social development is at a high level. This difference between what he knows, understands, and can do when he is about six and his level of competency at the beginning of this period is due in part to the developmental conditions that lead to his ability to communicate verbally, to his acquisition and use of language.

The great importance of language as a distinctively human phenomenon, its significance to thought, and its function as a frame of reference for the classification of experience require its consideration here. The reader should note that although language is included in this section, which deals with the period when the child "learns to speak," the actual beginnings of his use of language occur with his gradual recognition of himself as an entity apart and distinct from his surroundings and with his awareness of the differences among sounds. The beginnings of speech are to be found during infancy, but language development continues into the adult years.

Of course the human being is not the only animal that communicates with others of his species. In the presence of danger various animals may "signal" warnings by emitting sounds or by giving off particular scents. The male peacock prefaces his mating behavior by spreading his tail plumage and thus reporting—communicating—his sexual readiness. Nevertheless, speech as we know it seems to be a characteristic distinguishing between man and the lower species. It has long been believed that man is the only species possessing the capacity for combining sounds through control of his diaphragm, vocal apparatus, tongue, lips, and facial muscles to form words and combinations of words. This does not answer the question of whether man learns to speak because he has contact with other speaking people or whether his ability to speak is due to a superior physical endowment, or whether both factors are equally important.

In order to investigate the factors responsible for the development of speech, two psychologists raised a chimpanzee as they would have reared a child (27). During the three years of the study, the chimpanzee, named Viki, was cared for, fed, dressed, talked to, and treated as a child. The chimpanzee has a physical structure similar (but not identical) to that of human beings in terms of the vocal, muscular, and neural apparatus required for speech. Because of this anatomical similarity it was possible to test the hypothesis that adequate duplication of the social conditions to which the human infant is exposed would enable a chimpanzee to acquire speech. Viki's reactions to the treatment she received during the first three years of her life have been described in an informative and entertaining book, *The Ape in Our House* (26). The record of Viki's development covers not only speech, but many aspects of self-care and social competence. Viki walked upright and learned to hold a cup and to drink from it at an earlier age than do most children. Furthermore, Viki correctly learned to use the words *cup, mama,* and *papa.*

This study demonstrated the significance of the social environment and early experience in establishing a primitive use of words in a species previously considered beneath even this rudimentary level of attainment. Of related interest are the studies of children who have been abandoned or reared in isolation or semi-isolation. Such cases are very rare, but those that have been reported indicate that speech is retarded or lacking in these children. The student who consults the descriptions of the "feral" children reared among animals or by themselves will be rewarded by fascinating accounts of these unusual cases.

Many questions about the acquisition of language are raised by these studies. Could a more intelligent chimpanzee raised as a child for a longer period of time acquire the ability to use sentences for communicative purposes? What factors in the environment were most influential in this acquisition of language? Does the use of words even at a very primitive level imply an ability to think at a correspondingly primitive level?

Language as a Clue to Cultural Expectations

During their development children acquire not only a vocabulary but also an increased knowledge of the categories of experience to which the words refer. Thus, it is said that "When one can identify the referents for words he can make use of the expectancies common in his culture" (6). An example is that of the child who has learned the word *knife* and who has also learned to categorize knives as sharp objects having a particular shape. With the learning of the word *cut,* and of the category of experience associated with it—bleeding, pain, and so on— it is possible for a common cultural expectation to be transmitted to the child by the statement "Knives will cut."

Language provides the opportunity for the learner to generalize from his own sensory experience to the experience of others. He acquires knowledge of areas of possible gratification or danger without personally having to repeat all the actions leading to either. He learns to heed the

What is "human"?

Are people human because they are reared by other human beings—or are they human because they inherit the potential for specifically human activity, such as the ability to communicate verbally?

Viki, shown on the opposite page, was reared as any human infant might be—with diapers, baby bonnets, baths, naps, and feedings in the high chair. She was toilet trained earlier than most human infants, displayed excellent coordination, and developed motor skills rapidly. She followed simple commands and was curious, jealous, and affectionate. She learned to utilize three words appropriately. However, in spite of her remarkable achievements, toward the end of the three-year experiment it became increasingly difficult to "humanize" her, and Viki more frequently sought her freedom, climbed trees, and in general demonstrated the limitations of social experience in itself in altering species-determined behaviors.

words of persons with experience, experience which they also have acquired largely through language. For example, as part of his examination the physician talks with the patient about his complaints and symptoms or about his history. Although he uses a stethoscope to increase his sensitivity to heart sounds, the sounds have meaning for him only because he has learned about the sounds of other hearts, sick and well, from the words used by his teachers and written in his textbooks. The sounds themselves can be described in special words, which can be transmitted to another physician who can then comprehend what the first physician has heard.

There are many aspects of this complex process of integrating physical, motor, sensory, perceptual, and psychological activities into the spoken language that is used to communicate meaning. The vocal apparatus is used so smoothly and "instinctively" that it is taken for granted by most people.

The very close relationship of the biological capacities of the organism and the opportunities for learning provided by the environment is observed in the child's developing capacity to speak. Most children who are free of physical defect or limitation and who are reared in situations that provide the stimulation and opportunity essential for learning acquire a vocabulary of a little under three hundred words by the time they are two years old. Results of studies of children's language development are conflicting, perhaps because it is sometimes difficult to determine what constitutes "knowing" a word. Smith found the greatest increase occurring after the mastery of certain motor skills. Between two and a half and three years, for example, 450 new words are added, and the average six-year-old has a vocabulary of 2500 words (46). And just as the number of words increases, so the child's speech becomes more articulate, integrated, and precise, with full, longer, and more complex sentences appearing about the age of four.

Contact with Other Persons

Although we do not know the precise conditions under which speech is acquired, it is obvious that speech and the use of language depend on the presence of other persons who not only correctly repeat the word-like sounds the infant makes but also reinforce the "right" sounds and the "right" associations. Such reinforcement is provided by caresses or other parental behaviors that enable the infant to experience pleasurable sensations. Later, through secondary reinforcement, the child will respond to the parent's words of approval in terms similar to those he exhibited when he was actually caressed or otherwise rewarded.

Children who are deprived of contact with parents and who are reared in institutional settings do less well in learning words and in speaking than do children of corresponding ages who have homes (52). Contact with others serves to facilitate learning by providing the occasion for verbal communication, by offering opportunities to hear adults use language, and by permitting the necessary reinforcement when the child's efforts to communicate are adequate.

A theory based wholly on the reinforcement principle has been put forward by Skinner. Utilizing research and analogies drawn from operant conditioning (p. 94) he suggests that the infant who possesses the physical capacity to emit certain sounds will do so. At first the specific sounds made by the infant have no particular meaning and chance determines what sound is made. The characteristic babblings or pre-speech sounds of the four- or five-month-old infant are of this order. Some of the sounds the infant makes will be responded to in ways that are pleasing to him. To the sound of *mama,* the mother may pet the child, or pick it up or make certain responsive sounds. Over a period of time the tendency to emit the rewarded sounds is greater than the tendency to emit the sounds that bring no reward. With the increasing tendency to emit the rewarded sounds, there is an increasing ability to associate particular sounds with particular objects or persons, as well as an increasing ability to refine the sounds themselves.

It might seem that the "generality potential" of language which we have described, its capacity for providing the individual with vicarious experience, is wholly desirable and satisfying. If through learning about the world of words, as Hayakawa has termed it, a person is better able to deal with the world as it is, then language has played a facilitating role in his development. But if his world of words creates a false impression of the real world, then his language only assists him in deceiving himself.

The crucial psychological point has been made that language is the repository of culture and the principle vehicle of culture transmission (6). For example, the Eskimo has many words for snow in order to distinguish among the different snow conditions that form so large a part of his life. Our culture has only one word, although we also encounter many kinds of snow conditions. Although the Eskimo child may not personally experience all the various kinds of snow, he is able to extend his knowledge of what the world is like so that he can recognize these types and can understand their implications for him. Information on the various snow conditions may have been accumulated over many generations and this knowledge may have been acquired through painful experiences, experiences which he is spared because he has learned the meanings of the various snow terms.

The accident of birth places each man in the world at a particular time, and his life span can encompass only a small fragment of the time span of the universe. He is limited in terms of what he can see and touch, and he starts his life with the same unawareness of his world that characterizes all the new babies ever born into the world. During his lifetime, however, he has under certain conditions the opportunity to know much more about the world than did any of his ancestors. Not only are technical aids to communication available to him, but also the records of history and of intellectual thought as they have been accrued in the experience of others and transmitted through the medium of the language.

A helpful distinction has been made by Hayakawa, who points out that the world as we learn about it through words should stand in relation to the objective world in the same way that "a map does to a territory it is supposed to represent." The map should not be confused with the geographical territory, nor should any word be confused with what it represents. *Chair* is a word used to represent a class of objects that have specific characteristics and that function as seats; the word *chair* should not be confused with the thing called "chair."

Not only can words be confused with things, they can also take on such strong emotional connotations that they are actually misleading rather than informative. When this occurs, language no longer serves the function of providing an accurate picture of the world of things and processes.

The word *pig* has been cited as an example of this point. It may be used informatively to provide a readily agreed upon concept, such as "mammalian domestic quadruped of the kind generally raised by farmers to be made into pork, bacon, ham, lard . . . ," or it may have an "affective connotation," may evoke a personal emotional response, such as "Ugh! Dirty, evil-smelling creatures, wallowing in filthy sties" (25, p. 84). The confusion of the word with the thing in affective terms may be seen in the delicate evasions of language pertaining to sexual or eliminative behavior. The negative emotional reactions often associated with bladder and bowel activity are avoided by using the words "rest room" to designate the toilet in a public place. Words having affective connotations may be applied to the people or things we like or dislike and may influence us in our reactions toward people and things with whom we have had no direct experience.

Semanticists and linguists as well as psychologists have been interested in the relationship of language to thought. One point of view contends that "each language is not merely a reproducing instrument for voicing ideas but rather in itself is the shaper of ideas" (51). According to this position, language exerts an active influence on the type and the content of the thinking for which it is utilized. For example, some of the aspects of language that we take for granted as reflecting the properties of nature, such as the division of the world into things and actions (nouns and verbs), are actually only properties of the language we use, but they in turn influence the interpretations we make as we observe natural phenomena. A similar process occurs when we utilize verb tenses to reflect a chronological or mathematical conception of time. There are other languages that have different reference points. The Hopi utilize a personalized conception of time that is not expressed in arithmetic units, but in terms of events that are momentary, continued, or repeated (51).

An even closer relationship of language to thought has been postulated by some who have concluded that thinking is actually unspoken speech. They have conducted investigations utilizing sensitive devices to record the electrical activity of the nerves that activate the vocal mechanisms and have obtained results which support the hypothesis that thought is implicit speech. Other investigations, however, have found that thinking may occur without the hidden use of speech or language. The precise nature of the relationship between thought and language cannot as yet be specified, but available evidence, derived in part from studies of the development of language and thought in children, points up their close relationship.

Although the studies cited in the paragraphs above deal more or less specifically with various aspects of language development in the individual, all of them inevitably touch deeply on the area of interpersonal relationships. Language is vital to the personal contacts that provide the child with his concept of humanness, a process that has been referred to as socialization.

Summary

As a physical organism, the infant shares with all other members of the human species physical characteristics and potentialities that develop regardless of training, culture, and environment; he grows, coordinates muscles, and blends (and differentiates) sensations and responses essential to such performances as feeding himself, controlling his bowels, and manipulating small objects. But the acquisition of new behaviors as a result of maturation is supplemented by the skills he acquires from experience. These learnings are rooted in the specific society and culture into which he has been born; they provide the behavioral customs and characteristics that distinguish the Samoan from the New Yorker.

The child's experiences during his first five years with those closest to him reinforce behaviors congruent with social expectations. Various rewards, such as food, holding, petting, words of approval, and smiles, facilitate the acquisition of new behaviors, behaviors that are reflective not only of the culture but also of the parents' values and standards. Thus, it is through the parent-child relationship that the culture exercises its influence on the young child. For him it is usually the relationship with his mother that is crucial to psychological and social development. It is believed that the quality of the "mothering" the child receives contributes crucially to both his physical and his psychological well being. The significance the mother has for the infant has been attributed to her role as the provider of food and the satisfier of his needs for intimate physical contact.

The emergence and definition of the ego processes are observed in the young child when he becomes aware that he is an entity separate from the rest of the world. This awareness that the world exists outside himself leads to understanding of the nature of the world and the people who inhabit it. From experiences with the significant persons in his life, the young child generalizes so that in addition to the specific skills and techniques developed to satisfy the wishes and expectations of others, as well as his own needs, the general attitudes of trust or fear of others also begin to appear.

The basis of the individual's psychological need to feel related to others has its origin in the conditions characterizing the infant's physical dependence upon others for his survival. As the young child matures physically and acquires additional experiences and new learnings, the available means and techniques to satisfy his need to feel in communion with others increase.

Language, one identifying achievement of the human species, plays an increasingly important part of the child's life during his early years. By the time he has passed through the fourth year and into the fifth, he has learned a considerable amount, including how to talk to and with other persons and how partially to control his impulses. He is then ready to journey outside the home, to enter school, and to have his peers and adults unrelated to him play an increasingly important role in his life.

References

1. Baldwin, A. L., Kalhorn, J., and Breese, F. H.   The appraisal of parent behavior. *Psychol. Monogr.,* 1949, *63,* No. 4.
2. Bernstein, A.   Some relations between techniques of feeding and training during infancy and certain behavior in childhood. *Genet. Psychol. Monogr.,* 1955, *51,* 3–44.

3. Blatz, W. E., Allen, K. D., and Millichamp, D. A.   A study of laughter in the nursery school child. *Univer. Toronto Stud. Child Develpm. Ser.,* 1936, No. 7.

4. Bonney, M. E.   Relationships between social success, family size, socio-economic home background, and intelligence among school children in grades 3 and 4. *Sociometry,* 1944, *7,* 26–39.

5. Brody, S.   *Patterns of Mothering: Maternal Influence During Infancy.* New York: International Universities, 1956.

6. Brown, R. W., and Lenneberg, E. H.   Studies in linguistic relativity, in Maccoby, E. E., Newcomb, T. M., and Hartley, E. L. (eds.), *Readings in Social Psychology,* (ed. 3). New York: Holt, 1958.

7. Carpenter, A.   The differential measurement of speed in primary school children. *Child Develpm.,* 1941, *12,* 1–7.

8. Cobb, E. A.   Family press variables. *Monogr. Soc. Res. Child. Develpm.,* 1943, *8,* 327–361.

9. Coleman, R. W., Kris, E., and Provence, S.   The study of variations of early parental attitudes: A preliminary report, in Eissler, R., *et al.* (eds.), *The Psychoanalytic Study of the Child.* New York: International Universities, 1953.

10. Dennis, W., and Dennis, M. G.   The effect of cradling practices upon the onset of walking in Hopi children. *J. genet. Psychol.,* 1940, *56,* 77–86.

11. Diamond, S.   *Personality and Temperament.* New York: Harper, 1957.

12. Dollard, J., and Miller, N. E.   *Personality and Psychotherapy.* New York: McGraw-Hill, 1950.

13. DuBois, C.   *The People of Alor.* Minneapolis: University of Minnesota Press, 1944.

14. Escalona, S.   Emotional development in the first year of life, in Senn, M. J. E. (ed.), *Problems of Infancy and Childhood: Transactions of the Sixth Conference.* New York: Macy Foundation, 1953.

15. Freud, A., and Burlingham, D. T.   *War and Children.* New York: Medical War Books, 1943.

16. Gesell, A., and Ilg, F. L.   *Feeding Behavior of Infants: A Pediatric Approach to the Mental Hygiene of Early Life.* Philadelphia: Lippincott, 1937.

17. Glick, P. C.   The life-cycle of the family. *Marriage and Family Living,* Feb. 1955, p. 9.

18. Goldfarb, W.   Effects of psychological deprivation in infancy, and subsequent stimulation. *Amer. J. Psychiat.,* 1945, *102,* 18–23.

19. Goodenough, F. L.   Anger in Young Children, *Univer. Minnesota Inst. Child Welf. Monogr. Ser.,* 1931, No. 9.

20. Gorer, C.   Themes in Japanese culture. *Trans. New York Acad. Sci.,* 1943, *5,* 106–124.

21. Guilford, R. B., and Worcester, D. A.   A comparative study of the only and non-only child. *J. genet. Psychol.,* 1930, *38,* 411–426.

22. Gutteridge, Mary V.   A study of motor achievements of young children, *Arch. Psychol.,* N.Y., 1939, No. 244.

23. Hagman, E. R.   A study of fears of children of preschool age. *J. exp. Educ.,* 1932, *1,* 110–130.
24. Harlow, H. F.   The nature of love. *Amer. Psychologist,* 1958, *13,* 673–685.
25. Hayakawa, S. I.   *Language in Thought and Action.* New York: Harcourt, 1949.
26. Hayes, C.   *The Ape in Our House.* New York: Harper, 1951.
27. Hayes, K. J., and Hayes, C.   The intellectual development of a home raised chimpanzee. *Proc. Amer. Phil. Soc.,* 1951, *95,* 105–109.
28. Hollenberg, E., and Sperry, M.   Some antecedents of aggression and effects of frustration on doll play. *Personality,* 1950, *1,* 32–43.
29. Jersild, A. T., and Holmes, F. B.   Children's fears. *Child Develpm. Monogr.,* 1935, No. 20.
30. Justin, F.   A genetic study of laughter provoking stimuli. *Child Develpm.,* 1932, *3,* 114–136.
31. Kellogg, W. N., and Kellogg, L. A.   *The Ape and the Child.* New York: McGraw-Hill, 1933.
32. Kluckhohn, C.   Variations in the human family, in Bell, N. W., and Vogel, E. F., *The Family.* New York: Free Press, 1960.
33. Levy, D. M.   Experiments in the sucking reflex and social behavior of dogs. *Amer. J. Orthopsychiat.,* 1934, *4,* 203–224.
34. Levy, D. M.   Psychosomatic studies of some aspects of maternal behavior. *Psychosom. Med.,* 1942, *4,* 223–227.
35. Mead, M.   *Cooperation and Competition among Primitive People.* New York: McGraw-Hill, 1937.
36. Radke, M. J.   The relation of parental authority to children's behavior attitudes. *Univer. Minnesota Child Welf. Monogr.,* 1946, No. 22.
37. Ribble, M.   *The Rights of Infants.* New York: Columbia University Press, 1943.
38. Roberts, C. S.   Ordinal position and its relation to some aspects of personality. *J. genet. Psychol.,* 1938, *53,* 173–213.
39. Roberts, E.   Thumb and finger sucking in relation to feeding in early infancy. *Amer. J. Dis. Child.,* 1944, *68,* 7–8.
40. Rosenow, C., and Whyte, A. H.   The ordinal position of problem children. *Amer. J. Orthopsychiat.,* 1931, *1,* 430–434.
41. Ross, S.   Sucking behavior in neonate dogs. *J. abnorm. soc. Psychol.,* 1951, *46,* 142–149.
42. Schachter, S.   *The Psychology of Affiliation.* Stanford, Calif.: Stanford University Press, 1959.
43. Sears, P. S.   Doll play aggression in normal young children: Influence of sex, age, sibling status, father's absence. *Psychol. Monogr.,* 1951, *65* (6).
44. Sears, R. R., Maccoby, E. E., and Levin, H.   *Patterns of Child Rearing.* New York: Harper, 1957.
45. Sears, R. R., Whiting, J. W. M., Nowlis, V., and Sears, P. S.   Some child-rearing antecedents of aggression and dependency in young children. *Genet. Psychol. Monogr.,* 1953, *47,* 135–234.

46. Smith, M. E.   An investigation of the development of the sentence and the extent of the vocabulary in young children. *Univer. Iowa Stud. Child Welf.*, 1926, No. 5, 3.

47. Spitz, R. A.   Hospitalism, in Fenichel, O., *et al.* (eds.), *The Psychoanalytic Study of the Child* (Vol. 1). New York: International Universities, 1945.

48. Spitz, R. A.   Hospitalism: A follow-up report, in Fenichel, O., *et al.* (eds.), *The Psychoanalytic Study of the Child* (Vol. 2). New York: International Universities, 1946.

49. Stolz, L. M., *et al.*   *Father Relations of War-Born Children.* Stanford, Calif.: Stanford University Press, 1954.

50. Strodtbeck, F. L.   Family interaction, values, and achievement, in McClelland, D.C., Baldwin, A. L., Bronfenbrenner, U., and Strodtbeck, F. L., *Talent and Society.* Princeton, N.J.: Van Nostrand, 1958.

51. Whorf, B. L.   Science and linguistics, in Maccoby, E. E., Newcomb, T. M., and Hartley, E. L., *Readings in Social Psychology* (ed. 3). New York: Holt, 1958.

52. Williams, H. M., and Mattson, M. L.   The effect of social groupings upon the language of preschool children. *Univer. Iowa Stud. Child Welf.*, 1937, *13*, No. 2, Part III.

53. Whiting, J. W. M., and Child, I. L.   *Child Training and Personality.* New Haven: Yale University Press, 1953.

54. Yarrow, L. J.   The relationship between nutritive sucking experiences in infancy and non-nutritive sucking in childhood. *J. genet. Psychol.*, 1954, *84*, 149–162.

55. Zemlick, M. F., and Watson, R. I.   Maternal attitudes of acceptance and rejection during and after pregnancy. *Amer. J. Orthopsychiat.*, 1953, *23*, 570–584.

Selected Readings

Carmichael, L. (ed.).   *Manual of Child Psychology* (ed. 2). New York: Wiley, 1954.

Erickson, E. H.   *Childhood and Society.* New York: Norton, 1950.

Gesell, A., *et al.*   *The First Five Years of Life: A Guide to the Study of the Preschool Child.* New York: Harper, 1940.

Mussen, P. H., and Conger, J. J.   *Child Development and Personality.* New York: Harper, 1956.

Sears, R. R., Maccoby, E. E., and Levin, H.   *Patterns of Child Rearing.* New York: Harper, 1957.

Watson, R. I.   *Psychology of the Child.* New York: Wiley, 1959.

7.

Childhood

As the child developed physically in infancy and early childhood, he was expected to fulfill parental expectations in regard to drinking from a cup, feeding himself, controlling his bowels and bladder, walking, talking, dressing, and washing. These developmental tasks provided one context in which the attitudes toward the self developed. They were accompanied by the development and balancing of the ego and superego processes and by the techniques and mechanisms necessary for maintaining their optimal harmony.

During childhood, from the age of five to thirteen, personality development is less directly related to the specific stages of physical development and the tasks accompanying these stages. The extension and enhancement of physical skills, the development of attitudes toward the self that accompany lessening physical dependency, and the acquisition of physical prowess are comparatively gradual processes during this period; they are less dramatic than those of infancy or of adolescence but are nevertheless of great significance to the individual's psychological development.

At five, the child weighs five or six times as much as he did as an infant and his height has more than doubled. At birth, his head represented one fourth of his total height, but by the time he enters childhood it is only one eighth of his total height and his bodily proportions have become closer to those of an adult. Although the rate of growth is less rapid during childhood than it was during infancy, between the ages of five and nine the child's height and weight increase steadily. He becomes longer-limbed and longer-bodied and his proportions of breadth to width gradually change from the roundness of infancy to the

174

flatter contour of the child. Toward the latter part of childhood, usually during the twelfth or thirteenth year, well-known physical changes associated with puberty become evident. At this time the rate of growth again accelerates, and he gains weight and grows taller more rapidly than he had during the previous four or five years.

Between the ages of five and thirteen, the child learns to sustain his attention for longer periods; motor skills are refined and extended to include the more complex skills of writing, handling tools, playing baseball. Speed of reactions continues to increase, with boys being slightly faster than girls. Fancy stunts on bicycles and roller skates are not uncommon, and because of the development of fine motor control, this is regarded as the best time for the child to learn to play a musical instrument.

PHYSICAL DEVELOPMENT, PARENTAL ATTITUDES, AND SELF-ESTEEM

The child's physical status plays an important part in the genesis of the beliefs and attitudes the person holds of himself. Beliefs and attitudes regarding one's worth, competence, and ability arise, in part, from experiences of confronting a new task or a new demand and from developing the procedures, approaches, or skills required to afford gratification, tension reduction, or relief from pain or the threat of pain. Childhood offers many challenges: caring for one's own needs, attending school and performing activities related to reading and writing, playing cooperatively and competitively with one's peers, and fulfilling the responsibilities expected within the family situation. Successes and failures in coping with tasks such as these contribute to an impression of one's own value and worth. Although it is an oversimplification to assume that there is a direct relationship between self-esteem and physical development, it is also unwise to overlook the role physical development often plays in contributing to the image the individual has of himself.

The parents' attitudes and their expectations of what the child should or could be like are often closely related to some aspect of physical development, appearance, or physical proficiency. In infancy and early childhood his dependence upon adults is taken for granted, but how well he can assume responsibility for himself in such matters as eating, dressing, and complying with rules becomes increasingly significant to parents as the child grows older. How his self-esteem is affected by the behaviors and attitudes of parents during childhood depends upon the level of expectation the parent holds for him as well as upon the child's proficiency. Thus, a child whose performance and proficiency are high will not necessarily hold himself in high regard, nor will one whose physical prowess is below average necessarily devalue himself.

The crucial factors in determining the extent to which the child measures his own worth in terms of what he can do physically are the responses that the significant persons in his life provide to his efforts. Parents who reinforce the child's efforts to cope with new tasks by providing encouragement and approval when he has tried, even though the outcome may fall short, and who acknowledge even modest gains in a positive manner will contribute to the likelihood that the child will continue to try. The parent who evaluates the child's efforts in terms only of what other children do or of some arbitrarily high standard probably contributes to a personal self characterized by feelings of inadequacy and incompetence.

This, of course, does not imply that parents should fail to provide guidance or instruction when their children require it; it does suggest that unusually high parental standards and expectations, criticism, and unfavorable comparisons do not contribute to the child's sense of competence.

Physical Development and Social Environment

Another aspect of physical development during this period is of particular importance. Usually by the time the child is four or five he has learned that males and females are constructed differently. He has had some opportunities to observe the bodies of his playmates and his parents and he is aware that women, in contrast to men, have breasts and lack a penis. As the physical differences between men and women become more clearly identified in the course of his development, a host of attitudes and impressions, many of which gain emotional components, are acquired. He learns that certain acts, related to urination and defecation, are performed privately, that certain subjects are not discussed openly, that some questions he raises are evaded by his parents. His acts of manipulating his genitals are discouraged, scolded, or ridiculed.

How he comes to think of himself and his own body, his own physical impulses and urges, the behaviors that he believes he should present for others to see and respond to, and what he believes he should or should not do with his body develop through experiences in which parents, peers, and teachers communicate their attitudes to him. Such communication often occurs in the form of direct reinforcement of the child's behavior; acts that receive disapproval are not only less likely to be repeated but in addition the parental disapproval sometimes generalizes to many issues pertaining to the body, to its natural functions, and to one's personal feelings of self-worth and value.

Since the relationship of physical development to the development of self-attitudes can be understood only in terms of the child's experiences with other persons, the discussion at this point shifts its emphasis to the child's social world. The very close interrelationship of physical, social, and psychological development is illustrated by the first topic to be considered in the next section, which describes how the child's sex, a biologically determined physical status, assumes its particular psychological significance through his relationships with other persons.

Physical, Social, and Cultural Environment

FAMILY RELATIONSHIP AND THE SOCIAL ROLE

The culture into which the child is born continues to exert a powerful influence upon his psychological development, but only as it is interpreted and enforced, first through the parents and then, with increasing significance through the child's associations outside the family. The child's developing concept of himself as a member of his sex, his expectations of appropriate behaviors, his attitudes towards his own body and his own impulses, are all related to the expectations held of him because of his sex by those with whom he mingles. These expectations, which are assigned to him and over which he has no control, relate to the behaviors that are associated with a particular position held with respect to the other members of the social group.

The Learning of Role Behaviors

The social positions that are defined in terms of the society may bear many designations. For example, the terms *doctor* and *lawyer* designate social positions, and the behaviors considered relevant to these positions are termed "roles." The role—the expected behavior—of the doctor is to care for the sick and of the lawyer to protect the rights of his client. Similarly, there are behaviors expected of the child because he is a child, and, more specifically, behaviors that are expected of him because of his role as a boy or a girl. The expectations of the various role behaviors depend upon a common frame of reference, such as language and customs, and upon judgments or attitudes that are shared in common by the individuals in a society.

A person may simultaneously occupy a number of positions. The nine-year-old child may fill the positions of a boy, a third grader, the oldest of three children in a family, and a cub scout. Each of his roles will depend upon his position in relation to others in his social environment; the activities associated with any given role will therefore depend upon the relationship of that role to others. Consider the relationship between role and position as it can be observed in the baseball situation. Second base is a position; the second baseman who fills the position is expected to adopt a set of behaviors appropriate to it. By virtue of his position and his knowledge of the role associated with it, he behaves in accordance with the social expectation. Some roles are assigned to individuals on the basis of physical characteristics, characteristics over which they have no control. Thus, racial background or conditions of physical disability or deviancy may evoke expectations in others because of the roles that are assigned to such persons in the society.

Of the many roles that individuals are assigned by virtue of their position in our society, few are as explicitly defined as the boy-girl roles. Some of the experiences enabling the child to learn the role expectations were mentioned in the last section, but here Sears' comment (17) regarding the importance of the parents' behaviors, as they interpret cultural expectations, is relevant.

> The sex of her child provides an important stimulus to a mother. It places the child in a social category that has enormous implications for training. She knows the many differences in the roles that apply to the two sexes; she has expectancies that are congruent with these roles. Even by the age of 5, the child elicits some kinds of behavior from the mother that are direct responses to the fact of the child's being a boy or a girl.[1]

Parents' Role Expectations

Sears and his associates have been concerned with the behavioral expectations mothers hold for their children, expectations that were related to boy and girl roles. In this study of child-rearing practices as they were reported by over 200 mothers of five-year-old children, it was found that maternal expectancies for sons differed from those for daughters. Some of these differences seem obvious. For example, girls were expected to help with the dishes by 28 percent of the mothers, but only 19 percent expected their sons to perform this chore. In the same study, 60 percent of the mothers of daughters reported affectionate behaviors toward their daughters while only 49 percent of the mothers

---

[1] Reprinted by permission from R. R. Sears *et al., Patterns of Child Rearing.* New York: Harper: 1957. Copyright, 1957, by Harper & Row, Publishers, Incorporated.

of boys reported such behavior. It was found that boys were treated more permissively than were girls when they fought with neighbors' children or when they were aggressive toward their parents.

Judging from these mothers' reports, the image of the male as a warrior and fighter is still prevalent. Thirty-four percent of the mothers encouraged their sons to fight back if attacked, while only 14 percent of the mothers of girls did so. The authors of the study illustrate the point that being "boylike" is seen as involving the ability to defend oneself and to be aggressive with one's playmates by the following quotation.

> *Interviewer:* How important do you think it is for a boy of Ted's age to act like a real boy?
>
> *Mother:* Very important, very important—I will repeat that. By a real boy, I mean not being a sissy; it is very important. I wouldn't want him otherwise—I would give him boxing lessons if I had to.
>
> *Interviewer:* Have you ever encouraged him to fight back?
>
> *Mother:* Oh, yes. I have told him if he can't fight back and take care of his own battle, I am not going out there. You see, that is another thing that he is going to have to learn: to give as well as take; and that is going to make him get away from these other feminine likes of his. But, you see, he runs away from it, which isn't good. This summer will be the test, because then he'll be six, and he'll be meeting up with the gang around here, and unless he establishes himself as being a good kid and a good boy in their eyes, he might feel it from that point on, you see. That is why I am playing up this big, strong angle. All the boy needs is confidence. I mean, if he can stop this youngster once and hurt him, that, I think, gives him so much confidence that he can do it again without being hurt himself too much. I am not one that goes out and just hits for the sake of hitting, but I think around here if a child hits you, you can't run home and cry to your mother; you've got to hit him back and learn to take it and give it too.[2]

The role of the male as the provider and the related need for his being trained for an occupation underlies the different educational expectations mothers reported for their sons and daughters. The general expectation was that sons would complete a college education, daughters, a high-school education.

Other differences in the reports between mothers of boys and of girls had to do with specific training techniques. Sears found that the

[2] Reprinted by permission from R. R. Sears *et al., Patterns of Child Rearing.* New York, Harper, 1957. Copyright, 1957, by Harper & Row, Publishers, Incorporated.

measures used to discipline young children involved greater physical punishment for boys than for girls, who were disciplined more frequently by "love-oriented techniques," such as withholding of approval, verbal expressions of disapproval, or offering of praise.

Differences in parental treatment of boys and girls are reflected not only in the ways cited above but in many activities so common that they are taken for granted. The issue of appearance is a case in point. The little girl who comes in from the street with a dirty dress, her hands and face streaked with mud, is apt to receive a scolding from her mother, not merely because she is dirty, but also because "little girls shouldn't look like that." Her brother may also receive a scolding, but it is likely to be tempered with some degree of acceptance because "boys are like that." Customs in dress or manner or speech also reflect the differential expectations held for boys and girls; some behaviors are considered "unladylike" and inappropriate for girls, while other manners and interests are considered effeminate if engaged in by men. Appropriate role behavior is reinforced also by the child's experience with his own age group or peers and will be discussed in detail in a special section.

Inhibition of Sexual Expression

During the preschool years and childhood, sexual as well as aggressive impulses are redirected and inhibited as a result of experiences with parents and others. It has been noted earlier that the basic biological drives and urges which have been grouped within the category of the id impulses will energize the individual into action. These impulses —or more correctly their psychological components, which in adult life are integrated and combined in the procreative behaviors—are evident in children in the forms of self-gratification, interests, curiosity, and sex play of the type in which children engage. Yet the culture in which we live is one of the most restrictive and punitive toward these childish expressions of sexuality. In accounting for the social mores that serve to restrict the child in his expression of sexuality, Sears (17) makes the following point:

> Our relatively high level of education, which is a prerequisite for such a complex industrial society, requires that young people in their late teens remain in school and become prepared for their careers. They are expected to postpone marriage and childbearing until a later age than would be common in many more primitive societies. Furthermore, our monogamous marriage system requires that young people be trained toward the cultural ideal of confining their sex interest to one partner. They must receive early

training in impulse control and must acquire the ability to postpone gratification of sex impulses.[3]

The learnings through which such control over sexual impulses is acquired occur within the relationships of parents and children, the parents in effect representing the culture and imparting the attitudes of the society through the controls they place on the behavior of the child. Sears notes that such controls do not allow sexual contact between a child or adolescent and any other member of the family group; they prohibit sexual self-stimulation and all forms of sex play with other children.

Of all the restrictions upon the child's sexual activity, the commonest in all societies is that against incest. Sexual relations between parent and child are taboo not only in highly developed societies such as ours but also in less complex and in primitive societies. It has been suggested that such controls are essential if the family is to function as a unit; without them the authority of the parent would be lessened and the husband-wife relationship weakened.

With respect to self-stimulation and sex play, however, our culture shares only with Western Europe its restrictive controls. These cultures differ from most others in that sexual self-stimulation and child sex play are quite expressly forbidden. Although the practice of self-stimulation or masturbation is usually viewed as a natural part of the child's behavior pattern and is permitted in public in other societies, here it is discouraged. Such discouragement can range from calling the child's attention to the fact that he is handling his genitals or asking him if he has to go to the bathroom, to severe physical punishment or frightening him by describing fictitious harmful effects of masturbation. Since most children during their first several years of life learn that rubbing themselves in the genital area is gratifying, most parents will have occasion to deal with the problem of masturbation, if they are concerned about communicating that which society expects. In Sears' study, one mother reported: "He did tell me that it made him feel good, because it made him ticklish, and I said I know it did but not to do it again as it wasn't nice."

The third area in which parents control the sexual behaviors of their child has to do with what has been termed sex play. The child will engage in various "games" with other children in which clothing is removed and the child exposes himself. In these games a child may play the part of a doctor who examines the body of another child, or may simulate the taking of a temperature rectally; in other games the child

[3] Reprinted by permission from R. R. Sears *et al.*, *Patterns of Child Rearing*. New York: Harper, 1957. Copyright, 1957, by Harper & Row, Publishers, Incorporated.

"You are a big boy now."

This means that you conceal your fears, that you push back the tears, that you don't flinch or show your hurt.

To be a big boy is to be a man and men are brave, strong, and unemotional. And even if you are only seven you know this; you have seen your parents' smiles when you have acted "right" and have caught their disapproval when you have let them down.

To be emotional is to let yourself down if you are a male, for "everyone" knows that men are not supposed to behave this way. Yet men do have their fears and their feelings. To run from danger, to avoid pain, to express one's emotions—these are natural characteristics of the human being, whether male or female. But social expectations are learned early in life, and to behave contrary to these expectations brings shame and humiliation. So be brave, "You are a big boy now."

Wayne Miller—Magnum

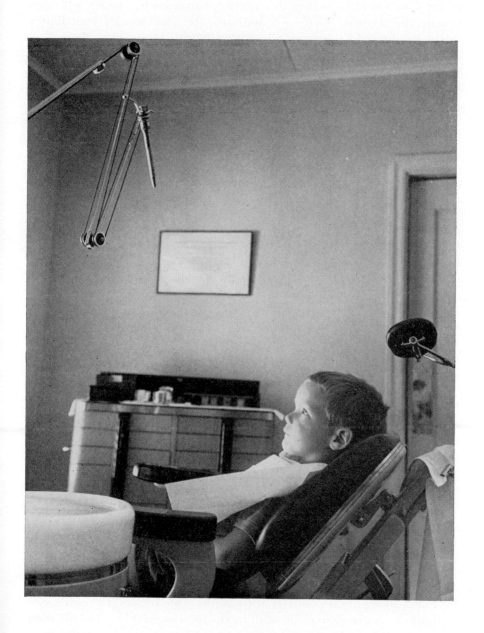

is dared to reveal himself or is challenged to a contest to see who can urinate the farthest. That such activities are done secretly contributes to the heightened excitement which they afford. In sex play, then, it is not merely the satisfaction of curiosity and the actual physical stimulation the child experiences that contributes to the pleasure of the situation but also the excitement of doing something forbidden or disapproved. The relatively common practice among children of preschool age and of first and second graders of going to the bathroom together probably has some elements in common with sex play of the type just mentioned.

The period of childhood is characterized by an expansion of the ego; information and knowledge are continuously being acquired about acceptable and unacceptable behaviors, and the attitudes of those who are significant in his life are related to the impulses he finds gratifying. The significance on a particular child of parental reinforcement of cultural mores and expectations is specific to the relationship that exists between the child and his parents. Within our culture, childhood sexual behavior is not condoned, and the parents communicate this to the child. But whether the child also learns that there is a degree of danger and threat in sexual gratification or interest, and whether he becomes anxious when he experiences his own sexual impulses depends upon several related issues pertaining to the parents (usually the mother's) feelings and the degree of anxiety she communicates in matters pertaining to sex. Closely related to this is the severity or permissiveness that characterize her efforts to reinforce the control of sexual activity.

Sears notes that the mothers in his study (17) who were rated as being nonpermissive with respect to the sexual activity of their children, also tended to prohibit their children from aggressing against them, were very strict in toilet training, often physically punished them, checked on their whereabouts often, were emotionally cold toward them, and were strict about their manners and care of property. The nonpermissive mothers also were concerned that their daughters should be "feminine" and their sons "masculine."

RELATIONSHIPS OUTSIDE THE FAMILY

As he grows older, the child spends increasing amounts of time outside the home, much of it in activities related to school, where he comes in significant contact with adults who are not his parents or members of his immediate family. In this process he begins to question the infallibility of his parents, learning—perhaps with some difficulty— their human failings. In addition, some of the essential learnings are acquired pertaining to self-identity in relation to the world about him; these learnings occur, in part, through contacts with his peer group.

In a study by Tuddenham (24), California children in the first, third, and fifth grades reported definite concepts of traits and characteristics associated with each sex. The typical girl was seen as tidy, quiet, friendly, not quarrelsome, and not a show-off. The typical boy was considered to be a show-off, wiggly, not bashful, good at games, and bossy. Tuddenham states:

> The picture of the typical boy and girl as conceived by children even in the primary grades seems to be almost a photostat of the common identification by adults within our society of aggressiveness, restlessness and daring with masculinity, and amiability, docility, and timidity with femininity.

The expectations that the child's friends hold toward behaviors appropriate to the two sexes is probably an additional factor accounting for behaviors adopted by boys and girls. The influence of the child's peer group is probably achieved through the responses that the members reinforce by their approval or disapproval, and those behaviors acceptable to the group, those that conform to expectations, will be reinforced, adopted, and strengthened; those that are inconsistent with expectations will be discouraged.

Researches involving social acceptance, such as the Tuddenham study, often utilize the "Guess Who" technique, in which a number of short descriptions of children in the group are given and the children are then asked to guess which member of the class is being described (24). Another technique, developed by Moreno, allows children to indicate preferences for classmates to serve on their committees, to sit next to, or to accompany on trips (12). This procedure, known as constructing a sociogram, allows the child to select or exclude members of the group according to the type of activity involved. Children's responses can be diagrammed in such a way that the "popular" as well as the "rejected" members can easily be identified by the teacher or psychologist. Studies using these techniques have led to reports that the characteristics involved in popularity tend to shift with age, from the quiet boy, for example, in younger groups, to the more athletic, aggressive "show-off" described in this chapter (10). It seems also that the characteristics essential for social acceptability are not the same for all economic levels.

INTERESTS

As the foregoing discussion has pointed out, the characteristics required of boys and girls if they are to be accepted and admired by their peers are reinforced in their contacts with these peers. These characteristics are reflected in the choices that children make of ways to spend their time. The pattern of masculine interests and activities will include the use of tools, playing with kites and marbles, wrestling, boxing, and football, while the girls' interests during the same period include playing with dolls, playing house, and cooking. Boys will be primarily concerned about their play activities, while girls may be chiefly occupied with helping at home. As children reach the sixth, seventh, and eighth grades their pattern of reading also reflects the effects of well-established differences in interests. Boys are interested in reading books of adventure, exploration, and travel, but girls tend to prefer stories of love, romance, and feminine activities. It should be emphasized that although sharp differences such as these are noted in some of the studies cited, masculine and feminine interests are better described as points on a continuum than as two distinct areas. Thus, some very "masculine" boys prefer quiet activities and some "feminine" girls enjoy sports.

The Social Self and the Perceived Sex Role

By the time the boy reaches the age of nine and until he enters adolescence at about the age of fourteen, his interests and his consciousness of himself with respect to the opposite sex result in a social self that is manifested by his not joining in a game in which he is an only boy and not showing a girl any particular attention, if he can avoid doing so. If he finds himself in a group of girls, he often tries to leave as quickly as possible. As he approaches the end of childhood, he may poke fun at girls and tease those of his friends who indicate an interest in them. He becomes aware of the physical aspects of sex and becomes very modest in undressing or going to the toilet in the presence of the opposite sex.

This pattern of self-consciousness about one's sex and accompanying modesty is duplicated in the behavior of girls, except that it begins and ends somewhat earlier, since girls enter their adolescence before boys; therefore, during the period from between her eighth and ninth year until about her twelfth year a girl tends to become increasingly interested in clothing and her physical attractiveness. She will not join a group of boys if she is the only girl and also will evidence a high degree of physical modesty.

During the period of childhood most boys come to value themselves for their aggressive and competitive skills, for their strength and competence in games, and for the things they can do and make. They develop ideas as to the type of work that is befitting a man and are disdainful of women's pursuits. Girls tend to share more in the responsibilities of the home and become increasingly conscious of the importance within this culture of feminine traits such as good manners, attractiveness, and competence in matters of dress and homemaking.

Through his peers the child comes in contact with various attitudes toward himself, toward adults, and toward those things that are to be valued or disregarded. He learns how to secure the recognition of his group, how to participate as one of its members, and how to avoid its displeasure. Many of his peer contacts occur in school; many indirectly involve adults as supervisors and teachers, or involve the imitation of adult standards. From the peer group the child learns modes of behavior that cannot be learned from adults. This contribution to the child's socialization—that is, to his development as a member of society —is accomplished in the peer group via its rewards when he complies with its expectations. His peers provide a model for him to follow.

From the group he also receives support for his wishes and for the stands he may take with his parents. Realization that he shares certain experiences and wishes with other children contributes to his feelings of relatedness and to the diffusion of his loyalties outside the familial relationships. Thus, as Martin and Stendler (11) have noted, the child acquires from his peer group (1) *rewards;* (2) *an identity;* and (3) *support.*

How he thinks of himself, as well as how he wants to present himself to others, initially depends upon his parental relationships; in these relationships being "love-worthy" is of primary significance to the child. In contrast, the period of middle childhood sees the development of self-esteem as being related also to his being "respect-worthy." White (28) comments in this connection:

> . . . It is fair to say that the crucial arena for self-esteem is the arena of one's age-mates. At home there is an age hierarchy. Even the siblings are bigger or smaller, so that differences of competence are expected. The home, moreover, continues to be the source of love and provision of basic wants, even when the child ventures forth to playground and school. At home he must be love-worthy; this may include being competent, but it is heavily weighted on the side of being good, obedient, and affectionate. On the playground the values are different: He must be respect-worthy, able to command respect because he shows competence and handles himself with ease. It is a sharp strain for many children when they pass from the atmosphere of a child-centered home into the competitive realities of even a friendly social group. They must now show what they have in the way of physical prowess, courage, manipulative skill, outgoing friendliness, all in direct comparison with other children of their age. The penalties for failure are humiliation, ridicule, rejection from the group.[4]

[4] Reprinted by permission from Robert W. White, *The Abnormal Personality.* Copyright 1948, The Ronald Press Company.

THE BEGINNINGS OF PREJUDICE

The group composed of the child's peers provides a context in which the child can acquire the experience necessary to evaluate the consequences of his own behaviors. He learns what is acceptable and unacceptable to the group and how to conform to their wishes. Although he acquires increasing ability to empathize with others—that is, to respond with sensitivity to the feelings and needs of others—he also becomes increasingly aware of his own ethnic background and class. This is the period when the awareness of differences in racial background and in religious convictions becomes evident as a basis in the selection or rejection of one's playmates. White children in the early grades will cross ethnic lines in selecting their associates, but by the fifth and sixth grades such a crossing occurs only rarely.

The formation of prejudice has been extensively studied, and this highly complex subject does not lend itself to a simple presentation. As far as school children are concerned, however, attitudes of prejudice appear to be learned and may have little relation either to personal experience or to direct knowledge of the persons discriminated against. In one study (15) it was found that white children do not change their attitudes toward Negroes even after having pleasant associations with them. This resistance to change in attitudes and beliefs is attributed to the fact that within the culture prejudiced attitudes are reinforced more often than nonprejudiced attitudes. In Chapter 12 the issue of prejudice is treated in more detail; it is introduced at this point merely to note that during the childhood period awareness of racial and ethnic differences becomes a factor in the choice of one's associations and that the emotional and value judgments which often are linked to the cognitive awareness of differences also become significant during this time. Many of these learnings occur in the school situation, a situation that is discussed later in this chapter in relation to the factors that contribute to extension, clarification, and refinement of ego processes.

Personality Development of the Child

THE SELVES AND INTRAPSYCHIC PROCESSES

Underlying the conscious self-images the child has during this period of development are the intrapsychic processes, which account for the child's selves. The peer group's importance in reinforcing sexual roles and in defining appropriate behaviors has been discussed. Learnings relative to sexual roles, reinforced by peers as well as by parents, contribute significantly to the development of the child's concepts of his personal, social, and ideal selves.

The distinctions between the role expectations of boys and girls and of men and women has significance not only for what the individual thinks of himself (personal self) and for what he wishes to show of himself in his relationships with others (social self), but also for the child's ideal self; that is, for what he believes he should be. The non-aggressive, nonathletically inclined boy whose interests are in music, art, or literature may in his fantasies perform marked feats of heroism or excel in athletics. In some cases, the disparity between the ideal and the personal self images is so great that the child will be dissatisfied and uncomfortable with himself and will have to rely upon various defenses to reconcile these incongruities.

With continued reinforcement of the behaviors associated with his sex role both at home and at school, it is not surprising that as the child proceeds through this period he acquires a clearly defined social self that includes those behaviors he feels should be presented in his relationships with others. These aspects of the social self are derived in large part from the expectations that others hold for those of the child's sex. Thus the social self is influenced by the ways in which his parents and friends expect him to behave.

DEVELOPING EMOTIONAL CONTROL

During infancy and the preschool years, the child becomes increasingly able to control his impulses. By the age of five he recognizes that some gratifications must be delayed, that the conditions of his situation will not permit unrestrained expression of his wishes, desires, and angers. The child has had a succession of encounters with his parents, other adults, and his siblings; their expectations and requirements of him, their attitudes and behaviors toward him, reinforce his tendencies to postpone immediate gratification and to inhibit the expression of his impulses.

It will be recalled that the Goodenough study mentioned in Chapter 6 reported that the preschool child often expressed his anger in an unrestrained fashion, by crying, screaming, and kicking, behaviors not necessarily directed against persons. After the child's second year, anger outbursts decrease in frequency, and, as he grows older, the incidents that trigger off anger responses become increasingly social in nature. The actions of others more often precipitate his anger, and the nature of his expression tends to become directed more specifically toward someone else. Direct physical attacks upon another person, however, give way to verbal attacks, such as taunts, sneers, or sarcasm, and anger shows itself in irritability, sulkiness, or "moods."

This trend continues throughout childhood; parents discourage the temper tantrums of their children and under most circumstances dissuade them from striking other children. By the time the child is two or three, he has begun to learn that open expression of anger is not condoned by his parents, teachers, and peers and that his self-interests are best served by restraining his impulses to strike out when frustrated.

Some research has been done on other emotional responses. A study by Pratt (14), for example, indicated that fears still plague the lives of older children; in fact, he found that rural children in the fifth to eighth grades reported a greater number and variety of fears than younger children. Jersild's investigation, involving reports from 1,000 fifth and sixth grade children, suggested that responses to fears tend to become more subtle and indirect, shifting to more complex derivatives. While some fears reported were realistic ones, a surprising number were in the realm of fantasy, such as fears of imaginary creatures, of being alone or in the dark. Eighteen percent of the subjects were afraid of being attacked by animals, yet only 2 percent had experienced such an attack (5, 6). England asked 100 seventh and eighth graders to make drawings of the most important events in their lives. Although he said nothing about fear while giving the directions, 88 out of 290 drawings were identified as depicting fear experiences, which suggests the extent to which fears persist even in the lives of older children (3).

As is the case for the period of earlier childhood, little research has been done on the expression of pleasant emotions. Another study by Jersild, however, suggests that older children identify social relationships and opportunities for self-discovery, realization, and improvement as being more joy-producing than younger ones do (7).

Anxiety and Sexual and Aggressive Impulses

In the discussion of the relationship between ego and id processes, it was noted that anxiety accompanies conditions that threaten the personality. Some of the id impulses have a sexual aspect; they strive for expression during this period, but society does not sanction their expression, as indicated by restrictions against incest, masturbation, and sex play. Expression of other feelings is similarly restrained, and the child slowly learns that satisfactions must be delayed. In this process of gaining control over physical expression of affection or aggression during the childhood period, the degree of danger or threat that his own impulses represent to the child will depend upon the degree to which the parents' anxieties about these behaviors are apparent in their own behaviors and attitudes. Just as the child's ego processes enable him to learn that some behaviors are frowned upon, so he can learn that some are upsetting and frightening to his parents. When he is unclear or uncertain about the nature of the act accounting for the anxiety or fear shown by the parent, then the potential for anxiety is greater than when the nature of the threat can be understood.

Sears makes the interesting observation that, with respect to his sexual organs and their function, the child may not be provided—as he is in other developmental experiences—with appropriate language, substitute skills, or alternative actions that can help him to cope with his own impulses and his parents' requirements. He notes that when the child is given misleading information, such as being told not to touch his genitals because they are "dirty," emotions may be associated with sexuality that can contribute to difficulties in the sexual area during both childhood and later life. In this connection it should be observed that the attitudes of childhood toward sex provide the basis upon which adult sexual attitudes are built. Parental emphasis upon sexual impulses as bad, upon undue modesty with respect to one's body, upon self-manipulation as causing mental illness, are all in some respects damaging to the child's development (17).

On the other hand, the parent, as the agent and architect of the ego in assisting the child to acquire a knowledge of society's expectations, cannot reinforce behaviors that would bring the child into severe conflict with the society. That the parent's position in matters pertaining to aggressive and sexual impulses is indeed difficult must be acknowledged. The best that parents can do is, perhaps, to reinforce the demands of reality by presenting the child with information he can understand, and to remain relaxed about the subject while they are doing so.

THE CHILD'S LOVE FOR THE PARENT
OF THE OPPOSITE SEX

Interest in the genitals is said to be magnified during the period from about the third to the sixth or seventh year, as evidenced by an increase in masturbation; sexual fantasies also mount, and there seems to be a stronger desire for physical contact with members of the opposite sex.

According to Freud, the central theme of this period is the child's love of the opposite-sexed parent. The Electra and Oedipus complexes pertain to the complex emotional relationship of the girl to her father (Electra complex) and the boy to his mother (Oedipal complex). The term Oedipal comes from the old Greek legend of Oedipus, who unknowingly murdered his father and married his mother. Psychoanalytic theory postulates that these Oedipal wishes diminish and that the adult can enjoy sexual and social relationships with members of the opposite sex because in the course of his development he manages to identify with the like-sexed parent. When such identification does not occur, the Oedipal situation is said to be unresolved and to form the basis of most adult intrapsychic conflicts. The hypothesis that the Oedipal and Electra complexes represent is difficult to test, however, and anthropological studies cast doubt upon the universality of the Oedipal conflict situation.

Freud's theory also holds that there is a period, roughly between the ages of six and ten, when the child's sexual impulses are dormant because of the repressive action of ego processes. Psychoanalysts refer to it as the latency period.

IDENTIFICATION

Whether or not one accepts the psychoanalytic hypothesis of the Oedipal situation, one must admit that identification is of primary importance in the development of the superego processes. Some attention will now be given to the type of learnings accounting for the development of conscience, internal controls, and self-reward.

Sears, who represents one point of view, postulates that identification results from learning without anyone's deliberately attempting to teach the child and without a conscious effort to learn on the child's part. In this type of learning, termed *role practice,* the child acts or pretends to act as if he were filling another person's role. Role practice occurs in fantasy, in daydreams, or in play behavior, and could be initiated by his desire to reproduce pleasant experiences. Sears notes also that the role-practice behavior can represent an attempt to reassure himself that he has his parents' affection and love. By assuming the parent role in fantasy or in his daydreams, he can give himself in an indirect way the affection he desires (17).

As the child grows older, the mother, the primary source of his affection, becomes, for one reason or another, no longer available to him for the attention and care on which he has depended; thus, following the period during which he attempts to regain her approval and attention by behaving in ways pleasing to her, the role-practice behaviors come to reflect her attitudes, values, and standards. By taking within himself (through role practice) these attitudes and standards associated with reward he provides himself with both gratification (when he does well according to these standards) and guilt and uneasiness (when he fails to meet them). The process of identification includes much more than the taking in of standards and values, however; it also encompasses many aspects of the adopted sex role.

THE DEVELOPING CONSCIENCE

Of major significance in the development of personality is the gradual emergence of the superego. This third intrapsychic process has its beginnings in the ego processes that operate during the preschool years, processes that involve the child's abilities to perceive the details of the external world, that permit him to recognize that some of his behaviors bring with them rewards and others punishment; and that through generalization and secondary reinforcement enable the child to associate parental attitudes and values with his own attitudes and behaviors.

The superego includes those ethical standards and values by which an individual assesses himself. By and large these standards are "borrowed" from the parents, but other adults and the child's peers also influence his perception and response to matters of ethics and goodness and badness. The superego processes are of particular significance in the socialization of the child, in that they enable him to function away from his parents or other adults in ways that still reflect the influence of their standards. Ego processes serve as a deterrent to some behaviors if there is a likelihood of discovery or of "getting caught," but the influence of the superego processes springs from their directing and inhibiting character, from the fact that the child has taken within himself the standards by which he is evaluated. When such standards are actually violated or their violation is threatened, the superego's restraining influence generates feelings of self-censure; this is the well-known experience of guilt. And when the individual meets or exceeds his own standards of rightness, he rewards himself by feelings of virtue and worthiness. The negative or restraining aspect of the superego is that which is commonly termed the conscience; the positive and rewarding aspect of the superego has been termed the ego ideal, and the conscious images that in part comprise the ego ideal are identical with the ideal self.

In the relationship between a particular child and his mother, the degree to which she disciplines by love and its withdrawal rather than by material rewards and physical punishment seems to be related to the strength of the developed conscience and the degree to which it provides inner controls over sexual and aggressive impulses. Sears points out that the actual content of the conscience—that is, the specific standards it enforces—will depend upon the parental (most often the mother's) behaviors, attitudes, and values, with the father's "voice of authority" reinforcing these (see p. 56). For example, in one study (9) it was

For the moment he is lord and master of all he surveys.

He is the big man, he gives orders that are instantly obeyed, he travels to far places. He has wealth and everyone respects him. Although fantasies of omnipotence occur throughout life, they have a special vividness and significance during childhood. For this boy, he himself is now the big man—he is trying out the feeling—he likes it and will adopt the "big men" of his life and time as his models. Their admired attributes become a part of him. To be like them for a moment, whether in fantasy or in actuality, is occasion for self-satisfaction.

Wayne Miller—Magnum

found that children identifying strongly with aggressive mothers were inclined in a play situation to evidence a considerable amount of aggressiveness; other children who strongly identified with nonaggressive mothers demonstrated a low order of aggressiveness.

Since the evaluative judgments that one makes of others may reflect the content of the conscience, the work of Piaget, who studied the development of moral judgments of children, is of interest. Piaget (13) noted that the four- and five-year-old child relies on parental morals and standards because they are the parents'. A violation of a standard of desirable behavior will call forth an unequivocal judgment from the young child, a judgment that reflects an absolute conception of what is right or proper. In contrast, the older child, who has been in contact with adults and other children outside the home situation and who has taken within himself the parental standards, no longer will evaluate in absolute and categorical terms merely because such evaluations are part of his perception of the parents' standards. Piaget notes that:

> . . . There are three great periods in the development of the sense of justice in the child. One period, lasting up to the age of 7–8, during which justice is subordinated to adult authority; a period contained approximately between 8–11, and which is that of progressive equalitarianism; and finally a period which sets in toward 11–12, and during which purely equalitarian justice is tempered by considerations of equity.

The development of the superego and eventually the conscience, is then, a gradual process. It first becomes apparent in older children whose behavior reflects inner controls, standards, and a sense of justice or "moral perspective."

THE CHILD AND SCHOOL

Although the transition from the home to the school situation is usually accomplished in such a way that the child spends only a few hours a day in the kindergarten—and even less time if he is enrolled in a nursery school program—the shift from the familiarity of home and mother to the less known and more impersonal group situation constitutes for most children a change of considerable psychological significance. For the majority who negotiate the change successfully, it indicates that they have reached a stage in their development in which many profound changes in self-concept and in ego functioning will be occurring.

The school reinforces many of the attitudes and behaviors that the child has learned at home. But in addition to existing attitudes and behaviors, the child will acquire new skills, attitudes, and concepts that stem from school experiences. These experiences center about his contacts with adults who are unrelated to him and who may be the first grown persons he encounters in close relationships outside the family situation. Through his contacts with teachers, his perceptions of the requirements of an adult world and of adults as helpful, friendly, hurtful, or unfriendly are reinforced, broadened, and tested.

The experiences of the school situation include that of being a member of a group. The behaviors learned at home and appropriate for the child in his relationships with his parents and siblings must be extended, for his mode of operation as a son within the family is not completely appropriate as a member of the class. He thus will acquire new self-concepts as a member of the group, as an individual functioning apart from his parents and outside the familiar confines of his home.

Children will respond to him and he to them in terms of his and their appearances, behaviors, attitudes, and skills. From them and with them, he will acquire a sense of his position or role with reference to the group, and this role may in part be related to ethnic, religious, or physical characteristics over which he has no control. He may find himself a member of a favored group or rejected because of characteristics he possesses through no fault of his own, and he may be unable to understand why he is responded to unfavorably.

With his entry into school he begins to learn adult skills. He learns how to read and write; he learns about his world and acquires techniques for utilizing the experience and the wisdom achieved by his predecessors. But in addition to the specific skills and knowledges that are learned in school, he acquires an awareness of what is expected of him as a student. Such an awareness, and the learnings that accompany it, add to his self-concept as a contributing member of society. Within the school context, he acquires the images of a worker, and eventually he comes to think of himself as functioning in some specific field of human endeavor.

It may sometimes seem that little is accomplished that relates to the child's eventual occupational and vocational choice during this period. However, the gratifications derived from investing his energies in school activity and from meeting his home responsibilities, or the absence of these gratifications, play a significant part in the attitudes he will hold toward himself as a worker. He learns that he is expected to be prompt, considerate, alert, reliable, and diligent. He learns to subordinate his immediate wishes and inclinations to the routines required of him and to commit himself to activities that are not of his choosing. With the opportunity for such learning, most children experience changes in their own feelings of importance and independence fairly soon after beginning school.

In one study (19), mothers of first-grade children were interviewed before their children began school and again after they had been attending school for two months. At the latter time, 86 percent of the mothers reported that their children were behaving in ways that reflected a greater degree of responsibility for themselves and a greater degree of self-control, and that they were more helpful and cooperative than when they entered first grade. Although these mothers provided favorable statements regarding the changes that occurred during the first several months of school, they also reported that a considerable number of the children (40 percent) occasionally did not want to go to school, and that 8 percent did not like school.

The Influence of the Preschool Personality

It is obvious that reactions to the school situation, what the child is able to get from it that facilitates his development, and the direction his behavioral patterns take as a result of being there, will depend in large part upon what he brings to the school. The child who has had trusting relationships with his parents will probably not be fearful of his teacher; the child who has been encouraged to care for himself will make fewer demands on his teacher for help; the child who is unsure of himself may feel threatened and intimidated by the number of other children in the classroom and may feel unable to compete; the child whose emotional outbursts have succeeded in intimidating his parents may rely upon such behavior in his dealings with his teachers, for he may lack more appropriate behavioral patterns for relating to adults. According to the results of one study (20), "rejected" children, whose parents failed to provide them with adequate protection, care, or affection, made a poor adjustment to school. They were rebellious, unable to comply with rules and regulations, and likely to play truant. In their academic work these rejected children had difficulty focusing their attention for sustained periods of time and were inclined to daydream and to be apathetic and indifferent. Other research studies support this impression.

However, although the child entering school will generalize the responses learned at home to his teachers and will bring with him a self-concept acquired at home, many responses emerge primarily from experiences in the school setting and are not to be considered solely as extensions of previously established behavioral patterns. Under appropriate conditions of response and reinforcement, the child learns to discriminate his teachers from his parents and to respond to them differently. When such discrimination occurs, behaviors also change; the child who has been rebellious often becomes cooperative; the child who has been apathetic becomes interested; and the child who has had little involvement with intellectual matters becomes stimulated to read and to acquire knowledge.

THE ACQUISITION OF KNOWLEDGE AND MASTERY OVER THE ENVIRONMENT

Included prominently in the learnings deriving primarily, though not exclusively, from the school situation are those relating to the processes of knowing and perceiving. Such processes are termed cognitive and include many of the activities assigned earlier to the ego: perceiving, thinking, naming, reasoning, abstracting, and communicating verbally.

The cognitive aspects of personality are sometimes described as if they were independent of the rest of personality. Actually, however, they are not separate. Even the seemingly solitary work of the student, whose activities are limited to study from his books and who may be preoccupied with solving complex and abstract problems in higher mathematics, is not separable from his emotions, motivation, and feelings. He is doing what he is because it is important to him, because his needs to maintain and enhance his personality are operating in such a way that he elects to pursue the studies at hand, and because such activity brings him closer to a feeling of relatedness with the world he values.

At the elementary school level the interrelationship between the cognitive and affective (emotional) processes is also evident. To learn the skill of reading, the child must feel some need to comply, to attend to what is being said by the teacher, to invest the necessary energy in the activity. The affective and motivational components of the learning process thus will influence the degree to which the child learns as well as what he learns in the school setting and elsewhere. And the child's cognitive learnings will in turn influence how he feels and what he responds to emotionally, will provide him with a means for categorizing the experiences he encounters. Although the school setting is usually thought of as being the locale where cognitive learnings occur, and although the focus in the following section is on the cognitive learnings acquired within it, the separation of cognitive and affective processes here is a matter of convenience, not a reflection of a dichotomy that exists in nature.

At school the child learns to read, to write, to deal with numbers.

He acquires knowledge of his past and of the world's past. His impressions of himself in relation to the rest of the world are extended and deepened, and with this differentiation or discrimination he acquires skills to master the environment and to fulfill the expectations that others hold for him. To the extent that he does acquire information about the world he lives in and the skills for coping with this world, his concept of himself will be influenced; under conditions of cognitive learnings, his sense of personal worth and adequacy will be positive. This is partially because he can master the tasks and problems with which he is confronted and because his successes in attaining these mastery skills are reinforced by parents and teachers.

A considerable amount of cognitive activity—and therefore of school learning—involves the manipulation of symbols. The reader will recall that symbols are shorthand devices representing events or experiences with which the individual himself may not have had direct contact. They are basic to activities of reasoning and thought. The learning of the symbols employed in reading, writing, and mathematics is useful to the individual as he thinks of himself in relation to future objectives. These symbols are "tools" of thinking and can range from direct representations of an object, such as a drawing of a chair, to highly abstract symbols that could express the relationships of the components of the chair in mathematical terms. The thinking process has been described as ranging from concrete to abstract; that is, from thinking which is confined to ideas pertaining to the highly specific and tangible aspects of life to thought which relies on abstracted properties of the different classes of events and experience.

Intelligence

Throughout the person's childhood, adolescence, and adult years his perceived and actual mastery of the problems presented to him by his environment will influence his self-concept. Environmental mastery depends, in part, on the individual's ability to manipulate symbols, to anticipate the consequences of his actions, and to profit from his experience. These abilities, which have a significant bearing not only on the child's school attainment but also on his personality organization and the content of his self-perceptions, can best be discussed under the heading of Intelligence. Because of its importance to these issues, the topic is given detailed consideration; however, specific points of relationship between intelligence and personality are touched upon throughout the text.

Since ancient times, observers of human behavior have noted that some people are alert, quick to learn, and able to grasp new relationships easily, while others are dull, learn laboriously, and seem unable to apply their previous experiences to new situations. In his description of a model state, Plato proposed to select and to train persons for the highest positions on the basis of what we would now call intelligence.

Although the fact of varied intelligence has been known for a long time, the systematic effort to study and measure intelligence did not begin until about the turn of the present century. In France, the public education movement was well under way by the early 1900's. Legislation provided that all French students who could benefit from public school were entitled to admission. Interpretation of the laws raised the question of which students could benefit from attendance. In 1904, a commission headed by Alfred Binet, a French psychologist, was charged with the task of developing procedures to identify students who could not benefit from the public school program (2).

The Binet Age Scale Intelligence Tests

Other psychologists had tried to utilize measures of simple reflex activity or sensory discrimination as indications of intelligence. Binet believed that their failures to find relationships between established performance levels and speed of finger withdrawal responses or accuracy of perception of weight differences resulted from their use of oversimplified measures. He postulated that the measurement of intelligence required tasks characteristic of the complex processes involved in the performance of intellectual acts.

Binet noted that as children grow older they also become more competent, more critical of their own performances, more able to recognize their surroundings and to offer explanations for their observations. In addition, they begin to apply previous experiences to the solution of specific problems not yet directly encountered. A child of three who can name a doll's nose, eyes, and ears but who is unable to count beyond three or four can, in the following year, not only count beyond his previous level but also perform a variety of tasks which had been beyond his earlier capacity.

Such observations led Binet to collect tasks and questions that were appropriate to children of given age levels. From these he selected items that could be passed by a majority of children at a given age level but that were too difficult for the majority of children one year younger. These items formed a test for children of the older of the two groups.

An item placed in Binet's scale at the sixth year level, for example, could not be passed by the majority of five-year-old children. The items located at the various age levels on the Binet scale characterized the competence achieved by the majority of children of that particular age.

Of course, a precocious child, whose rate of intellectual development was more rapid than those of most five-year-olds, might pass a six-year-old item and might even pass items located at higher points in the age scale. Thus, Binet's scales provided a means for comparing one child's performance level, and hence his developmental rate, with those of children of various ages. If his rate of development had been accelerated, his performance level would correspond to that of older children, and if his development was retarded, his level of performance would correspond to that of younger children. A child whose test performance corresponded to those characteristic of six-year-old children was said to have a mental age of six, while a child who could pass the items located at the ten-year age level on Binet's scale was described as having a mental age of ten.

This explicit means of identifying mental age made it possible to deal with some of the practical issues involved in the question of who could benefit from public instruction. If, for example, it were assumed that a first grade child required the competencies possessed by most six-year-old children, then the test could be utilized to determine whether the child had reached such a level of competency; moreover, the degree of a child's retardation could be assessed in terms of the age level of his performance. Such assessment has considerable importance for society, as does the early identification of unusually talented or gifted children whose intellectual attainments are characteristic of children older than themselves.

THE INTELLIGENCE QUOTIENT

Although the practical significance of identifying a child's mental age should not be underestimated, the mental age figure in itself does not provide a description of the child's "brightness." Such a descriptive index necessitates a consideration of the child's chronological age. A six-year-old child with a mental age of ten is identifiable as precocious, while a six-year-old child whose measured mental age is three is known to be retarded. The introduction of chronological age as the divisor of the ratio MA/CA led to the now famous intelligence quotient (IQ). Complete expression of the ratio is $IQ = MA/CA \times 100$. The multiplier of 100 is included in the expression simply to eliminate decimals; 100 is the average IQ.

The value of the intelligence quotient as a measure of intellectual development may be illustrated by an example of two children who attain similar mental ages of ten, but who do so at the ages of eight and ten years. The ten-year-old child's intelligence quotient of 100 ($MA = 10$, $CA = 10$) indicates a developmental rate that is similar to those of most children of his age. In contrast is the child of eight who also attains a mental age of ten, but who has an IQ of 125 (MA = 10, CA = 8), reflecting an accelerated rate of intellectual development. In a single statement, the intelligence quotient compares an individual's test performance to those of others of his age.

THE STANFORD-BINET INTELLIGENCE TESTS

The first large-scale use of the IQ as the ratio of chronological to mental age was in the 1916 revision of the Binet test made by Lewis Terman of Stanford University. Following Binet's approach, Terman developed and refined the procedures in the 1916 Stanford-Binet. In 1927 intensive work was begun on the refinement of the test, and in 1937, a revision was published by Terman and his associate, Maud Merrill; in 1959 the test was again revised by Dr. Merrill (22).

Philosophically, the Stanford-Binet tests rest on the view that intelligence develops with age and that test items at each mental age level should be based on the actual performance characteristic of children of that chronological age. The most important aspect of the test administration is that it must be given individually. This means that it is administered by a psychologist to a single child or adult, a procedure usually requiring from an hour to an hour and a half. A very specific procedure is followed by the psychologist, who must have extensive training in the administration of the test. This training involves not only the procedures for giving the test, but also those for scoring the responses and interpreting the results.

Since it is difficult to differentiate performance levels from one year to the next on nonverbal tasks, from the sixth year onward the Binet is essentially a verbal test. The term "verbal test" means that language is the vehicle of communication between the psychologist and the child. In most instances the individual being tested must respond verbally in order to meet the requirements of the test situation. Terman and Merrill have noted (21) the difficulty of devising nonverbal tests that differentiate the performances of individuals over six years of age.

At these levels the major intellectual differences between subjects reduce largely to differences in the ability to do conceptual thinking and facility in dealing with concepts is most readily sampled by the use of verbal tests. Language, essentially, is the shorthand of the higher thought processes, and the level at which this shorthand functions is one of the most important determinants of the level of the processes themselves.

An interesting problem in the construction of an age-scale intelligence test arises from the fact that the developmental rate of intellectual ability is greater during an individual's childhood years than it is during his adolescence and adulthood. The amount of knowledge and competence that the child gains between the ages of three and four is far greater than that achieved by the same individual between his thirteenth and his fourteenth year. The increases made by an individual between his twenty-third and twenty-fourth year are in turn less than those made during the adolescent period.

A number of studies have found, for example, that the most rapid rate of development occurs during the first six or seven years of a child's life. The rate becomes less rapid as the child grows older, and by mid-adolescence the increment from year to year has decreased considerably, although the individual continues to achieve gains through the period of the early twenties. From the early twenties to the late thirties there is a leveling off, and above the age of forty there is a gradual decline, which becomes more marked in the fifties and sixties. Because of this "slow-down" in rate, the chronological age divisor in the Stanford-Binet intelligence quotient formula has been statistically adjusted, beginning with age thirteen. After the age of sixteen, the divisor remains as a constant at sixteen.

This statement of the rate of intellectual development refers to a composite of all the specific abilities comprising the concept of intelligence; it is derived from studies of large groups of persons. For specific groups and individuals there can be differences in the curves that characterize intellectual development through the life period. For example, although performance requiring accuracy of vision or speed of hand-eye coordination may decline for the whole population of older persons, it has been found that performance on problem-solving tasks and proficiency at certain verbal skills, such as those measured in vocabulary tests, do not decline for those who possess high intellectual abilities and who work with language and verbal concepts (1).

THE WECHSLER INTELLIGENCE TESTS

A somewhat different approach is found in the tests developed by David Wechsler (25, 26, 27). These tests also are administered individually, but they include a number of items that rely less heavily on verbal abilities than do those of the Stanford-Binet. (One of Wechsler's tests is directed to an adult population.)

An interesting technical distinction exists between an age scale test such as the Stanford-Binet and a point scale test as exemplified by the Wechsler tests. In a *point scale test,* items are grouped not by age designation, but in terms of the type of task they represent; thus the Wechsler verbal test items are grouped in subtests identified as Vocabulary, General Information, General Comprehension, Digit Span, Arithmetical Reasoning, and Similarities. Wechsler also constructed five "performance" subtests: Digit Symbol, Picture Arrangement, Picture Completion, Object Assembly, and Block Design. In the Wechsler type of test, items are arranged in order of ascending difficulty, and an individual is given items from all the subtests. The examiner stops administering a specific subtest whenever the person being tested begins to fail consistently. It is possible to obtain composite scores for the verbal tests and the performance tests for a specific individual in addition to his total score for all the tests. The total score may be translated into "intelligence quotient" equivalents.

Although the construction of the Wechsler tests differs in certain aspects from that of the Stanford-Binet, both tests provide a basis for comparing a single individual's performance with that of other individuals. In the Wechsler tests there is also provision for comparing one adult with other adults of his own age group. Because of the gradual decline with age of some of the abilities measured by intelligence tests this feature is of value in the evaluation of the performance of adults, particularly those in their middle and later years.

Since each of Wechsler's subtests is a test in itself and yields a score, it is possible to note areas of especially good or poor performance for each person tested. This feature is useful in vocational guidance. Wechsler defines intelligence as "the aggregate or global capacity of the individual to act purposefully, to think rationally, to deal effectively with his environment," but it should be noted that Wechsler's verbal tests, like the Stanford-Binet, correlate higher with the usual measures of intellectual attainment (academic success, professional achievement, and position in the occupational hierarchy) than do his performance tests.

CHANGES IN INDIVIDUAL
INTELLIGENCE TEST RESULTS

One of the practical questions arising from the widespread use of intelligence tests is whether the child who scores relatively low during his early years will continue to perform less well than his peers, or whether there is a chance that he will "catch up." In the case of a retarded child plans for schooling must be made. It also is important in such instances to consider arrangements for future care and to predict as accurately as possible whether the individual can be expected to be economically self-sufficient.

If previous intelligence test scores for an individual fluctuate widely, then there is little predictive value in such measures; if they fluctuate relatively little, then credence can be given to the predictions that follow from the test scores. Although there is no categorical answer to the question of the stability of intelligence test scores, as a generalization it might be noted that intelligence test scores for an individual are most closely correlated when the time interval separating the two administrations is relatively short. If two tests are administered within a three-year interval, the scores obtained are most likely to be similar than are test scores ten years apart; furthermore, the relationship between two scores obtained on the same individual is more likely to be close if the first test is administered when the child is capable of using language. Tests given after the age of five or six are better bases for prediction than are tests administered when, for example, the child is two years of age, because the nonverbal test items in the preschool levels require skills that are different from those employed for the verbal items of the later levels. It follows from these statements that the later the administration of the intelligence test, the higher will be its predictive value for the level of adult intellectual functioning.

Predictions of adult intelligence level may be of great importance. If a child scores very low on an individual intelligence test and does so again on another intelligence test, then possible explanations for the obtained IQ must be considered. Physical factors, the child's opportunities to undergo the usual experiences of children of similar age in this culture, and the presence of emotional difficulties all require evaluation. A child with a sensory defect may be unable to hear adequately, although the deficit may be so slight that it is not evident to parents and teachers. Visual difficulties may account for an inability to acquire the usual experiences of children typical of a particular age, and they also may handicap the child in the actual test situation. Unusually lengthy periods of illness that isolate the child from his playmates may lower his level of performance. A child reared in socially or economically deprived circumstances, such as the child who comes from a home in which English is not habitually spoken, may also be handicapped in his day-by-day experiences and therefore in his responses to test items.

The contributions of psychological and emotional factors to a low level of attainment on an intelligence test should be carefully weighed in the interpretation of test results. The child who is anxious, tense, and angry must employ his energies in defending and maintaining his psychological self; consequently, he may have little energy available to direct to the outer world. Such a child also may misperceive the test items presented to him or interpret them in terms of the generalized threat that he perceives. Thus, the child who is emotionally upset or whose intrapersonal development has been disturbed may not be able to function any more succesfully in the intelligence test situation than he can in actual life situations that require him to demonstrate intelligent behaviors.

GROUP INTELLIGENCE TESTS

The cost and the time required for the administration of individual intelligence tests are such that group tests of intelligence are frequently employed for large-scale screening and selection. A group test may be administered to a large number of individuals at the same time. These tests are most frequently of a paper-and-pencil nature; the individuals being tested are given booklets and the examiner provides directions and times the test administration.

Group tests of intelligence are used for counseling and guidance purposes in schools and are also employed by industry for selecting new employees or for choosing those to be given special training or advancement. Perhaps the largest use of group intelligence tests occurred during World War II, when all individuals entering the armed services were given "classification tests." Only those who scored above certain "cutoff" points were admitted to special training programs, such as flight training or Officers' Candidate School.

Tests similar to the army classification tests are said to be performing a "screening" function. Persons whose test scores are so low that they probably will be unable to complete a given training program are screened out of the group selected for admission to the particular training activity. If an individual received a score of 140 or more on the Army General Classification Test, his chances of being graduated from Officers' Candidate School were better than nine in ten, while if he scored less than 110, his chances of being graduated were less than five in ten. This means that nine out of ten individuals who score 140 or better on the Army General Classification Tests were able to complete officer training, while fewer than five out of ten individuals who scored less than 110 were able to complete such training.

Group tests are used in similar fashion for college admission. One test that follows the general form of a group intelligence test is the frequently used Scholastic Aptitude Test (the SAT). This test is divided into verbal and quantitative sections and also yields a total score from which colleges are able to estimate the likelihood that an individual will be able to complete any particular academic program at their institution.

High schools often employ group intelligence tests to assign students to sections that differ in terms of the complexity of materials studied and the speed with which they are covered. The wise utilization of such test scores can spare individuals the frustration that accompanies failure and can prevent waste of energy and time by both the student and the school. Of course, factors other than intelligence may be associated with success in an academic or occupational program. Such factors have been discussed repeatedly in previous chapters and will be illustrated further in subsequent sections.

One of the most valuable uses of the intelligence test, particularly the individual intelligence test, is to identify the child who has the potential to profit from school experience but whose actual achievement level is low. This paves the way for those corrective educational or treatment approaches that can bring the child to his actual achievement level.

DEFINING INTELLIGENCE

The question of the meaning of the term *intelligence* may now be considered. This term has been variously defined as the ability to profit from experience, the ability to engage in abstract thought, the ability to be critical of oneself, and the ability to apply one's previous experience to novel situations. It has also been said that "intelligence is that which the intelligence tests measure." This definition is probably the most sensible, although initially it may seem to be evasive. What it suggests is that the content of any intelligence test must be examined very carefully to note what capacities, abilities, and aptitudes are measured in the specific test items comprising the scale. Viewed more comprehensively, the statement means that intelligence must be defined in terms of the activities and the proficiencies with which the test scores are correlated.

If those elementary school students who score high on intelligence tests are also most likely to do well in their academic studies, then it can be said that there is a high correlation between intelligence test performance and academic performance. In fact, for the tests cited, there is a correlation with school work that is high enough to permit general predictions of the later school work.

The question of whether intelligence is a unitary trait or a general ability, as it is sometimes expressed, is the same as the question of whether there *is an intelligence* or whether there *are intelligences*. Research on this issue has been conducted using a statistical procedure known as "factor analysis." This technique begins with a large number of intercorrelations of tests that have been administered to the same individuals. Those items that vary together (are positively correlated) are said to contain a "common factor." Factors are labeled in terms of the items or tests from which they have been derived. In studies conducted by Thurstone (23), the following factors of intelligence were named:

1. verbal comprehension—the ability to define and understand words;
2. word fluency—the ability to think rapidly of words;
3. number—the ability to do arithmetic problems;
4. space—the ability to draw and design from memory or to visualize relationships;
5. memory—the ability to memorize and recall;
6. perception—the ability to visualize details and to see differences and similarities among objects;
7. reasoning—the ability to find rules, principles or concepts for understanding or solving problems.

In addition, it was noted that various tests which had been developed specifically to measure different factors varied together to some degree. This supports the conclusion that there is a general intelligence or ability that runs through abilities such as those just mentioned, and that there also are specific abilities which, depending upon the tests and test items employed, may more or less resemble those indicated above.

To conclude this section, a final comment upon the nature of intelligence is relevant. Although it would seem that general intellectual ability is very closely related to verbal ability, there are other specific abilities influencing behavior which can be identified as intelligence. The nature of the device which is used to measure intelligence—that is, the specific abilities it taps—will influence the ways in which general intelligence and the specific intelligences are represented in the over-all score yielded by its administration.

The definition of intelligence as that which the test measures and the analysis of the intelligence test in terms of the abilities with which it correlates, are probably still the best and most helpful means of defining and describing intelligence. At present, the best single predictor for success in elementary school, high school, or college is the individual intelligence test. The prediction is far from perfect, but if wisely considered in conjunction with other measures, energy, time, and effort can be directed toward personal objectives appropriate to the individual's ability level.

School Achievement and Self-Concept

The extent to which children acquire academic skills and are able to use their abilities is a matter of considerable interest to society, for it will prosper to the extent to which all its resources, including those represented by the talents of its citizens, are utilized. The issue also possesses considerable significance to the individual, and the conditions under which he has the opportunity to acquire skills, such as those taught in school, will influence not only the extent to which he develops his abilities but also the way he perceives himself, the goals he sets for himself, and the tasks to which he commits himself.

In the elementary school situation, the child is exposed to experiences that are directed toward facilitating his learning of many new skills and attitudes. It has already been noted that his way of responding to his teacher will depend, in part, upon the relationship he has had with his parents; similarly, the attitudes he has toward the process of learning, toward the acquisition of symbols, and toward school itself will depend upon his parents' values and the extent to which academic pursuits are important to them. Children from socially and educationally deprived families have had little opportunity to observe their parents reading or writing, or even to participate in breakfast and dinner-table conversations with them. Such home situations are in contrast to those in which school is taken for granted, the acquisition of academic skills is valued, and the child's attainments in these areas are reinforced through attention and reward. The degree to which the child's self-concept will be influenced by his success or failure in the school situation is determined by the extent to which his parents value school attainment and the extent to which the child feels that his personal worth depends upon his achievement in this setting.

Although considerable evidence exists that many children from the lower economic and educational strata of our society do not include academic achievement in their self-evaluation and instead adopt their parents' values, for most children school achievement is an important measure of one's personal worth. The competitive aspects of this achievement are often symbolized by signs of special recognition, such as gold stars, special privileges, parental rewards, and grades. For children who conform to academic and parental expectations in school, who do well in their studies and compete successfully with their classmates, the rewards received reinforce the patterns of behavior that lead to school achievement. For those children who do not perform well, however, failures reinforce avoidant behaviors and the academic situation becomes one of frustration, boredom, and conflict with one's teachers and parents.

When intelligence test performance is utilized as a basis for evaluating academic potential, and the child's actual school attainment is considered relative to his intellectual ability, it is possible to describe school children in terms of under- and overachievement (also see Chapter 11).

Underachieving children are those whose academic performance is considerably beneath the level anticipated on the basis of their intellectual abilities; overachievers are those whose achievement is in excess of the level anticipated. In one study of 40 underachievers and 40 overachievers (8), the authors report that the groups differed significantly.

> Pride, confidence, affection, and interest of parents in their children as shown in instances in which parents read to their children, play with them, build for them, or attend school with them, appear to be in greater evidence for plus achievers [overachievers] than for minus-achievers [underachievers]. On the part of children, there is a tendency among plus-achievers to respect their parents, to take them into their confidence, to be concerned about pleasing them, and to return the love their parents show. Minus-achievers appear to have a comparatively limited place in the home. There does not appear to be so much exchange of affection, or mutual respect, desire to measure up to expectations. In fact, even expectations appear limited for minus-achievers.[5]

Causes of Underachievement

The explanations for underachievement should not be oversimplified, since children vary considerably in response to the competitive aspects of school and in the homes from which they come; the interplay among the preschool child's personality, his family relationships, and his school experiences, however, can be inferred from the finding that for boys whose academic performance was not commensurate with their measured aptitudes, underachievement was apparent in their first grade work, and the pattern became more evident as they proceeded through elementary, junior, and senior high school (18). Conditions operating before the child entered school—those that influenced his attitudes toward adults, his expectations of them, and his attitudes toward himself, his abilities, and his interests in attempting to conform to adult requirements—were such that his progress in school was far less than would have been anticipated on the basis of his intelligence test scores. The behaviors resulting in failure were apparently reinforced both at home and at school throughout the school period.

In another study, public school children, in response to the question, "What I dislike about myself," wrote themes in which school experience "were mentioned more often as a source of self-disparagement than as a

---

[5] Reprinted by permission from J. J. Kurtz and E. J. Swenson, "Factors Relating to Over-Achievement and Under-Achievement in School." *School Review*, 1951, *59*, 472–480. Copyright, 1951, by the University of Chicago.

The problem challenges—previous approaches won't work—new ones must be tried. Let's go to work and think it through once more. How about this? Yes, it might do—it DOES work! What a great feeling!

Tension, frustration, gratification—all are involved in learning. Learning is an active process. Even when the academic material to be learned is strictly symbolic, the motivation of the student, his previous experiences of success and failure, all influence his effectiveness. Thus, the intellect is not a disembodied entity, something that can be trained or developed like a muscle; rather, the intellectual life of man is to be viewed in the perspective of his total being. At the same time, man's capacity to manipulate symbols and to assign them meaning, to use language, to think, and to engage in intellectual pursuits places him in a favored position over all other species of life.

Wayne Miller—Magnum

source of confidence and good feeling toward the self." On the basis of such research Jersild concludes (4):

> . . . The school constantly and perpetually, day in and day out, year after year, reminds great numbers of children that they are not much good. To a large number of children who do not happen to have the kind of intellectual and conformist tendencies which are praised in most institutions of learning the school dispenses unfavorable comparison, reminders of failure, and implied rejection on a colossal scale. . . . What often happens is that when a person fails in a given test in life, such as an important assignment at school, it is difficult for him not to view this as a test of him as a person, a total test rather than just a measure of a limited facet of his worth. When a child is deficient in arithmetic or in reading, he will have a tendency, at least for the moment, to feel that he is just plain deficient in everything . . . [6]

Experiences that reinforce the child's feelings of inadequacy, such as those occurring when the child fails to compete successfully with his peers in school, may have subsequent effects on the goals the individual will set for himself, as is seen from the research of Pauline Sears (16). Selecting three groups of children who had earned different reading, arithmetic, and achievement scores, she studied the effects of success and failure experiences on the goals that the child would set for himself on his next attempt. Her "success" group had a history of having done well, the "failure" group of having done poorly, and the third group had a history of success in reading but none in arithmetic.

Each of the children in the three groups was given short speed tests in reading and arithmetic. After finishing, the child was told how many seconds the trial had taken and was asked to estimate how many seconds he would need to complete the task on the next trial. The study was designed to make it possible for the experimenter to provide success or failure according to a prearranged plan for the three groups. It was therefore possible to record both the immediate influence on goal-setting behaviors of conditions of success or failure, and the differences among the three groups pertaining to reactions to success and failure.

Sears found that in general, success in the tests tended to correlate with the setting of goals somewhat higher than the actual performance, and that these goals could be termed realistic. Experiences of induced failure also resulted in the setting of goals higher than the actual performance, but these goals were quite variable and were often unrealistically above the actual performance level.

[6] Reprinted by permission from A. T. Jersild, *Child Psychology* (ed. 4). © 1954, Prentice-Hall, Inc., Englewood Cliffs, N.J.

When the previous histories of the three groups were taken into account, the results indicated that students whose academic history had consistently reflected success set their goals slightly above their performance level. Thus they adapted their goals to their attainments on the test trials as they were reported to them. The failure group tended to respond to their performance by either dropping their goals or reporting unrealistic aspirations. The third group, which had a history of success in reading and lack of success in arithmetic, set goals on the reading tasks in a fashion similar to the success group; while on the arithmetical tasks their goal-setting behavior resembled that of the group with a history of failure.

From Sears' study it can be inferred that the child's self-esteem is influenced by success and failure experiences. Children with a positive self-concept modify their aspirations realistically in the light of their actual performance. Children whose self-concepts include feelings of being inadequate and unworthy will have to rely on various devices for protecting themselves from failure; they may set goals so low that success is inevitable; they may not commit energy to the attainment of goals (thus they cannot fail because they have not tried); or they may resort to fantasies about great attainment.

Reactions to Competition

The experiences of childhood in regard to success and failure contribute significantly to the child's self-concept. It should not be inferred—because of the cumulative pattern that seems to follow when a child does not succeed in school—that children are to be denied knowledge of their attainments relative to others. Rather, the issue is that of the separation of competitive achievement from feelings of self-worth. When parents and teachers can contribute to the child's feelings of esteem because he has tried, he has done his best, and when he feels sure that his parents value him not because of his attainments and his accomplishments, but because he is a human being, then the detrimental side-effects of unsuccessful competitive effort will be somewhat less than the present studies suggest they are.

The child's developing ego processes require information about his performance. This information, even when it is of inadequacies, can be communicated to him without his feeling that he is a failure. This is a matter not only of teaching technique but also of the basic orientation of the teacher and parent. If they value the child as such, then he can take performance results as a fact of life and can give consideration to appropriate remedial behaviors. On the other hand, when the child is made to feel that he is a failure because his performance level has been inadequate, there may be little incentive for him to continue to invest energy in further efforts to learn.

Summary

From his fifth to thirteenth year the child develops into a social being of considerable competence. He travels progressively farther from home, makes new friends, and has new and important relationships with adults other than his parents. He learns the expectations that are held for members of his sex and he acquires interests and skills consistent with these expectations.

At the beginning of the childhood period he starts attending school and during these years completes his elementary and junior high school grades. As physical growth and intellectual development continue he acquires new skills. His awareness of status and prestige distinctions develops, as do his own personal resources for achieving status within his family and his group. His peer group, gang, club, or clique creates its own special rules, rituals, and language. He becomes more cognizant of the views and opinions of others. At the same time his critical faculties become keener and the evaluations he makes of others may be harsh and uncompromising. As he nears the end of this period, he becomes aware of what he perceives as the shortcomings of his parents, and he may point out the inconsistencies between what they say and what they do.

The developing abilities to postpone immediate gratification, to perceive parental and peer expectations, and to control his aggressive impulses underlie the child's increasing social effectiveness. His experiences with the world outside the home bring opportunities for the acquisition of new skills, and these in turn extend the range of experience available to him. In addition to the knowledge and skills that are acquired during childhood, the personal and social selves become more complex and more clearly defined. With the incorporation of parental values and standards that provide a base for the child's judgments of himself, activities associated with the superego processes become more apparent. His behavior is modified by moral and ethical considerations and he feels guilty if he violates or considers violating his code; when he satisfies his own standards, he is able to reward himself by feeling worthy and virtuous. The development of superego processes is closely related to the clarification of the child's ideal self, of what he wishes he were and believes he should be. At the end of the childhood period the favorable state of balance that has obtained among his intrapsychic processes is altered by the physical, social, and psychological conditions accompanying adolescence.

References

1. Anastasi, A. *Differential Psychology* (ed. 3). New York: Macmillan, 1958.
2. Binet, A., and Simon, T. Methodes nouvelles pour le diagnostic du niveau intellectual des anormaux. *Année psychol.*, 1905, *11*, 191–244.
3. England, A. O. Non-structured approach to the study of children's fears. *J. clin. Psychol.*, 1946, *2*, 364–368.
4. Jersild, A. T. *Child Psychology*. New York: Prentice-Hall, 1954.
5. Jersild, A. T., Golman, B., and Loftus, J. J. A comparative study of the worries of children in two school situations. *J. exp. Educ.*, 1941, *9*, 323–326.
6. Jersild, A. T., Markey, F. V., and Jersild, C. L. Children's fears, dreams, wishes, daydreams, likes, dislikes, pleasant and unpleasant memories. *Child Develpm. Monogr.*, *12*, 1933.
7. Jersild, A. T., and Tasch, R. J. *Children's Interests and What They Suggest for Education*. New York: Teachers College, Columbia University, 1949.
8. Kurtz, J. J., and Swenson, E. J. Factors related to overachievement and underachievement in school. *Sch. Rev.*, 1951, *59*, 472–480.
9. Levin, H., and Sears, R. R. Identification with parents as a determinant of doll play aggression. *Child Develpm.*, 1956, *27*, 135–153.
10. Macfarlane, J. W. Study of personality development; in R. G. Barker, J. S. Kounin, and H. F. Wright, *Child Behavior and Development*. New York: McGraw-Hill, 1943.
11. Martin, W. E., and Stendler, C. B. *Child Development: The Process of Growing Up in Society*. New York: Harcourt, 1953.
12. Moreno, J. L. *Who Shall Survive? A New Approach to the Problem of Human Interrelations*. Washington, D.C.: Nervous and Mental Diseases Publishing Company, 1934.
13. Piaget, J. *The Moral Judgment of the Child*. London: Routledge, 1932.
14. Pratt, K. C. A study of "fears" of rural children. *J. genet. Psychol.*, 1945, *67*, 179–194.
15. Radke, M., Trager, H. G., and Davis, H. Social perceptions and attitudes of children. *Genet. Psychol. Monogr.*, 1949, *40*, 327–447.
16. Sears, P. S. Levels of aspiration in academically successful and unsuccessful children. *J. abnorm. soc. Psychol.*, 1940, *35*, 498–536.
17. Sears, R. R., Maccoby, E. E., and Levin, H. *Patterns of Child Rearing*. New York: Harper, 1957.
18. Shaw, M. C., and McCuen, J.T. The onset of academic underachievement in bright children. *J. educ. Psychol.*, 1960, *51*, 103–109.
19. Stendler, C. B., and Young, N. Impact of first-grade entrance upon the socialization of the child: Changes after eight months of school. *Child Develpm.*, 1951, *22*, 113–122.
20. Symonds, P. M. *The Psychology of Parent-Child Relationships*. New York: Appleton, 1939.

21. Terman, L. M., and Merrill, M. A. *Measuring Intelligence*. Boston: Houghton Mifflin, 1937.
22. Terman, L. M., and Merrill, M. A., *Stanford-Binet Intelligence Scale*. Boston: Houghton Mifflin, 1960.
23. Thurstone, L. L. Primary mental abilities. *Psychometr. Monogr., 1,* 1938.
24. Tuddenham, R. D. Studies in reputation: I. Sex and grade differences in school children's evaluation of their peers; II. The diagnosis of social adjustment. *Psychol. Monogr.,* 1952, *66,* No. 333.
25. Wechsler, D. *The Measurement and Appraisal of Adult Intelligence* (ed. 4). Baltimore: Williams & Wilkins, 1958.
26. Wechsler, D. *Manual for the Wechsler Adult Intelligence Scale*. New York: Psychol. Corp., 1955.
27. Wechsler, D. *Wechsler Intelligence Scale for Children*. New York: Psychol. Corp., 1949.
28. White, R. W. *The Abnormal Personality*. New York: Ronald, 1948.

Selected Readings

Carmichael, L. (ed.) *Manual of Child Psychology* (ed. 2). New York: Wiley, 1954.
Gesell, A., *et al.* *The Child from Five to Ten*. New York: Harper, 1946.
Martin, W. E., and Stendler, C. B. *Child Behavior and Development*. New York: Harcourt, 1959.
Mead, M., and Woltenstein, M. (eds.) *Childhood in Contemporary Cultures*. Chicago: University of Chicago Press, 1955.
Musson, P. H., and Conger, J. J. *Child Development and Personality*. New York: Harper, 1956.

8.

Adolescence

The teenage period is one of transition, of a physical, social, and psychological change-over from childhood to adulthood. In this period, termed adolescence, the behaviors and self-expectations of the child gradually give way to those of the adult.

For purposes of convenience, the first phase of adolescence, puberty (from the Latin *pubertas,* "age of manhood"), is usually defined as the beginning of menstruation in girls and the appearance of pigmented pubic hair in boys (5). By this definition, about 50 percent of boys reach puberty between the ages of 14 and 15.5 years, and about 50 percent of girls between the ages of 12.5 and 14.5 years. There may, of course, be considerable variation from the average; some girls menstruate as early as 9 or 10, others do not until they are 16 or 17.

The physical changes associated with puberty mark the onset of adolescence, and the attitudes and concerns of the adolescent often focus on some aspect of his physical appearance, his bodily functions, or his sex role. Since the significant psychological issues involving emancipation from his family and the development of adult skills and roles are intimately related to the adolescent's physical development, the discussion begins at this point.

PHYSICAL DEVELOPMENT

Popular belief accepts the term "weaker sex" as rightfully referring to women. Although this stereotype is pervasive in our culture, the facts do not give it much support. Even the beginnings of life belie such a distinction. Although approximately 20 percent more males are conceived, only 5 or 6 percent more boys than girls are actually born, for the prenatal mortality rate of males is considerably higher than that of females.

During infancy, the death rate of males continues to be higher. The male is more susceptible to many illnesses and hereditary defects. Each body cell in the female contains twenty-three pairs of identical chromosomes, one pair of which (the XX pair) carries sex-linked characteristics. Every cell of the male has twenty-two parallel pairs of chromosomes, plus a nonidentical pair of sex chromosomes (the XY pair). This difference has been cited as a possible explanation for the greater prevalence of physical defects among men than among women. Since the female has two X chromosomes, the opportunity exists for an inherited defective characteristic (a gene) to be counteracted by a healthy gene in the parallel chromosome. But the male cell has only one X chromosome, which is paired with a dissimilar Y chromosome containing relatively fewer genes, so there is less likelihood that a defective gene could be counteracted by a healthy one.

Other physical differences between men and women are genetically determined. At birth, the male weighs approximately 5 percent more than the female. This weight difference increases, so that at the age of twenty men are more than 20 percent heavier than women. Height differences fluctuate but also increase with age. By the age of twenty, men are on the average 10 percent taller than women.

In addition to being generally taller and heavier, males develop a heavier musculature and a greater lung capacity. These physical differences may account in part for the interests and abilities of males in vigorous games and mechanical activities. Studies by cultural anthropologists indicate, however, that even when an individual's physical abilities may seem to favor one line of endeavor over another, social custom and cultural tradition can still be decisive in accounting for his choice of activities. Certain roles characteristically assigned to men and women in our society are reversed in other societies, such as the Tchambuli, in which the male performs the household duties while his wife toils as the breadwinner (7).

As previous chapters have pointed out, physical differences in the genital and reproductive systems of men and women assume specific meanings for children as they grow older. These meanings obtain their dimensions from values in the culture, the interpretations that the society places upon maleness and femaleness. The young child's naive discovery of his structural differences from the opposite sex and his subsequent questions about his own body and those of other children are natural and healthy. How such curiosity is dealt with by the child's parents, what information is provided and what is concealed, reflect both the attitudes prevalent in our society and the emotional abilities of his parents to deal with the issue. Efforts to misinform children about the nature of differences in physical structure and function or to prevent their asking questions can create the impression that there is something mysterious and even bad about sexual matters. Such feelings of badness may be generalized to apply to the entire area of sexual activity and sexual impulses and, in some cases, to other physical functions as well.

The possession of a penis by the male has been considered by some psychological theorists to have an important effect on the psychological development and attitudes not only of males but also of females. According to these theories, possession of a penis makes the boy feel superior to females, and also may lead him to believe that the girl's lack of a penis is the result of punishment for misbehavior. The young boy may draw the frightening conclusion that indiscretion or misbehavior on his part can cause him to lose his penis in a similar manner. In support of the hypothesis that the possession of the penis by the male accounts significantly for differences in the self-concepts of men and women, various data have been assembled. These include analysis of sexual humor, anthropological reports of the use of the penis as a symbol of strength and virility, and studies of young children's questions about their bodies. As yet, however, those data which do support this hypothesis should not be overgeneralized to support the assumption that the absence or presence of the penis is the critical feature accounting for *all* the facets of one's self concept.

PHYSICAL DEVELOPMENT IN ADOLESCENCE

Although the signs of the onset of puberty appears at about the same age for boys and girls, the significence given to these signs is arbitrary, and it should not be assumed that the physical, social, and psychological development of boys and girls are similar during adolescence.

There are marked differences—both quantitative and qualitative—in the growths of boys and girls. Onset of menstruation and enlargement of the breasts appear for most girls between the ages of eleven and fourteen. The physical changes marking the transition from boy to man occur later, more gradually, and probably with less psychological impact than is the case for females. As far as height and weight are concerned, girls reach their period of most rapid growth two years before boys, and by the age of fourteen most girls have achieved 96 percent of their adult height. The growth rates of girls are most accelerated between their ninth and twelfth years, but boys, in general, do not show the "growth spurt" until their eleventh to fourteenth years. During this "spurt" the average girl has grown from 4 feet 2½ inches tall, weighing 57 pounds, to 4 feet 9 inches tall, weighing 100 pounds. On the average, boys at the age of eleven stand 4 feet 10 inches tall and weigh 86 pounds, but by the time they are fourteen, they are 5 feet 4 inches tall, about 90 percent of their adult stature, and weigh 119 pounds (19). Since boys and girls are together in the same grades when they are the same ages, the difference in their sizes is often very noticeable during the years immediately preceding their entry into high school and during their freshman year. The early maturing girl may appear to herself and to her classmates as a veritable giantess, the late maturing boy as a miniature edition of a high school student.

With the onset of puberty, the adolescent's arms and legs become proportionally longer and his facial features lose their round, babyish appearance and become more adult-like. By the time he is about fifteen, his head has assumed adult size. With rapid change of proportions during the early adolescent years, there is also a marked increase in the individual's musculature. While approximately 20 percent of the average eight-year-old child's body weight can be attributed to his muscles, at sixteen this percentage reaches 44 (4).

As the proportion of muscle tissue increases, there is, of course, a corresponding increase in the individual's strength and speed of movement. Although the adolescent's ability to coordinate his body as a result of increased muscle tissue is steadily enhanced, there may be periods in which he has not as yet accommodated to the growth of his extremities. Because of his inexperience with his newly acquired strength and with moving limbs that are longer than they had been, the familiar awkwardness of adolescence may occasionally be observed.

Although it may be said that girls, as a group, acquire their adult physical characteristics earlier than boys, it cannot be assumed that all girls or all boys follow the pattern or the developmental rates of their groups. Individual patterns of physical development are so varied that knowledge of the developmental history of each individual is necessary in understanding his interpersonal behavior. Sometimes the adult's personal self-concept may seem to be inappropriate to the observer unless he is acquainted with the details of the individual's physical development.

BIOLOGICAL ASPECTS OF SEXUAL BEHAVIOR

It is during adolescence that the youth becomes physically capable of sexually reproducing. Many behaviors of a physical sexual nature that are linked with male or female roles are not biologically determined, however. Although they are often discussed and reacted to as if they were necessary results of physical structure and functioning, it is important to distinguish between those physical role behaviors that are directly or only indirectly based on sexual biology.

The human sex drive is initiated by the activity of the sex glands, or gonads, which produce the reproductive cells and, in combination with certain other endocrine glands, account for what are termed the secondary sexual characteristics. These include the growth of bodily hair and beard, changes in voice pitch, and the changes in the shape of the body occurring during adolescence. Male secondary sexual characteristics cannot develop if the testes are removed, diseased, or functionally defective prior to puberty, for they produce testosterone, the male sex hormone. In the absence of this hormone, the individual's voice remains high, his beard fails to develop fully, the shape of his body is characterized by softness and roundness, and he fails to develop the expected sexual drive. The female who is deprived, prior to puberty, of her ovaries, which secrete the female hormone, estrogen, is unable to develop feminine secondary sexual characteristics, and she also lacks the expected sex drive.

A structurally adequate reproductive system prior to puberty is therefore necessary for the emergence of the sex drive. Once the secondary sexual characteristics have been developed and the drive has become manifest, removal of ovaries or testes does not have the marked effect on sexual characteristics and behaviors that it does prior to puberty. Nor does removal or degeneration of these glands, such as occurs in the change of life, necessarily result in diminution or loss of the sex drive. Individuals who have lost their gonads during adult life and are sterile are able to maintain sexual activity, provided that the psychological consequences of the loss do not interfere with or inhibit sexual interest. This continuation of sexual activity indicates that stimuli other than those produced by specific biochemical actions of the endocrine system— habit patterns, interests, and behaviors associated with physical gratification—can take over the function of stimulating the individual to sexual behavior.

The intensity of the sex drive varies. In some persons the drive is so compelling that it dominates the individual's thoughts and energies. In others, the drive is of such low intensity that even its presence might be questioned. Although it is known that certain conditions such as illness or drugs can diminish the intensity of the drive, explanations for instances of prolonged and intense sexual excitement (nymphomania in women and satyriasis in men) or of frigidity and impotence are probably to be found in nonphysical causes. The denial or repression of sexual impulses may reflect id–superego conflict originating in early childhood experiences, in which such expressions were forbidden, disapproved, or ridiculed. Intrapsychic conflict can also contribute to heightened sexual drive, for it may produce doubts as to individual value and adequacy, causing an unending search for reassurance and physical gratification.

Individuals also vary in the directions in which the drive is expressed. In the usual course of psychosexual development, as the previous chapter pointed out, the individual finds sources of pleasurable activity in various areas of his body. In the developmental process, these so-called erogenous zones shift and eventually lose much of their significance as major sources of gratification. The lips, mouth, and tongue, however, may still be sources of gratification in the expression of the adult sex drive. Thus, kissing is evocative of the sex drive and is considered one of the preliminary acts leading to intercourse in our culture. Since kissing is not universally practiced in all cultures, its potential to evoke sexual desire is viewed as learned rather than instinctual.

As the physical development of adolescence proceeds, the person in most cases identifies with his parent of the same sex, thus partially achieving his own personal identity. This identification includes some aspects of the sexual role. How firm the person's identifications are with his own sex and how satisfactorily he fulfills his own sexual role depend upon the nature of his previous experience, his physical well-being, and the character of his social situation. When the identification process has been disturbed, sexual tensions may, according to some theorists, be evoked and gratified through means other than sexual activity with the opposite sex. Such individuals are sexually aroused and stimulated by objects, animals, or members of their own sex. The broad range of possible ways in which individuals can channel their sexual drives is determined not biologically, but as a result of their social and psychological experiences.

PERCEPTIONS OF THE SELF AND PHYSICAL DEVELOPMENT

Of the many factors that influence the person's evaluation of himself in relation to his sex role, the experiences associated with physical development may be of primary importance. These experiences may center about reactions to a physical characteristic, such as a disability or irregular features, or to developmental rates and thus be more subtle in their psychological significance.

An example of the latter was provided by an attractive young woman who sought psychological assistance. She was unable to believe that the young man whom she had been dating for several years actually was in love with her. Although he was ardent and insisted that she marry him, and although she believed that she loved him very much, she refused to agree to marriage. She stated that she hesitated to accept his proposal because she doubted that anyone could really believe her to be attractive.

In discussing her attitudes toward herself, she revealed that she was the oldest of three girls. Her two sisters, who were identical twins, were only fifteen months younger than she. They had always been petite and graceful, while she had been large and physically mature for her age. She reported feelings of being awkward and clumsy and of embarrassment at being the largest child in her seventh and eighth grade classes, and she recalled her mother's comparing her unfavorably with her sisters. It was not until her junior year in college that she had her first date, although both her sisters were married within a year of their finishing high school. Thus, regardless of the obvious acceptance she received as an adult, she still maintained the negative feelings about herself and her acceptability as a woman that had developed in her childhood, feelings that were changed only after prolonged counseling.

The pattern of physical development also may have definite psychological implications for males. The early developer, the big boy who possesses the physical size and strength of a man, is often expected to exhibit the social, emotional, and judgmental characteristics of an adult. The late developing boy may be confronted with special problems because he is small and weak in relation to the other boys in his class. Derogatory references by classmates to a girl's height and boy's smallness can lead to much unhappiness. Although both early and late maturers have special problems and concerns, the anxieties of the late maturer are somewhat more intense and pervasive than those of the early maturer (1). The uncertainties of knowing whether he will ever "grow up" or whether he is a physical anomaly may cause the late developing boy considerable distress. Since he is at a disadvantage athletically and socially, doubts about his future can compound the dissatisfaction he experiences about his present physical status.

Physical, Social, and Cultural Environment

SEX ROLE

Psychological reactions and attitudes toward self are influenced by the degree to which the individual believes he fulfills his sex role. If the issue is put solely in terms of physical attractiveness, it becomes oversimplified and confusing. The belief that a body attractive to the opposite

sex is the definitive indication of masculinity or femininity is a prev--
alent but erroneous one in our society.

The term "sex role" may be thought of as including two components. One pertains to the physical sex role, the person's anatomic and
physiological ability to participate in an intimate, conjugal relationship.
The other pertains to the social sex role, which is made up of those
behaviors and characteristics associated with each sex and expected of
its members. Although the two parts of the role are related, they are
sufficiently independent to merit extreme caution in predicting physical
sex role from data pertaining to social sex role and vice versa. No sweep-
ing inferences can be made about the state of an individual's adjustment
from the fact that he may or may not fulfill some aspects of the role.
For example, failure to fulfill the physical aspects of the role may be due
not to physical limitation but to lack of opportunity or to conscious
choice.

Physical "Attractiveness"

People frequently make judgments of sex-role adequacy on
the basis of culturally determined aspects of physical attractiveness.
Persons reared in our culture may find it difficult to admire the Ubangi's
extended lips or the enlarged ear lobes of these natives of French
Equatorial Africa. Their welted tattoos also may represent something
other than masculine strength and virility to us. These symbols of sexual
adequacy are learned and they depend upon the customs of the culture
in which they occur. It is important to recognize that physical attractiveness as a symbol of sexual adequacy is at best a sign, a sign which may
relate more to the conventions of the culture than to intrinsic qualities
of masculinity or femininity.

Many individuals base their self-concepts largely on physical appearance, and they esteem themselves in terms of the closeness with which they
conform to socially determined standards of beauty. Many young people
consider the Hollywood concepts of physical attractiveness as the models
of femininity and masculinity, without regard to other social and cultural
standards of behavior. The acutely self-conscious adolescent or young
adult may feel that his value as a human being depends upon whether he
has broad shoulders or a muscular physique, and he may experience
unhappiness about real or imagined "shortcomings."

Certain focal experiences growing out of the physical differences
between the sexes provide the occasions in which the attitudes of significant persons can influence a person's attitudes toward himself and his
learning of what is good or bad, proper or improper, modest or im-
modest. The emotional quality of the situation in which the young child
inquires about sexual matters or sexual differences, the reactions of his

parents during the toilet training process, and their own concealment or display of their bodies, all may influence the child's feelings about himself and about what is expected or considered desirable of him relative to his sex. Attitudes toward the menstrual period or toward sexual impulses are determined by the attitudes of those with whom the individual has contact and with whom he has identified. Cultural standards and values reinforce in varying ways the individual's early concepts of desirable sexual behavior and appearance.

Since the male in our society frequently values physical strength, prowess in athletics, sexual attractiveness, and virility, he sometimes engages in activities that contribute to such achievements or feelings of achievement. Identifications with sport heroes or use of provocative or "tough" language can provide substitute gratifications for the person who does not fulfill the role of the athletic or attractive male. These substitute behaviors influence not only how he feels about himself and how he perceives himself, but they also partially account for his behaviors toward women. The person who doubts his adequacy as a male will, through the workings of the compensation mechanisms, sometimes seek—or boast of—many conquests. He has to "make out" on every date, and he may be unable to enjoy lasting relationships with women because he is preoccupied with a need to demonstrate his adequacy in the sexual-physical area.

The woman who equates femininity with physical attractiveness, or has it equated for her, has a similar need to demonstrate her adequacy by being sought after. She invests her energies in behaviors that will make her appear attractive to men and is satisfied with relationships from which she gains little. Some women who have had inadequate opportunities for identification with their own mothers are confused about their roles as wives and mothers. Their concepts of the attractive women who achieve husbands after dazzling successions of boy friends or romantic experiences often fail to include any realistic expectations of the demands or the requirements of marital roles. The roles associated with marriage and parenthood will be discussed in detail in Chapter 9.

The Body Image

The psychological significance our bodies have for us has been noted by a number of authorities. Their investigations have been concerned with what is termed the "body image." The body image is a person's mental picture of himself. The body image of the young lady mentioned did not correspond to the actual picture she presented to others, but rather to an image of herself formed many years before. Although there may have been a factual basis for her early feelings, her adult belief that she was awkward, clumsy, and undesirable because of her size represented her own self-evaluation. Since the significant individuals in her life had tended to devalue her, it is not surprising that she devalued herself and that she interpreted the comments and criticisms of her former peers as "evidence" that she possessed little worth.

The significance of the individual's concept of the adequacy of his own body was emphasized by Alfred Adler, one of the early associates of Sigmund Freud. Adler believed that those who felt that they were inadequate would often try to compensate for their inadequacies through the development of talents or skills in areas related—but not always in some physical aspect—to those in which they felt limited. Illustrations of compensatory reactions to disability include those of Theodore Roosevelt, who became a boxer, hunter, and sportsman following a childhood marked by illness and physical inadequacy, and Glenn Cunningham, the famous runner, who suffered serious burns on his legs during childhood.

Compensatory reactions can occur also in other areas: the boy who is not adequate as an athlete may focus his energies on achieving academic distinction; the unattractive girl may develop literary interests and talents. Compensatory reactions can be thought of as motivated by needs to achieve self-esteem when the individual is deprived of the most desired sources of self-esteem. According to this use of the concept, individual physical limitations may or may not be the occasions for the quest of additional sources of self-esteem. One cannot make psychological inferences purely from observations of the actual state of an individual's physical condition, for a person is not necessarily impaired psychologically because of a physical disability that may have presented him with special social problems. The significant issue involves the individual's specific sources of self-esteem that determine his attitudes toward himself and his own feelings of worth. These, of course, may or may not be involved in all persons whose physical appearance or functional ability departs from the socially valued norm.

Thus the role the adolescent perceives as appropriate for him and the sexual role that he attributes to members of the opposite sex have their origins in his previous experiences. These experiences have occurred at home where parents have reinforced the behaviors they responded to as appropriate to his sexual role. Parental attitudes, in part, reflect the attitudes prevalent in the society, and attitudes can differ markedly from one culture to the next.

Social Expectations and Sex Role

The behaviors associated with the role of a man or a woman in our society are significant influences upon the individual's expectations of himself. On first consideration, the question, "Are there social factors that account for differences in interests, activities and values of men and women?" might evoke reactions such as, "Of course not; men and women are physically different, and therefore all other differences are obviously due to these physical differences." This quick answer does not seem unreasonable. Boys are treated the way they are because they are boys, and they do the things they do because they are boys. Put in this way, the statement reveals an obvious logical fallacy; that boys are biologically male does not necessarily account for their actions or for the responses made by others to their conduct.

In Sears' study of child-rearing practices discussed in the previous chapter (12), for example, it was found that maternal expectancies for sons usually differed from those for daughters. Boys were treated more permissively when they were aggressive, but they were more frequently disciplined by physical punishment. Girls were expected to perform domestic chores, were treated more affectionately, were disciplined more by love-oriented techniques, such as withholding or offering approval and verbal expressions of dismay. They were expected to be ladylike in their appearance and behavior.

The behaviors of boys depend upon the treatment they receive, what their parents expect of them, the activities in which they are encouraged to participate, and the rewards they receive, the games they are taught, and the models their parents provide for them. Does this statement imply that only those behavioral differences involved in reproduction and excretion are directly attributable to the differences in physical structure? Before this question is considered, another should be asked. Are there differences in attitudes, activities, and behaviors of men and women other than those related to the reproductive system? Of course such differences do exist, although they are not necessarily due to either biological or societal influences. The emotionally charged nature of this issue was most clearly demonstrated during the days of the woman suffragist movement. The feminist position, which held that no differences existed and that therefore equal voting rights were justified, was countered by the equally extreme anti-suffragist position, which maintained that women were biologically inferior and therefore inept and incapable of assuming the responsibilities for full citizenship.

INTERESTS

What differences are actually found in the interests and attitudes of men and women in the United States? Twenty years ago, Terman and Miles undertook an intensive study of this question (16), and their essential results were duplicated in subsequent studies. That the findings have held up with time is not only a comment on the scientific adequacy of the investigation but also a suggestion that there is a considerable degree of stability in the roles of men and women, even during periods of unrest and social dislocation. These investigators reported that men were very much more interested in adventure than were women. Outdoor and physically strenuous occupations involving the use of machinery and tools appealed to them. Activities related to science or invention and interests in physical phenomena were decidedly characteristic of men, who were also distinguished by their interests in business and commerce, although to a lesser degree.

Women were reported to have marked interests in domestic affairs and in matters of art and appearance. They preferred working indoors and at occupations that were sedentary rather than active. They were most interested in occupations having to do with taking care of the young, the helpless, or the distressed. The investigators reported certain more subjective impressions that men were more self-assertive and aggressive, more fearless, rough, and hardy in their manners. Women gave the impression of being more compassionate, sympathetic, timid, and fastidious. The authors believed women to be more sensitive, more generally emotional, and more concerned with moral issues.

Interests in music, poetry, or the arts are considered by many persons in our culture to be activities unsuitable for men. The implication is that such interests are "unnatural" in men and are therefore signs of feminine sexual identification. This misconception warrants closer examination, for its connotation is that men who are interested in activities which in our culture are ascribed to the feminine role, are maladjusted or abnormal. It has already been noted that men and women do differ in regard to the interests they express. In general, women in American culture more frequently express interests in literary, artistic, and musical subjects, while men more frequently express interests in outdoor and mechanical subjects. But studies of the talents and aptitudes of men and women in these areas suggest that the interests are determined largely on the basis of customs prevalent in the culture rather than in terms of sexual differences in native ability.

It is therefore apparent that the social roles of men and women touch many areas of activity that are not direct products of biological difference. Writing poetry is an activity pursued more frequently by females than by males. This does not mean that either the activity or the poet is feminine, even though the social expectation is not being fulfilled. Since the standards of normal development adopted in this text are not those of the statistical concept of normality, an evaluation of the poet's adjustment would be made on grounds other than the degree to which he fits the pattern expected of all men.

There is a sense in which an individual must and should consider

the social expectations related to his occupational choice. Role behaviors of men and women are determined in large part by the opportunities afforded them by their society for the expression and development of their talents and interests. There are pressures that encourage
men to achieve in some areas and women in others, but the existence
of prejudices against women in certain fields and against men in others
need not be the determining factor for the person who is highly
motivated and who possesses definite abilities.

Although the study of Terman and Miles reflected the interest
patterns of adult men and women, these interests, as well as the attitudes
and values associated with them, are shared by adolescents. Studies
of adolescents emphasize the differences between boys and girls in their
patterns of interests, and show that the adult patterns are deeply imbedded in the culture and are probably acquired prior to adolescence.
According to such studies girls prefer to engage in sedentary activities,
such as reading or talking to one another, while boys prefer active sports.
In one study (9), girls stated that they believed their most valuable high
school subjects were English, commerce, and home economics. Boys
indicated that mathematics was their most valuable subject. Although
individuals' patterns of interest shift somewhat as they grow older, these
responses suggest that the adolescent's interests and the activities he
anticipates engaging in are geared to his sex role.

In studying the wishes of adolescents, Washburn found (18) the
familiar pattern of differences between boys and girls. Boys more frequently wished for cars and airplanes, wealth, and athletic skill; girls
for clothes, good looks, travel, academic proficiency, visiting, and going
to parties. Differences in interests among boys and girls are associated
also with intellectual level and the family's social and educational backgrounds; in addition, the rate of an individual's physical development
can influence his interest patterns and sets of self-attitudes.

TOWARD INDEPENDENCE

The attitudes and self-perceptions acquired during childhood
are only slowly and partially abandoned in the period of adolescent
change-over. Adult behaviors are achieved after experimentation and
experience; consequently, the adolescent at times feels a keen sense of
aloneness and is hard pushed to attain and maintain a satisfying integration of the constituent selves and processes comprising his personality.
As a result of his quest for intrapersonal integration during this period,
he slowly and at times painfully attains a greater degree of reliance upon
himself; he becomes less dependent upon the advice, direction, and
supervision of his parents, and although he may sometimes overtly resist

their efforts to direct him or to limit his "rights" and prerogatives, he will at other times desire their direction and imposition of control.

The progression from dependency to self-responsibility is expected in our culture to occur within a relatively short time, and it necessitates modification of behavioral patterns that have been rewarded and reinforced throughout most of the person's life. At the age of seventeen, the adolescent's parents may give him an allowance. set a deadline for bedtime, arrange a homework schedule for him, and establish the conditions under which he may drive the family car, and the law may prevent him from purchasing tobacco, liquor, or from owning property. Yet within a few years this same person is expected to be economically self-sufficient, following or in training for an occupation or profession, and capable of fulfilling the responsibilities of a citizen and parent.

In many societies the amount of independence expected and the privileges granted with the attainment of specific phases of development are clearly enunciated by special rites and ceremonies. In our culture, changes in status and role are for the most part unheralded, unobserved, and accompanied by uncertainties and anxieties on the part of the adolescent as well as of his parents and the adult community. It has been noted by Tryon (17) that:

> In our society, children do not achieve adult status through the succession of rituals and observances . . . that mark development in many societies. In some contemporary primitive societies certain culturally valued individual accomplishments are recognized with feasts and ceremonies, and new, more clearly adult privileges and responsibilities are thereafter accorded the boy or girl. In other words, the beginning and the end of various culturally described stages of development are observed with similar ceremonies and rituals, followed for the individual by a new status. In this way, individuals or groups of individuals are inducted into their adult roles.[1]

The adolescent finds little uniformity among the expectations that various groups hold for him. Not only do his parents, teachers, employers, and peers expect him to demonstrate different degrees of independence, but the same individuals will be inconsistent with respect to the degree of adult responsibility they expect and allow him to assume. One sixteen-year-old boy reported, for example, that his parents told him to think for himself with reference to his occupational choice, yet they insisted upon participating in his purchase of a new pair of slacks.

[1] Reprinted by permission from Caroline M. Tryon, "Evaluations of Adolescent Personality by Adolescents." *Monogr. Soc. Res. Child Develpm.*, 1939, *4*, No. 23.

Since many parents are unclear about the responsibilities and details of the roles they themselves are expected to fulfill, it is not easy for them to provide their adolescent children with either clear-cut guide lines or statements of their expectations that are logical and comprehensible to the adolescent. Three explanations—not necessarily mutually independent—can account for the doubts and confusion of parents in their attempts to contribute to the adolescent's development toward independence.

The first is that the parent is uninformed about the nature of the adolescent's subculture. He may respond to the adolescent's demands for increased privileges or freedom from supervision in terms of the conditions that prevailed when he was an adolescent some thirty years earlier. When the parents were reared in the traditions of foreign lands, additional complications are sometimes presented. The second explanation is that the doubts and confusion on the part of the parents stem from their conflicting needs. They may simultaneously hold conscious wishes that their children be able to assume adult roles and responsibilities and have subconscious needs to hold their children by not allowing them to relinquish their dependency. Children often represent a source of gratification for parents, gratification which may have been denied or limited in other areas of their lives. When parents have not had the love they desired from their marriage partners or when they have failed to fulfill their aspirations in other significant aspects, the child's emancipation from them represents a threat to one source of gratification and self-esteem that they are unwilling to relinquish. Meyers (8) makes this point.

> Allowing a child to achieve emancipation will be difficult in proportion as the parent has achieved satisfaction, knowingly or not, for his own wants by loving and controlling his child. If the child is providing gratification and compensation for frustration arising elsewhere, he will be surrendered reluctantly, surrendered at a cost, or not surrendered at all.

It has also been noted that in some instances parents may be unconsciously jealous of the child's opportunities for gratifications which they missed in their childhood. A mother whose child enjoys popularity in high school may try to restrict her activities to an unreasonable degree because she resents these successes. Or a father who had unsuccessfully wanted to be a football star may refuse to allow his son, who shows such potential, to play, saying that "It's too dangerous."

The third explanation has to do with the nature of the developmental process of the adolescent himself. As he observes the consequences of his own decisions and the effects of his own behaviors, the adolescent learns what he can and cannot do; but in this process he will evidence considerable conflict about the freedom he feels able to assume. At the same time that he may feel the need for parental guidance and the intervention of adult authority, he may vigorously protest that he wants to be allowed the right to make his own decisions.

Thus the ability to assume adult responsibility does not develop smoothly and equally in all areas; in some aspects of behavior the adolescent may function for a long period of time without seeming to make much progress. A seventeen-year-old boy may be well on the road to success in a chosen occupational or professional field, yet be painfully shy and embarrassed in the presence of girls. Within the area of activity in which his progress is slow, he will at times be unwilling to discuss his difficulties with his parents or other adults, but at other times he will welcome such discussion; he will both want and reject efforts to help him. It is this characteristic of the adolescent's psychological development that often causes parents to feel their child is unpredictable, volatile, and impossible to understand—an attitude that, of course, does nothing to contribute to the adolescent's willingness to seek counsel, even when he may want it very much.

Many of these areas of disagreement between parents and adolescents are familiar. In a well-known study (2), Block compiled a list of grievances that adolescents frequently reported as the cause of their difficulties. All the complaints stemmed from conflicts between the adolescents and their mothers. This list was submitted to 528 junior and high school boys and girls. They were asked to place a check mark after each problem that caused them serious trouble or unhappiness, and to add any unlisted problem. The results revealed fifty problems of which the following three were most frequently marked by both boys and girls. Over 75 percent of the boys and of the girls complained:

"Insists that I eat foods which I dislike, but which are good for me."
"Scolds if my school marks aren't as high as other people's."
"Insists that I tell her for exactly what I spend my money."

Another investigation (11) showed that "social life and friends" was the most frequently reported cause of quarreling between adolescents and parents. "Economic factors relating to work and spending money" had the second highest frequency. Although such complaints are indeed common, their significance can be understood only in light of the nature of the adolescent's relationships with his parents and the degree of psychological integration he has attained.

RELATIONSHIPS OUTSIDE THE FAMILY

As the adolescent comes to depend less upon adults, the reliance he places upon the opinions and attitudes of his peers increases. From his associates he learns much about his sex role, getting along with others, and techniques of competition and cooperation. Although he will rebel against parental authority, he capitulates willingly to the demands of the group. These demands can dictate what clothes he should wear, his style of language, and his patterns of activities and interests. Many of the learnings from his peers cannot be acquired in his contacts with teachers or parents, but the significance of peer relationships during adolescence is not limited to the information acquired from them.

From these relationships he receives considerable support as he turns away from his parents. With others who are similarly experiencing feelings of parental lack of understanding and parental limitations, he can share the hostility and irritation he may be unable to express directly to his parents. He experiences a relatedness to the group, and his identification with them becomes highly significant to him. Their approval and recognition of him substitutes in part for the approval and affection he previously attempted to acquire from his family. In addition to their support and teachings, the peer group thus provides a source of prestige, gratification, and reward for the adolescent.

In view of the considerable need he has for this support, encouragement, and reward, it is not surprising that the adolescent's behavior and thought are often markedly influenced by the group standards and by the specific relationships he has with his age mates. In some instances, when the adolescent is unusually beset by intrapsychic conflict, there may appear to be an almost total rejection of parental values, and the standards of the individual's peer group appear to be the primary source of the judgments that the individual makes of himself and his own worth. It must be remembered, however, that the values and attitudes acquired from the parents continue to exercise a directing force through superego activities.

RELATIONSHIPS WITH THE
OPPOSITE SEX

It has already been said that sexual impulses and drives assert themselves during this period and that the adolescent begins to think of himself in terms of his adequacy as a member of his sex. Becoming a man or woman has many social as well as physical meanings for the adolescent; it includes how one calls for a girl on a date, how one

The clash of parent and adolescent!

To the adolescent, the parent is unfair, inconsistent, restrictive, old-fashioned, unreasonable, and lacking in understanding. To the parent, the adolescent is unfair, inconsistent, impulsive, unreasonable, and lacking in understanding. How difficult this period can be for both! Each is learning to accommodate to the adolescent's ability and desire to extend his range of personal decision—and this often can be accomplished only through trial and error. The parent who has experienced the consequences of error finds it difficult not to intervene when he believes that his child is acting foolishly. And the adolescent finds that his parents seem to be forever disapproving, hypercritical, and lacking in respect for his judgment.

The significance of the conflict between the adolescent and his parents varies from that which is unavoidable in the developmental process of both parent and child to the type of prolonged struggle that may never be satisfactorily resolved. When the parent-child relationship has been built through the years upon mutual trust and respect, then the infrequent moments of intense crisis will be weathered without damage to the relationship.

Wayne Miller—Magnum

responds to a boy's interests, and how one dresses, speaks, and acts. In addition, adolescence is a time of preparation for the roles one assumes as an adult, that of husband or wife, worker, and parent. Although the learnings constituting one's self-identity have been in process for a long time prior to adolescence, the individual's physical and social development has progressed to the point where he is now able to enter into heterosexual relationships both for the direct gratification they afford— that is, for the relationships themselves—and indirectly, for the status acquired in the peer group as a result of dating, being seen together, or going steady.

While the adolescent's heterosexual relationships may be viewed as a part of the preparation for adult sexual roles and responsibilities, for him such relationships are central to self-esteem and are viewed not in terms of a long-term process of learning or preparation but in terms of the immediate situation; of whether one will have a date and how one will be rated by the peer group. The role of the peer group is important in several respects to adolescent heterosexual activity. By rewarding the adolescent for heterosexual behaviors that conform to those it values, the peer group will increase the likelihood that the individual will repeat such valued behavior. The peer group affords the arena for heterosexual experience and his "school" for learning how he should acquire such experience, what techniques he should employ in relationships with the opposite sex, and what is ethically permissible, socially proper, and realistically possible.

While the adolescent is in high school, he will raise many questions with his peers and with himself about such matters as whether to double date, what clothes to wear on a date, what to talk about with a date, and whether it is permissible to neck on dates. Many of these questions will center also about choice of an eventual marriage partner and the nature of the love relationship: "Will I find a person who will love me? How will I know when I am in love? What are the differences between love and infatuation?" Questions pertaining to marriage also occur frequently in the thoughts and discussions of adolescents. They ask, "What kind of person should I marry? Can I trust my intuition or should I be guided by the advice of other people when I choose a person to marry? Should I marry before I am well established in my profession?"

College students also spend a considerable amount of time discussing such topics. Issues pertaining to the sex role provide a frequent subject of discussion during college "bull sessions." These topics include "moral questions related to petting, trial marriage, the nature of true love, birth control, the wisdom of marrying someone of a different cultural, religious, or racial background." In this section those aspects of the adolescent's sex role related to conditions which prompt him to raise such questions are considered.

DATING

The effect of expectations associated with the sex roles is evident if we consider the stage of dating, which for most persons begins in adolescence. During adolescence, rules of dating are usually followed rigidly. In some groups, for example, a girl does not ask a boy to go out, nor does she show an unabashed interest in him or accept a date for the same night that it is extended. These rules constitute the expectations defining the sex role. They vary with the age of the individuals as well as with the social, economic, and ethnic composition of their groups. But they do exist for all groups, and they influence the form in which the interpersonal relationship is manifest. Although these rules are implicit —they are neither verbalized nor written—the adolescent holds tenaciously to them because he fears loss of status within his group if he does not conform. Some of the rules presently serve a function that was once provided by a chaperon or by supervising parents.

It has been suggested that the customs and mores surrounding the dating behaviors of high school and college students are such that the boy who wants a date is seeking a special situation more than he is seeking a special girl. The date serves to maintain or enhance the status of the boy or the girl. The value of each is determined by the approval and recognition that is received from the peer group; it is a desirable and good thing to date someone who rates high in the estimation of the group. This rating is merely a reflection of the peer group's values, which reflect, in turn, the values of the culture.

In the rating system, a high premium is placed upon a boy's appearance, his approach, his "line," whether he is a campus figure such as an athlete or member of the right fraternity, whether he has the "right" kind of car, wears the "right clothes," and in general conforms to the group's idea of a "popular" person. A girl's desirability as a date depends on her popularity and the extent to which she is known to be desirable by other boys. To a large extent her desirability will depend upon her physical appearance and the degree to which she conforms to the group stereotype of beauty.

A high rating as a "date" is achieved by a boy or girl partly by having a large number of dates with many different people. The girl who has five invitations to the senior prom may feel, and may be considered by her group to be, superior to the girl who has but one invitation. Since the rating is determined by the group's knowledge of the details of the date, a considerable amount of information is passed on by the persons concerned. It is also important for the couple to be seen by members of their group at the dance, movie, or drive-in. Although a participant in the rating and dating procedure may feel strong physical attraction toward a member of the opposite sex, the emphasis in such relationships is usually upon gratifications in terms of the social approval which comes to them for "doing well," or the gratification which they receive from the attentions of their partners.

Dating relationships are not love relationships as the term will be defined here; they are transitory and superficial, but they do constitute reality for young people. The person who "rates" low, the unattractive girl or the unpopular boy, may suffer pangs of loneliness and feelings of isolation in the dormitory on the night of the school dance or when a hoped-for invitation fails to materialize. This type of hurt is difficult for any young person to deal with, for the unattractive and unpopular share the same values with the attractive and popular. Those who are not dating will consider themselves less valuable than their peers, and in sessions with their friends or counselors they will "confess their social failures."

The hurt experienced by the unattractive or the unpopular boy when he is bypassed or turned down is particularly keen, because in addition to the social stigma inflicted he feels personally rejected. This event calls forth the emotional residuals or leftovers from earlier experiences of devaluation or rejection by those of importance to him. Some individuals who have experienced a considerable degree of rejection in early life develop defensive reactions to protect self-esteem. One boy may proclaim himself a "woman hater" and voice scorn for his friends, whom he says are "being taken for chumps." In order to protect himself from failure, he will publicly announce that he is not in the competitive market. A girl may be critical of the boys whom her friends date, implying that they do not meet her standards. Such defenses are, however, usually inadequate protection against the feelings of frustration, anger, and anxiety that underlie them.

It is not unusual for individuals who felt rejected during their early formative years to be particularly vulnerable to distress and emotional upset when they are socially rejected as adults. They may so doubt their intrinsic worth and desirability that they need symbols of social approval and acceptance to maintain their self-esteem. The person who is fairly sure of his own value may be disappointed when he is "left out," but he can deal with such rejection with less disruption and with less need to deny or distort the meaning of the situation for him.

As a social form, then, dating per se is not courtship. It is an entertainment that has a gamelike character; nevertheless, the game does have definite sexual implications, and success in dating is construed as success in fulfilling the expectations of the sex role. Sometimes it is erroneously believed that dating success can be used as a basis for predicting success in marriage. This assumes that to date means to be a man or woman and that not to date is a demonstration of masculine or feminine inadequacy. These interpretations are unfortunate, since failure or success in dating may have little relation to the degree to which the individual is actually capable of fulfilling the responsibilities of marriage or possesses true masculinity or femininity. An individual's success in dating, however, influences his impressions of his own sexual adequacy and also his evaluation of his chances to become a spouse and parent. Within our culture relatively little emphasis is placed upon psychological characteristics and the relationship between them and the ability to love, to be concerned about others, or to fulfill the role of a husband or wife.

"Going Steady"

Previously, the dating period provided opportunity for individuals to have experience with many persons of the opposite sex before pairings of particular boys and girls developed. Following a period in which a couple was "going steady," a formal engagement was announced. In recent years, the "going steady" relationship has become widespread among younger persons. One aspect of the "going steady" relationship is that it protects both persons from exposure to the uncertainties of the dating situation, such as the risk of not "having a date," of dating someone whose status is low or with whom one would have to go through the process of becoming acquainted. It also allays any doubts that the participants may have about their own adequacies and their opportunities for eventual marriage.

Obviously the advantages or disadvantages of the "going steady" relationship cannot be generalized, since the meaning of the relationship varies for different persons. Whether "going steady" can be termed a love relationship also cannot be answered categorically. Sometimes the relationship is not unlike the engagement relationship, and there is often a tacit assumption that "someday" a formal engagement will be announced which will eventually be followed by marriage.

During the dating period, the meanings, memories, and emotions that accompany "being in love" are often thought of in terms of decisions about marriage. Although the person may be confronted consciously for the first time with the specific issues reflected in these questions, he has been preparing for an adult sex role from childhood. His identifications with his sex and the meanings of this identification in terms of role

The world has suddenly changed!

Another person has become someone very special—someone to talk to, to think about, to thrill to. The world is now viewed through perceptual prisms that carry the special one's imprint. Ideas and feelings are shared, time spent together slides by quickly, and all experience takes on an added dimension— that of living through the experiences of another person as if they are your own. Though there will be other loves, the first can never be matched, for it carries with it more than the discovery of someone else. It brings to full awareness the meaning that another person can possess and the emotion that he or she can arouse.

Wayne Miller—Magnum

expectations as they have developed through childhood and adolescence have already been discussed. Sexual identification includes the expectation of assuming the role of husband or wife. In the process of growing up, the person becomes aware of the behaviors that lead to marriage. This awareness is transmitted to him in the form of social expectations, which include the belief that he will progress through a sequence of stages in his relationships with the opposite sex. These stages involve an early childhood period when there is no preference for playmates as far as their sex is concerned, a period when only like-sexed persons are acceptable, and an adolescent period when the first tentative and self-conscious efforts are made to establish relatively enduring relationships with members of the opposite sex. The dating pattern of adolescence is followed by the courtship and the marriage phases.

During these stages of the relationship, not only do the physical and social aspects of the individual's sex role play an important part in what he does or feels he should do, but they also influence the timing of his behaviors. There is a time when it is considered appropriate to turn away from close friends of the same sex, the gang or clique, and to walk home from school with the boy or girl friend. The movie date, the school dance, the first present given or received, mark points in the development of heterosexual relationships. The times of "going steady," becoming engaged, and getting married are set by the expectations that accompany the sex roles. Since part of the sex role involves the man's being able to provide for a wife, most marriages occur when he has become sufficiently established to be able to do so.

Personality Development and the Control of Sexual Impulses

The relationship between the attitude and values of the society and the superego and ego processes of individuals may be discovered from a closer examination of the psychological aspects of dating behavior. The implicit rules of conduct of high school and college students serve as aids to the ego in controlling or keeping the sexual impulses from having to be discharged through sexual intercourse. The role expectation of the girl, for example, is that she will stop the boy during a petting session from "going too far," and that, as part of his role, the boy will accede to the girl's wishes. The boy may attempt to stimulate her sexually, but he expects that she will stop him at a point prior to intercourse.

To a large extent, the enforcement of conduct that is valued by the group is presently left to the young people themselves. So great a degree of mobility is possible that dating and courtship activities no longer occur in the home. The automobile provides not only transportation but a place where the boy and girl can get to know each other and where they can engage in some degree of physical contact with each other in relative privacy. This freedom to interact without supervision, without the reliance upon others to enforce the rules, places considerable responsibility upon the persons themselves and may engender conflicts of varying intensity. The responsibility to act properly—to do the things that bring the approval of the peer group and to secure maximum personal gratification with minimal risk and guilt—may result in dilemmas for the individual that can be related to conflicts among cultural values.

This type of conflict is illustrated by the fact that independence, achievement, and physical attractiveness are highly valued in our culture, as are the ideas of virtue, chastity, and the avoidance of sexual intercourse until marriage. While being reared in a society that has prohibitions against premarital sexual intercourse as part of its ethical and moral code, the individual is also exposed to sexually provocative advertising and entertainment. That which is ethically disapproved is also glamorized and romanticized, and the individual who is uncertain about the degree of sexual freedom which he may or should allow himself is apt to feel considerable frustration no matter what he does. Persons who are clear about their ethical and moral positions may experience somewhat less frustration.

Young people are biologically capable of physical sexual behavior many years before most of them are economically or socially able to marry, and in most young adults strong physical and sexual impulses are readily aroused. In our society, however, it is expected that these impulses will be satisfied prior to marriage without physical intercourse with members of the opposite sex. It is expected that outlets will be found for redirecting physical energies into socially sanctioned and approved activities, such as athletics, music, or any form of work. Young persons are expected to control and redirect their sexual tensions, and they usually hold these expectations to be desirable; consequently, many adolescents welcome these redirecting activities, since they also feel the need for expending physical energies in time-consuming and socially approved ways.

Probably most persons in our culture have behaved in socially disapproved ways. They have attitudes acquired from parents and from the institutions of our society that sexual expression is unnatural, bad, or at best something special, appropriate only in special situations. These attitudes, which are frequently reinforced, exert a considerable emotional force, so that even the "enlightened" individual may be unable to disregard their influence. Stated in other terms, the person reared in our culture will probably be troubled by his own sexual impulses. His uneasiness is intensified by the restrictions and secrecy that surround sexual matters and by the emotional climate in many middle class families, which discourage open manifestations of feeling. The acquired standards of the superego can evoke anxiety and can prevent direct expression of sexual impulses.

Although it is outside the scope of the science of psychology to provide a set of moral pronouncements relating to sexual behaviors, several comments can be made relative to the assessment of psychological development and to conditions that minimize intrapsychic conflict. These statements cannot provide a substitute for the ethical considerations that religious and philosophical systems offer as guides to individual behavior.

That one's sexual impulses are a natural part of the individual's humanness must be acknowledged, but recognition of the compelling and human nature of these impulses does not imply that they are entitled to immediate and capricious gratification. In the discussion of the ego processes it was stated that the abilities to delay gratification, to take cognizance of all the factors in a situation, and to act in terms of one's own self-interest, in the broad sense, are essential to a strong ego and an effective personality. Such an ego has neither to deny nor to repress the fact that sexuality is one aspect of life that warrants consideration.

A strong ego enables an individual to accept his sexual impulses as facts of life, just as he accepts his superego, which has been influenced by society's attitudes toward sexual matters. The person who is able to recognize the guilt, depression, and torment that can result from the violation of the injunctions of his superego is psychologically wise not to place himself in the position of transgressing against his own conscience. In his rebellion against what is perceived as domination by parents and other adults, the adolescent may behave in ways that serve to test his ability to reject their standards. This behavior can be seen more accurately as a type of self-testing, involving the self-assignment of capabilities, the learning of the limits that exist in the external world, and the establishment of self-imposed limits. In the best of developmental situations, the adolescent becomes aware that part of his struggle is really with himself. Consequently, he can face his own superego, and, in the case of sexual behavior, can avoid the situations that cause him to feel most unworthy.

For most young people, premarital sexual behavior will at best afford only temporary gratification at the cost of persistent guilt reactions. Such behavior destroys the cultural value of sexual abstinence until the marital relationship, and although the value placed on this condition may be either defended or attacked, it does exist psychologically and may be strongly held by the potential marriage partner. For some persons whose ties to reality are strong, the risks of pregnancy, disease, and discovery are sufficient reasons for rejecting the immediate gratifications of premarital sexual intercourse. Additional reality factors may include the loss of social acceptance within the peer group for the girl who earns the reputation of being sexually promiscuous. In this connection girls who value status within the group recognize the needs of insecure boys to boast of their conquests. These boys' needs for self-esteem and for reassurance about their own masculinity may cause them to inform their friends of their sexual successes without concern for the girls involved.

A state of intrapsychic conflict is avoided by the actions of the ego, which prevents the individual from gratifying impulsive inclinations that would lead to punishment by the superego. In such a case conflict between the ego and the id is inevitable, and tension-releasing activities must be provided. These tension-reducing activities, which can take many forms, usually serve to bring the adolescent into play and work contacts with his peers and they often result in the expenditure of considerable physical energy. This is not to say that the sexual drive is depleted by physical activity per se. Rather, the point is that time and energy expended in activity that partially satisfies the person's relatedness need will tend to decrease the quest for other means—including sexual gratification—of enhancing feelings of communion with others.

In his efforts to control his sexual and aggressive impulses, to fulfill new role expectations, to attain gratification, and to protect against anxiety, the adolescent also relies upon fantasy and identification mechanisms. *Fantasy* may help to control drives by providing a means of anticipating gratifications and the risks involved in the overt expression of these drives. In the daydreams of the adolescent, the desires, the sexual conquests, the glorious triumphs, and the aggressive assaults against restrictive, punitive adults and other enemies are safely and privately expressed. In some instances, the adolescent's fantasies are part of a process that culminates in actual role experimentation or in decisions. Fantasies serve mastery as well as defensive functions; the adolescent may picture himself in different work situations, in relationships with members of the opposite sex, and in various activities that follow from one decision rather than another. Fantasies about what the responses might be to the ways that one asks for a date or applies for a position, for example, are preludes to action and to the planning essential to decisions.

The mechanism of *identification* often becomes a prominent aspect of the ego processes during this period. The adolescent will take within himself characteristics of those peers or adult figures he admires. Or without his conscious awareness, he may adopt the manners and attitudes of other persons in order to enhance and maintain his self-esteem. In this case it is as if he is "borrowing" the strength and the prestige of the individual with whom he identifies.

Identification figures significantly in his expectations and aspirations relative to the sex role and is also an important aspect of his peer-group behavior. Conformity to the mores, manners, and attitudes of his peers in preference to those of his family represents identifications that are essential to his eventual emancipation from his parents. The quest for the approval and support of his peers by conforming slavishly to their standards may reflect the operation of very strong identification mechanisms serving to keep at a minimum anxieties associated with separation from parents and rejection of parental values and standards.

The adolescent also identifies with esteemed public figures, such as television or sports personalities, and to a lesser extent with successful political, military, and business executives. These figures provide him with a basis for the hero worship frequently observed during this period. In addition, they provide him with nonparental adult models that can be consciously emulated. He can thus continue his rebellion against his parents without being deprived of adult leadership. The figures with whom the adolescent identifies may be significant in the construction of the ideal self and in the ego-ideal processes. When the adolescent overtly or in fantasy attains or approximates behaviors or characteristics similar to those of the "model," he bestows rewards upon himself for having done well.

In clarifying his self-concepts, the adolescent sometimes rejects vehemently persons with whom he has identified, when they demonstrate imperfections and frailties. The severity of the adolescent's reactions to weakness may stem, in part, from his considerable need for models who are perfect rather than human. The intolerance and lack of mercy often reflected in the adolescent's evaluations of others arises from his inability to tolerate ambiguities in his self-concepts. The adolescent will seize upon evidences of immorality or dishonesty, citing them as a basis for rejection of the adult culture or of a specific person. He requires his identification models to be clearly defined, to be readily classifiable in absolute categories, and in his judgments there is little margin for apparent contradictions, inconsistencies, compromising, or temporizing. In this connection, he may classify himself and his associates into categories, such as "wheels, brains, quiet ones, outsiders, drips, dopes, and wild ones" (6).

The need for specificity is apparent in the other aspect of the adolescent's superego processes, those relating to the "conscience." Values are reviewed intellectually, are tried out behaviorally, and are accepted or rejected in terms of whether they provide an absolute basis whereby one can judge and justify his own behavior.

In addition to his use of these mechanisms and unconscious activities in coping with increased intrapsychic conflict, the adolescent may engage in masturbation as a means of discharging sexual tension. But he has learned that to be observed by parents brings the scolding, "Don't play with yourself," or punishment, or even the threat, "If you keep that up, we will cut it off." The feelings of shame accompanying the child's being apprehended in the act of manipulating his sex organs blend into the feelings of guilt with which, with the development of the superego, he punishes himself for such activities. As the child grows into adolescence, he may be told that masturbation causes illness, acne, or even insanity. That these statements are false and have no legitimate medical basis does not affect their power to reinforce the feelings of shame and guilt evoked by masturbation. Masturbation, like premarital sexual relationships, may be avoided out of recognition that superego processes can engender sufficient guilt to cause feelings of unworthiness and depression; moreover, additional reality factors indicate that the energy and time involved in excessive masturbation may be diverted from more constructive pursuits.

From the standpoint of personality development, it is not the individual's departure from role expectations that is significant, so much as his emotional and intellectual reactions to the differences between his behavior and the social role. Does he see himself as inadequate and undesirable because he does not fill social expectations? If so, then the effects of such devaluation and lowered self-esteem will be apparent in his intrapersonal adjustment and interpersonal relationships. Such a person might attempt to demonstrate his value by entering marriage for the sake of being married to someone—anyone. On the other hand, a person unable to fulfill a physical sex role may recognize and accept his situation without loss of self-esteem. Having attained a high order of psychological development, he experiences no persistent internal conflict or interpersonal stress resulting from his inabilities. He may not be happy or satisfied with his limitations, but he can face them as facts and can enjoy compensating activities that enhance his self-esteem. In these activities he fulfills many of the requirements of the social sex role and obtains significant and enduring gratifications. There are also persons who are able to function physically in their sexual roles but who cannot demonstrate the social aspects of their roles; a physically adequate female might be unable to be sympathetic and supportive, or a male might be unable to be protective and provident.

Adolescence and Personality Trends Relating to Work

Another important aspect of development during this period is the adolescent's concern about his identity as a worker. For this reason attention will now be given to factors that influence his occupational decisions and his attitudes toward himself as a contributing member of society. In the age range of fourteen to seventeen, there are approximately eight million boys and girls; 90 percent are enrolled in high school and of these, more than 62 percent receive diplomas. Among those completing high school, about half take some advanced training, four out of five of these entering college on a full-time basis, and one out of five on a part-time basis.

All adolescents, those who complete high school and those who do not, give some attention to the problem of earning a living. The complex social, economic, and psychological determinants of work will be discussed in the next chapter, but here we should consider certain attitudes toward work and toward the individual as a worker that are consolidated during adolescence and are reflected in decisions required at that time. Academic programs, future occupations, college or post-high school training, opportunities for work in preference to further training, and part-time employment represent some of the choices available to the adolescent. Sometimes these decisions are made deliberately, as in the case of the high school student who elects to enter the military service rather than complete his high school studies; sometimes they are taken for granted, as in the case of the student who chooses college "because everybody in my family goes to college." Since the adolescent's decisions relative to work reflect, in part, his self-concept, which has been developing since early childhood, an understanding of him and his perception of himself as a worker necessitates a detailed review of pre-adolescent experiences that relate to this aspect of his personality.

PRE-ADOLESCENT EXPERIENCES AND ATTITUDES TOWARD WORK

Single incidents do not account for the formation of the child's attitudes toward himself as a worker or for the attitudes he will later hold toward those encountered as work supervisors or employees. Instead, these attitudes derive from the intricate pattern of relationships he has had with adults during his developmental periods. Whether he will perceive supervisors as persons with particular responsibilities who are available to him as helpers, or whether he sees them as enemies, will depend upon the early experiences he had with his parents. The child who can secure parental attention or approval only when he "earns" it may become an adult who is highly motivated to achieve or who is excessively anxious about his adequacy as a worker and easily threatened in any work situation. Another child who is not given opportunities in the preschool years to do what he can for himself fails to develop the skills and knowledge required to master new situations, and because his dependent behaviors are reinforced, they will be carried over into adult work situations.

The emotional "climate" in which the child struggles to achieve new competencies is another important factor in his later perceptions of himself in relation to his work. The child whose parents encourage and help him to try difficult tasks and who provide affectionate reassurance when his efforts do not succeed will approach difficult and challenging tasks with more confidence and enthusiasm than will one who is scolded for failure or who is not encouraged to try new activities. Adults with intense anxieties related to failure can perform only those activities with which they are familiar; they are unable to take the risks involved in changing positions or in entering activities requiring a variety of judgments or behaviors.

Parents sometimes fail to understand the issues involved in a child's learning to take responsibility for himself. They make demands which he is physically, socially, and emotionally unable to meet. The reader will recall our remarking that the anxious parent who fears his child will not be able to take his proper place in society because he lacks competence in some activity, such as reading, may unwittingly contribute to the child's difficulties in acquiring that competence. A parent who nags, scolds, and punishes a child when he fails certainly does not contribute to the child's enthusiasm for new activities; the risk of failure is always greater for tasks requiring new skills and behaviors than it is for previously learned tasks. If the child is to be able to profit maximally from his experience, he must be aware of the adequacy of his performance; he must know when he has failed as well as when he has succeeded. Knowledge of failure need not mean punishment or parental displeasure. If he knows what constitutes inadequate performance, the child is able to correct or improve his performance. Simple as it is, this point has important implications for the attitudes that the individual will carry into his work life. The adult who can tolerate neither criticism nor helpful suggestions from his colleagues and supervisors is often responding as if such suggestions or criticism imply a failure for which he will (or should) be punished.

As previous chapters have indicated, the child gradually learns that certain behaviors are expected of his sex while others are discouraged. As they are perceived by children, sex roles prominently feature the work that men and women perform; little girls imitate their mothers as they play at keeping house and tending their dolls. Such imitative play can be seen as constituting preparation for the work they expect to perform as women. Boys perceive their sex roles as including more active physical work than do those of women. They observe their fathers doing the repair work about the house, tending the garden and fixing the car, and in many ways they are made aware that fathers, as the breadwinners, deserve special consideration. Although boys of this age sometimes have nebulous or incorrect images of the actual work performed by the fathers away from home, it is impressed upon them that fathers have a special status as workers and income earners.

In addition to learning general behaviors expected of them, during this period children also acquire general orientations or predispositions toward work through identification with parents. Children begin to develop conceptions of work either as a satisfying activity or as a burden engaged in only as a matter of sheer necessity.

Another characteristic of the preschool period is that the child is left to his own devices for greater and greater periods of time. The opportunities for such independent and solitary activity and the circumstances that surround his being allowed to fend for himself may play a considerable part in the skills and interests he develops. Later, attitudes toward being by oneself and working alone may be further molded by the opportunities the child has to take responsibility for himself during childhood.

The elementary school years are of special significance in the development of the attitudes, skills, and behaviors necessary to work. During the early part of this period, the child extends his activities to engage in those of his school. In this situation he encounters other children with whom he must learn to work and play cooperatively and with whom he must learn to compete. Another adult figure of significance for him— in addition to his parents—enters his life, his teacher. He begins to acquire many of the skills and learnings that assist him in the mastery of his world by providing him with knowledge about it.

The child's impressions of the world may play a vital role in determining the occupation to which he aspires and the one he will actually enter. These knowledges and skills are included in what has been described earlier as ego processes. The child begins to acquire skills that are of special interest to him and in which he can excel. The skills that he acquires easily and rapidly and that are valued by his teacher and his parents bring him reward and special recognition, and it is through this process that specific interests and talents are developed.

The child may be rewarded and recognized for his abilities in such areas as literature, music, art, carpentry, or athletics. Because of the recognition he has received and the encouragement with which he has been provided, he may pursue work in these areas with special enthusiasm. In like manner he may acquire, through negative reinforcement, an aversion to a specific work activity, or he may go through his early school years without developing special interests or cultivating any particular talents.

It is during the elementary school years that the child acquires general attitudes toward academic learning activity. While one child may become resistive to all "book learning," another may discover in books and periodicals a rich source of interesting information. During this period a teacher can provide the child with an image with which he can identify, and adult interest patterns can often be traced back to the teacher and his special interest areas. As adult figures, teachers are agents both of the ego and of the superego; they reinforce the moral standards to which the child is expected to conform as well as acting as guides to the objective aspects of the real world.

As this chapter has emphasized, the child must acquire certain learnings from his peer relations, not from adults. These relationships are important in the development of his ability to work and associate with other people. The degree to which he can cooperate and compete successfully with others is related to his early associations with his classmates as well as to his experiences within the family. In the school setting, a child acquires the techniques that bring him the acceptance and recognition of his group. He learns that certain behaviors and attitudes bring him into favor with his peer group and that other behaviors bring the group's displeasure. Here he learns the consequences of nonconformity—what can result from his being different or behaving differently from the group. The acquired techniques that bring acceptance and recognition become a part of the child's role behaviors in group situations, and the adult who adopts a particular and unvarying role in group and work situations, whether it be that of the buffoon, the leader, the scapegoat, or the authority, is acting out a role originating in his childhood peer interactions.

The degree to which any individual acquires the ability to interact cooperatively depends also upon the specific quality of his peer relationships. Here it should be noted that the onset as well as the quality of his cooperative behavior in the peer-group situation will depend in part upon his ability to communicate. For example, the child with superior intelligence whose verbal level exceeds that of his companions may have difficulty in being understood by them. Such difficulties can have a bearing on the degree of cooperative play and activity in which he is able to engage. In addition, the extent to which he actually desires to work with or for others in a group setting depends upon the quality of his relationships. The child who has found his peer group a source of pain or who has failed to receive gratification from it may elect solitary, isolated, or independent occupations, or he may try to compensate in his work situations for the deficiencies of his earlier relationships.

It has already been noted that during the elementary school years the child goes through his most rapid rate of formal academic learning and understanding of himself and his relationship to the world. In addition to the skills he acquires that contribute to his ability to mediate between his own inner urges and the requirements of the external world, there is a host of learnings concerning the standards he will adopt as parts of his personal and ideal selves. These standards are reflected in the individual's attitudes and behaviors in the work situation. For example, the child has taken within himself the attitude that "anything worth doing is worth doing well" will feel guilty as an adult when his efforts are less than excellent or when he fails to complete his work. When his work meets the desired standard, he will experience a glow of satisfaction. Both the avoidance of guilt as self-inflicted pain and the quest for the sense of self-reward or satisfaction may influence the direction and manner of a person's energy output.

Of course, the specific conditions or circumstances that surround a child's acquisition of values (incorporated parental attitudes) occur in the total context of the parent-child relationship. The meaning of an episode, such as one in which a child disappoints or angers his parent by failing to perform his chores, will depend upon the quality of the general relationship with the parent. These incorporated moral and ethical values contribute to what the individual evaluates as the good life as well as what he considers the characteristics of the good worker.

ADOLESCENT EXPERIENCE AND ATTITUDES TOWARD WORK

By mid-adolescence, although the individual may not have decided on a specific career, his image of himself as a productive and responsible worker is usually firmly established. In one study (13), tenth and twelfth grade boys and girls were asked what they would do if they had a guaranteed income that would provide them with everything they and their families wanted. They indicated that they would work at either full-time or part-time jobs anyway, or that they would pursue activities of special interest to them; only 3 percent of the girls and 2 percent of the boys stated that they would "not get a job at all."

Although adolescents expect to work, and although this expectation seems on the basis of the study cited above to be somewhat independent of economic motives, their occupational plans are frequently vague and unrealistic. Decisions regarding areas of work are likely to change during adolescence. In high school adolescents may elect certain areas of academic preparation, such as college preparatory or business, but their plans are often not accurate forecasts of the work to which they will devote themselves as adults. There is evidence that the specific wishes of adolescents during high school are too optimistic. In one study (13) it was reported that 34 percent of boys and 30 percent of girls wished to enter some area of professional activity. Since only about 8 percent of the total working population is employed in professional and technical fields, many of these students will actually enter other fields. It should be noted that the students in this study were also asked which occupation they *expected* to enter, and that twenty-three percent of the girls and 22 percent of the boys responded to this question by selecting a profession. Although fewer students expect to enter professional work than wish to, the difference between their numbers and the percentage of professional workers in the population is still disproportionately large.

Certain experiences contribute to the adolescent's perception of work and to his perception of himself as a worker. Work performed after school or during vacation has considerable psychological significance, for it provides a student with an opportunity to check his expectations against the actual experience of working. An adolescent's employers have a relationship with him that is different from those of his parents and teachers. He is evaluated by his employer in terms of the work he is able to perform. His parents have treated him largely in terms of their previous perceptions of him, but in the work situation he is treated on the basis of his present status. Although the caliber of his performance and his attitudes toward his own standard of work are derived from previous experience, he may alter them when he has the opportunity for "checking them out" in the actual work situation. Work contributes to the adolescent's perspective by allowing him to extend the range of his experience and test reality, but for some adolescents it is merely another context into which they can project the acute problems they are facing. These basic struggles or conflicts are then expressed in terms of such issues as what work to choose, what training to seek, whether to obtain a college education, and how to regard all higher education.

In his effort to establish his own identity as an adult, an adolescent may resist or reject the well-intended decisions his parents make for him. Sometimes a father disapproves of the ways in which his son spends his time, money, and energy and feels that his son is failing to act "wisely." The son may begrudgingly acknowledge that the father is right but may prefer to deal with his own problems in his own way. These disagreements influence the adolescent's work decisions and his attitudes to varying degrees. If he needs to allay self-doubts and the anxiety precipitated by parental control, he will probably resist whenever possible his parents' wishes, including their occupational ambitions for him. A son who is expected to enter his father's business may elect not to do so for psychological reasons rather than for logical ones, and parents who press an adolescent to enter a specific occupation are often disappointed and hurt when their "wishes are not considered."

In some cases the struggle between an adolescent and his parents reaches such intensity that the adolescent leaves home, quits school, and goes to work in order to "be independent." In other instances, defiance of parental control, a defiance that accompanies the quest for self-determination, may be more subtly manifested. An adolescent who is coerced into attending college when she would rather be "on her own," working as a secretary, may attain her objective by failing to maintain the required college grade point average even though she believes that she is trying not to fail. Such subtle rebellions have more far-reaching effects than do the violent, overt clashes between generations, because they are less likely to lead to an understanding by the adolescent of his conflicts and to a subsequent resolution of them.

Although rejection of parental choice is frequent, the adolescent's identification with his parents and their social class is usually reflected in the decisions he eventually makes. Thus, the teen-ager who violently rejects entering his father's profession usually decides in the latter part of his college program that he is really interested in that profession or one closely allied to it. The occupations most likely to be entered are those that are in the same or adjacent brackets in the occupational hierarchy.

Planning by the Adolescent

In contrast to earlier years, adolescence is a period in which the future, and planning for that future, must be consciously considered. As part of such an appraisal, the adolescent must assess his abilities and reach decisions pertaining to training and work. Whatever his decisions about his future program, they will have some reference to work and will represent an effort to combine within one role the expectations he has for himself and the expectations others have for him. How well the individual's chosen career synthesizes his various self-perceptions will depend upon the extent to which the situation affords him an opportunity for a choice of careers as well as upon the degree to which he is able to take advantage of his potentialities.

In the process of arriving at career decisions, the adolescent or young adult tries to marshal all the pertinent information about himself and the available opportunities. Systematically or haphazardly, he attempts to "inventory" his abilities, intelligence, and interests as well as the situation in which he finds himself. He attempts to translate the results of this inventory into implications for his future occupation. He asks himself in what activities he excels and what areas of behavior constitute his weak points. He wonders what importance to assign to his enjoyment of some activities and his dislike of others. He questions his intellectual abilities and his possession of aptitudes for specific training or academic programs. To the consideration of these questions each person brings different amounts of accurate information and erroneous convictions about himself and the general nature of interests, abilities, and intelligence.

The self-assessment of these qualities is particularly characteristic of our culture, and the effective utilization of ability is a distinguishing aspect of adequate personal development. Psychologists, in their efforts to assist in the process of self-assessment, have developed various procedures for measuring interests and abilities, and most adolescents in our culture have had some experience with them. Since many of the adolescent's concerns about his future activity are expressed in the context of his interests and abilities, the next section is devoted to these topics.

An individual who is considering various occupational possibilities frequently wonders whether he will "like" the work or the training required in a specific field. Liking a particular work activity is, of course, not the same as doing well in it. Although these questions do differ and must be considered separately, there is usually a close relationship between them. Liking an activity, preferring to invest one's time and energy in it, is related to what will be termed *interests*. Doing well in an activity, demonstrating proficiency in it, is related in large part to what will be termed *abilities*. Preferences for certain activities can be discussed in broader terms than merely those of whether an individual prefers one occupational activity to another. When the entire pattern of an individual's preferences is considered, when all his likes and dislikes are evaluated, it is possible to make inferences concerning the motivations that may impel him toward one objective and away from another. As an avenue to understanding the individual and his motivations, the study of interests has been one of the most productive approaches available to psychological research.

INTERESTS AND THEIR RELATION
TO WORK

According to Super (15), the term "interests" can be given four distinct meanings. For example, a young man may tell his college counselor that he is very interested in automotive engineering. This is an example of an *expressed interest*. If the young man has actually spent time working on cars, then his activity reflects *manifest interest*. Another approach to the assessment of interest is illustrated in the testing of an individual who has an expressed interest in automotive engineering. His *tested interest* is measured by an objective test covering information from the available literature or from experience on the job. *Inventoried interests* represent a fourth approach to the measurement of interests. This method, which has been studied extensively by psychologists, requires the individual to respond in terms of liking, disliking, or being indifferent to many different activities. The measured interest level is based upon an analysis of the entire pattern of responses.

In the Strong Vocational Interest Test, probably the most famous of interest inventories, an individual's pattern of preferences is compared to the patterns reported by individuals who have succeeded in various occupations. It should be emphasized that in this type of inventory the items to which the individual responds are not necessarily directly related to the work performed by any occupational group. Thus, deep sea fishing may be "liked" by most physicians and "disliked" by most lawyers. The point is that actual preferences obtained from various occupational groups provide a basis for the identification of group patterns, even though there is no logical relationship between the preferences and the work of the group.

The test can be scored for 45 occupations on the men's form and for 25 occupations on the women's form; thus, the individual can be shown how nearly his pattern of interests corresponds to those of many occupational groups. In practice, all scores are considered rather than the one occupational group whose pattern resembles the testee's most closely. If an individual's highest score is in a professional occupation such as architecture, and if he also has high scores in the categories of designer and artist, a counselor may recommend that he consider work in several artistic and design occupations as well as in architecture. Since there are approximately thirty thousand known occupations, it is necessary for the counselor to be able to respond in terms of families of occupations.

The question is frequently raised as to the value of stated preferences having no logical connection with the work actually performed by the occupational group. The practical value of the interest inventory depends upon its accuracy as a predictor, and the similarity of an individual's interests to those of successful persons in various fields has proved to be a sound basis for several types of prediction. It has been found that the patterns of interests evidenced by adults are remarkably stable over long periods of time. Strong, who followed the individual careers of a large number of persons for almost twenty years after they left college, noted not only that their basic interests had remained stable, but also that the results of the inventory accurately predicted the actual occupations the individuals entered (14). Another study, conducted at the University of Minnesota (10), found that the pattern of interests yielded by the Strong test was the best predictor of the major field any individual would select during his college career.

Another frequently utilized interest inventory is the Kuder Preference Record. In this inventory the results are expressed not in occupational categories but in general areas of interest, labeled mechanical, scientific, outdoor, persuasive, social service, clerical, literary, artistic, musical and computational.

Super (15) has suggested that the following represent the basic interest groupings:

1. scientific: interests directed toward the understanding of phenomena.
2. social welfare: interests in people and a concern for them.
3. literary: interests in the utilization of words and in process of verbal communication.
4. material: interests in working with tangibles (as compared to working with ideas).
5. systematic: interests in the systematic recording and presentation of data.
6. contact: interests in dealing with people for one's own advantage.

As an individual acquires experience and knowledge, his range of interests tends to be extended, while at the same time his degrees of interest in different activities will change. This total pattern of interests becomes more stable as he enters his young adult years, and accordingly, by the time a person reaches the young adult years, the transitory interests of adolescence have been sifted through experience, and the short-lived enthusiasms that captured youthful energy and attention are replaced by the interests of the adult years. Although patterns of interest may shift between the ages of 15 and 20, it is often true that specific adolescent interests do carry over to the adult years; the boyhood interest patterns of outstanding scientists, for example, have often foretold their later professional occupations.

The Timing of Occupational Choice

Most adolescents are likely to shift occupational choices, and once out of high school they may shift actual occupations frequently. Although such changes in occupational choice or in jobs may be anticipated, the adolescent is frequently asked to make an early and specific statement of his occupational plans. It is probably more reasonable for him to decide first on his general objectives in regard to work areas, such as those of the sciences, the professions, or business. Whatever general area of preparation he chooses, he should make a deliberate attempt to acquire as much general knowledge drawn from other fields as possible. Shifting jobs or vocational objectives sometimes occurs because the individual does not have a broad enough range of experience upon which to base his decisions, and only through exposure to a variety of situations can he acquire the experience necessary to make a sound final choice. In some instances individuals who are unable to reach decisions regarding their preferred areas of training and work may wish to confer with a counselor or a psychologist.

Although many adolescents are not able to make firm decisions with respect to their life work, the present trend, accentuated somewhat by the increasing competition for admission to the name colleges, is to force such decisions upon them. The high school senior must designate his anticipated "major" program at the time he applies for college entrance. The college freshman often finds it difficult to defend a program of liberal arts or of general education to his parents and friends, who believe that he would be wiser to embark without delay upon preparation for earning a living. In addition to these social pressures, the length of time required for training in many professional areas makes it difficult for young people to achieve the desirable broad range of experience. An individual may feel that he cannot afford to delay his decision too long or he will be too old before he can begin working.

It is clear that interests in themselves do not provide a complete guide to how an individual will expend his time and energy in vocational or recreational pursuits. Predicting any individual's reactions to his work requires knowledge of his abilities. Consider a high school senior who has demonstrated a high degree of expressed, manifest, and inventoried interest in playing the piano. He has tentatively decided upon a career as a concert pianist. What information would his counselors and teachers require before they could encourage him to undertake the career he has chosen?

The question, "How well does he play the piano?" would probably be the first one to be answered. An evaluation of his performance relative to the length of time he has studied would provide essential data, and it might also be desirable to take into account certain physical characteristics related to proficiency in this field, such as ability to distinguish between tones and to identify rhythms, along with finger dexterity and hand-eye coordination. His counselors might wish to know whether he is able to practice for extended periods of time and to understand what others communicate to him, and how readily he can apply his previous experience to new situations. Having this much information about the young man, they would probably decide whether to encourage him in his career.

Thus, even when manifest, expressed, and inventoried interests in a given activity are high and it appears that a person is currently highly motivated toward a particular occupation, it is still important to obtain additional information about his ability, aptitudes, psychological characteristics, and intelligence. The questions suggested by the above example are typical of those raised by an individual or by those close to him, when he is considering specialized training programs or work of a technical or artistic nature. Since tests are sometimes helpful in formulating answers, the types of tests available for occupational assessment will now be examined in more detail.

PRESENT PERFORMANCE IN THE PREDICTION OF FUTURE ATTAINMENT

The Achievement Test

An individual's present performance or achievement level can be assessed by comparing his level with those of other persons. In many areas of activity this comparison is facilitated and the possibility of error and misinterpretation is reduced through the use of achievement tests. An achievement test yields an objective measure of attainment in a given field, area, or subject, and a person's test results can then be evaluated with reference to what is known as a standardization population. If the reading ability of a high school senior is tested through the use of one of the reading ability examinations, his performance or score will be compared to those of the high school seniors who were the reference group in the development of the test. Detailed descriptions of the persons (sample population) upon whom the test was standardized are provided to those who administer and interpret the test so that its appropriateness for any given individual may be determined.

Many achievement tests of school subjects have been standardized upon such large groups of representative students that statements such as the following are sometimes made: "Compared to all high school seniors, Joe's reading comprehension is superior, exceeding that of 92 percent of the national sample," or "Compared to the Norm Group, Joe's performance is at the ninety-second percentile." This means that Joe's performance exceeded those of 92 percent of the group upon whom the test was standardized. Tests given in school to evaluate progress in specific courses are examples of achievement tests, but usually there are no national or local norms against which to compare the results; consequently, the teacher will have to develop his own norms, or he will compare each student to the rest of the class.

Knowledge of the achievement level of an individual is particularly helpful when the level can be considered in terms of his opportunities to learn the material on which he is tested, his motivation to learn, and his ability to learn. On a vocabulary achievement test, a student who has recently arrived from a foreign country with little knowledge of English may do poorly compared to students who have always lived in the United States. In terms of the time he has lived in this country, however, the student may have demonstrated a considerable capacity to learn a new language. It can then be said that although his achievement level compared to native born students is low, his aptitude for learning English is high.

The Aptitude Test

A test that is utilized to predict an individual's future level of attainment, that assumes the appropriate opportunities for learning are available, and that provides a basis for inference from present performance level is termed an *aptitude test*. Sometimes these tests are designed to measure knowledge or abilities that are assumed to be available to all individuals comprising a given population. A college aptitude test is one that attempts to predict an individual's probable level of college attainment by testing his present achievement. The Scholastic Aptitude Test mentioned in the previous chapter, for example, measures a person's attainment in two areas related to performance in college, verbal ability and mathematics.

Factor analysis has been used to identify abilities and aptitudes that "go together." These are called special abilities and may then be measured by appropriate tests that can be considered in relation to each other. One such combination of tests of special abilities is the General Aptitude Test Battery (GATB), developed by the United States Employment Service. It is used in counseling individuals who seek assistance with occupational planning and is given without cost to the clients of the Service. The battery takes about three hours to administer and consists of ten parts, each constituting a test in itself. The abilities measured by the GATB may be inferred from the names of the constituent tests: General Intelligence, Verbal Ability, Numerical Ability, Spatial Ability, Form Perception, Clerical Perception, Aiming, Motor Speed, Finger Dexterity, and Manual Dexterity. The counselor notes the client's profile of scores on the various tests and adds this information to the other data in assisting him to arrive at an occupational choice.

Abilities such as those tested by the GATB are much narrower than those generally assumed by people who speak of an "aptitude for teaching" or an "aptitude for engineering." Aptitudes for occupations frequently involve a great many specific abilities in particular combinations. In many industrial or business situations, the special tests used to identify individuals who can be trained successfully do not directly measure the abilities required for the position. Instead, "criterion groups" are chosen to serve as standards or models for what the test is required to predict. There may, for example, be criterion groups of successful and unsuccessful bank clerks or of excellent and poor air stewardesses. A tentative test is made up of questions or tasks that distinguish successful employees from unsuccessful ones. These items are then tried out on all new employees, not for selection purposes but so that the test can be "tested." If the test proves to be a good predictor of the later success or failure of entering employees, its validity is reported to be high and it is ready for use in selecting new workers. This second step in trying out the test items is called "cross-validation."

A test developed according to this kind of procedure is termed an *empirical test,* and since it may include any item or task that has differentiating value, it will not necessarily measure specific aptitudes or special abilities. The accuracy of such a test in selecting successful workers or in predicting their performance is termed "empirical validity." Tests of performance that can be used to predict capacity to learn are available in many different fields of activity, including the mechanical, clerical, and academic.

It has been suggested that the degree to which a student interested in music will apply himself to his studies and will persist in practicing, the readiness with which he might become discouraged or depressed, and the extent to which he will be able to evaluate realistically the criticisms of his performance, all reflect psychological characteristics that are not measured by tests of interest, achievement, or aptitude. These aspects of motivation can sometimes be tapped by personality tests. These tests, frequently termed "inventories," yield measures reflecting an individual's attitudes toward himself, his skill and social presence in his relationships with other persons, and certain motivational characteristics. An example of such a test is the California Psychological Inventory (3).

The example cited at the beginning of this section suggested that the young man's ability to comprehend what others communicate to him and his ability to apply his previous experience to new situations also was important in assessing the wisdom of his occupational decision. Information of this type is provided by intelligence tests (see Chapter 7) which measure the abilities related to the learning of verbal and abstract concepts.

The Consolidation of the Self-Concept

Toward the end of the adolescent period, the images the individual has of himself achieve a greater degree of congruence; he is able to perceive himself more clearly in relation to other persons, to his future, and to his own capabilities and aspirations. This process is far from complete, however; the adolescent carries into his young adult years many of the questions and concerns about himself of his teen years. Within the context of work and love experiences to be encountered in his early twenties the consolidation of his personality continues; issues of his interests, abilities, and satisfactions to be derived from his occupational activity continue to be important to him and the significance he attaches to work will continue into the next period of his life.

Reflecting the consolidation of his personality processes and self-concepts is the gradually shifting nature of his relationships to members of the opposite sex. With his increasing ability to direct his energies and concerns to others, he becomes interested in the prolonged and more intense emotional commitments that accompany marriage. In both areas, work and interpersonal relationships, the continuing integration of his personality occurs with no sharp break as he leaves his adolescence and enters the adult phases of the life cycle.

Summary

At the beginning of adolescence and again when he enters adulthood, the individual will possess a greater degree of harmony among the components of his personality than has been the case during the in-between adolescent years. The relative stability of the childhood period diminishes as a result of the physical and social changes of puberty, changes that necessitate the development of new patterns of behaviors appropriate to newly acquired physical capabilities and to the expectations others hold of him. In addition to the acquisition of the skills appropriate to his changes in size and shape, there are necessary adaptations to the new experiences, impulses, and sensations associated with the development of his sexual drives.

Ethics and morals, completely accepted previously because they came from unquestioned authorities, may now be criticized and challenged. Adult views of propriety are often flaunted in the quest for experiences upon which to base independent judgments of what is proper. Many activities interpreted by adults as defiance involve attempts to achieve mastery over impulses that make the adolescent anxious. Expression of his sexual or aggressive impulses may represent his efforts to test himself and to test his ability to deal with the threats evoked by such expressions.

In fantasies involving his ideal self, the adolescent sometimes adopts cultural symbols denoting virtue and success. A large discrepancy may exist between his concepts of himself as he is and of the person he wants to be. This discrepancy changes as the individual more clearly identifies himself and more definitively settles on an ideal image of himself. Fluctuations in self-esteem are sometimes triggered by what appears to be the slightest positive or negative reactions of associates. In the adolescent's world, the sought-after, popular person is the successful person. Such approval must come from his group, since in relinquishing his childish dependent relationship with his parents, his need for the approval of the group is great. He utilizes his peers as a mirror, and he partially evaluates his own worth through their reactions to him.

For many adolescents the teenage period is difficult. They are frequently in conflict with parents, teachers, or friends. The internal conflicts they experience are reflected in extreme sensitivity to criticism, defiance of authority, and a paradoxical mixture of adult wishes, attitudes, and behaviors with childish ones. The adolescent achieves his own self-identity in the process of achieving the ability to fulfill the adult role; that is, he learns, albeit painfully, that he can never be fully independent of others. He usually finds that he can live within the rules and regulations of his society without having to fight endlessly against it. He finds that he does not have to be completely dependent upon his peer group for his self-esteem, since he can freely make his own decisions and can accept their consequences.

His development is characterized by the clarification of his concepts of himself as a worker and as a marital partner; in each of these areas he gradually acquires experiences relevant to his future roles and becomes involved in choices concerning his academic and occupational programs and in decisions with respect to the persons with whom he will associate.

References

1. Ausubel, D. P. *Theory and Problems of Adolescent Development.* New York: Grune & Stratton, 1954.

2. Block, V. L.　Conflicts of adolescents with their mothers. *J. abnorm. soc. Psychol.*, 1937, *32*, 193–206.
3. Gough, H. G.　*California Psychological Inventory*. Palo Alto, Calif.: Consulting Psychologists Press, 1956.
4. Hurlock, E. B.　*Adolescent Development*. New York: McGraw-Hill, 1949.
5. Jersild, A. T.　*The Psychology of Adolescence*. New York: Macmillan, 1957.
6. McGuire, C.　*Adolescent Society and Social Mobility*. Unpublished Dissertation, University of Chicago, 1949.
7. Mead, M.　*Sex and Temperament in Three Primitive Societies*. London: Routledge, 1935.
8. Meyers, C. E.　Emancipation of adolescents from parental control. *Nerv. Child,* 1946, *5,* 251–262.
9. Poll No. 13, Institute of Student Opinion, *Scholastic Magazine,* 1946.
10. Porter, J. K.　Predicting the vocational plans of high school senior boys. *Pers. Guid. J.,* 1954, *33,* 215–218.
11. Punke, H. H.　High school youth and family quarrels. *Sch. and Soc.,* 1943, *53,* 507–511.
12. Sears, R. R., Maccoby, E. E., and Levin, H.　*Patterns of Child Rearing.* New York: Harper, 1957.
13. Social Research Service, *Youth and the World of Work,* East Lansing, Mich.: Michigan State University, 1949.
14. Strong, E. K.　*Vocational Interests of Men and Women.* Stanford, Calif.: Stanford University Press, 1943.
15. Super, D. E.　*Appraising Vocational Fitness by Means of Psychological Tests.* New York: Harper, 1949.
16. Terman, L. M., and Miles, C. C.　*Sex and Personality: Studies in Masculinity and Femininity.* New York: McGraw-Hill, 1936.
17. Tryon, C. M.　Evaluation of adolescent personality by adolescents. *Monogr. Soc. Res. Child Develpm., 4,* No. 4, 1947.
18. Washburn, J. M.　The impulsions of adolescents as revealed by their written wishes. *J. juv. Res.,* 1932, *16,* 193–212.
19. Watson, E. H., and Lowrey, G. H.　*Growth and Development of Children* (ed. 2). Chicago: Year Book, 1954.

Selected Readings

Crow, L. D., and Crow, A. (eds.)　*Reading in Child and Adolescent Psychology.* New York: Longmans, 1961.
Erikson, E. H.　*Childhood and Society.* New York: Norton, 1950.
Farnham, M. F.　*The Adolescent.* New York: Harper, 1952.
Heyns, R. W.　*The Psychology of Personal Adjustment.* New York: Holt, 1958.
Mead, M.　*From the South Seas: Studies of Adolescence and Sex in Primitive Societies.* New York: Morrow, 1939.

9.

The Young Adult Years: Work

During the twenties and early thirties, the individual achieves his peak of physical performance; he is vigorous and his energy level is high. His new roles of worker, marital partner, and parent are demanding and are accompanied by their characteristic stresses and crises. Yet he has been preparing for the responsibilities of being a husband and parent for many years, and he has been developing the skills and attitudes appropriate to his occupation. He is now closer to being responsible for himself and able to care for others. The consolidation of his intrapsychic processes and the clarification of his self-concept are at the points where he wants to direct his energy and attention to his work, his mate, and his family.

The activities, relationships, and responsibilities of young adult life are readily subsumed under two major headings. Freud alluded to these when he described a normal person as one who is able to work and to love, and this chapter and the next relate to these central concerns of the young adult. Implicit in Freud's comment is his realization of the need for the individual to utilize his interests, aptitudes, talents, intelligence, and skills in goal-directed activity that he finds personally satisfying and that society identifies as consistent with its purposes. As a criterion of psychological development, the optimal utilization of personal resources in satisfying and socially acceptable activity is as important as are the criteria of within-self harmony and the ability to enjoy satisfying interpersonal relationships. The issue is then not just whether one works, but the degree of satisfaction the individual receives from working and the extent to which his capacities are utilized within his particular job.

267

Work and Its Psychological Significance

Although most men spend more of their time at work than in any other activity and often devote a good part of their lives to preparation and training for it, the purposes of work and its significance to the individual are usually oversimplified or taken for granted. For the young adult, feeling the pressure to be economically independent and having to delay marriage (or if married, having to delay beginning a family), work and its meaning will understandably center about the earnings it will provide. But work has many meanings and provides an important vehicle for self-expression as well as a means of income.

NONECONOMIC ASPECTS OF WORK

Statements that men "work to make money" or to "provide for their families" may seem acceptable and fairly complete explanations, but these statements account for only some of the reasons that impel individuals to work. Instances of workers who prefer to continue their jobs rather than take advantage of retirement benefits, and of wealthy persons who are engaged in gainful employment, suggest that the economic motive is not a complete answer to the question. This is suggested also by a number of studies of working conditions that contribute to satisfaction and affect the quality and quantity of the work done.

Although studies have revealed the importance to some individuals of aspects of the work activity itself, such as the skill it requires and the freedom for self-expression it affords, friendly and pleasant relationships with one's fellow workers and with supervisors and administrators are frequently mentioned by workers as a greater source of work satisfaction. In a study of the attitudes of General Motors Corporation employees toward their jobs (4), it was found that these relationships were considered more important to the workers than the wages or salaries.

The importance to workers of congenial associations is related to the opportunity the work situation often provides of achieving a sense of relatedness, of being in communion with others. Persons engaged in the same work will probably share other interests. In their attitudes toward politics, education, family life, books, and television programs, they will be in closer agreement with each other than with workers in different fields. It may be hypothesized that the underlying social and psychological experiences accounting for similar work choices are sufficiently similar to facilitate communication among persons performing the same work. The most satisfying situations are those in which the workers have an *esprit de corps*—a feeling of camaraderie, a sense of belonging. In such cases, the work situation means more to a person than a place in which he performs certain activities in return for money. His identification as a member of the particular group has a special meaning for him, and his own personal pride and self-esteem are enhanced by his belonging to the group and by being known as a member of it. Such groupings can include the people who work in his profession or trade— carpenters, doctors, or airline pilots—or the people in his department, crew, plant, or company. The groups with which an individual affiliates psychologically are numerous, and those involving his identification as a worker are especially important.

The individual's reactions to his work situation, the gratifications he receives from it, and the specific nature of his identifications will depend upon the measures he employs in maintaining, protecting, and enhancing himself psychologically. If he is easily threatened and per- sonally insecure, he may be quarrelsome, aggressive, or manipulative in his relationships with fellow workers. He may respond quickly if he perceives that his employer, supervisor, or a colleague is taking advantage of him. On the other hand, if he is an individual who must always be humble, ingratiating, and subservient, the work situation will probably elicit those behaviors.

The work situation however, affords more than an opportunity to react to others. In it the individual has the chance to fulfill unmet or unsatisfied needs that have their origin in earlier experiences, as well as to test himself and his own ability to enhance his self-esteem. It may allow him an opportunity to demonstrate his talents and capacities and to make contributions independent of family help. Just as the work situation provides a context in which the individual can demonstrate his personal and social inadequacies, so it can also afford him an op- portunity to satisfy his creative desires and to gain mastery over some areas of self-doubt and conflict.

OCCUPATIONAL PRESTIGE

In assessing the psychological significance of a work situation, it is helpful to consider the prestige factor. Although there is no simple relationship between individual self-esteem needs and the amount of social prestige received from being in a specific occupation, the respect and value the public attaches to various occupations have considerable significance for the individual and for what he thinks of himself in relation to his work.

The prestige factor associated with the various occupations exists as a social fact, operating as a labeling device for an individual and his family. This label is the most widely accepted and the most usable single index of the social and economic status of a family unit. The members of a family whose father is in one of the professions will, other things being equal, be held in greater esteem than those whose father is a manual laborer.

These differences in community acceptance of high and low prestige families can result in differences in economic and educational opportunity. In addition, they may have psychological effects upon the self-concepts of persons who encounter community acceptance or rejection, based upon who they are rather than what they do. Public expectations or attention may be injurious to the children of fathers in the high-prestige occupational groups, the children of the physicians, businessmen, and ministers of the community. They may encounter special psychological and social problems and may be pressured by parents to maintain higher or more rigid standards of achievement and conduct than those expected of children of less prominent citizens.

The first step in measuring the degree of prestige the public assigns to various occupations involves selection of the people to be questioned. Although they might be selected on a random (chance) basis, a more satisfactory method of selection involves what is known as *stratified sampling*. In such a sample, individuals from particular segments of the population would be included to the extent that they are represented in the general population. Thus, the stratified sample is a small proportional representation of the general population.

In one such study (11), 2,920 persons selected as constituting a cross-section of the national population ranked 38 male occupations on the basis of the prestige assigned to the occupation. Near the top of the list were such occupations as physician, college professor, natural scientist, architect, and chemist. At the lower end of the list were such occupations as unskilled worker (railroad), restaurant waiter, dock worker, night watchman, and janitor.

Other studies of occupational prestige also have found that "The top prestige ratings consistently go to public officials, business executives and managers, and the standard professions; and the bottom ratings consistently go to unskilled and menial types of work" (16). Results of additional studies have been summarized by Thomas (16) as follows:

1. Ownership of a business, even if the occupation involved is only a skilled manual trade, tends to be rated in prestige alongside such professional occupations as teaching and nursing.

2. Representative occupations from the skilled crafts, clerical work, and sales work tend to overlap completely in the middle ranges of prestige.

3. Supervisory occupations, even in manual labor, tend to be rated higher than nonsupervisory employment in both white-collar work and manual labor.

Studies indicate that no single factor, such as income, accounts for the degree of prestige assigned to the occupation. The nature of the work performed, the degree of responsibility it entails, and the amount of education and training required to achieve competence in it also are related to the prestige it carries. An occupation in which the worker manipulates symbols by thinking, talking, or writing is apt to be rated higher than one in which the person works with tools or materials. The amount of authority the individual has over others, the size of the group for which he is responsible, and the amount of control he has over them, as well as the number of individuals to whom he must answer, also are determinants of occupational prestige (3). Additional factors include the social class attributes of the occupation and the income it provides. Social class attributes include the public's tendency to associate white-collar clerical activities with the middle class and laboring activities with the lower classes. Although income is one of the factors associated with prestige, it is not only the amount of money the worker earns which is significant, but also the certainty of his receiving a regular income.

PRESTIGE FACTORS, OCCUPATIONAL DECISIONS, AND JOB SATISFACTIONS

The psychological significance of occupational prestige is experienced by the individual in a number of ways. In his everyday behavior he demonstrates his respect—or lack of respect—for his employers, his teachers, and others with whom he comes in contact. His behaviors toward his doctor and his newsboy are not the same; for each of them he holds certain particular expectations and toward each he reacts in particular ways. Although his specific reactions are determined somewhat by his attitudes toward them as individuals, they largely reflect his recognition of what they are and who they are. And it is not surprising that prestige factors influence his decisions about the occupational activities he wishes to pursue.

It is neither unusual nor unhealthy to desire the respect of one's fellow men, and quite naturally, high prestige occupations are more attractive than others. Occupational choices may be made because the person enjoys the work itself, he may also enjoy its prestige value, or an individual may be influenced in his occupational choice by its prestige without being aware of the effect of these needs upon his decision.

The influence of the prestige factor upon young people's occupational decisions can be inferred from the results of the studies previously cited indicating that high school students prefer the professions to a degree that is not justified by their abilities. Thus, many high school and college students, impressed by the social status and prestige afforded professional persons, will try to enter college and training programs for which they are poorly equipped in terms of ability and interest.

Since it is known that individuals who are satisfied with their work tend to be more successful than those who are discontented, on-the-job satisfaction can be related to initial motives for entering work. The person whose entry into a training program or an occupation is determined primarily by prestige considerations and not by his talents or interests is therefore at a disadvantage in competing with his more talented and highly motivated colleagues and cannot expect to achieve the same degree of success.

The interaction between social influence and individual need is not necessarily recognized consciously by the person as he makes his decisions about the work he will perform and as he engages in it. If he is unsure of his own adequacy and desirability, he sometimes requires status symbols in order to reassure himself. The individual's social background and experience determine the specific symbols of adequacy that satisfy his psychological needs.

The youth reared in the upper economic and social strata will contemplate college attendance, and even attendance at certain specific colleges, as almost a matter of course. Failure to gain admission to the college of his choice or to qualify for admission to any college may be a greater personal disaster to him than to a young man from a laboring background in whose family attendance at college is a rarity. These class differences between values and objectives in education and occupations are, however, less distinct than they were fifty years ago; the tradition of upward social mobility within our society, the greater availability of higher education, and the tendency for gifted individuals to rise on the economic and social ladder have all operated to reduce the differences among social classes in the objectives to which their children aspire.

Prestige and social status do have a definite relation to the type of occupation in which the individual engages. This does not indicate that a necessary relation exists between the individual's occupation and the extent or degree to which he esteems himself, but it does suggest that lack of self-esteem may be reflected in choice of occupational activity and in many aspects of the work performed.

The intimate and complex relationship between individual status needs and occupational activity is evident in still another form. Work may be performed because of its instrumental character; that is, work may be the instrument whereby needs are met or goals achieved. For example, an individual may satisfy needs related to his physical maintenance by his work, its nature being secondary to the function it serves for him. In this sense he may work to acquire the symbols of prestige his fellows recognize (or which he perceives them to recognize) in their evaluation of him. Although the prestige that is directly related to his occupation may be relatively low, his work may be still instrumental in his acquiring prestige symbols. Symbols such as a large car, fine clothes, the type of house he owns, or the manner of his entertaining may provide considerable incentive for the energy he expends in his work.

GRATIFICATIONS INTRINSIC TO WORK

In addition to the economic, prestige, sustenance, and secondary (instrumental) factors that account for man's motivation to work, there are other issues to be considered. Some hypotheses suggest that work in and of itself affords man the opportunity for satisfactions. Perhaps the most direct statement of this hypothesis is to be found in the principle of *functional autonomy* (1). According to this principle, the motives accounting for specific behaviors can change so that an activity originally engaged in for one set of reasons eventually affords satisfactions in its own right. The behaviors and their motives are now functionally autonomous, for they are no longer linked to the conditions that originally activated them.

A simple example of the functional autonomy of motives could be found in an insurance salesman who learns to play golf because he believes it will provide him with opportunities for meeting prospective clients. Upon learning the game, he comes to enjoy it and plays golf for the pleasure it affords him. He no longer goes to the links to extend his business contacts but rather to play golf. Or in the work situation, the individual who initially entered an occupation for the purpose of earning a livelihood becomes engrossed with the work itself and invests his energy in it for satisfactions that he receives directly from the activity.

Although the concept of functional autonomy of motives has been criticized as representing an oversimplification of the process whereby motives change, its ready applicability to the behaviors observed in everyday life has kept this popular, though controversial, principle alive in the psychological literature for over twenty years. Under some conditions at least, psychological means do become ends.

Another hypothesis that may account for gratification directly derivable from work states that physical and sensory processes themselves require and lead to activities. The need for such activity is seen (10) as deriving from the inherent nature of the human body's physical structure and as being met within the work situation. This idea can be related to individual differences in sensory domination. One person may rely more heavily upon hearing and another upon seeing because of differences in their physical endowments. Such differences in physical capacities and needs may be reflected in work situations that give opportunities for muscular exercise or for specific types of sensory experience.

The hypotheses of functional autonomy and of activity and sensory needs both suggest possible motivations to work springing not from the instrumental character of the work but from the gratifications derived directly from it.

At some point between the two situations, the one in which an individual works to attain goals unrelated to the work performed, the other in which the work activities have become ends in themselves, there is the case in which a person is motivated to achieve through work. The motive to achieve has been studied extensively by McClelland and his associates (9) and is apparently reflected at a fantasy level as well as in overt behaviors. This motive relates to accomplishment, success, attainment, and the avoidance of failure.

In studies of the achievement motive it was possible to classify individuals as having high or low achievement needs on the basis of the content of their fantasies (imaginative stories). The significant finding of this research is that persons classified as having high achievement needs on the basis of fantasy materials *also* expended the greatest amounts of energy and exhibited the strongest drive toward achievement on tasks performed in the laboratory. For example, high and low achievement persons differed in their tempos of activity in an experiment in which they were required to solve anagrams. The high achievement persons solved the puzzles in progressively decreasing amounts of time, but the low achievement individuals used about the same amounts of time for all the puzzles they solved (9).

McClelland's research supports the beliefs that people differ in the extent to which they are motivated to achieve and that this will be reflected in their behaviors. For persons with high achievement needs, work activity can provide the context in which this need may be met. The achievement studies suggest that for some persons the work performed is merely instrumental to the attainment of the appropriate objective. These results may also be interpreted in terms of "functional autonomy": whatever the initial motivations, for certain persons achievement becomes the end objective rather than merely the means of attaining other objectives. A third possible interpretation, that achievement and self-esteem are closely related for some persons, receives support from McClelland's findings, since persons demonstrating high and low achievement needs differed significantly with respect to family background and early experience. Work and the possibilities it affords for achievement would therefore be an instrument whereby the individual might enhance the respect he has for himself.

The relationship between achievement and attitudes toward work is not a simple one. The studies on the achievement motive do not eliminate the possibility that the low achievement need person may value achievement highly even though the theme does not figure prominently in his fantasies or in his behavior. If such a person feels unable to achieve, he may protect his own self-esteem by avoiding competitive activity and by denying his own impulses to behave aggressively and competitively. McClelland defines high achievement need persons quite appropriately as those who exhibit achievement themes in their fantasies, but the assumption that these individuals value attainment more highly than do low achievement need persons has not been proved. It may be only that high achievement need persons *demonstrate* their achievement values more readily in both fantasy and behavior than do the others.

The self-concept of the middle class member of our society includes achievement values that are expressed in terms of the culturally acceptable symbols that individuals associate with their work, the products of their work, or themselves as workers. Although several generalizations about work and self-esteem are offered below, it is not possible to provide a precise statement of this relationship that can be applied to all persons. The measures an individual employs in assessing his own work, as well as the emotional overtones related to these measures, depend upon his particular pattern of experience and the nature of his identifications during his childhood and adolescence.

In our culture a person cannot avoid being influenced by a value system that equates work with virtue. The equations of work with virtue and of idleness with sin have their origins in the history, philosophies, and religions of our cultural heritage. To be able to work and work well is seen as highly desirable. Parental approval and affection are bestowed upon the child who performs his chores well and who is diligent in his school work.

> He that gathereth in summer is a wise son; but he that sleepeth in harvest is a son that causeth shame. PROV. 9:5

The child learns that his parents value work and that they believe rewards come to those who work hard. This acceptance or identification with parental values does not necessarily mean that the parents provide a behavioral model for the child; they may reinforce the values without exhibiting the appropriate behaviors. But whether or not the parents work hard and whether they gain the world's rewards, the value orientation transmitted to the child in our culture is that to work is good. This value orientation has both a moral connotation and a realistic basis.

> He becometh poor that dealeth with a slack hand; but the hand of the diligent maketh rich. PROV. 9:4

The specific superego demands that the individual experiences in regard to the standards he "should" maintain include those pertaining to work. How he evaluates himself depends in part upon the concept he has of himself as a worker. Persons who are unable to work by virtue of disability, age, or restricted employment opportunities may experience severe loss of self-esteem and depression.

Some persons experience marked parental pressure to become self-reliant before they are physically, socially, or emotionally prepared. For such persons being dependent has a threatening meaning, as well as a positive one, and conditions that place them in an obviously dependent relationship with others, or that may possibly do so, will activate defenses to protect their self-esteem.

In the course of an individual's development, he has encountered a number of transitional points in his progress from great to less dependency. As he has become more self-reliant and less dependent he has found that he has increased his range of opportunity to express himself in the ways he desires. Increased opportunity for personal choice is gratifying, and conditions such as unemployment or inability to work threaten the individual with a loss of these gratifications. In part, men may esteem themselves for their ability to make personal choices about how they live and what they do; work is instrumental to this ability to make choices, and dependency upon others limits the individual's opportunities to choose how he will arrange and conduct his life.

WORK AND SEX ROLE

As previous chapters have pointed out, the self-esteem that comes from work is closely tied to an individual's image of himself as a man, or of herself as a woman, and to beliefs about the work that is appropriate to each sex role. It is not surprising, therefore, that the inventoried interests of men and women differ markedly. Men prefer active physical activities, politics, selling, and scientific and mechanical work. Interests in art, music, literature, people, clerical work, teaching, and social work are more characteristic of women (13, 15). Analysis of the inventoried interests of women suggests that they are less clearly focused than are those of men, and that they are not concentrated in the professional occupations. This may result in part from the cultural values that tie a woman's worth less directly to her occupational activity than is the case with men, and from the cultural expectation that a woman will not be the primary wage earner in her family.

These comments are generalizations about large numbers of people and, of course, some individuals will pursue occupational objectives and possess interests characteristic of the opposite sex. Some men are employed as elementary school teachers, nurses, social workers, musicians, cooks, and artists; some women are physicians, engineers, and bus drivers. The reader will recall that the possession of interests associated with the opposite sex, whether they be vocational or avocational, cannot be taken as an indication of the individual's actual sex identification. Inventoried interests are not a measure of sex identification per se.

In studies comparing the interest patterns of fathers and sons, a higher-than-chance degree of similarity was found (14). In the childhood identification process, the child acquires not only the general values and attitudes of his sex, he also emulates his own parent's preferred activities.

Public perceptions do not actually define the areas of masculine and feminine ability, since the skills and aptitudes of men and women overlap considerably, and the explanation for the public stereotypes is not to be found in actual capacities and talents. Convention and custom contribute to beliefs about the proper work for men and women, and these, in turn, have their bases in the conditions influencing the perception of the roles of men and women in general.

At the turn of the century, most people did not consider office work a fitting and proper activity for a woman. Because of the advent of the typewriter and the need for more clerical and office workers, and as a result of industrial growth, women presently occupy 97 percent of all clerical positions and approximately one third of all women who work are classified as clerical (and kindred) workers.

Although there is little relationship between popular stereotypes and the actual abilities of men and women, these stereotypes are reflected in the opportunities for training and education available to the individual who seeks to enter a field that is viewed as the proper domain of the opposite sex. The woman who seeks to enter engineering, medicine, or law often finds opportunities for training and employment limited because of her sex.

Stereotypes also exercise a less obvious but quite pervasive psychological influence. A child may be subtly encouraged by parents and teachers to perform activities and to think of occupational choices that society sees as appropriate to his sex role. A boy with artistic talents and interests is sometimes encouraged by his parents to engage in more active pursuits, or is discouraged from thinking of art as a career; the girl whose interests are mechanical may be encouraged to participate in more "ladylike" activities.

The person who persists in training for a career that is considered within the province of the opposite sex can anticipate that at the very least he will be dissuaded and discouraged by some persons. Depending upon the individual's motives for his occupational choice, the extreme possibility exists that in response to social opposition and ridicule, he may identify with others who adopt pseudo-Bohemian behavior in their efforts to cope with criticism. Because they have not resolved their intrapsychic conflicts, these individuals allay their anxieties by "acting out" in angry, defiant, unconventional behaviors.

Cultural expectations related to sex role also may influence an individual's behavior within his profession or his occupation. If a man is aggressive, direct, competitive, and dominant, he may be rewarded, but a woman will probably be criticized if she behaves similarly. In many work situations women are at a disadvantage because they are expected to take a secondary role to men. Such expectations will tend to limit the opportunities of women with superior talents and abilities. One way in which cultural expectations affect masculine and feminine work roles is shown by the fact that in some occupations and professions women are paid less than men who perform the same work.

CHARACTERISTICS OF WORKERS IN DIFFERENT OCCUPATIONAL AREAS

It has been suggested that workers within similar occupational areas may share certain psychological characteristics. Such similarities probably occur because the patterns of the person's developmental experiences influence the decisions he makes in regard to work and account for his attitudes toward work and toward himself as a worker. Before the research bearing on this point is summarized, the distinction between an occupation and an occupational area must be made explicit. The occupational area includes a whole family of occupations, all of which have certain attributes in common. Roe (12) has presented the following occupational area groupings.

1. *Service*. These occupations are primarily concerned with serving and attending to the personal tasks, needs, and welfare of other persons. Included are occupations in guidance, social work, and domestic and protective services.

2. *Business Contact*. These occupations primarily involve face-to-face sale of commodities, investments, real estate, and services. Also

included are such occupations as demonstrator, auctioneer, and some kinds of agents.

3. *Organization*. These are the managerial and white collar jobs in business, industry, and government.

4. *Technology*. This group includes occupations concerned with the production, maintenance, and transportation of commodities and utilities. Here are occupations in engineering, crafts, and the machine trades, as well as transportation and communication.

5. *Outdoor*. This group consists of agricultural, fishery, forestry, mining, and kindred occupations; the occupations primarily concerned with the cultivation, preservation, and gathering of crops, or marine or inland water resources, of mineral resources, of forest products, and of other natural resources; and with animal husbandry.

6. *Science*. These are the occupations primarily concerned with scientific theory and its application under specified circumstances other than technology.

7. *General Cultural*. These occupations are primarily concerned with the preservation and transmission of the general cultural heritage.

8. *The Arts and Entertainment*. These occupations include those primarily concerned with the use of special skills in the creative arts and the field of entertainment.

Roe notes that the Service groups are typified mainly by an interest in dealing helpfully with people. Persons working in the service occupations have values that are religious and social, and their interests correspond more to those of the feminine stereotype than they do to the masculine one. In the Business Contact group, interests in working with people are also dominant, but instead of being focused on help they are characterized as serving the individual's own needs and purposes. Persons in the Organization group also have strong interests in interpersonal activity, but they have a more marked clerical interest than other groups, and they possess primary values in the economic areas. None of these three groups, Service, Business Contact, and Organization, possesses strong interests in intellectual and artistic activities.

Individuals in groups labeled Technology, Science, and Outdoors show less interest in working with other people than do the first three groups. In the Technology group, mechanical aptitudes and interests play an important part and are more significant than in the other occupational groups. Psychological data on individuals in the Outdoor occupational grouping are quite limited, and Roe finds it difficult to generalize about them. The Science group is notable for intellectual interests; persons in this group do not have dominant artistic inclinations and interests. The exact patterning within this group of individuals may vary considerably with the specific scientific area, and it is possible—though there is no research report to substantiate it—that individuals in the biological, physical, and social sciences may differ in their psychological characteristics.

Similar to the occupations in the Science group, but with somewhat higher verbal interests, are those within the General Cultural category. Physical abilities play an important role in the Arts and Entertainment category, and intellectual ability is less directly related to success in this group than in several of the others.

The psychological characteristics of individuals in the various occupations are closely related to the ways in which they perceive their areas of work. How an individual sees the choices available to him may significantly influence his occupational decisions. Having made a choice, he then perceives the occupation in ways that will allow him to serve best his needs to maintain, protect, and enhance himself psychologically. The ways in which different individuals working in the same field view their endeavors can vary considerably. Some engineers may think of their specialty primarily in its scientific aspects; others may think of it as a social welfare enterprise.

As Roe presents them, within each of the groups specific occupations may be located on one of six levels of function representing the degree of responsibility, capacity, and skill the work requires. For example, an occupational group such as Organization includes a top level of responsibility, illustrated by the President of the United States, and a second level of professional and managerial activities, containing business and government executives. The third level of function includes accountants and owners of small businesses. Cashiers and sales clerks are in the fourth level, and file clerks and typists in the fifth. Positions of least responsibility, requiring least training and skill, are in the sixth level and are represented by messenger boys. Thus there may be a great variety of work activities or specialties and subspecialties. A lawyer may be involved primarily in the presentation and preparation of cases in court, or he may be involved primarily in research and the preparation of briefs. Some doctors may function as surgeons, who must exhibit great dexterity and unusual hand-eye coordination, while others work as psychiatrists, whose work involves an understanding and talent for interpersonal activity. Within a given occupational group the range of activity is sometimes so great that certain specialties may have more in common with other occupational groups than they have with their own. The psychiatrist who functions as a psychotherapist (see Chapter 14) and the social worker or psychologist are probably more similar in terms of the talents required by their work than are the psychiatrist and surgeon, though both are physicians.

PREVIOUS PSYCHOLOGICAL EXPERIENCE AND REACTIONS TO THE WORK SITUATION

An individual's ability to derive gratifications from his work—and the quality of those gratifications—will depend upon the needs he must satisfy as well as upon the characteristics of the work situation itself. A study of eighty persons who presented themselves to a vocational agency revealed that those who had records of high work adjustment, who did well in their work and derived satisfaction from the energy they expended in it, came from strongly knit families (5). The persons whose work adjustment records were considered poor came from families that were disorganized and in which the individual members were not psychologically close to one another. The poorly adjusted work group possessed more antagonism toward parents and siblings than did the high work adjustment group. The high adjustment group had been more independent of parental supervision during childhood years. A difference was found also between the two groups in regard to reactions to schooling. Those with satisfying records of work adjustment had found school satisfying, while those in the other group reported that they had felt rejected by their peers. Suggestive but less clear-cut differences were found in regard to feelings toward mothers, the religious values stressed, the "out-goingness," and the amount of formal education and special training received. Those in the high group indicated more positive reactions to their mothers (as well as to their fathers), had experienced less family disruption, reported backgrounds in which religious values were stressed, and recalled a higher degree of communication and interaction with others.

The authors of this study suggest that the worker's expectation of his job, the demands he makes within the work situation, and the specific satisfactions he requires from it will all depend upon the gratifications he received or failed to receive during his earlier years. If childhood deprivation underlies the individual's efforts to "make up" for what he lacked earlier, his work situation may afford him the opportunity to satisfy those psychological needs, even though they have little actual relation to the work situation.

The findings of this study do not relate achievement to work satisfaction, but they indicate that unrealistic occupational expectations stem from intense, unmet psychological needs and that these needs contribute to dissatisfaction in the work situation. Thus, the effects of past experiences are reflected in vocational development, as they will be manifest in other aspects of psychological and social development.

OTHER CONDITIONS AFFECTING
VOCATIONAL CHOICE

Just as a person's vocational choice is affected by his past experience and relationships, his particular psychological needs, sex role, and other factors, so his physical and intellectual competences significantly influence the numbers and kinds of opportunities available to him. Physical limitations or disabilities imposed by illness, injury, or structural defect affect the individual's work opportunities. The person who cannot walk is forced to consider work that does not demand walking, running, or jumping. The person with a hearing deficiency cannot choose work that requires a high degree of auditory acuity. Such instances of physical limitation represent aspects of an unfortunate reality that may have profound psychological and social significance. The psychological ramifications of limitations imposed by physical disability will be considered more fully in the next chapter.

In addition to physical or intellectual limitations, social and economic events may have profound and widespread effects on the work and training opportunities available. The individual cannot control economic conditions or the political conditions that lead to war or peace, yet economics, wars, and technological and social change have great impact upon him.

In times of depression it is more difficult to gain entry into more professional and technical fields. One study (8) of the graduates of a liberal arts college found that during depression years of the 1930s only one half of the graduates gained entry into professional, managerial, or clerical occupations, whereas three fourths of predepression graduates of the same institution had begun their careers within these categories. The effects of a depression upon the subsequent pattern of the individual's life are shown in this same study: four years later, when economic conditions had improved substantially, only one tenth of the depression group had shifted into the categories that the majority of predepression graduates had entered. On the other hand, there are certain fields that have difficulty recruiting qualified individuals during prosperous times. These tend to be occupations that offer "security" as one of their inducements. Thus, during a depression there is more competition for the available teaching and civil service positions than in prosperous years.

The opportunity to enter a particular occupation may be influenced also by technical changes and by large-scale social and economic forces over which the individual has no control. Within the last twenty-five years, opportunities for work in the New England textile industry have declined as the industry has moved to the South in search of cheaper sources of labor. An example of technological change that affects the opportunity of the individual for work is seen in the shift from piston-driven aircraft to jet planes. Changes in the number of persons required to fly such planes and differences in the engines will have a marked influence upon the numbers and types of pilots and flight engineers required. Junior pilots and flight engineers may have reduced opportunities for employment; consequently, the individual will find himself in a situation in which his opportunities are dependent upon forces over which he has no control.

The use of machines and electronic apparatus to perform work previously performed by human beings results in changes in employment opportunity. Although workers are displaced when their jobs are taken over by machines, these changes also result in the creation of new positions related to the building, maintenance, and "feeding" of the machines. The advent of the electronic computor, which stores and performs many calculations involving vast amounts of data with incredible speed, will eliminate many positions, but new positions are required in the preparation of information for the machine and in its maintenance and development.

Of all the impersonal events that affect every aspect of the individual's life, including his occupational opportunities, there is probably none whose impact can surpass that of war. In time of war, the personal wishes and choices of large numbers of men and women must be subordinated to the demands of the national situation. The student with talents and interests in music may be trained to fight as an infantry soldier, the girl who wanted to be an elementary school teacher may work as a riveter in an airplane factory. The ravages of war in terms of lives lost and physical injuries have a marked influence not only upon the occupational decisions of the individuals directly involved but also upon those of their families. The young mother whose husband is killed overseas evaluates her situation and the occupational opportunities open to her in the light of her need to support herself and her children. The athletic coach blinded in combat must re-evaluate his opportunities for work as he seeks new ways to earn a living.

In addition to the dramatic and obvious influences of war upon the opportunities for employment, there are important but less obvious social and psychological results. Through contacts with persons and places that would otherwise have been inaccessible, many men acquire a deepened awareness of the nature of the world and the people in it. Although these experiences are side products of war, they may alter individual life patterns and introduce some men to new occupational possibilities. Consider, for example, the many men who took advantage of veterans' educational benefits to acquire technical or academic training that was not previously available to them or in which they had not been interested.

In addition to war itself, the preparation for war also may facilitate changes in industry or develop new occupations and opportunities. The development of atomic energy for peaceful purposes has been brought closer by the development of the atomic and hydrogen bombs, and the fields of atomic energy now offer occupational opportunity for individuals whose talents, abilities, and interests lie in many areas. Twenty years ago, or even ten years ago, these same persons would not have had such opportunities available to them. Comparable examples could be cited in the fields of rocketry and in the various specialties concerned with the conquest of outer space.

Less obvious than the effects on men's occupational lives of large-scale forces, such as wars and depressions, are the arbitrary restrictions the members of a profession, school, or union may place upon entry to their ranks. Such restrictions may make it difficult or impossible for members of certain racial or religious groups to obtain necessary training, regardless of their abilities and interests. When, through no fault of their own, persons are denied access to the training or occupation of their choice, they are bound to feel dejected and to experience many of the reactions that accompany frustrations. The form and effects of these reactions will depend upon the individual's self-concept and his emotional and personal resources, as well as the alternatives available to him. Impersonal events must be accorded considerable importance in assessing an individual's level of psychological development, and occupational restrictions provide very real sources of stress and threat to the persons encountering them. In the assessment of development, reactions to restrictions, as well as the fact that restrictions are encountered, are evaluated. In this connection it should be noted that the pattern of potentialities for each individual suggests that success and satisfaction are available, not in just one occupational activity but in a number of them.

Leisure

The typical American spends less time at his work than did his father, and his father spent less time at his work than did *his* father. In 1850 the average work week was about 70 hours; in 1950 it had dropped to 40 hours, and the trend is expected to continue (7). As the number of hours committed to work decreases, the significance of non-work hours in the life of the individual increases. The typical American worker will soon have available, exclusive of sleeping, eating, and body care, eleven hours for every eight he spends at work (7). He can devote himself to a variety of pursuits; he may watch television, garden, go to

a symphony, play with his children, read, or talk to his friends. Whatever his inclinations, he has more time to pursue them, and he can look
forward to a progressively increasing proportion of nonwork hours.

The individual is at leisure when he is not at work and when he is
doing whatever he chooses, free of any sense of obligation or duty. From
his leisure activities he achieves satisfactions great enough to cause him
to think about and arrange periods of time to engage in these activities.
Leisure activities may be active, such as participation in a sport or in
artistic creation, or they may be passive, such as engaging in spectator
sports, attending concerts, or visiting museums and art galleries. Leisure
activities can include solitary pursuits such as reading or quiet contemplative activity, or they can bring the individual into contact with other
persons with whom he converses or with whom he participates in a sport
or activity. Some aspects of leisure activities are creative in that they
allow man to develop his potentialities and to employ his talents and
skills in new ways. Leisure activities often have a re-creative function.
They enable man to renew his energies, to restore himself, and thus to
prepare himself to again confront the demands of his everyday responsibilities, including those connected with his work.

In his leisure time the individual explores and experiments with
experiences that are outside those available to him in the usual course
of his work or occupation. The office worker who enjoys refinishing
furniture and the physician who derives satisfaction from playing the
cello are extending their experience beyond what is available within the
limits of their professions.

The demarcation between work and leisure activity is not always
clear, however. One instance of difficulty arises in the categorization of
those work activities having a strong obligatory character. For example,
many individuals engage in nonwork activities out of a sense of compulsion or duty in order to comply with expectations associated with the
various roles they fulfill. An individual may work in his garden, repair
his house, or tutor his children out of a sense of obligation to his home
and family; he may fulfill his role as a member of the community by
serving as a Civil Defense Warden or as a member of the Town Planning
Commission. An element of obligation also permeates those nonwork
activities performed in order to advance one's career. The lawyer and
salesman may join certain social groups to meet prospective clients. A
carpenter may invest time in study to obtain a contractor's license, and
individuals in technical and professional areas may spend hours reviewing
the latest developments in order to "keep up" with their fields.

Another problem in classification arises in the categorization of
activities performed during work time that are of paramount interest
to the individual and in which he would rather expend energy and

time than he would in any other pursuit. The craftsman, for example, performs his work not out of a sense of obligation but out of a feeling of achievement and gratification with the product of his efforts. His intrinsic commitment to himself, to his skill, and to his work activities is of such a nature that his preferences lead him to extend his skills and knowledge, and he freely elects to follow pursuits related to his craft rather than take advantage of alternate opportunities for the investment of his time. Even though it is difficult in all instances to distinguish work from leisure activities, the general distinction that leisure involves nonobligatory activities performed during nonworking hours has sufficient value to be used in discussing the issue of leisure in relation to psychological and social development.

With increased time available for nonwork activities, the worker often will feel a sense of responsibility for deciding how he will spend his time. In addition, under the influence of a persisting and somewhat Puritanic cultural belief that work is virtuous and idleness, play, and leisure are sinful, the person often feels guilty when he is not at work or when he is not spending his time doing "worthwhile" things. He thus will respond to values acquired early in life and feel that activities engaged in for their own pleasurable value are, if not immoral, somewhat improper.

When leisure is considered in the context of the retired worker, there is often the implication that questions pertaining to the use of nonwork time did not exist prior to his retirement. This prevalent belief is incorrect, for the range and depth of the individual's interests as he goes through his entire developmental span will determine how he utilizes his nonworking hours, just as it will determine how he invests of himself during his working hours.

The use of leisure time not only reflects the developmental stage the individual has achieved but also plays a vital role in contributing to the level of his psychological development. To the degree to which the individual is able to extend his awareness, to further his skills and achieve gratifications that are not ordinarily available within his work experience, to this extent psychological development is facilitated through leisure activities. This is not to say, however, that all activities undertaken during one's nonworking hours, such as gambling, excessive drinking, and indiscriminating contacts with others, are necessarily conducive to psychological development. Some leisure time activities, such as television viewing, spectator athletics, movies, and card playing, contribute more to the maintenance of the personality than to its extension and development; these primarily involve the re-creative, relaxing, restful, or diversionary functions of leisure in contrast to those that are creative and developmental. Even though they do not necessarily make a positive contribution to the extension and development of the personality, such pursuits serve significant psychological, physical, and social functions, and most individuals need such activities.

The creative and enriching utilization of leisure time gradually emerges from the experiences of childhood and adolescence. In the child's play behavior there are many opportunities to experience vicariously the roles he will ultimately be expected to fill. During adolescence activities are often undertaken on a trial-and-error basis, as the teenager seeks out areas of gratification and interest that he later may explore more fully. It is during this period of life that new experiences in art, music, drama, journalism, athletics, or debating are included in the school program. Such experiences can generate sufficient interest and motivation for the individual to pursue them voluntarily, although the mode in which he expresses the interest will sometimes change. For example, a high school student may acquire sufficient appreciation of the technical facets of an activity as a participant for him to adopt the role of an observer or a passive participant when active participation is no longer appropriate.

During the young adult years the issue of leisure becomes clearly delineated, largely because leisure and work stand in close relationship to one another. Without work there can be no leisure, for leisure, by definition, has to do with nonworking and nonobligatory experience in which the individual is free to elect how he will spend his time. In conditions of unemployment or enforced idleness, there is no leisure. Most young adults first engage in full-time employment during this period of their lives, and the value of time becomes increasingly apparent to them. The young adult gives careful consideration to how weekends, evenings, holidays, and vacations are to be spent.

Often he is subtly pushed by social forces within his community and among his friends toward conforming to patterns of utilization of nonworking time. Not to go along with the group can invite loss of prestige and peer approval, while compliance with the group pattern of activity often removes the quality of leisure from such participation. This occurs when the individual compulsively and ritualistically engages without pleasure in the group's leisure activities. Commercial interests, through popular media such as television, often exploit such tendencies toward conformity by emphasizing the value of their products or services, which are geared to the vacationer, the prospective traveler, or the person who is interested in improving his appearance.

Concern has been expressed about whether the nation's schools have been neglecting the development of appropriate leisure time activities. This concern has been heightened by the greater emphasis in recent years on the so-called solid or academic courses, which often provide the student with little opportunity to extend experience. The schools have also been critized for attempting to undertake too broad a responsibility, and it has been suggested that they should increase their emphasis upon academic areas of training. Such criticism often fails to take into account the fact that the amount of time available to most individuals for non-work activities is increasing. Many leisure activities constitute a part of the cultural heritage that is not included in the rather narrow academic and technical programs offered and emphasized in most high schools; therefore, if students are not provided with the opportunity of sampling the gratifications to be achieved from art, music, and citizenship activity, it may well be asked where these would be acquired. It is naive to assume that many students have families that would or could provide them with sufficient exposure to these cultural areas.

The leisure activities selected will depend, of course, on the values and previous experiences of the individual. The point is that the psychological function served by the activity is of greater importance than the modality of expression. For this reason it is not appropriate to list desirable activities; rather the desirability of the individual's questioning his own leisure activities from the standpoint of his own self-interest should be emphasized.

Erich Fromm has declared (6) that much of man's activity in the highly complex industrial society of the western world has "alienated" man from himself. Applied to the present context of leisure, Fromm's point is that man may invest his energies in ways that prevent his getting close to himself or to others. If there is a wish for distance from the human situation, then leisure time activities can provide the individual with a vehicle for accomplishing this. On the other hand, if there is the need and capacity to move toward others and oneself, then there are leisure time activities that can provide the context in which such movement can occur. And when large segments of the population have the urge to engage in ritualistic behaviors that will occupy their time, enabling them to be in close physical proximity to one another while at the same time obviating the chance for psychological closeness, then the society can be counted on to provide structures within which such needs can be met. The contemplative, speculative consideration of the times and the issues of life that may occur in solitude or in discussions with a friend is, for example, far less prevalent than formerly; it is regarded as an unnecessary luxury. The contemplative questioning of one's personal values is out of keeping with the tempo of our complex society, which leads one to be on the go whether at work or at play, to be attuned to the outside world, and to believe that responses to one's own needs or quiet consideration of personal issues are outside the accepted scope of leisure time patterns.

By this time the reader must be well aware of the role that personal values play in the utilization of leisure time. The individual who values himself and others highly will engage in activities that are apt to be quite different from those favored by individuals who have little esteem for themselves or anyone else. The person who values himself highly or (to put it in the terms we have utilized throughout the text) who has achieved a high level of psychological development will be relatively free of the compulsion to engage in "recreational" activities for the sake of conforming to the dictates of his group. Such an individual is able to arrive at his own decisions about the activities in which he will invest himself and his energies. He will be able to protect himself from intrusion when he feels the need to be alone. The individual who values himself highly engages in activities that are personally satisfying and that extend his experience and further his psychological development.

Since the person we are describing holds himself in high regard, he also holds others in high regard; some of his activities with people will therefore be gratifying and profitable for both himself and them. When such activities are engaged in, however, they will not have an obligatory quality. Rather, the time he elects to spend with children as a Sunday School teacher, scout leader, Little League coach, or hospital volunteer worker constitutes a source of satisfaction through the contribution he makes to the development of others. The uses made of their leisure time by individuals who have achieved a high order of psychological development not only brings them gratifications and contributes to other individuals, but the society, as a whole benefits. Within his leisure activities the citizen can to the fullest extent be himself while at the same time enjoying the responsibilities of citizenship. He has the time and the inclination to invest of himself in his local, state, or national government through an active interest in the issues and in the political actions appropriate to such issues. Through his leisure time he is able to direct his attention and energies both to himself and to his environment in such ways that his alienation from his own humanity and from the humanness of others is diminished.

Man's work and leisure activities together provide in large measure a picture of his life. They reflect what he has learned about himself and what life contains of value to him. In this connection the views of Charles K. Brightbill, one of the leaders in the field of recreation, are of considerable interest. In his book, *Man and Leisure* (2), he expresses a philosophy that eloquently sums up the relationship of leisure to man's development:

If there is a key to *satisfying living,* it is not easily found. We can only hope, even though we may be unable to define it, that when we come upon it, we can recognize it. Surely it is, to some degree at least, to be found along the path of humility and the realization that much as we want to be at the center of the good and sparkling world, we are only an infinitesimal part of a larger pattern. We are only somebody in relation to somebody else, only something in relation to something else. If we expect too much, we shall inevitably clash with the expectations of others. This secret to happiness, if it is a secret, is certainly to be discovered in affection given and service rendered, in using our capacities to grow, in knowing and preserving beauty, and in not abusing our bodies and minds or dissipating our energies. The key may also be found in the feeling of kinship toward all living things—including man—and in the inner man in tune with his universe. For leisure ought to be the time for cultivating ourselves in the whole of creation. We can be truly happy only if we enjoy life and establish such a state as being not only desirable but indispensable; otherwise we are as lumps of clay. It is the life often contemptuous of worldly success and characterized more by simplicity than by luxury, more by understanding than by monetary gain.

Latent in leisure are tremendous potential forces for good that are ready and awaiting that time when our social thinking and action mature to unleash them for the benefit of all humanity.[1]

Summary

The crucial experiences in the life of the young adult involve his work and his love relationships. Work affords him not only a means of livelihood but also contact with others of similar interests and various opportunities for the maintenance and enhancement of his self-concept. Work itself may be the primary source of satisfaction, as well as an instrument through which various needs can be fulfilled. It not only satisfies the body's need for activity, but enables the individual to fulfill the psychological needs of relatedness to others, achievement, and prestige. Intellectual and physical abilities, psychological characteristics, sex role, and social and economic factors all affect vocational choice. The effects of previous psychological experience are reflected in an individual's vocational development. In our culture, man's motivation to work should not be oversimplified, for no single explanation is adequate; rather, a number of motives account for his occupational activities, activities to which he devotes the major part of his life.

[1] Reprinted by permission from C. K. Brightbill, *Man and Leisure: A Philosophy of Recreation.* © 1961. Prentice-Hall, Inc., Englewood Cliffs, N.J.

As the number of hours that man is required to spend at his work declines, his opportunities to pursue his own interests increase. His nonworking time will include some activity that is obligatory: activity performed because it is expected of him as a parent, citizen, or member of a profession. He will also engage in a wide range of leisure activities that are chosen freely and performed without obligation. He may be an active participant in an athletic contest or a passive television viewer; the activity may be relaxing and restore his energies or it might deplete them.

Leisure activities both contribute to and reflect the individual's developmental level. The tradition linking nonwork activities to sin has tended to obscure the importance of leisure activity in the development of the individual. Man must have time and opportunity if he is to approach the fulfillment of his potentialities.

References

1. Allport, G. W. *Personality: A Psychological Interpretation*. New York: Holt, 1937.
2. Brightbill, C. K. *Man and Leisure: A Philosophy of Recreation*. Englewood Cliffs, N.J.: Prentice-Hall, 1961.
3. Caplow, T. *The Sociology of Work*. Minneapolis: University of Minnesota Press, 1954.
4. Evans, C. E., and Laseau, V. N. My Job Contest. *Personnel Psychology Monograph #1*. Washington, D.C.: Personnel Psychology, Inc., 1950.
5. Friend, F. G., and Haggard, E. A. Work adjustment in relation to family background. *Appl. Psychol. Monogr. 16*. Stanford, Calif.: Stanford University Press, 1948.
6. Fromm, E. *The Sane Society*. New York: Holt, 1955.
7. Kaplan, M. *Leisure in America: A Social Inquiry*. New York: Wiley, 1960.
8. King, M. A comparative study of follow-up procedures in high school and college. M. A. Thesis, Worcester, Mass.: Clark University, 1939.
9. McClelland, D. C., Atkinson, J. W., Clark, R. A., and Lowell, E. L. *The Achievement Motive*. New York: Appleton, 1953.
10. Murphy, G. *Human Potentialities*. New York: Basic Books, 1958.
11. *National Norms on 96 Occupations*. College Study in Intergroup Relations, Detroit, No. TM-55, Mimeo. No. E5556, 1947.
12. Roe, A. *The Psychology of Occupations*. New York: Wiley, 1956.
13. Strong, E. K., Jr. *Vocational Interests of Men and Women*. Stanford: Stanford University Press, 1943.
14. Super, D. E. *Appraising Vocational Fitness*. New York: Harper, 1949.
15. Terman, L. M., and Miles, C. C. *Sex and Personality: Studies in Masculinity and Femininity*. New York: McGraw-Hill, 1936.
16. Thomas, L. G. *The Occupational Structure and Education*. Englewood Cliffs, N.J.: Prentice-Hall, Inc., 1956.

Selected Readings

Anderson, N.   *Work and Leisure.* New York: Free Press, 1961.

Kleemeier, R. W. (ed.)   *Aging and Leisure.* New York: Oxford, 1961.

Kaplan, M.   *Leisure in America: A Social Inquiry.* New York: Wiley, 1960.

Roe, A.   *The Psychology of Occupations.* New York: Wiley, 1956.

Super, D. E.   *The Psychology of Careers.* New York: Harper, 1957.

10.

The Young Adult Years: Love

Of all the relationships an individual experiences in his lifetime, none commands his attention more fully than love and marital relationships. His reactions to the stresses and uncertainties of the premarital period and to the challenge of entering a love relationship constitute some of the most difficult tests of his interpersonal development. The love relationship is given special emphasis in this book because it has broad application to many interpersonal relationships and because it has acute significance for young adults who are in the process of selecting, wooing, or marrying the person of their choice; furthermore, the topic of love assumes vast social significance in these times. The Biblical injunction, "Love thy neighbor as thyself" takes on special meaning in a world that now possesses the technological capacity to destroy itself, even though the word *love* does not usually call forth thoughts of international politics.

The Love Relationship

In its general sense, loving is an active process in which the loving person achieves his own personal fulfillment and deepest sense of gratification through his contributions to the self-fulfillment and gratification of another. Sullivan expressed a similar concept when he said that love is a state in which "the satisfaction or security of another person becomes as significant as one's own satisfaction or security" (10). The mother engaged in a loving relationship with her child achieves gratification from contributing to his development and welfare. Such love is

295

unconditional; the mother does not require the child to earn that love. She provides him with affection, concern, and care, not because he is cute, cuddly, or precocious, but because as her child he requires these attentions, and when she administers them, they provide her with feelings of pleasure and self-fulfillment. In love relationships between parents and children, which will be discussed in detail later, the greatest development of the children is possible; it is this type of relationship that is considered most desirable from the standpoint of personal development, for such love does not have to be bought by behaviors or achievements that please and satisfy the parent. The child receives the feeling that as a human being he is worthy and valued by the persons who are important to him; he does not have to perform for this love, because it is there under all conditions, at all times, and without qualification.

Loving has as its central characteristic the giving of one's energy, one's time, and most important, one's emotional commitment. As it has been noted, this quality, the giving of oneself, is quite different from that implied by the idea of "being in love" or "falling in love," which emphasizes *receiving* the energy, attention, and affection of someone. In the passive concept of love, Erich Fromm points out, the major objective is to find the right object, the person who will provide the desired gratifications, rather than to develop one's own ability to contribute to the gratifications and self-fulfillment of another person.

It should be clear that the act of giving which characterizes the love relationship is not undertaken for the purpose of enhancing self-esteem through acts of self-sacrifice and martyrdom, nor is the giving undertaken for the purpose of presenting oneself to the public as a generous or good person, or bribing the loved one into returning that love. The giving is not motivated by the desire to allay anxiety or expiate guilt by doing good acts. The person able to love gives spontaneously; it is a natural way of relating to other human beings and comes easily and appropriately. The ability to give love requires attention, perception, sensitivity, and integrity, and the general concept of the love relationship is one that applies to all human relationships; to the love that a person may have for his parents, for his children, or for his friends.

Friendship

The first of the two broad categories of relationships subsumed under the generic term of "The Love Relationship" is friendship. It is followed by a discussion of Sexual Love Relationships.

In the following characterization of friendship its significance as a love relationship is quite evident.

Friendship exists between two human beings who seek to relate to each other; to the observer it appears the two have special enjoyment when they meet, they are interested in each other and their relation resists adversity. In time of need either will lend a helping hand to the other. When separated there is a desire to return and to take up the joys of their intimate association. If one is maligned or comes upon misfortune, the other will defend and lend support. Over a period of time, communality of thought and quick understanding are testimony to their psychological proximity. There are no commitments, no duties to the other, only a strong liking that each feels for the other and a want instead of an obligation. The expression of two selves becomes enhanced and enriched with the creation of novelty. From the one, the other learns and so they develop together through the history of their relationship.[1]

Another example of the similarity of friendship and love is found in the responses of young women to the questions "What do you mean when you say 'friend'?" and "What, in general, do you expect of your friends and they of you?" Their answers included: "Someone who wants the best for you. . . . Someone you get along with, do things with and who will help you. . . . Someone who will let you know when you are doing something wrong. . . . Someone you can be yourself with." A friend was further described as considerate, tolerant, understanding, trustworthy, loyal, and able to keep secrets. (1).

The meanings generally assigned to love and friendship usually do not make clear their common identity. This is because both love and friendship are usually defined very narrowly. Love is most often thought of as a sexually oriented relationship between a man and a women, and friendship as a nonsexual relationship between two people who enjoy one another's company and exchange minor confidences.

The belief that all love relationships are primarily sexual and that all friendships are nonsexual suggests incorrectly that deep and significant relationships between persons of the same sex must be based on sexual interest, or that relationships between members of the opposite sexes *must have* a sexual component in order to qualify as love relationships. While sexuality is an important feature of one type of love relationship, it is not a basic requirement of all love relationships.

Friendship as a love relationship is a highly rewarding human experience. The trust, affection, and respect that friends hold for one another provides many opportunities for each to contribute to his own and the other's development. Consider, for example, the statement that

[1] Reprinted by permission from M. Nesbitt, *Friendship, Love, and Values: A Technical Report*. Princeton, N.J.: Educational Testing Service. Copyright, 1959.

"a friend is someone you can be yourself with." In other words, with a friend one does not have to be on guard or "put on an act." The psychological implication is that people need a respite from their daily attempts to maintain and enhance their personalities and the opportunity to be with someone and at the same time to let down one's defenses is doubly welcome. Because the friend is trusted not to capitalize on our weaknesses or in any other way hurt us, we feel free to air our fears and exhibit our weaknesses as well as show our "good side." A friend's criticism is therefore not perceived as a threat to our self-esteem but is accepted as evidence of his concern.

Since friendships develop over a period of time, it is often believed that friendship can be explained solely on the basis of the amount of time persons spend together. This belief is found to be an inadequate explanation of what occurs in the acquaintance process, a process studied intensively by Newcomb and his associates at the University of Michigan (7, 8). Seventeen male transfer students who met as strangers and who lived in the same student house were carefully studied during their first semester together. For four or five hours each week data relevant to their degree of attraction for one another were obtained by interviews, questionnaires, and tests. This experiment was repeated a year later under comparable conditions with seventeen new subjects.

It was found that proximity or opportunity for contact helped the students to become acquainted with one another by allowing for the exchange of mutually rewarding information, thus it is not merely the amount of time spent together that is important but rather whether the communication taking place is rewarding. In general, the results of Newcomb's study indicated a relationship between attraction and perceived similarity of attitudes. Subjects tended to like those whom they thought agreed with them on important and relevant issues. For example, they liked those who perceived them as they perceived themselves—they tended to like those who agreed with their own positive and negative impressions of their self-image. Other findings showed that subjects tended to like the persons they believed liked them, and that as the students came to know one another, those who shared similar attitudes toward other house members became more attracted to each other. It appears that, on the whole, increased knowledge about a friend's attitudes causes one to feel closer or withdraw, depending on the extent of attitude agreement. In some instances, however, individuals ignore or distort information regarding those they consider highly attractive in order to retain contact with them.

While many persons are drawn together by similarities, there are also persons who become friends because their differences complement one another. A timid person and an outspoken one may find in each other's contrasting qualities elements that balance or complete their own systems. The timid person may draw courage from his partner's aggressiveness while the outspoken one may gain self-restraint from his friend.

There is another relationship that is frequently termed "friendship" yet fails to qualify as such according to the interpretation followed in this text. Its basis is admiration. A person is esteemed because he meets a standard set quite apart from considerations of his personal and social characteristics. An example is that of a college man who, valuing athletic prowess, greatly admires a "friend" for his sports achievements. Should the successful athlete lose interest in sports and redirect his energies to other areas, he would lose his status as "friend" with our college man because he no longer conforms to the standard. Here, intrinsic worth is secondary to extrinsic characteristics. The individuality of the friend and the quality of attachment to him are of less significance than in love relationships. In addition, the admirer may be seeking vicarious satisfaction by identifying with an individual who possesses the qualities lacking in himself. Moreover, if the friend responds in any measure, the admirer feels his worth to be enhanced because he receives attention from such an admirable person. The admired one, in turn, may need the adulation and approval that a bevy of admirers provides him because of an inordinate need for recognition. Therefore, although these relationships are not love relationships, they serve psychological purposes and can be of great significance to the participants.

Friendship as a love relationship can characterize the attitudes and behaviors of persons of the same or different sex toward one another. It is differentiated from the sexual love relationship in that friends do not engage in sexual behavior with one another. When a love relationship has as one of its aspects overt sexuality, then for purposes of categorization the term "Sexual Love Relationship" is appropriate.

Sexual Love Relationships

THE HETEROSEXUAL LOVE RELATIONSHIP

In this section issues relevant to the marital relationship are given primary attention. This is not to say that heterosexual love relationships outside of marriage do not occur. It also does not imply that all sexual relationships within marriage are love relationships—and the concept of love indicated expressly does *not equate* sexual behavior and love.

Since the individual usually decides for himself whom he will marry, without restrictions imposed by tradition, convention, or custom, the basis upon which his decision is made warrants careful attention. If one were to ask young people the question, "Upon what will you base your decision to marry?", he would receive comments such as, "My decision to marry will be based on whether or not I am in love with the person." If he then inquired about the meaning of the term "being in love," he would probably be told that the question was a difficult one, since love cannot be easily defined and has a different meaning for everyone. Others might point out that there is a stirring emotional quality to the state of being in love; that physical desire and the individual's attractiveness contribute to this emotional state; that the "loved person" possesses all the virtues and few, if any, of the frailties; that there is little interest in being with anyone other than the loved person, who provides a sense of well being and can be talked with for hours about the most confidential of matters. Finally, it might be stated that shared activities take on a special meaning, and that time spent with the loved person is pleasurable, regardless of what is done.

If being in love is as described, what then accounts for the high incidence of marital unhappiness? Is it that the persons change? Or can it be that somehow the person who was once seen as the epitome of perfection is now seen differently? Is it that the marriage partner is perceived as a human being with the strengths and weaknesses of a human being? Or do the vicissitudes of life and the stresses that are products of family life, involving children, budgeting, illness, disappointment, and responsibility, account for marital failure?

Although it is probable that each of these contributes to the disenchantment that many people experience after marriage, two in particular require elaboration: the tendency to misperceive the "loved one" prior to marriage, and the expectations of the marital relationship. Several possible sources of this misperception can be cited:

1. The person had been known only in certain situations that called forth his "best" behavior. Dating and courtship involved "having fun," being entertained, and other activities in which the persons were not required to evidence responsibility or deep concern for one another. They knew each other under the most favorable circumstances, and, at best, these circumstances provided only a limited basis for knowing the many aspects of individual make-up that are important in the marital relationship.

2. The need to be loved by a perfect person resulted in the distorted perception of the loved one as being that person.

3. The loved one was regarded as possessing the actual or wished-for qualities of persons who had been loved in the past.

Distortions of the second and third types also serve the function of enhancing self-esteem, for if the perfect person loves one, then one must be a very worthy person. Such projections can also have a quality of near-desperation. It is as if the person says, "This is *the* perfect relationship, for if it isn't, then there will never be a better one." This desperation is sometimes related to anxieties about remaining unmarried, which are common in our culture. A marriage that is initiated by a "love relationship" based on such perceptual distortions has a shaky foundation.

In addition to providing the basis for the family structure, the marriage relationship creates the social unit through which children are brought into the world. It provides one of the deepest and most meaningful of all human experiences, for it presents to those who are capable of taking advantage of it the opportunity for the greatest possible satisfaction of the need to feel related, to feel in communion with another human being, and to participate in the total range of the behaviors encompassing the essence of being human. If "being in love" does not provide an adequate basis for entering into this kind of marriage relationship, what type of love relationship will provide an adequate foundation for an enduring marriage?

The answer to this question is that the best basis for marriage is a love relationship reciprocal in character and entered into by persons possessing the ability to love. Such a relationship differs from the popular conception of "being in love" and it requires a great deal of the participants. In the meaning here given to the term *love*, not everyone possesses the ability to love, nor is everyone capable of entering heterosexual love relationships.

Two important qualifications in the interpretation of the term "the ability to love" must be noted. *Ability,* as the following discussion indicates, refers to *abilities,* to many skills, attitudes, and characteristics, not to a unitary capacity. For purposes of convenience the collective form of the noun is employed. Second, these abilities, both demonstrated and potential, will range from minimal to ideal, hence the ability to love is a matter of degree, it is not an "either you have it or you don't" proposition.

Within the heterosexual love relationship, both persons are concerned about each other, and each participates in the effort to contribute to the other's self-fulfillment; each receives his maximal gratification from efforts expended on behalf of the other person, and the self-interests of each become inextricably linked to the self-interests of the other. Within this merging of self-identities, there is no pressure for the loss of individual integrity; the partners can treat one another with mutual respect, and the relationship is not characterized by the dominance of one member and the submission of the other, nor by the loss of the integrity of one through the other's subjugation. In such relationships there is a capacity for sharing and no need for manipulation, indirection, or deceit.

In considering the sexual aspect of this love relationship, we must not make the error of equating it with a relationship that exists solely or primarily to afford the participants relief from their sexual tensions. The term "to make love" is popularly interpreted to refer to sexual intercourse, and this usage reflects a cultural tendency to equate love with sexual intercourse. When the relationships between men and women are characterized by the term "heterosexual love," it has an important sexual component, but a sexual relationship is not necessarily a love relationship. Sexual relationships may spring from the individuals' physical needs for sexual outlets and from psychological motives having to do with self-esteem. Marriages based upon sexual relationships alone fail to fulfill their participants' deepest needs, since the mutual ability to provide temporary relief from sexual tensions will not form the basis for an enduring relationship within which there is the opportunity for maximum gratification of the relatedness need.

In the sexual relationship without love the individual is concerned with his own immediate needs, and his own wishes and desires are of primary importance to him. His partner is only an instrument for providing gratification. Although in its early phases the sexual relationship may be an exciting and thrilling experience in which the elements of conquest, lust, and demonstration of one's own powers all play a part, such a relationship loses its potential to excite after a period of time, and partners seek others who hold greater promise of gratification.

To say that sexual intercourse comprises one aspect of the heterosexual love relationship is not to discount the importance of the physical aspects of the love relationship, but rather to suggest that it is not, as is sometimes supposed, the major issue of the relationship. The physical aspects of the love relationship between husband and wife provide the opportunity for each partner to contribute to the gratification of the other. The sexual component of the love relationship is one in which mutual concern, sensitivity, and affection result in the merging of both the psychological and the physical selves. It has been said that sexual incompatibility is a major cause of marital discord. Since sexual incompatibility is usually a sign that one or both of the individuals are unable to demonstrate the maturity required by the love relationship, the mere perfecting of sexual techniques is for most persons an inadequate solution to marital difficulties.

HOMOSEXUAL LOVE RELATIONSHIPS

Love relationships may develop between persons who, as a result of their identifications during childhood, are sexually aroused by members of their own sex. It must, of course, be noted here, as in the case of the heterosexual relationship, that the defining characteristic of love relationships is not found in sexual activity per se. For the homosexual as for the heterosexual, the degree of gratification received through the contribution to the partner's development constitutes the decisive determinant of the love relationship. Because the homosexual may have unusual difficulties for both psychological and social reasons in many interpersonal experiences, including love relationships, some additional information is provided here about the homosexual.

Social and psychological problems confronting the homosexual are frequently compounded by society's failure to provide the assistance he requires. In place of treatment, such persons may be punished and ostracized for transgressing the moral codes of the community and for behaving in ways not in keeping with role expectations. The topic of homosexuality evokes such strong antipathies and raises so much anxiety that its open discussion rarely occurs. As a consequence, the erroneous belief persists that homosexuals are all child molesters or drug addicts and are given to wearing the clothes or adopting the mannerisms of the opposite sex.

The view is often expressed that all individuals have some characteristics associated with the opposite sex. If women are characterized as sensitive and sympathetic, it can be expected that men also will show such characteristics. Sometimes this point is extended to suggest that both men and women have greater capacities to respond physically to members of their own sex than is generally supposed. That there may be a degree of latent (unexpressed) homosexuality in many persons who usually fulfill heterosexual roles is given some support by the behaviors of individuals who are restricted by outside forces to association with members of their own sex. In sexually segregated situations, such as prisons, residential schools, or remote service outposts, where there is minimal contact with members of the opposite sex, the incidence of homosexual behavior is higher than in nonsegregated situations.

The person whose sexual identification is confused or whose identification is with the opposite sex is apt to experience considerable difficulty in both his intrapersonal and his interpersonal relationships. In metropolitan areas such individuals may drift into relationships with other homosexuals and become members of small and highly self-contained segments of the community. They confine their social relationships to others like themselves, and their subculture takes on many of the characteristics of other minority groups. Although their interpersonal relationships are limited, they may feel a greater degree of relatedness than is possible for the person whose homosexual tendencies necessitate his isolation from other persons.

Homosexuals may experience profound feelings of guilt, unworthiness, and depression. They may feel morally corrupt even though they are able to control their impulses toward members of their own sex. In social situations they may feel called upon to fill roles that they are emotionally unable to do; they may date and have relationships with the opposite sex in their efforts to conform to social expectations. They may be deeply troubled by their inability to respond emotionally, and may become disturbed when their partners make affectionate overtures toward them. Emotional reactions of revulsion, panic, or acute anxiety may occur, and eventually the individual may avoid relationships with members of the opposite sex, or may engage only in those that offer little possibility for emotional involvement.

The Person Who Possesses the Ability to Love

The person who is able to love possesses the characteristics of intrapersonal development that will be described in detail in Chapter 12. Warmth and spontaneity characterize the interpersonal relationships of the individuals who are able to give and receive affection, but such characteristics are not necessarily evident in all interpersonal contacts of the individual, since they are more than affectations or mannerisms; they are reflections of the ways the individual feels toward those with whom he has developed close and meaningful relationships, and he can be identified by the behaviors he shows in these relationships.

The person who approaches a high level of psychological development can give and receive affection; he is able to attend to the needs and wishes of others and to perceive them clearly. He is able to relate to others in ways that reflect his respect for them and for himself. Fundamental to the ability to love are those psychological factors that account for self-esteem and self-respect. Erich Fromm has pointed out that before an individual can love others, he must be able to love himself. Contrary to popular opinion, to love oneself is not selfish, conceited, or egotistical. If the individual continually devalues himself, how can he value others? If he cannot accept his own strengths and weaknesses, how can he accept those of his associates? If the selfish person esteemed and respected himself, he would not need to be continually defensive and protective of his own interests. And because he is so preoccupied with his own needs, he can only take from others without being truly able to give. To be capable of loving oneself, as Fromm uses the term, implies a regard for oneself as a human being and the possession of a sense of self-value and importance. Those who love themselves have little need to "prove" their worth, value, or importance in their relations with others; they do not have to impress, manipulate, or control other people. They do not deceive themselves or others as to their significance, nor do they use other people in achieving status or their own ends. The person who loves himself respects his own integrity as a human being, so he has no need to violate the integrity of any other person; he is able to respect the rights and dignity of his fellow men while at the same time asserting his own rights and dignity.

The individual who possesses the ability to love is able to focus his attention upon the needs, wishes, and feelings of others. This implies that he is sufficiently free of preoccupations with himself to be able to turn his energies toward others. He can be interested, concerned, curious, and attentive in his relationships with other persons, for he has the available energy to do so.

To persons who are chronically in a state of intrapsychic conflict, little energy is available for love relationships. When they almost continually direct this energy toward themselves, to enhance their self-esteem, they may be described as narcissistic. The psychological concept of narcissism was taken by Freud from the Greek myth of Narcissus, whose indifference to the feelings of others and whose rapturous self-admiration led the gods to turn him into the flower that bears his name. Persons who are narcissistic to a marked degree cannot attend to the feelings, wishes, or needs of others, because their psychological development has been retarded; they can turn their attention to other people only when they hope to gain something for themselves. It is apparent that such persons are quite different from those characterized previously as having self-confidence and self-respect.

In addition to the intrapsychic conflicts that sap an individual's energy and cause him to be preoccupied with his own needs, defenses (denial, projection, rationalization) that function to protect against anxiety also can reduce his ability to turn his attention toward other people and can distort the way he perceives them. The individual who is able to love can perceive others realistically; he sees them neither as malevolent or depraved beings nor as beneficent or saintly creatures, but as individuals with the strengths and weaknesses of human beings. He can meet and face people as they are, for he has no need to impute to them his own unattainable wishes or intolerable impulses. His perceptions of people are such that he can meet and form his judgments of them on the basis of observation rather than of prejudice or stereotype. He does not have to fear the wishes and motives of others, nor does he have to misperceive them.

In addition to his being aware and perceptive of others, the person who is able to love can be responsive to them; he allows others to be themselves and to find self-fulfillment in their own ways, for he has no need to make people over in his own image. He needs neither to dominate nor to submit in relationships; he is neither sadistic nor masochistic. He has no need to punish people, and he does not enjoy seeing them suffer. He does not have the need to be punished in order to feel that he is gaining his maximum gratification. He is not manipulative or seductive in his relationships, because he has no need to demonstrate his power by getting others to do what he wants nor does he feel that he must always comply with what others want from him.

Finally, and perhaps most important, the person who has the capacity to enter a love relationship is able to give and to receive affection easily and without being self-conscious. He is able to respond to other persons readily and naturally and is neither ashamed nor embarrassed by the demonstration of his or their feelings. He views his own feelings as being a natural product of being human; he is not afraid of them nor does he need to exploit them. When he receives affection, he does so with pleasure and does not feel that he is unworthy or that the affection was received "under false pretenses." When he gives or receives affection, he is able to do so in ways that embarrass and humiliate neither donor nor recipient.

Such a person has his feelings available to him. Since he does not repress or deny his own emotional experiences, he is aware of how he feels toward other persons. In the process of giving or receiving affection, he is not threatened or frightened when his emotional impulses are activated to the point of requiring either direct expression or control. In such situations he has no need to withdraw by running away or denying the significance the experience has for him. Erikson's point (4) that variation exists in the degree to which persons approach the ideal state of development implied in the preceding pages is worth noting.

> Individuals will vary in the degree of intensity, depth, richness, and fulfillment they experience from loving another person. The variations reflect differences in the development of the intrapsychic processes as a result of a person's interaction with his social environment. The stronger the ego and the less intrapsychic conflict, the greater an individual's ability to love himself, and thus to receive

as well as give love spontaneously, appropriately, and without self-consciousness. The stronger the ego the less the fear of loss of ego through abandoning oneself to others.

MARRIAGE

The young adult inevitably either marries or considers marriage. Such considerations are usually in the context of a specific relationship with a specific person and are viewed in terms of the individual's needs and his feelings for and response to a member of the opposite sex. Although a subsequent section will focus upon the factors involved in an individual's deliberations about questions of when and whom to marry, it is necessary first to note that marriage may be viewed not only as an intimate personal love relationship, but also as a social institution and as conferring a highly valued status.

As a social and legal institution, there are laws pertaining to entry into a state of marriage and to its dissolution. For example, many states require that individuals not only have a license in order to wed but that they submit medical certificates attesting to their freedom from venereal disease. Many states further require a waiting interval between the issuance of the marriage license and the actual performance of the ceremony. Society takes such measures to increase the probability that the resulting family unit will survive and that the children born in such a family will have its protection and not become dependent upon the community. In part, and for similar reasons, society discourages divorce. The legalized aspects of marriage reflect the value that is placed upon marriage, a value partly derived from tradition and religion and partly from awareness of the society's need for stable family units within which children can have both parents available to them. Traditional aspects of the social conventions pertaining to marriage are well known; the ceremony itself, the wedding reception, and the roles of best man and bridesmaids do not have to be elaborated here. It is necessary merely to underline the point that these conventions are part of the ritual relating to marriage as an institution.

In our culture, marriage is monogamous. One man is married to one woman, and the nuclear family structure consisting of the husband, his wife, and their children is typical, even if relatives of the husband or wife, such as aged parents, sometimes live in the house and play a part in the family affairs. Monogamy and the nuclear family, however, are not as universal as is sometimes assumed, nor are they inherent products of the biological relationship of man and woman. In some societies one man may have several wives (polygyny), and in other societies one woman may have several husbands (polyandry), all of whom may live within the family and share the same shelter.

However, although the form of the family structure may differ from society to society, it exists in all societies and is essential for the care of children. The monogamous form carries with it the expectation that the man and woman will live together and provide for their children. The incidence of divorce and marital unhappiness in our society is great, but persons contemplating marriage expect that their relationship will be a permanent one. In addition to the legal restrictions mentioned above, this expectation is further enforced by its strong support and endorsement from the Protestant and Jewish religions and by the Catholic church's prohibition of divorce. Within the culture, divorced persons are frequently questioned and criticized, or it may be whispered that they are perverse or licentious in behavior.

This emphasis upon the preservation of the family places a high premium upon making the correct decision as to whom to marry. In our society this decision is left to the two persons who will enter into the relationship, unless they are underage. The custom of allowing young people to decide for themselves whom they will marry without formal interference is by no means universal. In other societies such decisions are made by parents, often in consultation with marriage brokers. Considerations of class position, status, health, family background, or dowry often enter into evaluations of marriage suitability and determine the arrangements. How the individuals feel toward each other and the emotional commitments that they have to others may be considered unimportant or even irrelevant.

In some societies in which individuals are permitted to decide for themselves whom they will marry, the available choices are rigorously limited to persons with similar social positions, background, and religion. Aside from some laws prohibiting racial intermarriage, in our society there are few such legal restrictions, and it is not unusual for persons of different religious faiths to marry or for persons to "fall in love" who have been reared in very different traditions, with different educational experiences and values. Considerations that enter into decisions regarding whom to marry are far less determined by tradition than is the case in cultures where class lines and family "place" are more rigidly defined.

When persons marry who differ in ethnic identification, educational level, cultural background, political affiliation, and economic status, special problems can be expected to occur. These problems may range from those of a seemingly trivial nature, such as the emphasis to be placed upon having a neat and clean house, to more serious issues such as where to live, how to distribute the family income, whom to befriend, and how to raise the children.

Marriage not only represents a valued social institution in our culture, it also confers a valued status upon its members. The roles of husband and wife carry a degree of prestige and are a source of self-esteem to the individuals who have "achieved" such statuses. Although one out of ten men and at least one out of every seven girls in our society will never marry, both the expectation and the hope of most men and women is that they will marry and remain married. The psychological problem of the unmarried in our society is a serious one. It is, for example, known that men tend to die at an earlier age than women, that men traditionally marry women who are somewhat younger than themselves, and that the estimated number of women in our population who have never married or who are presently divorced or widowed runs as high as eight million (9). Many individuals are therefore bound to experience disappointment with respect to a major goal in their lives, and the statistics that exhibit higher rates of suicide, alcoholism, and earlier deaths among both single men and single women are of concern to society.

Within the culture and at various points in the individual's development, the idea of the worth and value of marriage is reinforced in many ways. Young people hear stereotyped labels, such as "old maid." Parents often become anxious when their children do not "date" and subtly communicate their anxiety, frequently nonverbally. One's marital status sometimes is a consideration in a job promotion and advertisers attempt to sell soap, deodorant, mouthwash, and hair oil by associating them with one's attractiveness to the opposite sex. The prospect of remaining unmarried, even for the individual who does so as a matter of personal choice, can evoke anxiety and fear. For many persons, the prospect of living one's life alone without the guarantee of physical and psychological closeness to another is depressing.

The situation for an unmarried woman is more difficult both psychologically and socially than for a single man. According to the mores of our culture, the woman's role is a passive one; the man is expected to take the initiative in the relationships between the sexes. A difficult dilemma is posed for the unmarried woman; she faces the frustration resulting from passively hoping that she will be noticed by men who will then make the proper social overtures to her. If she takes too active a course, she risks social disapproval for taking the initiative, risks the disapproval of the man or men she hopes to impress, and, most importantly, risks her own disapproval of herself for violating a deeply ingrained social rule of the game of man-woman relationships. Some women, often with great subtlety, successfully interest men through appearances and behaviors that are carefully planned and carried out for the purpose of taking the initiative without appearing to do so. Such maneuverings are not always successful, however, and for many women, the duplicity and the skills required are so alien to their own concepts of proper role behavior that they cannot engage in this form of competition.

Not only does the unmarried woman frequently have personal feelings of devaluation and of being unfulfilled and deprived of the opportunity for motherhood, but our society tends to reinforce such devaluation. Rarely is it assumed that the unmarried woman has chosen to remain single because she has not found a man with whom she can participate in a love relationship as described in the previous section. Jokes that feature the spinster lady or the old maid reflect this devaluation of the role of the unmarried woman. Thus, for many women, attracting a husband constitutes a signal achievement, a mark of feminine adequacy, and a public statement that social expectations have been fulfilled. That single men and women encounter these difficulties should not lead us to think that they are denied the possibility for meaningful relationships with others, challenging work, or full and rewarding lives.

The high positive regard afforded those who marry does not stem completely from the fact that marriage as an institution fulfills a special social function and hence may be valued as being "good" for the society. Rather, the value attached to marriage by the individual is a very personal matter. It assumes some degree of desirability as a personal objective because as a status it is valued by most persons in our society. The psychological significance the individual attaches to the state of being married will depend on many factors, including his sources of self-esteem. For the person to whom marriage is primarily a means of enhancing self-esteem the always difficult choice of the right person to marry is even more difficult. The selection of the proper marital partner even when the person is not driven to marriage as a means of satisfying self-esteem needs is a complex and difficult process. As previously noted, in this culture this significant decision is made by the persons involved. While in some societies the couples would have been matched on the basis of background and interests, and with the active participation of the parents, here they are responsible for making their own decisions, mainly in terms of their physical reactions to, perceptions of, each other. The possibilities of distortions of the "loved one" that have been cited, along with lack of clarity concerning the marital roles and the absence of psychological readiness for mutual love relationships, account for the fact that many marriages turn out to be something quite different from the ideal union the couples dreamed of during their courtship.

During the period immediately following the Second World War, there was one divorce for every three marriages. Although the outlook for those presently marrying is somewhat less depressing, it must be noted that there are many marriage failures which never end in divorce, and these failures are defined in psychological rather than in legal or sociological terms. In this sense, a marriage fails if the relationship does not fulfill the criteria of a love relationship between husband and wife. Such a marriage may be a failure from its beginning, although it never ends in divorce, and the structure of the family may be preserved until the relationship is ended by the death of one of the members.

The extent of divorce and marital unhappiness means that their causes are worthy subjects for investigation. Although numerous studies have been undertaken, it is difficult to apply their results to any particular couple contemplating marriage, because there are many cases that are contrary to the general findings. Furthermore, marriage involves two persons and the nature of this relationship depends upon the level of development of the individual personalities and their unique interaction.

Psychological studies of marital happiness support the general statement that individuals who are reasonably capable of loving, as it has been defined in this chapter, will have successful marital relationships. Studies also have indicated that the couple's chances for a successful marriage are best when their social, educational, and class backgrounds are similar. Differences of religion and national origin have been found to be related to marital discord, providing a context in which hostility toward the mate can be expressed. The attitudes toward the marriage held by the couple's parents, the degree of happiness the couple experienced as children, and the success of the parents' marriages have all been found to be related to marital happiness. Also, persons who are dissatisfied with their sex roles are less successful in their marriages than those who express satisfaction with them.

For the person contemplating marriage who is ambivalent about his potential partner, the reports of studies such as those cited above often contribute to doubts and confusion. One research finding that does have considerable relevance for the person contemplating marriage, however, related the success of the marriage to the length of time the individuals were acquainted prior to marriage (2). It was found that individuals who knew one another for considerable periods of time were more apt to have successful marriages than those whose period of acquaintanceship was short. These data indicate that the better two people know each other, the less the likelihood that they will be disappointed or surprised at the behaviors and attitudes of their mates after marriage. During short periods of courtship it is possible to show only one's "good side," but this becomes more difficult over longer periods of time. Heyns (5) has noted that a person should not enter marriage hoping that the partner can be reformed, or that defects in his character can be corrected. It is likely that traits and characteristics which are found irritating and obnoxious to the partner before marriage will not only continue but will seem more unpleasant following marriage.

PARENT-CHILD LOVE

For persons who marry and who possess the ability to enter into the heterosexual love relationship as it has been described, marriage offers one of the greatest opportunities for self-fulfillment in human relationship. With the advent of children, the opportunities for gratifications through contributions to the development of another are extended, the opportunity for love is broadened, and the base for the husband-wife relationship deepens.

The birth of the first child presents young parents with new stresses and new opportunities for gratification. Much has been written of the stresses: the sleepless nights, the endless diaper changes, the constant vigilance and attention to the needs of the infant. Although the gratifications of parenthood have been eulogized in sentimental fashion, usually by individuals who are observers of the parent-child relationship rather than participants, the basic relationship between the parents' activity during this period and what has been termed the love relationship has probably been given insufficient attention.

Before describing parent-child love, it must be recalled that the needs of the infant are ever present; they cannot be delayed or postponed, and they are often irrational and incomprehensible to the parent. Infants do not take into account the needs of their parents for rest, tranquility, and time for each other, and their desire for some social life outside the home. For the young couple attempting to establish themselves economically and to adapt to the marital relationship and its roles and responsibilities, the birth of the first child is an event of great significance, which will markedly influence the pattern of their lives and alter the character of their relationship.

In parent-child relationships, the parent's unconditional love is required, for he must give of his time, his energy, and himself without opportunity for immediate gratification, sometimes even without the opportunity for future gratification. He is called upon to perform as a parent because he has become a parent. The parent-child relationship

about who he is, what he represents to others, and what he wishes to become. He employs more effective defenses and mastery mechanisms, and he is less often enmeshed in struggles with his parents and other authority figures.

Although they continue to cause him some concern and anxiety, sexual and aggressive impulses have generally become sufficiently integrated within his total personality to be controlled, directed, and sublimated. While providing him with gratifications, the outlets he has found for these impulses will tend to be appropriate to his situation and will not jeopardize his safety, and like the controls and defenses he employs, they tend to reflect his increased capacity for coping with his environment. His increased ego functioning is reflected also in the skills he has learned that relate to people as well as to work, in the knowledge he has acquired about others as well as about himself and in his own capabilities. Since his own values and superego standards have become clarified, the ego and superego processes are now in more harmonious balance with the primitive and impulsive aspects of his personality than they were in adolescence.

Although functioning at a higher level of intellectual and physical efficiency and with a greater degree of stability, the individual's specific modes of response to adult roles will depend upon the nature of his personality integration and self-concepts. The generalization we have just made concerning his personality status can be supplemented by another pertaining to the pattern of events of special significance in the lives of young adults. Such generalizations, of course, may not apply to many persons.

The beginning of the adult years finds about half the high school graduates of the nation in some form of advanced training. For those pursuing a professional career, one that requires graduate training beyond the four-year college program, stresses from several sources may complicate their lives. Pressure to perform well, to secure the grades and recommendations required to enter graduate school, may be felt, along with decisions about whether to marry or to defer such plans until closer to the completion of training. For those whose plans are still indefinite—and a large percentage of college students either have not selected a major or have made only a tentative choice—the usual questions of career will become of increasing importance as the end of their college program approaches. Often the issue of motivation for study and the question "Why am I here?" become important to the college student who is unable to apply himself to his studies. In such instances his academic courses will have little significance or relevance to the issues that concern him in his daily life. Studying may seem to consist of memorizing dull facts in order to be able to pass an examination that, once out of the way, is soon forgotten. His teachers are often far removed from him and even if they are enthusiastic about their courses, they still may fail to communicate their enthusiasm to him.

Virtually all young adults eventually come to some decision about a career, whether it be to complete the training already begun or to go immediately into the labor market. When they do decide, they will find varying degrees of gratification in their work, depending upon the level of their ability and the opportunities available to them. In general, however, the pattern of gratifications for the unskilled worker can be expected to be somewhat different from the individual who, by virtue of a college education, is able to enter the "white collar" ranks. Not only do professional and managerial workers (including the self-employed) indicate a greater degree of satisfaction with their jobs than do manual workers, but they express different goals for themselves in relation to their work. The professional and managerial groups state that they want opportunity for self-expression, independence, and interesting experiences in their work activity, while the manual worker group more frequently cites security and independence as being important to them (11).

Depending upon the nature of the work performed, the individual will have different degrees of opportunity for gratifications intrinsic to the work. Thus the instrumental function of work as a means to valuable ends may be part of a pattern related to the extent to which the individual has invested of himself in preparation for his job, as well as to the nature of the work itself. Young adults will be concerned about their "future" and the opportunities related to advancement, and the "blind alley" job will hold little appeal even to those who see their work only as an instrument whereby they can achieve other ends.

Related to questions about the future prospects of the individual's work, the income he is able to command, and his financial outlook are questions about marriage, having a family, settling down, and achieving the gratifications derived from a continuing and deep emotional commitment to another person. These decisions are frequently tied to the wage earner's income. A person entering a profession that requires many years of graduate study, for example, must decide whether to marry during his training period. If he does so, the would-be physician or research scientist begins his married life under the additional stresses imposed by the rigors of his training and his limited finances.

Even in the best of situations, marriage imposes upon both husband and wife many responsibilities for which they will be only partially prepared. For some, marriage affords opportunities chiefly for self-gratification, but since the marital relationship also provides many opportunities for each partner to express his concern for the other and to experience the quality of gratification achieved through contributing to the satisfaction of another, it may gradually become the type of heterosexual love relationship we have described.

In the early years of marriage, most men and women afford their partners more revealing pictures of their personal selves than are offered to any others with whom they maintain adult relationships. This self-revelation includes the sharing of hopes and plans and the communication of attitudes and thoughts. It occurs in the process of living intimately with another person. Thus the weaknesses and limitations that may not be apparent to the more casual observer are revealed to the marriage partner.

Discovery of the partner's weaknesses can be reacted to by denying them, by giving them great emphasis, or by using them to manipulate or to hurt the partner during moments of anger. Depending upon the level of his psychological development and the patterns of his previous experience, the person who cannot hide such weaknesses from his partner may employ various measures for protecting his self-esteem. Face-saving mechanisms may run the gamut from projection to rationalization, but for the person who accepts his own limitations and his partner's knowledge of them, the gratifications derived from fully sharing experience and self with another provide a richness and meaning to life that is otherwise unattainable.

Summary

Love can characterize many relationships; the love of a parent for a child; the love of friends; the love of a man and a woman. Too often in our culture the meaning of love is equated with sexuality. Such a restricted view is blind to the fact that in its general sense loving is an active process in which the loving person achieves his own personal fulfillment and deepest sense of gratification through his contributions to the self-fulfillment and gratification of another. It has as its central characteristic the giving of one's energy, time, and emotional commitment —the giving of oneself. The person who is able to love has progressed from earlier stages of development in which his needs for dependency were predominant to a stage in which he is concerned about others and able to care for them.

The love relationship may have a sexual component, as in the case of the heterosexual love relationship, or it may lack an overt sexual component as in the case of friendship. Loving is an active process that requires many abilities. It is not, as is sometimes supposed, a state one "falls" into, nor is it a passive process, as suggested by the term "being in love."

Dissatisfactions with marriage (reflected, in part, by high divorce rates) can be attributed to the inability of one or both partners to enter into love relationships. Insofar as the partners possess the ability to love, their relationship is characterized by mutual concern, acceptance of the other's integrity, and freedom from artificiality and the use of the partner as only a means to one's own gratification. The ideal expressed by this concept of the mutual love relationship is indeed high and for some may be unattainable.

During the young adult years, the various processes of the personality achieve a greater degree of consolidation and balance, and many of the adolescent conflicts diminish in intensity. The physical vigor and enthusiasm of the young adult serve him in good stead as he confronts the demands of this period and the stresses associated with the learning of new roles and responsibilities.

References

1. Archibald, K.   Quarrels in friendship: A theoretical model. M. A. Thesis, University of Illinois, Urbana, Ill., 1961.
2. Burgess, E. W., and Cottrell, L. S.   *Predicting Success or Failure in Marriage.* Englewood Cliffs, N.J.: Prentice-Hall, 1939.
3. English, O. S., and Pearson, G. H. J.   *Emotional Problems of Living.* New York: Norton, 1945.
4. Erikson, E. H.   *Childhood and Society.* New York: Norton, 1950.
5. Heyns, R. W.   *The Psychology of Personal Adjustment.* New York: Holt, 1958.
6. Nesbitt, M.   *Friendship, Love, and Values: A Technical Report.* Princeton, N.J.: Princeton University and Educational Testing Service, June, 1959.
7. Newcomb, T. M.   *The Acquaintance Process.* New York: Holt, 1961.
8. Newcomb, T. M.   The prediction of interpersonal attraction. *Amer. Psychologist,* 1956. *11,* 575–586.
9. Scheinfeld, A.   *Women and Men.* New York: Harcourt, 1944.
10. Sullivan, H. S.   *Conceptions of Modern Psychiatry.* Washington, D.C.: William Alanson White Psychiatric Foundation, 1947.
11. Thomas, L. G.   *The Occupational Structure and Education.* Englewood Cliffs, N.J.: Prentice-Hall, 1956.

Selected Readings

Becker, H., and Hill, R. L. (eds.)   *Family, Marriage and Parenthood* (ed. 2). Boston: Heath, 1955.
Fromm, E.   *Man for Himself.* New York: Holt, 1947.
Fromm, E.   *The Art of Loving.* New York: Harper, 1956.
Jacobson, P. H.   *American Marriage and Divorce.* New York: Holt, 1959.

11.

The Adult Years

The period of the adult years is arbitrarily defined as beginning sometime in the middle thirties and ending only with death. For purposes of convenience, this span of time, which often encompasses a period of forty or more years, will be divided into the middle years, the period between the middle thirties and the middle sixties, and the later years, the period after the mid-sixties. Such designations do not imply that the individual is noticeably different physically or socially after he makes a transition from one period to the next, for the aging process is gradual and its direct and indirect effects upon the individual, his self-concepts, and his skills and abilities are evident only over considerable time intervals.

The Middle Adult Years

By the time an individual reaches his late thirties and early forties many of the problems that had occupied his attention and absorbed his energies have been solved; partially resolved problems or those for which circumstances have not permitted solutions no longer hold the significance for him they once did. During the adult years he maintains a more harmonious relationship with himself. His intrapsychic processes are more stably balanced, he maintains deeper and more satisfactory relationships with others, and he approaches an optimal utilization of his skills and talents.

Many of the crises of earlier years exist for him now as indistinct memories. He may at moments recapture the intensity of emotion that at one time characterized his struggle to establish himself in his sex role, as a marital partner and parent, and as a worker. But for the most part his attentions are now directed toward the ongoing process of carrying out the responsibilities associated with the roles he has acquired. And it is in these activities, as he contributes to the development of others, that his own self-development reaches its furthest point. The energies previously bound up in his defense against anxiety and in the struggle to achieve his social and economic goals are now partially available to him as he deepens his patterns of interest and invests of himself in his family, his work, and his activities as a citizen.

Although the adult years are accompanied by a decline in physical prowess, the relationship of physique to psychological functioning is less pronounced than it is in childhood and adolescence, when changes in self-concept are often initiated or closely related to changes in the individual's physical status. The adult's response to his own body depends in large part on the extent of his psychological development and the sources of his self-esteem.

PHYSICAL CHANGES DURING THE MIDDLE YEARS

Our society has been characterized as one in which youth is highly valued. The attractiveness, strength, and virility of the young adult are considered the prerequisites of "the good life," and the changes that accompany aging are considered undesirable. Within our society the compensatory gains of experience and wisdom occurring with age are not valued as such, at least not by most persons. In many other cultures, age is respected and the physical attractiveness and vigor of youth are given a lesser value. Thus, many persons in our culture are concerned about whether they retain their youthful appearance and attempt to be as active and vigorous during their forties and fifties as they were during their twenties.

Although illness and disability increase with age, such increments are not abrupt. The body loses some of its resilience in recovering from damage or illness, and it has been estimated that for each five years of life, one can add a day to the period of recuperation from illness or disability. Visual acuity gradually declines, and there may be some slight losses in auditory efficiency, as well as in muscular strength, physical endurance, and general energy level. When persons of various ages are systematically tested and compared with reference to abilities likely to be affected by the passage of time, the most pronounced differences are found on tasks involving visual perception (23). As persons grow older, they also perform less well on tasks that may require them to organize unfamiliar events or experiences. In tasks requiring motor skills, such as hand-eye coordination, muscular activity, and speed of response, middle-aged persons perform somewhat less adequately than young adults. Again, it must be noted that the rate of loss of effectiveness is gradual and is even less than is "generally supposed" (19).

In a study of the effects of age upon motor skill, Welford (23) found that many of the results which demonstrated decline in motor performance did not stem from a decline in motor skill; that is, in physical strength, coordination, or muscular tonus, but rather from less effective methods of "sizing the situation up" or, to put it in psychological terms, of perceiving the nature of the task and the best approach to it. Welford also found that older persons can compensate for their declining abilities to such a degree that their performance level is unchanged, if they are given an opportunity to modify their approach to their work.

How well do older persons perform on tasks that involve physical strength? A study of industrial workers indicated that the decline in physical strength between the ages of twenty and sixty is very gradual. As a group, workers of sixty were capable of exerting physical strength that was only 16.5 percent below the average of the group of twenty-year-old workers (11).

These samples of the results of aging upon physical performance show that the changes occurring in physical proficiency are gradual and slight. In addition, considerable variation exists among individuals in their rates of decline. In general, however, losses in physical performance and in worker competence during these years are appreciably less than is generally supposed. The psychological impact upon sexual, intellectual, and social functioning of the physical changes that do occur must be considered in the light of the individual's psychological structure. Some persons will overreact to the loss of even moderate degrees of effectiveness.

SELF-PERCEPTION AND THE
SEXUAL ROLE

It was noted earlier that the sex role includes both a social and a physical set of expectations. The sex role for the woman, for example, places considerable emphasis upon physical attractiveness; for the male, upon strength and athletic prowess. In each instance many aspects of the culture have reinforced the equation of these characteristics with femininity and masculinity. For many persons who have accepted the "equation," such effects of aging as facial wrinkles, gray hair or baldness, and the accumulation of fat are considerable sources of concern. Maintenance of self-esteem by retaining a youthful appearance through dieting, using cosmetics, or resorting to surgery may constitute a major preoccupation for the individual who does not accept himself and whose sources of self-esteem are limited.

The equation of physical attractiveness with femininity and strength with masculinity is the result of certain assumptions about the individual's physical abilities to perform sexually. Such assumptions have little basis in fact, but this does not prevent their having profound psychological significance. Many persons value themselves, react to others, or are reacted to in terms of beliefs such as those equating the degree of sexual drive with appearance, or the ability of a woman to fulfill the role of a wife and mother with her resemblance to a glamorized Hollywood version of the female. The loss of youthful appearance does not necessarily mean that the individual has lost his sexual drive or his ability to respond sexually to a member of the opposite sex. Although the amount of drive that persons manifest does decline gradually with age, it is less rapid than is generally assumed and does not terminate for women, as is often believed, with the menopause.

The menopause, the "change of life" that marks the end of menstruation and of ability to conceive and bear children, usually occurs between the forty-fifth and fiftieth years. Along with the cessation of ovulation and the gradual atrophy of the uterus and mammary glands, women will sometimes experience vasomotor and neuromuscular symptoms. The woman's reactions to this physical discomfort may be considerably affected by the degree to which she psychologically responds to such changes as signaling an end to her chances of "being a woman" or to her self-valuation in terms of her child-bearing potential. Although some women are less interested in intercourse at this time, such a reaction is not physically but psychologically conditioned. For most women the sexual drive persists throughout the menopause and there is little stress or self-devaluation associated with the period. The woman's reaction to her change of life will depend upon her personality structure and the degree to which she has approached her optimal psychological development.

In men, the decline in sexual drive is gradual and there is no dramatic "change of life" at which the capacity to impregnate ceases. The psychological effects of the aging process are very variable, however, and men who engage in compulsive sexual activity to reassure themselves that their youth has not departed or that they are "as good" or "better than ever" are well known to psychologists and others who work with emotionally disturbed or psychologically ineffective persons.

LEARNING AND PERFORMANCE DURING THE ADULT YEARS

In addition to the individual's concern about physical and social powers during the middle adult years, there are several other issues that require consideration. These pertain to the abilities that are involved in learning new activities, in the utilization of talents, and in the various matters relating to the changing roles and responsibilities in the adult's family situation.

As indicated in previous chapters, the development of intelligence, as defined and measured by tests, has been a subject of considerable interest to psychologists. When different age groups are compared, these tests generally suggest that the highest order of functioning is achieved during the early twenties, and that the rate of decline is gradual following this peak period. In evaluating these results, however, it is necessary to remember that the test items often place a premium upon specific types of performances. When viewed in this fashion, it seems that the gradual decline can be better explained by the reduction in sensory proficiency, speed of response, and motor skill. The items involving the comprehension of principles, vocabulary, and arithmetic abilities show the least decline; furthermore, there is evidence suggesting that when individuals of above average intelligence are retested over the years, they show progressive gains in performance involving these kinds of abilities (2).

In one study comparing the performances of different ability groups, it was found that the relative positions of the groups never changed; that is, the group scoring highest on the initial tests still scored higher on a retest than the other groups (18). It was also noted that the seventy-year-old individuals who had postgraduate college training scored higher, on the average, than the twenty-year-olds who had only an elementary or high school education.

When we attempt to apply these general observations on the decline of intelligence with age, the person's initial level of ability is seen to have a considerable effect upon how he performs at any point in the age span; moreover, it must be remembered that the above results are based upon group performances; an individual's level of performance is not dictated by the performance of his group. One might question whether the findings mentioned suggest that persons in their middle years cannot learn new skills and extend their range of knowledge. Although this is a popular belief, there is considerable evidence to suggest that such a conclusion is not justified. As Anastasi has noted (1), one of the obstacles to comparing the learning of older persons with that of younger individuals has to do with the conditions under which the learning occurs. The motivational aspects of learning, the time available for learning, and the distractions to learning are different for young persons and adults. When the material to be learned can be related to former experience, the older person may have a special advantage. In stenography and typewriting, in learning Esperanto, or in university courses, the progress of older persons equals or sometimes even excels that of younger persons.

New learning that is contrary to what has been previously learned may present some special problems to the older person, not because of his age but rather because of the principle of interference or negative transfer. According to this principle, the previous learning impedes new learning to the extent to which there are elements common to each that require in the two instances separate and different associations. There is also evidence that the decline in rate of learning with age may be less for meaningful material than for material which has no logical meaning.

Lehman found that individuals of scientific and literary talent made their most significant contributions during their thirties (15). This does not necessarily mean that these individuals did not make significant contributions later in their lives or that there is a decline in creative ability; it may mean that the pressures of other responsibilities operate to prevent the demonstration of ability. In some fields, such as politics, Lehman's work indicates that on the basis of their experience and contacts, older persons in their fifties will be more likely to attract the public's attention and to be elected to public office than will men in their thirties. Thus, the demonstration of talent and ability will depend partially upon the field of activity as well as upon the level of ability and the individual's age.

Although research studies indicate that the individual's decline in abilities may be very gradual through the middle years, and that it does not in itself account for marked alterations in his behavior, the psychological effects of such changes for some persons may still constitute a significant issue. In some instances persons may perform better on some tasks than they did at an earlier age, yet their image of themselves may be that they are less adequate than previously.

The pattern of the individual's responses to aging will depend upon his personality structure and hence upon his previous experiences as well as upon situational factors. However, several points can be noted. Change in itself can provoke anxiety. When one has to modify well-established behavioral patterns, when one has to adapt to a new situation, the consequences of one's actions may not conform to the expectation, which is threatening to the self and thus a source of anxiety.

Although representing relatively minor changes in the individual's body or in his effective utilization of it, some of the changes occurring in the middle years may signal future difficulties that are of major significance to the person and his family. The construction worker who develops minor arthritis may be profoundly troubled by the possibility that this condition might progress to such a degree that he will be unable to earn his livelihood in his accustomed manner. For a teacher or an office worker, the same condition may be less disabling and less provocative of threat. But again, the actual threat resulting from loss of ability must be distinguished from the individual's response to expectations, projections of the future or, as is often the case, to the unresolved feelings of inadequacy that are activated by change.

CHANGES IN FAMILY ROLE AND RESPONSIBILITY

A significant source of change occurring during the middle years is to be found in the nature and quality of the individual's relationships and responsibilities involving the members of his family. The demands that he makes of them and that they, in turn, make of him are directly related to the point in their respective developmental patterns at which such demands occur. These relationships have as one feature the responsibilities of the husband or wife to each other and to their children, and as another, what is received by each member of the family unit from the others in the group.

Both the roles and the responsibilities of the family members spring from the functions the family serves. A study of 250 cultures (20) has led to the suggestion that four functions of the family are basic to social life: the sexual, the economic, the reproductive, and the educational. Although there may be variation in the manner in which these functions are served, and although familial units may differ considerably from one culture to the next, these functions are sufficiently identified with familial life as we know it throughout the world for their universality to be likely.

In some instances, such as the special social organization known as the kibbutz in Israel, there are patterns of parent-child responsibility markedly different to those in this culture (21). In the kibbutz, the economic and social life of the community is organized on a cooperative basis. Families, in the sense of individuals who live together as a unit under the same roof, have been replaced by a system in which the children are reared in their own houses (dormitories) and have special nurses and teachers to care for them. This does not mean that the children have no contact with their parents; they do and they show this by addressing them as "father" and "mother." It does indicate, however, that in the kibbutz the responsibility for socializing the child and for providing his education is entrusted primarily to special persons selected for their skill and training in these matters. Children may spend the evenings with their parents, both of whom work during the day, in the quarters their parents share, but the quarters are owned and provided by the kibbutz and are not planned to provide for the children's living with their parents. Even so, kibbutz children do have close relationships with their parents, the quality of these relationships depending upon the personalities of the parents as well as the organization of the community.

In a culture such as this, familial roles and responsibilities differ markedly from those found in our culture. Here it is anticipated that the children will live with their parents under the same roof and that parents will have the responsibility of supporting their children as well as of providing for their socialization and education. However, for the individual family member in our culture, there may be considerable variation in how the parental roles and responsibilities are carried out. Whether the father is dominant and the mother submissive, whether the father provides the economic support and the mother cares for the children, whether the mother is able to be nurturant and the father a source of strength to the children will depend upon their personalities.

The point in the life cycle achieved by the parents will also account for which set of role expectations is appropriate and possible in the light of the parents' personalities. Finally, special situational factors that affect the fortunes of the family can change the pattern of relationships. When the father is unemployed and the mother is forced to work, when there is chronic and severe illness of either parent, or when the family is broken by death or separation, the relationships among the members of the family are influenced in unpredictable ways. For our purposes, the focus will be upon those changes within the family structure that may have particular psychological significance to the adult and to his family. As the adult's children grow older, his responsibilities to care for them and to provide for their well being, education, and vocational training continue, but the specific form in which these responsibilities are carried out will differ as they proceed through infancy, childhood, and adolescence.

THE MOTHER'S CHANGING ROLE AND RESPONSIBILITIES

When her children are young the mother's role is well defined. Hers is the responsibility to care for them, to counsel with them, and to be alert to their needs. Although such demands upon the mother are at times almost overwhelming, partially because she does not usually have anyone available with whom she can equitably share them, such responsibilities bring gratifications. She is needed. Her efforts are recognized (or should be recognized), with the result that her children conform to the cultural expectations and that their behaviors and appearances reflect credit upon her. In addition to enjoying the recognition she receives through the attainments of her children, she is gratified by her awareness of the contributions she is making to their development. To some extent the mother loses opportunity for such gratifications as her children become older. As they become less dependent upon her and move out of the orbit of the home into the world of school and their peers, and eventually when she "loses" them to college, marriage, or the service, her feelings of esteem based upon the contribution she is making to their lives must lessen.

These feelings of no longer being needed or being important have been dramatized as reflecting the mother's reactions to the child's going away to college or as typifying the period when the child marries and the mother becomes peripheral to the family established by the child. However, such events only provide a context for the expression of feelings that develop and build throughout the adult years. After the child has entered elementary school, his increasing abilities to manage for himself, his interest in making his own decisions, and his struggles toward independence during adolescence make the parent's role increasingly superfluous. As her children go through their childhood and adolescent years, the parent becomes aware that they will be able to survive and manage without the assistance they required when small.

The awareness that they eventually will be capable of functioning independently will evoke various reactions within the parent. Even one whose psychological development has been of a high order and whose major gratifications have come through her contributions to the development of her child will feel twinges of loss and moments of nostalgia for the dependent child she once played with and cared for. Mothers whose psychological development was inadequate, whose children provided a means of bolstering self-esteem and were viewed as objects instrumental in satisfying needs for recognition, may adopt various behaviors and attitudes to retain the child, to forestall the feeling of loss by encouraging a continuation of the dependent relationship. When such is not possible, claims of being unappreciated are often heard. Sometimes the natural developmental process, during which the child asserts his independence, results in maternal attitudes of criticism, hostility, and rejection. The only way the child, who may now be an adult fulfilling the role of a worker or marital partner, can appease such a parent is through efforts at capitulation. Such efforts cannot succeed, because they run counter to the child's needs and fail to provide the parent with what is required: the resolution of the intrapsychic conflict that gave rise to the insatiable need for retaining the child as a means of protecting against the anxiety associated with change, loss, or loneliness.

Interests Outside the Home

Many women in their middle forties whose lives have been devoted to their children have not developed the community interests, contacts, or resources that could afford them with the means of fulfilling their need for creative activity. Neither have they had the academic and professional training commensurate with their abilities. For example, although 30 percent of undergraduate college degrees awarded go to women, less than 10 percent of graduate degrees go to them. One interpretation is that the careers of women of ability and talent are interrupted by marriage; at a later time such women find themselves unprepared for the work or activity in which they were once interested. At the point in their lives when it might be possible for them to invest energy and time in work they lack the requisite training and experience to do so; consequently many women find activities either beneath their levels of ability or outside the range of their major interest.

At an age when the personality has become less flexible, when change in established patterns of activity is resisted and is apt to be anxiety provoking, women may be confronted with the necessity of finding something to do with themselves and their time. This developmental crisis sometimes coincides with the menopause, and the physical and psychological reactions to the change can accentuate feelings of loss, not only of the woman's children but also of her feelings of significance and of womanhood. Some women of this age group find comfort in associations with others who are in the same situation and devote themselves to various social rituals (afternoon bridge clubs) that stave off the sense of uselessness and the feelings of isolation that envelop them when they are alone. Needless to say, such activities offer little opportunity for gratification, and they tend only to reinforce the bitterness felt. Since they do not often contribute to the development of others and are not socially recognized as worthwhile, most women will find them basically dissatisfying, although they are unaware of the reasons.

The stereotype of the middle-aged woman devoted to her bridge and "social" clubs is, like all stereotypes, a caricature. For most women whose children are grown, work outside the home provides an outlet for their energies and is a constructive means of satisfying needs for recognition and creative activity. Work performed either voluntarily or for salary affords women an opportunity to contribute to the development of others while enhancing their own range of knowledge and experience. Volunteer work in hospitals, schools, and community agencies provides women (and men) with the sense of positive accomplishment that is derived from performing significant service.

In recent years an increasing number of women have become involved in local community affairs and political life. In their roles as school board trustees and as members of the town council and city planning commissions they are able to devote the required time and energy for carrying out adequately the responsibilities of public office. For those women whose family responsibilities shunted aside the actualization of their artistic and creative interests, the middle years afford, in part, the time and freedom to develop the skills associated with those earlier interests. The opportunity to read, to study, and to participate in organizations such as the League of Women Voters provides satisfactions accompanying self-development and the extension of experience and awareness.

The Complex Role of the Working Mother

Although the preceding section describes the situation in which the mother's role is primarily that of housewife, for many women in this country there is the additional role of wage earner. When a mother whose children are in the preschool or school years accepts employment outside the home, the pattern of family relationships may change radically. In addition to the possibility that her working will threaten the father's status and prestige derived from his fulfilling the traditional role of wage earner, the mother's absence from the home can have a considerable impact upon her children. It may complicate the child's psychological development through the anxiety created by separations from her. Disturbances in the usual process of identification also can be anticipated when the mother does not fulfill the expected role. As Maccoby (17) points out:

Child training is made up of thousands of episodes in which an adult caretaker distracts a child from undesired activity or interests him in desired activity; physically stops or prevents an act; guides a child's early performance of a skill; punishes or rewards an action which the child carries out spontaneously; "reasons" with the child by labeling actions and events and their possible consequences clearly, so that the child will be able to recognize their recurrence and be able to act appropriately in the future.

Mothers who are on the scene all the time will differ widely in how they care for their children; when they are away part of the time, whether the child is better off will depend upon the nature of the relationship the child has with his mother and with the substitute mother. But whether the child is better off or not—a question which cannot be answered categorically—it is fairly evident that the child's life will become somewhat more complex because his care will be entrusted to more than one woman. The degree to which the caretaker respects the mother's authority, the similarity between her values and those of the mother, and the setting in which the care is provided all will influence the child's relationship with its mother.

One of the surprising observations reported earlier about kibbutz children was the degree of attachment that the natural parents had for their children, even though their association was limited. In this connection, there is a related issue pertaining to the degree to which the child is made anxious by separation from the mother. The effects of maternal deprivation on the child's development were noted in a previous chapter, and it might be reasonable to question whether the working mother who absents herself from her child is, in effect, depriving her child of affection.

Here the quality of the relationship between the mother and her child must be differentiated from the amount of time they spend together. There is no linear relationship between spending a great deal of time with one's child and the amount of affection that will be afforded him. In some instances, of course, the mother's motivation to seek outside employment may reflect dissatisfactions with her familial role and responsibility, and such dissatisfactions in turn relate to her intrapsychic integration, which makes it difficult for her to respond to her children with warmth and love.

An interesting study of the degree of anxiety that the mother's working may precipitate in her children is reported by Heinicke (14) in England. Two groups of two-year-olds were observed for three weeks. One group lived in a residential nursery, remaining there day and night; the other group were brought by their mothers in the morning to the day-care center and taken home in the evening. Although the children in both groups seemed equally distressed their first day, crying about the same amount and rather excessively, the day-care center children almost completely stopped crying for their parents during the three-week interval, while the residential children continued to do so. In addition, the residential nursery children were more hostile and seemingly less reassured when they did have contact with their parents. The findings of this study support the view that children who are separated from their mothers for long periods are apt to find such experiences more anxiety-provoking than children who are regularly "given over" to someone else while the mother works.

Working Mothers and Delinquency

The effects of the mother's working on delinquent behavior of boys was studied by the Gluecks (13). In this study, five hundred delinquent boys were compared to a group of nondelinquents. The two groups were similar with respect to intelligence, ethnic background, age, and economic status. The last factor is, of course, crucial when the effects of the mother's working are to be considered. It was found that both groups had about the same proportions of regularly working and nonworking mothers; thus, regular work by the mother does not seem to influence the likelihood of delinquent behavior in the son. There was, however, a significantly higher proportion of mothers of delinquent boys who worked occasionally. The most reasonable interpretation of these findings is provided by Maccoby (17), who suggests that "the emotionally disturbed and antisocial characteristics of the parents produced both a sporadic work pattern on the part of the mother and delinquent tendencies in the son."

Other studies that have attempted to assess the relationship between the work status of the mother and the social and psychological development of her children are difficult to interpret because it has been impossible to control accurately the economic status and the psychological development of the parents in comparing families with and without working mothers. The question of whether the mother's working is in itself a cause of disturbed psychological and social development cannot be answered, and the possibility must be considered that both her working and the emotional disturbance of the child have their origins in other issues involving the amount of tension within the household or the inadequate psychological development of one or both parents.

When mothers enter employment because of economic necessity or when they do so to fulfill needs that are not met at home, they may experience guilt. Our culture does not sanction the mother's turning over the care of her children to anyone else, despite the fact that a large percentage of mothers are gainfully employed. The extent to which such guilt presents a problem for the mother depends upon her intrapsychic integration. When her superego is essentially harsh and punitive and she is inclined to feel unworthy and inadequate in many of her relationships, working will provide a context for her to feel that she is also unworthy as a mother.

For the working mother, the husband and wife relationship is of considerable psychological significance. Again, the circumstances that lead to the mother's employment, the personalities of husband and wife, and the immediate situational factors must be considered in evaluating any specific family. In a general way it can be noted that the employment

of the wife will necessitate changes in the traditional roles of husband
and wife which, though not necessarily for the worse, are apt to complicate their lives.

In addition to these role changes, a change in the more subtle aspects
of familial relationships occurs when the mother is out of the home during her work periods; the father will probably have more direct contact
with his children and more direct responsibility for their physical care.
Such contact with the father may be beneficial or detrimental to the
children and to the father, depending upon the parents' capacity to
adapt to the changes in roles and the degree to which the father's self-
esteem is not jeopardized by the necessity of taking up responsibilities
that are usually assigned to the feminine role. Instances in which the
financial plight of the family necessitates the mother's working, or in
which the father, through illness or disability, cannot provide for the
family may precipitate a marked emotional reaction on his part that
relates to the loss of one of the richest sources of male self-esteem in
our society, his status as a worker and provider for his family, a status
intimately related to the content of the male sexual role.

It is important to note that the status of the male whose wife works
is not jeopardized by the fact that his wife works but rather by the
implication that he cannot fulfill the masculine role. Thus the circumstances that account for the wife's decision to work will be crucial to
the husband's reaction. At the present time there is much greater social
acceptance of wives working outside the home than had been the case.
In many cases the decision for the wife to work is agreed upon as best
for the family even though children may be quite young and the additional income not crucially needed. In such instances, when the wife
pursues her own career or when the decision reflects primarily the
recognition of her need for more varied experience than the role of
housewife permits, the family's interests are served as well or possibly
even better than if the mother were forced to remain at home.

THE FATHER'S CHANGING ROLE
AND RESPONSIBILITIES

While the social and psychological issues of the woman in her
middle adult years center about the home, family, and responsibilities to
her children, the male's focus of activity is split between his work situation and his family. Men have usually committed themselves by their
thirties to an occupation or style of vocational life. Although within a
particular occupation, such as salesman, they may change the organization
for which they work, their place of work, or even the products they sell,

their self-image still includes the constellation of characteristics of one who sells. With such commitment and with the experience accruing from practicing at one's work, the level of attainment during the thirties often rises, so that the economic status of the family improves and some of the concerns that were present during the early adult years disappear. The young couple who saved for the down payment on a home may be in the home a decade later.

For many men, however, achievement during these most productive years may fail to bring them the level of economic reward and the degree of recognition to which they had aspired. With his increasing psychological development, the adult who is forced by circumstances to modify or abandon the once cherished ambitions does so without despair or depression. It is characteristic of the life process that the progression toward higher levels of psychological development is marked by an increasing ability to confront oneself honestly. Thus, during the adult years the disappointments that are an inevitable product of life are accepted as such and the bitterness or vindictiveness that may have been characteristic of the person's response to frustration during an earlier period of his life is not at this stage as intense or disruptive.

During these years the adult acquires a more philosophic, less hurried attitude, and a greater awareness and appreciation of his family and friends. As the man finds his work less likely to bring him the fulfillment of his wishes, he may not only turn to his family for increased opportunities for gratification, but also extend the range and depth of his interests. Although studies of men during this period indicate a narrowing of interests, they also indicate that the interests that have been retained are likely to be engaged in more deeply.

Occupational Competition and the Older Man

The middle adult years are apt to bring greater economic achievement, but this period is not necessarily one of feeling economically secure. The arrival of younger men who are viewed as—and in many cases actually are—competitors presents both a perceived and a real threat to the man in his middle adult years, particularly one who has reached his mid-forties. The younger man is often perceived as vigorous, bright, and energetic by the older man and, in a derogatory vein, as being ingratiating to the boss, currying his good will by being a "yes man" or by "apple polishing." In addition, the older man is often threatened by the younger man's more recent advanced training and his technical proficiency. As new methods and procedures are introduced, the changes that occur in the work situation contribute to the man's sense of uncertainty and to doubts about his abilities and his capacity to cope with the requirements of his work situation.

These changes in the work situation impinge upon one of the characteristics of the aging process, the decreasing ability to reorganize concepts and principles and to shift one's mode of thinking. Thus, new routines are apt to be resisted by the older man, partly because learning new ways of doing things necessitates the investment of energy and effort, and partly because old learnings and old ways of perceiving and manipulating situations interfere with the required new learnings.

For some men, work during the middle adult years continues to offer expanding opportunities for the investment of their energy and time and for the enhancement of self-esteem. For these individuals, work and the creative activities related to it provide an avenue whereby their needs to feel in communion with others are well satisfied. For many other men, however, work is merely instrumental to the attainment of certain ends—an adequate income, for example. For these men, hobbies, fraternal organizations, friends, and their families become increasingly important to them.

The Father and His Children

The man in the family is typically viewed as playing a dominant role that includes the provision of economic necessities. By its very nature, such a responsibility requires that he spend a considerable part of his time away from the family. The amount of direct care he provides his children and the amount of direct responsibility he has for their guidance and supervision is usually considerably less than that provided by his wife. During the middle adult years the father's role as provider of the necessities of life for his family continues. Within the family, his involvement and investment of energy in his relationships with his children is probably at its high point during his children's infancies, when the demands upon his wife are considerable and may necessitate his sharing them with her. He will join them in outings and in activities around the house, and may sometimes become involved in their scout or athletic activities.

Through time, however, he can become increasingly distant from his children, and as they grow, he may at times resent the fact that he is not listened to with the respect that he feels his position as "head" of the household warrants. Because of his lack of closeness to his children, he is sometimes unclear about the details of their schooling and may not know how they spend their time or with whom they associate. This lack of knowledge places him at a disadvantage when they seek his advice or when their misbehavior commands his attention. Often fathers are called upon to discipline their children, and the mother will hope that the threat of his intervention will be frightening enough to stop the child's misbehavior.

While the father's relationships with his daughters often continue to be characterized by affection and attention, his contacts with his sons tend to change during their adolescence. Earlier they may have imitated him and sought his company and his assistance with their athletic and academic problems, but the relationship between the teenage boy and his father is often characterized by a struggle in which it seems to the latter that his will is being flouted and that he is being defied without reason. His son's behavior—especially his flare-ups—will seem irritating and unreasonable. In some cases the father, like the mother, will unconsciously evoke the boy's unacceptable social behavior in the course of satisfying his own repressed impulses, or he will attempt, in effect, to force him into a position of committing errors or getting into trouble in order to demonstrate the child's continued need for his assistance.

The father's strict surveillance of his adolescent daughter's social life can spring from fears about what may happen to her that reflect his recollections of his own impulses during adolescence. In some instances, severe restrictions upon the girl's freedoms, such as having to be home at a very early hour or give a strict account of all that occurred in her contacts with boys, have their origins in the father's incestuous wishes toward the daughter.

As he goes through his middle years, the father may commit himself progressively less and less to his work and to his family, so it is not surprising that during this period he often becomes active in professional organizations or in community affairs. He may take a part in the affairs of a service or fraternal organization, and his evenings "out with the boys" sometimes becomes a part of the family ritual as well as a family joke.

That such organizations provide him with the feeling of belonging to a club or group is easily recognized, as is the degree to which such activities contribute to his self-esteem. Some organizations make it a point to bestow this recognition through their rites and the offices members hold, offices that often require the wearing of special robes or the learning of special rituals. By being regularly scheduled, these activities also provide a continued ordering to the way he spends his time. Such regularity fits in well with the routines that he comes to value during this phase of his life. Service and fraternal organizations may also perform useful social services and thus provide him with gratifications from contributing to the welfare of others. During the middle adult years men will sometimes increase their interests in spectator sports and become more knowledgeable about their favorite athletic teams; they will identify with them to the extent that they are elated when they win and dejected when they lose.

As they may find less gratification in the development of their children during the middle years and become sexually less responsive to their wives, men may go through the experience of testing their masculinity by flirting with younger women and by "making passes" at those who attract them. Less overt expressions of their concerns about diminishing masculinity are fantasies and off-color and sexually provocative stories and jokes.

DIVORCE IN THE MIDDLE ADULT YEARS

Whether because the romantic aspects of the marriage relationship have dimmed, or because the demands of life have increased, or because the changing roles and responsibilities have contributed additional strains to the relationship, many couples are divorced during the middle adult years. It has been noted that "though our current [divorce] rate is far below what it was in 1946 and 1947, it is still more than twice what it was in 1900" (9). Thus, the impact of separation and divorce upon children and their parents represents a considerable social as well as psychological issue. In 1955, for example, 1.4 million persons (including children) were receiving some assistance from public agencies because of the absence of the father from the home for reasons other than his death.

The family problems occasioned by separation and divorce arise not only because a divorce has occurred, but also because of the psychological development of the individuals concerned, the tensions, conflicts, and conditions that have led to divorce. One aspect of the problem that represents an exception to this generalization, however, involves the complications arising for the individual because of his divorced status. (The reader will recall the discussion of this topic in the previous chapter.) Both men and women who divorce often remarry. "Half or more of those who divorce have at least average success in a remarriage" (4). The marriage rate of divorced women of thirty years of age is higher than that of any other group, regardless of past marital status. Perhaps part of the explanation of the high marriage rate among divorcees can be found in the social disapproval encountered by the divorced person. Part of the explanation also may lie in the divorced person's awareness of the value of companionship, with marriage being seen as a solution to feelings of isolation and loneliness. When children are involved, the divorced mother may want to provide a father to assist in their care.

Following a divorce, persons often experience a sense of personal inadequacy and guilt over the failure of their marriage; sometimes they are considerably shaken because the beliefs and perceptions they had held prior to and during the early period of their marriage have proved to be so wrong. If experienced by individuals whose self-esteem is low and whose ego processes fail to provide them with adequate defenses, such feelings may result in their avoidance of any intimate or close relationships with members of the opposite sex. When projection is a major mode of defense, the former partner will be blamed for all the difficulties and disappointments of the marriage. This bitterness may actually increase with time, in contrast to the usual course in which the partners come to view their marital experiences and their former perceptions of one another with greater objectivity. The emotional upheaval that accompanies the decision to divorce and the sense of loss that separation brings can cause most persons who have had such an experience to look at marriage in a less idealistic fashion than they did in their initial marital encounter. At the same time, they may be hesitant and cautious about committing themselves to a second marriage.

The divorced woman may be concerned over the passage of time. She feels, and correctly so, that her chances for remarriage diminish as she grows older. Her awareness of the values placed upon appearance and youthfulness by our culture increases her belief that she is at a competitive disadvantage with younger women. She must also contend with the fact that the number of eligible bachelors of her age group is considerably smaller than when she was in her early adult years, and that they are often interested in women who are younger than themselves.

For many persons the prospect of a future alone is depressing; consequently, marriage during the middle years—or in the case of divorce, remarriage—sometimes has a desperate and driven quality to it. On the other hand, marriages of persons at this time also may reflect their greater experience and their more realistic expectations of what can be expected from their marital partners. The chances of success of a marriage during this period, as in the early adult years, will depend upon the capacities of the individuals involved to engage in a reciprocal love relationship.

In addition to sharing some of the common concerns cited, the woman who has children from a previous marriage will be concerned about the relationships her children might have with a prospective father; she must evaluate the prospective father's ability to relate to her children and their willingness and readiness to relate to him. On the other hand, the man who is considering remarriage often has the financial responsibility for children by a former marriage; if he must also pay alimony, he may find himself in a poor economic position to assume the responsibilities of another family. From a man's standpoint, the economic aftermath of a divorce may be a source of frustration and a realistic obstacle to remarriage.

THE UNMARRIED PERSON IN HIS
MIDDLE ADULT YEARS

As was noted in Chapter 10, the status of the unmarried person in our culture is not an enviable one. The unmarried person who goes through his thirties and forties relies more and more upon the methods that he has developed for adapting to his single status. These methods range from commitment of energy and time to work, avocational activity, and the development of special talents and interests, to the acquisition of a special role in relation to one's relatives or friends. Some persons may, for example, actively play the role of the aunt or uncle—adopted or real—to their relatives' or friends' children. Certain fields of work offer individuals special opportunity to participate in the lives and development of other persons. Such activities are sometimes a partial substitute for one's own children and a marital partner. Nursing, teaching, and the medical and social service professions, in particular, provide such opportunities.

Often the unmarried adult in his middle years may develop a few significant and continuing relationships with friends of the same or opposite sex that have many of the characteristics and qualities of the love relationship, and in some instances are in fact love relationships. These relationships offer much to the individual who otherwise would have to experience the moving and deep human emotional experiences either through the lives of others or through the media of literature or the theater. Although the unmarried person's position in this society sounds bleak as it has been stated here, two considerations must be borne in mind in interpreting this section. The common assumption that any married person possesses the relationship which the unmarried person desires and lacks is to be avoided. Marriage is a legal and social form, but the quality of the personal relationship maintained in it is a psychological dimension. Many married persons may experience feelings of loneliness and lack of fulfillment not unlike those experienced by some unmarried persons. Finally, one must avoid the assumption that because the unmarried person's situation in this society is complex and difficult there is little opportunity for the single person to live a productive and gratifying life.

The Later Years

The second phase of the adult period of life is arbitrarily defined for our purposes as beginning in the individual's mid-sixties. Many businesses and industries make this the age of mandatory retirement, and sixty-five often identifies the beginning of the "aged" period in sociological discussions. From a psychological standpoint, however, it cannot be inferred that an individual will necessarily feel that he is an old person even though he has reached the age of 65. In one study (6), for example, only half the men and women interviewed who were between the ages of 80 and 84 considered themselves "old," and of those who were in their nineties, less than 40 percent thought of themselves as "aged."

Because of improved medical care and the control of certain contagious diseases, the proportion of our population in their later years is constantly increasing. "Since 1900, the population of the United States has doubled but the number of persons in the 45 to 65 age bracket has tripled while the number 65 years and older has quadrupled" (10). In 1900, there were three million persons over 65 living in this country, but by 1950, that age group had grown to fourteen million or 8 percent of our population. During that period, the life expectancy at birth increased from 49 to 68. At the beginning of it, one person out of every 25 was 65 or older; today, one out of every twelve persons is in this category (10).

As the proportion of citizens over sixty-five increases, the society is forced continually to examine its retirement regulations and the provisions made for housing and medical services for these older citizens. The social and political implications of this sizable segment of "senior" citizens in the adult population is, of course, considerable. Not only are legislative matters that directly affect this group (such as medical care for the aged) apt to evoke their political support, but the nation's political life in general will reflect their influence as their numbers increase.

Many communities have established housing and recreational and educational programs for older persons; however, as yet the role of the person over sixty-five in this society is not clearly defined. Linton, an eminent anthropologist, has commented (16) on the variability of treatment afforded the aged in various societies:

> In some cases they are relieved of all heavy labor and can settle back comfortably to live off their children. In others they perform most of the hard and monotonous tasks which do not require great physical strength, such as the gathering of firewood. In many societies the old women, in particular, take over most of the care of the younger children, leaving the younger women free to enjoy themselves. In some places the old are treated with consideration and respect; in others they are considered a useless encumbrance and removed as soon as they are incapable of heavy labor. In most

The return of the future!

There are some satisfactions that can accrue only in the later phases of life; among these, perhaps the most deeply rewarding comes from participation in the development of one's grandchildren. In the drama of successive generations the aging adult achieves a sense of linkage to the future in his closeness to the small child; once again he is significant to a growing and developing being, but the experience is much more than a reactivation of his experience with his own children. It possesses a mellowness, a depth, and a richness that is possible only because he has lived through much and can value the child as a child. He can see in the child innocence, promise, and hope.

Wayne Miller—Magnum

societies their advice is sought even when little attention is paid to their wishes . . .[1]

Within American society there is much variability in the life patterns of the aged. The very fortunate older person enjoys an assured place within his family and society. His wisdom and advice are respected. He feels needed, and in turn has his family and friends in whom he can confide his fears and hopes. He can bask in the achievements of his children and grandchildren. Hours of solitude are balanced by hours of companionship. He is able to enjoy life perhaps as never before and perceives this period of his life as one of contentment and joy. In less fortunate situations, an older person may be defeated by the problems of the aged. The decline in physical abilities, illness and disability, reduced economic level, loss of status within the family and as a worker, and increasing separation and isolation may complicate his life and contribute sources of frustration to the "golden years." Although these complications will be given attention in the pages that follow the reader is reminded that this stage of life has its joys and satisfactions as well as its sadness and frustrations. And as in earlier stages, the level of psychological development achieved contributes significantly to the quality of the life he leads.

The older person's role and responsibility within the family structure today are appreciably different from those of fifty years ago. At that time the family consisted of units larger than merely the husband, the wife, and their children. In many families of several generations ago, sons and daughters lived their married lives within the parental household or were sufficiently close to be more dependent upon their parents than is now the case. The senior members of the family retained their roles as heads of their households, and their assistance was sought by their children and grandchildren. They provided not only advice and guidance, but also attended to the needs of the newly arrived infants and participated in rearing their young grandchildren. Having been active in the affairs of the family for many years, the grandparents could be accommodated when circumstances necessitated their dependency upon their children, and they continued to have a "place" in the family.

In the present century, the family structure and the roles of aged parents are different, partly because persons marry earlier and tend to move away to establish their own homes and assume charge of their own households. Under these conditions grandparents may have minimal contact with their grown children or their grandchildren. If circumstances necessitate their moving into their children's household, they

---

[1] From Ralph Linton, *The Study of Man.* Copyright 1936, D. Appleton-Century Co., Inc. By permission of Appleton-Century-Crofts, Inc.

arrive as strangers whose place is poorly defined. The tragic complaint of the mother-in-law that "They don't let me help" reflects far more than a simple disagreement about the division of labor in the household. The modern family sometimes reacts with irritation and feelings of frustration to the grandparents' sudden entry into a functioning household and may perceive them as "set in their ways," bumbling, slow, and disapproving of the manner in which the children are being reared. In turn, the grandparents may feel that they are unwanted and unneeded, that the wisdom they have accumulated is rejected, and that they have no place where they belong or where they can go. The grandparents' awareness that they do not fit into the household intensifies the keenness with which they feel separated and isolated from the pattern of life they had enjoyed.

In other situations, grandparents who had not been physically close to their children or grandchildren, may, upon retirement, take up residence nearer their family or visit them more frequently and for longer periods of time than they had previously been able to do. Often the discovery of mutual respect and affection that is built upon the much earlier and different relationship of parent to child is a source of deep satisfaction to the parents and their adult sons and daughters. In their new relationship there is a depth of mutual understanding and appreciation for one another that the circumstances of their lives and roles had not previously permitted.

THE ROLE OF THE WORKER IN THE LATER YEARS

A central source of self-esteem, one that is related to the individual's concept of himself as a productive and contributing member of society, is his status as wage earner and worker. When this status shifts as a result of retirement from his work during his later years, an event of considerable psychological significance takes place. Contrary to the popular impression that everyone dreams of the days when he can retire, studies indicate that only a relatively small percentage of individuals withdraw from work voluntarily. Bernard notes (5) that "in a study by the Bureau of Old-age and Survivors Insurance, only 5 percent of retired persons were found to have retired voluntarily."

Despite the unwillingness of the worker to withdraw from his job, the conditions of the labor market and the development of pension and retirement programs are forcing an ever-increasing number of persons over the age of sixty-five to change their status to nonworker. In 1953, about 43 percent of the men over sixty-five years of age were working.

At that time they represented between 4 and 5 percent of the labor force. By 1975, however, it is estimated that the percentage of individuals sixty-five and over who will be working will have decreased to about 36 percent (5).

Although there is evidence that older workers have more difficulty than their younger associates in adopting new methods and procedures, they also demonstrate a greater concern with accuracy in their work and have a fund of experience upon which to draw that younger workers lack. In view of this situation, there appears to be considerable justification for the feelings that many older workers have about "being put out to pasture" when they could still perform useful services for their organizations. Although the compulsory retirement age of sixty-five is generally adhered to, there are some notable exceptions—some companies and institutions evaluate the person's performance and base retirement on criteria other than age. One well-known West Coast school of law has attracted national attention by its policy of employing distinguished professors *after* their retirement from the faculties of other law schools.

The significance of work to the individual has been shown to be far more than economic, and the other purposes that it serves are keenly missed even by the worker who for years looked forward to retirement as a time when he could do what he wanted. Although there is a heightened interest in hobbies during the later years, for many persons such activities may be unsatisfactory substitutes for the work that brought them into contact with others and that enabled them to feel productive. It seems doubtful that society will be able to devise systems that will fully protect the retired person from feeling this sting of separation. Preparation for retirement is not something the older worker carries on apart from all the rest of his life; rather, the breadth and the depth of his lifetime interests, the sources of his self-esteem, and the friendships he has available to him, all influence how he will react to retirement.

When the older person is forced to withdraw from work because of illness or disability, several additional stresses are experienced that also contribute to his feelings of isolation and separation. The impact of disability is felt economically and psychologically by individuals of all age levels but for the person in his later years it has special significance.

REACTIONS TO DISABILITY[2]

Blanket generalizations about the disabled, convenient as they may be, are apt to be in error by virtue of their oversimplifications.

[2] Adapted from L. S. Levine, The Impact of Disability, *J. Rehabilitation,* November–December 1959, pp. 10–12.

Many people assume that the greater the physical disability, the greater the psychological consequences of the disability, and some are convinced that specific disabling conditions produce specific psychological results. These popular beliefs are not supported by the available data. The impact experienced by each individual is related to the significance the disability possesses for him. This, in turn, will depend on the pattern of events in his life that have contributed to the values he holds, the way he perceives himself in relation to the rest of the world, and the form his reactions to stress take.

In fact, there are no simple psychological characterizations of the disabled that can be validly applied to all members of the group. The disabled share with the nondisabled hopes, fears, ideals, and superstitions; as a group they cannot be characterized as brave, or intelligent, or sensitive. A review of the research comparing the psychological and social characteristics of disabled and nondisabled persons only reinforces the impression that the range of human variability is great indeed. Such research reveals similarities in the social and psychological characteristics of disabled and nondisabled persons to be far more evident than their differences.

The factors known to be related to an individual's reactions to disability include his place in the economic and social milieu, the nature of his disability, the point at which it occurs in his life, the circumstances of its onset, the treatment procedures that are required, and the course and the prognosis of the disabling process.

Even though the adult's reaction to his disability is conditioned by the total experience he has accumulated during his lifetime, some general statements can be made about its impact. At first the individual's energies are mobilized and focused on his immediate hurt and on his uncertainties about his physical welfare. During this initial period the world is contained within the walls of his own skin, and it is only with the abatement of immediate pain that he becomes able to consider himself in relation to his surroundings. He may then worry about how the persons dependent upon him will manage, or he may become preoccupied with the question of why the fates had to deal him this particular blow. He begins to become aware, vaguely at first and then more clearly, that he has acquired a new status—one that he did not ask for and does not want and one which he did not and does not value.

The disabled person is forced to modify his image of himself. This image includes not only what he looks like in the mirror of his mind's eye but also what he thinks of himself as a human being. In many respects this new status, or self-image, remains indefinite. Not only does he lack the experience required to know what he can expect of himself; he does not know what attitudes and reactions to expect of others. The

What work am I fitted for? What training will I require? What are my chances of employment?

These questions are asked by most young adults. For the young adult with a physical disability, such questions have special significance. The special status in society of a worker brings with it a degree of independence; it also carries with it the respect of others and is contributory to self-respect. Yet for the person with a physical disability the status of a worker is often not easily achieved; even when the limitations imposed by the disability have been offset by special training and when he possesses special skills for specific work, the person with a disability may find himself at an occupational disadvantage. Employers who recognize the economic advantages that accrue to the society when the disabled are provided the opportunity to work, and who realize that the disabled have less absenteeism and better production and safety records than nondisabled workers are still apt to resist hiring disabled workers. The reasons for such resistance are to be found in a complex combination of social and psychological factors that are presently only partially understood. Research goes forward to better understanding of the nature of this resistance, and meanwhile the excellent efforts of many private, state, and federal agencies, such as the state and federal Offices of Vocational Rehabilitation, continue to assist persons with disabilities to attain the treatment and training essential to employment.

Courtesy Oklahoma Division of Vocational Rehabilitation.

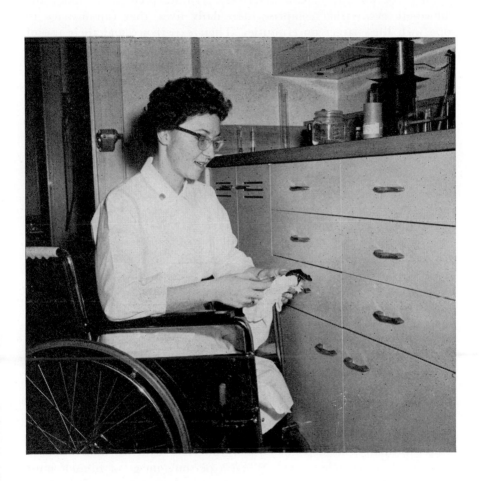

eventual outcome of his treatment and the extent to which he will be rehabilitated are questions that frequently remain unanswerable for considerable periods of time.

All persons have some difficulties in dealing with the uncertain character of life. By making relatively accurate predictions about the immediate events that comprise their daily lives, they can manage to cope with life's larger uncertainties. Their experience and their use of such experience are usually sufficiently relevant to the situation at hand to afford an appropriate basis for their expectations. The newly disabled person, however, may find that his previous experience is an unsatisfactory basis for the forecasts he now wants to make.

The disabled person will pursue his quest for certainty wherever he can, but his opportunities to do so have become narrowed and restricted. As he struggles to reorganize his self-perceptions, he must deal as best he can with the uncertainties that are presented to him by virtue of his changed status. To himself and to others he will point out the signs that he believes signify improvement or restoration of function, and he may make light of—or even fail to recognize—the negative implications of his condition. The degree to which any individual distorts or misperceives his situation will depend, in part, on the extent to which he has had to rely on such distortions in the past in order to bring the world into line with his wishes. It will also depend on the information available to him and the manner in which such information can be communicated to him.

As the individual values the image of himself as a worker, so he values his image of himself as a self-reliant and independent person who can contribute to the satisfactions and needs of others. The equation of self-reliance with virtue is deeply ingrained in most persons in our culture. The disabled person who finds himself forced to revert to dependent behaviors that had been gradually abandoned years before is confronted with a particularly difficult situation. If he does not accept a dependent role, he may be denying the actuality of his situation; but if he capitulates, his dependency may interfere with his motivation to achieve a less dependent level. When a person's image of himself must shift to allow for his greater reliance on others, the characteristic measures he has utilized to protect and maintain his self-concept are brought into play. These same measures also serve to protect him against being overwhelmed by anxiety. Imposed dependency enables some persons to gratify unresolved needs emanating from deprivations of their childhood. Dependence on others may provide them with the "secondary gain" that comes from the attentions and ministrations of others.

Some disabled persons blame themselves unduly for their disabilities; in the age-old fashion they equate misfortune with misbehavior. Such persons may experience a degree of self-blame which moves from guilt into depression—a depression which is different from a mourning for that part of one's self that has been lost or from that which is represented by acute feelings of isolation. Other reactions to disability include blaming others for one's misfortunes. These angry and hostile reactions may be accompanied by a denunciation of the world for having inflicted the hurt and the disability.

The degree to which an individual will experience separation from others is not a direct reflection of the extent of his physical disability. Along with many other circumstances, changes in physical functioning and physical appearance can contribute to the feeling of being apart and distant from others. This sense of loneliness and isolation does not depend on whether there are other persons actually close at hand, but rather on whether the disabled person feels that the persons about him understand him, value him, and love him. A person who says, "Unless this has happened to you, you can't really understand" is expressing his need to communicate his feeling of separation and difference to someone who can share the experience with him at an emotional level.

When disability occurs, it occurs to a person who shares with all people the need to feel related, and who shares with them the need to develop the hope and spiritual strength that will be available during life's vicissitudes. Like everyone else, the disabled person endeavors to avoid pain, whether it be the pain of the body or that which comes with social isolation and loneliness. Like everyone else, he possesses the need to feel acceptable and to be a valued participant in the human enterprise. Like everyone else, the disabled person may have remarkable resources and strength and great resilience—and like everyone else, he utilizes these in dealing with life's adversities.

SEPARATION EVENTS AND FEELINGS OF ISOLATION AND LONELINESS

Throughout this discussion, various references have been made to the conditions and events that elicit feelings of loneliness and isolation in the older person. Events that involve the abandonment of previous patterns of behavior, previous relationships, previous physical settings, events that accelerate the progression from the known and the familiar to the unknown and the new are termed *separation events*.

These are not necessarily evident at a moment in time but may be the result of changes occurring gradually throughout a considerable period. When the interests and developmental directions of friends differ, they become separated, not in the physical but in the psychological sense of having "grown away." In some instances, separation results from changes accompanying the aging process itself, when, for example, the individual becomes separated from the image that he once held of himself as an athlete or as a young man.

Each new stage in the developmental process involves a transition from a familiar pattern of behavior to an unfamiliar one. Because the rewards offered by the new behavioral patterns associated with the next developmental level are often sufficient to offset the experience of loss that separation brings, the person is able to make the progression. Although the freshman college student longs for his friends, his parents, and the familiarity of home, he remains in college.

Feelings of loneliness and isolation often accompany the experience of separation, but these feelings are not necessarily associated with the fact of being by oneself; they may occur when a person is in the midst of a crowd, as at a football game, or when he is sitting with relatives and associates whom he knows well. The reader will recall that the need to feel in communion with others was noted as basic and derived from the physical conditions of infancy. At that time, the presence of others close at hand to attend to needs was associated with tension reduction, and their absence with discomfort and pain. Because of the conditions from which it emerges, it can be hypothesized that anxiety reactions will be manifest when the psychological need to feel related is frustrated or threatened. Thus, separation experiences evoke feelings of loneliness and isolation as well as anxiety reactions.

Feelings of loneliness are to be differentiated from the individual's reactions to solitude, to being quietly by oneself and contemplating one's position in the vastness of the universe. Such feelings of solitude and aloneness may be awe-inspiring rather than anxiety-provoking, and unlike loneliness, they are usually under the individual's conscious control. Loneliness and isolation feelings, on the other hand, are involuntary and can reach such intensity that the individual suffers acutely and is so shut off psychologically from the world around him that his perceptions become distorted and he may even evidence the characteristics of the severely disoriented schizophrenic patient.

The ability of isolation to stimulate and supplement intense fear reactions has been observed in dramatic and unusual context, the situation referred to as "Voodoo Death" among primitive peoples (7). In response to a violation of a taboo or an edict pronounced by the witch doctor, the victim, who accepts the "verdict," demonstrates a sequence of reactions including signs of acute terror, the solitary wait for death, and the loss of interest in food or water. Cases are on record in which the victim, who had been in good health, actually did die within a short interval of time—from one to several days—after accepting the pronouncement of his impending death. While he was waiting for death, the community, his relatives, and friends withdrew from him and behaved as if he were, in fact, already dead. In some societies, the group who had withdrawn from him returns at a point before his death to prepare for the rites of passage from this world to the next.

The physiological effects of intense fear or hopelessness are exceedingly complex. Here we are concerned only with the individual's response first to the loss of communion with others, and then to their reactions to him as one who is about to depart. Warner, who studied the phenomena of voodoo death among the Aborgines in Northern Australia (22), writes:

> An analogous situation in our society is hard to imagine. If all a man's near kin, his father, mother, brothers and sisters, wife, children, business associates, friends and all the other members of the society should suddenly withdraw themselves because of some dramatic circumstance, refusing to take any attitude but one of taboo and looking at the man as one already dead, and then after some little time perform over him a sacred ceremony which is believed with certainty to guide him out of the land of the living into that of the dead, the enormous suggestive power of this two-fold movement of the community, after it has had its attitudes crystallized, can be somewhat understood by ourselves.[3]

Of course, most feelings of isolation or threats of separation evoke reactions far less dramatic and unusual than those noted above. In the later adult years it has been observed that persons are apt to be more conservative and less amenable to change; they are inclined to be intolerant of those who are different. Of course, intolerance of differences in customs or peoples is not confined to older persons; it may be observed in people of any age. Rejection of those who are different can represent an attempt to reduce the threat of isolation that difference symbolizes. The realization that people do differ and that many "stand apart" can precipitate anxieties having their origin in reactions to the fact that life in the form that it has been experienced has a terminal point. While the older person must protect against his separation anxieties in whatever ways are characteristic of him, it is interesting to note that he himself evokes the same anxieties in younger persons, hence their treatment of him often involves segregating him from the family.

It is essential to note that separation events and feelings of loneliness and isolation are neither unique to the later years nor are they an

---

[3] Reprinted by permission from W. L. Warner, *A Black Civilization: A Social Study of an Australian Tribe.* Copyright, 1941, by Harper & Roe, Publishers, Incorporated.

inevitable preoccupation of the older person. During the later adult years more time is often available for family and friends that makes possible, though does not ensure, greater communication. There is during these years a deeper appreciation for friendship and a broadened perspective that intensifies the sense of identification with all of life. And for some older persons there are new areas of service; new and younger friends may desire the guidance and counsel of respected elders. Finally, for the older person there are the patterns of life he knows so well and enjoys, that serve him well as a shield against the unknown. From his old friends and family as well as his new and younger friends the older person receives respect, recognition, and satisfaction. Having achieved a tranquility and wisdom born of a long and varied life experience, many an older person is able to attend to the feelings and needs of others, reducing his moments of loneliness to a minimum.

DEATH

The relatedness need underlies the behaviors through which an individual attempts to achieve and maintain the feeling of communion with others. In childhood there is a gradual awareness of the discontinuity of life. This realization frequently occurs in the context of grief and pain. The child's questions about death may be evaded or incompletely answered, and his feelings of terror are frequently reinforced rather than reduced by his attempts to learn why people die and what it is like to be dead. Because death represents the point of no communion with others, most persons must deal individually with the issue in whatever ways are available to them. At a conscious level, religious and philosophic positions offer explanations of death and provide a basis for some individuals to manage the anxieties associated with it; however, the vast anxiety-provoking potential of death generally evokes psychological reactions to death that are expressed indirectly and unconsciously.

No matter how primitive or how civilized, all societies have beliefs about death, its causes, and its significance as a part of their cultural heritage. All societies have prevailing customs and rituals pertaining to the disposal of the dead, from burying or burning the corpse to abandoning it, and various beliefs prevail about the nature of the dead person's spirit and the possibility and form of life after death.

An anthropological report (3) concerning the death and burial customs of the peoples of the world, which was published thirty years ago, indicated that practices varied not only among societies, but that within a society the specific customs followed depended upon the individual's sex, age, social position, and the physical condition of the body. Differences in the elaborateness of the ceremony may depend upon the rank the deceased held in the community, for example. According to one observer, Melanesian burial practices about the turn of the century varied with rank in the following manner:

> At Saa, the burial of common people is extremely simple; an inferior person is buried immediately; an ordinary man is buried the day after his death. However, men of rank are not buried for two days. . . . If a very great man dies, or a man much beloved by his son, the body is hung up in the son's house either in a canoe or enclosed in the figure of a swordfish.

The burial practices and customs of a culture contribute to the images and ideas that an individual utilizes in thinking about the death of others and his own death. In considering the psychological aspects, three forms of an individual's behavior in regard to death may be apparent. First there is the situation in which a person wishes that another person were absent. In this instance, the wish to remove or destroy him is manifest as a desire to kill. Such death wishes may be directed toward another person for a fleeting instant or for a long period of time; they may be held consciously or unconsciously, and they may be expressed directly, as in the case of deliberate murder, capital punishment, or warfare, or indirectly through displacement or fantasy. The popular television themes of violence and murder, for example, suggest the extent to which the public requires such "entertainment" in order to express indirectly its destructive impulses.

When the dead person is one who has been loved or esteemed, the second form in which a person deals with death can be observed. In this case, a profound separation situation occurs. The bereaved person may experience overwhelming grief, grief which includes not only the experience of loss of the beloved or esteemed person but also that of detachment and isolation. Grief can include mourning for the deceased, as well as mourning for oneself. Such self-mourning is due to the loss sustained, to the stimulation of one's own anxieties about death, and to the plight of the survivor who must get along without the assistance of the deceased. Another important component of grief comes from the survivor's identification with the dead person. A mourner's remark after the death of a loved one that, "It is as if a part of myself had also died," is not uncommon. Such an experience is understandable when one recalls that through the identification mechanism one person may take as part of himself the attitudes, values, and characteristics of another. When this person dies, part of the self is separated from its model, and the mourner grieves for both the deceased and himself.

Sometimes the death of a parent, sibling, or close friend results in intense mourning and a marked depression which does not lift even with time; it has been speculated that a depression of this degree may spring from the conviction that death wishes held many years before had somehow caused the death. Such convictions are below the individual's conscious awareness, so that his depression may seem to have little identifiable content; he is extremely depressed, but it seems to him that his reaction is quite appropriate considering the extent of his loss. In other instances, the bereaved experiences considerable guilt and may berate himself for having been unkind to the deceased, feeling that he could have done more to prevent the death.

Suicide

The conscious killing of oneself in suicide represents a seemingly paradoxical event. If separation by death is evocative of anxiety, then suicide appears to be unlikely behavior. The relatedness need is expressed psychologically, however, and for some persons physical separation or isolation from others represents their only form of achieving a feeling of communion with them. The extreme step of suicide can be a bizarre and irrational effort to establish some desired reaction from others, and in this sense "relate."

It is difficult to know what meaning suicide actually possesses for the individual, and no single explanation can be expected to apply equally well for all cases. In some instances, it could be inferred that the individual who is generally hostile and destructive in his interpersonal relationships carries out by committing suicide the most hostile act possible against those close to him. In other instances, an individual possessing an intense hatred of others turns the hatred against himself. There may be cases in which a person has experienced such severe and acute feelings of isolation that he views suicide as a chance to regain a feeling of communion with others who have died. In some situations, the prospect of prolonged illness or pain may lead the individual into suicide, since the mounting anxieties associated with death cannot be tolerated. Such a psychological state is frequently encountered in more commonplace situations when the person says, "I no longer care what will happen just so it happens soon." The person with a severe and fatal illness may decide logically to commit suicide rather than to expose himself and his family to the strain of a long and costly period of hospitalization and treatment.

To account for suicide, explanations emphasizing social, economic, and physical factors as well as psychological ones have been presented. Research concerning the causes must account for the differences in suicide rate for different age groups, for men and women, for married and unmarried persons, and for various ethnic groups. Over half of all suicides are committed by persons over the age of forty-five, for example, while only 3 percent are accounted for by persons between the ages of fifteen and nineteen. For every three men who commit suicide, there is only one woman who takes her own life. In 1940, the highest rate was among the Chinese, with 45 suicides for 100,000 persons, while the lowest rate was among Negroes with 4.1 suicides. Widowed and divorced persons commit suicide more frequently than do married persons. Rates fluctuate with the seasons of the year and with the national economy; there are more suicides in the spring of the year and fewer during wartime and financial depressions (8). Even casual consideration of these figures suggests the variety of researches that would have to be undertaken to learn more about the causes and meaning of suicide.

One's Own Death

It has been noted that the individual may have contact with death as a state inflicted actually or in fantasy upon someone else or, in the special case of suicide, upon oneself. Now the third form in which the individual deals with death will be considered. Death as an event that will occur to the person himself is difficult to think about, not only because of the anxieties the topic is apt to elicit but also because the images and symbolic representations required in thinking about it are not available. When the individual focuses his attention upon the prospect of his own death, he can visualize only the ceremonies and symbols associated with death or the burial ceremony; he cannot conceive of what it is like to be dead, nor can he think how it will be when the affairs of the world will be conducted without him. Death seems to be an unnatural event terminating man's existence, and although individuals will readily grant intellectually that it occurs to all persons, they also harbor the belief that somehow they will be spared.

How the individual responds to the prospect of his own death represents, in itself, his life as he has lived it. The extent to which fear and anxiety are precipitated by the prospect of the separation of death depends, in part, upon the degree to which he has achieved a sense of communion with others in close and significant interpersonal relationships. But all persons will deal in their own particular manner with the anxieties associated with the fact of death. Some persons find in their religious convictions deep and lasting comfort in the certainty of a life hereafter; consequently, they may have little conscious fear of death. For many persons the anxieties are displaced and repressed, and for the most part the issue is denied access to their conscious awareness.

A few persons who have approached the highest order of personal development may attain a sense of identification with all of life. They may receive gratification from an experience of communion not only with other persons but also with all that is natural. Such identification and unity with all of life often does not appear until the middle or later years, since its development requires considerable experience and the satisfaction of most of the criteria of psychological development. This sense of oneness with nature does not depend upon the immediate reactions of others to the person; he responds to dying as a natural event that is inextricably related to the process of living. For such persons death is not feared, dramatized, or denied. Dying is experienced as a natural event that need be reacted to neither cynically or fatalistically. It is an event that is considered deserving of the dignity properly attached to all the valued activities of life. Death is seen neither as an avenging tyrant nor as a bountiful parent offering repose; rather, it is an expected and accepted part of life itself. The poet Gibran (12) expresses this view in his lines:

> If you would indeed behold the spirit of death, open your heart wide unto the body of life.
> For life and death are one, even as the river and sea are one.[4]

Summary

For many persons the middle and later adult years will approximate a span of half a century. During their early thirties, men and women are active and vigorous and they have attained some of their earlier aspirations; marriage, a family, and some economic security. In his work the man has developed skill and proficiency, and in some fields the thirties represents the period of the greatest personal productivity and creativity.

With time, the adult's roles and responsibilities in his family and work situation shift, and changes in self-perception and in the opportunities for self-esteem occur. Their children's increasing independence can have many complications for the parents in the middle years. He sees his children in their own homes, with their own families. Women who have been preoccupied solely with their families and who, at the time of the menopause, no longer feel needed by their children may undergo a period of painful adaptation to an unfamiliar and uncomfortable status.

In this society age itself is not culturally valued as it is in a number of others; consequently, adults in their middle years may be troubled about the loss of youthful appearance. The unmarried woman's concern

---

[4] Reprinted by permission from Kahlil Gibran, *The Prophet*. Copyright, 1923, by Alfred A. Knopf, Incorporated.

about the effects of aging upon her chances for marriage are not un-realistic, and self-comparisons to younger women may cause her to feel at a competitive disadvantage. As the society devalues the position of the unmarried, many aging single persons experience feelings of loneliness and isolation.

As the person enters his later years, he may have to relinquish his role as a worker because of compulsory retirement rules, physical dis-ability, or infirmity. Forced retirement may be threatening to the self-esteem that one has had as a worker and contributing member of society. And if the aged person's family no longer relies upon his advice or holds open a place for him, such feelings of reduced self-esteem may be reinforced.

Changes in opportunities for self-esteem encountered by the aged need not present insurmountable obstacles for self-gratification. The person who has attained a high order of psychological development values himself not only for what he has accomplished during his lifetime but, more importantly, because he exists. Diminishing contacts with others and increasing physical debility need not be a cause of personal devaluation or of fear. Rather, he acknowledges these changes as inevit-able phases of the aging process and reaffirms his faith in himself by furthering his own "becoming."

The separation events of life activate feelings of isolation and the anxieties associated with death. Individuals deal with the prospect of death in various ways, just as they deal with all threats to their related-ness. He who has attained a high level of personal development recognizes that anxieties are sometimes unavoidable and reflect the human condition; rather than be overwhelmed by them, he resolves to conquer them. He does not dwell on thoughts of death and decay, but accepts wholeheartedly his role in the great adventure of life and its counterpart death. Whether he looks to eternal life or to oblivion, he does not await death with fear and foreboding. As a result of his high level of personal development, he is apt to experience a sense of identifi-cation with all of life and the wisdom and equanimity that can come only with age. He views life and death as a unitary process, enabling him to embrace the future as well as the past.

References

1. Anastasi, A. *Differential Psychology* (ed. 3) . New York: Macmillan, 1958.
2. Bayley, N., and Oden, M. H.   The maintenance of intellectual ability in gifted adults. *J. Geront.*, 1955, *10,* 91–107.
3. Bedann, E.   *Death Customs: An Analytical Study of Burial Rites.* New York: Knopf, 1930.

4. Bernard, J. *Remarriage: A Study of Marriage.* New York: Holt, 1956.
5. Bernard, J. *Social Problems at Mid-Century.* New York: Holt, 1957.
6. Burgess, E. W. Personal and social adjustment in old age; in *The Aged and Society.* Madison, Wis.: Industrial Relations Research Association, 1950.
7. Cannon, W. Voodoo death. *Psychosom. Med.,* 1957, *19,* 182–190.
8. Clinard, M. B. *Sociology of Deviant Behavior.* New York: Holt, 1960.
9. Davis, K. Divorce downswing. *New York Times Magazine,* May 8, 1955.
10. Federal Security Agency, Committee on Aging and Geriatrics. *Fact Book on Aging.* Washington, D.C.: U.S. Government Printing Office, 1952.
11. Fisher, M. B., and Birren, J. E. Age and strength. *J. appl. Psychol.,* 1947, *31,* 490–497.
12. Gibran, K. *The Prophet.* New York: Knopf, 1923.
13. Glueck, S., and Glueck, E. Working mothers and delinquency. *Ment. Hyg., N.Y.,* 1957, *41,* 327–352.
14. Heincke, C. M. Some effects of separating two-year-old children from their parents: A comparative study. *Hum. Relat.,* 1956, *19.*
15. Lehman, H. C. *Age and Achievement.* Princeton, N.J.: Princeton University Press, 1953.
16. Linton, R. *The Study of Man.* New York: Appleton, 1936.
17. Maccoby, E. E. Effects upon children of their mothers' outside employment; in Bell, N. W., and Vogel, E. F., *The Family.* New York: Free Press, 1960.
18. Miles, C. C., and Miles, W. R. The correlation of intelligence scores and chronological age from early to late maturity. *Amer. J. Psychol.,* 1832, *44,* 44–78.
19. Miles, W. R. Psychological aspects of aging; in E. V. Cowdry (ed.), *Problems of Ageing.* Baltimore: Williams & Wilkins, 1942.
20. Murdock, G. *Social Structure.* New York: Macmillan, 1949.
21. Spiro, M. E. Is the family universal?—The Israeli case; in Bell, N. W., and Vogel, E. F., *The Family.* New York: Free Press, 1960.
22. Warner, W. L. *A Black Civilization: A Social Study of an Australian Tribe.* New York: Harper, 1941.
23. Welford, A. T., *et al. Skill and Age: An Experimental Approach.* New York: Oxford, 1951.

Selected Readings

Anastasi, A. *Differential Psychology.* New York: Macmillan, 1958.

Drake, J. T. *The Aged in American Society.* New York: Ronald, 1958.

Thomas, L. G. *The Occupational Structure and Education.* Englewood Cliffs, N.J.: Prentice-Hall, 1956.

Welford, A. T. *Aging and Human Skill.* New York: Oxford, 1958.

White, R. W. *Lives in Progress.* New York: Holt, 1952.

Wolff, K. *The Biological, Sociological and Psychological Aspects of Aging.* Springfield, Ill.: Thomas. 1959.

•

PART THREE

•

The Psychology
of Effective Behavior

THROUGHOUT his life man is actively directing his energies and talents to maintaining, protecting, and enhancing himself and others. To the extent that he succeeds in doing so, he is effective; to the extent that he fails, he is ineffective.

In the following four chapters effective behavior is considered as it is evidenced in the individual's perceptions, thoughts, and emotions, in his social behaviors, and in his learning. In the final chapter man's relation to his government is considered and the mutual dependence of the democratic and developmental ideals is outlined.

12.

Effective Intrapersonal Behaviors

In approaching an explanation of the specific qualities of humanness that mark a person as a being different in some respect and degree from all other persons, it is necessary to explore the person's private world of perceptions, thoughts, and emotions. This private world is approached only through inference; it is not directly observed or recorded, and the processes that comprise perception, thought, and emotion intervene between stimuli and the responses associated with them. As well as accounting for the distinctive patterns of humanness, these intervening processes also provide in part a basis for evaluating the level of development that has been achieved. These within-the-person processes provide clues to the degree of harmony the individual maintains within himself. They are evaluated as indices of development in conjunction with the nature and quality of his interpersonal relationships and his utilization of his resources in worthwhile activity.

Intrapersonal behaviors at their best enable the individual to perceive the world without distortion; to think cogently and logically; to anticipate the consequences of his own behaviors; to express and direct his affections; to organize and, when necessary, to reorganize his perceptions and beliefs in order to achieve solutions to problems. They include both his rational decisions and the emotional commitments essential to execute those decisions—they are a composite of the intellectual and emotional facets of life.

Perception

Throughout his life man is exposed to an ever-changing world of sights, sounds, smells, movements, and temperature and pressure

359

fluctuations. And throughout his life he relies on the meanings that patterns of stimuli on his sensory receptors have acquired and that identify the objects, persons, and events of his world. He learns to impute these special meanings to certain patterns of stimuli so that, for example, the marks on this text appear as words rather than as a pattern of black and white, and a series of sounds are responded to as a specific message. He also learns to identify the patterns of stimuli that have special significance to his survival and to the maintenance of his personality. His interpretation of the stimuli impinging upon him will determine the specific behaviors to be elicited from his repertoire of responses. He will formulate his expectations, make predictions, and act in response to stimuli that are in themselves only quanta of physical energy impinging upon his specialized receptors, the sensory organs.

Meaning is not intrinsic to the stimulus object but is the result of a subjective process within the individual. The perceptual process—the interpretation of stimuli—depends on the interaction of the perceiver and the stimulus object; the nature of the interaction in turn depends on the history and structure of the perceiver. Although we are inclined to assume that the world is precisely as we see it, students of perceptual processes point out that as perceivers we will interpret stimuli so that objects will be "seen" as the same object irrespective of the visual angle of viewer to object, and that the sizes as well as the shapes of objects are seen as roughly constant irrespective of their distance from the viewer. (The taller person is still seen as taller than the shorter even though he is sixteen feet from the former who is only three feet away from us.)

The continuing stream of perceptual information has the function of providing the individual with a sense of a real and stable environment. From given bits of information, the individual inductively forms generalizations about the situation. He learns the significance of various stimuli, and he then responds to these interpreted perceptions. Included within such learnings are those pertaining to people and to the reactions of people to him, so his perceptions will involve not only the world of things about him but persons as well. The individual also learns to perceive himself in relation to others, and these self-perceptions form the basis for the personal, social, and ideal selves as they were presented earlier.

The perceptual processes assist the individual in responding adaptively to his environment. They partially account for the direction of his behaviors and serve to organize his resources, energies, and skills selectively and in combinations necessary to satisfy his needs and to guard against threat. In the individual whose intrapsychic processes are functioning harmoniously, the perceptual processes provide a "world in which we feel at home because we know what to expect, and what to expect does not disagree too much with what we want . . . [when the components of personality are not functioning harmoniously] the world may be a capricious and terrifying place, where all that we do is uncertain and dangerous, where we do not learn what to expect, where what we find is never satisfying" (10).

In the person functioning effectively, the organization and orientation of the perceptual processes, which are functions of ego activity, enable him to maintain contact with his environment. As a result, his judgments of a situation, of his capabilities, and of the consequences of his behaviors are congruent with the data available to him. When these judgments are inaccurate, he is able to make suitable modifications of his expectations.

PERCEPTION AND PREPARATORY SET

The expectation of the runner crouching at the starting line is one example of preparatory set. He awaits the sound of the gun and is literally "set" for it in the sense that he is ready to respond on the instant. He is prepared both for the sound of the gun and for his own response. Persons whose experiences have provided them with certain expectations will tend to perceive in terms of these expectations even when the specific situation does not provide them with an objectively adequate basis for so doing. Frequently their resultant behaviors are appropriate, and perceptual set serves its important stabilizing function, relieving the individual of the need to judge each situation individually and independently of previous experience.

Sometimes a preparatory set is provided by instructions or rules. A young man employed in a department store, for example, was given instructions on how to carry out his new job as a floorwalker. The manager carefully briefed him about methods of identifying shoplifters and emphasized the need for vigilance, since the store had recently suffered heavy losses attributed to shoplifting. As a result of his "set," the young man believed, during the first several days of his new work, that every customer he observed had just stolen something or was in the process of hiding some article. In this case, the young man's behavior was exaggerated, but not seriously so; at other times, however, a person's "set" can lead to inappropriate behaviors.

NEED-DETERMINED PERCEPTION

The type of observational distortion that occurs when the observer is predisposed or set to make a particular response is very similar to another kind of distortion that has been called *need-deter-*

mined perception. As the term implies, the observer's need or set of needs influences his perception of a person or a situation. For example, hungry persons tend to give a higher than normal percentage of food responses to ambiguous stimuli.

The influence of needs on perception is even more pronounced when human behavior is being observed. In one study (6) a tachistoscope, which exposes a picture for a short interval of time, was used to measure differences in the ability of the subjects to recognize the pictures flashed on a screen. When the pictures were selected to be distressing to some of the subjects, these persons were unable to recognize the pictures as quickly as those whose conflicts were not represented in the pictures. This type of research finding has been offered in support of the contention that the ego may protect the individual from anxiety by blocking from conscious awareness stimuli which would precipitate anxiety if perceived. Related research pertaining to the mechanism of projection illustrates how individuals with characteristics considered undesirable tend to perceive other people as possessing the same characteristics. Since we tend to think that what we perceive *is* the way things really are, it comes as a surprise to many students of psychology that their perceptions of other people are partially reflective of their own personalities rather than objective images. Everyone will to some extent perceive his environment in terms of his needs, but sometimes an individual is so beset by internal conflicts that he consistently does so. He then distorts the environment and the intentions and actions of others in the effort to minimize threat and anxiety; consequently, without being aware of it, he has deceived himself. Effective perception occurs when the individual's self-interests are not jeopardized by gross and persistent self-deception.

Absence of Relevant Cues

Sometimes the absence of essential cues causes errors in perceiving the meaning of the situation. For example, Mrs. Smith left her seven-year-old twins in the car while she went across the street to the drugstore. She was alarmed when she looked out the window and saw the twins in the car wrestling with each other. She could see their red faces and the tears streaming down their cheeks. On the basis of the visual cues, which she perceived correctly, but in the absence of auditory cues, Mrs. Smith inferred that her boys were battling with each other. Had she been able to hear the shrieks of laughter, she would have known that they were having quite a good time tickling each other.

A failure to consider all relevant cues, with the resulting perceptual errors, is, of course, a common occurrence. However, when such failures are characteristic of the individual's activity, and when they often place him in difficult positions at work or in his relationships with others, his behavior must be considered ineffective, and the possibility of developmental inadequacies must be raised. Gross and consistent perceptual distortions may suggest a serious state of personality disorganization known as schizophrenia (see page 386).

EFFECTIVE SELF-PERCEPTION

Since human beings are able to function simultaneously as both perceivers and as objects of their own perceptions, a discussion of the characteristics of the self-perceptions of individuals evidencing high levels of personal and social development is appropriate at this point. One source of information is studies of individuals who have moved toward greater degrees of personality development and effectiveness as a result of specialized psychological assistance. In summarizing the changes in self-perception apparent in these individuals, Rogers comments (16, p. 316):

> The essential elements would appear to be that the individual changes in three general ways. He perceives himself as a more adequate person, with more worth and more possibility of meeting life. He permits more experiential data to enter awareness and thus achieves a more realistic appraisal of himself, his relationships and his environment. He tends to place the basis of standards within himself, recognizing that the "goodness" or "badness" of any experience or perceptual object is not something inherent in that object but is a value placed on it by himself.

The tendency of persons to impute their own unfavorable characteristics to others has already been discussed (page 106). It will be recalled that this projection is unconscious and is most frequent in persons who have been rated by their associates as possessing undesirable characteristics.

Anxiety and Perceptual Effectiveness

Closely related to perceptual distortion is the degree to which an individual can tolerate ambiguous situations, which do not permit definite and clear-cut judgments. Studies have shown that children whose tolerance for ambiguity was low held a higher degree of prejudice toward "outsiders" (minority group members) than children who could tolerate ambiguity (8). One interpretation of the results is that the ambiguous situation holds different degrees of threat for different persons, depending upon their personality structure. Persons who were considered "rigid" personalities required clarity rather than accuracy in their perceptions, because they were unable to tolerate the seeming lack of knowledge and control required when one suspends judgment, acknowledges one's uncertainties, or recognizes the complexities inherent in situations involving judgments of other persons. According to the definition proposed in this text, these persons are not functioning effectively so far as their intrapersonal perceptual behaviors are concerned.

Factors other than anxiety and the inability to tolerate ambiguity may operate to reduce perceptual effectiveness. Although the research available does not provide a basis for fully understanding the processes whereby people deceive themselves when making judgments of others, interesting data demonstrate that the judgment one makes of oneself is apt to be a more significant influence on the judgments one makes of others than are the actual characteristics of the person judged. In studies comparing a person's self-concept to his impressions of others, it has been found that friends are more likely to be perceived as being similar to one's personal and ideal selves than are nonfriends, even though nonfriends were actually neither more nor less similar in personality characteristics (20). Friends and other persons are, in other words, misjudged in ways that tend to minimize the observer's anxiety.

ASSESSING PERSONAL PERCEPTIONS

Psychologists assessing personality utilize "projective" techniques, which sample the person's manner of seeing his world and his associates and of organizing the stimuli that impinge upon him. The Rorschach and the Thematic Apperception Tests are two of the best known procedures of this type.

Approximately fifty years ago, Hermann Rorschach, a Swiss psychiatrist, devised a procedure in which ambiguous images resembling ink blots were presented to the persons being studied. They were asked, "What might this be?" Rorschach's initial purpose was to identify the individual's characteristic mode of perceiving and organizing stimuli as a practical short-cut for arriving at inferences concerning his personality structure and function. Today the original intent of the examination remains, although his procedures have been somewhat modified, and an elaborate method for evaluating responses in terms of their content, the factors prompting them, and the modes of organization utilized has been added.

The Thematic Apperception Test, developed by Henry Murray of Harvard University, consists of a series of pictures, most of which involve human figures, about which the individual is asked to tell stories. Since no information is provided, the hero of each story has to be identified, a plot supplied, and the preceding events and outcome specified. Although they provide a more clear-cut and recognizable set of stimuli than do the Rorschach "ink blots," the pictures still allow a considerable latitude of response. The person taking these tests is told that there are no "right" or "wrong" answers, and he often feels less threatened and freer to respond than he would in more conventional tests of intelligence and achievement. The assumption is that he will "project" into the pictures his own characteristic attitudes and feelings, which he may be unaware of or unable to discuss openly.

Both the Rorschach and the Thematic Apperception Test are widely used in schools, clinics, hospitals and, in recent years, in industry. Many researchers have studied their value in the diagnosis of socially and psychologically ineffective persons and in differentiating known groups of persons, such as delinquents and nondelinquents. Since these techniques are still in the developmental stage, however, they are best utilized by skilled psychologists. When psychologists make predictions about future behaviors on the basis of projective test results, good practice requires that they also use information obtained from interviews, historical, medical, and other test sources.

Thought

Together with perception, thought enables the individual to organize his experiences and to maintain, protect, and effectively extend himself in his negotiations with the world about him. Thought processes are made up of symbolic representations of events, objects, or relationships to which the individual has responded. While perceptual processes are operative mainly in the immediate present (the light turns red and the driver stops his car), thought processes involve the past and the future as well. Man's ability to symbolize, which distinguishes him from other animals, enables him to think about past events and to anticipate future experiences.

In thought, the individual utilizes symbols to represent events he has experienced. Sometimes a symbol is a visual image of an experience or object, as when the word *chair* evokes a "mental picture" of a particular chair. As previous discussions have indicated, the word *chair*, as a symbol, stands for a class of objects fulfilling the functions assigned to the chair. This activity of classification is an important aspect of the thought process in that it enables the individual to order his thoughts and experiences with reference to other thoughts and experiences sharing the salient or central features of the class. Ordering and

classifying is an essential aspect of living, since it would be exhausting—
if not impossible—to respond to each event separately, as a new and
different stimulus requiring analysis.

An individual who possesses a high order of intrapersonal effectiveness is able to form generalizations from particular instances; that is, he
is able to abstract the common elements from different experiences and
thereby develop a relatively consistent pattern of responses that can be
applied to future events and problems. As an individual matures, his
ability to recognize relationships and to classify events increases. The
young child, for example, requires the aid of objects, blocks, or coins
that are concrete, that can be manipulated and grouped or felt and
seen, as he develops his abstract numerical concepts. He must first think
of the number of *four* as *four of something* before he can learn the
category of *four* as an abstraction and can utilize it in relation to *four
of anything*.

The abstracted category—the idea—that captures the common
quality or characteristic of a group of objects, events, or relationships is
termed a *cognitive category*. This term emphasizes its symbolic feature
and identifies it with the thinking processes. Such cognitive categories
provide the individual with his personal frame of reference, and one
psychological theorist, in order to tie the perceptual processes closely to
those involved in the representational aspects of thought, has extended
the meaning of "category" to that of "construct" (12). Kelly writes of
"personal constructs" when he considers how people think of their past,
present, and future and how they utilize these categories or constructs
as a personal frame of reference. Kelly maintains that if one is to understand another person well enough to be able to predict his behaviors, it
is essential to know how that person "construes" the world; that is, how
he perceives and thinks of it, what he knows about himself and about
the environment. In these terms, the effectively functioning individual
would be one whose personal constructs enable him to fulfill his own
developmental potential and to satisfy his needs through the type of
contacts he maintains with the world about him. When such constructs
or categories are congruent, when they are consistent, or, as one psychologist has expressed it, when they are "consonant" with one another,
the individual may experience a state of comfort, while the presence of
cognitive dissonance results in a state of discomfort and leads to activity
directed toward reducing the dissonance (7).

The purchase of a new automobile, for example, is usually a
rather important decision for a person. Considerable dissonance
should exist for a new car owner immediately after he has bought

his car; all "good" features of the makes he considered, but did not buy, and "bad" features of the one he bought are now dissonant with his ownership of the car. He should also attempt to reduce this dissonance.

To test the hypothesis that new car owners would attempt to reduce the dissonance by acquiring cognitions supportive of their purchase while avoiding inconsistent cognitions, a group of psychologists studied the car advertisements read by 65 new car owners (5). The results were in accord with the hypothesis: *after* buying their cars, the purchasers read more advertisements about the car they purchased than about other cars.

Cognitive Dissonance and Behavioral Change

The relationship between cognitive dissonance and effective functioning is interesting. Although research data are presently not available to document the position, one hypothesis suggests that the presence of some cognitive dissonance may be essential in activating an individual to achieve his full potential. For example, unless there is some degree of inconsistency between one's image of himself and what he wishes to be, there may be little reason for wanting to change and little reason for expending energy in attempting to effect such a change. On the other hand, when the dissonance is great, when the cognitions are in gross contradiction to one another, the behaviors or the other cognitions adopted in resolving the dissonance may be inappropriate or bizarre. In the effort to resolve dissonance, the individual may be activated either to utilize his abilities and resources in seeking active solutions to the problems he encounters, or to resort to behaviors and beliefs that serve to resolve the conflict but do not necessarily lead to the desired objectives. The high school boy who is not achieving but who aspires to enter a college noted for its high scholastic standards may resort to defensive and protective mechanisms to resolve the cognitive dissonance rather than studying more diligently. Thus he may be able to "explain" his inadequacies by condemning the teachers for being incompetent.

The individual who is functioning effectively will have available to him behavioral patterns that will assist in the resolution of dissonances. These patterns represent efforts at mastery rather than defense; they are directed toward active solution of problems or attainment of consonance through changes either in belief or in self-concept.

The individual who is evidencing optimally effective intrapersonal behaviors will also have available to him the cognitive categories essential for the classification and ordering of the vast array of stimuli, facts, and data that impinge upon him. Research is currently under way on the categories that individuals utilize in their perceptions of others, but at this point one possible explanation for some of the difficulties that individuals or nations have in understanding one another is that the cognitive categories they utilize in ordering their experiences differ. The communist view that capitalist economies require war to sustain them, for example, leads the Russians to interpret American actions as precipitating war. In turn, our knowledge of the missionary aspect of communist doctrine encourages us to perceive their actions in a similarly hostile fashion.

PROBLEM-SOLVING BEHAVIORS

The thought process that ties together events, learnings, and experiences occurring at different times is closely related to the function of thought that represents overt behavior by symbols, images, and categories. Through the thinking process it is possible to consider alternative routes to one's objectives without having actually to traverse each alternative. This process, in which consequences can be anticipated and evaluated without the time and energy required by a trial-and-error approach, is a central feature of effective problem-solving behavior. In many problem situations, however, the behaviors resorted to are a combination of random trial and error efforts and the more systematic symbolizing process of thought. The person unsuccessfully attempting to start his car, for example, may repetitively step on the starter, jiggle the keys, and move the gear shift lever, while he questions whether the gas gauge could be incorrect in its reading.

Varying the Perception of the Problem

Persons differ in the approaches they take toward a problem. Some will formulate the problem in a way that precludes its solution; they will try steps and procedures that have proved to be unsatisfactory, as one sometimes does in looking for a lost object. One may endlessly search through one's pockets and wander randomly through one's home repeatedly looking under books or cushions, even though the procedure has already proved fruitless. Others whose intrapersonal behaviors are more effective will shift readily to a different formulation of the problem and will consider alternatives in terms of various possible perspectives of the problem.

The importance of being able to reformulate the problem and to shift set is demonstrated in the task in which the subject is given six match sticks and asked to make four equal triangles. So long as he formulates the problem in terms of only two dimensions, he cannot solve it. When he shifts to consider the possibility that the solution may require the use of three dimensions, he is well on the road to its solution.

The tenacity with which some persons cling to patterns of thought and to characteristic modes of perceiving problems has caused some observers to wonder whether such tendencies are a product of intellectual or personality limitations or both. Although more research is required in this area, it appears that there are characteristic modes of intrapsychic functioning which are associated with rigid and inflexible patterns of perception and thought, and that these characteristics are almost unrelated to high intelligence. Thus, persons scoring high on intelligence tests are not always flexible and readily able to reformulate problem situations. On the other hand, persons who test low on intelligence tests usually have characteristic difficulties in shifting set and in thinking of a problem in new ways.

Effective problem-solving behavior involves the formulation of the problem and of its possible solutions. In the formulation stage effective behaviors result in perceiving the problem in its entirety. This means that the issue or question to be dealt with is first given attention as a whole. The precise nature of the problem is formulated before attention is directed to any specific aspect or to the approaches to its solution. The cliché of "not seeing the forest for the trees" is applicable to problem-solving behavior in which attention is directed at the beginning to some element or detail of the total issue.

Following the formulation of the problem in its totality—as a whole —effective problem-solving behavior involves the identification of the constituent aspects of the problem and of their relative significance and interrelationships. Finally, the details of the problem are given attention. This same sequence is helpful in the clarification and consideration of the alternatives that hold promise as possible solutions. The student interested in becoming familiar with the strategy of problem solving should consult the work of Mursell (15), who has suggested what is known as the *W-E-D* system (*W* represents the whole; *E*, the elements; and *D*, details).

Problem Solving and Anxiety

Although individuals need adequate information for both the formulation and the execution of the problem-solving sequence, for motivational and emotional reasons they often do not seek it. For example, the acquisition of knowledge may be threatening because it raises questions about childhood beliefs, or because it places the individual in competitive roles that carry additional responsibilities. When motivation to solve the problem is low, little energy or interest is available for seeking out the essential data; on the other hand, if the motivation is great, the individual may act impulsively to find a solution. Similarly, when the problem situation activates unresolved intrapsychic conflict, engenders anxiety, or is associated with emotionally charged meanings to the individual, there is the danger that available information will not be adequately evaluated. In some instances, when the emotional significance of an aspect of the problem situation is sufficiently strong, self-deceptive defenses or perceptual distortions are resorted to and will impair the objectivity of the thought processes.

Effective problem-solving behaviors include special efforts to secure the available information and to ensure its objective consideration. These efforts involve a voluntary and conscious decision to keep oneself open to alternative actions, by not prejudging the issue and by not acting until the required evidence is available. Effective problem-solving behaviors will frequently also include the use of disinterested but competent friends or authorities to review the formulation of the problem and the evaluation of the alternatives.

The final phase of the problem solution involves translating decisions and accepted plans into action. Such translation necessitates the energy available to carry out the plan. The degree to which one's resources are available for action will depend, in part, upon the extent to which the individual is free of internal conflict, as we have described; the amount of energy required to protect against anxiety; and the degree to which the decisions made are congruent with the individual's goals as he perceives them.

CREATIVITY

As the term is used here, creativity implies a characteristic of ingenuity in the individual's problem-solving behavior. In essence, this involves a freedom to depart from the conventional approaches to a problem and to formulate novel or unique solutions. There is considerable flexibility in shifting set and in the ways in which the individual characteristically perceives himself in relation to his situation. Bronowski (3) provides the following view:

A man becomes creative, whether he is an artist or a scientist, when he finds a new unity in the variety of nature. He does so by finding a likeness between things which were not thought alike before, and this gives him a sense both of richness and of understanding. The creative mind is a mind that looks for unexpected likenesses. This is not a mechanical procedure, and I believe that it engages the whole personality in science as in the arts.

The most dramatic advances in science and the greatest artistic masterpieces have been made by persons who combine intelligence, ability, aptitude, and interest with the personality characteristics implied by the term *creativity*. Society depends on such persons for its vitality and its progress, and their development has always been a subject of much interest and speculation. Where do creative persons come from? How do they develop? How are they different from their fellow human beings? Centers such as the University of California's Institute for Personality Assessment and Research have sought answers to these and similar questions. Persons identified as "creative" by their professional colleagues come to the Institute for three-day periods to be interviewed, tested, and observed in various situations. The first groups assessed were painters, writers, physicians, biologists, economists, anthropologists, architects, research scientists, and engineers. In reporting some of the findings, Barron (1) concludes that these individuals are characterized by their independence of judgment. They are not readily influenced by the pressures of the group; they are able to maintain their positions in the face of considerable opposition. They have little need to conform for the sake of conforming; they value their own assessment of an issue or a situation.

Although most of these individuals are quite unlike the stereotypes of the erratic scientist or the mad artist, they appear to feel under little pressure to conform to the social rituals or prejudices of the majority of their neighbors. Neither do most of them need to flout the rules of society; they can conform to the laws governing the social structure. They do not defy the social order as a means of expressing the hostility that originated in familial relationships. Although they do not strive merely to be "different," they often exhibit an unusual degree of freedom to act, to function effectively, and to focus their energies and efforts.

Since some very talented and creative individuals do show unmistakable signs of emotional disturbance, observers have wondered if this is an essential facet of creativity. It seems more plausible to assume that the creative works of Van Gogh or Dostoevsky were achieved in spite of emotional disturbance rather than because of it. This assumption seems to be consonant with most observations of human behaviors and motivations. The creative individual can probably be described as satisfying the criteria of psychological effectiveness as presented in this text, more completely than do most of his fellows.

LEVEL-OF-ASPIRATION BEHAVIORS

The goals a person sets for himself, the level of attainment to which he aspires, and how he reacts to his performances—that is, to his successes and failures—provide one measure of psychological development. In the process of setting goals, whether they be those of the high school boy who hopes to attain a varsity letter; the college student, an outstanding academic record warranting admission to graduate school; or the young father, a better paying position; the entire personality is involved. His ability to judge his environment and himself and to utilize such judgments in the setting and modification of his goals are not only significant indicators of the adequacy of his ego processes. Such abilities are also in effect the product of his total history.

Individuals who have attained a high level of personal development will set goals higher than those they have now achieved. In the light of the individual's ability and opportunity, however, the hoped-for level of attainment is not outside the realm of possibility. In the process of the individual's self-evaluation, assessment of his opportunities, and clarification of his objectives, rational consideration of available evidence and clarity of thought are required. Persons who must rely on self-deceptive mechanisms will often set goals far above or far below those warranted by their abilities. The relationship of ability level to actual achievement also results from goal setting, decision making, and problem solving, and the degree to which the individual can think rationally about himself and his opportunities plays an important role in determining the degree to which the ability and achievement levels are in accord.

Both underachievement and overachievement can represent efforts to resolve intrapsychic conflict and to maintain, protect, and enhance the self. Studies of failing high school and college students suggest that underachievement is related to unsatisfactory experiences with parents, particularly those who place an excessively high value on achievement. In part, this inference is based on the finding that the underachieving student is more hostile than the achiever. In many instances the underachiever cannot recognize his own hostility nor can he directly express it to either or both parents. Underachievement is self-defeating, for the individual hurts himself even though the effort represents a need to accomplish just the opposite. This kind of behavior is psychologically comprehensible, however, for by striking back, in the psychological sense, at the parent who "failed" him, the student not only inflicts hurt upon the parent (who may no longer be present or even alive), but also differentiates his own values from those of his parent and demonstrates his own range of control over what he will and will not do. Such adaptive mechanisms are particularly inconsistent with the self-interests of the student, who incorporates his parents' achievement values even though he vigorously resists them. He fails to achieve, but at the same time he is greatly distressed and anxious over his inability to do better work.

Another interpretation of underachievement as related to aspiration level is that it represents an attempted protection against feelings of failure. This paradox arises from the human being's ability to deceive himself. A person desperately desires to succeed in a given activity but he fears that he will fail, so he denies the significance of his own activity. Since he therefore cannot commit his energy and ability to the activity, he does, in fact, fail. He then rationalizes his failure by saying, in effect, "Had I really tried I would have succeeded."

Learning How to Learn

Some instances of academic underachievement are caused not by intrapsychic conflict or inadequate motivation but rather by a failure to learn how to learn. In assessing the factors responsible for underachievement, it is necessary to evaluate the individual's work and study habits, his knowledge of sources of information, and the many matters that pertain to the techniques of work and study.

In the case of overachievement, the individual acts as if the acquisition of status and achievement symbols will enhance his regard for himself. The tendency of some parents to require the child to behave in certain approved ways before he is loved, discussed in Chapter 8, is relevant here. The overachiever, whose relationships with his parents have created uncertainties as to his own worth and value, attempts to demonstrate his value by achieving. Not only does he often derive little satisfaction from the learning process itself, but his goals are probably so high they can never be reached and, in effect, he denies himself the satisfaction of ever experiencing success. If a great amount of tension is involved, overachieving behavior should be regarded as ineffective, since it has a "driven" quality to it and eventually can be detrimental to the individual's health and his interpersonal relationships.

INTELLIGENCE AND EFFECTIVE BEHAVIOR

One of the more prevalent misconceptions of intelligence is that individuals with superior intellectual ability are psychologically unstable. In one of the classical studies of psychology (17), Lewis Terman selected more than 600 elementary school students with intelligence quotients above 140. They were followed for a period of over forty years, and their emotional stability, as well as their achievement and their physical health, was compared to that of the general population. In the four volumes of his "studies of genius" Terman and his associates demonstrated that throughout their development, individuals with superior intellectual ability achieve not only higher than average levels of physical and social development, but that they also have a far lower incidence of mental illness. It was found that this group of individuals had contributed far more than their "quota" to society.

The Terman studies raise the socially significant question of whether individuals of unusual intellectual endowment are receiving the educational and social attention that their abilities warrant. The social as well as individual waste of unusual ability constitutes a major problem, one that unfortunately has been highlighted only by concerns over the technological achievements of our nation compared to those of other countries. In individual terms, the studies indicate that persons of high intellectual ability who are provided with opportunities for full development will probably be able to attain higher standards of living, more satisfying occupational activities, higher incomes, and healthier and longer lives than their contemporaries.

In a study (11) of gifted children of the very highest order of tested intelligence, Hollingworth observed that those with intelligence quotients above 180 exhibited less adequate social adjustment than did children whose intellectual levels were lower. This is understandable in terms of differences in general language levels and communication skills among children who have markedly different mental ages. A six-year-old with a mental age of ten or eleven has interests, skills in communication, and a vocabulary that might well create serious problems in his social relationships with average six-year-olds. A child of unusually high intellectual ability can take advantage of special educational programs, but when such opportunities are not provided there is a considerable chance that he will become bored, restless, and disruptive. Unfortunately, the public schools have not given sufficient attention to students who are intellectually gifted.

During his adolescent years the individual with superior intellectual ability often finds it difficult to communicate and maintain common interest levels with his peers. If he abandons his own interests in order to conform to the general interests and attainment levels of the peer group, he is accepting a solution involving underachievement and ineffective personal behavior. Individuals of high intellectual ability who pursue their own interests and who seek out individuals with whom they can communicate are more likely to utilize their abilities effectively.

Intellectual Effectiveness of the Mentally Retarded

Persons with intellectual levels lower than 70—and therefore in the bottom 5 percent of the population—are frequently referred to as mentally retarded. They should not be confused with persons characterized as "mentally ill," whose behaviors are primitive or erratic but whose previous levels of attainment have been higher. The mentally retarded person is one whose intellectual development has been appreciably slower than that of most persons of his age. Thus, a fully grown man can have the mental age of a five- or six-year-old child. Such persons are frequently capable of socially useful activities and may be able to work and live with moderate or minimal supervision. Although the problems of the mentally retarded individual in our society are indeed great, such a person can meet the criteria of psychological development as they have been presented here. A severely mentally retarded person sometimes requires considerable assistance and supervision even in the activities related to self-care, but for the majority of the mentally retarded, activity within an appropriate range of abilities can be found. It should be noted that the problem of underachievement can also exist for the mentally retarded, since in many instances it is assumed that the retarded individual's abilities are less than is actually the case. In some instances parents of moderately retarded children, out of a lack of understanding of the child's condition or as a result of anxiety about the child's failure to demonstrate the expected level of attainment, will push their children toward objectives that are impossible of achievement. Such situations result in great frustration and anguish; and when the child "fails" to satisfy the parents' wishes, such children are often rejected by their parents.

The Emotions and Effective Behavior

Anger, affection, joy, sorrow, guilt, and grief are profound human experiences known to all men. Yet to define these and the many additional emotions is not a simple matter. Who can describe the experience of an individual who has just broken a world's record or observed a terrible disaster? Who can verbally capture the feelings of the patriot who sees the enemy's troops marching into his country, or the mother who finds her child dead? In Part Two, the expression of emotions at various stages in the child's life was described. With increased experience, physical growth and maturation, and learning, the number of emotional states available to the individual increases from the limited patterns of the infant to the large number of feeling states of the adult. To introduce a discussion of emotions within the context of effective intrapersonal behaviors, we will cite a system of classification suggested by Krech and Crutchfield (14), because it is particularly applicable to our treatment of personality.

1. Primary emotions: joy, fear, anger, grief
2. Emotions pertaining to sensory stimulation: pain, disgust, horror, delight
3. Emotions pertaining to self-appraisal: shame, pride, guilt
4. Emotions pertaining to other people: love, hate, pity
5. Appreciative emotions: humor, beauty, wonder
6. Moods: sadness, anxiety, elation

The reader can easily extend the list of emotions included within the six classes, and also he can categorize the emotional states as positive or negative depending upon their congruence with the maintenance and enhancement needs.

Interaction of Personality and Situational Factors

A close relationship exists among the individual's physical state, the feelings he is experiencing, and the behaviors being elicited by the situation. A tired person seated in a theater next to persons who weep as they watch a tragedy is more apt to feel sadness than if he were seated at home watching his favorite comedian on television. In this example, it is apparent that not only are the immediate situation and the physical condition of the individual important influences on the feeling state experienced, but also that perception and thought are closely intertwined with the emotions. The nature of the situation, the memories and meanings it evokes, along with internal feeling states, will to an extent be consciously recognized, and it is the awareness of these factors that determines the quality and intensity of the experienced emotion.

The influence the emotional state has on what is perceived and responded to, however, also is evident in the everyday experiences of daily life. The irritated driver who has been delayed for forty-five minutes by highway construction will tend to perceive the discourtesy of another driver who enters his traffic lane without signaling as far more than a breach of good manners. He may perceive the other driver as an enemy, a public menace, and a criminal.

The emotional, perceptual, and thought processes that interact to determine the meaning a person sees in a given situation, and the feelings associated with this meaning, are, of course, all manifestations of the total personality. The complex interactions of an individual's id, ego, and superego processes account for the emotions experienced and expressed. Whether a breach of social etiquette brings feelings of shame or guilt, or both (or neither), for example, depends on previous experiences of failing to fulfill expectations held (usually by parents) and the consequences of such failures, as well as the values and standards the person has internalized as part of his superego. Whether feelings of grief or remorse, of sadness or depression, or of elation or euphoria are experienced in a given situation depends upon the experiences that have contributed to personality development.

Not only are the subtle "selections" among emotional states determined by the factors accounting for personality development, but gross differences in emotional reaction are similarly attributable to the interaction of the personality processes. A person experiences understanding and compassion or anger and scorn when encountering human suffering, depending on the activity of his total personality in the specific situation.

The primary role of the personality in accounting for the emotions experienced and expressed has been emphasized so far, but situational elements also play a part in accounting for an individual's emotional behaviors. The man who was unmoved by the deaths he observed during war often becomes nauseous and faint upon encountering the fatal aftermath of an automobile accident. Within a culture the commonly shared, learned behavioral patterns include a repertory of "appropriate" emotional responses to different situations. The solemn mood of the church service, the festive feelings appropriate to a party, the grief at a funeral all represent learned behaviors that include the identification of the situation as well as the feelings to be associated with it. These commonly shared learnings provide what have been termed the "shared norms" and afford a basis for one standard of effective emotional behaviors.

The appropriateness of an individual's emotional responses to a situation must be weighed both qualitatively and quantitatively. "Qualitatively appropriate" means that the response fits the situation as the observer views it, while "quantitatively appropriate" refers to the intensity or strength of the expressed reaction in light of the "shared norms." The distinction between emotions experienced and emotions expressed has been made in the preceding pages. This distinction highlights two aspects of effective emotional behaviors that have been implied throughout this discussion; one pertains to the range of emotional experience available to the person; the second to the ability to both express and control these emotions.

The person functioning effectively not only can experience a wide range of emotional response, but also is aware of himself and his feelings, and consequently is able to know what others mean when they make subtle distinctions between emotional states. Awareness of his own broad range of emotions contributes to a zest for living, and an avoidance of "sameness" and shallowness of his feelings. The person's accessibility to his own feelings depends on the degree to which they engender threat and have to be walled off. For the person functioning at a high degree of effectiveness, little energy is committed to blocking off, denying, or avoiding emotions.

Possibly because of religious traditions that tend to equate emotions with sinfulness, the ideal of the Stoic, the strong and unemotional figure with "nerves of steel," has been widely held within our culture, particularly among members of the middle class. People who equate strength with lack of emotional expression ignore the fact that emotions are a natural aspect of man and that feeling states themselves are different from overtly expressed behaviors. So prevalent is the belief that it is weak and feminine to experience emotions that in the training boys receive at home and at school, they are rewarded for being "unemotional" and reproved when they cry or indicate strong feeling. Because of this reinforcement, the experience of compassion, sympathy, empathy, and esthetic appreciation will often evoke guilt. There is another trend in the American culture involving the emotions associated with aggression and destruction. This is the widespread refusal to believe that all human beings have at times unexpressed murderous angers and irrational passions, even though there is daily exposure to reports of violence. The television programs featuring sadism and murder are among the most popular; yet when individuals commit such crimes they are regarded as inhuman and deserving of extermination.

Unless society recognizes that man's emotions are part of his being human and run the gamut from feelings of concern for his fellows to anger and destructiveness sufficient to account for the most bestial of behaviors, there can be no adequate provision for protecting man from himself. The horrors of the Nazis' systematic elimination of millions of men, women, and children testify not to the fact that the Nazi leadership somehow fell outside the range of what could properly be considered human; rather, it points to the potential within all men for hatred and the emotions which are associated with destruction and murder. Unless these emotions are recognized and controlled, men cannot function effectively in their own behalf and in accordance with their own self-interests.

Controlling emotion requires recognition of the feeling states and the channeling of their expressions in ways that are not harmful to others or to the individual himself. By recognizing one's emotions, one achieves the first step in their productive control and use. Control and direction of emotion imply that the conditions required for the ego process to function well have been met. In Chapter 14 we shall consider avenues of activity available to those whose ego activity is falling short of integrating the conflicting demands of id and superego processes and who therefore face a disruption of their emotional life.

Ineffective Intrapersonal Behaviors

DISORDERS OF THE SYMBOLIC PROCESSES

In the process of thinking, ideas or images that represent fragments of previous experience may be joined or related to symbolize behaviors that are not overtly expressed. Inferences about the nature and content of the thought processes of another person are made on the basis of what he says and what he does in given situations. Appropriateness of thinking processes is evaluated in terms of the logical relationships that bind the images together (the internal consistency of the ideas), and the logical relationship of the ideas or images to the external situation that stimulates their production. Consider the following incident that occurred during a psychological examination in which the person was asked, "How far is it from New York to Paris?" After indicating that he did not know and being encouraged to figure it out, the subject provided the following reply.

Well, it takes about a week to get from Paris to New York. There are seven days in a week and twenty-four hours in a day; so multiply 24 by 7 and you get 161 which equals the hours in seven days or one week. Now there are twenty blocks in a mile; so multiply 161 by 20, and this gives you 3,220. The distance from Paris to New York is 3,220 miles (19, p. 167).

In evaluating the thought process reflected in this sample, the reader might attempt to identify the ideas he himself utilizes in arriving at an answer to the question. Do the ideas in the example progress from one to another in an orderly and logical fashion? Do they lead systematically toward a correct solution of the problem? Are there errors in the reasoning process?

Consistency among Ideas

The internal consistency of an individual's series of thoughts and the adequacy of his ability to reason are important indicators of the degree to which he is free of internal conflict. Individuals who are experiencing great conflict must utilize their reasoning abilities to protect themselves from anxiety; consequently, their thought processes are sometimes qualitatively inappropriate. For these persons, protection against anxiety is accomplished by a misinterpretation of the external situation or by thought that appears to others to be disconnected or illogical.

Adequacy to think is defined here in terms of the degree to which the thought process is logical, systematic, and valid. In assessing development, we must consider the extent to which an individual is able to utilize the ability he has been born with, but in assessing intrapersonal effectiveness, we are interested—at least partly—in the internal consistency of ideas rather than just their brilliance or profundity.

Fantasy and Daydreaming

At this point the reader who has carefully followed the preceding section may wonder whether the label "inappropriate thought" can be applied to seemingly unrelated and illogical ideas, experienced especially during moments of reverie. Or he may ask whether the type of thinking that occurs when his attention wanders could be called an internally inconsistent sequence of ideas.

The answer to these questions is that the inappropriateness of a sequence of ideas is defined not only by the process itself but by the circumstances and conditions under which the process occurs. When the solution of problems or the accomplishment of personal objectives requires task-directed thinking, the important issue is whether the individual is able to think logically, systematically, and cogently. The ability to think appropriately is related to the ability to control and direct one's thoughts. If the ideas are logically tied together and are relevant to the issue, then there is no question about the qualitative appropriateness of the person's thought processes. But if the ideas are illogically related or inconsistent, then the qualitative inappropriateness of the process has relevance to the assessment of intrapersonal development.

Less difficult to identify than the internal consistency of ideas are those disorders of the thought processes resulting in behaviors that are contrary to or inconsistent with social expectations. In their gross forms such disorders are seen in hallucinatory, delusional, and withdrawal behaviors and are easily recognized as signs of marked personal disorganization. They will be discussed later in this chapter in connection with schizophrenia.

It is impossible to draw a clear-cut line of demarcation between the phenomenon of daydreaming and that which we have described as qualitatively inappropriate thought. As the previous discussion has indicated, the distinction depends upon whether the thought occurs in situations calling for goal-directed behavior or during moments of relaxation when no concerted effort is being made to sustain or direct attention. Whether daydreaming is classified as a qualitatively inappropriate thought reaction thus depends on the situation in which it occurs, the function it serves, the degree to which it substitutes for action, and whether it contributes to a distorted perception of the individual's relationship to the world and people around him. For example, an individual who is daydreaming has transitory thoughts of an imaginative character. He is later aware that he has "drifted off" and has had a fantasy. There is no doubt in his mind as to whether it actually occurred or not.

Daydreaming has been described as being realistic or unrealistic. In realistic daydreaming the fantasy or imagined event conforms to the person's life situation. He may think through an event that occurred during the day and say to himself, "Now if instead of doing this, I had followed this course of action, it may have had different results." The person may then envision the consequences of the alternative action. This type of daydreaming has its source in the factual circumstances, allows for the consideration of various actions or contingencies, and is probably an essential part of constructive thought. In a sense it represents a kind of functional thinking, since it allows for a type of "trying out" or anticipatory action, as described in problem solving, without requiring overt behavior in order to experience the consequences.

In "realistic" daydreaming the person is able to pull away from the fantasy at will, and he experiences no difficulty in distinguishing actuality from fantasy. In some instances, such thinking through, when it pertains to an event that has actually occurred, may provide an opportunity to achieve a feeling of completeness or mastery over the occurrence. The events leading to and precipitating anxiety, for example, may be thought about repeatedly. The actual process of thinking back through the events helps to minimize the anxiety and to enable the individual to cope consciously with some of the features of the situation that initially elicited the anxiety. In anticipated experiences the daydream aids the individual to prepare for the demands that may be made upon him in a problem situation. The person thinks, "If it goes this way, then I will want to say or do this; if it goes the other way, then I should say or do such and such." Everyone engages in "realistic" daydreaming and we should consider it constructive fantasy, and not include it in the category of qualitatively inappropriate thought.

Qualitatively Inappropriate Thought

It has been emphasized that the line between qualitatively inappropriate thought and daydreaming is impossible to identify clearly. The division is roughly the same as that between behaviors resulting from realistic and from unrealistic daydreaming. Unrealistic daydreaming is considered to be qualitatively inappropriate thought, for in enabling the individual to allay frustration through envisioning satisfying resolutions to his difficulties, it departs from reality. In such fantasies the situation may be altered in any way to produce the most satisfying result. The slightly built, nonathletic boy can picture himself intercepting a forward pass during the last moments of a football game with his school's arch rival. He sees himself scoring the winning touchdown, in a display of brilliant open field running and to the cheers of thousands. The unattractive girl can envision herself being "discovered" by a Hollywood talent scout and transformed into a glamorous movie queen. Such fantasies, which are engaged in to greater or lesser extent by all persons, enable the individual to counteract momentarily the actual dissatisfactions and frustrations of his situation. For a moment a boy can enjoy the gratification that would be his if he were the school's athletic hero, or the girl can put aside the realization that she is physically less attractive than the other girls in her class. Daydreaming of the unrealistic type is a matter of concern *only* when it becomes a habitual substitute for action. When the daydream becomes so satisfying that energy and effort are not expended in the usual activities associated with the pursuit of self-interest, then this type of qualitatively inappropriate thinking is significant as a sign of intrapersonal conflict.

In talking to a psychologist, the worried mother of an eighteen-year-old girl said, "I have come to you after talking to our family doctor. Frankly, I just don't know what to do about Betty. Her father and I have tried reasoning with her and scolding her, but nothing seems to help. She refuses to leave the house to go to school or to see her friends. If I didn't insist that she get out of bed in the morning, she would stay there all day. The school people have been very patient, but I know that she will not graduate with the senior class if she doesn't start back to school soon. It's not that she wasn't a good student. Though she didn't make top grades, she did have about a B or a B plus average. She just seems to be thinking about something all of the time. She doesn't seem to be unhappy, but when we interrupt her thinking and try to get her to do something, she will become very angry and scream at us to leave her alone. She refuses to tell us what she is thinking about, but whatever it is, she is thinking about it most of the time."

In his discussion with the mother and later in his psychological examination of the daughter, the psychologist tried to judge the degree to which the girl was able to perceive herself and her relationship to other people without distortion. In making this judgment, he was interested in learning whether the girl was experiencing delusions or hallucinations.

Hallucinations

A hallucination is a sensory impression that is not caused by specific external stimuli, such as light or sound. The person who has the hallucination usually believes at the time that the experience is an objective event which can be shared with other persons. Hallucinatory reactions can be stimulated by a personal "set" or, in some instances, by agents that affect the central nervous system, such as drugs or alcohol.

A common type of hallucination was experienced by a twelve-year-old boy who was returning home on Hallowe'en night after an evening of pranks. Because of the lateness of the hour, he elected to go home by a shortcut that followed some disused railroad tracks. The path and the tracks were flanked on both sides by steep banks and at one point they crossed an old cemetery. A local legend, which the boy had heard in vivid detail earlier in the evening, featured an engineer who had been run over by his own train along the same stretch of tracks. According to the legend, the engineer's train had been taken over by a ghostly figure who had stopped the train by waving it down with a red lantern. As the boy approached the cemetery area, he felt his skin prickle and his heart begin to pound against his chest; his eyes and ears strained for every sight and sound. He wanted to run, but he did not do so until he heard a rustling sound behind him that grew louder and louder. When he turned, he saw a ghostly figure slowly coming up the tracks waving a red lantern. The boy raced wildly for a qarter of a mile, then, exhausted and unable to run more, he looked behind him again and saw some old newspapers being blown along the tracks by the wind. As the papers came closer to him he heard the rustling sound, now barely audible.

If hallucinatory reactions do not interfere with the ability to function in relationships with other people, and if they are not persistent or of a quality that prevents the furtherance of one's self-interests, they can usually be dismissed as a personal idiosyncrasy. Hallucinatory reactions that interfere with the person's ability to deal with other people or that occur frequently enough for the person to be recognized as one responding to stimuli that are not perceived by others are considered signs of intrapersonal conflict. An extreme example is seen in the behaviors of the person who responds to voices that cannot be heard by others, or who has visions. The behavior of the alcoholic in acute delirium tremens offers a dramatic example of reactions to visual and auditory hallucinations. Pronounced hallucinatory reactions occur frequently in individuals diagnosed as schizophrenic and are often accompanied by marked delusional or withdrawal reactions.

Delusions

A delusion is a belief or a set of beliefs held with conviction but inconsistent with verifiable experience or events. The person who insists that he is a military hero of a bygone era will not be dissuaded from his belief that he is Caesar or Napoleon. In fact, such a person might present quite a plausible explanation to account for his masquerading as an ordinary citizen or to explain his "disappearing" from history.

Cameron (4) has classified delusions into the following types:

1. Persecutory delusions: the person feels that he is being victimized or persecuted. He feels threatened or the object of attack or that he is the victim of a conspiracy.
2. Delusions of influence: the person feels that external agents or forces account for his behaviors and reactions, that his will has been taken over, and that he is no longer in control of his thoughts or actions.
3. Grandiose delusions: the person believes himself to be possessed of great brilliance, power, or strength. He may identify with some great personage in history or assume the role of benefactor to mankind, savior, or tyrant.
4. Self-deprecatory delusions: the person believes that he is worthless, sinful, and rightly deserves to be punished or castigated.
5. Delusions of body change: the person believes his body or parts of it are being transformed or are functioning very differently. His complaints may include beliefs that his brain is missing or that his stomach has shriveled up or that his intestines are turning to stone.
6. Delusions of unreality: the person is distressed by the belief that the familiar has become strange and that which was once known well has lost its character of reality.

One characteristic of a delusion is the tenacity with which it is held. Logic, written evidence, and glaring contradictions will not shake the deluded person in his conviction. An illustration of this point is provided by Korzybski (13), who tells of a patient who believed that he was dead. To demonstrate to the patient that he was alive, the doctor stated, "Dead men don't bleed." The patient was then pricked with a needle and when blood appeared, he looked at it for a moment, and shaking his head, stated, "Dead men do bleed." A delusional system is an elaborate set of beliefs that all fit together. The person under the influence of a delusional system may imagine a great many people engaged in a conspiracy against the organization or country he represents. He may keep records of elaborate codes and may to such an extent live within the delusion that he invests all his time and energy in the maintenance of the venture.

Although the clear-cut delusion, easily recognized by the layman as a serious psychological disorganization, is encountered rather infrequently, behaviors having a delusional quality may often be observed in everyday life. Thinking may have a delusional quality (although not as unusual or dramatic as the examples above) if it is unyielding in the face of all contrary evidence or results in bizarre and unfounded interpretations and explanations of events or phenomena. These less dramatic instances of inappropriate thinking are similar to delusions, for they are well systematized, rigidly maintained, and are not readily modifiable. In the evaluation of inappropriate thought, the rigidity as well as the nature of the beliefs must be considered. If a person is able to keep an "open mind," even about issues on which he has strong convictions, he is less likely to make use of inappropriate thought in the protection of his self-concept or the maintenance of his self-esteem than is the person who is unreceptive to information that is inconsistent with his beliefs. A fixed belief or set of ideas serving the purpose of protecting self-esteem may be very different in content from the strange convictions of the deluded hospital patient, but its delusional qualities can be seen in the following example.

Miss Brown had many complaints about the people at work. She felt that they were very critical of her appearance and, in general, were quite unfriendly. During the four months that she had been working as a bookkeeper in the accounting department of a large organization, she had related to her family numerous instances in which she felt she had been slighted or made to feel inadequate.

She spoke mainly of her supervisor, Mrs. Thomas, who had been with the company for many years. Mrs. Thomas, a conscientious, businesslike person, had the responsibility of reviewing Miss Brown's work and had several times provided Miss Brown with information about office procedures. Miss Brown often tried to engage her supervisor in pleasant conversation about issues unrelated to the office, but Mrs. Thomas had avoided such discussion, since she was conscious of the amount of work that had to be taken care of. Miss Brown was convinced that the supervisor's behavior was intended to indicate her incompetence and to discredit her in the estimation of Mr. Jack, her employer. Miss Brown also believed that she was being given more than her share of work and that her supervisor was assigning her the hardest and most unpleasant tasks.

She explained to her family that the injustices she was encountering were "because Mrs. Thomas has it in for me." When she told several of the girls in the office that her supervisor disliked her, they disagreed, pointing out that Mrs. Thomas had recently recommended that she be given a raise, and that Miss Brown was not being treated differently from the other girls in the office. Miss Brown then decided that these girls also had it in for her, and she made it a point to avoid them. Although Miss Brown received a raise, she decided to quit the job at the end of the month and seek employment in a situation where she would receive better treatment.

It is of interest to note that Miss Brown had been employed in seven different offices in the three years following her graduation from business college.

The reader has probably already noted the relationship between inappropriate thought having a delusional character and the mechanisms of defense referred to earlier. Projection, repression, and to some extent, rationalization and intellectualization can defend against the anxieties engendered by intrapsychic conflict by enabling an individual to deceive himself. The deception is accomplished by the delusion or by beliefs having a delusional quality and is directed toward the protection of the concept of self, or it may have a wish-fulfillment function. This function consists of the denial of unsatisfactory realities and the substitution of a fixed belief that somehow the wished-for state of affairs does exist.

SCHIZOPHRENIC REACTIONS

In its extreme form, delusional thinking is a symptom of serious personality disorganization. Delusions and other signs of inappropriate perception, thought, and emotion may have considerable significance in the diagnosis of the group of disorders known as schizophrenia. Although not all persons classified as schizophrenic evidence delusions, many of their behaviors can be interpreted as inappropriate to their own self-interests and as incompatible with social expectations.

The frequency and severity of schizophrenic reactions may be grasped by realizing that over one half of the hospital beds in the country are occupied by persons with this diagnosis. The incidence of schizophrenia is so great that everyone will probably have contact during his lifetime with someone—a friend, relative, or acquaintance—who reacts in ways characteristic of this disorder. For this reason the informed person should know something of the nature of schizophrenic behaviors, but it is important to note that the information provided here represents only a minimal treatment of this highly complex problem.

In 1911, Eugene Blueler, a Swiss psychiatrist, originated the term "schizophrenia" to describe the splitting of the various psychic processes. According to Blueler, a person whose emotional reactions were incongruous was demonstrating a split between his emotional and intellectual processes. A psychiatric patient, upon being informed of the death of a friend, for example, would appear indifferent and uninterested. This lack of integration between the intellectual and emotional processes seemed to be a common characteristic of patients who demonstrated a wide range of behaviors. Bleuler believed that this was a more satisfactory term than "dementia praecox," which had been coined earlier by Kraepelin, a German psychiatrist, to characterize the same reactions. Kraepelin believed that the common element was the "precocious" appearance of a deteriorative process which led to gross personality disorganization. Later work has indicated that schizophrenic reactions may appear at any time during a person's life and that they do not inevitably lead to a chronic state from which there is no recovery.

Schizophrenic reactions are often readily identified by the layman as "odd," "eccentric," or "crazy." The facial movements, strange gestures and postures, the incoherent speech, the inappropriate smiles or rages, the peculiar beliefs—any of these alone or in combination—can cause the observer to feel that there is something gravely at fault. Sometimes a friend or relative behaves differently, less predictably than previously, and his associates express concern, wondering what is happening to him. At first he may seem preoccupied or inattentive, but for a time he continues to maintain his work schedule. Eventually, to the dismay of his friends and family, his reveries become more pronounced, and he begins to respond to voices that others do not hear and sights that others do not see. He may expend his energies on mysterious projects, such as preparing a secret code book or communicating with persons from outer space. If his delusional system becomes well established, he will act upon it, announcing that he is some powerful potentate or some well-known personage. Or he may behave as if he is the object of a search by hostile agents who are out to kidnap or harm him. Finally his behaviors result in so marked a disruption of his life that he can no longer work or carry out his usual social and familial roles. Persons who were once close friends may now be responded to as enemies or may not even be recognized.

Often the personality disorganization and the associated deviant behaviors reach a point that necessitates the patient's institutionalization. While in the hospital he will be examined and his treatment will now usually be by drugs instead of by insulin and electric shock, as was once common practice. If the institution has the resources and believes it to be important, he will also receive psychotherapy, a specialized form of personal relationship in which the professionally trained person attempts to facilitate the patient's psychological rehabilitation (see Chapter 14). Approximately one third of the persons hospitalized with diagnoses of schizophrenia are able to return to their homes, and many are able to resume their work and familial responsibilities. Some will have recurrences, but others will be able to function outside the hospital, even though their behavior may still be eccentric.

Although schizophrenia is represented by a syndrome or pattern of particular behaviors, not all the elements just described will be present in each case. The variation, both in degree and in the types of combinations that can appear, is too great to discuss in detail. Instead, one might say that the schizophrenic will generally exhibit one or more of these characteristics: lack of correspondence between emotional and intellectual reactions, marked withdrawal to a private fantasy world, hallucinatory experiences, and rigid and complex delusional systems. Sometimes the onset of the symptoms of disorientation, disorganization, and confusion is sudden; sometimes the individual becomes progressively more disorganized over a period of many years. Bower and his associates (2) studied the high school performances of a group of veterans later diagnosed as schizophrenic and compared them with the records of a control group of nonhospitalized men who were classmates of the patients. They found marked evidences of ineffectiveness in the group later diagnosed as schizophrenic, even in high school. They were less able to direct their abilities to goals valued by society; they received poorer grades, were less likely to complete school, to participate in extracurricular activities, and to demonstrate adequate intrapersonal relationships than those in the control group. In many instances, teachers and counselors had expressed concern about their behaviors.

The search for the causes of schizophrenia has been diligently pursued, but research in biochemistry, physiology, anatomy, psychiatry, psychology, and sociology has not yet provided a definitive explanation. One of the more promising points of view holds that several disorders having different causes might account for the patterns of withdrawal, loss of contact with reality, hallucinatory and delusional behaviors which provide the basis for the diagnosis of schizophrenia.

From a psychological point of view schizophrenia is often viewed as a disorder in which the customary reality-mediating functions of the ego processes break down under acute and prolonged intrapsychic conflict. In his efforts to maintain himself with a minimum of anxiety, the individual resorts to defenses that result in bizarre behaviors and loses contact with the external world. The behaviors demonstrated are often described as regressive in the sense that they correspond to primitive behaviors typical of earlier stages of the individual's development.

Various biological explanations of schizophrenia have also been put forth; studies of metabolism, circulation, and brain activity have been undertaken to account for the cause of these disorders. As yet, however, no single psychological or biological hypothesis accounting for schizophrenia can be accepted without reservations. In addition to the possibility that there may be several different disorders or diseases, each with its own set of causal factors, that are mistakenly grouped under the one category of schizophrenia, there are two other problems in the diagnosis of schizophrenia. The first is that some organically determined disorders such as general paresis, epilepsy, and brain tumors can result in behaviors resembling those associated with schizophrenia. Second, the layman who reads about schizophrenic reactions can easily and erroneously conclude that many of his friends are schizophrenic. The difficulty of establishing a specific diagnosis of schizophrenia is such that the layman is best advised to refrain from the temptation of labeling all nonconformist behaviors as "schizophrenic."

MANIC-DEPRESSIVE REACTIONS

Extreme and persistent responses of elation or depression suggest the presence of manic-depressive reactions. In the manic phase of the disorder the person is overactive. This overactivity sometimes reaches only a mild degree of elation or euphoria. The individual talks faster, acts more quickly, and feels as if he is thinking more rapidly and effectively. He may believe that he is delightfully witty, that the world is a wonderful place, that all people are his friends. His friends may even feel that he is "changing for the better." Persons who are usually reserved and who do not openly express their feelings may appear to be more social and gregarious. In its severe forms, the activity level of the manic phase is so high that a person may talk too rapidly to be intelligible; his restlessness becomes extreme and continuous. Persons in states of manic excitement may need medical and protective measures, such as sedation or confinement, to prevent them from harming themselves or others.

This manic phase may last for a period of hours or weeks. Gradually the overactivity subsides and is replaced by listless behavior in which the person appears "slowed down" and feels depressed. He feels unworthy, that life is not worth living, or that he has committed unpardonable sins and is utterly despicable. The severely depressed person is markedly unresponsive to what is going on about him and may sit for hours refusing all efforts to engage him in conversation. He may weep, sigh, or give other evidence of profound depression.

The cyclic character of the manic-depressive reaction is not present in all cases. Not all persons who experience the periods of great elation or of profound depression, for example, will show a shift from one to the other.

Manic-depressive reactions should not be confused with the relatively mild variations in emotional mood that are characteristic of all individuals The essential differences between manic-depressive reactions and those that are within the bounds of normal mood fluctuation lie in the qualities of intensity, persistence, and appropriateness. The manic-depressive reaction is more intense, more persistent, and less appropriate than are the reactions we consider reflective of mood fluctuation. Even the untrained observer can detect gross distortions of reality and overt expressions of irrational feelings and behaviors in the manic-depressive. Such a person may convincingly describe a scheme that will make a million, but close examination will reveal its flaws. Or in his depressive states he will paint so hopeless a picture of the world and will wallow in such self-condemnation that no amount of "reason" will convince him that he is exaggerating.

The manic-depressive disorders represent a serious mental health problem, since approximately 14 percent of all patients admitted to psychiatric hospitals are so diagnosed (18). Although it is very difficult to obtain accurate statistical information about diagnoses, recovery rates, and effectiveness of treatment, certain general conclusions can be deduced from reports in the professional literature. They cannot, however, serve as a basis for the prediction of the chances for recovery of any *specific* patient.

Most patients who are hospitalized with manic-depressive reactions may be expected to achieve enough control of their emotional responses to allow them to return to their homes. Approximately 65 to 75 percent are able to return to their former activities. On the other hand, approximately 40 percent of those admitted to hospitals for the first time with this disorder have recurrences that are severe enough to necessitate their readmission. The length of time for hospitalization or special treatment varies from several days to many years, but as the statistical information above indicates, most manic-depressive patients are able to return to their homes and resume their usual routines. One outstanding characteristic of this disorder is that following periods of mania or depression there is no loss of intellectual ability.

The use of electric shock treatment is frequent in the manic-depressive disorders and much publicity has been given to this type of therapeutic procedure. The procedure involves passing electrical currents through the brain so that a convulsion is produced in the body. The patient is unaware of the convulsion, since consciousness is lost as soon as the current is turned on. Following a period of sleep, he awakens feeling stiff and slightly confused. Several hours later, no ill effects of the shock can be observed, and in some instances the patient will behave in a manner characteristic for him before the onset of the disorder. The number of shock treatments required before the manic-depressive reactions disappear may range from less than ten to twenty or thirty. This treatment seems to have benefited individuals in the depressed phase of the disorder more than those experiencing manic reactions. The term "benefit" is used in the sense that individuals receiving shock treatment may be able to leave the hospital sooner than those who do not receive such treatment, but we are still not sure how long this benefit lasts, as well as of the physiological explanation of the benefit.

Since the early 1950s there has been an increasing interest in the use of certain drugs as influencers of perceptual, thought, and emotional processes. These so-called "psychoactive" drugs have been utilized in the treatment of severely disturbed persons, schizophrenics and manic-depressives. Although the amount of improvement resulting from the administration of these drugs has not matched the enthusiastic expectations that greeted their discovery, they have made the management and treatment of the hospitalized psychiatric patient less difficult. In addition to their use in the treatment of hospitalized patients, drugs (tranquilizers) have been widely used to reduce anxiety and tension in persons with less severe psychological difficulties.

Due to the widespread use of drugs in psychiatric hospitals there has been a decline in the amount of electric shock therapy administered and in the number of patients requiring physical restraint.

NEUROTIC REACTIONS

In the preceding pages, two sets of reactions indicative of profound degrees of personality disorganization were described, the schizophrenic and the manic-depressive. These behaviors are often designated as "psychotic," in contrast to "neurotic," which is applied to behavioral symptoms of lesser disorganization. In psychotic conditions delusions, hallucinations, and disordered thought are often quite apparent, and the person usually cannot function in society without supervision and must often be institutionalized to protect him and others from himself. In contrast, the neurotic often has some insight into his difficulties and usually does not require institutionalization, since he is able, although with some difficulty, to continue with his work and his familial and social life. Since delusions and hallucinatory reactions are usually absent, neurotic behaviors are not necessarily apparent to the observer, even though the individual experiencing them may require special assistance in achieving more satisfactory levels of personality integration.

The use of these frequently employed terms, *neurotic* and *psychotic,* quite incorrectly implies that persons can be readily placed in one or the other of these boxlike categories and that there are clear-cut differences between them. Actually, the differences between psychotic and neurotic behaviors are of degree, not of kind. In general, it is helpful to think of human behaviors as extending on a continuum from completely effective to completely ineffective. At the effective end are those behaviors reflecting a high order of personal and social development; at the ineffective end are those reflecting a marked degree of personality disorganization, the *psychoses.* Below the effective and at the upper range of the ineffective behaviors fall those that are termed the *neuroses.*

In attempting to describe behavior it must be remembered that the culture and the times exert considerable influence upon what is considered to be psychotic and neurotic behavior. By today's standards, certain bizarre behaviors would be labeled psychotic, but fifty years ago they would merely be considered "odd." Similarly, an individual who communicates with his dead ancestors or who lays claim to having experienced certain visions would be commended in some societies or presumed to possess enviable powers, and in some cultures the competitive, aggressive male is thought to be deviant. Thus, each culture provides a range of established, recognized, approved behavioral patterns.

Innumerable texts have been devoted almost exclusively to the subject of neuroses, and it is beyond the scope of this book to present a complete and detailed description of them or of the theories concerning their causes and treatment. In this discussion, mention will be made of some of the major defining qualities of the neuroses, and the reader who is interested in a more detailed discussion is encouraged to explore the references cited at the end of the chapter.

MAJOR CHARACTERISTICS OF THE NEUROSES

One of the major qualities of the neuroses is the presence of anxiety, which is experienced as an unpleasant emotional state involving vague feelings of dread, oppression, or panic. Severe anxiety states may last several hours or only a few minutes and often are accompanied by physical reactions such as trembling, rapid breathing, profuse perspiring, and quickened heartbeat. Milder states may involve less intense but persistent feelings of discouragement, uneasiness, or tension.

In general, these anxiety reactions are precipitated by threatening events and experiences in the past, the memories of which are no longer consciously available to the individual. These experiences cause a disturbed development of the intrapsychic processes, with the result that adequate balance and integration of the components of personality are not achieved. One interpretation of neurosis is that it represents unresolved intrapsychic conflict and that the personality processes are, in effect, at war among themselves. In a neurosis the ego processes are operative to the extent that the individual maintains an orientation to the external world sufficient for his behaviors not to be considered bizarre although they are ineffective.

The protective and defensive behaviors initiated by threat and directed to warding off and controlling anxiety necessitate a considerable expenditure of energy and may take diverse forms. Some of the behavioral patterns were described earlier as mechanisms of defense. They may have a repetitive and seemingly senseless character.

> An example of this type of behavior was shown by Patrick, a young English boy who was evacuated to the country when extensive air raids began during World War II. He was so upset by being separated from his mother that he was returned to her after a few days, only to be separated again when he caught measles. After a stay in the hospital he was placed in a war nursery to insure his recovery, and his mother promised that she would return to visit him often.
>
> The anxiety aroused by the second separation from her was so great, however, that Patrick was unable to enter into any relationships with the staff or with other children. He refused to eat and would stand in the corner compulsively carrying out stereotyped gestures and talking to himself, "She will put on my overcoat and my leggings, she will zip up the zipper, she will put on my pixie hat," he said over and over again, and even when asked to stop, he sulked and continued to move his lips and nod his head. When his mother did return and he was permitted to stay with her in the air raid shelter for several days, his stereotyped behavior ceased. When he later returned to the nursery, he showed fewer signs of anxiety, seemed more contented, and was able to play with the other children.

The important point of the illustration, provided by Anna Freud and Burlingham (9), is that Patrick's stereotyped behavior did not eliminate his anxiety, but in a nonlogical way it enabled him to maintain himself in the situation. At the same time it interfered with new learnings and with his obtaining satisfactions through contacts with others. Only when his anxiety level decreased was he able to respond to those around him and to become a part of the group.

The Avoidance of Anxiety

The modes of behavior utilized in the avoidance of anxiety are varied and complex. Patrick's stereotyped behavior represents but one common pattern, that of dealing with the existence of threat through compulsive and ritualistic behaviors. Another pattern frequently adopted to protect the person from experiencing the direct and full impact of his anxieties employs the mechanism of displacement and is seen in the well-known phobic or acute fear reactions. In these reactions the anxieties associated with threat are not related to their original events or symbols but to a different stimulus, with the result that the person may experience unreasonable fear of high places, animals, or any other "convenient" object. When a person is in the presence of these feared objects, profound anxiety reactions occur even though he is consciously aware that his safety is not jeopardized. Sometimes such phobic reactions seem to have their beginnings in very specific experiences. For example, a young woman who became terrified in the presence of cats could vividly recall a childhood experience in which a cat jumped on her in a dark theater. In most cases, however, phobic reactions are not totally explained on the basis of a single event or experience, and they are extremely resistive to change.

Some persons, through displacement mechanisms, focus their anxieties on some aspect of their bodies or their health. The prevalence of these so-called hypochondriacal reactions is reflected in the estimate that about half of those seeking medical attention in the United States have no physical basis for their complaints. Some persons utilize so much energy in avoiding anxiety by maintaining elaborate systems of defense that they are literally exhausted or may be depressed to such a disabling degree that they are unable to concentrate or work effectively. In more dramatic forms the neurotic may disassociate himself from his conflict by actually losing his identity through loss of memory or consciousness, or he may convert his fears to physical symptoms, such as functional paralysis or blindness.

Even in forms less extreme than those cited above, the debilitating effects of prolonged defense against anxiety constitute a considerable problem for the individual. So much energy is expended in maintaining and protecting himself that the individual's physical as well as intellectual efficiency is reduced and he can no longer direct sufficient energy to mastery of his external environment.

At this more extreme level, damage occurs in the physical tissues of the body. The gastrointestinal and the circulatory systems are particularly vulnerable to breakdown. Instances of ulcers, hypertension, and heart ailments have been attributed to excessive and prolonged anxiety and stress. Although it is necessary to caution against attributing every case of ulcer and heart attack to such causes, available evidence is sufficient to justify the position that anxiety intensely experienced over long periods of time will impair the efficiency of the body.

In addition to these effects, the excessive use of some of the mechanisms of defense results in distortion of the individual's perceptions of himself, of the situations he encounters, and of the persons with whom he has contact. Neurotic individuals may perceive themselves as victims of circumstance, of the malevolence of others, or they may unduly pamper themselves and be concerned with imaginary injustices. Such persons are highly sensitive to any aspects of their perceived environment that are anxiety-provoking; hence many of their reactions to an observer seem illogical or caused by incidents too trivial to be a basis for concern.

THE TRAUMATIC NEUROSES

It should not be assumed that ineffective personal behaviors are demonstrated only by individuals whose personality development has been impeded or whose intrapsychic processes have failed to achieve adequate integration. Since ineffective behaviors may result also from the stress with which an individual is confronted, the situation as well as the individual's personality structure must be considered in accounting for the source of such behaviors. Persons who have attained a high order of personal and social development may be able to withstand considerable situational stress before their behaviors become ineffectual. On the other hand, individuals whose psychological development has fallen short may reflect ineffective behaviors under conditions of moderate or slight situational stress.

That each person if exposed to sufficient stress has a "breaking point" and will then begin to show signs of ineffectual behavior and personality disorganization is dramatically illustrated by cases of so-called "battle fatigue" during wartime. It was found that experienced combat soldiers who had demonstrated high levels of personal development and effectiveness would nevertheless become temporarily neurotic if exposed to sufficiently prolonged and intense stress or to a profound personal shock, such as the loss of a close friend. The civilian counterpart of such findings occurs when persons involved in accidents and fires in which they have escaped physical injury are unable to sleep or eat and experience periods of overwhelming tension and anxiety for a considerable period of time after the disaster. These reactions have been called the *traumatic neuroses,* the term emphasizing the situational shock or blow as the primary agent accounting for the ineffective personal behaviors.

DEGREES OF EFFECTIVENESS

As one reads of the fears and conflicts and the resultant behaviors of the psychotic and neurotic, he cannot help seeing something of himself in them and may thus question his own effectiveness. Here the continuum again becomes an important concept, for effective and ineffective behaviors are perceived in terms of degrees, not categories. The world of today is complex, uncertain, changing. It presents many problems, and to live successfully in it the individual must have considerable strength, resilience, and flexibility. To some extent he is bound to experience fears and anxieties, depression and conflict. To some extent, he will employ defense mechanisms. But when such defenses markedly interfere with his ability to establish meaningful relationships, to realize his full potential, socially and intellectually, and to express his feelings appropriately, then the well-being of the individual and of those with whom he has contact necessitates further evaluation of his effectiveness and personality development. An examination of the individual's self-concept in relation to his effectiveness is of value in this connection.

Personal Effectiveness and Self-Concept

The hypothetical individual who has been favored with conditions and experiences that have resulted in a harmonious balance among his intrapsychic processes, and whose selves are well integrated, shows certain characteristic approaches to perceiving himself, to responding emotionally to himself and others, and to thinking about himself and the events that he experiences.

The possession of a respect for oneself, an awareness of oneself and one's own feelings, and a positive and definite self-concept constitutes a state attainable in varying degrees. The person possessing these attitudes esteems himself as having worth and value and is able to live his life without continually expending energy in proving his adequacy to himself or to others. He is able to perceive his own strengths and weaknesses with considerable accuracy. This type of self-awareness differs from the acute "self-consciousness" experienced by those whose anxieties lead them to believe—painfully and incorrectly—that they are the focus of attention in groups or interpersonal situations.

The person who is relatively free from intrapersonal conflict does not cut himself off from his own experiences; he has no need to rely heavily upon mechanisms such as repression, denial, or projection. He is able to experience deeply and to retain in his awareness the memory of these experiences. He is therefore able to perceive and to evaluate the nature of the world, so that he can deal more effectively with it than if the operation of his defense mechanisms resulted in perceptions that were distorted or provided unreal impressions.

The hypothetical individual we are describing feels free to express affection, love, irritation, and anger, and he recognizes that the impulse to express feelings is a natural and human characteristic. At the same time, he is able to control the direct expression of his emotion when it would cause others discomfort, embarrassment, or pain, or when it would interfere with the accomplishment of his own objectives.

His actions will be appropriate to the situation and will reflect not only his needs but also his conscience. He is able to make decisions and to act purposefully without doing harm to himself or others. He is able to approach challenging situations directly, to consider a variety of alternatives, and to attempt those most suited to the problem at hand. When blocked in his efforts, he is able to try alternative solutions, and he does not persist in employing unsuccessful behaviors. He has available a fund of previous experience that can be relied upon in new situations.

The psychologically effective person is able to think in terms of the future. He will establish long-range goals as well as immediate ones, and he will be able to delay immediate gratifications in favor of the anticipated satisfactions associated with the accomplishment of the more distant objective. As additional information about his situation or himself becomes available, he will modify his objectives when necessary; otherwise, he will be able to pursue the activities leading to his goals diligently.

The person free of internal conflict has a definite impression of himself and what he represents. He knows who he is. He has an awareness of his own beliefs and attitudes and is able to control his own impulses appropriately without having to punish himself. Although free of pervasive and continuing feelings of guilt, he has a definite and frequently explicit set of ethical beliefs that guide his conduct. His self-concept is such that he is able to respect and esteem himself when his behaviors conform to the standards he values. This sense of achievement, it must be observed, springs from a personal value system, and gratification is not dependent on the approval of others.

His impression of himself is not far removed from his ideal self.

In individuals whose self-components are well integrated there is a sufficient difference between the personal and the ideal selves to serve as a motive for self-improvement and at the same time the person feels that he is a desirable human being. The individual with a positive self-concept takes pride in himself. He enjoys the challenges life presents and without loss of self-esteem is able to deal directly with life's adversities, which are unavoidable at times for everyone.

Summary

How a person perceives himself in relation to others, how he thinks of himself and the world about him, and how he responds emotionally to himself and to his situation reflect his personal development. Behaviors indicative of high orders of personality development and organization are termed effective and are apparent in the perceptual, intellectual, and emotional activities of man.

Levels of personal development and effectiveness are inferred from intrapersonal and social behaviors and from the use the individual makes of his abilities and aptitudes. The degree to which he maintains meaningful relationships with other persons and the extent to which he is able to utilize his personal resources in work depend in large measure upon his personality organization and his intrapersonal integration. When the intrapsychic processes are in internal conflict, the energies required to maintain and defend the personality and to protect against anxiety reduce the individual's ability to cope with the current demands presented by the external environment; moreover, in his self-protection and defense, he will deceive himself, thus further impairing his ability to function in maximally gratifying ways, consistent with his goals. In some instances, not only do the self-deceptive processes affect the individual's ability to further his own self-interests, but the perceptions, thinking, and emotions are so disrupted that for his own protection and the protection of others his social movement must be restricted and he has to be institutionalized.

Effective intrapersonal processes are those that result in accurate perceptions of the self and others, clear and cogent thought, and the availability of a wide range of emotions with the controls essential for their appropriate use. Such a person is able to commit himself and his energy to personal objectives and challenging new problems that he can specify and that require the attainment of skills, knowledge, and learnings not too far beyond the possibilities of attainment.

Like all persons, the individual who has attained a high order of psychological development will exhibit ineffective behaviors if he is subjected to overwhelming stress. When such traumatizing experiences occur, however, his ineffectualness will not be so prolonged as in the case of one whose general personality integration is less adequate.

References

1. Barron, F. The psychology of imagination. *Scientific American,* 1958, *199,* 151.
2. Bower, E. M. *High school students who later became schizophrenic.* Sacramento: Bulletin of the California State Dept. of Education, 1960, *29.*
3. Bronowski, J. The creative process. *Scientific American,* 1958, *199,* 63.
4. Cameron, N., and Magaret, A. *Behavior Pathology,* New York: Houghton Mifflin, 1951.
5. Ehrlich, D., Guttman, I., Schonbach, P., and Mills, J. Post-decision exposure to relevant information. *J. abnorm. soc. Psychol.,* 1957, *54,* 98–102.
6. Eriksen, C. W. Perceptual defense as a function of unacceptable needs. *J. abnorm. soc. Psychol.,* 1951, *46,* 557–564.
7. Festinger, L. *A Theory of Cognitive Dissonance.* New York: Harper, 1957.
8. Frenkel-Brunswik, E. Personality theory and perception; in Blake, R. R., and Ramsey, G. V., *Perception: An Approach to Personality.* New York: Ronald, 1951.
9. Freud, A., and Burlingham, D. T. *War and Children.* New York: Medical War Books, 1943.
10. Hilgard, E. R. The role of learning in perception; in Blake, R. R., and Ramsey, G. V., *Perception: An Approach to Personality.* New York: Ronald, 1951.
11. Hollingworth, L. S. *Children above 180 I.Q.* Yonkers: Harcourt, 1942.
12. Kelly, G. A. *The Psychology of Personal Constructs.* New York: Norton, 1955.
13. Korzybski, A. *Science and Sanity* (ed. 2). New York: International Non-Aristotelian Library and Publishing Press, 1941.
14. Krech, D., and Crutchfield, R. S. *Elements of Psychology.* New York: Knopf, 1958.
15. Mursell, J. L. *Using Your Mind Effectively.* New York: McGraw-Hill, 1951.
16. Rogers, C. R. Perceptual reorganization in client-centered therapy; in Blake, R. R., and Ramsey, G. V., *Perception: An Approach to Personality.* New York: Ronald, 1951.
17. Terman, L. H. (ed.), *et al. Genetic Studies of Genius.* Stanford, Calif.: Stanford University Press, 1925.
18. U.S. Department of Commerce. *Patients in Mental Institutions, 1942.* Washington, D.C.: U.S. Government Printing Office, 1945.
19. Wechsler, D. *The Measurement of Adult Intelligence.* Baltimore: Williams and Wilkins, 1944, p. 167.
20. Wylie, R. C. *The Self Concept: A Critical Survey of Pertinent Research Literature.* Lincoln: University of Nebraska Press, 1961.

Selected Readings

Anderson, H. H.   Creativity in perspective; in *Creativity and Its Cultivation*. New York: Harper, 1959.

Blake, R. R., and Ramsey, G. V.   *Perception: An Approach to Personality*. New York: Ronald, 1951.

Cameron, N., and Magaret, A.   *Behavior Pathology*. Boston: Houghton Mifflin, 1951.

Coleman, J. C.   *Personality Dynamics and Effective Behavior*. Chicago: Scott, Foresman, 1960.

Jourard, S. M.   *Personal Adjustment*. New York: Macmillan, 1958.

Kimball, R. R., and Wing, R. L.   *Education for Effective Thinking*. New York: Appleton, 1960.

Lindgren, H. C.   *Psychology of Personal and Social Adjustment*. New York: American Book, 1959.

Morgan, C. T., and Deese, J.   *How to Study*. New York: McGraw-Hill, 1957.

Shaffer, L. F., and Shoben, E. J.   *The Psychology of Adjustment*. Boston: Houghton Mifflin, 1956.

13.

Effective Social Behaviors

Man's social behaviors are in part responses to his immediate situation, but they also reflect all his previous encounters with human beings and their social institutions. He perceives and responds to others on the basis of their special meanings for him, and he treats them in ways that can be understood only in terms of the specific details of his lifelong developmental pattern. Now we turn directly to some aspects of his behavior that reflect his developmental progression as it is observed in his treatment of people, the uses he makes of others, and the roles he assumes in relation to them. These behaviors are intimately related to his personality development and to his intrapersonal activities. They are of most immediate concern when a person evaluates his own effectiveness and questions how others perceive him.

Because man's developmental experiences occur through his contacts with other people, and his self-perception largely depends upon the way others have thought of him and treated him during the period of his development, it is not surprising that an individual will think essentially in terms of his social behaviors when evaluating his own effectiveness; moreover, in view of the social origin and character of man, it is also understandable that he is *concerned* about his social effectiveness. Such concern has been reflected in the amount of current literature devoted to the topic and is exemplified by Dale Carnegie's book, *How to Win Friends and Influence People.* In the popular treatment, the degree to which an individual can manipulate or influence others or become a social success is accepted as a measure of his effectiveness. Popular literature directed toward improving social effectiveness gives first place to the techniques useful in evoking positive reactions from others.

In contrast to this emphasis upon techniques, psychologists interested in effective social behavior direct their attention to the extent to which the person can recognize and assume the role behaviors expected of him and the degree to which he can and does assume responsibility for them. Psychologists evaluate social effectiveness in terms of the *quality* of the interpersonal relationship, the way people treat one another, and whether the relationship fosters the development of the persons involved.

The characteristics of effective social behaviors are discussed in this chapter. As the behaviors that directly and indirectly involve others are discussed, the close relationship between them and the person's thoughts, perceptions, emotions, and mechanisms of defense will be evident. However, the situation that evokes the behavior also plays a part in accounting for the individual's actions. The teenage boy who earlier had engaged in an unrestrained wrestling match with several of his friends will probably be quiet, shy, and polite when he talks with his girl-friend's parents.

The close relationship between personal and social aspects of behavior is also worth noting. For example, the child whose early experiences with adults brought unsatisfactory consequences subsequently views all persons as sources of potential threat. As an adult he will probably deal with the anxieties aroused in his personal contacts by being careful, withholding communication, or resorting to defenses that will cause his behaviors with others to appear aloof, indifferent, or perhaps suspicious and hostile.

In studying the behaviors of persons in relation to one another, the interactional effects must be recognized. If the behavior of two persons in a given situation is to be fully understood, it is necessary to know not only the personality structures involved but also the effect that each has upon the other. The individual's social behavior will depend upon his perception of the other person and his reactions to this perception; his self-perception partially depends upon the other's perceptions of and reactions to him. Parents and teachers of young children frequently find that two children interact so that in the presence of each other they behave in ways that individually would be considered quite "out of character." Since the most important component of social behavior is recognition of and response to the expectations others hold, the first considerations relevant to the characteristics of effective social behavior are the social roles that the individual fills.

SOCIAL ROLES AND EFFECTIVE BEHAVIOR

Earlier (page 178) it was noted that within the social group various positions, such as father, son, doctor, and second baseman, could be identified by title, and that associated with these positions are the group's expectations of appropriate behaviors. These shared expectations were designated as *roles*.

The Conflict of Role Responsibilities

The reader will recall that the adult fulfills a number of different positions and is a member of various groups; he may simultaneously be a lawyer, a father, a husband, a Democrat, a Kiwanian, and a church deacon, as well as a neighbor and a member of the city council. The behaviors expected of him differ from role to role. Because of these differences, he sometimes experiences conflicting expectations. In a study of the behaviors of persons during disasters, for example, it was found that those in positions carrying the expectation of their serving the community during a crisis, men such as policemen and firemen, are torn between their community and family responsibilities. They have assignments to carry out during a period of acute social stress. At the same time, their concerns about the safety and welfare of their own families and friends are compelling, and they are tempted to abandon their official roles. This role conflict is reflected in the statement of a police officer in a town that had suffered a tornado (12).

> As I drove around town after the tornado had passed I realized that the best thing I could do was to try to make contact with the outside and get help from there. I started out to drive to the next town and try to call from there. As I drove out of town, people I knew well would call me by name and ask me to help them find their relatives. Driving by and not stopping to help those people who were looking to me as a friend was one of the hardest thing I ever had to do.

Sometimes several groups will have different ideas about the behaviors they expect the person occupying a specific position to fulfill, and the person who must satisfy contradictory expectations of a role can experience situational conflict. In the case of a school superintendent, for example, different groups in the community hold various views about the appropriate behaviors of the superintendent on issues such as salary increases for teachers. The PTA and teacher groups expect the superintendent to push for the highest possible salaries, while taxpayer associations and similar groups expect him to take positions favoring the least possible increases.

Another clear instance of conflict emanating from the different expectations that groups hold for their leaders is demonstrated in a study of attitudes toward U.S. Army noncommissioned officers. In response to the item, "A noncom should not let the men in his squad forget that he is a noncom, even off duty," 81 percent of the officers agreed with the statement, while only 39 percent of the privates agreed with it (22). Although social positions carry with them general role expectations, it cannot be assumed that all persons will have the same ideas about how an individual occupying a particular position should behave. An individual's position relative to the positions of those he is perceiving will account, in part, for the specific role behaviors he will expect to be fulfilled.

Since most persons hold membership in many groups and thereby assume a number of different roles, it is not a simple matter to determine the degrees of effective social behavior they demonstrate. In general, it could be said that effective social behavior is evidenced when the individual is aware of the behaviors associated with the roles he has chosen to fulfill, when he is aware of the roles that others are fulfilling, and when he can move readily from one role to another with a minimum of conflict.

The preceding statement implies that a person voluntarily chooses the positions he occupies within the society, but it is obvious that some positions, such as that of man or woman, a minority group member, or a disabled person, are imposed rather than voluntary. These imposed social positions, based upon age, sex, ethnic origin, and physical status, carry with them group expectations and actions that tend to define the opportunities the individual will have to develop and demonstrate his abilities and talents. For example, a person who is refused admission to a teacher-training program because he is physically disabled will have fewer alternatives available to him than the nondisabled person of equal ability. The restrictions imposed upon the individual by such imposed social positions must be considered when his performance is evaluated. Appropriate behaviors for both imposed and voluntary roles, however, are dictated to a considerable degree by group expectations. For both kinds of positions the degree to which the individual is aware of the expectations associated with the position—and the degree to which he can fulfill these expectations—are relevant as indices of effective behavior.

Intrapsychic Conflict and Social Behavior

The nature of an individual's intrapsychic conflict, the measures he employs to defend and maintain himself, and the content of his personal, social, and ideal selves are all reflected in his role behaviors. Persons whose perceptions of others are distorted by intrapsychic conflict will have difficulty in evaluating social situations clearly and in identifying the roles they are expected to assume. Some persons are limited in their ability to perceive the roles assigned to them because of preoccupations with themselves and with what they hope to obtain from the group, as the following example illustrates.

> Roger had recently transferred to State. On his second day in physics class, he skillfully mimicked the instructor when the latter left the room for a few minutes. Roger was quite surprised when the student sitting next to him told him to "knock it off." When his habitual assumption of the clown role did not produce the desired effect, he mistakenly thought that his imitation was not good enough. Roger not only misperceived the role expected of him as a newcomer to the class, but he also failed to perceive that his classmates took their roles as students seriously and preferred to use the few minutes available to them to check over the current assignment.

For the same reasons that he fails to interpret correctly the roles expected of him, an individual may misperceive the roles which the members of the group have assumed. Had Roger understood more clearly the roles of the instructor and of his classmates, he might have made his bid for the approval of the group in some other way. As it was, he failed to receive the gratification he sought, and he probably found the subsequent criticisms still more confusing and dissatisfying.

Some individuals who are driven to win group approval perceive what is expected of them and comply almost automatically, without attention to whether their actions are consistent with their beliefs and values. Pressures on the adolescent to "go along with the gang" and the social demands of clubs or fraternities are examples of tests of an individual's intrapersonal development. The individual who is evincing effective social behavior does not assume a role that is contrary to his own ethical principles; he will not buy popularity at the cost of his own self-respect. If he accepts a position in an organization, he carries out its duties and does not shirk responsibilities or cut corners in fulfilling the role he has chosen. Persons demonstrating effective social behaviors are sufficiently flexible to assume any of a variety of roles, depending upon the situation. Maslow (17) describes the self-actualizing individual as one who is spontaneous, but not unconventional in the usual sense of the term. "Apparently recognizing that the world of people in which he lives could not understand or accept this [his personal convictions], and since he has no wish to hurt them or fight with them over every triviality, he will go through the ceremonies and rituals of convention with a good-humored shrug and with the best possible grace."

The roles such an individual assumes do not exact abnormal penalties, such as exhaustion or psychosomatic conditions. If the role requirements are incompatible with his values and beliefs, he will attempt to change his situation, when possible, to make different and more compatible roles available to him. In general, the individual who maintains satisfactory interpersonal relationships experiences a sense of self-fulfillment and gratification from the positions he assumes. This implies that he adopts roles which provide him with an opportunity to work toward his own objectives, and that he is able to carry out role behaviors which are congruent with his psychological structure.

As workers, parents, neighbors, and friends, most adults occupy social positions whose role behaviors contribute to the development of others. This is not to say that all persons who fulfill these positions are making the contribution the role demands, or that they achieve personal gratification from sharing responsibilitity for the development of others. When holding social positions that require concern, consideration, and care of others, however, the person who functions effectively will demonstrate such behaviors.

THE LEADERSHIP ROLE

In our culture the individual who has attained a high level of personal and social development is able to recognize the role expectations of leadership. If he assumes such a position, he is able not only to help the group achieve its goals, but also to help the members derive personal satisfaction from participating in the group's activities.

Are leaders born or made? Are the qualities of leadership such that the person who possesses them will emerge to take responsibility and initiative regardless of circumstances? Do the times and conditions make the man, or does the man make history? These questions cannot be answered with conviction on the basis of the research data available, but they have many immediate implications. If leaders will be leaders whatever their times and circumstances, then society's task is to identify such individuals early in order to utilize their talents most effectively. On the other hand, if leaders are products of the circumstances and situations in which they find themselves, effort should be directed toward understanding the group conditions that facilitate the emergence of leadership and the techniques that make it most effective.

Research is going forward on both of these fronts; individuals possessing leadership qualities are being studied in a variety of situations and in terms of the personal and developmental experiences that differentiate them from followers. Studies of the behaviors of groups, the organization and purposes of such groups, the lines of communication, and the "psychological atmosphere" that affect the leadership behaviors of the members have increased considerably in recent years.

Leaders can be identified in any child or adult group situation. Groups may function over a long or short period of time, on a national or local level, on a formal or informal basis. Sometimes leaders can be easily identified as formal officials who have been elected or appointed to responsible positions. Whether they are effective in such roles, however, and are perceived by their "followers" as actually carrying authority and influence is apparent only after careful and extensive observations of group behaviors and the reactions of individual members. Often sociometric techniques (which were described in Chapter 7) are used in such studies, and leaders are identified after the complex positive and negative responses of the group members have been analyzed. Perhaps the leader is best defined not as a person possessing specific qualities, but rather as one "who takes a specialized role in a group whose members share a set of norms" (18).

Thus, one of the primary determinants of the leader's role is the purpose for which the group exists. A second determinant is the extent to which the group believes the leader's role is essential for the accomplishment of its objectives. Although, for example, the conductor of a symphony orchestra and a football coach may be expected to have similar qualities evoking the respect of those with whom they work, their tasks differ because the nature and purposes of the groups they lead are different. Each would be presumed to know his field and to be able to contribute to the group's competent performance, but the specific behaviors expected of them reflect the distinctive purposes of their respective groups.

In considering the nature of the situation and its influence upon the emergence of a leader, the characteristics of the followers are also an important factor. Marked differences between the followers and the leader with respect to intelligence, personality, and attitudes will lead to the group's rejection of him as their leader. Sanford (21) found, for example, that leaders whose approach was direct and dominant and who focused upon the job to be done rather than upon the persons involved were desired by followers who themselves were characterized as "authoritarian." Followers who were described as "equalitarian" preferred leaders who were sensitive to "human relations."

The tendency to equate leadership with particular characteristics of the leader can be observed in popular writings, in which the qualities of the leader's behaviors are described in magical terms: "People followed his orders as if hypnotized," for example, or "His followers worshipped him as a god." Actually, the leader's traits are more varied and specific to the situation than is generally believed. When individuals move from one group situation calling for leader behavior to another, the same persons will sometimes assume both leadership roles succesfully. When this happens, however, the relationships between the leader and follower roles in the two situations and the functions of the groups are essentially similar. Perhaps the most general statement that can be made about the characteristics of leaders, apart from a discussion of the group situation, is that intelligence, initiative, self-confidence, responsibility, and clarity of self-concepts seem to be associated with persons occupying leadership positions. Even this generalization, however, is subject to many exceptions, depending upon the function and structure of the group and the needs and personalities of its members.

The role of the structure and organization of the group in determining the leader's function has been studied in terms of the flow of communication. The participants were assigned a problem to solve and were seated in such ways that different patterns of communication had to be followed. In one study (14), they were seated in a circle and thus could communicate only with persons on either side of them, or in a line, one next to the other, or in a "wheel," with one person in the center and the participants able to communicate with other members only through the person at the "hub." When the participants identified the leaders of their groups, the individual handling the greatest number of messages was so identified. Findings such as these lead to the hypothesis of the importance of the structure and organization of the group in locating the leader.

The "Psychological Atmosphere" of the Group

Leaders vary in the degree to which they share their leadership responsibility with other members of the group. In one series of studies (16), groups in which the leaders assumed strong control by directing activities and assigning specific tasks to individuals were compared to groups in which the leaders led through "democratic" procedures. Generally it was found that the "authoritarian" leader might achieve a fairly high degree of efficiency from his group under certain circumstances, but that the by-products of the authoritarian atmosphere included a greater incidence of aggressive and apathetic reactions. The aggressive behaviors usually occurred in the leader's absence and were directed toward others in the group, while the apathy seemed to be associated with fear of the leader. These reactions were more apparent when the group had encountered some specific difficulty without being able to produce constructive solutions.

In democratically controlled groups, which were given wide latitude and responsibility for their decisions and task and role assignments, the morale was generally high with infrequent aggressive incidents. When such groups encountered obstacles, they focused upon solutions rather than upon bickering with each other as was the case in the leader-directed groups. Again, these results should not be overgeneralized. All the studies following this type of procedure were conducted within this country, and the values of initiative, responsibility for self, and participation in the democratic process are reinforced by many agencies of American culture. This is a particularly important point, for it suggests that the reactions to democratic leadership may be quite different in cultures in which other values may predominate. Foreign students who come to this country to study, for example, are often confused by—and sometimes quite disdainful of—what they perceive as the "waste and inefficiency" of our system.

Responsibility, Self-reliance, and Reliance upon Others

The popular impression of any responsible person, leader or follower, includes as an important element the degree to which he can be relied upon to do his duty, to perform his work, and to be available when needed. According to this view, responsibility is a characteristic an individual demonstrates in a variety of situations. That persons rated as responsible in one situation are likely to be similarly rated in others has been demonstrated in psychological research. Rather than focusing upon the factors related to responsibility as an individual characteristic, however, this section directs attention to the interpersonal implications of the concept.

When a person demonstrates his reliability and trustworthiness, he does not disappoint his associates; he fulfills their expectations of him. In this sense the role of the responsible person is one that arises from the interdependent nature of all men. The term *interdependent* suggests that even though in the course of his development man progresses from total reliance upon others to a state of lesser dependency, he is never completely self-reliant; others make his clothing, prepare the food he eats, and provide many essential services. In any society, "no man is an Iland, intire of itself." Since men must depend upon each other, it is important to consider the degree of self-reliance an individual exhibits in relation to the degree to which he contributes to the needs of others and assists in their development. The socially effective person fulfills the role of the responsible person.

The use of the concept of *interdependency* also implies that high levels of personal and social development are characterized not by independence of others and separation from them, but rather by mutually constructive participation with them. Thus, the life progression is from a state of total reliance upon other persons to one of competence in caring for others, in contributing to their development and at the same time being able to accept and utilize their assistance.

THE DEPENDENT PERSON

Everyone relies physically, socially, and psychologically upon other persons. Thus, to some extent everyone is dependent in these three areas, but not necessarily to the same extent. To distinguish among these related spheres of human activity in which individuals rely upon others, each will be given consideration.

Physical dependency may be defined as the need that a person has for others to attend to his physical requirements. The infant who must rely completely upon others to feed, dress, and protect him plays a physically dependent role. As previous chapters have indicated, he progressively discards the role, if his parents allow it, because he is increasingly able to attend to his own physical needs. An important exception to this pattern of development was noted in the discussion of the disabled person who, because of accident, illness, or congenital disability, continues to play a dependent role so far as his physical needs are concerned; it does not follow, however, that he requires advice or assistance from others in matters pertaining to choices and judgments involving his personal affairs.

Just as the complexity of modern society makes complete physical independence impossible, so it is true that socially and psychologically no man stands alone. Although he may value the feeling that he can make his own decisions, can maintain his dignity and self-respect in his dealings with others, and can follow the dictates of his conscience, and although he may enjoy the belief that he is the captain of his soul and the master of his destiny, he never achieves this degree of independence without contact with others or reference to them.

A particularly close relationship exists between socially and psychologically dependent behaviors. *Social dependency* is defined as the need to have other people to whom to relate, with whom to live, work, and communicate. This type of dependency is sometimes related to the characteristics of gregariousness, of wanting to be with others, to share activities with them. In this sense, it is universal in its application, although individuals differ considerably in the extent to which they depend upon such social contacts. Some people enjoy frequent contacts with others on both deep and superficial levels; others seem to require infrequent contacts and are quite satisfied to engage in many activities alone.

Of particular importance in assessing the effectiveness of interpersonal behaviors is the extent to which an individual is perceived as playing a psychologically dependent role. *Psychological dependency* is described as the need to be reliant upon other people for direction, advice, and the prescription of attitudes and values. Such reliance is vested in individuals who represent authority figures for the person. Initially this function is served by parents, later by significant adults outside the family, and then by peers or other individuals or institutions that symbolize authority.

The psychologically dependent individual uses others as his *major* source of self-esteem and looks continually toward the reactions of people to him so that he will be able to gauge "how well" he is doing. He constantly needs the approval of his group, and his failure to achieve it results in a major loss of self-respect. He consistently requires the psychological support of others to maintain his morale and to enable him to function. Sometimes sociopsychological dependency is revealed in the behaviors of the unassertive, compliant person who cannot register open dissent, who readily yields on all issues, and who "goes along" with whatever is suggested. Such a person expects and wishes to be taken care of. He not only wants to be told what to do, but he *has* to be told what to do. Because of his helplessness, he is frequently able to elicit not only the sympathy but also the assistance of his associates. Thus, he is able to capitalize on his wish to be taken care of by looking as if he is appealing—and sometimes beseeching—for aid. He may borrow notebooks, copy homework assignments, or stand by while his friends fulfill his responsibilities.

Although the passive person's manner often appears to be quite different from that of the overtly angry and aggressive individual, considerable hostility is frequently concealed beneath the quiet, nonassertive impression he creates. The same conditions that account for his dependency reactions make it dangerous for him to express overtly the hostile anger he often feels. The passive-dependent person who is angry is more likely to express his anger indirectly than to reveal it openly. He will agree, or seem to agree, while he expresses his hostility through noncooperation and subtle negativism.

The dependent role frequently has a possessive quality to it, as seen in the actions of the young child who resents other children's efforts to gain the attention of his parents, who scolds another child who has made such an advance by screaming, "Don't do that; he is MY daddy." Within adult relationships the person who is psychologically dependent says, in effect, "I need you; you can't desert me. I cannot share you with anyone else, for I need you too much." The need to be the "best" friend and to have first call on the friend's time or activities, and the tendency to be jealous or resentful of attention given to anyone else are behaviors which have a possessive quality to them. Persons who behave in this manner can engender considerable feelings of guilt in their associates, causing them to feel as if they were committing a wrongful act by devoting time and attention to someone else. Such possessive-dependent behavior often occurs within the relationships of men and women, and the intensity of possessiveness or of dependency can be erroneously considered a sign of the love the individual has for the loved one.

Closely related to the passive and possessive qualities of the dependent role are behaviors in which one person consistently relies upon another for the approval of his plans, decisions, attitudes, and efforts. Frequently a person will say to a friend, "Tell me what you think of this idea," when actually he means, "Tell me that this idea meets with your approval," or even more basically, "Tell me that you approve of me." The key to the distinction between the dependent use of others' evaluations and judgments and the sound procedure of obtaining relevant information before commitment to a course of action is to be found in the underlying motivational situation and in the use that is made of the opinion. A person behaves in a dependent fashion if he is seeking support, not advice; thus what is dependent behavior in one person may not be in another. The spirit and motivation characterizing and accounting for the request for advice determine whether the behaviors are dependent. Sometimes individuals who wish to be dependent on others are made uncomfortable and anxious by being dependent or by the prospect of being dependent and will hence reject almost all advice or help offered to them.

Persons who must conceal their dependent feelings from others and from themselves often achieve their successes at considerable cost to themselves. This cost may be calculated in terms of physical health or of the effect upon interpersonal relationships. For example, the incidence of ulcers or alcoholism is higher than normal for dependent persons who cannot accept their feelings as natural and who must "show the world." Other persons are known to their associates as being unable to accept any type of help even when it is required. The person who must pay for everything that he receives to avoid feeling obligated or helpless and the person who cannot accept physical assistance illustrate the extent to which the denial of dependency can be carried.

The individual who consistently and inappropriately resorts to socially and psychologically dependent behaviors is not behaving effectively. Lacking the capacity to mediate between the demands of the external environment and his own impulses, the dependent individual finds his greatest source of safety in utilizing the resources and strengths of others; hence he must consistently rely upon them for direction, advice, and the evaluation of his own behavior. Such behavior is inconsistent with the demands of adult life. The person who approaches a high level of social development is able to rely physically, socially, and psychologically on others when it is appropriate to do so. He is aware of his needs and accepts them, realizing the interdependence of man.

CONFORMITY BEHAVIOR

In our complex society an individual must acquire considerable knowledge about the behaviors and attitudes that are permissible and those which are discouraged or forbidden. As previous chapters have emphasized, these learnings are communicated not only by parents, but by peer groups, schools, and law enforcement agencies, and they include knowledge of society's rules, regulations, and laws. The laws essential to the protection of health and safety are adhered to by most persons, and many less explicit regulations, called folkways and mores, carry considerable weight, for they relate to behaviors considered socially proper and desirable even though they are not legally enforceable.

Respect for Others

It should be noted, however, that conformity to laws protecting the health, safety, and rights of citizens does not present a problem to the individual who has attained a high level of interpersonal development. He conforms to such regulations because he believes in the purposes behind them and because he is aware of the protection that such a system insures. Because he identifies with other human beings, he feels it proper and necessary to afford them protection as well as to obtain protection for himself from them. He has internalized ethical standards of behavior toward his fellow men that deter him from inflicting harm on others or taking advantage of them; therefore, he is not in conflict with the laws that discourage or prohibit such behavior. This kind of compliance does not constitute conformity for the sake of conformity, although compliance with internalized standards (with the demands of the superego) results in behaviors having a conforming appearance.

Through the governmental process, society presents the individual with its requirements in terms of taxes, military service, and the like. In such instances, the individual meeting the criteria of interpersonal development is able to comply with what he sees as a just—though possibly an inconvenient and irritating—demand on him. When he considers such demands unjust or inapplicable, he uses the legal means available to him for review or redress. Although he may be neither happy about nor in agreement with governmental demands, still he is able to comply, for such compliance is with a principle. Riesman's description (20) of the autonomous character applies also to the person described here as socially effective. "He can cooperate with others in action while maintaining the right of private judgment."

Fears of Being Different

Although compliance with law and formalized social regulation results in conformity, the more conventional use of the conformity concept has to do with compliance to the tastes, judgments, manners, and attitudes of others. A high value can be attached to conformity as an end in itself. A person who values conformity to this extent will determine the goodness or badness of beliefs, behaviors, esthetic effects, and people solely on the basis of whether they reflect the opinions or characteristics of the reference group, the group that is significant to him. When this occurs, the significance of any specific judgment does not lie in *what* is being conformed to, but rather, that conformity is being evidenced.

The degree to which our culture values conformity is debatable. Riesman (20) has characterized American culture as one in which "other directedness" is predominant. By this term he means that many persons in our society are so directed by the opinions, judgments, and values of others that the measure of an individual's adequacy is in terms of group opinion and acceptance. If our culture is characteristically "other directed," then the individual who can function in terms of his own beliefs and values, who does not blindly conform, would be in the minority. In contrast to Riesman, another careful observer of the American scene, Lerner (15), is impressed with the opportunity for individual expression and the freedom afforded the "marginal man"—the person who does not conform.

Probably the culture cannot be characterized in terms of either extreme; large segments of conforming behaviors manifested by all persons are taken for granted. Certain aspects of our way of life are characterized by a quest for sameness, while other traditions within our society support the quest for individuality.

SOCIAL FORCES AND CONFORMING BEHAVIOR

At this point we turn our attention briefly to some of the social conditions in America that initiated and continue to reinforce conformity to attitudes and behaviors generally characteristic of our society. How large-scale events and movements of the past have contributed to the cultural content—a content that is incorporated as part of the individual's psychological self and then expressed in his behavior, attitudes, and values—can only be suggested, and the reader should consult the references at the end of the chapter for a more detailed analysis of the American culture.

Material Success

The conditions associated with the acculturation of new citizens and their children and with their accompanying rise on the economic and social scale have contributed importantly to the positive values attached to conforming behavior in the United States. The term *social mobility* refers to a rise in social and economic position from one genera- to the next. It is reflected in the progress of the son of immigrant parents who hopes for, works for, and eventually attains a "better life" than his parents had. In his eyes the "better life" is usually made up of greater economic security and a more respected social position that that achieved by his parents. In the case of immigrants the chances for a better life and for upward social mobility depend on becoming "Americanized," but the acculturation process is not restricted to newly arrived citizens. In the past, the midwestern farm boy who migrated to the city to work or to study was also confronted with a new and strange culture, and he was required to adopt these customs and behaviors if he wished to succeed.

This emphasis on success in material terms is the historical product of the geographical, technological, and economic development of this nation. Individuals did rise from humble circumstances to positions of great wealth and power because of the opportunities this country afforded them. The fruits of success were great indeed and the striving for this success motivated the life works of many Americans. The great popularity of the Horatio Alger series, which were built on the theme of "poor boy makes good" through honesty and diligence, testified to the wishes of Americans for themselves and their children.

The search for material success had, however, the side effect of putting a high valuation on conformity. That the worship of conformity was the product of a period when the individual was able to capitalize on his individuality in business and technical ventures is an interesting historical paradox. This valuation of conformity has carried over into the present and is represented by the slogans, "Give the customer what he wants," "The customer is always right," and their counterparts that relate to human beings and what they should look and be like. The person with a "marketing orientation," who, as Fromm termed it, "sells" himself, tries to become—or more accurately, to look like—a person wanted and accepted by others. "Selling oneself" implies that characteristics and manners are chosen which will most efficiently bring one into the good graces of one's associates. The person with a marketing orientation thinks of himself as a product whose value is determined by the reactions of others toward him. If this orientation is characteristic of the culture, then the people within it will be confronted with the need to conform to the group's dictates in matters of taste, attitudes, and morals.

Social Institutions and Conformity

One of the outstanding achievements of American society is the system of public education and the concept of education for *all* the people rather than only the children of the economically favored. This objective has necessitated a curriculum far broader than that offered in private schools, whose students come from similar backgrounds and usually intend to go from school to college.

In addition to serving all the students, regardless of their ability to pay the costs of their education, and offering them courses appropriate to their interests and abilities, the public schools have another characteristic feature that has a close relation to the conformity issue. This is their tendency to mirror the convictions and the attitudes of their communities. Private schools may or may not have directors or governing boards who reflect the point of view to which the school is dedicated, but all public schools are governed by boards who represent the local community. Local control is the cornerstone of public education; in principle it reflects the essential democratic tenet that the government and its agencies shall serve the interests of the people and shall be responsible to them.

Since schools are bound to give the community what it wants, the decisions of the school board about both the quality of the program and the content of the curriculum will be in accord with the tastes and attitudes, the competencies and weaknesses, of the community. The absence of objective criteria for the "good" school, superintendent, or teacher also contributes to the high value attached to "fitting in." This regard for conformity is shown in the school's need to avoid controversy, to maintain good community relationships, and to adhere closely to the tastes and prejudices of the politically powerful groups in the community. Although all public schools do not necessarily enforce conformity for its own sake, nor do all students necessarily succumb to such pressures, the dilemma presented by local school control does have social and psychological meaning for all students who attend public schools.

Other forces that have contributed to the emphasis upon conformity include the highly developed media of communication, which make it possible for individuals in all sections of the country to know immediately any changes in style or thought that are made by the style setters—the group of individuals that serves as the public's model. In the past, the traditions of a locality or the customs of an ethnic group were less open to the assimilative pressures of movies, television, magazines, and newspapers. The circular process of developing and nurturing conformity is seen in the type of television programming that strives to attract the kind of viewers who will respond favorably to the advertiser's message. People are given what they want, or what the advertiser thinks they want, in the way of entertainment, and this results in their being treated to entertainment that reflects their own interests and attitudes. There is little chance that the general level of knowledge or tolerance for difference will be raised by such a process. Its effects are to reflect and to reinforce the existing pressures toward conformity.

In 1956 it was found that elementary school children spent about as much time watching television as they spent in school (23). Because of the commercial nature of television, it tends to reinforce values that center about the traditional concepts of success, expressed mainly in materialistic terms that can be conveyed within a half-hour or hour. Adult TV fare generally consists of programs that are noncontroversial, inoffensive to any group, and sufficiently appealing to sexual and aggressive interests to capture high ratings.

Whether television is considered a positive influence because it provides an acceptable fantasy outlet for aggressive impulses, or a negative influence because it places emphasis on violence, cannot be argued with conviction one way or the other since little appropriate research data are available. Analysis of television programming and of the values symbolized in the highly rated programs make it clear that the value of conformity receives greater reinforcement than do those values which emphasize individuality, creativity, intellectual activity, knowledge for the sake of knowledge, or virtue for its own sake.

Digest versions of news reports, magazine articles, and works of literature are becoming increasingly popular. Although these are advertised as having educational value, they can also be seen as a constrictive force that reduces individual latitude in selection of reading material and in response to the material read. The condensed presentation of news can often do little more than capture selected highlights and when a glib style characterizes the summary, oversimplification of issues inevitably results. Any digest necessarily reduces the number of stimuli presented to the reader, and these stimuli may be changed in quality as well. Such a simplification of stimulus pattern will elicit individual reader responses that are less internally varied than would result from the original works. Digest magazines capitalize on the conformity needs of the public by claiming to contain material that informed persons "should" read. When this appeal to conformity is successful, it produces additional conforming behaviors.

To assist wives and mothers to do the "right thing," "slick" paper women's magazines offer suggestions on homemaking, child care, budgeting, decoration, and family relations. Such magazines provide the middle class woman with standards for self-evaluation and her judgments of her neighbors. The partial effect of such material is to reinforce the value of doing the "right" thing because everyone else is doing it.

PSYCHOLOGICAL FORCES AND CONFORMING BEHAVIOR

It must be remembered that social institutions, such as the educational and communication agencies reinforcing the positive valuation of conformity, do not influence all individuals to the same extent. Research indicates that individuals exhibit considerable diversity in the amount of conformity they manifest in situations where such diversity is feasible. Because of this variety in individual reactions to a group pressure to conform, it becomes important to identify the psychological factors that differentiate those who conform under these circumstances from those who retain their individuality.

The research cited has both a social and a psychological character. In studies by Asch (3) and later by Crutchfield (5) an ingenious situation was devised requiring a subject to make simple judgments, such as choosing the longest of three lines. These judgments were made in the presence of other individuals who were apparently making equally spontaneous judgments, although they were actually giving pre-set responses, some of which were clearly wrong. The judgments of the other participants were made known to the subject prior to his response. The simplicity of the task was such that subjects need not have experienced difficulty in making the correct determination, but many subjects gave incorrect answers in order to make them correspond to the answers of the other participants.

The tendency to conform to the pressure of the group was measured by the individual's compliance with the stated judgments of the other participants. Those who consistently presented the group judgment as their own were termed "high conformers." "Low conformers" retained and presented their own judgments even though they differed from those of their group.

In Asch's study it was found that about one third of the subjects were markedly influenced to make incorrect judgments in conformity with the group, and that increasing the size of the group contributed to the tendency to conform. When only one other person presented erroneous judgments, the subject tended to hold to his own opinions; when two persons presented inaccurate judgments, however, there was a considerable tendency to conform, and when three or more people presented a unanimously contrary judgment, there was high conformity to the incorrect group judgment. It was also found that support in the form of another person's agreeing with the subject's judgment decidedly reduced his tendency to conform. As might be anticipated, the difficulty of the task itself influenced an individual's confidence in holding to his own opinion. These results applied to a task in which the correct judgment could be made easily; when the task became more difficult, the tendency to conform to the group judgment became more marked.

In addition to its size, several other characteristics of the group influence conformity reactions. The perceived attractiveness of the group influences the effort and energy that the subject will expend to conform (13). Thus, conformity behaviors are most likely to occur if the person has positive attitudes toward the group. Individuals who believe that they are not accepted by the group will be more likely to conform if they think the attitude of the group toward them may change, and they will be more conforming than persons who are quite confident that they are accepted.

The research in this area generally supports the belief that individuals low in self-esteem and self-confidence are relatively susceptible to being influenced by others. In one comprehensive study (13), for example, it was found that individuals able to retain their individuality and hold their own position in the face of group pressures to conform possessed the following characteristics:

1. Intelligence, as measured by standard mental tests;
2. Originality, as manifested in thought processes and problem solving;
3. "Ego strength," that is, the ability to cope effectively despite stressful circumstances;
4. Self-confidence and absence of anxiety and inferiority feelings;
5. Optimal social attitudes and behavior, such as tolerance, responsibility, dominance, and freedom from disturbed and dependent relations with other people.

The studies described also suggest that the individual who has to conform tends to exhibit anxiety and that his conforming behaviors provide a means for defending against anxiety and feelings of insecurity. By relying on the authority and paternalism of the group, he achieves a measure of closeness and an illusion of being strong. For him conformity is a means of avoiding unpopularity, and he will not willingly threaten the group by presenting it with alien behaviors or beliefs.

Socially Ineffective Behavior

DELINQUENCY

In the discussion of social behavior the effect of the individual's behavior on other persons has been emphasized. Behaviors that contribute to the well-being and development of others are evaluated as effective to various degrees and those that are harmful are to various degrees ineffective. The determination of what constitutes behavior that is harmful to the development of another person cannot be made easily except in extreme instances, as when one person physically assaults another. Generally an individual's social behavior is considered ineffective when it interferes with the developmental processes of other persons.

Some behaviors have been recognized and legally specified by society as being contrary to its orderly function and to the self-interests of its citizens. When these laws are violated and the offender is apprehended and convicted, he is legally defined as a delinquent. Although the legal definition of delinquency covers a narrow range of interpersonal behaviors, it is utilized here as an explicit, though extreme, example of socially ineffective behavior.

In 1950, over three fourths of a million persons were imprisoned in state and federal reformatories. The number of persons confined to prisons and reformatories exceeds the population of San Francisco, the nation's eleventh largest city. Thus, it is not surprising that the magnitude of the delinquency problem commands the attention of law officers and welfare officials as well as students of society and human behavior.

Social, Psychological, and Physical Factors in Delinquency

The delinquent population comes chiefly from the less favored economic and social classes, the highest incidence of delinquency occuring in urban slum areas in neighborhoods that are undergoing general decline. Although some delinquents have normal or superior intelligence, their average intellectual level is below that of the general population. Not enough research data have yet been assembled to support any comprehensive statement of the causes of criminal behavior, but the social environment of the delinquent has frequently been mentioned as directly or indirectly contributary. Although poor housing, poverty, and inadequate social and economic opportunity can result in individual frustration and anger, such deficiencies cannot be considered as the sole causes of delinquency, since relatively few persons who live under such conditions actually become delinquent or criminal.

One line of speculation concerning the causes of delinquent behavior springs from the frustration-aggression hypothesis (page 71). According to this view, the frustration engendered by limitation of opportunity culminates in aggressive impulses that most people restrain or direct toward safe outlets. Some persons, however, lack the ego and superego strength to hold their impulses in check or to foresee the consequences of their behavior, and their aggressive impulses are expressed in antisocial behavior.

Another psychological theory holds that delinquent behavior represents the externalization of intrapsychic conflict. This means that an individual attempts to allay anxiety by "acting out" his conflict in the social setting. Anxiety precipitated by authority figures might be dealt with through physical attack on individuals who symbolize authority to the attacker. This view is supported by studies (9) which found that the psychological test performances of boys who become delinquent resembled those of adults with pronounced psychological disturbances. Other studies indicate that delinquent youths do less well in school and seem to have fewer psychological defenses available to them.

If delinquent behavior is caused partly by intrapsychic conflict, then the delinquent population is probably characterized by more family instability and by a greater number of disturbed parent-child relationships than is the nondelinquent population. The Gluecks' comparison (7) of 500 delinquent boys with 500 nondelinquent boys in the Boston area supported these assumptions. There were higher rates of divorce and separation among the parents of the delinquents, greater hostility in the delinquents' relationships with their parents, and more likelihood of their being reared by persons other than parents.

Although various additional psychological and sociological explanations of delinquency have been proposed, they tend to be speculative. At this point the best conclusion seems to be the general one that social and psychological factors combine to account for delinquent behavior.

The Punishment Principle

It has been estimated that from 60 to 90 percent of persons imprisoned for delinquent behavior will later be convicted of other crimes and returned to prison. Experts in the field have suggested that society could be benefited by drastic changes in the procedures for dealing with criminals and their return to society. At present, institutionalization is viewed as punishment, with the hope that confinement will by itself produce some change in the individual's attitudes. Available evidence (10) indicates, however, that the longer prisoners are confined, the more pronounced their signs of intrapsychic conflict become. The rate of

Man's inhumanity to man!

Aggression, the act of hurting another, is often perceived as one of the primary and basic human characteristics—a view supported by the history of man's brutality. Whether the impulse to violence is innate or is a product of social learning and a response to frustration is an open question. Irrespective of its origin, man's potential for violence and destruction should not be underestimated. But neither should his capacity to control these impulses. His potential to inflict harm on others should be viewed in the perspective of all his characteristics, including his ability to act rationally and constructively.

Under stress, men will often act like small boys—resorting to aggression or threatening to aggress against those who frighten them; and in such instances, like small boys caught up in the heat of the moment, they will give little consideration to the conditions that evoke the behavior of their adversary or the emotional origins of their own desires to destroy him.

Wayne Miller—Magnum

recidivism demonstrates the degree to which the punishment theory has failed.

One change in the treatment of delinquents, which is in effect in some reformatories, is the institution of a detailed medical, social, and psychological study of the prisoner upon his arrival. His program within the prison depends on the findings of this study and includes the appropriate treatment for his emotional, social, and psychological problems. At the same time he is given educational and occupational training. In support of this position, Dr. Karl Menninger, former president of the American Psychiatric Association, suggests that the concept of punishment be abandoned and that the delinquent be remanded to prison for an indefinite period, being released when he is considered socially and psychologically able to conform to the laws of society.

Proposals such as this are designed to consider each individual separately in all his psychological complexity, and they reflect views of human motivation and behavior that are similar to those of this book. They often fail to gain public support, however, for the punishment theory is an old and often appealing one. Antisocial behavior is one of the most difficult symptoms of maladjustment for society to treat rationally.

DISCRIMINATION

Discrimination has been defined as behavior that denies equal treatment to an individual or to a group of persons who desires and deserves such equality. Discriminatory behaviors most often occur on the basis of sex, race, ethnic background, and religion, and result in exclusion from or limitation of social and professional group memberships, occupational and educational opportunities, suffrage, and housing and recreational facilities. They are ineffectual in the sense that they hurt those against whom they are directed, and they are not contributory to the self-development of the individual who practices them. In addition, discriminatory behaviors lead to conflict between groups and individuals, or they provide the conditions from which such conflict emerges.

The psychological origins of discrimination are to be found in the conditions responsible for a type of thinking known as *stereotyping* and in *prejudice,* an emotionally laden bias. It must be recognized that individuals may engage in stereotyped thinking and hold steadfastly to their prejudices without showing socially discriminatory behaviors. In some instances, as in response to group pressure, individuals will even discriminate against others without being prejudiced, but a close relationship exists among discrimination, stereotyped thinking, and prejudice.

STEREOTYPING

The expectations that govern one's attitudes and behaviors toward others often stem from beliefs that are not based upon direct knowledge or evidence about the person as an individual, but rather upon his membership in an ethnic, racial, religious, social, or other specific group. A short-cut procedure that may or may not be accurate is employed to provide a quick and almost automatic basis for expectations about the individual. One may often be told that women drivers, as a class, are incompetent. A commonly shared belief such as this may be inaccurate, but it provides a basis for judgments about any woman who drives. This short-cut process whereby one is assigned qualities or characteristics because of his group membership is termed *stereotyping*. Stereotyping thus is (1) a biased generalization about a class or group and (2) the assignment of the traits considered characteristic of the group to all persons identified as group members.

If, for example, an individual believes that all persons with high foreheads are intelligent, he will attribute the trait of intelligence to any person he encounters who has a high forehead and will probably assign to this person whatever other characteristics he associates with intelligence. Whether the judgment based upon the stereotype is correct depends upon objective evidence and not upon the fact that it is a widespread belief.

In one study which used photographs (8), it was found that individuals with high foreheads were rated as being more intelligent than were individuals with low foreheads. In fact, the academic averages of the two groups showed a slight trend in the direction opposite to that assigned by the stereotype.

Many of the commonly held stereotypes regarding racial, religious, or ethnic groups cannot be examined so easily as the example we have mentioned. Since objective evidence regarding the accuracy of many commonly accepted stereotypes is lacking, they provide a poor basis for generalizing about people. Judgments based upon assumed relationships between characteristics or upon meager information about specific individuals are very likely to be in error. Although this caution appears obvious, there is considerable evidence to indicate that stereotypes do influence almost every person's judgments.

In an interesting study (19), college students were asked to rate photographs of thirty girls for general likeableness, beauty, intelligence, character, ambition, and charm. Two months later the same students were again asked to rate the photographs for the same characteristics. This time, however, surnames of Jewish, Italian, Irish and "Old

American" origin were added to each picture. A considerable change in ratings occurred: for example, girls labeled with Jewish names received noticeably lower ratings in likeableness, slightly lower ratings in beauty and character, and higher ratings in ambition.

The popular belief, and its exploitation in comedy, that the Scotsman is an unusually thrifty person, represents another stereotype. In 1932 at Princeton, students were asked to indicate the characteristics they associated with ten nationalities (11). They attributed the following characteristics most frequently to the various groups: Germans, scientifically minded, industrious, stolid; Italians, artistic, impulsive, passionate; Negroes, superstitious, lazy, happy-go-lucky; Irish, pugnacious, quick-tempered, witty; English, sportsmanlike, intelligent, conventional; Jews, shrewd, mercenary, industrious; Americans, industrious, intelligent, materialistic, ambitious; Chinese, superstitious, sly, conservative; Japanese, intelligent, industrious, progressive; Turks, cruel, religious, treacherous.

A technique for measuring the extent to which the raters were in agreement was utilized to yield an "index of definiteness." The same index was applied in a similar study conducted eighteen years later at the same university. Although the results in the second study indicated that essentially the same descriptions were applied to the various groups, the agreement among the students had dropped considerably. For example, in 1932, 75 percent of the students had described Negroes as being "lazy," while in 1950, only 31 percent used this adjective; 47 percent of the students rated the Jews as being shrewd in the second study, as compared to 79 percent in 1932. Other such changes were also noted, and on the basis of this study it appears that the stereotypes, though relatively unchanged in character through the years, had lost some degree of sharpness and strength.

In addition to influencing the type of judgment a person makes, stereotypes can influence what he thinks he sees. For example, Southern children were shown a picture of an expensive home. After the picture had been removed, they were asked, "What is the colored lady doing?" Many of the children responded that she was cleaning. Since no colored lady was in the picture, the response was consistent with the stereotyped role of the Negro as a domestic.

When oversimplified though widely shared beliefs about groups are utilized as a basis for perceiving and thinking about individuals, errors in judging inevitably occur. Social behaviors based upon stereotypes rather than upon the individual's actual behavior and evidence available about his personal characteristics will fail to provide a basis for satisfactory relationships. For this reason, they are considered to be ineffectual.

PREJUDICE

According to some definitions, one may be prejudiced to respond favorably, with positive feelings, toward a group or member of a group. The term here, however, relates to the negative, rejecting attitudes in which one person is "against" members of groups. The effects of prejudice are divisive to the society; they are detrimental to the individual because they isolate him from new experiences and relationships and often represent irrational or arational thinking.

Personal Experience and Prejudice

Although it can conceivably have its origins in actual experience of an unpleasant nature with a member or members of the group involved, group prejudice more often derives from the parents' attitudes, from the child's identification with the parents and his response to their teachings. Since prejudice is usually a product of contacts with persons who hold the prejudice rather than a product of actual experience with the "victims," the conditions that support the development of prejudice have been of considerable interest to social scientists.

Attention has been directed to the general social and economic conditions and their relationship to prejudice. It has, for example, been suggested that the frustration engendered by conditions of poverty and unemployment results in aggressive and hostile feelings that are then directed to an identifiable, though weak, "scapegoat."

Another interpretation of the conditions that create prejudice focuses on the family as the unit of society having the most marked influence upon the child's development. In a classic study of reactions to authority, it has been found that passive submission to a dominating parent engenders hostility which is eventually directed to despised and distrusted persons; moreover, conditions requiring passive submission to authority seem to engender a tendency to oversimplification and intolerance of ambiguity.

These studies found that strongly prejudiced persons were unusually anxious, unclear about their self-identities and their own ethical and moral standards. They had difficulties in getting along with others and placed considerable value upon conformity to the standards of their group. Some research points to excessive concern about status and the projection of hostile motives to others as contributing to prejudice (1).

Although explanations of prejudice emphasizing the "scapegoat" theory and beliefs that it is a manifestation of disturbed parent-child relationships can be defended, the interpretation of prejudice in terms of learned attitudes requires careful consideration. This interpretation points out that stereotypes are not only learned through experience with parents but also reinforced by peers and the popular media of mass communication. The addition of the negative and hostile emotional components to the stereotypes that constitute prejudice occur as a result of the individual's vulnerability to perceived threat and experienced anxiety. By this interpretation, the significance of prevalent shared beliefs and the individual's need to defend himself against anxieties activated by human differences plays an important role.

The cultural reinforcement of stereotypes was demonstrated by a study of some 900 fictional characters featured in 185 short stories that appeared in eight well-known national magazines. Berelson and Salter (4) found that nine tenths of them were marked as Anglo-Saxons, while the remaining one tenth played unpopular roles of a menial or antisocial nature. In the words of the investigators:

> American short story writers have made "nice people" synonymous with Anglo-Saxons. Such characters are written as intelligent, industrious, esthetic, democratic, athletic, practical, frank, lovable. . . . The non-Anglo-Saxons were usually pictured as the "villains," domineering, immoral, selfish, unintelligent, cowardly, lazy, sly, cruel, stubborn, nonesthetic, weak. . . . The behavior of these fictional characters could easily be used to "prove" that the Negroes are lazy, the Jews wily, the Irish superstitious and the Italians criminal.

Self-deceptive Mechanisms

The prejudiced person will often have recourse to the mechanisms described as behavioral patterns for defending himself against anxiety. Thus, the prejudiced person can find "facts" to fit his beliefs; he can rationalize his discriminatory behaviors and can "see" his own unacceptable wishes and motives in the behaviors of the scapegoat. He is alert and sensitive to human differences, since these constitute a source of threat to him, and he can identify minority group members from pictures somewhat more accurately than nonprejudiced persons (2).

Knowledge of the role of the family and of patterns of response to authority is essential in an understanding of how socially sanctioned and reinforced stereotypes become prejudices. In one of the major investigations in this field (1), conducted by Adorno, Frenkel-Brunswik, Levinson, and Sanford at the University of California and published as part of *The Authoritarian Personality*, considerable evidence is provided to support the view that prejudiced individuals have certain identifiable characteristics which can to some degree be specified.

In this study children were classified as "prejudiced" and "less prejudiced" according to their responses in test situations. Many aspects of their personalities and of the personalities of their parents were carefully studied and significant differences were found between the two groups of children. For example, parents of prejudiced children placed considerable emphasis upon strict discipline and unquestioning obedience in their childrearing practices. At the same time, they were concerned about how the children of other parents behaved, whether their own children created a favorable impression and performed adequately according to society's standards of how the "good" child (thus reflecting the "good" parent) behaves.

Their extensive reliance on conforming behaviors could be viewed as a means of allaying the anxiety raised when they were forced to "stand alone." Thus, their lack of self-esteem and confidence seen in their need to accept authorities—and, in turn, to be accepted by them— was reflected in their preoccupation with the status and monetary success they felt they had not achieved. They apparently tended to project their feelings of inadequacy to their children, as indicated by the hope that their children would achieve what they had not, and they *then* implied that this would not be accomplished by superior performance or by hard work but passively, through "luck," "fate," or by the fulfillment of an almost childlike fantasy, such as an inheritance from a rich, and usually unknown, uncle.

The hypothesis that identification is a process through which children acquire value structures similar to their parents' is supported by this study. When asked to describe certain "ideal" people, prejudiced youngsters responded in a manner significantly different to that of the less prejudiced group. For example, they consistently indicated their acceptance of common stereotypes, particularly with reference to sex roles, and they mirrored their parents' definition of success in terms of status and monetary symbols.

Their attitudes toward authority were, however, less consistent than those of their parents', for while they described the ideal father and teacher as "strict" and insisted that their own fathers were ideal and that the "perfect" boy or girl obeys adults, projective tests revealed that adults were actually perceived as being rather unpleasant and as more punitive than helpful. In contrast to the less prejudiced group, none of them chose a parent as a possible companion if stranded on a desert island or said he would voluntarily discuss a personal problem with an adult.

In keeping with the "scapegoat" theory that passive acceptance of authority fosters hostility which is displaced upon innocent victims, prejudiced children's stories were dominated by concern with aggressive impulses and the punishment that the offender incurred; moreover, "the passive characters in their tales were invariably attacked because of their weaknesses."

Effective Social Behavior and the Interpersonal Relationship

As with other behaviors, social behavior is considered to be a product of the situation and the personality; therefore, a close relationship between those behaviors described in the chapter on intrapersonal activity and those expressed in relationships with other persons can be anticipated. How a person thinks of himself, how he perceives himself in relation to others, and the types of adaptive mechanisms he employs in defending himself against anxiety and in mastering his environment will all play important parts in determining how he acts in the presence of other persons. The perceptions that an individual has of himself in relation to his associates, and the behaviors that follow from such perceptions, will elicit reactions from others, which, in turn, will be responded to. Thus there is reciprocal interaction between situation and personality. The term *reciprocal* is appropriate because it indicates that the situation (that is, the behaviors of other persons) is not independent of the observer's perceptions and actions.

QUALITATIVE ASPECTS OF INTERPERSONAL BEHAVIOR

Behavior may be characterized in quantitative and qualitative terms. One's speech, for example, can be specified as varying in quantity, the number of words utilized, and as varying in kind or in quality; thus, one may speak at length in a friendly fashion. Similarly, social actions may be described in adjectives relating to behaviors that can be counted or ordered on some dimension of time or intensity, and these behaviors may also be described in terms of their kind and quality, such as friendliness, warmth, and communicativeness.

The social behaviors of an individual who has reached a high order of personal development reflect certain characteristic qualities. They are considered to be a typical part of the ideal state of development and, as such, are offered not as a standard in the statistical sense, but rather as a hypothetical "ideal." The person who attains so high a level of psychological development would demonstrate a capacity for friendliness, an ability to recognize the feelings and needs of others, and a respect for his own integrity as well as for the integrity of those with whom he has contact. These "ideal" characteristics are elaborated below.

FRIENDLINESS

The individual who fulfills the criteria of interpersonal effectiveness does not necessarily possess many close friends, nor does he form his deepest personal relationships quickly. His friendships develop gradually to a level of mutual respect and understanding; neither person is dominant, and neither uses the relationship for personal gain. This type of friendly relationship assumes a minimum of self-deception and misperception of one's friends. The participants do not need to conceal their faults, nor do they need to idolize each other.

The individual whose interpersonal development is of a high order perceives others as people, not as objects to be manipulated or used for his own selfish advantage. Neither does he see himself as an object to be advertised or sold. He is not concerned with mere appearance, for he can be sincere, honest, and straightforward. He is capable of expressing the feelings he has toward others; he can express love and affection, and he can become angry when his own rights or those of others are attacked. Although the person who demonstrates desirable interpersonal adjustment feels a kind of kinship with mankind, he can be selective about his most intimate relationships. He can enter reciprocal love relationships with a member of the opposite sex and can experience profound pleasure when he gratifies his partner.

The psychologically healthy person experiences feelings of oneness with all men, for he is not frightened or disturbed by the ways they differ from him in custom or appearance. An individual who is sensitive and aware of others' feelings is able to empathize with them and, even in brief encounters, his empathy is a basis for his friendliness and for his respect for others.

RESPECT FOR SELF AND OTHERS

Since the healthy person can feel related in many ways other than that of physical closeness, he has the ability to be by himself. When he prefers his own company to that of others, it is not because he disdains them but because he has a clear concept of himself. If he appears self-contained and self-reliant, it is not because he is unfriendly or fearful of others. The person who is a back-slapping good fellow or the life of the party is not necessarily a participant in any deep or enduring friendships. The quality of detachment that may characterize the individual who is able to maintain satisfying interpersonal relationships is considered by some to be a means of maintaining psychological integration in a society with a high incidence of psychological disturbance.

The person functioning effectively accepts and demonstrates his dependence on others at the same time that he pursues his own objectives in a self-reliant manner. His initiative is not destroyed by the lack of interest or disapproval of others. With full awareness that he is physically and emotionally bound to others, he can still obey the dictates of his own conscience and he measures his conduct first in terms of his own clear standards of right and wrong. The person who is free to act on his own convictions and in his own interests seldom finds it necessary publicly to defy established customs and manners; he does not become a social "character" and violate the rights, needs, and feelings of others.

This hypothetical person does not have to substitute the word of an authority or a hero for his own thinking, since he does not need to rely on other people, as mirrors, to see how well he is doing. He is an individual in his own right. He can accept the dependence of others without irritation, although he does not get lost in their problems or accede unquestioningly to their demands. He does not have to exploit his subordinates, make the "right friends," or test established friendships. He gives of himself freely without being taken advantage of, and he can avoid or withdraw from relationships in which he is exploited. Such a person respects others for what they are, and he is aware that no man stands alone. He is more impressed with the implications of the common brotherhood of man than he is with the differences that can be observed among the peoples of the world. He judges individuals on the basis of their adequacies as human beings and not in terms of stereotypes of ethnic, religious, or national groups. He has relationships with persons on the basis of their individual characteristics, and his friends may include persons of varied interests, backgrounds, and cultures.

Summary

The socially effective person is able to comply and conform to the needs and wishes of others when it is appropriate to do so; at the same time he maintains his own personal integrity and freedom from the group. The evaluations and judgments he makes of others are based upon the evidence at hand and are revised as additional information becomes available. He is aware of the tendencies of all men to stereotype others, and he attempts to avoid generalizations about persons on the basis of their appearance, color, or ethnic derivations. The presence of others who are different from himself does not cause him to become frightened, anxious, or hostile.

The personal relationships that the effective person maintains are not superficial or ritualistic; they are characterized by friendliness, warmth, spontaneity, and the giving and receiving of affection. At the same time, he has little need to be always in the presence of others. While he avoids hurting others, he has no need to allow others to hurt him. He is aware of the responsibilities associated with the roles he chooses to fill. He is perceptive and responsive to the needs and feelings of others and can respect them, just as he expects others to respect his needs and feelings.

In the course of his development, man never reaches a point where he is totally independent. Rather, as he achieves levels of lesser dependence on others, he becomes increasingly able to assist others, to allow them to be dependent upon him, and to contribute to their development. To the extent that he makes this contribution, he is evidencing socially effective behavior; to the extent that he does not contribute to such development, his behavior is socially ineffective.

References

1. Adorno, T. W., Frenkel-Brunswik, E., Levinson, D. J., and Sanford, R. N. *The Authoritarian Personality*. New York: Harper, 1950.
2. Allport, G. W., and Kramer, B. M. Some roots of prejudice. *J. Psychol.*, 1956, *22*, 9–39.
3. Asch, S. E. Studies of independence and submission to group pressure: 1. A minority of one against a unanimous majority. *Psychol. Monogr.*, 1956, *70*.
4. Berelson, B., and Salter, P. J. Majority and minority Americans: An analysis of magazine fiction. *Public Opinion Quarterly*, 1946, *10*, 168–190.
5. Crutchfield, R. S. Conformity and character. *Amer. Psychologist*, 1956, *10*, 191–198.
6. Gilbert, G. M. Stereotype persistence and change among college students. *J. abnorm. soc. Psychol.*, 1951, *46*, 245–254.
7. Glueck, S., and Glueck, E. T. *Unraveling Juvenile Delinquency*. New York: Commonwealth Fund, 1950.
8. Goring, C. *The English Convict*. London: Darling & Sons, Ltd., 1913.
9. Hathaway, S. R., and Monachesi, E. *Analyzing and Predicting Juvenile Delinquency with the MMPI*. Minneapolis: University of Minnesota Press, 1953.
10. Jacobson, J. L., and Wirt, R. D. Characteristics of improved and unimproved prisoners in group psychotherapy. *Group Psychother.*, 1958, *11*, 299–308.
11. Katz, D., and Braly, K. Racial stereotypes of 100 college students. *J. abnorm. soc. Psychol.*, 1933, *28*, 280–290.
12. Killian, L. M. The significance of multiple group membership in disaster. *Amer. J. Soc.*, 1952, *57*, 309–314.

13. Krech, D., and Crutchfield, R. S. *Elements of Psychology*. New York: Knopf, 1958.
14. Leavitt, H. J. Some effects of certain communication patterns on group performance. *J. abnorm. soc. Psychol.*, 1951, *46*, 38–50.
15. Lerner, M. *America as a Civilization: Life and Thought in the United States Today*. New York: Simon and Schuster, 1957.
16. Lippitt, R. An experimental study of the effect of democratic and authoritarian group atmospheres. Univ. Iowa Stud., 1940, *16*, 43–198.
17. Maslow, A. H. *Motivation and Personality*. New York: Harper, 1954.
18. Newcomb, T. M. *Social Psychology*. New York: Holt, 1950.
19. Razran, G. Ethnic dislikes and stereotypes: A laboratory study. *J. abnorm. soc. Psychol.*, 1950, *45*, 7–27.
20. Riesman, D., *et al. The Lonely Crowd*. New Haven: Yale University Press, 1950.
21. Sanford, F. H. Research on military leadership; in Flanahan, J. C. (ed.), *Psychology in the World Emergency*. Pittsburgh: University of Pittsburgh Press, 1952.
22. Stouffer, S. A., Guttmann, L., Suchman, E. A., Lazarsfeld, P. F., Star, S. A., and Clausen, J. A. *The American Soldier* (Vol. IV). Princeton: Princeton University Press, 1950.
23. Witty, P. A. A seventh report on T.V., *Elementary English,* 1956, *33,* 523–528.

Selected Readings

Adorno, T. W., *et al. The Authoritarian Personality*. New York: Harper, 1950.
Allport, G. W. *The Nature of Prejudice*. Boston: Beacon Press, 1954.
Bernard, J. *Social Problems at Mid-Century*. New York: Holt, 1957.
Fromm, E. *The Sane Society*. New York: Holt, 1955.
Newcomb, T. M. *Social Psychology*. New York: Holt, 1950.
Riesman, D., *et al. The Lonely Crowd*. New Haven: Yale University Press, 1950.

14.

Effective Learning

Human development is an on-going and dynamic process. It involves the continuous organization and reorganization of perceptions, skills, and knowledge as well as the modification and remobilization of attention and energy in response to the continually changing aspects of the environment. In this process the person extends his behavioral repertoire. He acquires new insights into the nature of the physical and social world, and he sees his relationships with others in new and different terms. He achieves greater proficiency in old skills and masters new ones. In short, the process of human development consists in large part of the learning of new patterns of behavior.

Not all behavioral changes are learned, however. Some are the products of maturation or of a process termed "imprinting," in which the complex interaction of specific stimulus and the individual's physical structure at a given point in his development results in the acquisition of behaviors that are particularly resistant to modification. Nor do all learned behaviors further the individual's development. Some acquired behaviors are self-destructive: learned fears can prevent the productive and gratifying use of talents; learned prejudices can stand in the way of satisfying personal relationships.

The range of learned behaviors is indeed broad, covering the intellectual, emotional, and social life of the individual. These behaviors involve the acquisition not only of new symbols and new meanings for previously familiar symbols but also of new skills, such as typing or driving a car, and new modes of social response, such as how to act at a reception. In addition, fears are learned—and so are means of dealing with them.

The range of behavioral change that can properly be attributed to learning is so broad that we can discuss only two settings in which learning occurs. The first is the academic. In this situation some of the symbols, facts, knowledge, and skills essential to living and working within society are learned. The activities associated with their acquisition involves what is generally thought of as "book learning." These are the activities that generally come to mind when the words "learning" and "studying" are used in everyday conversation. Yet such learning has motivational and emotional components, and it is not limited solely to the acquisition of symbols.

The second setting is the psychotherapeutic situation. In this setting troubled persons attempt, with the assistance of a counselor or psychotherapist, to learn new patterns of behavior. Since these new patterns of behavior emerge from changes in personality organization and function, they involve not only verbal and symbolic learning but also complex learnings of a motivational, emotional, and perceptual nature.

The section "Learning in the Psychotherapeutic Situation" emphasizes the contention that the learning process includes much more than "school" learning. This section illustrates how in one setting man's beliefs about himself, his behaviors toward others, the values to which he aspires, the goals he sets, and the psychological limitations that prevent the fullest expression of his potential are all subject to modification. Such modifications are among the most significant of all learnings to both the individual and his society. Psychotherapy is included in this chapter, not because it is the only route to personality modification but because it is explicitly directed to such an objective.

Learning in the Academic Setting

The psychological and social significance of the child's school experiences were described in Chapter 7. In the academic situation he extends his awareness of the world and acquires additional knowledge and skills necessary for maintaining and coping with his environment. Since more than half of all high school graduates go on to some form of additional academic or technical training, a brief consideration of some factors related to effective learning at this level is appropriate.

Effective learning in the academic setting implies more than preparing for one's career; it also implies the discovery of relationships among events the individual has personally encountered or drawn from the experiences of others. Through his abilities to communicate via symbols he acquires knowledge and skill; he becomes aware of events and their significance without personally developing and discovering the relationships, principles, and facts. It is through his symbolic abilities that man achieves his greatest proficiency in mastering his environment. Consider the state of affairs if there were no recourse to the developments and the knowledge of the past. Each generation would then start afresh from the beginning and be limited to the progress possible within one generation.

The symbol-using abilities that are so necessary in academic learning provide a focus for the present discussion. Although some mention will be made of specific learning techniques, the reader is encouraged to consider the general principles that are discussed and adapt them to his own particular situation. For those students interested in a more detailed discussion of techniques of study, the references listed at the end of the chapter will be helpful.

Motivation

Individuals will learn most readily when they feel a need to master some challenging aspect of their environment. Unfortunately, a considerable amount of the information presented in academic programs is remote from the immediate concerns of the student. Some studies may be instrumental to the attainment of long-range goals, as in the case of a course in chemistry for a pre-medical student. However, some required programs or parts of them appear to have little bearing on the student's objectives, either short- or long-range. Studies of motivation suggest that learning will occur in proportion to the individual's desire to master the material studied and his interest in it. Consequently, the student who clarifies his objectives and perceives the relationship between his long-term goals and his present activities has an advantage over the student whose immediate and long-term goals are nebulous. When this relationship is unclear, the student will often be motivated by such "instrumental" aspects of the task as attaining a good grade, remaining in the teacher's or parent's good graces, or receiving a good recommendation.

It is believed that, in general, learning is accomplished most effectively when the mastery of a new skill or the acquisition of additional knowledge relates directly to an experienced need, rather than when such learning is secondary to the attainment of some goal to which it bears no logical relationship. From the student's viewpoint, however, much of what is learned in the academic situation is instrumental, representing in many instances a necessary evil, a hurdle to be surmounted as part of a degree program, or a course of study that stands as prerequisite to another closer to the student's immediate interests. The student who deliberately attempts to stimulate his interest in the material at hand and to relate his courses to his own interests and needs, and who develops the need to acquire knowledge for its own sake will learn more effectively and retain more of what he learns than if he approaches his courses as mere means to unrelated ends.

Often, of course, a student cannot identify a goal, for interests do not normally stabilize until the twenties. Thus, it is not uncommon to hear undergraduates say, "But I don't know what vocation I want to prepare for," envying their classmates who "know" they want to be engineers or accountants. Parents sometimes heighten their concern by saying such things as, "But you can't just keep taking courses that are useless. You must decide upon a major."

Such statements reflect the popular concept of a college education as vocational preparation, leading a student to feel that he must see some specific utilitarian value in each course he takes. And if he has not yet identified a specific goal, he is bound to minimize an interest he may have, so long as it seems to have only "cultural" value. A student should feel justified in taking courses simply because they represent unexplored areas of knowledge or because they contribute to his general understanding or enjoyment. If students believed that such reasons were legitimate ones, they would have greater motivation to learn.

The importance of the student's allowing himself enough time for self-analysis warrants mentioning at this point. As previous chapters have emphasized, aspects other than interests are important in vocational choice, and the student needs time to identify relevant personality traits, values, and needs.

Reinforcement

As was noted earlier, the reinforcement that follows a given response increases the likelihood of the repetition of the response. In academic learning individuals will learn most rapidly and most effectively when they receive—or, in a sense, bestow upon themselves—recognition for their attainments. It is therefore essential that the individual have a clear picture of the adequacy of his performance. Unless he knows whether he is performing in the expected manner, there is little opportunity either for correction of inadequate responses or for reward and the resulting reinforcement.

The operation of reinforcers is much more subtle in the human learning situation than in simple animal experiments. As was described earlier in connection with operant conditioning, the animal who makes the desired response, such as pressing a lever in a cage, receives a pellet of food as a reward. In the human learning situation, the process is more complex because of the individual's capacity to bestow rewards upon himself and because of the complex and intangible nature of many rewards. For example, the student completing an assignment is able to say to himself, "I did well," and experience a glow of self-satisfaction.

If interpreted psychologically, the cliché that nothing succeeds like success suggests that the individual who experiences a degree of success is hence more apt to behave in ways which, in turn, will contribute to additional successes. By indiscriminately cutting classes, ignoring assignments, or missing tests, he deprives himself of possible success experiences.

Although knowledge of the adequacy of one's performance is considered essential if reinforcement is to be effective, it should not be assumed that learning cannot occur with minimal reinforcement or seemingly minimal motivation. In some situations persons acquire new skills or form new associations among events, symbols, or ideas without any conscious intent to do so. Although the extent of learning without intent or awareness is generally minimized because men cherish the conviction that they are aware of and control the significant events of their development, the importance of this type of learning should not be underestimated. The individual's self-concepts, his values, his biases, and irrational fears are primarily learned not as the result of a deliberate effort but through the occurrence of events overlapping or succeeding one another in time and the simultaneous presence of conditions serving as subtle reinforcers. It is, however, necessary to treat with some skepticism the claims made for procedures that capitalize on incidental learning processes. The advertisements claiming that languages can be learned during one's sleep, for example, are not supported by research.

The student desiring to capitalize on his potential to learn unintentionally will give careful attention to his associates and his surroundings. He will deliberately seek contact with those whose knowledge and skills exceed his. In his choice of roommates, friends, employment, or vocation he will consider their possible contribution to his incidental learning. Some students deliberately decide not to room with close friends because they realize the distractions involved. Others choose part-time or summer jobs that will give them experience in an area of interest, even though they may pay less money than jobs that cannot contribute to their future goals. Some colleges and universities have organized overseas centers where their students can spend one or more semesters pursuing their studies, one reason being the assumption that the language, customs, and culture of the land will be acquired incidentally, as well as intentionally.

APPLYING PREVIOUS LEARNINGS
TO NEW SITUATIONS

Various measures can be used to evaluate an individual's learning effectiveness in an academic situation, such as the length of time required to demonstrate a satisfactory performance, the number of efforts at learning within a given time interval, and the length of time following learning during which the newly acquired skill or knowledge can be appropriately applied. In most instances of academic learning such measures will yield information not only about the present performance but also about the effects of previous learnings. Let us suppose that after three lessons one clarinet student is significantly ahead of another. If the difference can be attributed to the fact that the superior student knew how to read music before beginning the clarinet then a "positive transfer of training" from an earlier learning situation to the present one has been demonstrated. Much of man' attainment can be attributed to his ability to apply what he has previously learned to the acquisition of new behavioral patterns, skills, and knowledge. The value of positive transfer in the learning of new material is recognized in the old adage that in teaching one starts with what is known and then moves to material that is unfamiliar.

Within recent years society's interest in educational problems has increased. Newspapers and magazines have featured descriptions of the shortage of college facilities, the lack of qualified teachers, and the relatively small number of persons being trained in the physical sciences. These reports have often been accompanied by critical evaluations of the national effort in education, and by such slogans as "Education for Excellence." Particularly relevant to the present discussion is the revival of an assumption that was questioned early in research on the transfer of training: that the "mind" is like a single muscle and that any type of rigorous activity can "strengthen" it. According to this view, learning difficult subjects, such as ancient languages and advanced mathematics, contributes to the individual's ability to think, to reason, to utilize critical judgment, and to excel in other studies. Actually, research results have discredited this position. They do suggest, however, that positive transfer may occur—not because the mind is "strengthened" but rather because there may be a carry-over of certain principles or procedures that the new learning situation shares with the previous one. When motor skills such as those involved in typing or driving are learned, a high degree of similarity between the old and new situation with respect to the stimuli and the required responses will produce the greatest amount of positive transfer.

When the stimuli presented in the new situation are the same or similar to those involved in previous learning but the new required responses are different, the resulting interference with learning the proper response is attributed to "negative transfer of training." Negative transfer effects are minimized by delineating, identifying, and separating the learning to be acquired from previous learnings. This would be the case with a football coach who wants to teach his team a new play and who provides them with a new signal for it instead of using one that has been identified with an old discarded play.

In the academic situation, the student who is aware of the principle of positive transfer will be alert to the elements that new tasks share with those previously learned. In addition, he will deliberately apply appropriate learned principles, procedures, and techniques in new learning situations and he will avoid such application when they are inappropriate. In the absence of obvious applications, as the use of mathematics in an engineering drawing class, the student will need to seek such relationships actively. For example, economic principles can be related to historical periods, sociological forces can be dovetailed with psychological principles of behavior, the roots of a current event can be seen in early political forces, a principle of physics can be applied to a problem in perception.

Perhaps the most important implication to be drawn from transfer-of-training research is that the individual confronted with the challenge of learning something new is best advised to focus directly on what he wants to learn. The student who wants to acquire a speaking knowledge of French, for example, will do better studying French for three years than studying Latin for one year and French for two. Similarly, the pre-law student who takes courses in mathematics in order to improve his ability to think critically and to argue effectively would increase the opportunity to transfer by joining the debating team.

Learning is facilitated when the individual is motivated, when his "correct" responses are reinforced, and when he is able to apply previous principles and learnings to new situations. In addition, effectiveness is influenced by the way the learner approaches his studies and the conditions under which the learning is attempted. These are considered in the next section.

SUGGESTIONS FOR STUDYING

The conditions under which individuals learn most effectively vary considerably from person to person. Some poorly motivated individuals learn relatively little under the most favorable conditions, while highly motivated individuals can learn under circumstances that are far from desirable. In general, the conditions that are most conducive to effective study are those of minimal distraction, such as might exist in a quiet room where a person is seated at an orderly desk without pictures or mementos that can evoke daydreams. The significance of the work situation is emphasized by research indicating that students who did their studying in the school library performed better than those who studied elsewhere (2). A good place for studying should diminish the time spent in getting ready and in shifting from one subject to the next. These two difficulties, along with the complaint that they do not get as much studying done as they intend, constitute the three major problems that students report about their studying (7).

Some experts suggest that the student who wishes to improve his work habits should schedule his time in a definite fashion. Such a schedule would include the specific subjects to be studied at specific times, with allowances made for leisure time activities and for recreation. It has been found that students with the most time available for study do not necessarily do better work than students who have less time because they are also employed (6). Research has indicated also that students who spend the most time studying are not necessarily those who get the best grades (1).

Although individuals develop their own characteristic approaches to the learning of academic material, most students can profitably take inventory of their own techniques and consider whether they can be improved. The following general suggestions apply to techniques appropriate for the learning of academic subject matter. In beginning any assignment a student is advised to scan the material to be studied (7). At the outset of a course it is usually profitable to go through the textbook, noting its organization, the material that is presented, the chapter titles, and the subheadings. If there are chapter summaries, these should be read as part of the scanning phase. The value of the scanning phase will depend, in part, on how well the student is able to identify the pattern that is followed in the development of the subject.

After scanning the material, the student can begin to read with an intent to remember, and he should question himself in detail on the content of his assignment. When he has mastered the material, he should be able to provide a statement of the content, of its highlights and its significant details. In general, meaningful material is most efficiently studied by the "whole" method, not sentence by sentence or paragraph by paragraph. The student should include active recitation as an important part of his learning procedure. This means not only a silent self-examination, but a type of conversation with oneself. Research has indicated that students who devote as much as 80 percent of their study time to recitation do better than those who do not recite at all (3). Recitation is valuable probably because it forces the student to focus his attention on the material at hand, requires him to conceptualize it in a fashion clear enough for verbal expression, and allows for the correction of errors or misperceptions.

Throughout the learning of new material students should seek out the relationships among the facts presented, and if such relationships are not clear they should be pondered and worked out. Meaningful material is learned and retained better than material that is acquired purely through rote memorization.

Closely related to self-examination procedures are those that enable the learner to make an immediate evaluation of his efforts. "Teaching machines" utilize the principle that immediate knowledge of the results of one's efforts will expedite learning. In many automatic instructional programs the student cannot proceed to the next "frame" until he has mastered the previous one. In addition, the student's correct response is often reinforced through some self-reward procedure, such as being allowed to star the response as correct by pressing a special button or lever. A common example of a technique that embodies the basic principles of the automatic teaching device is the "flash" card. Children learning arithmetic are shown cards, one side presenting the problem, such as $4 - 2 = ?$, and the reverse side containing the correct answer, 2. Immediately after the child's response, he is shown the correct answer. This flash card procedure is employed to good advantage by foreign language students to increase their vocabularies. Whether or not the student is in an automatic teaching program, he should make provision for frequent self-quizzes. Although the forms of these self-quizzes will vary, depending on the subject matter, they should share the important feature of providing for an evaluation of the student's performance.

Active review of material learned is another essential factor in efficient learning, for many investigations (7) have shown that a considerable portion of any learned material is rapidly forgotten unless it is reviewed. Review is usually most effective when it closely follows initial learning and when it is followed, in turn, by brief additional reviews that are spaced appropriately. A more intensive review is usually made just before the examination.

RETENTION OF LEARNED MATERIAL

The issue of review relates directly to the problem of retaining learned material, a problem which to some extent differs from that of the effectiveness of learning. Memory for what has been learned is evident whenever we attempt to recall, recognize, or relearn something. *Recall* is the re-entry into conscious awareness of that which was previously learned. The instructor who asks a student to repeat a point made in the previous lecture is testing the student's retention by the method of recall. If the same question is contained in a multiple choice examination, the student's retention is tested in terms of *recognition*. If the student encounters the same point in a different course two years later, he may neither recall nor recognize it. But if he requires less time to *relearn* it than he needed initially, he shows some degree of retention.

It is more difficult to recall material than to recognize it (5). Consequently, the student preparing for a recall type of test should "overlearn" his lesson; he should learn it beyond the point of immediate recall. It has been demonstrated that overlearning can markedly increase the amount of retention of recall material (4). Overlearning is less necessary when retention is to be tested by recognition or relearning, but it is still a practical safeguard for examination purposes. The student who learns his lessons beyond the point of a perfect immediate performance, who reviews and continues to study after he has once learned the material, is least likely to forget over long periods of time or to "draw a blank" at examination time.

Here it should be noted that forgetting is less influenced by the passage of time than by the experiences intervening between the time of the learning and the time of the test of retention. For example, studies show that persons who spend a period of time awake after learning material tend to forget more than do individuals whose learning is followed by an equal period of sleep. The theory that forgetting occurs when subsequent learnings interfere with the old learning is termed the *theory of retroactive inhibition*. The best way to offset this retroactive inhibition is to review systematically the material to be retained. A person who wants to retain skill in a foreign language, for example, will make provision to read, speak, and hear the language after he has finished his academic training.

Forgetting can also be attributed to unpleasant associations with some aspect of what was learned. Pleasant experiences are recalled more easily than unpleasant ones, and these differences in recall of pleasant and unpleasant events are attributed to the operation of various defense mechanisms, of which repression is the most prominent. If the learner can derive pleasure from what he learns and can associate the conditions of the learning situation with pleasant and satisfying activities, his retention will be increased. On the other hand, if the learner's associations to his task evoke feelings of threat and require him to defend himself against anxiety, then forgetting is more likely to occur.

THE ACADEMIC EXPERIENCE AND PERSONALITY DYNAMICS

We have been discussing learning in the academic setting as a topic separate from the other events of significance in the individual's life. In actual life the behavior of an individual in the academic situation is a reflection of his personality and the specific meanings the academic situation possesses for him. In the academic setting, as in all others, he will respond in terms of his characteristic modes of perception; he will attempt to maintain, protect, and extend his self-concept, and in doing so he will rely on the defense and mastery mechanisms he has acquired over the years.

The student who deceives rather than confronts himself will continue to do so in the academic setting. His learning difficulties will be attributed to the inadequacy of the instructors, the behavior of his roommate, or the lack of library facilities. Rather than accepting responsibility for his own actions and performance, the student whose defenses distort his assessments of the situation will believe that the instructor is persecuting him and that his classmates are hostile and enjoy his difficulties.

The disorganization and lack of motivation that characterize the study efforts of many students do not reflect a lack of knowledge of how to study. Rather they reflect the confusions pertaining to the student's own self-identities and a failure to understand how their immediate activities relate to long-term objectives. Some students are so entangled in the struggle for self-identity and so involved in achieving a delayed stabilization and balance among their intrapsychic processes that the ego processes essential for effective studying are invested elsewhere: in the maintenance of the personality, in keeping impulses under control, in trying to clarify the nature of the social world, and in meeting the demands of daily life. For such students the opportunities the academic situation offers for the learning of new patterns of emotional and social behavior are of paramount importance; mastery of academic material is of secondary significance to them.

For most students their academic experience—and more specifically their college experience—affords the opportunity for marked personality development. College experiences as a whole provide, in addition to academic learning, a host of new emotional and social learnings. Exposure to different ideas and to persons of different beliefs and backgrounds provides the student with an opportunity to extend the range of his awareness. The structure and organization of both the curricular and extracurricular activities and the student's relative freedom to decide for himself how he invests his time and energies within the structure afford the opportunity for new mastery experiences. The relationship between one's actions and their consequences is often more clearly perceived in the away-from-home college setting. With parental restraints removed, the student also has an opportunity to develop his own resources for impulse control and for the clarification of his own ethical and moral standards.

Learning New Emotional and Social Behaviors

In the encounter with his physical and social environment man extends his range of skills, he acquires new means of mastering the challenges confronted, and he modifies and adapts his behaviors to new conditions. And in this process he learns new patterns of response, new ways of perceiving himself and others; some features of his life that were significant to him become less so, and others assume new significance. He acquires experience and knowledge and as he develops he becomes less afraid, less superstitious, and less prejudiced. Most of what man learns during his life is not academic, although the intellectual component is often prominent, and his capacity to rely on symbolic representations of events, experience, and expectations serves him particularly well as he relates the signals the environment presents to the reactions that bring him satisfaction. He learns what is expected of him by others in countless situations, and he learns what to expect of others. He learns the behaviors, perceptions, and emotions appropriate to these expectations, and he learns how to evaluate the adequacy of his performance, how to recognize his failures, and how to enjoy his successes. He learns to try new patterns of behavior when his efforts have been unsatisfactory and to repeat those that were rewarded. Much that is learned he is only partially aware of; some of the learning occurs completely outside his awareness. Before considering how new patterns of emotional and social behavior are acquired in one specific situation, the psychotherapeutic, several general features involved in such learning warrant attention.

Some dissatisfaction, discomfort, or desire that activates the individual to respond must be present as a basic condition for new learning to occur.[1] It was noted earlier in connection with developmental fixation (p. 69) that in the presence of total gratification little impetus to change can be anticipated. The totally satisfied adult has no need to invest energy in attempting new patterns of response. This degree of self-satisfaction is rare, however, and most adults experience various degrees of dissatisfaction with themselves or their situations. Even such unimportant behaviors as a decision about which fingernail polish to purchase can be influenced by the association of a particular product with the "need" for it. An axiom in advertising which recog-

---

[1] Incidental learning has neither this condition nor the reinforcement requirement considered basic for the formation of new associations. Whether such learning is an actual or only apparent exception to the present statement cannot be decided at this time.

nizes this principle is that a "need" must be developed before the advertiser sells the product.

The individual's activation to the point of response can be considered evidence of a tension state and therefore of the presence of a drive. Dissatisfaction with one's income, the discomfort associated with physical labor, and the desire to be respected in the community, for example, might combine to account for the drive to change one's pattern of work activity.

If behavior patterns are to change, the second requirement is that a reaction or pattern of responses actually be elicited. Something must take place behaviorally, some effort must be expended, some movements either overt or covert, either external or internal, are essential in the learning sequence. Although drives and the states prompting them give rise to the reactions associated with new learning, they do not provide the direction that is often essential. This is found in the signals and stimuli experienced by the individual. It is the association of stimuli, signals, or cues with the responses made to them that constitutes what is learned. Thus, to new challenges represented by the environment, behaviors will be associated with certain cues and not with others. The closeness of association of stimulus to response, and the amount of learning, will depend on the last phase of the learning sequence, the occurrence of reinforcement during or following the response.

These phases are more difficult to identify in the life situation than in the laboratory learning situation. For example, consider how the adult who has acquired a prejudice against all members of a minority group would learn new patterns of perceiving and responding to them. If in such a situation prejudiced references to the minority group bring disapproval from one's valued associates, then behaviors more directly related to satisfying needs for approval and recognition will be attempted. In this case such behaviors may be merely inhibitory: the prejudiced remark is withheld, the reinforcement provided by maintaining the favor of one's associates is forthcoming, and the tendency to refrain from derogatory or disparaging remarks is strengthened. To this extent no new patterns or attitudes toward the minority group have been acquired, although significant learning has occurred pertaining to the expression of these views in the presence of one's associates. However, because the person has become aware of the unacceptability of prejudice and has learned to inhibit his expression of it, it is possible that he will have more contact with persons whom otherwise would have been shunned, and that eventually his basic attitudes toward the minority group will change.

It is apparent that a complex relationship exists between the behavioral pattern and its emotional significance. Changes in behaviors do not necessarily imply changes in feelings and attitudes, or in the personality structure. On the other hand, such changes are in themselves significant and at times do relate to or set the stage for emotional, attitudinal, and personality change. In addition to discomfort, desire, or dissatisfaction being necessary for change, the accustomed patterns of response in adults have been reinforced over such a long period of time that new learning may not occur even when moderate dissatisfactions with existing response patterns are present. Sometimes new social and emotional learning is made difficult by the anxieties precipitated by either the prospect of change, which may be threatening, or by the content or subject itself. In such instances defense mechanisms may function to obstruct the learning and blame for the experienced problems may be projected to some specific person or feature of the environment. The academically unsuccessful student may cite his inability to find a good place to study; a wife may hold her husband responsible for her unhappiness; an unsuccessful businessman may blame his associates for his failures.

By externalizing the causes of one's difficulties, it is possible to protect valued self-concepts, even though such concepts may be distorted and may contribute to some of the person's difficulties. In some instances, asking friends and associates for advice is an indication of the person's need to maintain and protect his self-concept. Without necessarily realizing it, he may merely be seeking confirmation of his own beliefs regarding the origin of his problems, thus reinforcing his proposed solutions.

Learning in the Psychotherapeutic Situation

Psychotherapy is a psychological process that facilitates the learning of new modes of perceiving and responding to oneself and one's physical and social world. This learning is accompanied by changes in personality functioning and organization and is essentially accomplished within the personal relationship of one individual, a therapist, to another, a client or patient. The events that transpire within the relationship between therapist and client provide the basic components of the psychotherapeutic process. In the relationship the therapist is particularly attentive to what the client expresses and experiences, emotionally as well as verbally. The role of the therapist is to facilitate learning, but in doing so his actions differ markedly from that of the teacher who lectures, provides information, and is primarily attentive to the students' intellectual activities.

Although the reasons that impel a person to seek help show wide variation, they have in common dissatisfaction with one's emotional, social, or occupational condition, situation, or status. For example, a graduate engineer after working for six years felt that he was interested in coming into close contact with more persons than his present occupation permitted. He considered a shift to sales work within his firm. However, if he made such a move, he would exchange a stable and sure salary for an uncertain return based on the commissions received from sales. Since he was married and the father of two small children, the decision had a number of implications not only for him but for his family as well.

Miss Baker was referred to a psychotherapist by her physician. She had been experiencing increasingly intense and prolonged periods of depression and was preoccupied with morbid and unhappy thoughts. She often felt like crying but was unable to tell the therapist any specific experiences in her life that might account for her feelings. She stated that everything at work was going well, but the fact that her associates thought well of her only made her feel guilty.

The principal of the elementary school suggested that Mr. and Mrs. Smith meet with a counselor to discuss their son's learning difficulties. Bobby, a fourth grader, was experiencing marked difficulties in learning to read and in doing arithmetic. Since his intelligence was above average and he had had the usual opportunities for learning, the cause of the learning problem was not clear. The mother believed that Bobby was generally very unsure of himself; she attributed this state to the fact that the father's work required that he be away from home for considerable periods of time and that when he was home he had little time to spend with Bobby. The father took the position that Bobby was pampered by his mother and that the boy's difficulties were due to her indulgence. He believed that Bobby "lacked discipline" and raised the question of whether Bobby would not do better if he were sent away from home to a military school.

On the recommendation of the Juvenile Court judge, a therapist saw a fifteen-year-old boy who was apprehended while serving as a lookout during an unsuccessful robbery attempt by a gang of older youths. During his first visit, the boy stated that he did not have any problems and was seeing the therapist only because the judge forced him to do so.

Other problems for which individuals seek assistance may relate to marriage, to some specific behavior such as drinking, or to extreme shyness in social situations. Individuals are often referred for psychotherapy when they have physical complaints, such as sleeplessness or stomach difficulties, for which no physical basis can be identified. In some instances the problem may be related to a physical ailment that the referring physician believes is accentuated by stress or intrapsychic conflict. Persons with ulcers, high blood pressure, and asthma may be included in this category.

When individuals seek help, some degree of anxiety usually accompanies the dissatisfaction. The person often feels that he is at a critical point in his life: "I have tried everything else and nothing has helped"; "Something has to be done." The person seeking help is usually aware of his uncertainties and anxieties and his doubts and feelings of depression, but he is unclear as to their origin, significance, or remedy. This was the case with Carol.

Carol White: A Student Needing Help

Carol, a nineteen-year-old college sophomore, came to a college counselor on the advice of one of her instructors. The counselor knew from Carol's entrance examination scores and from her high-school record that Carol's failing college grades were not due to a lack of ability or intelligence. From observing the listless way she entered his office and her barely audible responses to his questions, he also concluded that she was depressed. As Carol became able to talk about her own feelings, she said she believed that there was no point in continuing her college program. In a voice that was almost too faint to be heard she said, "I am so discouraged that everything seems hopeless. I know that whatever I try will flop. It's not just the school work, though that's part of it, but it's everything. Everything is a mess. My mother is all upset that I am flunking, and the other girls in dorm think that I am a pill, and even Frank doesn't come around anymore."

In the appointments that followed, Carol told her counselor many things about her background, her family, and her feelings toward her parents. She described experiences that had occurred during her childhood which she had not thought of for many years. At times Carol became obviously upset by the memories which she reported; at other times she felt a great relief in being able to confide in someone.

The picture that emerged indicated clearly the conditions under which Carol's standards were acquired and how they had affected her self-concept. She described her small home town as a typical suburban community. She had lived there all her life and had never been away from home for an extended period before coming to college. Initially Carol described her parents as "average" people who were about the "same" as everyone else's father and mother. After she had seen the counselor a number of times her picture of her parents changed. Carol's mother, Mrs. White, had come from a small rural town. In the second year of her teacher-training course at the State Teachers College she met and married Carol's father, who was just starting his own business. Carol was born two years after the Whites were married, at a time when the business was still struggling to survive. Carol could recall many tense and unpleasant quarrels about money during her early and middle childhood.

Her father's business had never really prospered, although in recent years it had become sufficiently stable to provide the Whites with a comfortable home and a steady income. Mrs. White had resented moving to Centerville and she continued to feel that the community afforded her little opportunity to develop her interests in art and music. She felt that she had little in common with many of her neighbors and that she was restricted by lack of money. Mrs. White had a high regard for people who achieved success in the academic and literary world.

Because of a series of family quarrels, Mrs. White, an only child, came to have very little to do with her own father and mother. She felt that her husband was too good-natured and easy-going, and that he could have been far more successful in his business had he tried. She often compared his modest success with that of more successful friends who, she felt, were less capable. Mrs. White, an intelligent and aggressive woman, was critical and often openly disdainful of men. She regarded them as dependent, lazy, and interested mainly in the gratification of their physical needs. She was a very rigid person who believed that things were right or wrong, good or bad, black or white. She made up her mind resolutely, and her convictions were unchangeable. Mrs. White had very definite ideas about child care and applied them in rearing Carol, the Whites' only child.

In her relationships with Carol, Mrs. White was an efficient and driving teacher. She set high standards for Carol's behavior and insisted upon their maintenance. Although Carol had never been spanked or shouted at, she could recall numerous instances during her childhood when she had been terrified by her mother's displeasure. Carol recalled her mother as being affectionate toward her only on certain occasions, such as the time she won the county spelling bee in the fifth grade. The few instances when her mother was genuinely pleased with her performance were vivid in Carol's memory. Carol also remembered a great many episodes in which she had felt let down and even worthless following "constructive" suggestions about how she might have done somewhat better. At such times Carol would feel that she could not really satisfy her mother's expectations no matter how hard she tried or how well she did. Although she seemed to have little chance of satisfying her mother, it was easier to keep trying than to face her reproof and disapproval.

Carol told the counselor that she was not sure just when she had begun to doubt her ability to achieve the level of performance that her mother expected. Without saying so directly, Carol indicated that she had introjected her mother's standards and values. Since she could rarely satisfy her "own" wishes to achieve or to do the right thing, she gained little gratification from her attainments. Her excellent grades did not alter her feeling that any recognition she received was obtained under false pretenses.

Mrs. White closely supervised all Carol's activities and friends through both elementary and high school. She had a keen concern for what was the "proper" thing, insisted that Carol's friends in school be limited to those from the "right" families, and viewed with distrust and disdain those friends whom Carol selected for herself. She described Carol as being "her child" and frequently made the comment that if she had allowed Mr. White to influence the way in which Carol had been reared, she would never have developed into the best student in her class.

Carol described her father as a kindly person who was very quiet at home, though he was talkative at work. Although Mr. White seldom disagreed openly with his wife, Carol was aware that her parents were at odds on many fundamental issues, including how she was to be disciplined, whether she was to go to college, and how she was to choose her friends. She believed that her father sided with her and understood her, even though he was unable to take issue with Mrs. White. Carol commented that her father always seemed somewhat preoccupied and aloof, and that she had never felt close to him.

Carol was also aware that her mother did not respect her father or any other man. Mrs. White warned her daughter that men could not be trusted and that the proper attitude toward them was one of guarded alertness. Mrs. White's basic attitudes toward sex were that it was evil and that all sexual impulses were evidence of personal immorality. She was convinced that men were lustful and that Carol had to be very careful lest they take advantage of her. Carol's attitudes toward men and her introjected belief that sexual impulses were wicked often caused her to feel "bad" and unworthy and contributed to her uncertainties in her relationships with boys.

Her doubts of her own value and goodness were intensified during her freshman year. In this new situation she could no longer rely on her mother to make decisions for her. Now she had to decide for herself what she would wear, how she would write a theme, and with whom she would associate. Not only were there many girls in her dormitory whose ideas of right and wrong were different from hers, but the information she was receiving in courses in social science and philosophy seemed contrary to her own strongly held beliefs. And she had met and come to like Frank, a member of the junior class.

Frank was an intelligent, attractive, and capable person and he liked Carol. Since she had told him that she liked him very much and that she thought of him all the time, he failed to understand why she was so angry whenever he became affectionate. Nor did Carol understand her reactions. She had no doubt that she was in love, for she had never felt this way about any boy; nevertheless, after almost a year of steady dating, she still became very upset when he touched her or tried to kiss her. Frank had finally stopped seeing her, and Carol found that nothing had much meaning. She could not concentrate on the professor's lectures, and she did not care very much whether she passed or failed her exams. She became depressed and, until her English professor suggested she seek help, she believed that there was very little that she could hope for.

She came to the counselor as a last resort with a desperate desire to be given the answers to all her difficulties. She soon found that the counselor did not prescribe or advise. He listened carefully while she talked, and from time to time he asked a question or offered comment. She found that she sometimes reacted to the counselor in ways that seemed to have very little to do with him or what he did. At these times her reactions were based on her deeply rooted expectations of men. At other times she reacted to the counselor on the basis of what she expected of adults in general, and particularly of people whom she perceived as having control or authority over her.

Gradually Carol began to understand the nature of her intra-psychic disunity. Even more important to Carol than knowledge of the origin of her difficulties was the fact that she now was able to function more comfortably with other people, and that she was less likely to feel guilty. She had come to have greater respect for herself and to be able to think and act without having to punish herself.

The following hypotheses suggest explanations of Carol's behavior. Carol's feelings of guilt and unworthiness were the possible result of the critical and moralistic attitudes she had introjected during her childhood. Her inability to tolerate or return Frank's demonstrations of affection reflected internal conflict between id and superego processes. She was attracted to Frank and wanted to be responsive to him, but her impulsive inclinations to do so evoked guilt over being immoral. Because of the conditions under which her concepts of right and wrong had been acquired, Carol's fears of being bad were overwhelming; her rejection of Frank's demonstrations of affection represented rejection of her own desires for physical gratification. This rejection was essential for Carol since her self-esteem was directly dependent on meeting her mother's high and uncompromising standards, which in turn had become her own standards. The conditions under which Carol had acquired these standards provided little opportunity for her to feel secure and loved. As a result her attitudes toward herself and her expectations of others provided little basis for feelings of self-esteem and confidence.

In light of her experiences and the problems confronting her, Carol's counselor perceived his responsibility as the provision of a learning situation for Carol in which she could clarify her feelings about herself. The counselor anticipated that in this process Carol would learn that she could exist independently of her mother and that many expectations based upon previous experiences were not appropriate to the present circumstances.

The Settings of Psychotherapy

Many colleges and universities maintain counseling centers or psychological or psychiatric clinics to which students with personal, social, or academic difficulties are referred. Some large industrial organizations also are now providing these services to their employees, because they believe that the efficiency and morale of their workers are important to the organization as well as to the employees. Many communities support public mental health clinics, and psychotherapy is also provided in city, county, state, and federal hospitals. In addition, the services of therapists are available in their private offices.

THE PSYCHOTHERAPIST: HIS PROFESSION AND TRAINING

Many different specialists practice psychotherapy and counseling: psychiatrists, psychologists, social workers, counselors, and psychoanalysts. Since both physicians and nonphysicians are qualified to practice, there is considerable confusion about what constitutes proper training in this field.

The psychiatrist is a physician with specialized training in psychiatry. In addition to his work as a psychotherapist, he is qualified to prescribe drugs, conduct physical examinations, and perform the work of a medical doctor.

The clinical or counseling psychologist is a specialist trained in the science of psychology. His doctorate is a Ph.D. and he has had from two to four years of supervised internship or field experience. Along with his qualifications as a psychotherapist, he is competent to formulate, conduct, and evaluate research in the area of his specialization and to provide personality assessment. To assist the public in identifying the psychologist qualified to offer psychotherapeutic and other services, many states have enacted legislation stipulating the requirements that must be met before the individual can practice as a psychologist.

The social worker who has had at least two years of graduate work also will provide counseling and psychotherapy in some hospital and clinic settings. The social worker often carries the major professional responsibility for bringing the resources of the community to bear on the patient's practical problems, such as those involving housing, medical attention, public assistance, and employment.

In many academic, vocational, and rehabilitation settings persons trained as counselors at both the master's degree and doctoral (Ed.D. or Ph.D) levels provide services to students and clients. The occasion for the seeking of help in such settings is often quite specific, such as an unsatisfactory academic performance or need for vocational direction. Although counselors may in such instances see their clients fewer times than when the focus of therapy is on modification of self-concepts and shifts in defense, the basic processes of counseling and psychotherapy are considered essentially similar.[2]

THE PSYCHOTHERAPEUTIC PROCESS

Whatever their professional identifications and approaches psychotherapists attempt to provide for their patients a situation that will maximize the opportunity for the learning of new behaviors and perceptions. One psychologist, Dr. Carl Rogers, in discussing his goals in the psychotherapeutic interchange, identifies certain trends or directions of development to which these new learnings contribute.

> The individual moves toward being, knowingly and acceptingly, the process which he inwardly and actually is. He moves away from being what he is not, from being a façade. He is not trying to be more than he is, with the attendant feelings of insecurity or bombastic defensiveness. He is not trying to be less than he is, with the increased feelings of guilt or self-deprecation. He is increasingly listening to the deepest recesses of his psychological and emotional being and finds himself increasingly willing to be, with greater accuracy and depth, that self which he most truly is.

As previously indicated, a person may be dissatisfied with the progress he is making in his vocational career, or he may be unhappy about the relationships he maintains with others, or he may feel persistently depressed or that he is gaining little from life. Such feelings represent dissatisfaction with learned patterns of behavior and the effort to seek assistance constitutes an effort to find (to learn) more satisfying

[2] For a contrasting view see L. Brammer and E. Shostram, *Psychotherapeutic Psychology*. Englewood Cliffs, N.J.: Prentice-Hall, 1960.

behaviors. When individuals seek assistance, however, it is not often with the conscious intent of learning new patterns of response. Since most of the issues that are of concern to individuals directly or indirectly involve their relationships with other persons, the experience with the therapist will either reinforce the existing modes of behavior or provide a basis for some degree of new learning. The primary factor in facilitating new learnings is thus the relationship between the therapist and the individual seeking help.

Whatever the therapist's professional identification may be, the client will perceive him in terms of his own previous encounters with other human beings, particular the significant ones in his life; consequently, the experience with the therapist, as it varies from the client's expectations, provides an extension of his social experience and may be of considerable significance to him.

In the early stages of the psychotherapeutic relationship, the person seeking help learns that he can express himself freely and fully to another person. What he says will be heard, and regardless of how reprehensible he may believe his "secret" fantasies, wishes, and impulses to be, his therapist will listen and will make the effort to understand him. He learns that within the psychotherapeutic situation he will not be censured, criticized, or rejected for the beliefs and feelings he describes. In the sixth session with her counselor, Carol White describes this awareness.

> *Carol:* I have been thinking about what you said to me last time. You said I could discuss whatever I wanted to.
> *Counselor:* There are things you would like to mention but you are not quite sure it would be all right.
> *Carol:* Well, no, that's not the way I feel now. The first couple of times I saw you I wasn't sure what you wanted me to talk about. But now I see that it is important for me to talk about myself and my feelings and that you aren't going to tell me what I should and should not think. But even though I know this I still have a hard time expressing some of the things that I spend a lot of time worrying about.
> *Counselor:* You want to talk about some things yet you seem to be unable to do so.
> *Carol:* Yes, that's about it.

> (LONG PAUSE)

> *Carol:* There may be another reason why it is hard to talk about these things here. I never could talk with my father either. He didn't criticize me but he would act like it bothered him or that he wished he were doing something else.

The realization that one can relate openly and without the need to deceive either oneself or others is generalized in successful therapy from this one relationship to persons other than the therapist, and the behavioral changes associated with this shift are in the direction of greater development and effectiveness. The patient brings to this relationship attitudes, values, and expectations as well as his characteristic modes of perceiving and responding to others. He will respond to and perceive the therapist in a manner consistent with his previous experience. If he has had to defend himself by being aloof, by concealing his beliefs and feelings from others, and by "playing his cards close to the vest," then he will respond to the therapist in that way. If he has relied on his ability to control and dominate others, then he will attempt to do so in the therapeutic situation. Such patterns of relating and of protecting and maintaining the personality have been learned; the therapeutic situation offers conditions that make it possible to learn new modes of perceiving and responding to others.

Carol anticipated attack and criticism when none was forthcoming; in the early sessions with her counselor she could not acknowledge that she was physically attracted to Frank; her denial defenses are reflected in this excerpt from the tenth session.

> *Carol:* Frank and I got along with each other very well; we could spend hours together just talking.
> *Counselor:* You had a great deal in common.
> *Carol:* Well, yes, but we had one big problem and I guess that's what led to his not coming around any more. He would always want to get affectionate and when I wouldn't let him he would get angry.
> *Counselor:* It was hard for you to understand why he reacted this way?
> *Carol:* Well, yes, I told him many times I wasn't raised like that.
> *Counselor:* Raised like that?
> *Carol:* You know what I mean, I couldn't let him take advantage of me.
> *Counselor:* Even though you wanted him to be affectionate, and you felt affectionate toward him, you had to hold him off or otherwise it would have made you feel evil?
> *Carol* (with much feeling): No, that is not it at all! I didn't want him to try to kiss me, and the only way I felt at the time was very tense, so tense, I would cry, after all. . . . (At this point Carol wept for several minutes, then with difficulty continued). . . You are just like my mother, always accusing me of having bad feelings. . . .

In the "accepting" environment of the relationship the degree of general threat the client experiences is to an extent reduced, and he becomes more able to differentiate between what is actually occurring in the relationship and what he is projecting into it. The objective appraisal of what transpires between himself and one other person—in this case, the therapist—is aided not only by the accepting conditions, which minimize the opportunity for anxiety arousal, but also by the therapist's reinforcement of the patient's effort to understand himself. The therapist's reinforcement of the patient's perceptions of reality and of himself as a person responsible for the consequences of his own behaviors also occurs in this process and is often accomplished gradually and subtly.

Several days following the previous episode, Carol appeared for her eleventh visit. Shortly after being seated she said:

> *Carol:* I have been thinking a lot about what happened here the other day and I am kind of ashamed of myself.
>
> *Counselor:* Ashamed? Why?
>
> *Carol:* Well, for one thing I had a hard time understanding why I became so upset. Then it occurred to me that I had very much wanted to respond to Frank, but I guess all I could think of was how wrong that was. Yet I guess it really wasn't very bad to feel that way.
>
> *Counselor:* Not as bad as your mother would have pictured it?
>
> *Carol:* Yes, and that reminds me, there is another thing that is kind of peculiar about last time. I thought you had accused me of being immoral, but when I was back in the dorm I realized you hadn't suggested that at all—I only thought you did.

In the course of his contacts with the psychotherapist the individual will often formulate more clearly the frame of reference whereby he can think and talk about himself and his own behaviors. This frame of reference may be considerably influenced by that held by the therapist, and since all therapists do not necessarily subscribe to the same personality theory, their techniques and practices will vary, as will the frame of reference they communicate to their patients and clients. Two prominent approaches to psychotherapy are psychoanalysis and client-centered therapy.

PSYCHOANALYTIC THERAPY

Psychoanalysts accept Freud's theoretical framework, placing considerable emphasis on the impact of childhood experiences. In orthodox psychoanalysis the patient reclines on a couch and does not see the therapist during some part or most of the session. It is thought that under such conditions he will be more relaxed, expressing himself more freely than if he faced the therapist and was distracted by his reactions. The client is encouraged verbally to express whatever comes to his mind—his thoughts, memories, impulses, irrespective of their coherence, organization, or meaning. He is thus required to say all that he is conscious of and to put aside the usual efforts to express only the well-organized and proper expressions that "make sense." In this process, known as free association, the patient will communicate perceptions of the therapist similar to perceptions of his parents. Often feelings of affection or hostility that had their origins in these earlier relationships will be directed to the analyst, and in this aspect of the relationship, known as the transference, the patient perceives and responds to the analyst in terms of the previous significant relationships in his life.

Through his relationship with the therapist the patient comes gradually to recognize the appropriateness and inappropriateness of his feelings, as well as their origins, and the situations and the symbols that evoke them. Memories of emotionally disturbing events are brought into awareness, and the anxiety-provoking potential of such memories and of the stimuli that evoke them is thus often reduced. Behavior changes occur, however, not only because many of these situations are brought into consciousness, but also because the patient, in effect, "relives" them with the therapist, and because conflict among the intrapsychic processes diminishes in the process. With the reduction of intrapsychic conflict, the person has more energy to direct toward others and less need to rely on self-deceptive and repressive defenses.

Contrary to the common belief that the therapist "tells the person what is wrong with him," psychoanalysis and other forms of psychotherapy assist in the developmental process by providing a psychological "climate" in which the person can activate his own potential for growth. In psychoanalysis this "climate" includes the emotional quality of the relationship between the patient and the therapist. Within this context the patient has the opportunity for emotional "relearning." The relationships that had to be avoided, the self-deception, and the aggressions against others, which are all related to the needs to maintain and protect the personality, become less necessary. Although the relearning process has its intellectual aspects, it occurs mainly as an emotional experience.

CLIENT-CENTERED THERAPY

The psychotherapeutic technique developed by Dr. Carl Rogers differs in several important respects from orthodox psychoanalysis. In his theoretical approach to personality, Rogers gives primary importance to the person's potential for "growth," for the achievement of greater degrees of personality integration. This growth takes place most often in nonthreatening environments. It is the Rogerians' view that the therapist's function is best achieved by establishing a relationship in which the client can express himself freely and fully. The Rogerian client is encouraged to talk about his concerns and to do so in his own way. The therapist does not evaluate or interpret what he is told, he focuses primarily on assisting the client to clarify his own feelings and self-perceptions, and he does this through his efforts to understand and experience what is being communicated to him.

Whereas the psychoanalyst directs the attention of the client to past events and experiences and to the emotions associated to them, the client-centered therapist permits the discussion to follow whatever direction the client chooses. Rogerian therapists attempt to avoid injecting their values and their frames of reference into the relationship. This follows from the conviction that development will occur when the client is able to consider himself and his situation in a candid manner and that this comes about when he learns he does not have to defend and deceive himself; that it is safe within the therapeutic relationship to say what he thinks and feels. The Rogerian therapist will explicitly indicate that he cannot provide solutions for the client; that his contribution is to assist in the client's clarification of his own position. The acceptance of the client and the role of the Rogerian therapist is reflected in the following excerpt from a therapy session reported by Rogers.[3]

> *Client:* I've never said this before to anyone—but I've thought for such a long time—This is a terrible thing to say, but if I could just—well (short, bitter laugh; pause), if I could just find some glorious cause that I could give my life for I would be happy. I cannot be the kind of a person I want to be. I guess maybe I haven't the guts—or the strength—to kill myself—and if someone else would relieve me of the responsibility—or I would be in an accident —I—I just don't want to live.
>
> *Counselor:* At the present time things look so black to you that you can't see much point in living . . .
>
> *Client:* Yes—I wish I'd never started this therapy. I was happy when I was living in my dream world. There I could be the kind of person I wanted to be—But now—There is such a wide, wide gap— between my ideal—and what I am. I wish people hated me. I try to make them hate me. Because then I could turn away from them and could blame them—but no—It is all in my hands—Here is my life—and I either accept the fact that I am absolutely worthless

[3] Reprinted by permission, from C. R. Rogers and R. F. Dymond, *Psychotherapy and Personality Change.* Copyright 1954 by the University of Chicago.

—or I fight whatever it is that holds me in this terrible conflict. And I suppose if I accepted the fact that I am worthless, then I could go away someplace—and get a little room someplace—get a mechanical job someplace—and retreat clear back to the security of my dream world where I could do things, have clever friends, be a pretty wonderful sort of person . . .

Counselor: It's really a tough struggle—digging into this like you are—and at times the shelter of your dream world looks more attractive and comfortable.

Client: My dream world or suicide.

Counselor: Your dream world or something more permanent than dreams . . .

Client: Yes. (A long pause. Complete change of voice.) So I don't see why I should waste your time—coming in twice a week—I'm not worth it—What do you think?

Counselor: It's up to you, Gil—it isn't wasting my time—I'd be glad to see you—whenever you come—but it's how you feel about it—if you don't want to come twice a week—or if you do want to come twice a week?—once a week?—It's up to you. (Long pause.)

Client: You're not going to suggest that I come in oftener? You're not alarmed and think I ought to come in—every day—until I get out of this?

Counselor: I believe you are able to make your own decision. I'll see you whenever you want to come.

Although only two approaches to individual psychotherapy have been mentioned here—the orthodox psychoanalytic and client-centered therapy—many other variants exist, depending on the personality theory to which the therapist subscribes, his own personality and value orientation, and the setting in which he offers his services. In addition to the variants of individual psychotherapy, several additional forms of the therapeutic process involving children and groups require mention. These are the subject of the next section.

OTHER PSYCHOTHERAPEUTIC APPROACHES

Child Psychotherapy

In contrast to adult psychotherapeutic practice in which the request for assistance is made by the patient, in child psychotherapy the parents, often at the suggestion of friends, school, or community officers, make the request that help be provided their child. Usually the request is prompted by specific behaviors that cause trouble for some adults, the parents, school officials, or police. These specific behaviors, such as bedwetting, school failure, fighting, or fire setting, are not the only reasons why parents who are concerned about the development of their children seek assistance. They may believe their child to be withdrawn, fearful, or excessively preoccupied with his fantasies—sometimes a parent will express concern that his child is unhappy or seems to be "different" than the "other kids his age." When the parents seek professional assistance, the psychologist discusses the problem with them. The child is then seen for a diagnostic evaluation. As part of this procedure the psychologist may administer intelligence and projective tests, and will usually—if the child is younger than eleven or twelve—observe him in a "playroom" situation. In this room the child is told that he can do anything he wants to with the toys that are available. How he behaves provides the psychologist with data that will be coordinated with the other information. Following the assessment, the decision will be reached as to the most effective alternatives that are available. When the child's problems stem from disturbances in his relationship to his parents, either one or both parents and the child may be seen individually. In such cases the common practice is for each member of the family to have his own therapist.

Therapy with a young child relies less on verbal communication than with adolescents and adults. By expressing himself through his activity in the playroom, the way he perceives and responds to his situation and to adults is gradually established. The child learns to distinguish his therapist from his parents—who may have been erratic in their treatment of him, who may have hurt him, or may have been indifferent to him. Such a differentiation is facilitated by the fact that the therapist is friendly, consistent, does not scold or punish, and gives him undivided attention during the session, which is usually about 45 minutes long and is regularly scheduled once or twice a week. In the course of the therapy the child learns that he can rely on an adult who attempts to understand him and shares with him his concerns. In this process the child learns new perceptions of himself and his situation and new response patterns appropriate to these perceptions.

Often the child completes therapy before his parents. Children are generally more amenable to treatment than adults, for their defenses are less rigidly established and they are able to express their feelings and emotions more readily.

Family Therapy

Based upon the hypothesis that the difficulties experienced by any individual member of a family constitute a problem for the whole family, a new psychotherapeutic approach has been developed in recent years. The family is held to be the natural unit within which to attempt to solve *its* problem; for this reason, all the members (except very young children) meet together with one therapist. During these meetings the interacting antagonisms and affections of the family members are expressed, and their feelings toward the "problem" member and his difficulties are discussed. This technique is termed *family therapy* and is closely related to another of the major psychotherapeutic approaches, group therapy.

Group Psychotherapy

As the name implies, group therapy consists of therapeutic interchanges between the therapist and from three to eight clients. Although it is not considered a totally adequate substitute for individual therapy, group therapy has several possible advantages over the individual therapist-client situation. A therapist can treat more clients in a given period of time than if he were to see them individually, and his fees are correspondingly less. The presence of other persons in the therapeutic sessions provides several valuable features. Since the client finds that others also have problems which may correspond to his own, he learns that he is not alone. The group setting provides an opportunity to learn new patterns of response to other persons. Within the group setting characteristic feelings and perceptions regarding the self and others emerge as reactions to the other group members. The group then becomes a segment of the individual member's social world. Because of this, the individual's awareness of the reactions he evokes in others can be validated or corrected by the group and generalized to other relationships.

The process of learning new interpersonal behaviors within the group includes both observation and discussion of the members' reactions to individual behaviors and discussion of experiences related by the group members. At times in this process the group leader will direct the discussion, make an observation, or give an interpretation of the group's behavior. The group leader's actions are aimed at reinforcing the awarenesses of the group members and at specifying the nature of their behaviors and their communications. Such reinforcement strengthens the efforts of the individual members to express themselves, to clarify their feelings, and to modify their behaviors.

EVALUATING THE RESULTS
OF PSYCHOTHERAPY

If persons who had experienced individual or group psychotherapy were asked whether they had benefited from the experience, most would probably say they had. Although this endorsement of psychotherapy cannot be dismissed, neither can it be accepted as scientific evidence of its value. There are many difficulties in evaluating a process that extends over a considerable period of time, that occurs concurrently with other events of significance in the patient's life, that depends on the relationship of the unique personalities of a therapist and a client. Further, the difficulty of providing a matching control group of patients who do not receive psychotherapy is almost insurmountable since the specific personality organization of each individual entering therapy is an important variable in accounting for behavior change or lack of change. Although such technical problems complicate the scientific evaluation of psychotherapy, research studies have been attempted in this area and considerable effort has been directed toward the study of psychotherapeutic processes, procedures, and results. Since present research data indicate that about two thirds of those who undergo psychotherapy are benefited, the most reasonable hypothesis is that psychotherapy is beneficial for at least some persons, possibly those who are highly motivated to learn new behavioral patterns, who are intelligent and articulate, whose ego processes are well developed, and whose defenses are still pliable and flexible.

Summary

The acquisition of new behaviors as a result of experience is a central feature of man's development. How well the individual copes with his physical and social world depends in large part on the content and effectiveness of his learning. Learning occurs in many situations and accounts for changes in behaviors, attitudes, and emotions, as well as in the assignment of meaning to symbols.

The motivation of the student and the reinforcements he receives from his efforts are significant elements of his effectiveness in learning in the academic setting as well as in other life situations. The student interested in improving his academic performance will relate his studies to his personal goals and to what he has previously learned. He will follow certain principles in his approach to studying, to the organization of the information to be learned, and to review and recitation.

Learning also accounts for the acquisition of new modes of perceiving and responding to oneself. The psychotherapeutic setting is specifically created to foster such new learnings for persons who are dissatisfied or troubled. Here a therapist, whose role and responsibilities are quite different from those of the teacher, attempts to facilitate the individual's development. In the various psychotherapeutic settings—individual, group, child, and family—there is little formal instruction or information. Rather, the therapist attempts to establish with the patient a trusting human relationship in which the latter will be able to express his own feelings, beliefs, and concerns. In this process the individual approaches an integration of intrapsychic processes and a more accurate perception of himself and his environment.

References

1. Bird, C., and Bird, D. M. *Learning More by Effective Study*. New York: Appleton, 1945.
2. Eruick, A. The significance of library reading among college students. *School and Society*, 1932, *36*, 92–96.
3. Gates, A. I. Recitation as a factor in memorizing. *Arch. Psychol.*, N.Y., 1917, *6*, No. 40.
4. Krueger, W. C. F. The effect of overlearning on retention. *J. exp. Psychol.*, 1929, *12*, 71–78.
5. Luh, C. W. The conditions of retention. *Psychol. Monogr.*, 1922, *31*, No. 142.
6. Remmlein, M. K. Scholastic accomplishment as affected by intelligence and participation in extra-curricular activities. *J. appl. Psychol.*, 1939, *23*, 602–607.
7. Robinson, F. P. *Effective Study* (rev. ed.). New York: Harper, 1946.

Selected Readings

Bennett, M. E. *College and Life* (ed. 4). New York: McGraw-Hill, 1952.
Bordin, E. S. *Psychological Counseling*. New York: Appleton, 1955.
Brammer, L., and Shostram, E. *Psychotherapeutic Psychology*. Englewood Cliffs, N.J.: Prentice-Hall, 1960.
Freud, S. *An Outline of Psychoanalysis*. New York: Norton, 1949.
Hall, C. S. *A Primer of Freudian Psychology*. Cleveland: World Publishing, 1954.
Robinson, F. P. *Effective Study* (rev. ed.). New York: Harper, 1946.
Rogers, C. R., and Dymond, R. F. (eds.) *Psychotherapy and Personality Change*. Chicago: University of Chicago Press, 1954.
Wrenn, C. G. *Studying Effectively*. Stanford: Stanford University Press, 1950.

15.

The Democratic Ideal
and Psychological Development

The content of this chapter requires that the reader be reminded that the truths of any science are only tentative truths; that the evidence available today may be replaced by tomorrow's findings, and that knowledge of personal and social development, like all knowledge, must stand not only the test of time, but also the tests of critical evaluation and rigorous re-evaluation. Thus this final chapter can offer no absolute solutions for man's personal problems—nor can it offer definitive answers for the resolution of national and international conflict. This last chapter is but a commentary—speculative, debatable, and, hopefully, provocative. Its content derives directly from the belief that human development is a desirable human objective, an objective which, though never totally achieved by any individual, constitutes a worthy goal for all individuals.

Human development has served in this text as a value orientation as well as an organizing framework for ordering life's events. It is therefore necessary to note that the value placed on the developmental "ideal" does not imply that findings from the study of the conditions that relate to man's progress toward this ideal are to be judged on any bases other than those prescribed by the scientific method. In this sense, the ideal of human development only points toward the end state; the routes to the objective are tentative and change as knowledge increases. Further, the imperfect and relative nature of knowledge concerning the events and conditions facilitating man's development precludes any specification in an absolute sense of the social conditions that contribute optimally to his development. This is not to say that the study of the optimal relationship of man to his society falls outside the domain of science; rather, it alerts the reader that any such commentary, including that which follows, is inferential and partisan.

The reader must also note in the discussion that follows that the concept of the Democratic Ideal is emphasized in contrast to the present practices of democracy. Here again, as in the use of the term "ideal" in connection with development, ideal means the "perfect" state—that which is striven toward; it is not to be equated with that which is presently observable.

According to the developmental view, man's progress toward the ideal psychological state is evaluated on the basis of an examination of his intrapersonal processes, his interpersonal relationships, and the degree to which he fulfills his potentialities in constructive work. In societies in which the developmental view of man is most applicable, the laws, customs, and social institutions promote the life and talents of all the people.

Man's highest order of development will occur in those societies that encourage human diversity; in such societies the range of differences in appearances, beliefs, backgrounds, and customs is viewed as natural to humanity and not frightening. In such societies the acquisition of knowledge is valued for its contribution to an individual's development and to his potential to contribute to others. Since the application of any knowledge to man's development cannot be prejudged, it must first be acquired and then tested logically and scientifically. For this reason the laws and customs of society must encourage investigations of all human phenomena, even investigations that challenge cherished convictions.

The society and the state that enable man to reach his highest order of development provide not only for the acquisition of all knowledge, but also for its free and open dissemination to the public. In this society the citizens hold beliefs about any aspect of human behavior, morality, or politics. Ideas can be expressed that are at odds with the prevalent and popular attitudes of their time. These ideas may or may not be consistent with the convictions of the majority; they may or may not be in accord with the position of the government. But in the open society, one that respects the individual and one in which the development of man is encouraged, these ideas are permitted expression and no man is restrained from expressing himself. In such a society respect for both the individual and the truth is such that ideas are not feared but are welcomed, and the people are considered to have the right of—and capacity for—judgment, the right to relate ideas to evidence and evidence to values. In his famous essay, "On Liberty," (10) John Stuart Mill relates individuality, development, and societal conditions.

> In proportion to the development of his individuality, each person becomes more valuable to himself, and is, therefore, capable of being more valuable to others. . . . Having said that the individuality is the same thing with development, and that it is only the cultivation of individuality which produces, or can produce, well-developed human beings, I might here close the argument; for what more or better can be said of any condition of human affairs than it brings human beings themselves nearer to the best thing they can be? Or what worse can be said of any obstruction to good than that it prevents this?

If a large number of citizens were asked, "What does living in a democracy mean to you?" some would comment on the freedom they enjoy, others on the opportunities available to them as "free and equal" citizens, others on the roles and responsibilities they assume as members of this society. Most, perhaps, would find it difficult to formulate an answer that relates their personal development to a political ideal. Man is usually forced by the demands of the immediate to focus his attention on narrow segments of his experience, to direct his energy toward solving his current problems; he is thus bound in time to that which is current, tangible, and personal. He has neither the leisure nor the inclination to think of himself in terms of the wide span of events and experience encompassed by the concept of development. Except at fleeting moments, he is unlikely to ponder the relationship between personal and political ideals.

The student of psychology is also unlikely to focus his attention on the interdependence of the developmental and democratic ideals. In his preoccupation with developmental detail the vital relationship between these ideals can easily evade him.

In the Democratic Ideal the philosophic basis for a society in which the human needs of men can best be met is contained within six central ideas: equality, humanitarianism, individualism, progress, majority rule, and freedom to dissent (8). These ideas are reflected in statements which affirm that man is the primary unit of the society, state, and government. Consider, for example, Jefferson's formulation in the *Declaration of Independence:*

> We hold these truths to be self-evident—that all men are created equal; that they are endowed by their Creator with certain unalienable rights; that among these are life, liberty and the pursuit of happiness. That to secure these rights, Governments are instituted

among Men, deriving their just powers from the consent of the governed.

In his writings, Jefferson explicitly acknowledged that government was the agent of the people and that the responsibility of the state is that of service to the people. This concept was enunciated by Lincoln in his Gettysburg Address when he referred to government "for the people, of the people and by the people."

The Democratic Ideal envisions a society that will meet man's physical and psychological needs. If the society is to move forward toward this ideal, a majority of its citizens must first understand that ideal and the fact that their self-interest is inextricably linked to its maintenance and extension. Second, if the Democratic Ideal is to survive, a majority of the nation's citizens must be able to act in accordance with this understanding. Knowing that man needs to feel in communion with others, the citizen, out of self-interest, should act to reduce barriers to communication between peoples. He must work toward the extension of educational opportunity and for the dissemination of all views, beliefs, and knowledge. Knowing that man needs to maintain and protect himself, the citizen's self-interest requires that he actively support all efforts, legal and social, that protect not only person and property but the integrity and dignity of all men. Knowing that all men need to enhance their abilities and widen their horizons, the citizen concerned with his own well-being should support the society's efforts to provide the individual with opportunities for the development of his special interests, skills, and talents. When the individual understands the conditions required for man to fulfill his human potentialities, he will view with vested interest the social and political process whereby the Democratic Ideal is translated into the laws and customs of the land. As man requires a free, open, and democratic society for his development, so the democratic society, in order to prosper, maintain, and extend itself, requires citizens of high psychological calibre. This point is crucial, for the Democratic Ideal is being threatened by coercive forces within the society and totalitarian forces abroad. The survival of the Democratic Ideal will depend in large measure on the reactions of citizens to domestic and international stresses.

National and International Events:
Perceptions and Reactions

Of the threats to the survival of the Democratic Ideal, the citizen is most aware of that presented by Communism. As he attempts to understand the degree of this threat and the best way of meeting it, the citizen is not sure what to believe, whom to support, or to what political program he should commit himself. His difficulty can be partly attributed to conflicting information, partly to the complexities of the issues, and partly to his lack of familiarity with his government and how it operates.

When the citizen, alarmed because his nation is threatened by an alien system, seeks guidance from the experts as to what course of action he should support, he may well receive conflicting advice. With respect to nuclear testing, for example, he hears one authority state (11):

> Testing of nuclear devices will increase the amount of [gene] mutations in humans by one percent . . . the man who gives the order to test a superbomb is dooming 15,000 children to a defective life.

On the other hand, another expert (16) offers the comment that, "Sober consideration of the facts makes it perfectly clear that we must continue testing nuclear weapons." The broader question of our national armaments policy elicits more expert advice for the citizen in search of the "facts" (15):

> The pivot of Western strategy must be the capability of with-standing psychologically the Soviet nuclear threat and to counter it with a superior capability of massive retaliation. This capability in turn must be based on the security of the launching sites of massive retaliation—i.e., their invulnerability to surprise attack—and on adequate military as well as civilian air defense. The conditions of a viable Western strategy are psychological readiness and military technological superiority, the resolution to stand up to the Soviet thermonuclear threat and superior force to counter it.

If the issue is pursued, an anti-armaments approach to security states (14):

> Whatever may be the purposes of a war, they will not now be achieved. Both East and West can give the world more of what they respectively consider desirable if they achieve peaceful coexistence than if they indulge in nuclear war. . . . Catholics and Protestants, in the course of 130 years, learned to tolerate each other's existence. Communists and anti-Communists have to learn the lesson of mutual tolerance more quickly, because wars have become more destructive. We can all live or all die. No other choice is possible.

As the citizen studies issues of armaments and disarmament, nuclear testing, and international negotiation, he develops a sense of urgency, a feeling that "something" must be done immediately, even though he may be quite unclear as what specific actions are desirable. As he contemplates the fact that his way of life is in jeopardy he wants to express his anger and fear, but the avenues of expression are often not available. As he considers the devastation, horror, and suffering that a full-scale nuclear war would inflict on his country, his city, and his family, he becomes frightened. Images of the destruction of cities and deaths of millions of persons by blast and radiation sickness are fraught with emotion.

Domestic issues are also a cause of concern and evoke reactions that are often contrary to the interests of his society and himself. Among the stresses that beset the society and to which many citizens react with great emotion are those emanating from the relations between the Negro and Caucasian communities. Repercussions of their opposing attitudes and beliefs have been felt in education, employment, and housing. The bitterness accompanying the school desegregation issue reflects the marked degree of frustration, anxiety, and threat experienced by both parties to the conflict. The stress engendered by desegregation results in the direct emotional involvement of large numbers of people, both Caucasian and Negro.

In contrast to the emotions engendered by the prospect of a nuclear war, the emotions stirred by desegregation are tied to highly visible actions having an immediate and clearly discernible effect on the lives of the parties to the controversy. As a consequence threat is experienced not in abstract but in concrete issues that can evoke fundamental emotional responses of anger and violence. Both integrationists and segregationists perceive their position to be in accord with democratic philosophy. Of marked concern to students of the American system of democracy is the fact that in some parts of the country large and influential segments of the population appear to be committed to preserving the customs of the region rather than to supporting the law of the land. The Democratic Ideal includes the principle that laws, even though unpopular or repugnant to some, will be adhered to until repealed by the actions of a popularly elected representative legislative body.

Also in relation to the domestic scene, many citizens are uneasy about their personal opportunities for occupational satisfaction and security. The changes being introduced by automation, the increasing importance of technical skills, the discrimination against the older worker and members of minority groups, and the difficulties of the small business man provide sources of concern and anxiety to many persons.

In dealing with such issues and the fears they evoke, the individual utilizes his potential for constructive and creative action along with his characteristic patterns of defense. The graveness of the issues and the person's relative inability to direct energies toward their solution in any seemingly significant fashion often place him in a psychological situation in which the stress is great and solutions to the problems are unclear. In such a predicament the individual often relies upon inadequate information, oversimplification, emotion, and prejudice in his efforts to solve the problems.

SOURCES OF MISPERCEPTION OF INTERNATIONAL EVENTS

The impulse to act when confronted with danger is a characteristic of both men and animals. Primitive reactions to the presence or expectation of danger consist of either a physical attack or an equally physical retreat from the dangerous object or situation. More complex reactions involve some consideration of the origins of the danger and the preparations necessary for self-protection. It is in this connection that the accuracy of self-perception and perception of one's adversary is crucial if one is to deal effectively with the threat. Unfortunately, as perceived threat increases, man's likelihood of perceptual error also increases. And as the threatening situation becomes more complex and less well defined, the likelihood of misperception further increases. In all threatening situations the nature of the threat and the appropriate measures to deal with it must be considered. How an individual *reacts* to perceived threat depends on what he perceives, and what is perceived will, in turn, depend upon many factors in addition to the objective situation. Of special relevance in the present context are the following sources of perceptual error.

1. The perception of any act is determined both by our perception of the act itself and by our perception of the context in which the act occurs.
2. Our perceptions of the external world are often determined indirectly by the information we receive from others rather than by our direct experiences.
3. Our perceptions of the world are often greatly influenced by the need to conform to and agree with the perceptions of other people.
4. Individuals attempt to perceive their environment so that it is consistent with their self-perceptions.[1]

Errors arising from these four conditions impair the accuracy of one's judgments of the behavior and intentions of others. Not only do perceptual errors occur in judgments of persons with whom one has personal contact, but they also occur in one's judgment of the behaviors

[1] Adapted from Morton Deutsch, Psychological alternatives to war; *J. soc. Issues,* 1962, *18,* 97.

and intentions of national leaders, both in one's own and in other nations. When the citizen evaluates the relations of his nation with other nations, these perceptual errors influence his conclusions. Because we perceive both the act and the context in which it occurs, the behavior of a friend will be perceived differently to that of a stranger or enemy who engages in the same or similar activity. In the same way, the espionage activity of enemy agents is held as overt evidence of their nation's hostility toward the United States and the espionage activity of the United States is perceived as a "necessary defensive" operation having no relevance to our military designs on anyone else.

Some observers have noted (1) that the Russians and the Americans hold a "mirror" view toward each other; that is, they each impute similar motives to the other which reflect a standard characterization of the "enemy" more than accurate perceptions of each other. In both countries, for example, there is the common perception that the leadership of the other country does not represent the people and that there is widespread dissatisfaction. The "mirror" belief prevails that the form of government in each country would be overthrown if the people were able to express their will and that it is only the fear of reprisal that prevents revolution. Each side perceives the other as the aggressor, each believes that the other government exploits and deludes the people. Each side believes the other cannot be trusted and that their policies verge on madness.

In our complicated world the citizen usually has no direct knowledge of national and international affairs; he must depend on others for this information. His beliefs and decisions as to the persons and policies he should support are dependent on the information he receives through the news media. As a consequence the wisdom of his political choices is partially determined by the amount and accuracy of the information channeled to him. Even with information readily available, it has been estimated that 20 to 40 percent of the American public is totally ignorant on any given political topic (8).

Three years after the United Nations was set up, and after it had held several well-publicized meetings in the United States, one out of every four Americans admitted that they either had never heard of the U.N. or had no idea of what its purpose was. In the middle of the 1948 presidential election, one out of three did not know that Henry Wallace was running for President, half could not name the vice-presidential nominee of either major party, twelve out of every hundred did not know that Dewey was the Republican nominee, and nine out of every hundred Americans did not know that President Truman was the Democratic candidate. Shortly after the 1956 presidential election, 6 percent of the Democratic voters could not identify Senator Estes Kefauver, their party's vice-presidential candidate.

The third source of misperception having special significance for the relationship between the Democratic and Developmental Ideals involves social and psychological pressures toward conformity. Although these have been considered in Chapter 13, at this point it is important to recall that there is a strong tendency in most people to agree (or at least not to dissent openly) with the attitudes that are popular; further, that unpopular ideas and beliefs are judged more critically than those of the majority; and finally, that attitudes, beliefs, and personal characteristics different from those of the majority are apt to incur criticism and rejection. Of course, the degree to which conforming tendencies are expressed behaviorally depends not only on the situation but also on the individual involved, his level of psychological development, and his methods of dealing with intrapsychic conflict.

Pressures toward conformity and perceptual error resulting from these pressures constitute a particular challenge to a democratic society. Justice William Douglas has said (8), "Full and free discussion has indeed been the first article of our faith. We have founded our political system on it." And political theorists have noted that the right to dissent is a central characteristic of democratic societies, in contrast to the control of belief and expression practiced in totalitarian societies. As stresses become more intense the pressures toward conformity and the intolerance and fear evoked by dissent can be expected to increase. During one period of recent history in the early 1950's, when allegations of Communist subversion were widely and loosely applied to all who dissented, high school students polled on questions that paraphrased the *Bill of Rights* showed a considerable lack of commitment to some of the basic beliefs comprising the Democratic Ideal (13). For example, only 45 percent of American teenagers agreed with the statement, "Newspapers and magazines should be allowed to print anything they want except military secrets." In another statement pertaining to freedom of speech, only 53 percent disagreed with the statement, "The government should prohibit some people from making public speeches." Only 60 percent of the nation's teenagers agreed with the *Bill of Rights* that, "Persons who refuse to testify against themselves (that is, give evidence that would show that they are guilty of criminal acts) should either be made to talk or severely punished."

In a similar study (7) conducted in 1960 and 1961, fewer students were in agreement with the *Bill of Rights* relative to freedom of the press, only 29 percent believing that newspapers and magazines should be allowed to print everything except military secrets. In their responses to other questions, the students polled in the 1960–1961 study were to a slight extent more in accord with the *Bill of Rights;* however, as the authors of the study note:

> The outlook for free communication of ideas is especially dark. Unless our homes, our schools and other educational media can effect changes in these attitudes it would seem that censorship will become even more prevalent and accepted as today's teenagers gain adult influence in our society.

The dissenter in a democratic society is often criticized and rejected. Even though his role may offer little personal gratification and is probably little appreciated by most of the members of the society, he can through open disagreement contribute to gradual social change. This contribution occurs through his reinforcement of the tendency to express dissent in those who believe they are alone in their convictions. The significance of one strong dissenter in mobilizing anticonformity sentiment has been demonstrated in conformity studies similar to those of Asch described earlier.

The fourth source of misperception arises from the operation of the defense mechanisms. We have already discussed these defenses at a personal and social level. Here only brief mention need be made of how the personal need to maintain and protect oneself psychologically may manifest itself in beliefs about national and international affairs. Many persons cannot confront the anxiety-provoking potential of the present world situation, since doing so would add an intolerable and overwhelming load to an already troublesome degree of discomfort. When the repressive and denial modes of defense predominate in such instances, then disinterest or a denial of the reality or significance of the threat occurs; views may then be expressed that issues such as nuclear testing, disarmament, and civil defense are given "too much attention" and are not "worth all the fuss."

Of course, many examples of the particular modes individuals utilize in defending against anxiety in the context of national and international events could be enumerated. However, only one additional common perceptual distortion arising from unresolved intrapsychic conflict requires mention here. This is the case where the individual must identify with the all-powerful authority (father-nation) and cannot accept the shift of the United States position from unrivaled world power to one whose supremacy is challenged. In such instances the belief is tenaciously held, in spite of information to the contrary, that the United States can easily prevail over all opposition. Sometimes, when the changed status is acknowledged, the belief is adopted that such a change could only have happened because of subversion in high places.

Misperceptions arising from these sources contribute to over-simplified formulations of the nation's problems and to oversimplified "solutions."

Oversimplification: One Response to Stress

The likelihood of misperceiving any situation increases as the elements of the situation become more numerous and as their inter-relationships become less apparent. Misperception of complex situations will further increase as the situation evokes increasing emotion in the observer. Thus, as situations become more complicated and provocative, individuals are likely to regress to relatively primitive patterns of perception and thought. Under such conditions unfortunate oversimplifications of the problem are likely to occur and quick, simple solutions will be presented.

The question of how the Democratic Ideal is to be maintained has exceedingly complex proportions. It involves issues at an international as well as a national level. These issues embrace economic, political, social, and psychological factors. Failure to solve the question of how to maintain the Democratic Ideal means the end of man's progress toward the society that would maximally facilitate his development. The emotion precipitated by the prospect of a failure to solve this question is aug-mented by the fear that in failing to achieve workable methods for approaching and dealing with their differences the East and West will become involved in a nuclear war which will bring not only vast death and destruction but also the loss of the Democratic Ideal. The citizen thus is confronted by a highly complex situation involving many tech-nical elements that possess great emotional significance for him. Unable to bear the anxiety precipitated by the uncertainties and ambiguities of the situation—including questions of what he should do and think— he deals with his discomfort by resorting to an oversimplification of the problem and its solution. Although such a process partially defends against anxiety, it has the considerable disadvantage of reducing the individual's ability to act in accord with his own self-interest.

When large numbers of citizens resort to oversimplified perception and thought in reaction to the complex crises posed by Communism, then a great danger exists for the survival of the Democratic Ideal. Out of the threat of Communism and through oversimplification the Demo-cratic Ideal may be surrendered even though no nuclear warhead is detonated. Because of the complexity of the emotionally laden crises and the danger that oversimplification constitutes for the survival of the Democratic Ideal, it requires elaboration.

The most common form of oversimplification is the easily recognized "either-or" thinking. In "either-or" thinking involved issues are reduced to simple terms; alternatives that logically would be worth consideration are dismissed since ambiguities of the situation have been dispensed with by imputing certainty and definiteness where none may exist. The reduction of complex issues to two diametrically opposed alternatives is an example of "either-or" thinking and is illustrated in statements such as, "We will either approve what the visitor to campus has to say or we will not let him speak"; "He either agrees with us or he is a Communist"; "We either drop the bomb now or we will lose out to Communism"; "We either totally and unilaterally disarm or we will be destroyed in a nuclear holocaust." Complicated situations should not be reduced to simple categorical formulations; to do so makes impossible the valid representation of the situation. When this occurs it is unlikely that adequate solutions to the problems can be reached. There are few domestic or international issues for which single categorical formulations are appropriate.

The danger of "either-or" oversimplified thought is that it precludes the consideration of a wide range of alternative solutions while appearing to provide *the* authoritative answer. Even though their ambiguity does create anxiety and a desire for immediate action, issues in a democratic society must remain open for discussion and the consideration of a variety of possible solutions. Consider, for example, the "either-or" statements above of "drop the bomb now" and "total unilateral disarmament." The position taken in each case is one of reaction to immediate stress in which the ambiguities and uncertainty of what we should do are resolved in a definite statement of immediate action. Critics of both positions will argue that advocates of neither position appear to have given adequate consideration to the consequences of their recommended actions, nor adequate consideration to the many alternatives to either the initiation of a "first strike" war or to total and immediate unilateral disarmament. Other alternatives are available. For example, the person who supports the position that in order to deter an enemy attack, armed strength sufficient to discourage such an attack is necessary, can offer many proposals for strengthening the military establishment; he does not have to simplify the situation by suggesting that the *only* way of maintaining our position in the world is to take the offensive in a nuclear war. On the other hand, the individual who believes that continued emphasis on military strength will lead to war does not have to conclude that the *only* solution to the problem is immediate disarmament with no attention paid to the position of the enemy. The person taking this position can logically support efforts to arrive at mutual disarmament agreements—or efforts to partially disarm —or efforts to reduce the tensions that lead to the need for armaments.

Scapegoating: One Form of Oversimplification

One specific form of oversimplification that is frequently resorted to in crisis situations is the technique of scapegoating. In this reaction to frustration and anxiety a particular person or group is held solely responsible for the undesirable state of affairs. For example, the difficulties the United States is encountering are seen not as a complex product of vast changes that have occurred in the total world picture but rather as due to the actions of subversive persons in high governmental positions. Presidents of the United States have been accused of being Communist "dupes" and the Chief Justice of the United States has been accused of "disloyalty." This type of thinking has in the past been represented by attacks on religious and racial minority groups or on "intellectuals" and "liberals." The Nazi utilization of German Jews as a scapegoat is a well-known example of how through oversimplification the woes and frustrations emanating from many complex sources were attributed to one ethnic group. The subsequent utilization of the scapegoat for purposes of mobilizing the latent hostilities of many persons in Nazi Germany is recorded in a tragic episode of history that revealed man's capacity to destroy life and his capacity for irrationality. The eventual annihilation of six million European Jews is but one example of how in crisis situations the combination of oversimplification and hatred can culminate in deeds that previous generations would not have imagined possible.

Wherever the Democratic Ideal has been attacked or feared by totalitarian groups or governments one particular scapegoat has been the object for especial attack. This scapegoat, who is termed "the intellectual," or more derisively, "the egghead," is usually a teacher, student, or writer, who devotes himself to the development and dissemination of ideas. The first attack of those who would change the democratic system is upon those involved in the educational process—those who can be singled out for not conforming to the beliefs and convictions of the "true patriot." Thus, in one highly publicized "anti-Communist school" the statement is made repeatedly that Communism is not related to conditions of economic distress, poverty, hunger, oppression, and inequity, but rather to the activity of intellectuals and students, and that therefore if one wants to stop Communism one must curtail the activities and influence of intellectuals.

Another illustration of "either-or" thinking that constitutes a danger to the survival of the Democratic Ideal is the reaction to difference which holds that, "Either the person looks, acts, and thinks as I do, in which event he is good, or he differs from me and is therefore bad." When individuals cannot tolerate the proximity of those who differ in appearance from themselves, when they cannot listen to and attempt to understand expressions of belief that vary from those they hold, we assume that they are functioning under unusual psychological handicaps and the matter would be dismissed as unfortunate or some thought might be given as to how they could be helped. However, the persons with "fixed beliefs" must be of concern to our society, not because they are psychologically underdeveloped but rather because they constitute a liability in a society that must confront the existence of difference among peoples and ideas and between patterns of thought required by the present and patterns appropriate to the past. Those whose fixed beliefs are of such rigidity that they are unable to modify them as new conditions develop and are insistent that outmoded approaches be retained are apt to place the nation in jeopardy if as a group they possess sufficient power to block the changes that the future requires. Thomas Jefferson once noted that men are apt to endure for a long time the worst possible arrangements simply because they are familiar with them. In his contribution to the Constitution he also foresaw the need for a document embodying democratic principles along with the procedures for assuring their flexibility and relevance through time. The existence of the United States as the world's oldest continuous constitutional government is testimony to the genius of those who, like Jefferson, enunciated the principles and then provided the mechanism for change. They did not fear progress or controversy and abhorred unwillingness to confront both the present and future.

From the foregoing it is obvious that the level of psychological development of citizens and the survival of the Democratic Ideal are closely interrelated. Insofar as knowledge is increased, valued, and used in ways consistent with the development of the individual and of his ability to contribute to the development of others, the maintenance of the Democratic Ideal will be made easier. And at the same time all citizens will become capable of efforts to bring the society closer to its ideal. At a time when the intellectual and humanistic qualities of man are required to a greater degree than ever before, the conditions that make for rational and humane action are conspicuously lacking.

How the individual is to act when confronted by multiple possibilities of action, how he is to evaluate the evidence before him, how he is to function in ways congruent with his self-interests, how he is to create the best possible social conditions for his development and for the development of others, cannot be answered simply. If answers to these questions are to be found, individuals will have to marshall all their psychological resources. Unless these answers are found, the Democratic Ideal may not survive. Assuming that an individual values knowledge and the fullest development of the human being and has achieved a high order of psychological development, he will be in a favorable position to consider and judge evidence, to evaluate the consequences of the decisions he makes, the opinions he holds, and the behaviors in which he engages.

If the Democratic Ideal is to survive, a large segment of our population must possess such a value orientation and the developmental level indicated; otherwise the present stresses will lead to the domination of emotion, ignorance, and hatred. If people act only in terms of stereotypes and prejudices, and if their actions reflect their lack of respect and concern for the integrity of all other human beings, decisions will be reached impulsively, irrationally, and without consideration of either the evidence or their own self-interests. If irrational action based upon unreasoned emotion prevails, the objective of maintaining national sovereignty to insure the survival of the Democratic Ideal may be lost through reaction to threat of war, as well as to war itself.

War

The universal destruction and suffering of nuclear war has been vividly and shockingly portrayed by proponents of both increased and decreased armaments. Of special concern here is one less publicized, though generally agreed upon, result of nuclear war: the termination—for many years and possibly forever—of man's progress toward the realization of the Democratic Ideal. The question of whether the best that man can hope for is a totalitarian society brought about by war or the threat of war leads us directly to a consideration of war and some psychological aspects of military preparation and of the search for alternatives to war.

It must be noted first that psychology and the other behavioral sciences do not yet have definitive solutions to the problems of averting war. And further, when research findings pertaining to the behavior of individuals are applied to the behavior of nations, there is a considerable possibility of error. Until recently the psychological issues related to war were apt to be overlooked, and those of a political, economic, and military nature given sole attention. Governmental decisions to prepare for and wage war can be understood only if the motives of men are given consideration. The decisions reached relative to the military establishment—whether to arm and how to arm or when and where to strike—depend on political and economic factors, but they also involve the leader's response to his perceptions, his motives, his ideals, and his fears.

WAR IS NOT INEVITABLE

The first point in our discussion of the psychological factors associated with war and peace is that there is a need for all citizens and their leaders to understand fully that war is neither inevitable nor beyond the control of man. There is a widespread belief that regardless of all efforts to the contrary wars cannot be prevented, and that all hopes for "enduring peace" are but the fantasies of starry-eyed idealists. Advocates of the inevitability-of-war doctrine often assert that wars have been fought throughout history and that as it has been, so shall it be. Their second and related argument is that man is by nature aggressive and warlike. Before examining these two assumptions, which form the basis of the inevitability-of-war doctrine, one significant point relative to the effects of widespread subscription to the doctrine requires attention.

The conviction that war is inevitable leads not only to the expectation of war but also to the view that the best time to strike is *now* and that it is wasted effort to seek peaceful solutions to East–West disagreements. For this reason, the beliefs associated with the inevitability-of-war doctrine—if held by large numbers of people or by national decision—can increase the likelihood of war. When people act on an initially false prediction their actions can contribute to the prediction coming true. Merton has called this the "self-fulfilling prophecy" (9). In considering the psychological aspects of war and peace, the concept of the "self-fulfilling prophecy" is especially relevant; Merton points out that through his beliefs man can influence his future in a subtle and sometimes indirect fashion, without being aware that he is doing so. Thus, widespread acceptance of the inevitability of war, the accompanying attitudes of resignation and despair, and the disparagement of efforts for peace can all contribute to the likelihood of war.

The inevitability-of-war doctrine can be criticized on the basis of the two assumptions upon which it rests. The first of these, that men have always resorted to war as one method of resolving disputes between nations, implies that since warfare has been a method of national foreign policy in the past, it must continue to be relied upon in the future. The belief that what man has done in the past he *has* to do in the present and future does not allow for the fact that the environment changes through time. With the development of weapons of great destructive potential for civilian as well as military targets; with the establishment of such tribunals as the United Nations and World Court (though often faltering and ineffective in settling international disputes), and with the move toward massive coalitions or power blocs and away from the independently acting sovereign national states, we have reached

an age when it is erroneous to believe that the past contains all the possibilities for the present and future. As has been shown repeatedly
throughout this text, man's behavior depends, in part, on the environment impinging upon him. International affairs now occur in a world
which is radically different from that before the atomic bomb, and man's
response should be to the world as it is, not to the way he saw it in the
past. In his writings on the subject Albert Einstein stated (6), "The
unleashed power of the atom has changed everything except our ways
of thinking. Thus we are drifting toward a catastrophe beyond comparison. We shall require a substantially new manner of thinking if
mankind is to survive."

The second assumption underlying the inevitability-of-war doctrine
is that man is basically an aggressive and warlike creature. As a strictly
psychological interpretation of man's nature, such a belief warrants
very careful consideration. Whether man is by nature aggressive and
destructive or whether these behaviors constitute partial reactions to the
frustration occasioned by the thwarting of his needs and wishes is a
debate that has waged long and fiercely in the literature of both philosophy and psychology. Whether man acquires his aggressive potential
genetically or as the result of learning, it cannot be denied that the
history of man is a record of warfare, brutality, and inhumanity. But
man's history also records his potentialities for cooperative and constructive action and his humanistic endeavors. The salient point here is
that although he may be impulsive, aggressive, irrational, and violent,
a total characterization must also include his capacity to control his
destructive impulses and to act rationally in terms of his own self-
interests. Man has the capacity to redirect aggressive impulses into constructive channels, he can find reasonable solutions to the problems be-
setting him, whether such problems are personal or international. He is
able to delay gratification, to plan for the future, and to take advantage
of past experience. Such central characteristics of the human being must
also be taken into account in any predictions about his future.

Accepting the fact that man is at times aggressive and barbaric, we
must nevertheless question whether modern warfare constitutes an outlet for these aggressive impulses. When aggressive and warlike characteristics are equated, there is usually a failure to note that modern
warfare is a highly technical and impersonal activity. In a nuclear war
the combatants do not see each other, and even in so-called conventional
warfare the combatants usually engage each other at a considerable
distance. The pilot dropping bombs or the naval officer giving an order
to fire does so without personal contact with the enemy. The trend is
toward armaments and methods of warfare that are increasingly

impersonal and technical; therefore, the assertion that war itself provides an outlet for man's aggressive impulses is not plausible.

While the belief that war provides an *outlet* for man's aggressive impulses is untenable, it is also true that some sadistic persons want to hurt and destroy in an effort to achieve satisfaction that they otherwise cannot experience. Consider, for example, those American youths who imitate and identify with the Nazis by adopting their symbols, rituals, and beliefs. Also it must be noted that war and weapons afford some persons with a context in which through fantasy they can annihilate their enemies; however, such fantasies do not require participation in war. They are as effective or ineffective in the maintenance and protection of the personality when they are stimulated by literature or by memories of past events, experienced directly or vicariously.

Aggression can be viewed as a response to frustration. This statement does not suggest that all frustration inevitably leads to aggression. It has been noted earlier in this chapter that the American citizen is beset with frustrations from a number of sources. One source is an awareness that the existence and activity of the Communist are threatening to him and he does not know what to do about it.

A conflict situation has been previously characterized as resulting from wishes or objectives that cannot be satisfied simultaneously; that is, the satisfaction of one set of wishes precludes the satisfaction of the other. Frustration is one of the concomitants of this type of conflict. When transposed to the international level, each of the adversaries—the Western and Communist coalitions—can be thought of as existing within a conflict situation. Each has its aspirations and objectives, which cannot be fulfilled because of the perceived presence, threat, or activity of the adversary. Thus the continued existence and the extension of the ideological beliefs of one is threatened by the other. It will be recalled that such a conflict situation is termed the "approach-avoidant." With both East and West bound in this type of psychological situation, the frustration and stress associated with perceptions of threat lead to oversimplified formulations of the situation and oversimplified solutions.

Reactions to frustration and stress that involve the primitivization or oversimplification of thought and the tendency to misperceive have been cited both in this chapter and earlier. Awareness of oversimplification as one response to frustration and stress can lead to a critical and questioning attitude whenever the implication arises that everything the West does is good, charitable, and honest, and that everything the East does is bad, selfish, and deceitful. A critical attitude toward such formulations will help the citizen arrive at rational decisions as to the persons and programs to which he can give his intellectual and political support. Efforts to avoid gross oversimplification and a noncritical evaluation of the West's role in the present international situation may be considered subversive, but equating critical evaluation with subversion reflects in itself the dangerous effects of oversimplification on the maintenance of the Democratic Ideal.

As one measure that can reduce the likelihood of oversimplification of the international situation, knowledge of the adversary's customs, history, politics, and language is, of course, desirable. Such knowledge, along with knowledge of democratic history and philosophy, extends the range of cognitive categories available to the individual as he evaluates the policies and programs pertaining to the international situation. From a psychological standpoint, knowledge of the dynamics of tension reduction and frustration are vital to all concerned about their own future.

REDUCING INTERNATIONAL TENSIONS

The clarification of our own objectives is of the utmost importance in the reduction of international tensions. If a primary objective is to maintain and strengthen the Democratic Ideal, the actions of the adversary must be viewed in the context of the degree to which they threaten or weaken the prospects for the fulfillment of the Democratic Ideal. If such an objective is clearly defined, a basis exists for the evaluation of our own actions as well as those of our adversary. In the conflict situation the perception of the enemy as thwarting the attainment of our objectives is central to the conflict and the resulting frustrations. It therefore follows that great care must be exercised to insure as accurate a perception of the adversary's beliefs, actions, and intentions as is possible.

Accurate perception of the adversary's motives and intentions is difficult to achieve. One complication is introduced by the self-fulfilling nature of the sequence in which Country A reacts with hostility to its perception of a hostile act on the part of Country B. Country B then reacts with hostility to its perception of Country A's hostile act. In this sequence both intranational and international frustration increase and the probability of achieving a nonviolent basis for dealing with the actual differences between nations decreases. In the situation in which ideological conflict between Democracy and Communism can be expected to continue for many years, programs which offer hope of reducing intranational frustration and international tension merit consideration.

In one program termed Graduated Reciprocation in Tension Reduction (GRIT) (12), developed by a psychologist, Charles Osgood, the nation would systematically initiate a series of actions that would tend to induce reciprocation from the adversary. These acts would have no immediate military implications and would be directed toward the alleviation of tensions by evoking conciliatory and friendly actions from the adversary. In this way we could, through a variety of measures, take advantage of certain psychological principles of the theory of reinforcement to reduce the degree of frustration experienced by both parties to the controversy. Easing travel restrictions on visiting Russians and making accessible to the Russians space in American newspapers or television time for whatever presentations to the American public they would wish, represent two implementations of this proposal. Such presentations might cover a wide range of areas: sharing nonmilitary scientific and medical information, personal exchanges, reducing trade barriers, diplomatic moves, and so on.

A key feature of this proposal is that the actions are undertaken in a series and would be graded in terms of the degree of risk entailed; at first only small risk actions would be taken, and only after publicity had been given to the fact that the United States was going to act in these specific ways, irrespective of the Communist reactions to them. In such a program the adversary would be invited to respond at the time the public announcement of our action was made. But the critical point is that regardless of his response, we would still carry out the announced action. In the event that such actions were reciprocated, then bolder action, still not affecting our military position, could be taken. In Osgood's approach the United States retains its nuclear weapons and its "second strike" potential, though if its efforts were sufficiently reciprocated, it might eventually offer actions involving the reduction of conventional arms. The degree to which such disarmament efforts would be offered for reciprocation would of course depend on the degree and nature of the adversary's reactions to our previous nonmilitary tension-reducing actions. Osgood, in describing his proposal (12), makes the following point:

> Unilateral actions should be planned in graded series and continued over a considerable period regardless of immediate reciprocation; given the cold war mentality early actions are likely to be greeted with cries "It's a trick!"—but as action follows announced action, it becomes harder and harder to deny the bonafideness of our intent. And finally, our unilateral initiatives should be deeds rather than words—unambiguous and susceptible to verification.

A program such as that proposed by Osgood is quite different from the previously attempted, occasional, ungraded, uncoordinated, and unpublicized unilateral actions directed toward tension reduction. One essential feature of this program is education of the public. The persistent provision of unilateral acts directed toward tension reduction could, ironically enough, be the cause of increased intranational frustration if the public were unprepared for the possibility that American efforts might go unreciprocated for considerable periods of time—or perhaps completely.

In efforts to reduce international tension, as in efforts to reduce tension between individuals or groups, the likelihood of success is greatest if areas of common interest can be identified. For example, in relation to the United States–Russia hostility, an all-out nuclear war would operate to the disadvantage of both adversaries. A possible basis for agreement would therefore involve procedures for minimizing the possibilities of an accidental war, one in which human or mechanical error results in an attack being initiated or being perceived as having been initiated. An unauthorized missile attack initiated by a submarine commander or an erroneous reading on a radar screen is possible. Further, it might be in the best interests of both Russia and the United States to prevent nuclear armament of countries not presently in possession of such weapons. Activities such as joint exploration of outer space might also be ventured.

The reduction of international tensions will have its greatest likelihood of success when the leadership and the populations of East and West recognize that the interests of both sides are inextricably linked. This new way of thinking considers the interests of both sides whenever programs are adopted and recognizes that the security of the Democratic Ideal involves the security of the rest of the world. This awareness of mutual security recognizes that the greater the frustration and stress the adversary experiences, the greater the perception of threat and the less capable he will be of working toward peaceful solutions to international issues.

In Osgood's program, actions toward tension reduction are taken unilaterally; they do not await the attainment of mutual trust. However, the goal of creating trust between East and West is a part of the long-range objective of a world without war. Psychological experiments have shown that the chances of working effectively toward mutual interests are best when the individuals trust one another (2, 3, 4). It is also known that two parties to a controversy who do not trust each each other can he helped to resolve their disagreements if a third, trusted party acts as mediator. This principle, drawn from studies of labor–management conflict, is difficult to apply to controversies between the two most powerful nations of the world. Even so, the principle suggests recognition of the need for the development of a world system of law and a clearly defined set of procedures for its maintenance and enforcement. Such proposals for world law often encounter fiercely emotional oversimplified reactions, such as that the United States must either maintain complete autonomy to act as it deems best or it will "sacrifice its heritage." As Deutsch (5) has noted, agreements pertaining to international postal procedures, trade, freedom of the seas, and ambassadorial rights have existed for many years without damage to the United States. The evaluation of the emotional reactions to such proposals requires an understanding of the origins of oversimplified thinking.

Because competition between different ideological systems cannot be expected to disappear, proposals have been made that

> . . . would enable the different nations of the world to reveal their achievements and progress in such fields as art, music, literature, the various sciences, space exploration, education, economic development, agriculture, sports, ballet, the theatre, cooking, architecture, medicine, women's fashions, the domestic arts, children's books, etc. The contests should be diverse enough to permit each national culture to display its unique attainments. The rules should require that the knowledge, skills, and techniques of the contest winners be made freely available to every nation. Awards might be granted on two separate bases; the relative level of absolute achievement and the relative amount of progress since the last contest. It is assumed that the societies who win many contests will be the ones who are effective in developing a culture that is richly creative and a populace who is educated, talented, and resourceful (5).

The absence of reliable knowledge appropriate to the reduction of international tensions is a problem of formidable proportions to those who wish to prepare programs that would accomplish this objective. Many scientific solutions to baffling problems have been found once a recognized need for solution has brought support for the necessary research. Examples are Dr. Jonas Salk's discovery of a poliomyelitis vaccine and the research required for man to orbit the earth. Such achievements were dependent on funds and efforts on behalf of the research. A major step toward the reduction of international tensions could be made if funds and efforts were provided for the study of the many issues related to international tension, alternatives to war, and conflict resolution. At present, in comparison with the funds being spent on armaments and preparations for war ($48 billion in 1961), the amount available in the federal budget for studies of arms control, disarmament, and tension reduction is very limited ($6 million in 1961). The ratio of funds for arms to those for disarmament and tension reduction is dramatically illustrated by the fact that of every $125 the government spends for armaments and the maintenance of the military establishment, less than two cents is allocated to the agency concerned with disarmament and arms control.

As the public becomes increasingly aware that war and the threat of war constitute a grave danger to the Democratic Ideal and the American way of life, it might be hoped that support will be forthcoming for an all-out program of research into the causes and treatment of international conflict. The urgency of the crises, in which each side increases its destructive capabilities, diverts attention from the need for the study of alternatives to war. Yet it seems quite clear that as man's efforts and intelligence have been utilized to develop his potential to kill, so it is now time to direct energy and intelligence toward activities that will enable man to live; research is one such activity.

THE CITIZEN'S ROLE

The apathy toward local, national, and international politics characteristic of the American citizen cannot be accounted for by any one explanation. Traditional images of ward politicians meeting in smoke-filled rooms represents stereotypes of the politician as unsavory and disreputable. The strength of the stereotype may prevent some people from actively participating or showing interest in politics, but it cannot account for the widespread lack of interest in, and ignorance of, their government exhibited by other citizens. Lack of knowledge, preoccupation with the details of daily life, and the fact that many persons have not attained a sufficiently high order of development to want to assume the responsibilities associated with citizenship have been considered as factors in political disinterest.

It is also possible that what appears to be apathy or lack of interest is rather an active turning away, an aversive response to the unpleasantness and complexity of many national and international issues. The international situation, for example, requires consideration not only of the grimly terrifying consequences of a nuclear holocaust; it also requires serious contemplation of the problems created by the ever-increasing rate of population growth. The disease, poverty, and hunger afflicting large segments of the world's population are of shocking proportions. Such issues are unpleasant, but it is doubtful that aversion to them completely accounts for the citizen's failure to involve himself in political activity.

Many citizens do not see or feel any connection between their beliefs and behaviors and international events. They ask, "What can I possibly do?" The citizen feels he is insignificant in the governmental process of decision-making. In part, this attitude arises from lack of knowledge about governmental operation and procedure. This suggests that the citizen's role is to be informed about his government and about political activity at all levels. He also has the responsibility as a citizen in a democratic society to be involved personally in political activity and to involve others in becoming informed and active. He needs to understand that the East–West crisis may continue for many years. He must examine and question the extent to which the various social institutions are fulfilling the expectations that derive from the Democratic Ideal. The citizen who is concerned about a world in which the Democratic Ideal can be fulfilled would be expected to take an active interest in the education of tomorrow's decision-makers. Are the elementary schools, for example, reinforcing the behaviors essential to a democratic society— those that reflect respect for the integrity and worth of all persons; respect for cooperative action; respect for the right of everyone to express his opinion and to dissent; respect for full and open inquiry; respect for knowledge; and respect for the fullest development of the human being, his special talents and skills, and his capacity to care about others?

The history of man's progress from a primitive and animal-like being to the cultivated, civilized, and enlightened individual found when he is at his best is a record of both human frailties and human potentialities. The well-known struggle within the individual to control and direct his aggressive and destructive impulses, to maintain a favorable balance of rational over irrational behavior, has its counterpart in the struggle of all men to live and work together, directing their collective energies into constructive action rather than unproductive conflict. As the individual has his times of terror, despair, destruction, and depression, so do societies have their times of chaos and war. The development of neither the individual nor his society is continuously upward; rather, it is irregular and erratic, a process of ups and downs. The psychological development of the individual and the well-being of his society are closely related and one point of departure for the person pondering this relationship is a consideration of his own developmental progress.

It is characteristic of man to consider himself in relation to his physical and social world, to be observant and curious about that which he sees but does not comprehend, and to invest energy in extending his knowledge and his control over the forces that impinge upon him. Within these potentialities lie, in part, the promise of a future for man and for his offspring. To be fulfilled, however, this promise requires men who not only value knowledge but who are wise; men who not only get along with people but who invest of themselves in contributing to the development of others. In short, the future of all men depends upon the level of personal and social development attained by each individual. The individual's concern about his own developmental progress is a starting point in his actively contributing not only to his own future but to the future of all men.

Toward Personal Development

To the complex person confronting a complex and changing world, experiencing the disappointments, the rejections, and the losses that are a significant part of being human, the earlier specifications of a high standard of development and effectiveness will have been helpful to only a limited extent. The reader will have matched his own impressions and feelings about himself against the descriptions provided. One general response to such self-evaluation is for the reader to feel that he still has some distance to travel in order to come near to the ideal presented, and he will wonder what he can do to facilitate his development.

The developmental ideal presented has clarified a goal that is approached, rather than achieved; it has not specified guaranteed solutions for developmental inadequacies. The particular meaning a person attaches to his humanity is a highly personal and private matter; what one person views as his ideal self and what particular shortcomings he wishes to offset may be quite different from another's. No clear-cut prescription for self-improvement can be provided either here or elsewhere.

THE EXTENSION OF EXPERIENCE: A ROUTE TO DEVELOPMENT

In making his progress toward higher levels of psychological development both easier and quicker, the individual will extend and deepen his self-awareness; he will widen his range of personal relationships, deepening the significance that some of them have for him; finally, he will increase the depths of his existing skills and the precision of his knowledge in order to master specific challenges that his environment presents to him. Thus, the extension of the individual's experience provides the context in which he develops as well as the basic condition of such development. It must be noted, however, that additional experience and participation in the lives of others will not necessarily ensure movement toward the goal of higher levels of psychological development. It has been remarked earlier that the capacity of the human being to deceive himself should not be underestimated and that he will misperceive what he experiences in order to protect his self-esteem and minimize threat.

One step toward accelerated personality development and behavioral change is taken by maintaining a conscious awareness of oneself, one's feelings, and one's past. Through such awareness the self-concept can be clarified, extended, and modified. Achieving this type of self-awareness is not an easy task. The degree to which the self-deceptive processes can disrupt accurate perceptions of self and others has been given considerable emphasis. For some persons the changes in established patterns of defensive behaviors can be accomplished only over considerable periods of time and with specialized assistance. For most persons the task of achieving higher developmental levels will be difficult but not impossible, so long as they have a conscious desire to change, make a conscious effort to improve the clarity of their self-perceptions, and are willing to expend the amount of energy necessary to do so.

Such an investment of energy is usually made only when problems are to be solved, when the stresses are high, or when the person feels frustrated because his wishes are thwarted. Out of such problem situations individuals may climb to greater heights of psychological development, and if the individual consistently and systematically expends energy in looking at and into himself the process can be accelerated.

If one is to approach the question of "Who am I," he must consider his beliefs about himself, his behavior, and the consequences of his actions with respect to his personal objectives. He must consider his goals, feelings, ideals, strengths, and weaknesses. Specifically, he will need to examine the degree of congruence between the goals he privately admits holding and the use he makes of his talents and energies. He will examine the picture that he presents to others as well as the impression he wants to convey to others, and he will examine the values by which he judges himself and other people.

If pursued, this process of specifying the nature of one's personal, social, and ideal selves will bring a greater awareness of all that is being experienced in the present. With such awareness, experiences tend to take on more richness, depth, and meaning; the shades and nuances of feeling become clearer and the individual perceives himself and his world with greater clarity and definition. At the same time, through such awareness his past becomes closer to the feelings and behaviors that are part of his present. The consistencies and inconsistencies among the selves tend to emerge more clearly. In some instances, when there is a great disparity between personal and ideal selves, the introspective process can result in feelings of unworthiness, guilt, and depression, because the person cannot measure up to his own standards and can never experience success. If he achieves one goal, he finds minute flaws in it or he sets up another. If a friend points out the unrealistic level of his standards, he disregards the advice, saying that such standards are necessary and challenging, that his critic is merely flattering him or is indifferent to standards.

In the process of self-consideration, the specification and assessment of personal and ideal selves constitute a first step in reducing the disparity between them. This is accomplished through a conscious shift in the impression that one has of himself, in the standards he feels he should fulfill, or in both.

From a developmental standpoint, the most favorable state exists when the individual recognizes areas of change essential to meeting his own reasonable standards; he will not feel complacent or smug, but rather he will be desirous of change and will be somewhat dissatisfied with himself as he is. Such dissatisfaction will lead to constructive action, however, not merely to debilitating feelings of guilt. The consideration of personal and ideal selves can lead to a recording of the ideals, standards, and values that provide the partial basis for these selves. Since many of these values and standards derive from parental attitudes and behaviors that may have been adopted without thought, the adult who reconsiders his personal value orientation and its implications for his every-day behaviors, as well as for long-range decisions, will find himself questioning many beliefs previously taken for granted.

Thus far the discussion has been focused upon the relationship between the personal and ideal selves, but the importance of integrating the concepts of the social self must not be overlooked. The differences between the intended representation of oneself to others and the personal and ideal selves can affect the individual's self-esteem in various ways. When he is not functioning socially in accord with his "true" self, or when he behaves contrary to his beliefs, then self-esteem will be low. The approach to reducing disparity between the personal and ideal selves involves the conscious and deliberate examination of the social self; in turn, answering the question of how one wishes to be perceived by others necessitates the examination of one's values.

Since the image that one wishes to present may not coincide with the image actually created in the eyes of other people, the individual who is examining his own effectiveness and who is interested in furthering his own development will attempt also to evaluate the degree to which the responses that he evokes from others and the relationships he has with them are consistent with what he believes he wants from these relationships.

The young adult often harbors memories of conflict and unpleasantness associated with his parents. In some instances, his feelings will be extremely hostile, and the parent will be held accountable for his misfortunes, inadequacies, and failures. The removal of deep-seated conflicts related to parental relationships will often require specialized psychotherapeutic assistance. For most adults attempting to resolve these residual difficulties, however, it is helpful to make a conscious effort to look at parents as people with human abilities and human frailties rather than to cling to childish perceptions of the parent as a special kind of deity.

To counteract the tendency to see the present through the eyes of the past usually necessitates a conscious effort to interpret immediate events and experience in terms of what is actually observed, rather than what is anticipated, feared, or wished for. Although awareness of one's self-deceptive tendencies affords some prospect for improvement in the accuracy of self-perception, the reader is cautioned against oversimplifying the problem. Certainly an individual does not suddenly behave differently because he becomes aware that his employer reminds him of his father. But by focusing clearly on the immediate situation, he is sometimes able to limit the operation and activation of defense mechanisms.

Such defenses generally tend to take the form of keeping people away, either through a withdrawal from them or through an attack upon them, and experience with others is thereby subtly and unconsciously curtailed. In contacts with other persons, as previous discussions have emphasized, the quality of the relationships, not the quantity, is important. The point emphasized here has to do with the importance of conscious and deliberate effort to examine one's situation, oneself, and one's relationships in terms of the evidence available.

Relationships provide a context in which mastery over previously threatening impulses and fears can be achieved. To the extent that new experiences with people are not in line with past expectations and to the extent that the consequences of these relationships differ from those which were anticipated, growth in the sense of finer perceptual discrimination and finer and more selective responses to people is possible. Experiences with individuals who are neither malevolent nor harmful can reduce the extent to which a person responds to all persons as potentially threatening. Thus, relationships with peers who are capable of giving themselves and of contributing to the development of others, and special relationships with friends who have achieved a high level of psychological development can provide opportunities for further psychological development. Such relationships contribute to growth by making possible the abandonment of inappropriate expectations, attitudes, and perceptual sets.

An attitude of inquiry into one's own motives, the question "Why am I doing this?", is appropriate within the context of interpersonal relationships. The intent to understand what it is that is wanted from another person constitutes the first step toward eliminating the utilization of others for the satisfaction of selfish needs that would result in manipulative and exploitative behavior.

For the person who desires to understand why he wishes to be perceived in certain ways, the awareness of his own need to feel in communion with others is essential. As noted earlier, this need is not to be confused with the desire to be in the presence of other people. The awareness of the need to feel in communion is, however, closely linked to the individual's possession of a sense of identification with some other persons, and the feeling that he is vital to their development and that his development is dependent upon theirs.

Additional experiences of close relationships with persons who possess the capacity to love afford considerable opportunity for the psychological extension and development of the individual. However, since the general culture, particularly that of young persons, does not often place a premium upon gentleness, concern for others, empathy, and understanding, there may seem to be few opportunities for relationships meeting these criteria. Because of this the individual may become discouraged and tend to be unselective in his contacts. Contact that is confined to persons having a need to exploit or hurt him does not contribute to his development. On the other hand, with self-awareness, experience with all persons provides the opportunity for focusing one's attention upon others and the opportunity to understand their behaviors, attitudes, and feelings. Even transitory contacts with other 'human beings can be growth-enhancing.

At times men must mobilize their physical and psychological resources to meet demands of the social, physical, occupational, and personal world. They will be forced to apply what they have learned to some novel situation, to address their energies to the solution of a problem or to the acquisition of a skill. At such times they may have to perceive themselves and their abilities in relation to their world in new and unaccustomed ways.

That man can mobilize his intellectual and emotional resources in response to the challenges his environment presents, that he can actively commit his energies and attention to finding new ways of dealing with new problems, and that he can evidence curiosity and the ability to evaluate evidence is an essential part of his nature and a central feature of his capacity for mastery. But while it is assumed that each man has a potential for growth, it does not follow that men are equal in their ability to cope with the problems which life presents.

Sometimes opportunities for development are presented in a totally new situation, and the individual may be faced with a decision involving a major change in his environment: a move to a new locale, a job entailing additional or different responsibilities, a similar position in another company and thus in a different social context. To contemplate such a change is often difficult for individuals who have enjoyed a degree of security in "the known," who have acquired a circle of friends with whom they feel comfortable, and who have experienced the confidence that comes from "knowing one's job." Although contemplated or actual change, constituting as it does the separation of oneself from one's past, is evocative of some anxiety, it also affords the chance to extend experience. Hence, the objective is not merely the avoidance of anxiety, rather it is the maximizing of conditions for development.

Within human potentiality there is a source of hope as well as despair; man has the capacity to love as well as to hate, to build as well as to destroy. He can relate to other human beings and he has the ability to act rationally and in ways consistent with his own development. Although they are often underdeveloped, these abilities exist as part of the nature of man, and the task of the future is to see to it that the total society both encourages and makes use of their fullest expression.

Summary

The Democratic Ideal and the ideal of psychological development both value the dignity and worth of the individual. The relationship between the two ideals is reciprocal. Man requires an environment that encourages his open inquiry into all the facets of his life and of his physical and social world. He requires a society that cherishes freedom of expression and facilitates the development of his resources. The survival of the Democratic Ideal requires individuals who can consider the needs of others and who can contribute to their development. To the extent that a society's citizens are committed to the Democratic Ideal and can react without oversimplifying the situation, can consider alternatives to aggression, and can perceive the origin of threat without distortion— to this extent the Democratic Ideal will survive.

Beliefs that wars are inevitable complicate the quest for alternatives to war; they increase the probability of war and hence jeopardize the survival of the Democratic Ideal. The belief that man is by nature aggressive and that war affords an outlet for aggressive impulses fails to account for the fact that an accurate characterization of man's nature must also include his abilities to control his impulses, to act rationally and in accord with his self-interests.

The citizen who is concerned about the contribution he can make to world peace often cannot perceive any connection between his beliefs and behaviors and national and international events. In addition to becoming more knowledgeable about his government and its affairs and becoming politically active, the citizen can contribute to a "better world" through extension of his own range of experience and through enhancment of his capacities to care for and contribute to the development of others.

The apathy of many citizens toward their fellow men, the disinterest that they exhibit toward social and political affairs, and their failure to comprehend the interdependence of all men not only constitutes a serious personal limitation, but also holds dire consequences for the survival of the Democratic Ideal.

Whether man achieves the full glory contained within the vision of the Democratic Ideal or falls back to the barbarism of the past depends on how fully he commits himself to himself, to his own development, and to the development of all men.

References

1. Bronfenbrenner, U. The mirror image in Soviet-American relations. *J. soc. Issues,* 1961, *17,* 45–56.
2. Deutsch, M. A theory of cooperation and competition. *Hum. Relat.,* 1949, *2,* 129–152.
3. Deutsch, M. Trust and suspicion. *Conflict Resol.,* 1958, *2,* 265–279.
4. Deutsch, M. The effect of motivational orientation upon trust and suspicion. *Hum. Relat.,* 1960, *13,* 123–140.
5. Deutsch, M. Psychological alternatives to war. *J. soc. Issues,* 1962, *18,* 97–119.
6. Einstein, A. *The New York Times,* May 25, 1946.
7. Franklin, R. D., and Remmers, H. H. Youth looks at civil liberties and the 1960 election; in *The Purdue Opinion Panel,* 1960, *20,* No. 1.
8. Irish, M. D., and Prothro, J. W. *The Politics of American Democracy.* Englewood Cliffs, N.J.: Prentice-Hall, 1959.
9. Merton, R. K. The self-fulfilling prophecy; in *Social Theory and Social Structure* (rev. ed.). New York: The Free Press, 1957.
10. Mill, J. S. On liberty; in *The Library of Liberal Arts,* No. 61. New York: The Liberal Arts Press, 1956.
11. Pauling, L. *Newsweek,* March 3, 1958.
12. Osgood, C. E. *Graduated Reciprocation in Tension Reduction: A Key to Initiative in Foreign Policy.* Urbana, Ill.: Institute of Communications Research, The University of Illinois, 1960.
13. Remmers, H. H., and Radler, D. H. *The American Teenager.* Indianapolis, Ind.: Bobbs-Merrill, 1957.
14. Russell, B. Unilateralism. *New Republic,* 1961, *144,* No. 10, 13–14.
15. Strausz-Hupé, R. Russia's "nuclear blackmail"—and how to meet it. *U.S. News & World Report,* 1959, *46,* No. 14, 86–88.

16. Teller, E., and Latter, A. The compelling need for nuclear tests. *Life,*
1958, *44,* No. 6, 64.

Selected Readings

Brown, H., and Real, J. *Community of Fear.* Santa Barbara, Calif.: Center for
the Study of Democratic Institutions, 1960.

Etzioni, A. *The Hard Way to Peace.* New York: Collier Books, 1962.

Fromm, E. *The Sane Society.* New York: Holt, 1955.

Fromm, E. *May Man Prevail.* Garden City, N.Y.: Doubleday, 1961.

Irish, M. D., and Prothro, J. W. *The Politics of American Democracy.* Englewood Cliffs, N.J.: Prentice-Hall, 1959.

Kahn, H. *On Thermonuclear War.* Princeton, N.J.: Princeton University
Press, 1960.

Osgood, C. E. *Graduated Reciprocation in Tension Reduction: A Key to
Initiative in Foreign Policy.* Urbana, Ill.: Institute of Communications
Research, The University of Illinois, 1960.

INDEX

Index